TURKEY

The Traveller's Guide

KW-467-605

Springfield Books Limited

SBL

Turkey: The Traveller's Guide
First English edition 1989
Translated from the third German edition

Published by Springfield Books Limited, Norman Road, Denby Dale,
Huddersfield HD8 8TH, West Yorkshire, England.
© **Copyright 1989, Michael Muller Verlag** , Erlangen, West-Germany.

Research	
JOCHEN GRASHÄUSER & LARS SCHMITZ-EGGEN HORST WEBER & CHRISTOPH KELLER	General Information, Getting Around in Turkey Thrace, İstanbul, North Aegean, South Aegean, Lycia, West-Anatolia
JOCHEN GRASHÄUSER & HELMUT FREISZLER MARCUS X. SCHMID HELMUT FREISZLER	South Coast Cappadocia, Hattuşa Konya, Ankara, History

Translation	DAVID CRAWFORD
Cover design	BRYAN LEDGARD
Maps	HELGA HORNBERGER, MICHAEL HAKEN
Photography	THE AUTHORS, M. MULLER VERLAG

British Library Cataloguing in Publication Data
Turkey: the traveller's guide.
   1. Turkey. Description & travel
   I.) Muller, Michael II.) Turkei. English.
   915.61'0438

ISBN 0-947655-45-X

The authors and publishers accept no responsiblity for accuracy of information contained in this book.
Printed and bound in West-Germany by Alfa Druck Ltd. Göttingen.

— CONTENTS —

General Information

Tips from A - Z 33

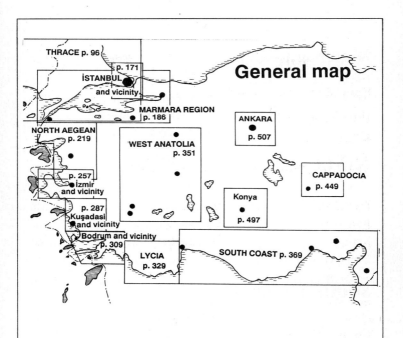

THRACE p. 96

p. 171

İSTANBUL
and vicinity

MARMARA REGION
p. 186

General map

ANKARA
● p. 507

NORTH AEGEAN
p. 219

WEST ANATOLIA
p. 351

CAPPADOCIA
● p. 449

p. 257
İzmir
and vicinity

Konya
●
p. 497

p. 287
Kuşadası
and vicinity

Bodrum and vicinity
p. 309

LYCIA
p. 329

SOUTH COAST p. 369

Marmara Region _____187

North Aegean _____218

South Aegean _____257

Lycia _____328

West Anatolian Backlands _____351

South Coast _____ 368

Cappadocia _____ 447

Anatolia _____ 493

PREFACE

Turkey is Tremendous

Field research consumes tremendous amounts of time. No one author
is capable of covering all of Turkey in the timely fashion required for
an up-to-date travel guide. For this reason, Michael Müller
Publications sent several teams of Turkey-wise writers to cover the
Land of the Half-moon.

Back at the office, with an unrivalled mass of information, they
produced a book of almost 600 pages, packed with details of
accommodation, connections, food, swimming, sights, history, and
excavation sites. This information is unfolded in a relaxed manner,
easy to find and understand.

Turkey is not the Lake District

Turkey's climate, traditions, food and religion are new to most
western visitors. For this reason we include 100 pages of background
information to help you get ready for your vacation and to help you
better understand a foreign land. You'll enjoy skimming through the
sections on Turkey's economy and religion.

In Short

This is a travel guide to Turkey which has something for everyone.
Backpackers with marginal means and tourists with higher standards
will find they have something in common. Whether you are a water
rat in search of a beach, or a cultural recluse in search of lost
civilizations, this is the book for you.

GENERAL INFORMATION

Encyclopedias could be written about the tremendous country of Turkey. You might be wondering why all the men wear a moustache, or from where you can get a bus to Çeşme? But let's start at the beginning.

Geography

780,580 sq.km - plate tectonics - geologically young!

Turkey is six times the size of Great Britain with 780,580 sq.km. Three per cent of the country is in Europe and the rest (generally called Anatolia) belongs to the Asia.

Location: Turkey is bordered from the west to the east by Greece, Bulgaria, the Soviet Union, Iran, Iraq, and Syria. The country stretches 1,570 km from west to east. The distance from north to south ranges from 450 km to 660 km. Situated between latitudes of 36 degrees to 42 degrees north, Ankara and İstanbul are on the same latitudes as Madrid and New York. With a longitude of 26 degrees to 45 degrees east, the entire country is in one time zone, three hours ahead of Greenwich Mean Time (8 hours ahead of US Eastern Standard Time). Time differences may vary in the summer time, since only some parts of Turkey use daylight saving time.

Geography / Geology: Most of Turkey - with the exception of a small section of the Arabian plateau in the southeast - belongs to the belt of mountains surrounding Europe and can be subdivided into regions. From the deep furrows of the Aegean coast in the west (whose offshore islands are the peaks of an underwater mountain chain), the terrain rises to 1000 m above sea level. Between 900 m and 1100 m above sea level, the central Anatolian Plain is bordered by the Pontic Mountains (2600 m) to the north and the Taurus Mountains (3900 m) to the south. In the east the Pontic Mountains and the Taurus Mountains fuse with the East Anatolian Massif. This range contains 23 peaks rising above 3000 m. The tallest of these is also the tallest in Turkey - Mount Ararat (5165 m) on the border of Iran and the Soviet Union.

Geologically speaking, Turkey is a very young region. During the tertiary era, 60 million years ago, a collision of the Eurasian and Arabian plates created a series of mountain chains. By the quaternary period the Aegean Sea had flooded the river valleys of the Bosporus and Dardanelles and the connection with Europe was broken. Volcanic activity is now extinct, although the earth is still unsettled. Three earthquake zones join in Turkey and powerful earthquakes continue to plague the country, particularly its eastern provinces, costing many lives.

Climate

Weather: Due to great differences in altitude, Turkey has a varied climate. The Aegean and Mediterranean coasts have long, hot summers and brief, mild winters. Summers are dry but some rain falls in the winter. The swimming season is April to October and the best months to visit Turkey are April, May, September and October, when temperatures range from 20 to 25 degrees Celsius. During the summer, average highs are 30 degrees Celsius with 35 degrees or more in wind sheltered areas.

Central Anatolia has a steppe climate: hot, dry summers and cold winters with heavy snow fall. Summer evenings are cool due to the altitude of 1000 m. Springtime is the rainy season.

Around the Black Sea: mild temperatures all year round. Lots of rain creates high humidity all year, becoming almost tropical in the summer. The Black Sea coast boasts the mildest temperatures and the most rain in all of Turkey. Winter brings only occasional frost and light snow.

CLIMATE TABLE

Mean Air Temperatures in Degrees Celsius:

	Spring	Summer	Autumn	Winter
İstanbul	11	24	15	6
Aegean	15	28	22	8
Mediterranean	15	31	23	10
Ankara	13	30	23	4

Mean Water Temperatures in Degrees Celsius:

	Spring	Summer	Autumn	Winter
Sea of Marmara	10	23	19	7
Aegean	13	26	23	10
Mediterranean	17	28	25	16
Black Sea	8	25	21	8

Flora

Steppe - sclerophyllous evergreen - fruit from 1001 nights - cotton - nuts

Turkey has lost its major forest regions. Central Anatolia is barren steppe. Livestock and wheat occupy large sections.

Only 14 per cent of the land is covered by forest, of which two-thirds is brush. The destruction of the forests has led to erosion: fertile earth has been carried away by wind and rains. Natural recovery of the soil has been prevented by intensive grazing of livestock.

The steppe becomes more barren as you move toward east Anatolia, with the parched vegetation presenting a uniform grey-brown colour during the summer. Cultivated plants such as apricots, cucumbers and eggplant need constant irrigation.

The historically important region of *Cappadocia* is like an oasis in the steppe. A rain of ash from the 3916 m volcano ERCIYAS DAGI, created the fertile soil upon which melons, apricots, grapes and other fruit flourish.

Along the *Aegean* and *Mediterranean* coasts, export fruits (figs, melons, peaches, lemons, bananas) are planted. Cotton also does well. Huge plantations are found in the Çukurova, a lowland plain around Adana. This is also a typical Mediterranean pine forest region. Along the coast, evergreen bushes (macchia) are common: oleander, holly, boxtree, myrtle, lavender, carob, and others. The predominant tree is pine and firs are found in Taurus forests along with an occasional cedar.

As in Yugoslavia, Greece and Italy, fires are hard to extinguish because of the dry forests. In 1985 a major forest fire near the coastal town of Kuşadası cost many lives in addition to causing great ecological damage.

In the precipitation-rich region along the Black Sea coast beechwood, lime trees, maple, oak, and at high altitudes fir, form a green belt along the Pontic Mountains. The underbrush features Mediterranean plants including cherry-laurel, holly and ivy. The major crops are tea, tobacco, hazelnuts, almonds, pistachio, and various fruits like mandarines, figs and plums.

The Sea of Marmara is also lined by forest. The European side, like central Anatolia, has a typical steppe climate with monotone macchia.

Fauna

Animals from Europe, Asia and Africa have flown, crawled or walked to Turkey and many exotic species have made homes in the various regions. Wild animals range from storks to flamingos, brown bears to jackals.

In the summer storks are easy to spot along Turkey's Aegean coast and in the European part of Turkey. The country is a paradise for them because they are protected by law. Hundreds of other bird species can be found, including several quite rare ones. Ornithologists flock to the nature reserve for birds on Lake Manya by the Sea of Marmara to watch flamingos, cormorants and pelicans. Predatory birds like eagles, hawks, buzzards and falcons are also native to Turkey.

Insects and reptiles (over 70 species) do well in the Turkish climate. Butterflies, bees, dragonflies, mosquitoes, cockroaches, tics and fleas thrive throughout the country and mosquitoes flourish in the warmer regions.

Among the reptiles are over 20 species of lizard, including the popular gecko. Turkish snakes (viper, sand boa, cross adder and sand adder) are quite shy and difficult to spot. Turtles feel at home everywhere in Turkey on land and in water. In the Mediterranean region you can spot an occasional chameleon, if its colour has not yet adjusted to its background.

Among the mammals: rodents include a ground squirrel closely related to the wood chuck, the energetic desert jumping mouse, and the endangered porcupine.

The countryside abounds with deer, fox, wild boar, badger, polecat, tree marten, rock marten, crop gazelle (in southern Anatolia), leopard (in the higher mountain regions of the east and southwest), chamois, bezoar goats and wild sheep (in the eastern highlands). Wolf, bear, jackal and lynx are found in the forest regions along the Black Sea. There is even a hunting season for wolf and bear. During winters with heavy snow, wolves venture into eastern provincial villages where they howl and search for food.

Domestic animals provide food (sheep, goats, cattle and fowl), transport (donkeys, mules, horses, water buffalos and camels) or produce (bees, silkworm).

ECONOMY

The Turkish economy has tremendous problems. The gross domestic product is increasing only slowly, yet the country desperately needs investment to modernize industry and improve infrastructure. This is being financed by international loans, which ever increase the national debt.

Another problem is Turkey's traditional east-west conflict. Investment is concentrated around İstanbul, the Marmara region, a few coastal cities and near Ankara. As a result, people are leaving the villages to find work in the major cities or abroad.

Government efforts to expand industry in central and eastern Anatolia have not met with success. Sparse population (and therefore a lack of purchasing power) and the long distances to cities and ports in the west make production there uneconomical.

In prosperous regions, factory chimneys spew smoke through day and night shifts yet the tea houses in central Anatolia are filled with idle men. This is a contradiction seen throughout the country.

Agriculture: this is the traditional mainstay of the Turkish economy, employing 60 per cent of the work force. Major crops include wheat, potatoes, beans, cotton, fruit, olives, sunflower seeds, tobacco, and sugar cane. Citrus fruits and vegetables (primarily tomatoes) are produced for export, as are tobacco (1983: 226,000 t) and cotton (1983: 1,35 mill. t). Legumes and grain serve domestic needs. One exception is the hard wheat used by noodle manufacturers which draws an exceptionally high price on the international market. In turn, Turkey imports less expensive wheat from the USA and Canada.

Another traditional export is hazel nuts, grown along the Black Sea coast. The harvest in 1980 was 280,000 t; 1978 300,000 t, approximately 60 per cent of world production. Since Chernobyl, however, export has declined considerably, while domestic consumption remains strong.

Livestock: on the high plains of Anatolia you'll find sheep, cattle and goats (including angora goats). Cattle are still sometimes used to work the fields, while cows supply the new demand for milk. Donkeys and mules provide important transport to isolated regions. Lack of pasture land and old-fashioned methods of raising livestock hinder herd expansion.

Over 80 per cent of Turkish farmers work less than 125 acres, making efficient use of machinery impossible. Although the government has made efforts to improve agriculture (land reform, replenishing topsoil), progress is slow. However, it has been possible to increase agricultural output to match population growth.

Minerals: Turkey is blessed with a variety of important minerals, but exploitation is slow as the poor transportation network means most mining is done near the coastal regions. State financing has resulted in the tapping of the resources in the east of Turkey.

Hard coal and brown coal are predominantly mined. Hard coal, mined mostly along the Black Sea, is used primarily by industry for power generation. Charcoal is produced throughout Turkey for use in private households.

Oil reserves, in south Anatolia and around Adana, supply 50 per cent of domestic needs. The Turkish government is energetic in its efforts to increase domestic output in order to reduce expensive imports.

Iron ore is mined mostly in east Anatolia (Divriği). Turkey is a major exporter of the raw material which is also consumed by domestic heavy industry.

Copper, chrome, borax, mercury, lead, tungsten, manganese, bauxite, silver and *antimony* are additional resources mined for export or domestic industry.

Regional limits and open-cast mining methods keep production levels modest. All large mining corporations are state-owned. There are also several hundred small private companies.

Industry: When Atatürk took over the government in 1923, he tried to push industrial expansion at a fast pace. Import of industrial goods, money and know-how was required (to be counterbalanced with income from exports). The only part of the economy in which Atatürk could make an impact was agriculture, which remains important even today.

The economic structure of Turkey is typical of a developing country, dominated by *food*, *produce* and *textiles*. *Metalworking*, *tool-making* and *car production* follow. (The tool-making and auto industries are primarily assembly-oriented, using imported parts).

Heavy industry is generally state-owned. Large corporations have not taken hold in Turkey, where small businesses still predominate. At present the trend is continuing - privately owned, medium size consumer goods industries are expanding.

Although agriculture employs more than half the work force, it produces less than 20 per cent of the GNP. Industry and mining produce 30 per cent of the GNP (a rise from 18 per cent in 1978) although they employ just 16 per cent of the work force.

The main trading partners for agricultural produce are West Germany, the USA, the UK, Italy and the USSR.

Imports (oil and machinery) considerably exceed exports, although this is partially counterbalanced by the annual transfer of one billion dollars sent home by Turkish workers abroad.

Economic expansion continues. In 1981 the Turkish government invested £490 million to develop the three major sections of the economy. Foreign aid from governments and banks had mounted to £1.3 billion by 1987. Of course Turkey was required to make concessions: open itself to the international market, encourage foreign investment, reduce tariffs and expand exports at the cost of domestic demand. In 1980, Turkey was almost bankrupt; today it is again considered a good credit risk. Inflation has dropped while exports increase. Turkey is on its own appointed road to industrialization - but the chosen road ignores eastern sections of the country, leaving a major problem for the future. It is not yet clear if Turkey will ever pay off its international debt. Only then would a healthy economy be possible.

POPULATION

"Go to the city, my son, there you will find your fortune!" The old woman hides her tears while embracing her youngest son. She doesn't want to see him go, but what can he do here? Mustafa is anything but sad. His eyes are sparkling with excitement: soon he'll be in İstanbul, the city of his dreams, where he can become rich. Gold will outweigh the cares of his mother.

There is little chance that this Turkish fairytale might come true. Population growth is not matched by economic growth. The result is increasing poverty and high unemployment, particularly in rural areas. People migrate from village to city, and then abroad in search of work.

In 1955, about 18 per cent of the population lived in cities. Today the figure is 55 per cent and rising annually at a rate of 4.1 per cent. A third of the urban population live in İstanbul, İzmir and Ankara. These cities attract newcomers who are housed in ghettos ("*Gecekondu*" - see the box in the Ankara section) on the outskirts of town. In İstanbul and İzmir over 50 per cent of the population live in Gecekondus, in Ankara it is over 70 per cent.

In 1986 the population of Turkey was 48 million (increased from 27.8 million in 1960). This figure does not include the estimated 2 million Turks living abroad.

According to UNESCO statistics, the population is growing at an annual rate of 2.4 to 2.7 per cent. Today 60 per cent of the population is under 25 years of age and the trend is continuing.

Population density is varied. İstanbul is the most dense with 900 people per square km. The under-populated regions of east Anatolia only have 15 persons per square km.

Ethnic Mix: Most of Turkey's population (almost 90 per cent) are ethnic Turk. Until WW I there were strong Armenian and Greek Christian minorities. These were practically eliminated: the Armenians were killed (see the box at the Kis Kalesi section), while Turkey's Greek population was exchanged for Greece's Turkish population. Today about 40,000 ethnic Armenians and 10,000 ethnic Greeks remain in Turkey - mostly around İstanbul.

The largest minority are the Kurds. Officially called "mountain Turks" they make up 7 per cent of the population but their high birthrate suggests that the percentage has increased. Concentrated in the southeast they continue to have problems due to their persistant demands for autonomy.

Ethnic Arabs make up 1.2 per cent of the population and that number is also on the rise. They are concentrated along the border with Syria. They suffer from the same problems as the Greek, Armenian and Kurdish minorities (see *Samandag - Alevi have Long Noses*).

Kurds and Arabs use their own languages. The Lasens, Cherkessens, Georgians, and Islamic Bulgarians also do, but these minorities are small.

EDUCATION

At the post office an elderly Turk picks up a package. Upon receipt, he or she asks the postal agent "Who is it from?" Most elderly Turks, particularly women, are illiterate.

As Turkey's population becomes younger, the rate of literacy is rising. In 1970 the rate of illiteracy was 31 per cent among men and 65 per cent among women. In 1980 these numbers had dropped to 20 per cent and 50 per cent respectively. In 1981, 49 per cent of men and 24 per cent of women received higher education.

The rise of the literacy rate in Turkey can be seen in the percentage of female school attendance. In 1960 it was just 58 per cent; by 1979 the figure had risen to 96 per cent. Today 30 per cent of the population remains illiterate (mostly the elderly).

Turkish children receive five years of basic schooling followed by an optional three years at middle school. After successful completion, pupils may attend a preparatory college or a professional school (hotel trade schools are popular). Students may enter a university after completing the preparatory schooling.

Children are required to take the basic schooling, Koran school is optional. While attendance of Koran schools has always been high, the rising strength of Islamic fundamentalism has increased attendance still further. Koran schools teach pupils the word and laws of the Koran, which remain important in Turkey despite laicism.

The east-west divide is again seen in education. The education system in the east lags far behind that of the west and the cities. The problems are not only created by single-room schoolhouses or learning by rote and rod, but also by the necessity for cheap child labour. Teachers face almost empty classrooms during harvest time. In winter, children find it difficult, if not impossible, to reach school from isolated villages. Some parents just don't see the need to put their children through the trials of education.

FAMILY

Turkey is not a welfare state. Few Turks receive a pension and there is no such thing as unemployment benefit. The average Turk cannot even comprehend what an old age home might be. Turks in need are cared for by the "aile" - the family.

Although family structure is similar to that in the West, the Turkish family has a much higher status than in other Western countries. It is the basis for all social life. The patriarch has the final word in both extended and nuclear families, although the grandmothers have great influence in extended families. In smaller families, the importance of women increases with their contribution to family income.

Rarely does a member of the family make individual decisions by himself. All major issues are discussed with the family. If the family decides against it - "Kismet", then it is so.

Marriage is a sober business undertaken by two families. Over half the marriages in Turkey are still arranged by the parents. If we give our daughter to your son, how much are you willing to pay? Terms are influenced by the appearance and education of the daughter, in addition to the means of the groom's family.

A sign of the times is the increase of marriage for love, particularly in the cities. If Süleyman loves Marya, and she loves him, then marriage is possible - if the families approve. City weddings are shorter, lasting just one day. In rural areas the festivities continue for at least three days.

The closest and strictest family tradition is practiced along the Black Sea coast. Don't even speculate what might happen if a family member should be insulted or a daughter lose her maidenhood. Conflicts are settled personally, rarely in court. Clan revenge is considered legitimate if honour has been lost, or injustice done.

Tourists rarely have the opportunity to see behind the facade of family life. An invitation to tea is common, but an evening meal is another matter. For Turks, the family is sacred. If you are invited into someone's home, be conscious of the value of the gesture.

VISITING

Western European visitors frequently seem like an elephant in a porcelain shop when visiting a Turkish home. The Orient has its own traditions. A few tips:

Bring a small present, nothing expensive, but something pleasant. Alcoholic beverages or foreign cigarettes usually achieve a smile from the men, while women approve of coffee, perfume, shampoo or sweets. The latter are appreciated by children.

Remove your shoes at the front door. If no slippers are available, make do with your socks. Pets, even the most faithful dog, are not permitted in the house - a house is no place for animals.

At the traditional double kiss of greeting - first the right, then the left cheek - kiss only members of your own sex! It is considered polite to kiss the hand of an elderly person and then raise it to one's forehead. It would be very impolite to speak loudly in the presence of older people (always respect the elder). If the head of the family arrives, you will be expected to rise.

It is considered impolite to refuse anything offered. Your host has certainly gone to great effort, sometimes at unusual expense, to please the guest. Perhaps just a plate of rice is something special in this household. The guest repays the honour by bravely consuming the food, or making use of the vacated bedroom. If you enjoy yourself, be lavish with your praise - something everyone likes, particularly Turkish hosts.

Sometimes at meals the men eat first while the family women have their meal later. If a European couple is invited to dinner, an exception is made: the woman is invited to join the men.

In general, be polite, patient and considerate. A few words of broken Turkish will work wonders. Loud singing is considered a sign of drunkenness. Blowing your nose loudly in public is shameful. However, small trespasses of etiquette will be forgiven.

Family structure differs greatly between urban and rural families. In the three major cities - İstanbul, Ankara and İzmir - the nuclear family (traditional in western Europe) is much more common than in rural regions. According to the official statistics of the Turkish Family Ministry, family structure in rural areas began a trend toward the nuclear family model in the 1960s. The four-generation family, from the new-born child to the great-grandmother, all living under one roof, is becoming rare. Only 5 per cent of Turkish households are organized along these lines.

The European model of parents and one child is also rare in Turkey. The exceptions are found in the three major cities, and generally only within the upper class.

A high birth rate is a common symptom of underdeveloped countries. The motives for a large family are the same in Turkey as in other less-developed countries, although Turkey is difficult to place in this category. In an agricultural society, children provide for their elders and the family, and there is prestige, at least for the father, in having a large family.

A high birth rate is also needed to compensate for a high rate of infant mortality. According to UNESCO statistics, infant mortality in Turkey was about 195,000 between 1975 and 1980. The health system improves from year to year, leading to lower death rates among children and longer life expectancy. The average life expectancy has risen from 51 years in 1960 to 62 years in 1981. In the United Kingdom, by comparison, it is 76 years for women and 72 for men.

WOMEN

"Men are above women because they were chosen by Allah", to quote the Koran. In other words, women are to do what men tell them. According to the teaching of the Koran, women are second-class people.

The woman's place is in the home, raising children. There she can exercise her skills as a hostess and manage the household finances. The family patriarch represents the family in public. He provides for and protects the family. This is what tradition, religious teaching and society expect.

In the 1920's Turkish women began moving toward equality. For the first time they were accepted as legal entities. However, these reforms were instituted from above, and found little grass-roots support. Turkish men and women have been indoctrinated for centuries with Islamic teaching. Men are expected to assume the patriarchal role. Women, locked into the traditional female role, make little effort to take advantage of their new rights. Women who do try to exercise their equality quickly discover that written theory is not practiced.

It should be noted that Turkish men are not better or worse than men elsewhere. Patriarchy is a way of life in almost every country on earth, only the leash upon which women are held is of varied length.

Also note that there is no such thing as the typical Turkish woman. There is a tremendous difference between the woman with baggy breeches and a kerchief who works in a field while her husband keeps watch on the donkey, compared to a bank employee in İstanbul who paints her fingernails while thumbing through fashion magazines. Then there is the woman from the Gececondu in Ankara, who struggles just to feed her family, while her unemployed husband sits around the house. Women do share their warmth and solidarity, however.

One thing is clear: Islam will not alter its position on women any time in the near future. As long as the *Koran* dominates the thinking of Turkish men and women, the role of Turkish women is unlikely to change.

RELIGION

"La ilahe ill Allah!" The voice of the muezzins preaches this day after day from every minaret. Five times daily, Muslims are called to prayer in the name of Allah. La ilahe ill Allah! - There is no God except Allah!

Islam is the youngest of the world religions and has around 700 million believers. About 99 per cent of the Turkish population is Islamic (meaning in Arabic "submit to God's will"). The remaining percent consists of Jews, Syrian Monophysites and Greek Orthodox, et al.

The Teaching of Islam: The most important tenet of Islam says: "*There is no god except Allah, and Muhammad is his prophet.*" Muslims do not revere MUHAMMAD, the founder of the monothetic religion, but only God - ALLAH. Muslims believe he is the only God, that he never had a son and that Muhammad was his last prophet - the bearer of his final message.

Muslims believe in a number of spirits - angels who serve God, even the Devil who rejected Allah and leads people into harmful temptation. Muslims are not permitted to worship angels. Prophets play an important role in Islam: to date, more than 2000 different prophets have proclaimed the will of Allah. Among the prophets recognized by Islam are Noah, Abraham, Moses, Jacob, David and Jesus. But they

were only a few of the many and only Muhammad has special importance, since he brought the last revelation of God.

MUHAMMAD

Muhammad lived from 570 AD to 632 AD. Born in Mecca, he
was left an orphan at the age of five and was raised in poverty.
He worked as a shepherd and camel driver until in 595 AD he
married a wealthy widow for whom he had tended the camels.
Suddenly wealthy, Muhammad enjoyed 15 carefree years. At
the age of 40, he began to hear the word of God. He received the
messages in a state of enlightenment, and passed the word on to
his followers.

The messages contained elements of almost unbelievable social
controversy in the Arab world. For example, slavery was condemned in one of the basic tenets of Islam but this was conve-
niently modified or forgotten: only faithful Muslims may not be
enslaved.

The poor population of Mecca was very enthusiastic about
Muhammad, and was the first to profess his faith. The wealthy
establishment was much less enthusiastic. They feared social
unrest and repressed the early Muslims. In 622 AD,
Muhammad emigrated to Medina. This is considered the year
"zero" in the Islamic calendar.

In Medina, Muhammad succeeded in making Islam the dominant religion. The fascinating new teaching was more than just
a religion; it provided guidelines for a whole way of life. His followers developed a powerful military organization, permitting
Muhammad to capture Mecca. This initial victory brought him a
number of new followers. By the time of his death, two years
later, the tribe of Arabia had joined the faith. The teaching of
Islam was carried from Spain to India. In the "Holy War" against
non-believers, all means were justified.

According to Islamic belief, Allah created the world, just like the
Christian God described in the Bible. For this reason the Bible, including the New Testament, is revered by Muslims as sacred literature. One fundamental difference is that Muslims do not see Jesus as
the son of God and the saviour of humanity. In the eyes of Islam,
Christianity is a predecessor of Islam. Christianity and the Jewish
faith are considered "book religions" which have accepted a part of
the true faith which achieves its full character under Islam.

Christians and Jews are considered persons of a different faith rather than polytheists or atheists (persons who believe in many Gods or non-believers). Heathens are damned by Allah, and have no right to expect humane treatment. People of a different faith have a special minority status under Islam. As long as they don't endanger Islam they are tolerated and permitted to practice their own beliefs.

Muslims, like Christians, face a day of judgment leading to Paradise or Hell. However, there is more than just one Heaven and one Hell, they are divided into different categories. Seventh Heaven, for example, is reserved for the most devout Muslims - and for those who die fighting for Islam in a holy war.

According to the teaching of Islam, fate is predetermined. Allah controls the world and each individual. A faithful Muslim accepts the will of Allah, submitting his thoughts and will to the laws of Islam. The result, difficult for Christians to understand, is the Muslim acceptance of fate: Kismet, the will of Allah, can't be changed.

The Koran: The word of God was written in *sura* making up the sacred Koran, successor to the Bible and Thora. Muhammad himself was illiterate; his followers put his words in writing. The Koran is considered one of the most poetic works in Arabic literature.

Originally the Koran was considered the only valid law. It was the basis for Islamic law, the *Scheria*. Every Islamic government, judicial system and scientific discipline was required to adhere to its tenets. Turkey is not the only country to dilute Islamic law with western jurisprudence. However, western ideas of justice are alien to conservative Muslims and meet resistance in Orthodox Muslim circles. There are conflicts concerning the position of women, sexual morality, prohibition of alcohol, western schools, and dress (particularly for women). Since the days of Atatürk, women are prohibited to wear a veil or kerchief in public buildings.

The popularity of Islam is on the rise in Turkey. In 1982, the religious classes banished by Atatürk, were returned to the schools. In 1984, consumption of alcohol was restricted by law. Cafés, kiosks and tea gardens located near mosques, schools or barracks are not permitted to serve alcohol (this does not apply to foreign tourists). Also, Turkish foreign policy, under pressure from strong domestic Islamic forces, has begun to seek cooperation with other Islamic nations.

Islamic Sects: Islam has split into two branches, each of which is again subdivided into numerous lesser sects. Ninety per cent of all Muslims are Sunnite, the remainder are Shiite. The majority of Turkish muslims are Sunnite.

For members of the *Sunna* (Arabic for habit) both the *Koran* and the *Hadith* (speeches of Muhammad), the second-most important book in Islam, are important. The Sunnites believe the heir of Muhammad, the Calif, must be elected from the direct descendants of Muhammad. The Shiites believe that the Sunnites have made a mistake in the electing of their leaders: they believe that ALI, the nephew and son-in-law of Muhammad was wrongfully deprived of his rightful position as heir. The Shiites chose their leader or *Imam* from Ali's line.

Five Pillars of Islam: The five basic tenets of Islam are accepted by both branches of the faith. These include public proclamation of faith *(la illahe il Allah. . .)*, the five daily prayers preceded by cleansing *(salat)*, giving to the poor *(zakat)*, fasting during the month of *Ramazan* and making the required pilgrimage to Mecca *(hacc)*.

Some of the tenets have restrictions which permit some variation: a Muslim is only required to make the pilgrimage to Mecca if he is financially capable. Cleansing is permissible without water, e.g. as a symbolic gesture.

Religious Behavior: Turkey is an Islamic country where western habits are generally tolerated, but not necessarily approved of. Increasing numbers of western tourists, particularly along the coast, have expanded tolerance, even inspired imitation by the local population. No Turk living along the Aegean coast is going to gawk if a tourist wanders past wearing shorts. But a similar display in an Anatolian village might result in hidden laughter.

Nakedness is considered immoral under Islam. The private parts of the body are strictly taboo. It is not proper to go swimming in the nude or to be seen naked in public, whether in a hotel corridor or on the way between tent and shower. If you risk it, count on an official complaint by an offended Turk resulting in several days imprisonment and a heavy fine (see *Tips from A - Z / Swimming*).

When visiting Turkey, don't forget that pork is absolutely taboo. Muslims are not permitted to touch pork, much less eat it. The prohibition is understandable considering the difficulty of preserving pork in high temperatures.

Alcoholic beverages are prohibited for strict Muslims. Still, many Turks turn a blind eye to the prohibition, as seen by the heavy consumption of beer and rakı. However, the rise of Islamic fundamentalism has led many pubs and beer gardens to stop serving alcohol.

In rural areas, Islam has permeated daily life for countless generations. Ancient religious traditions, long forgotten in the cities, are still important.

PRAYER CALL (EZAN)

Five times daily, faithful Muslims are called to prayer by the muezzin: morning prayer (Günes), noon prayer (Ögle), afternoon prayer (Ikindi), evening prayer (Aksam) and prayer at sunset (Yatsi). The call, of varied intensity, is always the same:

Allah is great! (4 x)	Allahu ekber Allahu ekber
	Allahu ekber Allahu ekber
I proclaim that there is no	Eshedü en la ilahe ill Allah
God except Allah! (2 x)	Eshedü en la ilahe ill Allah
I proclaim that Muhammad	Eshedü enne Muhammeden resulullah
is Allah's prophet! (2 x)	Eshedü enne Muhammeden resulullah
Begin to pray! (2 x,	Hay alassalat
faces turn to the right)	Hay alassalat
Begin to hail! (2 x,	Hay alalfalah
faces turn to the left)	Hay alalfalah
Allah is great! (2 x)	Allahu ekber Allahu ekber
There is no God except Allah!	La ilahe ill Allah

FESTIVALS AND HOLIDAYS

Every country has its national holidays. Everyone knows that at Easter, Christians celebrate the resurrection and children search for easter eggs. Why is the 29th of October a national holiday in Turkey and how is the Kurban Bayramı celebrated? This chapter will answer these and other questions.

Turkey celebrates national and religious holidays. In some cases they correspond. In rural areas, religion plays a more important role, lending importance to rural religious celebrations not seen in Turkey's westernized cities. However, Islamic fundamentalism might change city life in the near future.

Government Holidays

Friday is the Muslim Sunday, but western influence has made Sunday a day of rest in Turkey: shops, banks and government offices are closed. Tradition-conscious Muslims have difficulty with the practice, particularly in rural areas. The result might be that you'll find local shops open on Sundays and closed on Fridays. It is important to remember that the Islamic calendar views sunset as the beginning of the day. A Thursday holiday will actually begin at sunset on Wednesday. For major religious holidays, shops close at noon on the previous day.

1 January (New Year)

23 April (Independence Day, Children's Day) - the Parliament met for the first time in Ankara on this day in 1920.

1 May (Spring Festival, formerly Labour Day)

19 May (Day of Youth and Sport, officially "Parliament Day")

30 August (Commemoration of the victory over the Greeks in 1922)

29 October (Republic Day) - the Turkish Republic was proclaimed on this day in 1923.

10 November (Anniversary of Atatürk's death) - this holiday is only semi-official. A major proportion of the population stays away from work in commemoration of Atatürk's death. However, the date is not a legal holiday.

The two most important holidays are 23 April and 29 October.

Tile with the invocation to Allah (besmele) which is said before every committing act: "In the name of the merciful and gracious God."

Religious Holidays

Turkish religious holidays are based on the moon calendar, hence the dates change every year. The moon calendar has 11 fewer days each year than the Gregorian calendar used in the west. The result is that each year, religious holidays in Turkey are celebrated 11 days earlier. Few religious holidays figure in the official government calendar. Consequently, visitors to Turkey might not even notice that a holiday is being celebrated since all shops and services are open. Worth special mention:

Ramazan: In other Islamic countries the holiday is called "Ramadan". It is similar to the Christian period of Lent, with the difference that Muslims take it more seriously. For 30 days, strict Muslims fast from sunrise to sunset, obstaining from eating, drinking, smoking and sex.

As soon as darkness falls, all pent up frustrations receive quick satisfaction. Since the date of Ramazan varies each year, it is most painful when it falls during the hot summer months. In 1989 Ramazan begins on 18 April; in 1990 on 28 March.

During Ramazan you will be able to get food in shops or restaurants, but business hours may be restricted. By the way, the *Koran* expressly stipulates that pregnant women, the sick and travellers may break fast if necessary. Be respectful in strict Muslim regions!

Kadir Gecesi: On the night between the 23rd and 24th day of Ramazan, the revelation of the *Koran* is celebrated. Muhammad is said to have received his message from God via the Archangel Gabriel after this "night of strength" (direct translation) and special prayers are said in remembrance. Generally, Kadir Gecesi is celebrated during the month of June.

Şeker Bayramı (Sugar Festival): Marks the end of Ramazan. The festival takes its name from children going from house to house asking for sweets. Adults spend this time visiting relations throughout the country to rejoice at the end of fasting.

Because the Sugar Festival is both a national and religious holiday, all shops and offices are closed. Dates for the coming years are 7 May in 1989 and 27 April in 1990.

Kurban Bayramı (Sacrificial Festival): The four-day event is also a government holiday. This greatest of Islamic holidays is comparable to the Christian Christmas. The festival is based upon the biblical story of Abraham. It explains the meaning of the word Islam (submitting to God's will) and is briefly told like this:

God demanded that Abraham give his most precious possession as sacrifice. After much thought, Abraham concluded that this was his late-born son, Isaac. With a heavy heart, but in obedience to God's will, he led Isaac to the mountain of Moria, with the intention of sacrificing his son on the summit. He laid the boy upon the altar, took out his knife, raised it - and God intervened. Abraham was praised for his willingness to submit to God's will. God then showed him a ram caught in a nearby bush. Abraham sacrificed the ram instead of his son.

During Kurban Bayramı over 2.5 million sheep are sacrificed each year, but also cattle and oxen by the more wealthy. A third of the meat is given to friends, a third is donated to the poor, who are not able to afford their own sheep for slaughter, and a third is eaten by the family.

For weeks before the sacrificial festival, the bleats of sheep can be heard at bus stations and in residential neighbourhoods. The sudden presence of the animals has the same effect as Christmas decorations in the west. People are encouraged to go out and buy!

Economically this is the most important time of year for the shepherds. Bargaining is intense on the streets and at markets. If need be, transportation of the sheep is done by mopeds.

On the first day of Bayram the sheep is traditionally slaughtered by the head of the family after morning prayers. Then it is skinned, cut and prepared. The festival is celebrated with the family and relatives. The best from kitchen and cellar is offered. Many families skimp in the coming months in order to afford the high cost of the festival.

The sacrificial festival is celebrated in 1989 on 14 July, and in 1990 on 4 July. Public buildings are closed for Kurban Bayramı.

MUSIC

While Turkey is hardly a typical oriental country, its music does sound quite exotic to western ears: shrill-sounding instruments and unusual melodies. Oriental-style singing sets a mood, sometimes monotonous to untrained ears, but there is a great variety.

Classical Artistic Music: Whether Arabian, Persian or Turkish, the artistic Islamic music of the former Ottoman countries sounds much the same. Turkish music has greatly influenced all branches of oriental music. The roots of Turkish music go back to the thirteenth century. Patronized in the residential cities of Konya and İstanbul, it was the music of the Turkish upper class. The secular and religious music of the royal court in İstanbul dominated oriental music from the fifteenth century on.

Among Atatürk's reforms was the systematic Europeanization of classical Turkish music. Paul Hindemith (a German classical composer) was hired to reorganize Turkish music and musical training. The Ankara orchestra and opera were founded, based upon European models.

The present generation of Turkish composers can be divided into two groups: one utilizes only European-style music, the other works with a synthesis of Turkish and western elements.

The major instruments used in Turkish artistic music are the long flute (*ney*), the fiddles (*kemence rumi* and *rebab*), the lutes (*ud* and *tanbur*) and the zithers (*kanun* and *santur*). A number of European instruments are beginning to be utilized, including the violin (*keman*) and the cello.

Folk Music: Away from the royal court, folk music provided the creative inspiration for Turkish composers. Melodies and lyrics would be picked up by Turkish classical music where they would be refined and integrated into a "work". Turkish folk music is traditionally concerned with never-ending themes: birth, death, love (joyous and sad), but also everyday work. The most popular accompanying instrument is the *saz*, a percussion and plucked string instrument. Several types of dance - performances are becoming less frequent - are associated with folk music from different regions. Traditional costumes vary just as greatly, reflecting Turkey's ethnic diversity. Arabs, Jews, Kurds, Armenians, Greeks and others have all left a mark on Turkish folklore.

Besides the voice, string and wind instruments are important. Instruments, too, vary according to region. On the Aegean coast, the *ssipsi*, a flute, is popular. The *argun* is more common along the southern Mediterranean coast. The bagpipe (*tulum*) is seen mostly along the Black Sea coast. There are a number of flutes and shawms, plus other instruments. The most common instruments are the long flute (*kaval*) and recorder (*düdük*), tin drum (*deblek*), violin and long-neck lute (*saz*). The *kabak* (a stick violin) is rarely seen. At festivities, you'll often find gypsies playing the drum and oboe (*davul, zurna*).

ZEKI MÜREN

What, you have never heard of Zeki Müren? Shame on you! In Turkey everyone knows him/her and everyone likes him/her. Zeki Müren is an all-round artist, painter, actor/actress, poet, singer, composer. Since establishing his/her reputation with a series of films and old songs in the 1950s, all of Turkey adores him/her. Which might seem strange in a country with such a strict moral code. Zeki Müren wears long, colourful costumes. He/she is fat, adorned with jewelry, and dyes his/her combed up hair. Tourists can hear whispers of the true story: Zeki Müren is half male, half female - a hermaphrodite. Today Zeki Müren is a living legend, slowly growing old. For that reason, he/she only makes one public appearance each year, when his/her health permits. Come and see him/her during the Culture Festival in Bodrum from the 1st to 7th of September.

Pop Music: Turkey, like any modern country, has its share of pop stars. ÜMIT BESEN and AYSE MINE make music based upon familiar themes such as love. Much of the population, particularly bus drivers, seem to enjoy the hits. Cassettes play for hours at full blast. The melodies are traditional Turkish songs, presented in a modern style. The success of the hits is even more amazing when you consider how few of the fans can identify with the singers and their songs.

In Turkey you will rarely hear foreign pop music. If you can't do without the familiar sounds, foreign music (a few years outdated) is played on fm radio between 22:00-23:00 h. The latest hits are only available on shortwave from English broadcasts. (Bad reception!) English-language news is read daily on Turkish Radio's 3rd channel (TRT - 88-99.2 MHz).

TIPS FROM A - Z

Antique Sites

A wealth of ancient ruins can be found throughout Turkey. The well known tourist sites are generally open from 9:00 h to sunset (see local sections). There are also many sites, some quite impressive, which are always accessable.

Warning: The export of true antiques is strictly prohibited! However, customs officials pay little attention to the numerous coins sold near ruin sites as "original antique".

Barber/Hairdresser

Visit a *berber*, who, with years of concentrated experience, slices away your beard. Long blades, sharpended to a chilling edge, now belong to the past; today disposable razors are used. A shave is a pleasant Turkish custom when experienced at the hands of a master. Should blood flow, the barber will tend to it masterfully. Be sure to add a 15 per cent tip to the price of the shave.

Women may visit the *kuaför*, the coiffeur (hairdresser), who, with his employees, will tend to both hair and manicure.

Begging

Dirty hands reach out, particularly in the major cities: cripples drone out their monotone chant, mothers with children on their laps call aloud for a handout, or just sit quietly on the sidewalk. This show of poverty is difficult for tourists to ignore. Begging children are particularly good at awaking sympathy.

Beggars are the poorest of the poor; officially they don't even exist. Generally they are only driven away from the entrances to hotels and showy boulevards. They are quietly tolerated on the fringe of society, because the Muslim faith teaches the importance of giving alms. That is the way it is and always has been. Charity keeps these people without hope or a future alive.

Every tourist will react to this poverty in some way: you can turn your head and hurry past or give a donation. How you react is strictly up to your conscience. Keep in mind, however, that beggar children have no future. Their job is begging. If they are good and work at a good location, children can earn a comparatively good living. Because they are begging, however, there is no time for school. Time passes, the children grow and arouse less and less compassion. They can't read or write, nor have they learned a profession. The best part of their lives is over. The question is: how can one truly help?

Communicating

The most common second language in Turkey is German due to the large numbers of Turkish workers in West Germany. In recent years, knowledge of English has increased as English is the first language taught in schools. It is possible to speak English with any Turk who has graduated from high school (and usually never worked in Germany), or who works in the tourist industry. Still, it would be polite to learn just a few words and phrases of Turkish.

The common Turkish gestures are not easy for westerners to understand. "No" may be expressed with a slight lifting of the head and a tongue click. Shaking the head usually means "I did not understand."

Corruption

Government officials have been on the take everywhere in the world since the beginning of time. The difference between officials in western Europe and in the Ottoman successor states is that European officials don't do it in public, and are better able to live on their official income.

That is not the case in Turkey. As a minor official in Turkey, one's status is high, but one's income is minimal. An example: an official of the Tax Office in Ankara earns about £50 per month. The rent for his two-room flat is £20 per month. With the remaining £30 he must support his family. That is simply impossible. This is why a discrete exchange of envelopes is necessary to ease any bureaucracy.

This form of compensation for services rendered has been traditional in the Empire of the Half Moon since well before Atatürk. The modern Turkish state is just as miserly with its officials as the sultans of the past. The tradition remains, despite the signs of western-oriented Turks and European tourists irked at the prospect of paying money or western cigarettes to facilitate the bureaucratic process.

Crime

Toward the end of the 1970s, the number of politically-motivated offences rose dramatically. Today, at the end of the 1980s, most of the Turkish Republic is quiet. The mighty security forces have established law and order. Robbery and theft were never common crimes in Turkey. The unwritten law of hospitality to strangers prohibits it. Just as in the rest of the world, tourists will have to watch out for con artists ready to rip off vacationers, especially in cities and tourist centres. There are a number of tricks and countless variations.

1. The Already Closed Trick: Particularly popular in İstanbul. You are on your way to Top Kapı Palace when a young Turk approaches you just before you get there. He informs you, "Sorry, it is closed". So what can you do? He has a great idea, "We can all go to my brother's carpet shop for a cup of tea!" In this case it might be difficult to leave the shop without an expensive carpet under your arm. Only firm resolution will save you. Point out, "You are misusing your hospitality!" Another variation of this trick is called, "Do you have a few minutes?". It also ends at a relative's shop.

To avoid any misunderstanding: if somebody speaks to you on the street, and seems nice, there is no reason not to do something together. But if the topic turns to business or souvenirs, then caution is advisable.

2. The Exchange Trick: A friendly Turk explains to you that he works for an international company which pays him in western currency (dollars, pounds...). He has run out of lira and has difficulty exchanging at a bank - could you possibly help the poor guy? Once he has your lira in his pocket, he needs to change them in the next shop - before you receive your money, of course. Don't expect to see him again.

The variation - you give lira and receive hard currency - is much more refined than the old standard "need for dollars because my nephew is planning to go to America" trick. Should you decide to exchange money on the street or in a tea house, hang on to your cash like a mistrusting child: "We exchange at the same time, ok?".

3. The "It Belongs To Me" Trick: An angry Turk storms up to you and demands to be paid for the bracelet you took from him. He pressures you ever stronger. Perhaps his friends also get involved, and if you still won't pay - because you don't have anything of his - a call goes out for the police. Give support to this brilliant idea of calling the police; the guy will leave quickly.

The trick is all bluff, but it plays on your natural fear of getting involved in something unpleasant in a foreign country. The best way to end the hassle is to insist that the matter be settled at a police station. Explain to him what he can expect there - violent enforcement of the law.

There are a number of variations. The land on which you are camping can suddenly belong to an irate owner, who will only calm down in return for money. Note: Freely accessible stretches of beach are never privately owned.

Tips: Ask about the price before buying goods or services. Don't worry, it is the accepted way in Turkey. Always count your change immediately and speak up if you don't receive the full amount. If necessary, get help at the nearest police station, military post or tourist information office. You are sure to receive help. As a tourist, you are an honoured guest. You should be able to enjoy yourself.

Dress

If you picture Turkey as an oriental country where the men wear fez and kaftan while the women wear veils, you will only be partially correct - about the women. Since the reforms of Atatürk, it is forbidden to wear fez or veils. However a veil, or at least a kerchief, is common among women, even in major cities. Islam is slow to accept western reforms. Only in public buildings is it required to remove all head covering. Men have accepted European dress for 60 years; the former traditional costume (fez) is now only sold to tourists. In general, Turks place importance upon a clean, proper appearance.

What to Pack: For a beach holiday along the Aegean, take light cotton clothes. If you plan a tour of the country, be prepared for changing weather conditions. Along with a hat or kerchiefagainst the hot sun, carry a light sweater and rain gear. Comfortable dress should not be overdone. Shorts are tolerated, but are not considered in good taste 100 m from the beach. Turks say, "Only children wear shorts."

If you visit İstanbul in winter, be prepared for rain and possible snow.
Ankara may experience a lot of snow. Along the coast, the temperature is not very low, but there can be lots of rain during the winter.

Drugs

Illegal drugs available in Turkey include marijuana, hash, opium and
heroin. It would be best to avoid the subject entirely. The penalties
for import, export or consumption of drugs are very severe. Turkish
jails are famous world-wide for their lack of comfort. And don't expect
diplomatic help if you get into trouble!

Warning: Should you be asked by anyone to take a package home with you, be sure -
very sure - of the contents. Remember: many drug dealers work closely with the police.

Events

Camel Wrestling	- Selçuk	15-16th January
Traditional "mesir" Festival	- Manisa	21-24th May
Internat. Efes Art & Culture Festival	- Selçuk	5-12th May
Silifke Festival		20-26th May
Pamukkale Theatre Festival	- Denizli	25-27th May
International Bergama Fair		30th May-2nd June
Art & Tourism Festival	- Marmaris	8-17th June
Water Sports	- Foça	24-27th June
Tourism Theatre Festival	- Nevşehir	24-27th June
International Theatre Festival	- İstanbul	20th June-15th July
International Folk Dance Festival	- Samsun	1-31st July
Trad. Wrestling & Theatre Festival	- Edirne	1-7th July
Ihlara Theatre Festival	- Aksaray	2-6th July
Ocean Theatre Festival	- Çeşme	3-8th July
Nasrettin Hoca Theatre Festival	- Akşehir	5-10th July
Traditional Rose Competition	- Konya	7th July
International Art & Culture Festival	- Bursa	7-31st July
Trojan Theatre Festival	- Çanakkale	10-14th August
Art & Culture Festival	- Bodrum	1-7th September
Hittite Theatre Festival	- Corum	17-22nd September
International Fair and Festival	- Mersin	22nd Sept.-12th Oct
International Art Festival	- Antalya	1-9th October
St. Nicholas Theatre Festival Demre	- Antalya	3-7th Dec
Mevlana Memorial Festival	- Konya	14-17th December

Folk Dance

Every region in Turkey has a traditional costume still worn for the dance. Among the most popular:

Horon: This dance originates along the Black Sea coast and is performed by men wearing black costumes sewn with silver. The dancers move arm-in-arm to the tune of the *kemençe*, a simple stringed instrument.

Kaşik Oyunu: The "spoon dance" is popular between Konya and Silifke. Colourfully-dressed male and female dancers swing to the rhythm of pairs of spoons held in each hand.

Kiliç Kalkan: This dance with sword and shield symbolizes the Ottoman capture of the town Bursa. Men in traditional costumes dance to the rhythm of resounding swords and shields.

Zeybek: This Aegean dance is performed by men in colourful costumes, symbolizes bravery.

Halay: Performed in Erzurum, Erzincan, Urfa and Diyarbakır. Similar to "*Horon*", five male and five female dancers move slowly and deliberately to the sound of *zurna* (oboe) and *davul* (drum).

Folk Heroes

NASRETTIN HOCA: This humorist and wise man lived in the thirteenth century in Akşehir. His jokes are famous beyond the borders of Turkey. Here is just one of the stories told about him:

> One night Nasrettin Hoca is lying in bed but he can't sleep because his baby is crying. He asks his wife, "Why don't you rock the baby awhile?" She answers, "I am tired, why don't you do it?" "That is your responsibility," he calls. "The child is half yours," complains his wife. "That is true, but my half never bothers me," he answers, "Rock your half and leave mine alone!"

KARAGÖZ: The fourteenth century jester is said to have lived in Bursa. His fame continues even today as a shadow-play figure. KARAGÖZ is always able to outwit his boastful friend Hacivat. (See under Bursa).

"Greece"

Greek-Turkish relations are burdened by the weight of history. The Cyprus Crisis (see History) has intensified nationalistic feelings on both sides. Lately the conflict has spread to the Aegean. NATO member countries have been concerned about the conflict between the two member countries since 1964.

Health

There are no inoculation requirements when visiting Turkey these days. The exception would be if you are coming from a region infected with cholera. In that case you must prove your inoculation by presenting an International Health Certificate.

Preventive inoculations: Despite the regulations, it is advisable to have yourself immunized for hepatitis and polio before visiting Turkey. Even if the danger of catching hepatitis is not great in Turkey, the shot of gamagoblian strengthens the entire immune system, which gets run down by exposure to a new climate and food. The inoculation for polio lasts for seven to ten years, and is highly recommended for Turkey, since the virus is still wide spread. Be sure children have been immunized. Also recommended are tetanus shots, taken in three doses and good for ten years.

Malaria pills are advisable if you plan to visit swamp regions near Adana in summer. Beware of allergic reactions to the medication. Consult your doctor or nearest health institute.

First Aid Kit: There is little need to vary your standard kit. Antibiotics, which are available only upon prescription in western countries, are freely available in Turkey. Ask your doctor about medication against diarrhea. If you would prefer to avoid chemicals, unsweetened black tea helps against water loss. Warm soup restores lost mineral salts. If you like, try a *rehydration* beverage: a litre of water, three spoonfulls of honey, a quarter tea spoon of bicarbonate of soda and a quarter tea spoon of salt. Or try the old standard: one tea spoon dry coffee powder (Turkish mocca) and one tea spoon dry tea mixed with lemon juice. Cheers!

Don't forget something for allergies, burns, motion sickness, and water purification. Bandages are a must.

Health Insurance: Another matter to look into before you depart is health insurance. Check with your insurance company to determine if and how well you are covered while in Turkey. Information on the formalities for filing claims should not be forgotten.

Should you become ill, your consulate in Ankara can provide you with a list of doctors. Kızılay (Red Halfmoon) is the Turkish equivalent of the Red Cross. First aid in Turkish hospitals is unbureaucratic and frequently free of charge for minor ailments. Don't bother them with insurance formalities. Private doctors have a list of rates which they are certain to charge. The money you must pay for the doctor or chemist will be refunded by your insurance company at home. Be sure to get a receipt containing the stamp, date and signature of the Turkish doctor or chemist.

If you don't trust a Turkish doctor, you can visit one of the more expensive foreign hospitals in İstanbul. For extended hospital stays, it is recommended!

Addresses:

AMERICAN HOSPITAL	Güzelbahce Sok. Nisantasi, Tel. 1486030.
GERMAN HOSPITAL	Siraselviler Cad., Taksim, Tel. 1435500.
FRENCH HOSPITAL	"Pasteur": behind Hotel "Divan", Taksim, Tel. 1484756 and "La Paix", Büyükdere Cad., Sisli, Tel. 1481832
ITALIAN HOSPITAL	Defterdar Yokusu, Tophane, Tel. 1499751.

For minor ailments, it is not necessary to consult a doctor. Just visit any chemist's and get some advice. However, doctors are more likely to speak your language. Generally, any medication can be sold without prescription. Many foreign chemical companies produce medicines in Turkey or have licensed a local firm to do so. Most common products are available, although often under a different name, cheaper than imported medications.

Note: Some helpful health vocabulary can be found in the language section under "Health".

Hospitality

Talking with foreigners is one way in which Turks demonstrate their hospitality. When moving about, travelling on a bus, or in simple restaurants, it is possible that you will meet Turks who have worked abroad and might spontaneously invite you to tea or a tour of town. Sometimes they can't even speak your language, resulting in a funny conversation using hands and feet.

Sometimes the gestures of friendship can be a mite too much, particularly when it invades your privacy. In a small pension, the owner might knock on your door in the evening with a pot of tea, eager to speak your language and hear about your country. Be sure to be friendly, even if it is difficult.

Hygiene

Showers, sometimes only with cold water, are available in almost every hotel or pension. The toilets, however, frequently do not meet European standards. The squat toilet is common. Toilet paper is rare in rural areas; your own supply is recommended. A water faucet, or a jug of water, can be found on the left side of the toilet. The water is not only used for flushing, but also for cleaning the left hand which is considered the "unclean" hand in Turkey.

All your hygienic concerns will dissipate during a visit to a Turkish bath, or *hamam*. There you will be slapped, wrenched, rubbed and massaged until you feel like a new person. The procedure is as good for your health as for your cleanliness, particularly your circulation.

Import & Export Regulations

Foreign currency can be imported in any amounts. The same is true of Turkish lira, although the exchange rate is best on the domestic Turkish market. You must declare the export of more than US $3000. You may only export Turkish lira up to maximum US $1000. If at the end of your trip you have up to US $100 in Turkish lira, this can be changed without difficulty at any bank. To change back more than this amount, you will have to present the exchange slip you received from the Turkish bank when you bought Turkish lira.

It is possible to make a duty-free purchase upon arrival at İstanbul Airport. The selection, however, is modest. The duty-free shop for departures is much better stocked.

The following amounts may be imported duty free:

---

* 400 **cigarettes** or 50 **cigars** or 200 g **tobacco**.
* 1 kg **coffee** (additional 3 kg may also be imported after paying duty)
* 500 g **powdered coffee**, 1 kg **tea**, 1 kg **chocolate** or 1 kg **sweets**
* 5 l **alcoholic beverages**.
* **gifts** valued up to £175.
* portable televisions and video recorders will be noted in your passport.

You are permitted to export gifts in value up to 15,000 TL. For carpets, you will have to present the sales slip. By the way, you will have to declare carpets to customs in your home country. A tip: It is safer to have carpets shipped home.

Antique objects may be exported only with a written licence from a museum director. Antiques may not be exported. The export of tea, cocoa, coffee, and grains is also strictly prohibited, but nobody checks for tea! Minerals may only be exported with a license from the MTA institute in Ankara.

Pets: They will need to be inoculated against rabies (last shot two weeks before arrival) and an official health certificate with the confirmation dated within 48 hours of departure. Get this translated and notarized at a Turkish consulate in your country of origin, and present it upon arrival.

Vehicles: Drivers can bring in a vehicle for up to three months without customs formalities. If you plan to stay longer, you will need a Carnet de Passage from your automobile club or Turkish Touring. If you will be working or studying in Turkey, you can get a Turkish document permitting the duty-free import of your vehicle for up to five years. This law does not apply for minibuses. Upon departure, be sure that the car registration (placed in your passport upon entry) is invalidated.

In general, Turkish customs are very lax, particularly if you enter by rail or ship. Air passengers are also quickly processed. Upon departure, your luggage is frequently searched for drugs. Drivers, when leaving Turkey, can expect their vehicle to be thoroughly searched for drugs.

Mass Media

Press: Its modern form originated with the founding of the Republic. Party and commercial newspapers began in 1945. Freedom of the press is guaranteed in the new constitution. However, there are restrictions against treason, immorality, incitement, etc. There is no censorship; the police only keeps tabs on the content. Freedom of the press has been suspended in those provinces under martial law.

Newspapers are very popular in Turkey. Each day, millions of the large, colourful pages are thumbed through, crossword puzzles are solved, and scantily-dressed European beauties are stared at.

The only newspaper catering to the serious newspaper tradition is the *Cumhuriyet*, the Republic. The circulation of this paper has fallen from 500,000 to 100,000. Other papers are in the tabloid tradition, ranging from right-wing to slightly leftist. Total circulation of the tabloids is 3.5 million.

In order of circulation, the most popular paper is *Sabah* (Morning) followed by *Hürriyet* (Freedom) a left-of-centre publication. *Tan* (Morning) is into sex and violence, like many of its competitors. *Günaydın* (Good Morning) and *Bulvar* (Boulevard) lean to the left and right respectively, but both feature sex and hardcore crime. *Milliyet* (The Nation) is Social Democratic. *Tercüman* (The Translator) is the voice of the Nationalist Party - both with circulations of 200,000 to 250,000 and serious in style. *Son Havadis* is a conservative paper, while *Türkiye* is an Islamic orthodox religious paper.

The editorial offices for almost all major papers are in İstanbul. The only major regional paper is *Yeni Asır* (New Century), based in İzmir with a circulation of 200,000 daily along the Aegean coast.

Foreign visitors will be primarily interested in the Ankara-based Turkish Daily, published in English, available in all major Turkish cities. Foreign newspapers are available, several days late.

Radio: In 1964 a state-run program was inaugurated, *Türkiye Radyo Televizyon Kurumu / TRT*, using the BBC as a model. It offers domestic programs and a foreign service in 15 languages, in addition to monitoring local broadcasts. Two stations, TRT 1 and TRT 2, are broadcast on AM and long-wave.

Television: State-run TRT-TV was started in Ankara in 1968. Televisions are the most commonly used electric device in the country. Foreign travellers will enjoy the commercials, many of which are known from home.

Video is very popular in Turkey. Tea gardens offer television to attract crowds. A clever inn-keeper with the right selection of tapes can sweep 100 m of beach clean, even on a hot afternoon. What is a pleasant swim compared to a horror film?

Military

The Turkish military sees itself as the protector of Atatürk's legacy. In 1980 the military got tired of watching the politicians and seized power for itself. By November 1987 the situation was stabilized and the military was willing to permit free elections. The clear victor was the Justice Party led by Özal. General Evren, who led the coup d'etat, remains Prime Minister until 1989.

Military patrols, equipped with megaphones and machine guns, are common. In provinces under martial law, banks and government offices are well guarded; law and order is ensured by military presence.

Turkish men are required to perform 18 months of military service. There is no such thing as draft resistance in Turkey. By paying £7300 it is possible, however, to attend only the three-month basic training. Turkey is NATO's eastern flank, sharing a common border with the Soviet Union.

Tip: Be friendly to the soldiers! The Turkish army is well respected by the local population. If you talk to an off-duty soldier or jandarma, you may make a friend for life. Most likely he is far from his home and grateful for human contact.

Money

The Turkish national currency is the Turkish lira (TL), sometimes referred to as the Turkish pound. A lira is divided into 100 kuruş, which are only of historical interest today. Due to inflation, there is nothing for sale for less than 5 TL. There are no kuruş coins.

Coins are denominated in 5 TL and 10 TL, plus paper money of 50 TL, 100 TL, 1000 TL, 5000 TL and 10,000 TL. Coins are rarely seen.

Measured in European terms, Turkey is a cheap country to visit. If you are satisfied with a minimum of comfort, you can survive on £7 to £10 per day.

Changing Money: No problem at any bank or exchange booth. At the end of 1987 the rate was 1000 TL for £0.60, £1 gets you about 1620

TL. Exchanging money at home is less advantageous, as the best rates are offered in Turkey.

Note: The lira exchange rates are fixed in October, which means they are adjusted to the rate of inflation. The results are a further devaluation of the Turkish lira and rising prices for the locals. Always change money for only a few days at a time as the exchange rate always fluctuates.

Eurocheques & Traveller's Cheques: There are occasional problems. Not every branch office is authorized to accept them. In some major cities, you will have to visit several banks before you can get a check cashed. Plus there are a number of forms to be filled out (done by the bank clerk using your passport, you only have to sign). There is no difficulty in tourist areas along the coast. Sometimes the exchange rate is better for checks than for cash.

There is not much of a *black market* for money since the official exchange rate is reasonable. However, occasionally an İstanbul taxi driver or a private individual will ask to exchange money. Sometimes these people work for the police.

Mosques

Mosques are Islamic churches with a major difference: they are not considered sacred houses of God as in Christianity; they serve only for prayers to Allah. At prayer time, the *muezzin* (prayer caller) climbs the *minaret* (tower) and calls the faithful to prayer. In front of the mosque are the *sadirvan* (fountains or faucets) for ritual cleansing before the prayer. The mosque interior is practically empty. Carpets or straw mats cover the floor. A niche in the wall, the *mihrab*, points the direction to Mecca. Near the *mihrab* is the *minbar*, the preacher's chair. On Friday afternoon, the *minbar* is used for a formal sermon. Of course most Muslims pray at less elaborate sites than the ornate and extravagant great mosques.

There are two categories of mosques: the *ulu cami* (Friday mosques) and the smaller *Mescid*. Usually, only the *ulu cami* have a *mihrab* and *minbar*, since Friday services are held here. Not every *mescid* has a minaret, but a *ulu cami* will often have several.

The great mosques maintain a complex of buildings (*külliye*), which perform services offered by mosques since the beginning of Islam. These include the Koran school, library, guesthouse and *medrese* (theological college). Once upon a time, no külliye was complete without a kitchen for the poor, a hospital and a public fountain. The *türbe* (tomb, frequently of the mosque's founder) and the cemetery are also parts of the *külliye*.

Mosques are open to Non-Muslims - only at prayer time are tourists sent away. Should you visit a mosque at prayer time, keep quiet and off to the side; don't take pictures! Keep the dress code in mind: men should not show their arms or legs. A woman's dress should cover at least the knees and women should cover their heads (kerchief) and upper arms. Some of the popular mosques in İstanbul provide suitable clothing. Women should keep in mind that while they are required to wear a kerchief in a mosque, it is prohibited in government offices.

Moustache

You rarely see a Turkish man who does not sport fuzz under his nose. Whether bushy and luxurious or thin and functional, the banner of male pride is always tended to with loving care. For good reason: it is the moustache which makes a man a real man. Even today in many villages, the elder moustache wearers keep watch to ensure that no youngster sprouts growth before his time. It must be shaved until the youth is recognized as a man by age. This tradition has lessened in major cities. By the way: Turkish soldiers, who you see everywhere, never wear a moustache. For good reason: the Turkish army is infiltrated by lice.

Museums

Turkey is a land of many cultures. Museums have been established throughout the country to display finds unearthed at countless excavation sites. Depending upon the region, you will find monumental Hittite sculptures alongside Hellenist reliefs. Bronze Roman senators are set up alongside original Ottoman furniture. Every town of importance has an Atatürk Museum. There is lots and lots to see, but don't come on a Monday when museums are closed. More info (opening hours, admission fees etc.) in the local sections.

> **ATTENTION!** The latest news: the governement in Ankara has drastically hiked up **admission fees** for museums, mosques etc. in 1989! Calculate about 5 - 10 times the prices given in this edition (depending upon the fame of the sights; for instance: admission for Hagia Sophia rose from £0.30 up to £3 !)

Opening Hours

Banks: Monday to Friday 8:30-12:00 and 13:30-17:00 h, Saturdays and Sundays only at international airports and Sirkeci Railway Station (İstanbul).

Government Offices: Closed on Saturdays and Sundays; open weekdays 8:30-12:00 h and 13:00-17:30 h.

Shops: Open Monday to Friday 9:00-13:00 h and 14:00-19:00 h; Saturdays 9:00-13:00 h. Smaller shops keep their own hours - e.g. are open later than 19:00 h or don't open until 10:00 h.

Post Office: Open weekdays 8:30-12:00 h and 13:00-17:00 h; closed on weekends. In major cities some postal services (telephone) are accessable until 24:00 h and on Sundays from 9:00-19:00 h.

Photography / Filming

You will frequently be requested to take a picture of children posing with their friends. Women, however, rarely want to be photographed. Always ask permission and practice discretion. Female photographers have the best chance of receiving permission.

Men are proud to be photographed, but the spontaneity is lost completely when they strike their poses. For this reason, carry a tele-photo lens.

Be sure to bring enough film from home. Be careful about taking pictures of military installations. It is considered a serious matter, particularly on the border to Greece.

"That will be 10.000 Lira."

Police

The police and army are present everywhere in Turkey. Even the tiniest village will have a "*Jandarma*" station. The actual police - *polis* -

keep traffic moving, patrol on foot and in squad cars, taking care of minor offences. The *polis* officers (male and female) can be recognized by their green uniforms and white hats. When a squad car drives slowly through town with lights and siren flashing, it is their simple way of saying "Don't do anything foolish; we are here." (or so explained a Turkish friend).

Belediye Zabitasi wear blue uniforms and keep watch in towns. Tourists will rarely encounter them, unlike shopkeepers and market dealers. The "city watchmen" patrol shops and markets, ensuring proper measure of weights and quality of wares.

Jandarma are military-style units which handle security and combat crime. Jandarmas, patrolling the streets, wear green uniforms with steel helmets (no matter what the weather is like) plus a red armband with the word "Jandarma".

Tip: Always be friendly to the officers!

Post Office

Yellow signs with black lettering "PTT" (*posta, telefon, telegraf*) mark mailboxes and post offices. The General Post Office ("*Merkez Postahane*") is usually around the main square or, in major towns, in the banking or business quarter. In İstanbul it is in Eminönü; in İzmir at the harbour (Atatürk Cad.). You can receive mail addressed to you for holding at the main post offices in this manner:

Family Name, Christian Name
Postrestante
Merkez Postahane
City
Turkey

At the window, you must present your passport to receive mail.

Postal Charges: A 10 g airmail letter to England costs £0.17; airmail postcards cost £0.15. A telegram costs £0.10 per word including the address.

Student Discounts

Wonderful! Just present an ISIC, IYHC, YIEE or FIYTO card for discounts of up to 60 per cent. Students should consider their international student ID as important as their toothbrush and passport.

Cheaper By Air: On flights throughout Europe, THY (Turkish Airlines) offers discounts of 25 per cent for youths under 22 years and 60 per cent for students under 28 years. Students of any age receive a

10 per cent discount on all domestic flights. On flights between
Turkey and all Near Eastern or Middle Eastern countries, youths
under 26 and students up to 31 receive discounts of 50 per cent; to
Cairo 55 per cent.

Cheaper By Rail: The Turkish Railway (TCDD) offers students a
10 per cent discount on all domestic tickets. Frequently the ticket
clerks in small towns have never heard of the discount. There is no
problem getting discount tickets in İstanbul, İzmir and Ankara. Avoid
the hassle with a round-trip ticket.

Cheaper By Sea: Turkish Maritime Lines offers a 10 per cent discount on international routes to Italy, Cyprus and Syria; 25 per cent
on coastal ships and a 50 per cent discount on the Van Lake ferry in
eastern Turkey.

Also Cheaper: Museums, cinemas and theatres offer 50 per cent
student discounts. Several national bus companies offer student
discounts of 10-25 per cent.

Tip: To avoid difficulty getting your discount, consider buying a Turkish student ID.
Every ticket agent between the Bosporus and Ararat will be able to read it, if he or she
is able to read. The Turkish ID is issued in İstanbul at the TMGT office (İstiklal Cad. 471).
Also available at the Ankara office.

Few questions are asked when purchasing an international student
ID at the Student Tourist Office, Babiali Cad. 40, Caçaoçu, in
İstanbul. Any type of student registration form is accepted. Across
from the Blue Mosque in İstanbul, in the "Pudding Shop", counterfeit
student IDs are sold.

Swimming

Men in bathing trunks will have no problems. Women, however, must
keep in mind that a scimpy bikini might attract undue attention.
Swimming in the nude is improper for both sexes. Never assume that
a beach is isolated and lonely. The orient is full of hidden eyes, and
local people are always interested in what foreigners are doing, especially in isolated regions. If you are caught swimming in the nude, expect a jail term and a heavy fine (see Religion).

A word for women travelers: A scene repeatedly seen on tourist
beaches: a bare-breasted European woman gets a tan while Turkish
swimming trunks develop noticeable bulges. Turkish women try not
to look, and keep their curious children at a safe distance. The moral:
Turkey is not France. Nudism may have its place in Western Europe,
but Turkish culture has a very different interpretation for it. For
Turks, a naked woman is absolute filth, although, for some, very
desirable filth. By the way, rape is the most common violent crime in
Turkey, followed by murder.

Taboos

Books dealing with the following topics are not permitted to be imported into Turkey: Armenians, Kurds, political literature opposing the ruling party in Turkey, violations of human rights. For this reason readers won't be given information about the repression of political opposition and the persecution of ethnic minority leaders in this book. The result would be one less book permissible for importation into Turkey, namely this one.

Telephone

In the post offices there are telephone booths which require special coins (*jeton*). Regular coins are not accepted. Direct-dialling is possible in major cities and several tourist communities along the Aegean and Mediterranean coasts.

There is also an operator-assisted system. No matter what system you use, telephoning takes time. The best time to make a call home is in the early morning around 6:00 h. Long queues form in front of phone booths throughout Turkey.

If you are still determined to try the adventure, buy one or more **jetons** at any post office. The smaller jetons cost £0.08 and are good for a local call. The larger ones cost £0.25 and are used for long-distance calls. Now join the queue in front of a phone booth and wait. Once inside, insert a jeton in the slot. With older phones you throw in the jeton after the called number answers. Never throw in more than one jeton because the machines occasionally just eat the money. Keep trying until you get through. Unused jetons can be cashed in at the post office.

Telephones with which you can dial international calls direct are marked "*Milletlerarasi*".

Tipping

The oriental term for tipping is "*Baksheesh*" ("bahsis"). The term's many meanings include a donation to a beggar (obligatory for all Muslims) but also a payment for a special service. Baksheesh is much more prevalent in Turkey than in the west, particularly as an incentive.

These days in İstanbul, baksheesh is sought right on the streets. Normally a small tip is expected for a service, but never demanded. In addition to money, Western or American cigarettes make a valued tip. Don't be surprised if they disappear, unsmoked, into a pocket. They bring a good price on the black market.

The lust for baksheesh in Turkey has still not reached Egyptian proportions. In Cairo thousands of people live from performing small services like opening a taxi door! These hidden unemployed are not contained in official statistics. The acquisition of tips is their means of survival and their "profession".

Traditional sports

Yağli Güreş (oil wrestling): Every year the national championships of Turkey's most popular sport are held in Kirkpinar (near Edirne). Before the fun begins, the wrestlers rub themselves with oil, making a firm grip very difficult. Still, there is lots of violence. Heavy bruises, scrapes and broken bones are part of the risk. At local festivals, wrestling matches are often part of the entertainment.

Deve Güreşi (camel fights): Every year, in villages along the Mediterranean, camel stallions are matched against each other until one proves its dominance. In order to prevent serious injury, camels, these days, are usually muzzled.

Cirit Oyunu (capturing the spear): In eastern Turkey, daring horsemanship is demonstrated by two teams, each trying to capture a spear. These competitions are now becoming rare.

Travelling With Children

Except for the children, it is quite pleasant. As a travelling parent you are treated like royalty. Turkey is a true children's paradise, where spoiling children has a great tradition. Whether your child uses a restaurant plate as a frisbee or screams its heart out on a bus, nobody will mind. The broken pieces will be swept up with a smile and the child comforted. Its head will be stroked and it will be treated to a piece of melon. Or a sweet or a biscuit. That is the only problem: you might return home with a fat child that's used to getting sweets all the time.

Certainly children have more difficulty on long rides than adults. Keep them in mind when planning your itinerary. And bring along a pram, capable of surviving difficult terrain.

Women Travellers

The position of women in Turkey, thanks to Atatürk's reforms, cannot be compared with Arab countries. Still, daily life is dominated by men. This means that European women, travelling alone, will be confronted with a number of problems. Women are approached on the street, in tea houses or in restaurants. Many men cannot understand why a woman should be travelling alone. It is possible that the men are just curious, but often they have other motives. European advertising and films have led many Turkish men to believe that all European women are out for an erotic adventure. Turkish newspapers support these cliches (see Media). Reports of success by beach gigolos in the tourist centres have been spread throughout the entire Turkish male community.

Women travelling alone are advised to stay in *Ayle* hotels or pensions. They will not attract as much attention in these family accommodations as in regular hotels which are male domains. Any hotel will give information as to where to find the nearest Ayle-hotel.

The wrong dress - no bra, clinging T-shirts, tight jeans, short skirts - all support the theory that a woman travelling alone is just out for one thing. We recommend "demure" dress, avoiding eye contact with .nen and keeping your distance. Perhaps the simplest solution is to travel with a male companion.

Work

Foreigners are not permitted to work for pay in Turkey. If you are not interested in money but in intensifying your relationship with Turkish people by working with them, ask for work in any town. Skilled workers have the best chance of finding work, but don't expect anything beyond room and board.

SHOPPING & BARGAINING

"I'd like a magic carpet, but at a good price." Or would you prefer a bottle containing a genie? How about a magic ring to make you invisible? Open Sesame: you can find whatever you want in a Turkish bazaari.

Admittedly, genuine magic items are not for sale. But if you have a sense of humour and ask politely for any of the above, you are likely to be drawn into an entertaining conversation. If you want to spend some money, but can't really decide what to buy, visit a bazaar (*çarşi*). In these oriental department stores you can find car tires, food, furniture, household appliances, baby pacifiers and more.

In a *çarşi* you will meet carpet makers from the far-east of Turkey or tea merchants from the fertile Black Sea coast. The Turkish word *bazar* actually means a vegetable market where the stands are removed from time to time.

What you buy is much less important than how you acquire it. Bargaining applies to more than the wares, it also takes in all services. Before starting on a taxi ride, be sure to bargain the price before departure. The same applies to a tour through an archaeological site.

Usually you will not bargain in stores where the prices are already marked on the items, e.g. grocery stores.

Some souvenir shops mark their items with prices or claim to have fixed prices. These original prices are usually so high that even after intensive bargaining, the price is still higher than elsewhere. If you intend to buy a major item, check prices in a number of shops. This will take time, but it pays off in the end.

Rules of the Game

There are a few basic rules to keep in mind when bargaining: first and foremost, it is considered very rude not to buy an item after arriving at a bargained price. On the other hand there is no obligation to buy, even after drinking many cups of tea provided by the shop keeper. It is usual to invite customers to tea. The merchant will offer the foreigner several prices and ask the customer what he is willing to pay. If you are not interested in making a purchase, never name a price or agree to one. In the first case the bargaining has begun in earnest; in the second case the sale may already be legally concluded!

Bargaining for souvenirs is traditional. Every region has its own momentos. In Cappadocia, alabaster is very popular. The stone is worked into vases, bowls, ashtrays, etc. Carpets from Cappadocia are also often bought as souvenirs. But many other regions have excellent carpets. Each region is known for particular colour combinations and patterns.

If you are not a carpet expert, try to appear like one when making a purchase. An expert glance at the size of the knots and questions as to the number of knots per square centimeter will convey a good impression. Take the carpet out into the sunlight. Separate the threads to see if they are colourfast. Then the dealer will know that you are an expert.

If you want a leather souvenir, check along the Mediterranean coast. İzmir is famous for its leather goods. Other items of interest include copperware (particularly good in İstanbul), meerschaum pipes from Eskişehir, ceramics (tiles), jewellery and inlay work. In the Egyptian Bazaar you can pick up cheap sponges, tea, perfume and spices. These are everyday articles with fixed prices.

A carpetweaver near Burdur

PARTICIPATION SPORTS

Sailing

Lovely scenery, ideal weather and a wealth of historical sites right by the ocean makes Turkey a great place to cruise.

Foreign yachts may sail Turkish waters for only three months without importation formalities. You may receive permission from Turkish customs to extend your boat's stay for an additional three months. Ships which want to dock in a Turkish harbour must report to the harbour master and process papers with the proper authorities.

In Bodrum, Çeşme, Kuşadası, Marmaris, İstanbul or İzmir, you can rent a yacht. Prices vary according to season and comfort. Expect to pay £80 per day or more for charter fee, fuel, crew, and harbour tax. Provisions will be purchased locally for an additional fee.

The best season for yachting or sailing vacations along the Aegean and Mediterranean coasts is May to October. In July and August, beware of the *"meltem"*, a northeast wind which usually rises in the afternoon bringing high seas. During the rest of the year, watch out for the *"imbat"*, a wind which rises between 16:00 and 17:00 h.

A navigation chart at a scale of 1:100,000 costs £2 per page and can be ordered at the following address:

T.C. Deniz Kuvvetteri Komutanliği
Seyir, Hidrografi ve Oşinografi
Dairesi Baskanliği
Çubuklu-İstanbul/Turkey.

The chart shows dangerous reefs which should not be ignored when anchoring in inlets. The number of *marinas* is increasing each year. Their facilities can be compared with those in Europe.

Skin diving, Snorkeling, Surfing

Blubb, blubb, blubb, he's gone. You may skin dive off almost every stretch of coast. But removal of historical objects and treasure hunting is strictly prohibited.

Air compressors and tanks are not permitted. But if you just plan to snorkel or have amateur diving equipment (air tank, wet suit, mask, etc.) in order to do some underwater photography, you usually won't have any problem. You can refill your air tanks in many beach villages.

There is no difficulty importing or exporting surf boards, either by car or air. If you plan to rent a board in Turkey, a number of surfing schools scattered along the coast will be happy to serve you. But don't expect the latest models.

Skiing, Hiking and Mountain Climbing

Turkey is a wonderful place to spend a winter vacation. The mountains rise above 3000 m, and the lift lines are much shorter than in the Alps.

The best known ski region is around Bursa on the *Sea of Marmara*. The season here and elsewhere in Turkey is from January to April. The Après-Ski facilities (Hotels, Bars, Restaurants) measure up to those in the Alps. The sporting challenge (slopes of varying difficulty) is good.

Other ski regions include *Antalya-Saklikent* and *Bolu-Köroglu*. The facilities are standard: ski schools, lifts and rentals.

Hiking: During the warm seasons of the year, Turkey's national parks offer lovely scenery. The weather is uniformly good. On overnight excursions you can pitch a tent at campsites. Ask at any Turkish Tourist Office for a list of national parks.

Mountain Climbing: Turkish Tourist Offices provide tips for mountain climbers. The most enchanting mountains are in central and eastern Anatolia. Mount Ararat and the Cilo Sat peaks may not be climbed by foreigners without a guide, but you may join a group of Turkish climbers.

For detailed information contact the *Turkish Alpine Club*:

Dağcilik Federasyonu
B.T.G.M., Ulus İşhani, A-Blok
Ulus-Ankara / Turkey
Tel. 124150-328.

The *Turkish Ski Club* (Kayak Federasyonu) has an office in the same building (Tel. 124150/329).

LODGINGS

Plans call for mass tourism to bring much-needed foreign currency into Turkey in addition to providing jobs. In recent years there has been a real boom in the tourist industry, whose guests have to sleep somewhere.

The number of lodgings is tremendous and increasing year by year. The number of beds has been systematically expanded since 1963. The variety of establishments and luxury standards is also large.

You will find everything from luxury hotels charging £180 per night to bus station dives which let you in for just £1. Hotels with good to excellent standards can be found in the major cities (İstanbul, İzmir and Ankara), along the Aegean and Mediterranean coasts and in Cappadocia, Konya or Pamukkale. At Turkish Tourist Offices around the world you can receive a list of hotels registered with the Ministry of Culture and Tourism. Local tourist offices will have additional addresses which also meet quality requirements.

Turkish Tourist Offices can provide information about holiday villages along the coast. Club Mediterranée has facilities in Foça, Kuşadası and Kemer.

In İstanbul the Tourist Office has registered 70 hotels. They range from the HILTON to the SULTAN HOTEL in the old town. The metropol on the Bosporus certainly offers much more than "only" 70 hotels. There are numerous smaller pensions unknown to the ministry, but still clean. Here you will pay much less per night. Major hotels and hotel chains charge £25 and up per night in season. Prices are lower from September to May.

Pensions: Calculate £3.50 for a double along the coast, rising to £6 during high season. Don't expect a "Hilton" or "Sheraton" in this price range. You can, however, expect a friendly atmosphere, hospitable service and contact with local people. During the summer, many middle-class Turkish families spend their holidays in a pension.

Single rooms are not always available, but a discounted double will be offered. Triple-bed rooms and suites with space for a large family are common in regions frequented by Turkish tourists.

Almost every Turkish village, no matter how isolated or distant from the tourist trail, will have a small hotel offering rooms with shower/WC for just a few lira. If you aren't choosy, a room can be had for just £1. Such establishments will have the shower/WC in the hallway. Showers are usually available, but often cold. For a warm shower in cheap Turkish hotels, you will generally have to pay an additional fee.

Backpackers who are careful with their money will find Turkey an ideal country. Be sure to inspect the room offered in advance. Check whether the room can be locked, the bed is made with clean sheets and whether the shower functions properly.

Tourists who want to relax should get a room in the middle or upper category. The cheaper rooms are not comfortable for long-term stays.

Hotels and pensions are divided into several categories. From luxury to dive, the price usually fits what is offered. It is sometimes possible to bargain in the smaller cheap lodgings, but it is not looked upon favorably.

Tip: If a hotel has an adjoining restaurant, the food is usually uninspiring and expensive. This is not always the case in the best hotels. And keep in mind that bed bugs do not discriminate between luxury hotels and cheap pensions. (Islamic fatalism is required in respect to these beasts).

Youth Hostels: There are no official IYHF establishments in Turkey. Still, the Tourist Office can suggest a few addresses. These are actually student dorms which rent rooms during school holidays for £3 and up (too expensive). Since the "hostels" are away from the centre of towns, downtown pensions are preferable. Usually these hostels are open in July and August. Student dorms can be found in İstanbul, İzmir, Canakkale, Bursa, Bolu and Ankara. For more info, check with the Tourist Office.

Camp Grounds: The Ministry of Culture and Tourism is keeping watch here as well. The number of sites around the country is limited. The days of nomadic caravans is past. Western tourists introduced this type of holiday. A list of camp grounds can be obtained from any Turkish Tourist Office, or check in this book under the local sections. Licenced sites are situated along the coast (Marmara / Aegean / Mediterranean) and in Cappadocia. The BP-Mocamps meet European standards. Showers (warm water), kitchen facilities, electricity, restaurants and sometimes supermarkets are part of the standards. Occasionally you will find a swimming pool or discotheque. The better camp grounds are relatively expensive. The BP-Mocamps charge £5, otherwise calculate just £1 per person (plus £1 for your car or tent), varying with the length of stay and facilities offered. Most of the guests will be European.

Private camp grounds usually cater to Turkish campers since they are cheaper (£0.30 to £1.50) and below European standards. Westerners may not consider the hygiene up to par. Water is often collected from a well. Electric lights and showers have not yet been invented. Cleaning toilets or removing trash are unpopular, and don't expect shade. The sites were set up without great care and are hopelessly crowded during the Turkish summer holidays.

In recent years the numbers of such camp sites have increased as ever more Turkish families discover the pleasures of camping by the ocean. There are no lists of these sites as the tourist offices either don't know about them or consider them to be below standard. We list them under the respective local sections.

Only a few of the Mocamps are open year round.

Wilderness Camping: Try to avoid it. Alternatives are picnic areas (found in many national parks) where you will find trash cans, picnic tables, fireplaces and toilets.

Food and Drink - Refreshment

"The Imam fainted" when he was served "Women's Thighs" and "The Lady's Navel". "The sultan enjoyed it", when he was served the "Finger of the Vizier". You could write whole novels just using the names of Turkish dishes. They certainly show the great tradition and imagination of Turkish cooks.

In fact, Turkish cooking is an art of its own, equal without doubt to the French cuisine. It is based on the use of fresh vegetables, many of which are unfamiliar to Europeans. The spices used are not mysterious oriental treasures, but ordinary things like onions, peppers, tomatoes and parsley. Garlic, too, is used, but by no means in the quantities some would imagine. The usage of salt and pepper is measured to enhance, rather than bury, the taste of the ingredients.

In Turkey you can go out to eat in a *restoran*, a *locanta* or a *kebapçı*. A restoran offers nicer furnishings and a larger selection of food. It also has a liquor license. There is little difference, however, in the quality of the food compared with locantas or kebapçıs. It is not normal to look into the kitchen for a personal talk with the cook in a restoran, but you can ask the waiter to convey special requests to the kitchen. In cities, there is little difference between a restoran and locanta. Locantas (meat and seafood) and kebapçıs (only meat dishes) usually do not have a liquor license. Service is usually quick; the cash register is often at the exit. The food is good and cheap. You can select from a variety of pre-cooked dishes. You will almost always be asked to follow the waiter into the kitchen where you may ask to sample small portions of various dishes before making your selection.

The furnishings of locantas/kebapçıs are simple; linoleum floors and plastic table covers remind you of a canteen rather than a restaurant. Locantas/kebapçıs cater primarily to working people wanting to have a quick lunch or dinner.

A regular meal in Turkey will always include fresh water (*su*) and bread (*ekmek*). The water served in a locanta or kebapçı can usually be drunk safely. Bread is usually white bread or Turkish bread (a fresh, oval or round, flat white bread, often sprinkled with sesame seed) in which some dishes are rolled and served as a sort of sandwich.

Breakfast

Not every hotel includes breakfast in the room price. Many small hotels and pensions do not even have the facilities to serve breakfast. The standard breakfast includes fresh white bread, jam, butter, olives, sheep's cheese and tea. Variations are possible: you might get honey instead of jam or hot milk instead of tea. Coffee is not traditional. Local specialties: *pekmez* (thickened grape juice) is spread on bread with *tahin* (sesame-seed). You won't find ham or bacon on a Turkish breakfast table, nor eggs - they are too expensive. They can be purchased, however, in grocery stores or at the market.

The large hotels in tourist regions usually serve only a continental breakfast with coffee, cold meat and eggs.

Snacks

"**Kebap**" is the magic word with which you can do no wrong in a Turkish locanta. What is "Kebap"? Lamb, sometimes grilled or baked.

Döner Kebap consists of lamb roasted on a vertical spit, sliced off in strips. It is prepared by specially trained cooks, as skill is required to cut the meat from the spit with a sharp knife into thin strips.

Şiş Kebap are small pieces of lamb grilled on charcoal. Both Döner and Şiş are served with rice. If you trust your intestines, you might order a salad. This should either be made of spicy vegetables, or be liberally spiced in order to increase the strength of your stomach juices (to kill bacteria).

Rice (*pilav*): Both long-grained rice and brown (wild rice) are served. Often the two types will be mixed. Pilav is served at almost every meal in Turkey. Potatoes are occasionally seen.

"*Orman Kebabı*" is usually accompanied by potatoes. These are served with lamb and vegetables (e.g. tomatoes) in a clear meat broth. "*Patlican Kebabı*" is eggplant served with lamb. The eggplant is grilled over charcoal and served with the meat. Before eating, you must remove the burned (and therefore bitter-tasting) skin from the eggplant. You roll up the pulp of the eggplant and the pieces of lamb in a piece of Turkish bread and eat it with your hands. You can order a side dish of rice, although this is not normally done as *Patlıcan Kebabı* is a very messy affair.

Stuffed Vegetables: *Peppers* or *tomatoes* are stuffed with rice and ground meat. Also stuffed are *eggplant* and *zucchini*, the taste varying greatly as each cook has a secret recipe.

Fish: If you want to enjoy seafood in İstanbul, go to the fishmongers at the Atatürk and Galata Bridges - they sell fresh grilled fish right off their boats. The fish is taken from three seas (the Sea of Marmara, the Black Sea and the Aegean).

In the larger cities, "**Büfe**" stands for fast food. In İstanbul, around Sirkeci station, there are countless "Büfesi" serving sandwiches much like in Britain, only toasted. Or try some of the pastry. "*Lahmacun*" is a spicy pizza made of soft batter, with meat and tomatoes plus various spices. Obviously a Büfe would not be complete without refreshing drinks including fruit juices, lemonade or Coca Cola.

Full Meals

In any locanta, you can order a small meal of rice served with meat and vegetables, bread and water. For a full meal, Turks patronize restaurants with higher standards. Tourists may have difficulty finding such spots as they are often located in sections of town not frequented by foreigners.

We begin with an *appetizer*, perhaps a pastry with cheese and olives. Inexperienced guests should not eat too much of this appetizer as it is quite filling. Also popular are stuffed vine leaves served warm or cold.

Now we have a good basis for enjoying the second course. Along the coast, consider *seafood*. As travellers can frequently make little of Turkish names, you are invited to have a look in the kitchen to pick out a fish. Frequently served are *bass*, *plaice*, and *sardines*. *Tuna* is also served in a number of styles. In order to avoid a surprise, you can ask for the price in advance, a common procedure in Turkey.

Meat eaters can choose between a number of types of kebap in the better restaurants. Usually these are named for their "creator" or the town from which the recipe originates. Some examples are *Adana Kebabı, Bursa Kebabı* or *Urfa Kebabı.*

Adana Kebabı is very spicy, with lots of peppers and paprika. *Bursa Kebabı* only earns its name if yoghurt and tomato paste are mixed together with meat on Turkish bread.

Travellers are frequently astonished by *İskembeci*, which in addition to numerous indiscernible soups offer a number of other delicacies: grilled intestines, boiled sheeps' head, or roasted testicles.
As the third and last course, dessert is served.
Servings are generally small. But as a meal consists of several courses, each of which takes time, don't worry about starving.

Dessert

If you like it sweet, Turkey is the place for you! Start with *helva* (Turkish honey), also popular in Greece, and go on from there.

You can sample many of the delicacies without eating a meal first. Specialty shops lure passers-by with their seductive scents. In a **Muhallebici** you can enjoy all sorts of pudding for just a few lira. We especially liked *keskül*, the almond pudding, but there are also other flavors (vanilla etc.) available.The puddings are frequently soaked in syrup and topped with pistachio or grated coconut.

You can also get sweets in a **Tatlıcı**. Be sure to try the *baklava* which is super sweet. It is a sort of puff pastry with almonds, pistachios, and other nuts in between the layers. The rectangles are covered with syrup made of sugar, lemon juice and honey and served slightly warmed. There are so many different types of sweets that we can only cover a few. We suggest you visit a pastry shop or café and let yourself be surprised.

Turkey's *fruit* also makes a great dessert, ranging from melons in summer to citrus fruit in winter. Of course you can also find citrus fruit in the summer. In addition to melons, oranges, apples and grapes, you can enjoy bananas along the Mediterranean coast.

Be careful when selecting fruit. Today's pleasure might be tomorrow's stomach ache. Wash all fruit thoroughly, or better, skin it! Some books even advise boiling all fruit but that is slightly over the top and difficult to arrange. Be sure to be careful.

Drinks

Tea: There is no doubt that *çay* is the Turkish national drink. Çay is served everywhere: in the waiting room of the bus terminal, in carpet shops as a pleasant gesture during bargaining, or in the tea gardens frequented by men.

Turkish çay is black tea grown on plantations along the Black Sea coast, but available throughout the country. In the tea gardens it is brewed in samovars (*"semafer"*) and poured into 10 cm tall, bulbous glasses (*küçük çayı*) and hot water is added to the tea extract. Note: if you hold the glass at the top, you can drink without burning your fingers. A glass of tea usually costs £0.04 to £0.07.

Coffee: The famous Turkish mocca is still available, but it is no longer considered the Turkish national drink. Since the Ottoman Empire lost its possessions on the Arabian Peninsula, the cost of coffee has risen continuously, placing it beyond the means of the average population.

Should you be invited to visit a Turkish household, a small jar of Nescafé is a welcome gift which is difficult to procure in Turkey. So bring some along from home.

Water/Juices: Turkey's wells are famous for their excellent and pleasant-tasting water, noted for its healing powers. In restaurants water is placed on the table in large tin jugs so you can't tell where it comes from. You should be careful, but the danger of diarrhea is no greater than with other drinks. Sometimes you will be served water in sealed (safer) bottles. Additionally, you can find carbonated mineral water (only in 0.3 l bottles), lemonade and Coca Cola.

Fruit juices are almost always diluted with water and artificially sweetened these days. Depending upon the season, you can find street vendors selling fresh-pressed orange or grapefruit juice very cheaply. You can see for yourself that only pure juice reaches the glass.

Sour-tasting, but refreshing, is *ayran*, a drink of yoghurt, salt and cold water, served everywhere in glasses or metal goblets.

Alcoholic Beverages: Although the Koran prohibits the drinking of alcohol, large amounts of the hard stuff are consumed in Turkey. First off we should mention *rakı* which at 100 proof can put a whole crowd in a good mood. Rakı is an aniseed liquor, tasting strongly of liquorice, similar to Greek ouzo or Arabian arrak. Most Turks drink it diluted with water which gives the clear rakı a milky colour. Rakı is traditionally served only at meals. After every sip you chase it with water from an accompanying glass. It is almost an art to drink: a master rakı drinker will not get drunk, even after several glasses. Confirmed rakı drinkers believe it is a cure-all for any ailment. So there is always a reason to enjoy rakı.

Less powerful and less well known is Turkish *wine*. "Tekel", a state-owned monopoly, produces wine in several price categories. The most important wine-producing region is Cappadocia. The best-known table wine is "Güzel Marmara". Restaurants serve wines from private vineyards (Doluca and Kavaklıdere) including the white wine "Villa Doluca".

Many Turks consider themselves to be *beer* drinkers. Not every locanta will serve beer, but it can be arranged to please a guest. In some towns you can even find a beer garden, often lovely with a pleasant atmosphere. But the revival of Islamic fundamentalism has left its mark: today many pubs, including beer gardens, no longer serve beer.

There are three basic types of beer in Turkey. *Efes-Pilsen* is brewed in Turkey under the direction of European master brewers. The Danish *Tuborg* is widely sold throughout Turkey. Also brewed in Turkey, it is more bitter than Efes. And, of course, "Tekel" brews its own "*bira*", an insipid, foamless beverage which cannot compare with the two above. For a higher price you can get international brews, including Löwen-bräu, Düsseldorfer Spaten etc., but only in the cities.

GETTING AROUND IN TURKEY

By Air

"Welcome aboard the plane. In just a few minutes we will be taking off for Kayseri; our flight time will be about two hours. Captain Hizmet Güler has received the weather report: the temperature in Kayseri is 27 degrees Celsius. Please fasten your seat belts and extinguish your cigarettes!"

Turkish Airlines (Türk Hava Yolları - THY) provides more extensive service to the less developed eastern parts of the country than to the west where transportation via roads, railways and shipping is no problem.

Modern DC 9s, Boeing 727s and Airbus 310s connect İstanbul, Ankara and İzmir several times daily.

İstanbul is the centre for Turkey's international flights, while on domestic flights you must usually change planes in Ankara, the hub with connections throughout the Turkish route system. Smaller centres, with domestic service bypassing Ankara, include İzmir, İstanbul, Adana, Antalya and Dalaman.

The airstrip on northern Cyprus is served exclusively by Kibris Turkish Airlines, a 100% subsidiary.

Air traffic in the east is often delayed in winter due to snow and ice. Even Ankara can be affected. During the summer, some flights are booked up for weeks in advance.

Tickets are cheap. A flight from İstanbul to Ankara costs about £50, from İstanbul to Adana £80. Families and couples receive a discount of 10 % (students: see student discounts!).

The size of the country comes into perspective when you consider the flight times. From İzmir via Ankara to Van in eastern Turkey, calculate 155 minutes airtime.

There are direct flights from Ankara and İstanbul to Diyarbakır, Elazig, Erzurum, Gaziantep, Kayseri, Malatya, Merzifon, Sivas (only from İstanbul), Trabzon and Van.

Major Connections

ANKARA TO:

Adana -	daily (55 min)
Antalya -	twice weekly (50 min)
Dalaman -	weekly (85 min)
İstanbul -	7-8 times daily (55 min)
İzmir -	1-2 times daily (75 min)
Lefkose -	6 times weekly (65 min)

İSTANBUL TO:

Adana -	1-2 times daily (80 min)
Antalya -	twice daily (65 min)
Dalaman -	twice daily (75 min)
İzmir -	3-4 times daily (55 min)
Lefkose(Cyprus)	1-2 times daily (80 min)

İZMIR TO:

Antalya -	weekly (50 min)
Lefkose -	thrice weekly (85 min)

ADANA TO:

Lefkose(Cyprus)	thrice weekly (55 min)

By Ship

A pleasant way to travel and no longer dangerous: the pirates are long gone. You can enjoy the coastline from the railing and the harbour becomes your introduction to the town. So why not take at least one boat ride?

All year round passenger ships and car ferries cruise between the coastal towns. Major ship connections exist between İstanbul and İzmir and İstanbul and Trabzon. There is also the Marmara and Dardanelles Ferry Service.

İstanbul-İzmir: All year round a Turkish Maritime Line ship bound for İzmir departs from İstanbul on Mondays, Wednesdays and Fridays at 14:00 h. The ship arrives the next morning at 09:00 h. Departure from İzmir is on Sundays, Tuesdays and Thursdays at 14:00 h. Costs per person are £7-27, depending upon comfort on board. The ferry fee per car is £20.

İstanbul-Trabzon: The Black Sea Line departs from İstanbul once a week and runs between Sinop, Samsun, Giresun and Trabzon. The ferry leaves the Bosphorus on Mondays and arrives in Trabzon three days later. One-way, including a cabin, costs £10 per person, the ferry fee per car is £27. This three-day **mini-cruise** is a good way to get to know the almost unspoiled Black Sea coast. All four towns are of historical interest. We recommend a visit to Sinop and Trabzon.

Mediterranean Cruise: During the months of June to September, Turkish Maritime Line offers 11-day Mediterranean cruises. The round trip stops at most coastal towns of tourist interest, including: İzmir, Kuşadası, Bodrum, Datça, Marmaris, Fethiye, Antalya and Alanya. Costs £285 to £572, including room, board and day trips. Be sure to book early for this trip along more than 1000 km of coast (for address see below).

Southern Turkey - Cyprus: All year round, the modern ferry YEŞİLADA cruises between *Mersin* in southern Turkey and *Magusa* (formerly Famagusta) on Cyprus. The trip takes 10 hours. The ship departs from Mersin from early June to mid-September Monday, Tuesday, Wednesday, Friday and Sunday at 22:00 h. On Thursdays the ship is scheduled to depart to Lattakia, Syria. Generally, however, there are too few bookings to warrant the cruise, so that the YEŞİLADA cruises to Cyprus again on Thursday - ask when you book! During the off season, the YEŞİLADA cruises between Mersin and Magusa on Monday, Wednesday and Friday. The cost is £9 per person plus the harbour tax. Ferrying a car costs £12. Be sure to book your car and cabin passage early especially during summer. Deck passage is available until the last minute.

You can also get to Cyprus via Taşucu. Besides the ferry, you can take the hydrofoil BARBAROS for a fast cruise to Girne on Cyprus (see listing Taşuğu/Coming - Going).

The standard of living on Northern Cyprus is higher than in many regions of the Turkish mainland. Officially called *Turkish Republic of Cyprus* (since its declaration of independence in 1983), Turkey is the only country to recognize the state. Still, there are few hotels which can be compared to those in Southern Cyprus. It is not possible to cross over into Greek Southern Cyprus!

Ferries: On the Sea of Marmara there are three ferry connections serving Kartal, a village 20 km from İstanbul on the Asiatic side, and Yalova on the southern coast of the Sea of Marmara. Ferries cross the Dardanelles between Gelibolu and Lapseki every 90 minutes and hourly between Eçeabat and Çanakkale. Taking a car is no problem.

For more information contact the nearest office or agent of Turkish Maritime Line.

By Rail

Turks have never been enthusiastic about the railway system for passenger or freight service. Apart from the İstanbul Express to Europe, trains have never played an important role in Turkey. Even in the 20th century, the rail system has played only a minor role in Asia Minor.

The rail service to important tourist spots e.g. Konya, Bursa and Pamukkale is quite good but you shouldn't be in a hurry.

There are several good connections daily between İstanbul, Ankara and İzmir. Other than that, rail service is not very good: trains are infrequent and punctuality was never the strength of the Turkish Railway.

There has been little expansion of the sparse rail network since the end of World War II. Before the war, the Germans financed the laying of track from İstanbul via Konya and Adana to Bagdad as part of the legendary "Berlin to Bagdad" line. German development aid for the declining Ottoman Empire did have ulterior motives: the German Empire wanted to gain an economic advantage by obtaining better access to Persian Gulf oil and it hoped to get in on the imperialist expansion in the Near East. Work on the Bagdad Railway began in 1903 and was completed in 1940.

Few Turkish trains get up a good head of steam. The only real express is the **Mavi Tren** (Blue Train) between İstanbul (Haydarpaşa) and Ankara.

Mavi Tren: Daily from İstanbul at 13:30 and 22:50 h, arrives in Ankara at 21:00 and 06:20 h.
From Ankara at 13:30 and 22:50 h, arrives in İstanbul at 21:00 and 06:20 h.
Seat reservations and express surcharge are required even in 1st class; the route from İstanbul to Ankara is 578 km.

Daily Trains with Sleepers & Couchette

Depart İstanbul	Arrive Ankara
19:30 h	07:30 h
20:25 h	08:25 h
20:55 h	08:55 h
21:40 h	09:40 h
22:50 h	10:50 h

There are eight trains daily from İstanbul to Ankara and vice versa. Dining cars are usually available.

There are two trains daily from İzmir to Ankara (07:35 and 17:45 h) and one train to İstanbul (06:40 h, in Bandirma on the Sea of Marmara you have to get on the ferry). Tickets are available in the train stations; the clerks usually speak some English. Seat reservations are common on some trains and generally recommended. Sleeping cars and couchettes are often booked on weekends and holidays. If possible, travel during the week. With some luck you can get a couchette after boarding - ask the conductor.

From Mersin on the south coast, there are trains to Adana which continue on the Bagdad Railway Line to Syria and Iraq. From Adana, you might take the pleasant 16-hour ride to Ankara. From Adana to İstanbul the train takes 27 hours - if nothing happens along the way.

In general you can say that buses are faster, more punctual and more frequent. Trains, however, are more comfortable and cheaper. There is no rail service along the Mediterranean coast; along the Aegean coast there are connections only between İzmir and Söke.

By Car

Their ancestors - proud and aggressive, men to the tips of their moustaches - galloped their horses across the plains all the way to Vienna. The great, great, great grandsons - proud and aggressive, men to the tips of their moustaches - steer their horsepower across Anatolia, taking supreme pleasure in honking the horn.

Mysterious Asia! As you move east, the Turkish road system thins out as the quality of the roads deteriorates. Along the coastline and between major towns, there are about 25,000 km of paved roads in good condition.

Turkey's only limited-access intercity highway connects İstanbul with İzmit on the Sea of Marmara. A ring road has recently been completed around İstanbul.

Other highways move traffic through İzmir, Ankara, Adana and Antalya. There are usually no tolls. On the Bosporus Bridge, which is part of the İstanbul ring road, a toll is charged for cars crossing from Europe to Asia (£0.40, cheaper after 17:00 h). The volume of traffic is extremely heavy on the bridge since it is used by most of the traffic that moves from Europe to the Near East.

Around Town: Traffic is heavy in major towns. İstanbul is not a city for timid drivers. Parking problems, bumper to bumper traffic and reckless drivers are all problems you know from home. In Turkey you also enjoy endless concerts of horn honking, while streetlights and traffic regulations are, as a rule, ignored. For many Turks, the horn is the car's most important feature - the louder the better. Brakes, lights and turn signals are deemed of secondary importance. On sunny days, the left arm of the driver frequently replaces the left-turn signal. Few Turkish drivers find use for the rear view mirror - that is why an overtaking car always honks.

Country Roads: Outside the towns, traffic moves easily, although there is a lot of traffic between İstanbul and Ankara. This is because three major international routes share this stretch of road: European Road 5 to Syria, E 24 to Bagdad and E 23 to Teheran. You'll see a lot of Bulgarian trucks along the transit routes. Since the Gulf War, E 24 has filled with tank trucks. They transport oil via the land route to the Turkish Mediterranean port of İskenderun.

We strongly advise against driving at night: beware of poor lights on cars and trucks and totally unlighted oxcarts driven by farmers in dark attire.

And getting back to **horns**: In Turkey drivers usually honk before going into blind curves. If you don't honk, somebody might make the fatal assumption that the road is clear.

Other sources of danger include potholes, construction sites marked only by rocks and hordes of carefree children and careless adults, particularly as you enter villages.

Accidents: Should you be involved in a car accident, be sure to call the police (your insurance company will require a police statement before it pays damages). For additional tips, check with your automobile club. A word of caution. Often you'll be advised that if someone is injured in an accident, it is best not to stop but to step on the gas and proceed to the next police station. The reason implied is that European drivers risk being lynched. This is nonsense! Certainly there is nothing pleasant about being involved in an accident in Turkey as a foreigner - but don't expect to be hanged. You would be in real trouble if you left the scene of the accident: that is "hit and run driving", something police are very serious about, and not just in Turkey. It is advisable to get a police statement made even in case of small fender benders in which no other car is involved. If your car is undrivable, you will need certification from the nearest customs office (*gümrük müdürlügü*) in order to leave Turkey without your car.

This means that somehow you will have to transport the junked car to the customs office.

Papers and Insurance: You need a driver's license, car registration and a green insurance card. The insurance card has to be valid for all of Turkey, both the European and the Asian part. Get your insurance company to confirm in writing that you have the same coverage in all of Turkey as you enjoy in your home country! Otherwise, the company will only provide the minimum coverage required for Turkey, e.g. up to £2000 for personal injury and £250 for property damage. If they won't verify the coverage, it is advisable to buy additional insurance. If you do not have full coverage (which usually also includes the Near East) you may have to buy a short-term full-coverage policy.

If you are planning to spend more than three months in Turkey, you need a Carnet de Passage or a Triptik (issued by your automobile club).

Throwing Stones: In remote rural areas you may still come across children with stones in their hands demanding a toll - generally cigarettes. If you pay, you keep the tradition alive. If you drive by quickly you risk your windows. The best advice is to drive slowly, so if necessary you can get out of your car to chase the kids away. They aren't crooks but kids who still fear adults.

Traffic Signs

bozuk satıh	bad road
dikkat	Caution!
dur	Stop!
düsün banket	loose pavement
kaygan yol	dirty road
park (yeri)	parking lot
park yapılmaz	parking prohibited
şehir merkezi	town centre
tamirat	road construction
taşit gecemez!	no thoroughfare!
yavaş	drive slow
yasak	prohibited

Traffic Regulations: On the high seas, starboard over port is the first rule in right of way laws, but Turkish drivers recognize a different hierarchy: heavy vehicles (lorries, buses), then cars, motorcycles, bicycles and lastly pedestrians. Otherwise traffic regulations are similar to those you know from home. The speed limit in towns is 50 km/h (with a trailer 40 km/h). Outside of towns the speed limit is 90 km/h (with a trailer 70 km/h) or on a motorbike 70 km/h. The legal blood alcohol level is zero. You must carry two warning triangles to be placed in front of and behind your car in case of an accident. Local people often have only one triangle and place rocks behind the vehicle to signal car trouble.

Beware of *radar traps*! Occasionally you will notice a radar-equipped Renault 12 parked by the road, flanked by warning rocks.

Help: If you need assistance contact the Turkish Touring and Automobile Club (TTOK). The main office is in İstanbul (tel. 1314631-36), with a branch office in Ankara (tel. 317648-49). There is a close-knit chain of car breakdown services, particularly along E5 between İstanbul and Ankara. Vehicles of the *Turing Servisi* serve the Edirne-Ankara and Edirne-İzmir routes. On other roads you must frequently rely upon help from other drivers. Petrol stations equipped with garages and mechanics are located approximately every 3-4 hours drive apart.

The TTOK also has offices in İskenderun (tel. 17462), İzmir (tel. 217149) Mersin (tel. 20492) and Trabzon (tel. 17156).

The TTOK maintains information offices at the border crossings Cilvegözü (Syria), Dereköy (Bulgaria), Gürbulak (Iran), Habur (Iraq), Kapikule (Edirne/Bulgaria) and Ipsala (Greece).

Spare Parts: You'll have no problem if you're driving a Fiat, Renault, Ford or Mercedes; other types pose difficulties. Auto repair shops are usually located at the entrance to town. They will perform most services. Exhausts and oil pans are salvaged from junked cars, or molded from door parts and welded until they fit. Labor is cheap, and the mechanic usually makes a special effort to please foreign customers. You can also have replacement parts mailed from home but customs duties may be a problem.

Petrol: Expect problems if your car uses super-grade petrol, which is difficult to find outside of major cities. European cars all require Turkish super petrol, whose octane level resembles regular petrol in Europe.

In 1987 Türk Petrol began installing pumps with regular 91 octane petrol. Be sure to check the octane level before you fill the tank.

PETROL PRICES *(per liter)*

Regular	81 octane	£0.22
Super	94 octane (2 star)	£0.26
Diesel		£0.23

Lead-free petrol has not yet been discovered in Turkey. You'll find a mixture of local and brand-name petrol stations such as BP, Mobil and Shell. Petrol stations on the major highways are open round the clock, with mechanics and a restaurant nearby. Cross country buses make regular stops here.

Renting a Car

The major international car rental firms, e.g. INTER RENT, AVIS or HERTZ, have offices in all major Turkish towns and in tourist spots such as Kuşadası, Marmaris, Side, etc. You can rent a Fiat 124 (known as *Murat* in Turkey and the cheapest rental) or one of the popular Suzuki jeeps in the upper-middle price range. Prices vary little between the brand-name rental firms. In November 1987, AVIS offered the following prices:

A Fiat 124 costs £9.50 for one day plus £0.10 per kilometer. For two days you get unlimited mileage and pay £34 per day; for 3-6 days you pay £26 per day and after 7 days £25 are calculated daily. A Suzuki jeep costs £11 for one day plus £0.18 per kilometer. Two days cost £61, 3-6 days cost £47 daily, while after 7 days you pay £44 daily.

Car rental firms frequently inform customers only of the **base price**. Kilometer charges, 10 % tax, petrol and insurance come extra. In many towns a local rental firm will not have cars meeting the standards of international rental firms. In short: domestic firms are cheaper, but lower in quality. To rent a car you only need a driver's license issued in your home country.

ADDRESSES OF CAR RENTAL FIRMS:

Kayhan Turizm Seyahat Acentası
Mete Cad. 26/A, İstanbul-Taksim,
Tel. 1450766

Esin Turizm Seyahat Acentası
Cumhuriyet Cad. 47/2, İstanbul,
Tel. 1431515

Setur Seyahat Acentası
Cumhuriyet Cad. 107, İstanbul-harbiye, Tel. 1485085

Genso Seyahat Acentası
Atatürk Cad. 294/A İzmir, Tel. 211226

Zena Seyahat Acentası
1376 Sokak No. 10, İzmir,
Tel. 12540 & 125788

Konvoy Turizm Seyahat Acentası
Atatürk Bulvarı 233/8, Kavaklıdere,
Ankara, Tel. 137771 & 131536

Seltur Seyahat Acentası
Kumrular Sokak 6/A, Yenisehir, Ankara,
Tel. 254676 & 180477

By Bus

You will have no problem getting around in Turkey without your own set of wheels. This is the land of buses. Buses are for everybody: men, women, children and chickens. A good route system covers every region. Along the coast, connections are more frequent, with a greater number of bus companies serving the routes.

Buses between İstanbul, İzmir and Ankara run every few minutes. The number of bus companies is difficult to keep track of, but prices vary little. Calculate about £0.01 per kilometer. The Ankara - İstanbul route takes 8 hours and costs £5.50.

If you are willing to pay more for the ride, you can enjoy air conditioning, toilets, tinted windows, pillows, etc. These luxury bus companies provide service only on relatively few routes - so you won't get the ultimate in comfort on most trips. It is possible to board en route, if there are vacant seats.

Generally you will be riding a modern Mercedes bus, built under license in Turkey. One of the better companies, "*Superman Otobüsleri*" (don't be put off by the name) uses only Scandinavian-made "Scania" buses.

The following companies have a good reputation: *Edirne Ebirlik* for Thrace, *Kamil Koc, Pamukkale* and *Köseoglu* for Anatolia-West coast, *Akdeniz* for Anatolia-South coast and *Van Gölü* for East Anatolia. This does not mean that the other companies are necessarily bad - all companies usually use the same bus types:

Mercedes - Licence 0 302: Standard bus, acceptable to comfortable depending on maintenance.

Mercedes - Licence 0 302S/303: a little bit better, the seats are more comfortable.

MAN SuperMAN: Luxury bus with air-conditioning, rarely available, usually runs only between major cities.

Every major Turkish town has a **Central Bus Station**. These are frequently located several kilometers outside of town, accessible by local bus or taxi. Most of the major bus companies arrange to pick up passengers in small minibuses from their city offices for transport to the bus station. When purchasing your ticket, ask about this "*Dolmuş Servis*".

It is easy to buy a ticket, English is usually spoken. Before you pick up your ticket at the station, take a look at the firm's buses. Prices vary little, and a bit more comfort is worthwhile on an eight-hour drive.

İstanbul has two bus stations, *Topkapı* (not to be confused with the sultan's palace Topkapı Sarayı) on the European side, and *Harem* on the Asian side. Smaller towns frequently have only a collection of bus company offices near the market square or the centre of town. In this case, the buses will depart from there. Touts try to get customers for their company by storming up to prospective passengers at the entrance to the bus station. Don't let yourself be taken in by one. In order to get rid of them, just go with them to the ticket window and ask about departure times. If they are not what you want, try another company.

Ticket prices are posted in both the city offices and in the tiny offices at the bus stations. Your booking also includes a seat reservation: you can pick your own seat on a chart.

During the drive, you will be served by a - generally young - steward (*muavin*) who, at your call, will provide free drinking water or spray eau de toilette on your hands. This may help you survive the toils of travel and the smell of your neighbour's cigarettes. The buses are poorly ventilated, and summer heat and dust dehydrate passengers.

Every three to four hours the bus stops at a bus station with a restaurant or rest area. You will have enough time to get a meal, stretch your legs or just enjoy a cup of tea. Before the bus continues, passengers will be called to board the bus over a loudspeaker. But the call is only in Turkish! To be sure not to miss the departure, ask when leaving the bus how long the break will be or check with your fellow passengers.

By Dolmuş - *(Collective Taxi)*

"Müsait yerde!" a passenger calls from the back. Whether on the bustling Atatürk Bulvarı in a Turkish city or a lonely road in the Anatolian highlands, the dolmuş stops and the passenger disembarks. Because this is Müsait yerde - the right place.

The dolmuş provides an important service both in and between towns in Turkey.

Dolmuş means "occupied". This is one of its primary characteristics: a dolmuş doesn't depart until it is full (but conversely, it will not take on more than the legal number of passengers). Outside of towns Ford transit buses are used for transport. In İstanbul and other major cities old American cars (Dodge, Plymouth, Chrysler) are used as dolmuşes.

A drive in a dolmuş is a good way to get to know Turkey. Just choosing seats can take time, as women prefer to sit next to their husbands or other women. If you have a sense of humour and have acquired Turkish patience, you might have some amusing experiences.

Anamur. The bus, en route from Adana to Antalya, ends its run in Anamur - there aren't enough passengers. A dolmuş is quickly organized for me and two other passengers. That's all right with me, because it's faster and more comfortable for the same price; we are scheduled to leave in five or ten minutes at the most. Good. All of a sudden, there are a lot more people heading to Antalya, about 20 in all, with baggage and chickens and countless special requests concerning seating arrangements. Discussions ensue, a head count, a test sit, a recount, adjustments and a recount follow - but it just won't work. There are too many people and the Ford transit can't accommodate all of them. The first arguments erupt; an old woman shouts herself hoarse; the entire bus station takes lively interest. Four passengers get their money back and leave cursing. A new formation is tested - finally 16 passengers together with livestock and baggage are crammed into the vehicle. A miracle has been performed.

The driver boards and starts the motor. At a whistle, he gets back out and critically inspects the left rear tire while a group of "experts" gathers round him. He boards again, starts the engine and drives the bus about 50 m to the next petrol station - the left rear wobbles disconcertingly. 280 psi are pumped optimistically into the tire, but it is stubborn and remains flat. The old woman, by now completely hoarse, chain smokes cigarettes and talks a mile a minute. Respectful silence, everyone listens intently. A slow hobbling ride returns us to the bus station where we all disembark. The tire is changed. The reboarding goes off smoothly - we're experts at it by now. After two hours the ride begins; the old woman falls into an exhausted doze. Relaxed conversation starts up among the passengers whom fate has brought together in the dolmuş for a few hours.

Collective taxis frequently display their destination on a sign behind the windshield. Enjoy some tea while you await departure. In cities there are separate bus stations for departing dolmuşes running routes out of the city. Otherwise they depart from the market square. In larger towns there are fixed routes with regular stops, just like busstops. But you can also stop a dolmuş with hand signals and get on where you choose.

The prices (set by federal law) are slightly higher than bus fares. It is advisable to check the price with your fellow passengers before paying in order to avoid a tourist surcharge. Longer routes are split up into various fare stages. If you board in between, you pay only for the portion you actually ride.

Collective taxis can be recognized by yellow-black rally stripes below the window, just like a regular taxi ("*taksi*"). Before you board, be sure to ask if it really is a dolmuş.

Be careful when boarding a regular **taxi**, which charges much higher prices (insist upon the taximeter in İstanbul). If a taxi does not have a taximeter, or the driver insists that it is broken, be sure to negotiate about the price before departure. If you don't reach an agreement, try it with the next taxi. Taxis from the airport into town usually charge a fixed price about which bargaining is not possible.

By Thumb

You rarely see backpackers thumbing along the highway.

This has a lot to do with the fact that public transport is both cheap and reliable throughout much of the country. Hitchhiking is hardly worth it over long distances. In addition, the number of private cars is limited, particularly on secondary roads. Over short hauls, you might be lucky enough to get a lift. Tank trucks and agricultural vehicles usually stop for hitchhikers. Over long distances, try to stay on Turkey's three *European Roads* (see By Car). The big international lorries don't usually stop, but local lorries almost always stop. Your chances are good if you talk to drivers at rest areas.

Chances of getting a ride in Turkey also improve if you are properly dressed. But for many Turks, curiosity and their natural hospitality are the main motivation for picking up hitchhikers. Turkish drivers often invite you to tea at rest areas. As a gesture of friendship, be sure to carry a few cigarettes to offer your host. The helpful driver will be pleased and the next hitchhiker will have a better chance of getting a ride.

Women and girls without male companions, should avoid hitchhiking. If the obvious reasons are not sufficient, see "Family", "Religion".

HISTORY OF ANATOLIA
AND TURKEY

Turkey is an ancient land. There is evidence of numerous settlements dating from prehistoric times (since 7000 BC). Traces of early agriculture and crafts - clay pots, spearheads artfully made from obsidian, agricultural implements made of wood - have been found.

Certain locations were used as settlements for several thousand years, leaving behind cultural hills of rubble, called *hüyüks*, made up of debris from the wood and clay buildings. One of the most famous sites is *Catal Hüyük* on the Konya Plains (see Around Konya). It has been the most important hüyük for archaeological finds.

With the Hittite Empire, marking the Indo-Europeanization of Anatolia about 2000 BC, we move into recorded history. The Hittites, an Indo-European tribe, were very aggressive. Using brute force, they conquered the fertile Inner Anatolian steppe. Still not satisfied, they marched into Babylon (1531 BC) and to the border of Egypt. These "original inhabitants" of Anatolia probably invented the hook plow, the thresh board, and the single-axle cart - tools still used in the region today. The artistry of these people can be seen at the Hittite Museum in Ankara. ATATÜRK tried to raise the awareness of the Hittites being the original inhabitants of Anatolia by establishing various cultural institutions. Hattuşa, the Hittite capital, was located near the present-day village of Boğazkale (see Hattuşa).

In 1200 BC the fall of the Hittite empire was forced by the "Sea People", *Dorian tribes* from the west. We are now entering the time of the Greek heroic legends (Troy was destroyed in 1240 BC). Greek trading towns developed along the coast and steadily increased in power, while in Inner Anatolia regional nation states were formed again. The most important of these was the *Phrygian Empire*, which was founded about 800 BC with its capital at Gordion. The coastal towns gained control over the east-west trade, achieving tremendous wealth. With their fleets they controlled coastal commerce, forcing the merchants to pay taxes.

In the 7th century BC the Cimmerians, a mounted tribe from the steppes of southern Russia, entered Anatolia, ending the rule of the Phrygian Empire. Although the Cimmerians quickly faded from the scene, they did indicate from which direction the new rulers would arrive. But we still have about a thousand years to cover...

After the fall of the Phrygians a new star rose over Anatolia, the legendary Lydian king CROESUS. He conquered most of the Greek trading cities thus becoming the richest man in the world (inventor of Dagobertism and the minted coin). But then he overestimated himself and went to war against the Persian kings. He lost the war against Persia and Anatolia gained a new ruler.

The Greek coastal towns were not pleased with the new situation. They were eager to regain their accustomed freedom and the accompanying profitable trade. An attempt was made to join an alliance with the Greek city-states of Attica. The east-west conflict was in full swing. While the Greeks could prevent Persia from capturing Attica (Salamis and Marathon), Persia remained entrenched in Anatolia.

Hellenism and Rome

All this changed when ALEXANDER THE GREAT set out to conquer the world. Anatolia was the key because it controlled the military and trade roads to the East and to Egypt. The strategic position was the Cilician Gate, a natural fortress from which the major trade routes could be controlled. Alexander the Great won, and went on to conquer Persia and Egypt, pushing all the way to India. By the way,

Alexander's father, PHILIP II, was still allied with Persia against the Greek states.

After the death of Alexander (called Iskender in Asia Minor, where he is still greatly admired), Anatolia was again dominated by the Greek culture. Greek became the national language; the towns were relatively independent again aside from the usual conflicts between Greek military commanders (known from history books as the Diadochi Wars, diadoche = successor). The region experienced wealth and prosperity. The new neighbours to the east, the Parthians, were too weak to be a threat. For the next 1000 years, the region would belong to western culture.

In 133 BC Rome inherited the Kingdom of Pergamon, a small kingdom in western Anatolia, giving it a foothold in Asia (see Pergamon/History). In 88 BC MITHRIDATES, King of Pontus, attacked the Roman province. He was extremely brutal and let 80,000 Romans be slaughtered at the "Ephesian Vesper". That was too much. After heated discussions in Rome about how to deal with the situation - the government had been overthrown in another military coup - general SULLA took to the field, conquering Athens which had previously fallen to Mithridates. The disobedient Greeks were severely punished. Then Sulla returned to Rome where he became dictator. Rome was now the dominant power in Asia Minor.

In the meantime, Celts - Galatians - had settled in Inner Anatolia and were allied with Rome. The Armenian kingdom to the east also joined this alliance after persuasion on the part of Rome. Rome invested in the new province: roads for cross country trade were built, new harbors were established, aqueducts were built to carry water over great distances in lead pipes to the major cities, swamps were drained and extensive irrigation systems constructed. The ruins of these tremendous facilities can still be seen today. The later Ottoman Empire was not capable or willing to preserve all of this. As a result, malaria returned to the region, and the best agricultural land was reduced to steppe. More on that later.

At this point Asia Minor was the wealthiest region of the Roman Empire. Mighty cities including Antiochia, Caesarea, Ephesus and Pergamon were world famous (read the Acts of the Apostles in the Bible).

In 67 BC general POMPEIUS defeated the Greek states along the coast in a major campaign against "piracy". For the first time in history, all of Asia Minor was ruled by one empire. The people of Side were probably disappointed. The days of slave trading and ransom were over (see *Side/History*).

The Byzantine Empire

On 15 March 313 AD, Emperor CONSTANTINE THE GREAT renamed Byzantium Constantinople. From this day on there were two Romes: the Christian East Rome and the heathen West Rome, the latter under constant barbarian attack. With the loss of its affluent eastern provinces, West Rome could no longer finance the war against migrating Germanic tribes. Tales of the decadence and eccentricity with which Rome celebrated its decline are renowned. In Rome (East) law and order was supreme. It looked forward to a great future, having rid itself of the hedonistic West.

The first force to challenge this peace were the Huns, riding in from the great steppes to the east. Byzantium defeated their allies, the Goths, in terrible battles, resettling the weakened tribes in Anatolia. The cultural mix became increasingly diversified. The melting pot included the Hittites, Cimmerians, Gauls, Romans, Greeks, Persians and God knows who else...

By 391 AD Christianity had become the official religion. The days of religious freedom were gone. Christian religious dogma would not permit worshipping other gods. This marked a tremendous change in Asia Minor where religious freedom had reigned for thousands of years, permitting diverse peoples to live together in harmony. Other religions would later take a lesson from Christianity's intolerance. One cannot blame Constantine for this - he died in 337 AD.

Islam

After the previously mentioned 1000 years of inactivity, the East once again stirred. There was dissatisfaction with clerical Christianity and a new religion, just as unyielding and intolerant, was on the rise in the Eastern Mediterranean : Islam.

The 7th century brought the first attack by Islamic Arabs against Constantinople. Together with its Slavic allies, Byzantium was able to defeat the challenge. But pressure by other Islamic nomadic tribes was increasing. They did not attack with great armies of knights in armour which could have been defeated. Rather, they made quick raids against isolated farmers and disappeared like bandits. The border guards had to be increased which was a great expense. This forced taxes to be raised, creating greater dissatisfaction. Minds were open to a new religion.

Finally the *Turks* arrived. Nobody actually knows exactly where they came from. Perhaps they originated north of the Aral Lake (Turkmenistan). Many Turkoman tribes were driven west by the Mongols, others joined the enemy as allies. All the tribes shared the fate of losing their agricultural land, and being forced into a nomadic existence. With their herds they were very mobile and militarily superior to the stationary peasants.

Members of these tribes were recruited by the *Seljuk Empire* to serve as nomadic patrols along the northwest border of neighbouring Byzantium. The Seljuks, with their capital at Konya, built a mighty empire in Anatolia, where their architecture can still be admired today. The Seljuk empire preceded the Ottoman.

The Turkomans did their job well, continually extending the border to the west. They regularly raided villages and herds along the trade routes, thereby disturbing the economic basis of major cities against which a frontal attack would have been inconceivable. In the country-side, and eventually even in the cities, fear of these troops became so great that the population either fled west or joined the new rulers and became nomads themselves. In this way, the Turks increased their territory. The pre-Ottoman era had its high point about 1250 AD.

The nomadic expansion was aided by a Christian crusade against Byzantium in 1204 AD and by the Islamic religion which justified these attacks by calling them a holy war. Later, the Sultan had to engage in two military campaigns against neighbouring countries annually - it was demanded by his preachers.

The Ottoman Empire

Towards the end of the 12th century, the Mongols again attacked Asia Minor, weakening the Seljuk empire. It eventually disintegrated into a number of lesser Turkish kingdoms. The people of the sur-rounding mountains, many of whom had never been conquered, be-came stronger again.

This was the hour of the commander OSMAN (1281-1326), founder of the Ottoman Empire. He was emir of a small Turkish tribe which had fled from the Mongols to Anatolia in the 13th century. In 1301 Osman declared his independence from the Seljuk Empire. After subduing a number of Turkish tribes, he founded a small kingdom based in Bursa. Osman and his descendants turned to the west, since mounted Mongol troops were firmly entrenched to the east control-ling the whole of Inner Anatolia.

In 1354 Ottoman mercenaries crossed the Dardanelles. Byzantium, which needed help in its conflict with the Holy Roman Empire, had requested them. The Ottomans solved the problem in their own way: they defeated the crusader empire and established a firm stronghold on the European continent. The Balkan region soon became their new homeland because there was no serious opposition in this region. At this time Byzantium had raised its taxes to over 60 %, while the Koran prohibited taxation at a rate greater than 10 %. The Byzantine Empire was quickly reduced to the city limits of Constantinople.

MURAT I (1360-1389) was the real founder of the Ottoman Empire by way of his victories in Thrace and the Balkans. He took a Byzantine princess as his wife, and founded the Janissary Corps, a guard of Christian soldiers, who were to be the Sultan's guard for centuries. In 1361 he conquered Hadrianopolis (Edirne) which he made his capital four years later.

In 1369 King SIGISMUND of Hungary was defeated by Sultan YILDERIM BEYAZIT (THE LIGHTNING-FAST) establishing Ottoman domination of the Balkans. The foresight of settling in the Balkans paid off when the legendary Mongol Prince TAMERLANE invaded Anatolia as a step in his attempt to conquer Europe. Beyazit fought back with a mighty army, but the Mongol's war elephants and 100,000 troops were too much for the Ottoman army. Ankara, defended by 30,000 Armenian troops, fell to the Mongols; the Sultan was taken prisoner. This would be the only defeat for the Ottoman Empire in its first 300 years.

Tamerlane's warriors laid waste entire regions of Anatolia but the Mongols needed to regroup and withdrew to central Asia. The heart of the Ottoman Empire, the Balkans, was not captured. After the death of Tamerlane, the Mongol empire disintegrated. Civil war took hold of the Ottoman Empire. Religious unrest shook the very foundation of the state.

In 1413, Sultan MEHMET I was able to regain control of Anatolia from his European base using the bloodiest of means. His heir, MURAT I, consolidated Ottoman rule in the Balkans, ending the submission of the small Turkish princes in the region. Then MEHMET II (the Conqueror) achieved greatness in 1453 when his force of 300,000 troops took Byzantium by storm. Numerous reports show that most of the population was happy to surrender. There was little support for a strong defense. For this reason, Venice and Genoa sent troops to defend their endangered trade routes to India and China. With the ship and manpower reinforcement, Constantinople was able to resist. Then the Sultan ordered the casting of a cannon in Hungary, so heavy that 40,000 soldiers were required to maneuver it into position before the city walls. This, too, did not work; the city refused to surrender. At some point the people became tired of the siege. The gates were opened on 29 May, 1453. The disloyal neighborhoods were spared.

The international effects of this victory were greater than the Sultan could ever have imagined. Greek priests fled to the west (particularly to Italy, but also to Austria, Germany and France) bringing with them the inheritance of ancient Greece. So the age of Humanism began. In search of new trade routes to India, America was discovered while the patriarch of the Greek Orthodox church established residence in Moscow. So the foundation for the two 20th century superpowers was laid.

Now Turkey was a great European power. In the course of the next 60 years major regions of present-day Turkey, Syria and Egypt became provinces. Venice lost the eastern Mediterranean islands, thereby giving up its status as a major power. Genoa was equally reduced. Hungary became a Turkish province, France an ally. Turkish ships landed in Italy, challenging the red apple, the Ottoman term for the Pope.

The Blue Mosque - bulit on the pinnacle of power

With increasing wealth the Islamic religion became more liberal: the Christians were granted rights. If they surrendered, as in Byzantium, Christians could keep their lives, possessions and religion. The conquered land passed into Allah's ownership, as stipulated in the Koran; the Sultan was the administrator. The dervishes set official Ottoman policy. From 1517 on, the Sultan held the office of Caliph, combining religious and secular rule as Mohammed's representative.

SELIM I conquered the Caliphate along with Egypt. No private possession of land was tolerated, and use of its yield was granted only to outstanding commanders. The only road to success was by conquering territory and people to work the soil. There was no investment in agriculture, none in handicrafts, only in the military. Endless military campaigns were designed to increase wealth until the entire world had submitted to Islam. But they hadn't reckoned with the Austrians who did not see their future in Islam. In 1529 the first siege of Vienna had to be lifted. It was just too expensive to feed and supply 300,000 Turkish soldiers on Austrian soil over an extended period of time.

The Fall of the Ottoman Empire

The Ottoman Empire experienced its golden age under SÜLEYMAN THE MAGNIFICENT (1520-1566). His death brought the beginning of its decline. In 1571 Venice gathered its naval strength for a decisive battle near Lepanto which destroyed the Turkish fleet. With the military defeat, political dissatisfaction began to surface. The administration was sloppy; taxes were raised arbitrarily; the sultans frequently lost track of political realities.

Vienna was again besieged in 1683. Although even greater resources were invested in the attack this time, it proved unsuccessful again. It was a tremendous defeat for Turkey. With the seizure of the Turkish military treasury, Austria was suddenly wealthy and able to attack.

The Russian Tsar PETER THE GREAT quickly realized that Turkish territory was there for the taking. He called for a "Holy war of the Christians" against Turkey. In the coming decades Austria conquered part of the Balkans while Russia took Crimea.

The sultans now completely lost contact with reality, withdrawing increasingly from the business of government, and with MURAT IV (1623-1640) all active participation in military campaigns ended. Administration of the empire passed into the hands of slaves, members of the harem and eunuchs. The influence of the Janissary Corps increased. As the power of the sultan declined, the court became preoccupied with bribery and blackmail. With the decline of the central government, regional armies rebelled; entire provinces sought autonomy. The influence of Greek *Fanariots* - named for the *Faner* district (today *Fener*) of İstanbul where the Greek Patriarch had his seat - increased markedly after 1711.

Ascending to the throne under these conditions, Sultan SELIM III tried to institute major reforms. Acting upon the French model, he transferred administrative power to civilian authorities (secretaries).

However, they proved to be just as corrupt and inefficient as their predecessors.

Adding to the decline were the "Capitulations", trade agreements with France, England, and Germany. These agreements gave foreign merchants international rights, similar to diplomatic status. The Turkish economy became flooded with foreign goods and the domestic market was ruined.

During the Crimean war, Turkey was at the point of economic ruin, forcing the Sultan to pawn Egypt to England. This made the Ottoman Empire dependent upon foreign capital. The national government became bankrupt in 1876 when England and France cancelled credits. The term "Sick man of Europe" was coined.

Young Turks

Opposition mounted against the Sultan's autocracy and foreign interference in domestic affairs. Students and officers began forming secret societies including "Unity and Progress". Unrest resulting in bloody riots became frequent. In 1896, 70,000 Christian Armenians were killed in Samsun.

In 1908 the Young Turks came to power after a military rebellion at Saloniki led by Enver Pasha. But it was too late. The European powers had already decided to split the empire. In the Balkan War of 1912, Turkey lost most of the Balkans to Greece and the Habsburg Empire. The victors, however, could not agree on how to divide the land. Distrust on both sides was great; WWI was soon in full swing. Because England and France coveted the oil-rich provinces of Syria and Mesopotamia, Turkey joined the war on the German side and lost. Millions of Muslims fled to Asia Minor in fear of Christian reprisals.

The victors again set out to divide the spoils. The Greek Prime Minister received a mandate from the allies to restore order in Anatolia. A marauding Greek army plundered its way toward Ankara. Italy occupied the coastline along Antalya. France took Cilicia. Kurdistan and Armenia were to receive their independence. The Bosporus became an international mandate under British occupation. The Ottoman Empire now consisted of no more than Inner-Anatolia.

Mustafa Kemal Atatürk

In this hour of need, M. KEMAL ATATÜRK made his great entrance. He founded a National Assembly in Ankara and raised an army. He first moved against his weakest opposition: the Armenians were subdued

*Mustafa Kemal Atatürk -
he is still remembered
in Turkey today*

by the Turkish army in 1920-21. Many thousands were killed. Only a small minority, protected by the Red Army of the Soviet Union, was able to find refuge in the Socialist Soviet Republic of Armenia (SSR).

In 1921 the Greek army was defeated in a battle near the Sakaria River. American warships evacuated the Greek civilian population along with the remaining troops. After the Italians and French saw the fate of the Greeks, they voluntarily withdrew their own troops. In 1922 a truce was arranged. In 1923 Mustafa Kemal Atatürk declared the establishment of a new country, the Turkish Republic.

The new government was inspired by the west. The Caliphate and Muslim courts were abolished; religious orders dissolved. The legal foundation of the country was no longer the Koran but rather Swiss civil law, Italian criminal law and German trade law. All references to religion were removed from the constitution. It was now prohibited to wear a fez. Arabic and Persian, the languages of the Koran, were no longer compulsory subjects in the schools. Religious education was abolished. Other reforms included equality for women, reform of written Turkish (the Latin alphabet was instituted), changing the weekly day of rest from Friday to Sunday, and compulsory use of surnames. When Atatürk died in 1938 he left a healthy country behind.

He was the only revolutionary of the 20th century who brought his people (not including the Kurds and Armenians) something more than unhappiness. The Turkish people idolize him even today, as can be seen in the numerous portraits of Atatürk in Turkish shops, pubs and hotels. There are many monuments dedicated to him and streets bearing his name.

Atatürk's successor was ISMET INÖNÜ (another common street name). New political parties were founded during his régime. Inönü avoided bringing his country into WWII, permitting the expansion of Turkey's trade and industry. By the way, Turkey was one of the few countries in the world to accept religious and political refugees from Germany without reservation during the Nazi era.

Today the Turkish military looks with pride to the Atatürk tradition. The army considers itself to bear the special responsibility of preventing separatist ambitions on the part of ethnic minorities which might threaten national unity. Additionally, the military, in upholding Atatürk's reforms, stands in clear opposition to Islamic fundamentalists and radical left-wing groups.

The Turkish military has never been squeamish about expressing its feelings concerning matters of important policy. This has had an effect upon the state of Turkish democracy. The Turkish military executed Prime Minister MENDERES in 1961 due to his reactionary religious tendencies and his attempt at a re-Ottomanization of the country. The military was equally severe in the 1970s, when, under DEMIREL and ECEVIT, conflicts mounted between ultra-conservatives and left-wing groups. In 1980 the military dissolved parliament and prohibited the leaders of the two major political parties, the Conservative Justice Party and the Social Democratic Party, from engaging in any political activity. General K. EVREN became the new head of state.

Since 1982 the military has been carefully working toward restoring democracy. The old political parties are still prohibited. Only new parties approved by the military are permitted to present candidates for election. Islamic fundamentalists, however, keep the Turkish government under pressure. Democracy is no certain thing in Turkey.

Even so, the first free elections were held in November 1987. In the previous summer, General EVREN ordered registration of all eligible voters. A curfew was ordered to ensure that all potential voters would be found at home. The voters were asked to decide whether the former political parties should be permitted to resume their activities. The voters agreed that the old parties should be restored. The clear winner of the election held in November 1987 was ÖZAL and his Justice Party, who now hold the absolute majority of seats in parliament. ÖZAL received only one-third of the votes, but the electoral system, which was changed shortly before the election, suited his distribution of support wonderfully. The opposition parties, who received two-thirds of the votes, were granted only one-third of the seats in parliament.

National Structure

The Turkish Republic was declared in 1923. According to the constitution of July 9, 1961 (amended several times), Turkey is a "National, Democratic, Secular and Social Republic". The law-making body is the Great National Assembly. It consists of the National Assembly (450 representatives, who are elected to four-year terms according to proportional representation) and the Senate (150 directly elected members, 15 members named by the president and a number of life-time members). These in turn elect a president to a term of seven years (the president may not be re-elected). Executive powers are shared by the President and the Council of Ministers (which requires a vote of confidence by the National Assembly).

Turkey is divided into 67 administrative regions (*Il*), each administered by a governor. The legal system, as already mentioned, was reformed in 1923 with civil law based upon the Swiss model and criminal law based upon Italian law.

Turkey is a member of OECD (Organization of Economic Cooperation and Development), NATO, the European Parliament and is an associate member of the European Community.

The Cyprus Crisis

About 1230 BC: The southern portion of Cyprus was settled by the Achaeans. At the end of the 9th century BC the Phoenicians arrived. There were three Phoenician and seven Greek fortified settlements along the coast (ruled by kings). About 1200 BC, Cyprus (Alasia) belonged to the Hittite Empire.

58 BC: The beginning of Roman rule on the island, under which the island's economic development reached new heights. Missionary visits by PAUL the Apostle and BARNABAS consolidated Christianity on the island. By 325 AD there were three bishoprics on Cyprus. After the division of the Roman Empire in 395 AD, Cyprus belonged to the Eastern Roman Empire.

Crusader Era: After the Islamic conquest of Akkon in 1291 AD the island was the last crusader kingdom and a base for Italian city states engaged in oriental trade. From 1369-1498 the island attracted armies from Egypt, Genoa and Venice. None of these conquerors, however, were able to bridge the social and cultural gulf between themselves and the native Greek population. The Turks were greeted as liberators in 1570 upon their conquest of Nicosia. Under Turkish rule the Roman Catholic churches were converted into mosques while the Greek Orthodox churches were tolerated. Over the course of the coming centuries, Turkish soldiers, along with ethnic Turks from Asia Minor, were settled on Cyprus, forming a self-contained ethnic community.

1931: The desire of Greek Cypriots for annexation of Cyprus by Greece led to an uprising. After WWII further unrest and terror occured.

1955: An underground army, the E.O.K.A., led by General G. GRIVAS, began a guerrilla war against British colonial occupation. At the same time the E.O.K.A fought against the ethnic Turkish Cypriots.

16 August, 1960: Cyprus is granted independence and joins the British Commonwealth.

The two ethnic communities engage in a civil war, as the ethnic Turks feel their constitutionally guaranteed rights are being infringed upon by the government and bureaucracy. In March 1964 UN troops are stationed upon Cyprus as part of UNO-sponsored peace talks.

1964: Ethnic Turks establish a "Provisional Turkish Administration" which is never recognized by the government of MAKARIOS III. A conflict develops (about 1966) between General Grivas, who represents the ideas of Enosis ("Unity"), and President Makarios III, who speaks increasingly of Cypriot independence. Supported by a newly formed

E.O.K.A. (II), Grivas begins a small war against the government of Makarios III.

15 July 1974: Officers of the Greek Cypriot National Guard, with the aid of the Greek Military government and the E.O.K.A. II, overthrow the government of Makarios III who flees abroad. On July 20, 1974 the Turkish Prime Minister B. ECEVIT sends Turkish troops to the island, leading to the fall of the military dictatorship in Greece. Turkish troops occupy northern Cyprus up to the Lefka-Nicosia line. 200,000 Greek Cypriots flee south while 90,000 Turkish Cypriots flee north. In December 1974 Makarios returns to Cyprus where he resumes the presidency until his death in 1977. His successor is S. KYPRIANU. On 13 February 1975 the Turkish Cypriot territory is declared the "North Cyprus Turkish Republic" (KKTC) under President R. DENKTASH.

Until today there has been no breakthrough in negotiations between the two Cypriot communities. The Turkish Cypriots call for autonomous Greek and Turkish regions. The ethnic Greeks propose the division of the entire island into a number of cantons, each with cultural autonomy. There has been some agreement on humanitarian issues (resettlement). In 1983, under Rauf Denktash, the "Turkish Republic of Cyprus" was proclaimed, a government recognized to this day only by Ankara. The Cyprus Crisis has been extremely expensive for the Turkish government.

THRACE

The European part of Turkey - once the heart of the Ottoman Empire with its ancient capital at Edirne - was the mobilization point for the Turkish army during its campaigns in the Balkans.

Everywhere there is evidence of great history: the Selim Mosque in Edirne (built by Sinan), perhaps the most beautiful mosque in all of Turkey; the 1.4 km Ottoman aqueduct in Uzunköprü; the remarkable camel-back bridge, built by Sinan at Büyükçekmece on the Sea of Marmara.

Thrace is not a country of tremendous scenery. Gently rolling hills stretch monotonously to the horizon. There is little vegetation. The only forests are along the Maritza (Meriç) and Tunca Rivers. Sunflowers are harvested along with wheat and barley. Lovely and green in the spring, with the summer sun the landscape first turns brown, then black. It is not a picturesque countryside.

Thrace is a transit area. The access route to İstanbul becomes ever narrower. Everything moving from the Occident to the Orient must pass through here. Heavy traffic from the Balkans arrives on E 5, squeezing through Edirne along Thrace's extremely narrow roads, before reaching the eternal traffic jam up to the Bosporus bridge. Long-haul truck drivers do not like this region; it is slow to pass. Tourists also use it for transit. There are no great attractions. After a long tiring drive, and the difficulty of finding petrol in Bulgaria, few drivers have the time and energy to make a stop before İstanbul. The sea beckons, the oriental metropolis calls. What do Edirne, Havsa, Lüleburgaz have in comparison?

Thrace is a transit area even for the Turks. This is their last stop before departing to central Europe. Or their first taste of Turkey when returning for Christmas, summer holidays or the Sacrificial Festival. Anatolia is still far away. Few are at home when they reach Turkish territory at Kapıkule. Time is scarce - keep moving!

For this reason every stranger is happily received. Edirne is one of the loveliest of Ottoman cities. Mosques, bridges, and palaces combined with traditional Turkish hospitality are still unspoiled.

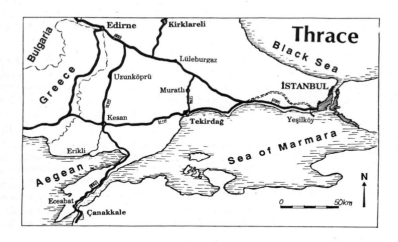

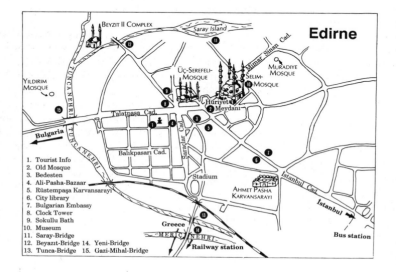

1. Tourist Info
2. Old Mosque
3. Bedesten
4. Ali-Pasha-Bazaar
5. Rüstempaşa Karvansarayı
6. City library
7. Bulgarian Embassy
8. Clock Tower
9. Sokullu Bath
10. Museum
11. Saray-Bridge
12. Beyazıt-Bridge 14. Yeni-Bridge
13. Tunca-Bridge 15. Gazi-Mihal-Bridge

EDIRNE *(pop. 83,000)*

**The geographical data is less than spectacular: a provincial
capital at the point where the Tunca and Arda Rivers flow
into the Meriç River. This is a market for the fertile
surrounding country, before it dries in the summer heat.
Local industries include perfume, textiles and tobacco.**

Once a year the city comes to life. *Kırkpınar*, traditional Turkish
wrestling, is extremely popular and an important media event. This
is the place for the most important tournament in the entire country.
But Kırkpınar includes more: the festival features horse races, a carnival and folklore events. The city bursts at its seams for an entire
week.

When the festivities end, typical oriental calm returns. Tradition is
very important here. Once the officers of the Edirnespor Soccer
Team tried to change the team's colours. Loud dissatisfaction was
voiced by the team's supporters - just about every resident of the
town. So Edirnespor continues to wear the good old red and yellow.

Tradition also plays a role in the restoration of Edirne's narrow
streets, bazaars, caravanserai and the oriental bridges which are
among the loveliest in central Turkey.

The city's aorta, the E5, pulsates steadily. Chugging in from the Bulgarian border at Kapıkule, 40-ton trucks roll up *Talat-Paşa-Caddesi* to
the central Freedom Square, squeeze past the Old Mosque and Selim
Mosque, then race on toward İstanbul. Scheduled freight, generators
for the Anatolian dam, supplies for the Gulf War, Mannesmann pipes
for Saudi Arabia - everything has to pass through the narrow streets.

The military presence cannot be overlooked. There are soldiers in
almost every tea garden, guarding every bridge, and at every place of
strategic importance. Edirne is the border town at the northwest tip
of Turkey. The Bulgarian border is 18 km away. Greece is just 5 km
from town. Neither Bulgaria nor Greece are friends of the Ottomans.

Tourists are rare guests. Art fans occasionally make a quick stop to
glance in the Selim Mosque, perhaps the prettiest in all of Turkey.
Even in a land of traditional hospitality, Edirne is a pleasant excep-

tion: the visitor is still king. If you have travelled a great distance, you will be welcomed with open arms. It is easier to meet local people here than in more traditional tourist towns where the profit motive reigns.

History

The Thracians themselves founded a settlement called Orestia here at the confluence of the Tunca and Meriç Rivers. Ships were able to sail up the Meriç to the gates of the city.

It is known that Hadrianopolis (Adrianople) was founded in 125 AD by Emperor HADRIAN as an outpost of Constantinople. As such it suffered the regular wrath of invaders forced to turn back at the impregnable gates of Constantinople.

In 314 AD and again in 323 AD Emperor CONSTANTINE I defeated LICINIUS, a successor to the East Roman throne, taking the fortress. First, in 378 AD, the Goths besieged the city unsuccessfully. The Avars could not pierce the walls in 586 AD. The Bulgarians were more successful: in 814, 922 and 1002 AD, after defeats before the gates of Constantinople, they pillaged Hadrianopolis on the way home.

The crusaders also took the opportunity to rape and pillage in 1101 and 1147. The city was spared during the Third Crusade. Emperor FREDERICK BARBAROSSA used the city as his base for six months in 1189 AD.

Conquest by the Ottoman Empire must have seemed like salvation. The Ottomans first crossed the Dardanelles in 1333, making quick conquests in the north before capturing the city in 1361. Edirne, as the city was now called, replaced Bursa as capital of the Ottoman Empire until the conquest of İstanbul in 1453. Edirne was thus a major garrison town and the departure point for Janissary troops who accompanied the Sultan on his campaigns through the Balkans.

The town remained as the "second capital". A period of peace lasting almost 500 years provided the basis for tremendous development. Although there were never plans to make Edirne a religious center, the city center and vicinity boast no less than 14 major mosques and over 300 smaller mosques. There were 53 schools, 16 bathhouses, 24 hostels and 124 wells according to the famous Turkish chronicler EVLIYA ÇELEBI. The most famous architect of his time, SINAN, displayed his ingenuity here as nowhere else (see box: Sinan).

The affluence ceased with the Russian occupation in 1828, which ended after the Treaty of Adrianople in 1829. In 1877 Russian troops again entered the city. The treaty of Yeşilköy required Turkey to surrender its entire territory in the Balkans beyond the present-day region of Thrace. Cut off from the backlands, the population declined from 120,000 to just 30,000.

In the 1st Balkan War the Young Turks lost the border fortress to Bulgaria after a long siege, but it was recaptured later the same year in the 2nd Balkan War. In WW I Greece took the opportunity to capture Edirne, but after the Treaty of Sèvres in 1922, the great powers insisted that Greece return the occupied regions of Eastern Thrace to Turkey.

After WW II a new era of economic and cultural development was sparked by transit traffic, new industries and the founding of Thrace University.

INFORMATION: Kültür ve Turizm Müdürlüğü, Hüriyet Meydanı 27, tel. 115 18. Friendly, competent advice. Edirne is an easy town to explore; the young team have all the facts in their heads. English, French, German spoken.

There is another Tourist Information Office at the Bulgarian border at Kapıkule: Hudut Sahasi, tel. 1019.

TELEPHONE AREA CODE: 1811

COMING - GOING: Buses every 30-45 minutes to İstanbul (takes four hours, sometimes with a rest stop). Hourly buses to Çanakkale and İzmir. Minibuses half-hourly to Uzunköprü, Lüleburgaz and Tekirdağ. It is a 30 minute walk from the center of town to the Otogar. The dolmuş station is in front of Rüstem Paşa Kervansarayı, behind the Old Mosque. Note: In İstanbul, buses departing for Edirne leave from Trakya Garajı (the quite small, northern station at Edirnekapı).

BY RAIL to İstanbul: Two trains daily, takes seven hours, not recommended.

CAR RENTALS: At the BP camp site (local).

TRAVEL AGENCIES: No air or ship agents. Bus offices at the Otogar.

SHOPPING: The bazaars are of little interest to tourists. For the best selection of postcards and souvenirs, visit Arasta Bazaar by the Selimiye Mosque.
There is a new shopping street below the Selim Mosque at Hüriyet Meydanı. Every Sunday there is a large Farmer's Market in the south of town, in the valley between the railway dam and the Tunca, with hundreds of horse carts selling juicy fruit in front of the bridge at good prices. Don't miss it!

POST OFFICE: On Saraçlar Caddesi, across from Ali-Paşa Bazaar.

HOSPITAL: Directly adjoining the bus station.

SPORTS & RECREATION: **Kapalı Spor Salonu**, across from the Otogar, a roofed sports center with indoor pool, boxing ring, weight room, low fees (£0.35). There is a jogging track at **Meriç Camp** and a **picnic area** (always popular in Turkey).

CITY LIBRARY: English, French and German books available.

MEETING PLACE: On Hüriyet Meydanı and the surrounding tea gardens. In the evening Saraçlar Caddesi is popular.

FESTIVALS: Kırkpınar Wrestling Festival (usually June or early July), a three-day folk festival plus three days of wrestling.

A Night's Rest

Sultan Otel: Talat Paşa Asfaltı (map); double £13.50. Rooms are clean and well furnished, usually with a balcony, all with warm-water showers. The rooms facing the back are much quieter. Large parking lot for guests, bar, best hotel in Edirne, tel. 1811 1372.

Kervan Otel: İstanbul Caddesi, diagonally across from the Old Mosque (Kadirhane Sok. 134); double £8. Good clean medium-priced hotel, but loud trucks. Garage, reasonable prices, tel. 18 11 1382.

Konak Hotel: Maarif Cad; double £2.70, simple, clean, separate showers & WC.

Saray Otel: Eski İstanbul Cad. 28; double £3.35, bare, clean, a bit quieter, only doubles and triples, tel. 18 57 1474.

Berlin Otel on Arif Paşa Cad. (double £2.70) has a good reputation. The Tourist Office also recommends Anıl Otel on Maarif Cad. and Otel İstanbul on Çilingirler Cad. (both double £2.70).

Camping

BP Kervansarayı: tel. 18 11 1290. The best site in Edirne, adjoining the bus station, costs £4 per person and tent. All the service you expect from a BP site, minimarket, restaurant, clean sanitation, warm water, electricity. The site is shady and looks nice. Bungalows available.

Meriç Camping: in the south of town, just behind Yeni Köprü on the way to the Greek border. Costs £2.70 per person. Lovely location by the Meriç River, swimming possible. Clean, warm water, electricity, minimarket, restaurant. The place appears desolate.

Fifi Camping: tel. 18 11 1554. 10 km beyond Edirne on E 5 toward İstanbul, no buses. Costs £2 per person and tent, bungalows £8.35. A small site without shade, rudimentary cold showers, small restaurant, for rugged individuals with a car.

Food

Along Saraçlar Caddesi are lots of locantas and köftecis, catering mostly to a local clientele. There are tea gardens around Hüriyet Meydanı. The best ice cream is sold in Roma Dondurma on İstanbul Caddesi, just behind the Old Mosque.

Meriç Restoranı: Karaağac Yolu, tel. 18 11 3505/6. In the south of town across Yeni Köprü on the Meriç (next to the camp site). An exquisite restaurant with evening entertainment, but expensive. Easier to recommend is the tea garden next door, right on the bank of the Meriç with a great view of the lovely Yeni Köprü. Surprisingly, few guests make it out here.

Other restaurants diagonally across from Sultan Otel (reasonable prices, sloppy service, catering to transit clientele), and between Tunca Bridge and Yeni Köprü (polite, friendly, good cook). From the terrace you can see the farmers driving horse carts to the market or working in the fields.

Kirkpinar

In 1988 the 627th *Edirne Kırkpınar Yaglıgüres* (or Kırkpınar for short) was held. During the festival, all of Turkey turns its attention to wrestling. It is a national event to determine the holder of the championship belt - the *Başpehlivan*. All of Turkey takes an interest in Kırkpınar.

There are as many legends surrounding Kırkpınar as there have been victors. The following legend is commonly told. At the time of ORHAN GAZIS, a horde of 40 warriors crossed the Dardanelles on rafts and conquered the Byzantine fortress at Domuzhisarı and a number of smaller fortresses in one sweep, taking rich plunder. Battle with the weak Byzantines was not much of a challenge, so on the way home they invented an outlet for their pent up energy. Near the village of Samona they decided to determine their strongest man in a wrestling match. The 38 weakest were quickly determined, but there was no separating the two strongest. They kept going at each other without a clear decision for several days. They agreed to meet on the 6th of May (date of the Ottoman Spring Festival) on the village green of Ahirköy for a final battle lasting until a victor could be determined. They fought from sunrise until well past midnight when they both collapsed and died.

The 38 weaker men buried the two victors under a fig tree. Years later, when they passed the spot at the head of another Turkish army, the grave site was marked with 40 springs (Kırkpınar means bubbling water). Forty is one of the most sacred numbers of Islam. The sultan and the warriors understood the omen from Allah. Since then annual wrestling matches have been held in the sacred grove. Such is the legend.

The games are sponsored by the *Kırkpınar Agası*, the Ağas. The Ağas are a group of wealthy organizers with sufficient means to finance the show.

The most important personality at the battle grounds is the *cazgır*, who acts as master of ceremonies and stadium announcer. He presents the individual contestants to the audience in well formulated verse.

And then there are the fighters, called *pehlivah*. These are the best fighters in Turkey who have qualified for the championships in local level competitions. They fight for the golden championship belt and the title of *Başpehlivan* (chief wrestler) in Turkey. Although the purse is modest, a Başpehlivan is usually a made man. The tremendous status of wrestling in Turkey ensures an affluent future.

Before the competition, tradition reigns. Each day begins with the greasing: first the right hand greases the left side of the body; then the left hand does the right. Then follows the *Peşrev*, the warming up ceremony. Drums and clarinets (*davul* and *zurna*) accompany the wrestlers' ritual exercises: touching the grass with their left knee, then touching the knee, lips and forehead three times with the right hand, eating stems of grass, shouting "*Hay da bre pehlivan*" (Go Man!) to cheer themselves on, jumping up and down. Everybody has their own method. Then the battle begins.

The wrestlers fight with naked torsos. All they wear is a *kispet*, a pair of tight-fitting black pants made of water buffalo or calves' leather. Before the competition these are soaked in oil and greased to prevent the opponents from getting a firm grip. During breaks in competition, the valuable Kispets are put in a *zembil*, a bast bag.

During the fight just about anything is permitted except biting, spitting, scratching, insulting the opponent, speaking with the opponent, or rigging the fight. The competition can end quickly. In addition to pinning the shoulders, there are five other methods of winning. The competition continues on an elimination basis. Only the victor goes on to the next round.

Sights

A tour of town should begin on Hüriyet Meydanı, the main square, around which most sights are located.

Selim Mosque *(Selimiye Camii)*

"Build me a mosque which will overshadow every other mosque in my empire. Let it crown the top of this hill, and proclaim to non-believers the greatness of Allah!" The command by Sultan SELIM II to his master builder, SINAN, in 1568 was obvious: the loveliest mosque in all of Turkey should be built upon the highest point at the center of town, visible to all, far and wide. There is little doubt that Sinan followed his orders exactly. The status of the Selim Mosque is best described by a saying which was already popular during Sinan's lifetime: Sehzade-Mosque in İstanbul was his apprentice piece; Süleimaniye - considered the loveliest mosque in İstanbul - was his journeyman's piece; while the Selimiye in Edirne was his masterpiece.

Enter the mosque from Edirne's main square, Hüriyet Meydanı. Through a small, lovely garden, you enter the *arasta*, a roofed bazaar at the foot of the mosque. The 225 m long bazaar was built 30 years after the mosque to finance mosque maintenance. The architect was Sinan's student, DAVUD AGA, who also built the Blue Mosque in İstanbul. In the center of the elongated arasta, a covered stairway leads to the front courtyard of the mosque.

The *interior courtyard* is crowned by an eight-sided *cleansing fountain* boasting lovely ornamentation. It is surrounded on all sides by arcades of pointed arches. The 16 Moorish-style columns (notice the typical transition between red and white stone) with stalactite capitals support 18 domes. The meticulous painting of the domes is remarkable, particularly in the dome above the main gate. Sinan plays with the visitor: not every dome is the same size. The largest is on the mosque wall; the smallest across by the arcade. Large and small arcades are altered harmoniously. The eye of the viewer is carried from dome to dome leading automatically to the main entrance and the mosque beyond.

The *main entrance* boasts a splendid stalactite gate. It was originally located in the Great Mosque of Birgi near İzmir where Sinan personally dismantled it and transported it stone by stone to Edirne in oxcarts.

The interior displays the unique ingenuity of the mosque: the sense of space within such proportions has never again been achieved in a mosque. The single dome is 31.5 m in diameter and 45 m high (even taller than the Hagia Sophia in İstanbul). It sits playfully, almost floating upon eight relatively thin columns, of which four stand free in the hall. Amazing light streams into the hall from numerous windows in the dome and walls. Only the perfectly balanced system of support permits the walls to be pierced with so many windows. The blue texture of the light stems from the painting of the dome.

Sinan placed the *tribune of the prayer leader* under the center of the dome to emphasize the symmetry of the building. The fountains under the arcades of the tribune are unusual: Sinan is thereby returning to an ancient theme. Cleansing fountains in the mosque were designed for purification, but also because the sound of splashing water intensifies concentration and meditation.

The *Sultan's Box* in the northwest corner is the loveliest of its kind. Constructed of twelve marble plates, it rests upon 3 m tall breccia legs, and is covered with costly faiences. The *mimber*, or pulpit, is second to none. It leans defiantly against one of the supporting columns impressing with its height, the huge suns on its sides and the extremely precise marblework. This mimber has been compared to a terraced throne, reinforcing the concept of closeness between Allah and his servants.

Adding to the breathtaking impression are the extremely slim and elegant *minarets* whose height of 71 m overshadows all others in the Islamic world. Every minaret has three galleries accessible via three separate sets of stairs. As a result, three individuals can be on the tower at one time without ever seeing each other.

Museum: The museum is divided into two parts. The smaller section is in the *medrese* behind the Selim Mosque; the larger is in a modern building a bit to the north. The former **medrese** (admission £0.10) houses a local museum featuring a *Kırkpınar Hall* (pictures of famous wrestlers, medals, wrestling paraphernalia), a large weapons collection, the obligatory İznik tiles, metalware, blankets and flags from the surrounding region. In the central courtyard is a row of interesting tombstones marking the resting place of famous wrestlers and unknown viziers.

OPEN: 9.00-12.00 h, 13.00-18.00 h, closed Mondays.

Modern Museum Building: North of Selim Mosque (admission: £0.20). A casual display in light-filled rooms of archaeological and ethnographical exhibits from Thrace. The archaeology department features a valuable coin collection, numerous busts and statue heads from the Greek and Roman eras, plus tomb artifacts from the pre-Christian era. d

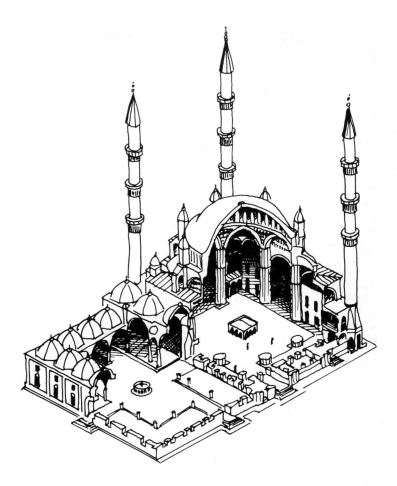

Just as interesting are the ethnographical exhibits which showcase
Thracian and Anatolian kelims, Gördes carpets, delicately ornamented bags, bath shoes, handkerchiefs and costumes, along with an
old Phaeton coach.

Old Mosque (*Eski Cami*): Below Selim Mosque on Freedom Square is the oldest large mosque in Edirne, built from 1404 - 1414 under Sultan MEHMET I by GENCI ALAEDDIN from Konya.

The Old Mosque is in the pillar-mosque style and (like the Great Mosque in Bursa) a direct descendant of the post-supported Seljuk nomad tent. But there are a number of new features not seen in the Great Mosque of Bursa. While 20 domes were installed in Bursa, the architect managed to get by here with nine much larger domes.

The entrance hall, dating from a later period, is less impressive. Only the calligraphy, which continues into the interior, is of interest, dating from the 19th century.

Inside, the four massive columns are decorated with ornamentation and calligraphy. If the Baroque era comes to mind, it is not without cause. The gaudy colouring, mostly blue, is from the Turkish Baroque period (Tulip Period). To give an increased sense of space, the three central domes were built slightly higher. The entrance dome is roofed with glass to let in more light. A treasured jewel is the stone by the window next to the prayer niche, said to be a piece of the Kaaba in Mecca. The mimber clearly depicts Seljuk motifs.

In 1987 a partial restoration was in progress. Hopefully there will be enough money and energy to restore the entire mosque, remove the mold from the walls and buy a new carpet.

Bedesten: The Bedesten or covered bazaar behind the Old Mosque is Edirne's third bazaar (in addition to the Ali-Paşa Bazaar and the Arast). Built between 1414 and 1424 AD, it is also the oldest. The building is a basilica, 65 m long and 32 m wide, covered by 14 domes. Although it is nicknamed the "Antique Bazaar", there are few treasures to be found inside. On sale are household goods ranging from garden hoses to washing machines, a few sweets, and junk. The quite modern appearance of the shops does not create a nostalgic bazaar atmosphere.

Rüstempaşa Karvansarayı: Also built by Sinan in 1560 as a guesthouse for travellers (caravanserai) on the orders of SÜLEYMAN'S Grand Vizier RÜSTEM PASHA. You are permitted to look inside if you ask politely. Restored from 1968 to 1972, the building is owned by the Turkish government.

Üç-Şerefeli Mosque: The "Three-Gallery Mosque" (1438-1442) received its name from the northwestern minaret. It was the first in the Ottoman Empire with three entrances, and at almost 68 m, it was the tallest in Turkey until completion of the Selim Mosque. The mosque has something of an experimental character as can be seen in the four very different minarets. In addition to the largest minaret with its Seljuk-style, red-white, zigzag pattern, the other minarets sport chessboard patterns, spiral patterns and fluting. It seems to be a test of the optical appearance of several basic styles.

Experimentation can also be seen in the *front courtyard*, which seems rather crowded: hardly any of the 21 domes are of the same size or diameter. These were probably designed to emphasize various sections of the courtyard.

The *interior* of the "Test Mosque" seems equally confining. The extremely flat dome (24 m diameter/29 m high) absolutely destroys a sense of space. But keep in mind that this is the first mosque ever built without the column style. The single-dome mosque was built before the conquest of İstanbul, that means before Ottoman architects could look inside the Hagia Sophia to see how it was done.

The mosque is worth a look if only for its valuable, blue-toned mosaic windows around the dome and side walls. Unfortunately, the steel supports needed during restoration completely destroy the sense of space.

Sokullu-Bath (*Sokullu Hamamı*): Set opposite the Üç Şerefeli Cami, this double bath (for men and women) was built in the 16th century, obviously by SINAN. It is in excellent condition, and both parts are still in use today. For a fee of £0.70 to £3.35, depending upon service, local people and travellers are invited to relax.

Clock Tower (*Büyük Kule*): Beside Sokullu Bath is the oldest structure in town, and one of the few remaining from the Byzantine era. Built on the order of Emperor JOHN III DUKAS in 1123, the tower served as the northeast bastion of the town fortifications of ancient Hadrianopolis. The wooden addition dates from 1866. From here the town wall ran along Saraclar Caddesi to the Tunca and from there westward to Gazimihal Bridge. On the bank of the Tunca, ruins of the fortifications can still be seen.

Ali-Paşa Bazaar (*Ali Paşa Çarşısı*): Another example of Sinan's work is the 150 m market hall across from the clock tower. Built in 1569 on the order of the Grand Vizier ALI PASHA, the Ali Paşa Çarşısı is the most important bazaar in Edirne. The main entrance on Talat Paşa Caddesi is easy to overlook. The long, narrow building runs parallel to Saraçlar Caddesi down to Balıkpazarı Caddesi (the former fish market, where a few fish stands are still located today) and is accessible from the street via several entrance gates.

The selection is not especially large, consisting of household goods and some junk. But a visit to the covered market is worthwhile, just for a look at the almost festive lighting.

Sinan

Ottoman architecture is tremendously well done at its best, but largely the work of anonymous architects. Mosques, palaces, aqueducts, baths are usually recorded with the names of the ruling sultan, who ordered the construction. The architect's name is rarely familiar to anyone other than the experts.

There is one exception: SINAN, chief architect under SÜLEYMAN the Magnificent, SELIM II and MURAT III. The Ottomans were the mightiest military power of the time: it was the golden age of the Ottoman Empire. This, of course, inspired cultural expression. The enthusiasm of the time provided Sinan with unlimited support for his projects. Money was no object during an era when the Turkish army was taking rich booty in the Balkans. Sinan had the good fortune to live at a time and a place when his ingenuity furthered the sultans' wish for showcase architecture.

Born in the heart of provincial Agirna in the tiny village of Vilayet Kayseri, he is said to have made a name for himself even as a child. His first works consisted of small huts, barns and water canals. In 1513, fate intervened: he was brought to İstanbul as part of a recruitment of youths for the Janissary Corps and pressed into the service of the infamous Greek renegade and Grand Vizier IBRAHIM PASHA.

During his apprenticeship he learned courtly manners while looking over the shoulder of the most famous architects of the time. As a Janissary, he participated in all the military campaigns, travelling to far away lands where he could study the architecture. He saw Persian memorials in Tabris, the pyramids in Gizeh, Roman aqueducts in the Balkans, and the most important mosques in the entire Islamic world.

His diligence and his ingenuity permitted him to rise quickly within the ranks of the Janissary Corps. He rose to the rank of Infantry Commander, then to Chief of Munitions and the high rank of Haseki - after he built the ships with which the army crossed the Van Lake during a Persian campaign. The sultan took notice of this talented man.

On 8 April 1536, at the age of 50, he was named Süleyman's Chief Court Architect. As such he had unlimited power over all buildings under construction in the entire empire. Subject to veto by the sultan, he was empowered to build any building he desired, or to tear down any structure not meeting his expectations.

His first great work was the **Sehzade Mosque** built in 1548 in
İstanbul. Then he solved the water supply problem in grand
style: a tremendous piping system transported well water to the
capital from the Belgrade Forest. In quick succession he adorned
İstanbul with palaces, mosques, medreses and mausoleums.

In 1550 he began construction of the loveliest mosque in
İstanbul, the **Süleymaniye**; in 1569 he immortalized himself in

Edirne with the even lovelier **Selimiye**. And in 1584 he fulfilled another dream by supervising restoration in Mecca of the domes in the most sacred of all mosques, the **Harem i-Şerif**.

In all, Sinan built or restored 84 major mosques and 52 smaller mosques, 57 medreses (Koran schools), 22 mausoleums, 17 ımarets (charity kitchens), 35 palaces, 3 hospitals, 20 caravanserais and 41 bath houses.

Despite his high office, Sinan lived modestly. As a man whose work spoke for itself throughout the Muslim world, he saw no need to build a mausoleum dedicated to himself. The greatest of Ottoman architects is laid to rest in a simple tomb in the Süleymaniye in İstanbul. He knew his work would survive his death for centuries to come, and his name would never be forgotten.

Muradiye Mosque (*Muradiye Camii*): Following the Mimar Sinan Caddesi past Selim Mosque and uphill, we come to Mosque Murat II, built in 1429 as a dervish monastery and later converted to a pillar mosque. The interior suffered greatly in an earthquake, losing much of its original appeal. The minaret was built in 1960 to replace its collapsed predecessor. Notice the tombstones of the dervish monks, recognizable by the tall dervish cap made of stone.

Seraglio Island (*Saray İçi*): North of town, easy to reach from both Muradiye Mosque or the centre of town, the island in the Tunca River was once the site of a sultan's castle. Edirne had its Seraglio long before İstanbul, built by MEHMET the Conqueror, who was raised here. The centre of attraction is a seven-story palace tower surrounded by look-out terraces. It remained one of Mehmet's favorite spots, even after the conquest of İstanbul!

The only account of the once splendid palace was given by the Austrian count **Philipp Franz Gudenus**, who in 1740 was one of the few Europeans ever to visit the Seraglio. He described the Seraglio of Edirne as an extensive building complex, divided by small walls into courtyards and gardens. The harem resided in splendid rooms with tiled walls, and cabinets inlaid with pearl, tortoiseshell, and silver. The Austrian described the buildings as "neglected". Not surprising, as the harem and Seraglio had served as a refuge for aging concubines and a place of banishment for fallen dignitaries since the 16th century. In absolute decay, the complex was blown up by the Turkish army in 1877 to provide a better line of fire against invading Russian troops.

All that remains is part of the *Justice Tower* (restored) dating from the days of Süleyman and the sparse remains of the palace of Mehmet II. The older of the island's two bridges, *Fatih Köprüsü*, dates from the time of İstanbul's conquest (15th century). Seraglio Island, with its shady trees, is also the site of the Wrestling Stadium (see Kırkpınar).

Complex Beyazit II. (*II. Bayazıt Külliyesi*): Financed by Sultan BEYAZIT II and built by HAYRETTIN in 1484-1488. The large mosque complex lies behind the dam on the Tunca River like a fairy palace in the lonely countryside. If the attendants are there - not always the case - you can visit the newly restored *Külliye* buildings in addition to the mosque.

The mosque itself is a less than spectacular rectangular building with a single dome 20 m in diameter. As in the Eski Cami, the paintings are baroque. Two domed wings (*tabhane*) served as overnight rooms for travellers. Today the house is a library for religious writings. The stone sultan's box set on columns taken from Ephesus is particularly interesting.

To the right of the mosque, the center of the Külliye is the *Medicine School*, consisting primarily of a courtyard with a *purification fountain* surrounded by arcades and the asymmetrical *hospital buildings*. The hospital consists of a courtyard with only one columned hall and an inner courtyard at right angles. At the back is the most interesting building of the complex, a hexagonal structure with a domed central hall and heated side rooms for the sick. In a niche across from the entrance, musicians would sit and play for the patients.

> The traveller **Evliya Celebi** writes that the mentally ill, hypochondriacs and melancholics were treated using humanist methods. Treatment here emphasized soft music, listening to splashing water, discovering beautiful flowers, and serving meals of fresh game, while in Europe the mentally ill were commonly restrained with chains.

To the left of the mosque are the newly restored facilities including the kitchen, storage rooms and a bakery.

The Külliye is an easy 20 minute walk from the center of town. A visit is worth it, since this is a now rare, perfectly preserved charity complex "set in a field" with no other buildings in the area.

Yıldırım Mosque (*Yıldırım Camii*): Its roots date back to the Byzantine era. Recently discovered maps and writings indicate that this was the site of an early church which was later modified. This explains why none of the four walls face Mecca and why the mihrab (prayer niche) had to be painted onto one of the columns. The interior is crowned by four domes supported by columns. According to the Tourist Information Office, the mosque will be restored in the near future.

> The Yıldırım Mosque is not easy to find. Follow Talatpaşa Caddesi toward Bulgaria, cross the Gazimihal Bridge and take the field path off to the right. After about 300 m you will reach an old Ottoman bridge undergoing restoration. From here it is just a few steps to the overgrown mosque district. During our last visit the interior of the mosque was closed, but this will hopefully change soon.

Bridges: Edirne is famous for its bridges, some of which were built or restored by Sinan.

Our favorite is **Yeni Köprü** (New Bridge), built in 1840 on the order of Sultan ABDÜL MECIT. The 263 m long bridge, supported by twelve arches, rises slightly in the center and joins with a stone canopy. It crosses the Meriç in the south of town, en route to the Greek border. By the way, it was designed as a railway bridge before the railway station was forced to move to the south of town in compliance with the Treaty of Sèvres in 1922.

The design of the Yeni Köprü was undoubtedly copied from the **Beyazıt-Bridge** in the north of town en route to Külliye Beyazıt II. Although it has only ten arches, it is just as long and boasts a canopy of equal beauty. Built by SINAN in 1488, the bridge is a masterpiece of structural engineering, with its weight supported not by columns, but rather by the abutment at both ends.

Gazi Mihal Köprüsü, restored by SINAN, probably dates from the Byzantine era. It crosses the Tunca west of town. Allah be praised that city planners routed traffic on E 5 toward the Bulgarian border via a parallel bridge of steel and concrete. Since then, the Gazi Mihal bridge belongs to its admirers.

Also of interest are the **Tunca Köprüsü** (1618) south of town (before the new bridge), the **Saray Köprüsü** (15th century) on the way to Seraglio Island, and **Sarachane Köprüsü** (1751) further west.

A quick word about photography. In the border region every bridge is closely guarded. Don't let yourself be deterred. No soldier will prevent you from taking a picture of any historic bridge. On the contrary, they will frequently ask to be photographed with the bridge! Avoid walking in the restricted areas on the banks beside the bridges - they are often mined!

Around Edirne

Hiking along the river meadows: A great idea. The meadows are particularly pretty between the *Tunca* and *Meriç* in the south of town just before their junction. Why not walk along the *Tunca* from the *Külliye Beyazıd II* to its junction with the *Meriç*? This involves rounding half the town, taking 2 1/2 hours, without ever losing sight of the Selim Mosque.

Lüleburgaz: A lovely country town with a real surprise; the *Sokullu Mehmet Paşa Külliyesi*. The complex was built by the ingenious 16th century master architect, consisting of a mosque, caravanserai, medrese (prayer school), hamam (Turkish bath) and a library. We particularly liked the *şadirvan* (cleansing fountain), in the front courtyard of the mosque, with its slightly waving roof, almost Chinese in style.

COMING - GOING: 74 km from Edirne. Minibuses or buses every half hour (bus toward İstanbul). From İstanbul it is 160 km (bus toward Edirne from the European Bus Station Trakya Garajı).

Uzunköprü: A regional market town (pop. 30,000). The town's name "Uzun Köprü" means "long bridge", referring to the 1.4 km aqueduct with 173 arcades in the north of town. While the aqueduct was not built by Sinan, it is still worth a look.

COMING - GOING: E 5 toward İstanbul to Havsa (20 km), then turn off toward Uzunköprü/Keşan. Minibuses and buses every half hour.

Keşan and Saros Körfezi: Keşan (113 km south of Edirne) a quiet agricultural centre without any major sights. More interesting is an excursion to **Erikli** on the still largely unfrequented strait *of Saros Körfezi*, 25 km away.

A NIGHT'S REST: **İşçimen Oteli,** Saros Körfezi, Erikli. tel. 22. Double £8, full board £15.35. 64 beds, all 30 rooms with shower and bath. Rooms are nicely furnished. The swimming pool opens on 1 June. Note: Guests wishing full board have preference. Guests wishing lodgings only must register in the evening.

İSTANBUL AND VICINITY

"I have seen the ruins of Athens, Ephesus and Delphi. I have wandered through a large part of Turkey, many parts of Europe, and some of Asia, but never have I seen a work of art or nature, which has left such a great impression upon me, as the view from both sides of the Seven Towers Fortress to the end of the Golden Horn."

LORD BYRON said it all. For poets, İstanbul, next to Venice and Rome, is the loveliest city in Europe and one of the most splendid in Asia. It is the only city in the world which is spread over two continents, separated by the Bosporus and connected by the Bosporus Bridge.

ATATÜRK established his capital at Ankara. But Ankara is a cold, technocratic upstart, lacking the flair and tradition of Byzantium/Constantinople. İstanbul controls the Bosporus, Europe's most strategic straits. İstanbul has the largest harbour, the greatest industrial potential, the largest population, the best soccer teams and the worst environmental problems in all of Turkey.

What would Turkey be without İstanbul? And what would a trip to Turkey be without visiting the Blue Mosque, the Hagia Sophia, the Galata Bridge, the Topkapı Seraglio, having seafood in Kumkapı, taking a trip to the Prince Islands or a Bosporus cruise? İstanbul has as many sights as most of the rest of Turkey. Nowhere else in Turkey can you shop so well or find so many hotels, youth hostels and pensions in every price category.

It takes a few days just to familiarize yourself with this Ottoman town. And when the city stress is just too much, do as the locals do: leave town for the beaches at Kilyos or Şile, cruise over to the Prince Islands, visit Hereke or Belgrade Forest.

İSTANBUL *(pop. 7,000,000)*

İstanbul's unique panorama is visible when landing at Yeşilköy Airport: an armada of heavy freighters in the Sea of Marmara, minarets of countless mosques, the dome of Hagia Sophia, the Blue Mosque, the Golden Horn, the Bosporus, a thousand cars on Galata Bridge, and seven hills (just like in Rome).

The drive from the airport into town is an unforgettable experience. Taxis honk their way through an obstacle course of donkey carts, porters loaded with huge piles of cotton on their backs, improvised markets directly on busy crossroads, the sound of ships' horns in the distance, and masses of people. There are shoe shiners on the street corners, T-shirt vendors on every curb, students, muslims en route to mosque, children, passers-by, soldiers, tourists, dancing bears waiting to be photographed etc.

Arriving by train: the empty beaches at *Florya* illuminated by the early-morning light, young boys fishing in lonely bays. The train glides past a cattle market, then through districts of old wooden houses down to the Sea of Marmara. Here you'll see a different İstanbul: small businesses, pipes for the planned sewage system and finally a view of *Galata* and its *Galata tower*.

You will detect the city's enormous problems only on second glance: no sewage system, torn up roads, blocked up drainage pipes, poverty and filth. Thousands of cars choke the main roads, Bosporus steamers pollute the air with black smoke. On the outskirts of town, the *Gecekondus* grow unchecked as peasants from Anatolia move to these shanty towns in hope of finding work.

The city is tottering, but it won't die. New settlements are built where factories have been torn down. Improvisation is a way of life and problems are put off until tomorrow. İstanbul is like its people: just getting by. Perhaps this is the fascination: old and new, side by side, ever chaotic, ever amazing.

History

People have inhabited the site of present-day İstanbul since the late Stone Age. The actual town, considering its strategic location, is still quite young.

About 1000 BC, a settlement called Semistra was founded at the end of the Golden Horn. These people later resettled at the tip of the seraglio, where the fishing village Lygos has been inhabited since the 9th century BC.

In 667 BC the Greeks arrived and settled the town of Byzantium. The Greeks quickly recognized the full strategic value of İstanbul's location: surrounded by water on three sides, only a narrow strip of land facing inland need be secured with towers and walls. In a strong position at the entrance to the Bosporus they controlled traffic between the Aegean and the Black Sea. Anyone travelling from Asia to Europe or vice versa was forced to pass through here.

The town quickly developed into a major trading centre famous for both its fish and wine. In 513 BC the great Persian commander DARIUS ordered construction of a large bridge across the Bosporus, led his army across it and captured the town which put up little resistance.

In the course of the Persian wars, the town was liberated by Spartan forces under PAUSANIAS. "Liberation" in reality meant integration in the Attic Naval Alliance and heavy financial obligations! Two uprisings in 440 BC and 411 BC faltered. Not until 356 BC were the Byzantines finally able to free themselves from Athens.

It would have been insane to ignore the strength of ALEXANDER THE GREAT. After his victory against Persia at Granicus (334 BC), the Byzantines voluntarily opened their gates to him. Under ALEXANDER the town remained unscathed by the Diadochan fighting: it was able to expand its trade and grew prosperous. But the city's wealth attracted envy: in 278 BC the town was conquered and plundered by the Celts.

Byzantium was required to pay tribute to the Gauls. In order to pay the annual duty, the city demanded a tax of all ships passing through the Bosporus. This, of course, did not please the neighbouring towns of Pergamon and Bythinia. Together with the equally affected fleet of Rhodes, they conquered the city and eliminated the toll.

Peace lasted for three hundred years, until the Byzantines angered the Roman emperor SEPTIMIUS SEVERUS (196 AD) by supporting his rival PESCENNIUS NIGER. The victorious emperor stripped the city of its privileges. Byzantium came close to sharing the fate of Carthage, but it found an advocate in the emperor's son (and future emperor) CARACALLA. Septimius softened his stand and permitted the reconstruction of the city - now twice its previous size - with solid city walls, the Hippodrome and splendid palaces.

BYZAS OF MEGARA

According to legend, this is the man who founded Byzantium. Before leaving Greece with a group of colonists, he is said to have consulted the Oracle at Delphi as to where they should settle. "Settle across from the blind" was the puzzling response. When BYZAS sailed through the Dardanelles and reached the Golden Horn, he noticed a colony on the Asian side called Chalcedon (today Kadıköy), founded shortly before by settlers from Megara. "The Chalcedonians must be blind!" he exclaimed, as they had completely failed to see the natural harbour.

Byzantium's greatest moment came on September 18, 324 AD, when Emperor CONSTANTINE made the city his imperial capital and named it Nova Roma. The name which stuck, however, was *Constantinopolis*.

CONSTANTINE immediately set to work to make Nova Roma a worthy site for his court. He himself chose the site for new, more secure city walls, which were constructed within four years. The size of the city was thereby increased five-fold. Like the original city of Rome, it now encompassed seven hills, and like its predecessor it was divided into thirteen districts. Wide boulevards, large squares and forums, a huge imperial palace and a number of churches were built within the Constantinian walls. Nothing remains of them today except the Constantine column (*Burned Column*). The city itself, now the centre of an empire, quickly developed, spreading beyond its walls even during Constantine's lifetime.

In 395 AD Emperor THEODOSIUS I divided the empire between his sons HONORIUS and ARCADIUS, the latter receiving the eastern half of the empire. This is how the history of the independent eastern Roman empire began. THEODOSIUS II expanded the land and sea fortifications (which are still well preserved today) making the city practically impregnable.

Constantinople enjoyed a golden age under JUSTINIAN (527 - 565 AD). The early days of his reign seemed foreboding. In his fifth year of rule, JUSTINIAN had to put down the Nika uprising at a cost of 40,000 lives and great destruction. The battle did free a lot of space upon which Justinian undertook extravagant construction. The showcase building was Hagia Sophia, the most splendid building in the ancient world!

HOW VLADIMIR SENT HIS CONCUBINES HOME

In 987 AD Grand Duke Vladimir of Russia decided to end his heathen ways. He sent out emissaries to explore the Roman Catholic, the Greek Orthodox, the Jewish, and the Islamic faiths. The Islamic Bulgarians were found to be too sad and too lazy; the German churches were too ugly. Only the Hagia Sophia and the Orthodox religious service were so impressive "they didn't know if they were in heaven or on earth". Vladimir sent his hundreds of concubines home and joined the Greek Orthodox faith.

Justinian instituted imperial reforms: Christian culture and architecture supplanted the Roman inheritance. Greek replaced Latin as the official language. His government became a rigid bureaucracy. The primary source of power was the Orthodox church which, since the days of Constantine, had recognized the emperor as its leader and patron. The east Roman emperor was thereby both the religious and secular ruler. Justinian's successors were equally skillful. They permitted the Avars - a warlike Balkan people descended from the Huns - to proceed unchecked to the gates of Byzantium, where the powerful Byzantine fleet and the impregnable Theodosian walls forced the invaders to leave empty-handed.

While the Persians and Avars proved manageable in the 6th century, a new danger arose from Arabia in the 7th century. In 674 an Arab army challenged Constantinople for the first time. The siege of the city lasted two years, then they withdrew with heavy losses. The attackers were worn down by hunger and illness and the tiresome and senseless storming of the walls as much as by the "Greek Fire", a form of napalm, fired with flame throwers from the Byzantine galleys on the enemy fleet. In 716 AD a new Arab fleet arrived at Constantinople only to meet defeat again. Of 800 Arab ships, only five returned home!

During the second siege of Constantinople, LEO II ascended to the throne. From the Arabs, he gained the belief that depictions of Christ, the apostles and saints were a sin. This brought a quick end to the love of icons, which were removed from the churches. For 120 years, the iconographic controversy imposed cultural stagnation in addition to weakening the empire by internal unrest. In 843, Empress THEODORA ended the controversy by ceremoniously "Restoring the Icons".

In previous centuries the Arabs posed the greatest threat to the city, but in the 9th and 10th centuries the Islamic Bulgarians were the most serious adversaries. Twice, in 813 and 924, they appeared before the gates of the city; twice they were defeated.

ENDLESS TROUBLE WITH THE BULGARIANS

In the 6th century the Bulgarians challenged the gates of Constantinople, but because their ally, Persia, was unable to cross the Bosporus and they themselves were too weak to storm the walls, they turned back in exchange for a large ransom and invited emperor HERACLIUS to join them in an extravagant farewell banquet. It was almost too late when Heraclius realized that he himself was part of the menu. He managed to escape on horseback but his entourage was captured and 250,000 Byzantine spectators were taken prisoner.

In 924 AD, the Bulgarians had to pay for this. Emperor BASILIUS II had 15,000 Bulgarian prisoners blinded. One man out of each hundred was spared one eye with which to lead 99 compatriots home. The Bulgarian Khan fainted when he saw the state of his returning army. Neither he nor his empire were ever able to recover from this shock.

At the end of the 20th century, there is trouble with the Bulgarians once again. Bulgaria insists on "Bulgarization" of its small Turkish minority. Travel restrictions and the required assumption of Bulgarian names have been imposed.

The Byzantine empire was at the height of its power under BASILIUS II. The emperor lived in almost inconceivable splendour, isolated from his people by an army of eunuchs and bureaucrats. When he died, no worthy successor could be found. The military, the economy and foreign policy were neglected. Large landowners gained such advantages that small farmers were forced to flee from their land to the cities. This deprived the Byzantine army of its primary source of recruits. For centuries, young peasants from Anatolia had been the backbone of the Byzantine defense forces. At the same time powerful enemies were gaining strength sufficient to seal the fate of Constantinople. The greatest danger was from the crusaders. After the defeat at the hands of the Turks in the Battle of Manzikert, Byzantium had sent out a call for help to France and Germany, but the emperor had surely not expected that a horde of barbarians would heed his call.

For centuries Byzantium had mixed with the peoples all around the Mediterranean and they got along well together. Lively trade and the common Greek culture provided a basis of understanding. But the knights who stopped to rest in Constantinople in 1096 en route to the Holy City did not speak Greek, nor were they of the Greek Orthodox faith; and they certainly possessed no manners. While Byzantium gave them its official support, providing transport to Asia Minor, the Byzantines looked down upon the loud and barbaric "Franconians". And the crusaders just hated the clever and shrewd Byzantines. A conflict was unavoidable.

The trouble came to a head after the massacre of Venetians and Genoese at Galata where they had maintained a trading post for centuries. In anger, Doge ENRICO DANDOLO hired members of the 4th crusade on their way to Egypt to perform a personal favour for him. In order to reach the Holy Land, the crusaders needed Venetian ships. These were promised only if the crusaders agreed to make a side trip to Constantinople for the purpose of destroying the Byzantine empire. And the job was done - thoroughly.

In 1204 AD the Venetian fleet arrived at Constantinople and conquered the city almost without resistance. For 53 days the crusaders plundered the richest city of those times, robbing and destroying art treasures of priceless value. It is reported that Orthodox priests were roasted at the stake and then eaten.

Afterwards the crusaders established a Latin empire in Constantinople. The wealthy Byzantine families fled to Nicaea (İznik) where they founded an imperial court in exile and consolidated their financial resources. Finally they convinced the Genoese (the Byzantines were historically the greatest diplomats) to assist in their plan to recapture Byzantium. In 1261 Emperor MICHAEL VIII Palaeologos led a colourfully mixed army back into the city, attracting the cheers of onlookers. The Palaeologan dynasty would manage to stay in power for almost 200 years. But Constantinople was no longer the queen of cities. The population had declined from almost a million to just 50,000. Palaces and churches were in decay. The once powerful empire was reduced to just a strip of land sheltered behind the Theodosian walls. On the horizon loomed the Turks, to whom the Byzantines were already paying tribute. By 1453, the Ottoman empire was ready to take Constantinople.

The Byzantines prepared for the deciding battle as best they could. Emperor CONSTANTINE XI ordered the Golden Horn closed with a heavy iron chain. Then he drummed up all the armed men available, a poor lot of 5000 Byzantines, 3000 Genoese under Admiral GIUSTI-NIANI, plus a small contingent of Ottoman deserters. The Turks took their time, however, choosing first to close off all avenues of access. On April 5, 1453, the Turkish siege began. The first actual attack was on April 18. Sultan MEHMET II commanded an army of 80,000, supported by the world's most powerful artillery. On the night before April 23, the Sultan ordered 70 warships from the Bosporus (at the site of the present-day Dolmabahçe Palace) to be pulled on soaped boards over the hills into the Golden Horn, thus avoiding the barricading chain. The city could no longer be defended! By April 29 the Turkish artillery had broken through the land wall, permitting entry by Turkish troops. Emperor Constantine was killed in battle. Giustiniani and the Genoese retreated onto their ships, where Giustiniani was soon to die of a wound.

After three days of looting - the usual practice in those days - the Sultan restored order and began with the reconstruction of the city which had experienced centuries of decay. His most significant constructions were the Topkapı Sarayı and the huge Conqueror's Mosque, second in size only to the Hagia Sophia. Grand viziers and pashas soon followed his example and erected smaller mosques and Koran schools throughout the city. Mehmet and his son BEYAZIT permitted the settlement of Genoese, Venetians, Greeks, Armenians, and Jews fleeing the Spanish Inquisition. They all enlivened the metropolis with money and trade.

The Ottoman empire experienced a golden age under SELIM I (1512 - 1520), the son of BEYAZIT II. His son SÜLEYMAN THE MAGNIFICENT (1520 - 1566) was famous even beyond the Orient for his tolerance, humanity, intelligence and righteousness. During his reign the empire achieved the zenith of its power and its greatest prosperity. Süleyman hired the ingenious architect SINAN who built 24 mosques, 27 medreses and about 80 other buildings in İstanbul alone.

The Ottoman empire had experienced a succession of outstanding sultans ever since the conquest of İstanbul. After Süleyman's death, however, the dynasty was not so fortunate. In 1571 SELIM II lost a sea battle at Lepanto. MURAT II has gone into history as "the drunk". His successors were strangled, poisoned, or deposed for reasons of mental health. The real government was in the seraglio. The eldest women of the harem exerted great influence on the young princes succeeding to the sultan's throne. Equally powerful were the Grand Viziers and the elite military corps of the Janissaries, which grew more and more rebellious.

The Napoleonic Wars provided Turkey with a needed break. Sultan MAHMUT II (1808 - 1839) instituted long overdue reforms. In 1826 he ordered the massacre in the Hippodrome of his own Janissary Corps which had bitterly opposed any reform for centuries. His descendant tried to follow in his footsteps but with little success. The Ottoman empire was saved only by a fortunate turn of events in which Russia lost the Crimean War (1853 - 1856), forcing the Tsar to relinquish his pressure on İstanbul (the key to the Black Sea). Still Turkey remained the "sick Man on the Bosporus", totally dependent upon the European powers. A number of semi-colonial projects, aimed at the "Europeanization" of Turkey (including the German-financed Berlin-Bagdad Railway) drained Turkish resources more than they improved its infrastructure. The sad result was the national bankruptcy in 1875 which resulted in the sultan's murder. The next sultan was quickly deposed, before the third, ABDUL HAMID II, could solidify his tyrannical reign which lasted for 30 years.

In 1889 the Young Turk Movement, a secret society within the officer's corps, was founded at the Military Medical Academy in İstanbul. In 1909 the Saloniki Section of the Young Turks revolted, leading to the downfall of Abdul Hamid. Institutional reforms, opposed by the sultan, were immediately implemented, but without success. Good trade relations with Germany and the help of German military officers in reforming and training the Turkish army under the Young Turks led to Turkey joining WW I on the German side. Allied military units occupied İstanbul and the territories surrounding the Sea of Marmara in 1919 after the defeat.

Turkish nationalists gathered under KEMAL PASHA ATATÜRK in central Anatolia. On April 23, 1920 they called a meeting of the "Great National Assembly" in Ankara. The right of the sultan to the Turkish throne was revoked in deference to the Turkish people. War was declared upon the occupying powers. In the ensuing battles the Greek army was soundly defeated, and the Allies evacuated İstanbul.

Since then history has more or less bypassed İstanbul. Atatürk made Ankara his new capital. İstanbul, however, remained the economic centre of the Republic, attracting masses of people in search of jobs. In the periods from 1939 to 1945 and 1956 to 1959, road networks

were built downtown to handle the traffic problem. In 1973 the new Bosporus bridge was opened. Yeşilköy Airport began service in 1984. In the same year BEDRETTON DALAN took office as mayor, with the goal of making İstanbul the most attractive city in Turkey. -
The latest news before going into print: B. Dalan lost his mayoral seat in the municipal elections of 1989. He wasn't spared the crushing defeat of the ruling Motherland Party (ANAP) whose candidate he was. It seems, that the people of İstanbul are more concerned about jobs and better social conditions than an "attractive" city.

INFORMATION: **Karaköy**, Maritime Station, tel. 149 57 76
   Hilton (Entrance), tel. 133 05 92 - 93
   Atatürk **Airport**, tel. 573 73 99
   Sultanahmet, Divanyolu Caddesi, tel. 522 49 03
   Gençtur **Student Travel**, Yerebatan Caddesi 15/3 (Sultanahmet), tel. 528 7 34 /526 54 09 (very helpful and competent!).
TELEPHONE AREA CODE: 1

Coming - Going

AIRLINES

TURKISH AIRLINES (Türk Hava Yolları/THY).
Main Office: Cumhuriyet Caddesi 131, Harbiye, tel. 147 13 38.
Aksaray Office: Mustafa Kemal Paşa Caddesi 27, tel. 386 75 14.
Sirkeci Office: Gar Karşısı, Doğubank, İşhanı altı, tel. 522 88 85.
Taksim Office: Hilton Hotel, tel. 147 01 21.

LUFTHANSA: Cumhuriyet Caddesi 179, tel. 146 51 30.
AIR FRANCE: Cumhuriyet Caddesi 6, tel. 143 24 24.
SWISSAIR: Cumhuriyet Caddesi 6, tel. 148 42 30.
AUSTRIAN AIRLINES: Cumhuriyet Caddesi 26a, tel. 146 88 03.

Yeşilköy Airport (18 km outside of İstanbul, international flights). Right next to the big airport are the more modest facilities for domestic flights. Special buses move people between the airport and the city (No. 96 and No. 31, 6:00-23:00 h). The "Eminönü" bus takes you all the way into the centre of town; if you take other buses you have to change in Aksaray and get on an "Eminönü" bus. Always keep a sharp eye on your luggage in the overcrowded buses! If you have a lot of luggage, it is worth the expense of getting a taxi. Warning: helpless tourists will frequently be charged extravagant prices. Keep the following prices in mind: one passenger (maximum £4.30), two passengers (maximum £5.30). It is essential to agree on a fixed price for the ride in advance.
THY buses depart from Sishane every half hour, at no charge to airline ticket holders. From the national airport (200 m from the international terminal) THY buses depart for downtown. The trip from downtown to the airport rarely takes more than 45 minutes.

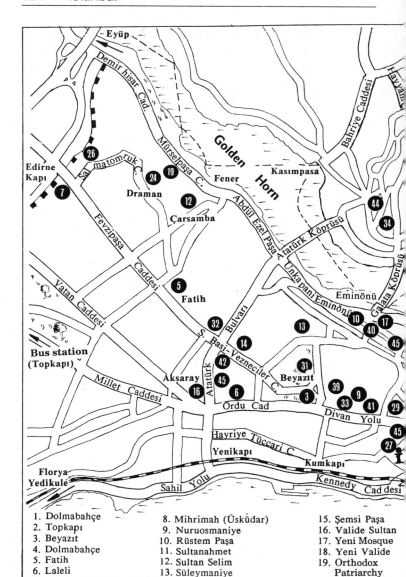

1. Dolmabahçe
2. Topkapı
3. Beyazıt
4. Dolmabahçe
5. Fatih
6. Laleli
7. Mihrimah (Edirnekapi)

8. Mihrimah (Üsküdar)
9. Nuruosmaniye
10. Rüstem Paşa
11. Sultanahmet
12. Sultan Selim
13. Süleymaniye
14. Şehzade

15. Şemsi Paşa
16. Valide Sultan
17. Yeni Mosque
18. Yeni Valide
19. Orthodox
    Patriarchy
    Fener

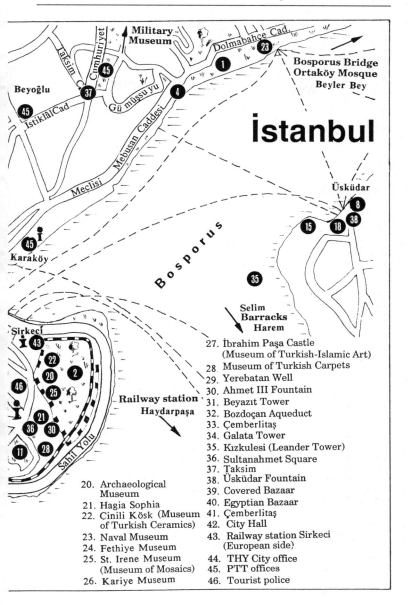

Military Museum

Beyoğlu

Bosporus Bridge
Ortaköy Mosque
Beyler Bey

İstanbul

Üsküdar

Karaköy

Bosporus

Sirkeci

Selim
Barracks
Harem

27. İbrahim Paşa Castle
    (Museum of Turkish-Islamic Art)
28. Museum of Turkish Carpets
29. Yerebatan Well
30. Ahmet III Fountain
Railway station   31. Beyazıt Tower
Haydarpaşa   32. Bozdoçan Aqueduct
                  33. Çemberlitaş
                  34. Galata Tower
                  35. Kızkulesi (Leander Tower)
                  36. Sultanahmet Square
                  37. Taksim
                  38. Üsküdar Fountain
20. Archaeological   39. Covered Bazaar
    Museum   40. Egyptian Bazaar
21. Hagia Sophia   41. Çemberlitaş
22. Cinili Kösk (Museum 42. City Hall
    of Turkish Ceramics) 43. Railway station Sirkeci
23. Naval Museum   (European side)
24. Fethiye Museum   44. THY City office
25. St. Irene Museum 45. PTT offices
    (Museum of Mosaics) 46. Tourist police
26. Kariye Museum

SHIP AGENCIES

All of your questions can be answered at **Turkish Maritime Lines**, Rıhtım Caddesi, Karaköy, tel. 144 02 07.

There are a lot of ships daily (departure usually hourly) from the harbour in Eminönü along the main routes: Karaköy to Kadıköy or to Haydarpaşa; from Eminönü to Kadıköy, Eyüp, Üsküdar from Sirkeci to Harem, Üsküdar Kabataş and Kartal Yalova. The ships depart from 06:00-24:00 h.

Warning: Always get your ticket in advance and be on time!

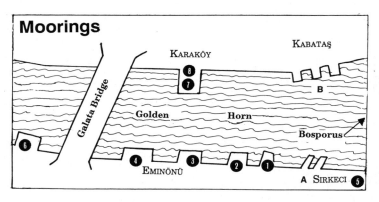

1 - Kadıköy, Bostanci
2 - Üsküdar
3 - Çengelköy, Kuzguncuk
4 - Bosporus

5 - Prince Islands
A - Sirkeci, Car Ferry
B - Yalova, Prince Islands, Marmara.

BUS COMPANIES

Numerous bus companies, all charging about the same prices, have offices on **Divan Yolu** (near Sultan Ahmet). Agencies offering tickets to Asia prefer locations around Beyazıt Square. Prices are posted in the windows. Gençtur offers good student discounts. However, they do not ask if you are a student. You will have to present your ID and ask for the discount. It is advisable to book your trip a day in advance. If enough passengers book a trip, the travel agency will provide transport to **Topkapı Bus Station** from where the buses actually depart.

Bus Station: International buses and domestic lines depart from **Topkapı** (6 km from town). Information on arrival and departure times is available from the bus agencies on Divan Yolu near Sultan Ahmet. There are several buses daily to practically every domestic destination.

LOCAL BUSES: Red city buses run frequently. Note: Buy your ticket before boarding! Most ticket windows close at 20:00 h. Children and elderly people will then offer tickets at slightly higher prices. But unfortunately, they frequently cannot be found where you need them. **Tip**: Always keep a reserve supply of tickets on hand (cost £0.07 each). Monthly tickets are available, but rarely used.

DOLMUŞ (Collective taxi): Collective taxis run like buses on established routes (even to distant towns). Marked with a white sign, dolmuş stops are usually located near a bus stop. Just yell "dolmuş" and the destination you want.

MINIBUSES: In İstanbul these are slowly replacing collective taxis. Minibuses provide transport to the major stations (e.g. Topkapı-Aksaray-Beyazıt, Sirkeci-Bakırköy), but also to more distant locations, cost £0.10.

TAXI: The fastest way around town. Taxis are recognizable by the double rows of yellow and black stripes below the windshield. On longer trips, be sure to fix the price in advance!

Addresses, Attractions, Tips

BANKS: There are numerous banks throughout town. Open: Monday to Friday 9:00-17:00 h. Note: Doors are generally locked 15 minutes before closing time. Checks are not cashed everywhere. We never had a problem with American Express and Swiss Banker's Travellers' Checks.

Also open on weekends are:
American Express/Türk Express, Hilton Hotel (9:00 - 20:00 h).
İş Banka, Hava Limanı, Yeşilköy (Airport) (8:00 - 20:00 h).
Denizcilik Bankası, Yolcu Salonu, Karaköy (9:00 - 17:00 h).
The Change Window in Sirkeci Train Station.
Tip: Much better exchange rates are frequently available on the black market. Although such channels are not encouraged, it is not illegal.

BOOK STORES: **Hasel Kitabevi**, İstiklal Caddesi 469, Beyoğlu, tel. 144 94 70, international literature. **Sander Kitabevi**, Cumhuriyet Cad. 280282, Beyoğlu.
English magazines are available along Divan Yolu near Hagia Sophia, in Sirkeci Station and - if you are lucky - on Taksim Square.

CAR RENTALS: **Avis**: Yedikular Cad. 4/A, Elmadağ/Taksim, tel. 141 29 17. Also in Divan Otel and in Hilton Hotel. **Hertz**: Cumhuriyet Cad. 295, tel. 141 53 23. Also in Sheraton Hotel, Taksim. **Budget**: İnönü Cad. 33/1, Taksim, tel. 149 57 14. **InterRent**: Cumhuriyet Cad. 203, tel. 147 92 49. **Esin**: Cumhuriyet Caddesi 472, tel. 143 15 15. **Kontur**: Cumhuriyet Caddesi 283, tel. 147 31 40.

In Taksim there are numerous other agencies offering the same price range.

CAR REPAIRS: If you have trouble with your car in İstanbul, try to fix it yourself first. For spare parts, try any of the shops on Tarlabaşı Caddesi (near Taksim Square). Here they can provide you with the addresses of specialized mechanics.

CARPETS: **Ali Katlan**, Yerebatan Caddesi 17 a, they have more carpets than you can imagine. Note: Decide first if you really want to buy a carpet. **Bazaar 54**, Nurousmaniye Cad. 54, Cağaloğlu, a member of the well-known and respected Bazaar 54 chain, good, but rarely the best quality. **M. Mavro's**, Tavukhane Sok. 2325, Sultanahmet (at the end of the Hippodrome), tel. 511 82 93, good service, reasonable prices, no bargaining.

CINEMAS: There are few cinemas worth mentioning in İstanbul, at best a couple in Taksim. Most films are in Turkish; few have subtitles. Occasionally an antiquated American film is shown.

128   İstanbul

Good international films do come to light during the **İstanbul Film Festival**. Some of the better films shown in recent years include Colonel Redl (Szabo), Love Streams (Cassavetes), Deprisa (Saura), A Passage to India (David Lean), Rumble Fish (Ford Coppola), Stranger than Paradise (Jarmusch) and Local Hero (Forsyth).

CITY TOURS: Not cheap, prices range from £10 per day to over £35 for "İstanbul by night", including a visit to a night club. **Sultan**, Cumhuriyet Cad. 87, Taksim, tel. 140 37 71. **Tura**, Cumhuriyet Cad. 129, Taksim, tel. 140 67 71. **Camel**, Dünya Sağlık Sok. Opera Ishani 41, Taksim, tel. 143 80 20.

CONSULATES: **GB**, Mesrutiyet Cad. 34, Tepebaşı, tel 44 75 40. **USA**, Meşrutiyet Cad. 104, Tepebaşı, tel. 43 62 00. **FRG**, İnönü Caddesi 1618, Beyoğlu, tel. 45 07 058. **NL**, İstiklal Caddesi 393, Beyoğlu, tel. 49 53 10. **A**, Silahhane Caddesi 59, Teşvikiye, tel. 146 37 69. **CH**, Hüsrev Gerede Caddesi 75, Teşvikiye, tel. 48 50 70. **BUL**, (transit visa!) Yıldızposta Cad. 15, Gayrettepe, Tepebaşı , tel. 26 66 05.

FESTIVALS: in the Atatürk Cultural Centre on Taksim Square you can pick up information on what is happening during your visit. The major annual events include: 20.6.-15.7. **Art and Culture Festival**. In April there is the International **Film Festival**.

HOSPITALS: In case of emergency, don't visit a doctor; go directly to a hospital. Your best bet is the **German hospital** where you are sure to receive good care. Here you will have a room to yourself and quiet. Turkish hospitals are frequently like family weddings, laughter and fun seem to replace good medical care. **German hospital** (Alman Hastanesi), Sıraselviler Caddesi 119, Taksim, tel. 143 55 00. **Austrian hospital** (Avusturya Sen Yorj Hastanesi), Büyük Medrese, Sok. 5, Karaköy, tel. 144 02 83/4. **First Aid Station** (İlk Yardim Hastanesi), Sıraselviler Cad., Taksim, tel. 1 49 30 00. Recommended in case of emergency. Here they speak English. They are set up to handle emergencies (appendicitis, colics, accidental injuries). **Dentist**: Yılmaz Aykaç, Lamartin Caddesi 16, Taksim.

LAUNDRY: Near Sultan Ahmet, at Yerebatan Caddesi 60 is a large laundry which seems trustworthy, open daily 8:00 - 20:00 h, prices: jacket £0.40, trousers £0.35, pullover £0.35, underwear £0.05, socks £0.08, sleeping bag £0.65.

LEATHER: **Kacar Leder**, Ordu Cad. 15, Beyazıt, tel. 522 31 07. A good selection of the best leather clothes! **Deri**, Silahhane Cad. 38, Tesvikiye, good and expensive.

PARKING (guarded): **Opera Garaji**, Taksim Square (near the Culture Palace). **Çukurova Garajı**, Şişli, across from Şişli Mosque. **Tepebaşı**, Meşrutiyet Cad., Tepebaşı, day and night. **Kabataş** (next to the car ferry), Arabalşı Vapur İskelesi yanşı, day and night. **Eminönü** (across from the Egyptian Bazaar, next to the Atatürk Bridge), Mısır Çarşısı, Köprü başında, only during the day.

POLICE: Foreigners with problems (theft or loss) should report to the tourist police: **Tourist Police** (Turizm Polisi), Sultanahmet, Almendar Caddesi 6, tel. 52 85 369. Contact with the "regular police" is usually involuntary, initiated by the other side.

POST OFFICE: Sirkeci, Yeni Postane Caddesi, open daily 8:00-20:00 h, passport required for Poste Restante.

SLIDE SHOW: In three languages in the garden of the Blue Mosque, daily from May to September if the weather is nice. There is another show by the Bosporus in Rumeli Hisarı castle, less crowded, nicer.

SPORTS: Don't expect much! The few golf courses and tennis courts are all in private hands. You cannot even rent a moped! Some water sport activities are offered on the Prince Islands.

TURKISH BATH: **Cağaloğlu Hamami**, Hilal i Ahmer or Yerebatan Cad. 34, Cağaloğlu (near Babiali Cad.) tel. 522 24 24, daily 7:00 - 24:00 h (women until 20:00 h).

Waiting for customers - shoe-shiners in İstanbul

The **Çemberlitaş Hamamı**, Divan Yolu, Vezirhanı Cad. 8, Çemberlitaş, tel. 522 79 74. Probably the best Turkish bath in İstanbul. A bath " Sultan style", costs £5 but it's worth the money.
Galatasaray Hamamı, Beyoglu, next to the Galatasaray Lisesi, the entrance is on a side street. For men (Erkek), Turnacıbası Sok 2, tel. 49 94 56, for women (Kadın) Capanoğlu Sok., tel. 49 43 42.

Night's Rest

In İstanbul there are countless hotels, but even more tourists. In high season you might have to look around a bit, but you will always find something. Cheap hotels, many just simple dives, can be found in *Sultanahmet District* and around *Sirkeci Station*. More expensive are the hotels in *Aksaray* and *Laleli* or along the side streets off *İstlikal Cad.* and *Tepebaşı.*

You can, of course, spend the night in one of the expensive luxury hotels in İstanbul like the "Hilton", the "Etap Marmara", the "Etap İstanbul" and the "Sheraton" (all near Taksim - double £70). But if you want a luxury hotel, how about one with history:

Perapalas Oteli, Meşrutiyet Cad. 98, double £70. Not as modern as the "Hilton", but with much more charm and elegance, turn of the century style. It is the oldest luxury hotel in İstanbul. A few of the guests: Greta Garbo, Josephine Baker, Mata Hari, Agatha Christie, King Ferdinand of Bulgaria, King Victor Emanuel of Italy, Kemal Atatürk...

Keban, Taksim, Siıaselviler 51; double £30, comfort befitting the price. tel. 143 33 10.

Midiat, Aksaray Tiryaki Hasan Paşa Cad. 33; double £18, WC in the rooms; very good. tel. 586 77 41.

Hotel Burç, Gençtürk Cad. Ağayokusu Sok. 18, Laleli; double £17; recommended, clean, friendly. tel. 520 76 67.

Nomade, Ticarethane Sok. No. 7, Divanyolu; double £16, lovely hotel, inviting, decorated with nomad utensils. Laundry service, recommended! tel. 511 12 96.

Hotel Neşet, Harikzedeler Cad. 23; centrally located in Aksaray on a small street off Ordu Cad. The rooms are small but the guests are international. There is a bar, a breakfast room and a small lounge. It is comfortable and the people at the reception are friendly and helpful. Double incl. breakfast about £13. tel. 526 74 12.

Efes, Mis Sok. 15, Beyoğlu; double £13, recommendable. tel. 143 02 28.

Bora, Sıraselviler Kazanci Yokuşu 14; double £11, nice rooms. tel. 149 64 20.

Hotel As, Bekar Sok. 26, Beyoğlu; double £11, price fits service. tel. 145 00 99.

Hotel Ay, Küçük Langa Cad., Sok. 56, Aksaray; double £11; good standards, recommendable and clean. Not the greatest view (courtyard). tel. 525 34 43.

Hotel Canada, Tiryaki Hasanpaşsa Cad.; double £9; relatively clean, quite loud, good sanitation and friendly service. tel. 145 10 88.

Sultan Tourist Hotel, Yerebatan Cad. 35; double £9, simple furnishings, but clean. Very good, multilingual reception. Bingo! Best known youth hotel in Turkey. International clientele. The people at the reception know every inch of İstanbul. tel. 520 76 76.

İpek Palas Oteli, Orhaniye Cad. 9; double £7; some rooms with showers, very clean, but thin walls (could rip if you cough). Hip atmosphere.

Pırlanta, Sultanahmet; double £7, free showers, multilingual reception, quite good. tel. 27 70 85.

Kont, İstiklal Cad. Mis Sok. 21; double £7; tel. 145 40 23.

Pamuk Palas, Sultanahmet; double £6, shower/bath extra.

Olimpiyat Hotel, Ebusuut Cad. 68; double £6; showers in hall, acceptably clean, quiet.

Holiday Hotel, Divanyolu Cad. 10, Sultanahmet; double £4.30; cheap hotel across from the Blue Mosque. Loud but clean. One of the best hotels in the district. International clientele. tel. 526 17 45.

Yörük Turizm, Sultanahmet; double £3.30, very simple hotel; a place for adventurers. International backpacker paradise; to use the toilet, you need command of the word "occupied" in at least twelve languages. Bring own sleeping bag.

Büyük Ayasofya Hotel, Sultanahmet, next to Yücel Youth Hostel (Caferiye Sok.); per person £3; hard, but hearty. International atmosphere, lovely garden, some hassles: water when the manager is in the mood, electricity only in emergency, bathrooms stink. A great place for burned-out people.

Manolya, İstiklal Cad. 10; double £3, very simple; tel. 143 10 38.

YÜCEL YOUTH HOSTEL, Caferiye Sok. 6, Sultanahmet. Double £8.30, dorm £3, roof £1.60. Almost as good as Sultan Tourist, but roomier, clean, modern sanitation. International clientele. Modern reception and lounge. Beautiful garden with fountains, cafeteria, library (international). Advance reservations recommended, booked up in the summer! tel. 522 47 90.

CAMPING

Florya Tourist Camping, Florya, tel. 57 37 99 1, right by the ocean, sandy beach, shady trees, warm water showers (problems), restaurant and mini market. Crowded in the summer. International clientele. Clean, but loud, acceptable sanitation.
Coming - Going: By local train from Sirkeci to Florya. By car on the E 5 to Florya, 2 km straight ahead, turn left behind the underpass, after 500 m it is on the right.

Camping Yeşilyurt, Yeşilköy, tel. 738 408. Shady trees, small dirty beach (used as a public beach), mini market, expensive restaurant, fast food stand. Loud, crowded, hot. Non-stop Turkish disco tunes. We did not like it.
Coming - Going: Turn off the E5 at the airport and follow the signs.

Camping Albatros, Büyükçekmece, tel. 76. Barren site, lovely beach, mini market, restaurant. Poor sanitation, bungalows available.
Coming - Going : E5 to Büyükçekmece (notice the camel bridge built by Sinan, see Thrace), then follow the signs. A long way from İstanbul.

BP-Mocamp Kervansarayı Kartaltepe, tel. 575 47 21. An excellent site, muggy, but very clean. Good sanitation, restaurant, mini market, petrol station, nice layout, roomy. The tents in the front are right on the main road. Unfortunately the site is not by the sea.
Coming - Going: On E5 toward Edirne, right on the road, you can't miss it.

Londra Camping, the site closest to İstanbul, very crowded, shady trees. Sanitation includes warm water, swimming pool. Hotel with adjoining restaurant. Buses and dolmuş to İstanbul-Aksaray (near Topkapı).

Food

There are countless restaurants the cheapest of which can be found in Sultanahmet across from the Blue Mosque, e.g. the legendary "Pudding Shop" (see box) or the "Vitamin Restaurant". Seafood is excellent and very inexpensive under the Galata Bridge and in Sarıyer on the Bosporus. The seafood in Kumkapı is even better - a five-course dinner costs less than £5.- including beer and local wine. The best restaurants in Kumkapı:

Hoş Seda, Balik Restaurant, Ördekli Bakkal Sok. 2, Kumkapi.

Köşem Cemal Restaurant, Samsa Sok. 1, Kumkapı Meydanı, tel. 520 12 29. The best seafood restaurant in İstanbul. We will take on any bets!

Canlı Balık, Sahilyolu 101, Kumkapı, tel. 160 00 71. Almost as good as Köşem Cemal.

NO CHICKEN IN THE CHICKEN SHOP?

It is a living legend: the Pudding Shop in İstanbul, diagonally across from the Blue Mosque.

At the end of the 1960s hair started to grow longer, Jimmy played guitar and Brian rolled his joints on the beach at Santa Monica. Psychedelic was a way of life... and so was India. If Daddy stopped sending his checks, you simply packed up and headed east. Some people moved through quickly, others got stuck in İstanbul where everyone got together at the Pudding Shop near Hagia Sophia. You couldn't miss it.

The Pudding Shop today: lokanta atmosphere, self service with stewed meat. The lights go out at 22:00 h. The clientele is made up of tourists standing in a queue with their trays - not a hippy in sight. Nothing is left of its turbulent past and nothing makes it stand out from the dozen other spots in the neighbourhood. But there was one question we had to ask: "Why is the Pudding Shop called the Pudding Shop?". They were ready with an answer: "After all, we do serve pudding. In Amsterdam there is a Golden Chicken Shop which does not even sell chicken!"

If you want international cuisine in Turkey, try:

Pizzeria Papillon, Akatlar 50, Yıl Çarşısı 21, Etiler. tel. 165 51 14.

Ancelo, Plaj Gazinosu, Ataköy. tel. 571 84 21.

Chinese Restaurant, Lamartin Cad. 22, Taksim. tel. 145 08 19.

Japanese, İstinye Cad. 92, İstinye. tel. 165 55 77.

Swiss Pub, Cumhuriyet Cad. 14, Elmadağ. tel. 149 80 49.

Rejans, Oliviya Gec. 15, Galatasaray. Russian. tel. 144 16 10.

Union Française, Meşrutiyet Cad. 233, Tepebaşı. tel. 144 43 64.

None are cheap.

ÇIÇEK PASAJI

Çiçek Pasajı is on İstiklal Cad. in the modern European section of Beyoğlu about halfway between the Galata Tower and Taksim Square across from Galatasaray Lisesi. Got it? The explanation is important because the passage entrance is difficult to spot, and you could easily walk past it and miss something special.

"*Çiçek*" means flower, and Çiçek Pasajı means flower passage. And that's what it was until a fire several years ago. Very few flowers are sold here today, but you can get excellent food.

No less than 15 restaurants have opened their doors in the rectangular passage. Here you'll find the best draft beer and certainly the best *meze* (appetizers) in İstanbul.

You may be disappointed if you visit during the day. Just a few tourists, sleepy old men, and a couple of business people from surrounding offices stop by. Things liven up in the evening. Musicians arrive from every part of town; drums, bongos, gypsies with violins and oboes, string instruments of all kinds. The audience, consisting of Turkish connoisseurs, students and tourists, spurs on the performers, clapping to the rhythm and calling for more. Each group of performers tries to outplay (drown out) their competition. Rakı and beer flow freely. And then there are the flowers, sold by children going from table to table.

In a city where evening entertainment is pretty rare, such a tip remains no secret. As the number of tourists increases, the Turkish crowd diminishes. Several tour companies include a visit to Çiçek Pasajı as part of their evening tour.

DISCOTHEQUES: Western-style discos are only found on Taksim: **Regine** and **Number One** (both on Cumhuriyet Caddesi) are the most obvious. International melodies are the norm with an occasional Turkish folk song. If you like it hotter, try:
Club 33, Cumhuriyet Cad. 18, Elmadağ, cool. **Hydromel**, Cumhuriyet Cad. 12, Elmadağ, the spot in 1987. **Quartier**, Valikonaği Cad. Pasaj 73, Nişantaşı, a lot of laser, disc jockeys with very bad taste. **Foliberjer**, Beşir Fuad Cad. 8, Tepebaşı, **Lunapark**, Vatan Cad. 79, Aksaray.
The most comfortable and most expensive nightclub is in the exclusive Galata Tower. You won't be admitted in jeans, a bow tie is the minimum.

Swimming

Of İstanbul's 36 beaches, 34 are considered health hazards. The beaches at Florya are also filthy.

We can recommend the beaches on the *Prince Islands* (see there), in *Kilyos* and *Şile* on the Black Sea.

Sights

> **ATTENTION!** The latest news: the governement in Ankara has drastically hiked up **admission fees** for museums, mosques etc. in 1989! Calculate about 5 - 10 times the prices given in this edition (depending upon the fame of the sights; for instance: admission for Hagia Sophia rose from £0.30 up to £3 !)

Theodosian Land Wall

Coming from the west into downtown İstanbul, you'll notice the ruins of the tremendous Theodosian Land Wall beyond the factory chimneys. The 6670 m long fortification connects the Sea of Marmara with the Golden Horn. A moat, almost 20 m wide and 6 m deep, formed the first obstacle. The outermost wall stood offshore, secured by 96 towers, each 10 m tall. A bit further back was the main wall, also secured with 96 towers (15-20 m tall). The 60 m wide wall was arranged so that even a heavy attack supported by artillery could be repelled.

The fortifications stood impregnable for a thousand years before the wear of time - and the building craze of the İstanbul population, who used parts of the wall for building material - weakened its mighty defenses. Today the ring of moats and walls is partially overgrown, inviting an interesting walk along the outskirts of town. There is a lot of activity along the fortifications: a shepherd guards his flock, small gardeners give loving care to a few heads of lettuce, newly arrived peasants from rural Turkey make a first improvised home near the wall.

About every 60 m you'll find the defiant remains of a watch tower. The wall is pierced by numerous city gates, the most important of which is the *Topkapı*. In front of this gate is the bus station of the same name, an important point of orientation for anyone driving in İstanbul; almost every major road passes through here.

On the southern end, at the Sea of Marmara, a marble tower (*Mermer Kule*) stands final guard. It dates from the reign of BASILIUS II and was part of a castle fortress.

Yedikule Fortress *(Seven Towers Fortress)*

The ring of walls south of the Theodosian Wall was constructed by MEHMET THE CONQUORER, using four towers from the original town wall. The site of the present fortress was once occupied by a triumphal arch dating from 390 AD, the *Golden Gate*. When victory parades became infrequent, the gate was simply walled shut. Two of the seven towers contained infamous dungeons. Other towers held the crown jewels.

The facility is in such good condition that you can climb the stairs inside, up to the battlements, where you can look down upon much of the fortifications.

The fortress museum contains a variety of torture devices and the *Fountain of Blood*, a water-filled bowl in which the heads of the executed were collected.

OPEN: Daily 10:00-17:00 h, closed Mondays, admission £0.15.

Mihrimah Mosque *(Mihrimah Camii)*

In front of Edirne Gate is the second mosque of MIHRIMAH, daughter of SÜLEYMAN the Magnificent (the first was *İskele Camii*). The architect, SINAN, chose the highest spot in the old town for his site. Completed in 1565, the building was severely damaged by two earthquakes before reconstruction in this century. The 37 m high vault is supported by four massive dome-crowned corner pillars made of pink granite and encloses a cube-shaped interior. The facade arches between the corner pillars are each pierced by a triple row of windows, permitting a "triumph of light" (Artemis) in the interior. The entrance hall is topped by seven domes. Only a few of the tombs in the *Külliye* are preserved. The lovely minaret, however, is remarkable.

Chora Monastery *(Kariye Camii)*

The mosque is in northern İstanbul, just inside the town walls. Part of the structure was constructed in the 11th century as a church. In the 14th century it was expanded into a mosque. Special attention was given to ornamentation. Care was given not just to the overall concept, as in the Hagia Sophia, but also to details: ornamental paintings, sills, niches, arches, and light sources were all carefully considered.

The most fascinating parts of the mosque are the mosaics and frescos of the Chora Church, masterpieces of the Palaelogic Renaissance.

The mosaics depict Biblical history from the predecessors of Jesus to the Day of Judgement.

The mosaics and frescos were painted over when the church was converted into a mosque. However, the "Byzantine Institute of America" was able to uncover and preserve the art works in a project lasting from 1947 to 1958.

OPEN: Daily except Tuesdays, 9:30-16:30 h. Admission £0.35.

Imperial Palace *(Tekfur Sarayı)*

The building dates from the 13th century and served as a residence in the last years of the empire. The three-story structure was built between the outer and inner Theodosian city wall. The lovely courtyard facade has been restored. The ornamentation includes the combination of red brick and white marble, and the geometrical setting of window arches and arcades. After the fall of the empire, the building was converted to a faience factory before being reduced to a simple glass factory.

Mosque of the Conquest *(Fethiye Camii)*

This mosque in the *Fener* section of town was originally built as a Christian Byzantine church (Church of St. Mary). For 130 years after the fall of Constantinople, the Orthodox patriarch resided here. The building has been restored and modified several times, finally as a mosque in 1591 in memory of the victories of Sultan MURAT III in Georgia and Azerbaijan. Renamed "Mosque of the Conquest", much was destroyed or disturbed in the modification process. After a costly and difficult restoration process, recently completed, priceless mosaics and frescos have been brought to light, including the *Parecclesion* (inner chamber). The magnificent dome mosaic depicts Christ Pantocrator.

Sultan Selim Mosque

Located about half-way between Fatih and Atatürk Bridge, high above the Golden Horn. The architecture is very simple, but still impressive. The slightly curved dome of the 25 by 25 m square makes the room appear larger than it really is. Colourful carpets and *İznik tiles* provide decoration. *Mihrab* and *mimber*, made of marble, accentuate the charm.

Fatih Mosque

On the fourth city hill, west of the aqueduct, the famous Apostle Church was torn down in 1453. Parts of it were used to construct a new mosque on the orders of MEHMET THE CONQUERER. An earthquake destroyed all but a few secondary buildings shortly after completion.

Today, part of the reconstructed mosque stands in a rectangle formed by the medrese. The opening along its length has been closed with a wall. In front of the mosque there is a courtyard whose 18 columns support 22 domes. The ornamentation on the dome arches is unique. The Koran inscriptions in white marble are inlaid on a green background (*verde antico*). Little effort was made in the restoration, the colours are dull. A *Drinking Fountain* can be found inside the mosque.

In the mosque garden are the tombs of Sultan MEHMET FAHTI and his wife GÜLBAHAR (Scent of Roses).

Tulip Mosque   (Laleli Cami)

This masterpiece of Ottoman Baroque, from the tulip period, can be found near Aksaray Square. MUSTAFA III assigned MEHMET TAHIR to begin construction in 1763. Just two years later the mosque fell victim to an earthquake, but was painstakingly restored.

The mosque has a lower level containing a bazaar and an upper level, supported by eight columns, with a fountain in the middle. The architect's intention was "to build it in the air" using just a few pillars. The tremendous dome is set on an octagonal frame supported by columns. The real splendor is revealed inside. Over 100 long ornamental glass windows, some decorated with valuable opals and emeralds, let the light shine upon the porphyrite walls. The *külliye* includes a *medrese* and the tombs of the founder and his murdered son.

Valens Aqueduct   (Bozdogan Kemeri/Arch of the Gray Falcon)

The aqueduct built during the reign of Emperor VALENS (364 - 378) bridged the third and fourth town hills and crosses the present-day Atatürk Bulvarı. The aqueduct is completely intact: over 900 m long and 27 m high. A museum employee in Topkapı insists that it could, in theory, go right back into service. The water from springs in Belgrade Forest was transported via the aqueduct to a fountain on Beyazıt Square from which it was channeled on to the Imperial Palace.

Şehzade Mosque

On Atatürk Bulvarı, not far from the aqueduct, is the huge *Şehzade Complex*, containing, in addition to the mosque, *tombs*, *medrese*, *hospital*, *charity kitchen* and a *primary school*. Sultan SÜLEYMAN THE MAGNIFICENT donated the mosque in memory of his favorite son and designated heir who died in 1543 at the age of 22 from smallpox.

The sultan commissioned the then unknown architect SINAN, who considered this structure to mark his coming of age. Sinan's concept was to merge all the lines together upon one spot. In the centre, standing on sturdy "elephant feet", is the 37 m high main dome, with four adjoining secondary domes. The main hall seems huge and empty. In contrast to this unusual interior design, the outside of the building is richly ornamented. The *mimber* of marble is one of the loveliest of its kind. In the garden is the octagonal tomb of Prince MEHMET. The interior is covered with pastel-coloured faience. Above the tomb is a nut tree canopy with carved ivory.

Beyazıt Square

You can't miss the square on *Yeniceriler Caddesi*. Its central location in front of the Great Bazaar and the university ensures bustle all day long. Vendors sell corn which masses of tourists feed to flocks of pigeons. This is a nice place to relax. The idyllic spot can be enjoyed from a number of perspectives, but most pleasantly from the large and shady garden restaurant behind Beyazıt Mosque.

North of *Beyazıt Square* are the university grounds, built on the orders of Sultan ABDÜL MECIT in 1845. For a long time the university was considered conservative, as it held firmly to tradition and gave little consideration to modern research. The declaration of the Turkish Republic brought an end to such thinking. Today it is attended by 30,000 students.

In the University Park is **Beyazıt Tower** (1828), successor to a wooden fire tower. The present-day tower is almost 50 m tall. Climb the 180 stairs for a magnificent view. The tower also serves as a meteorological station. Various coloured signals depict the weather forecast: green means rain, yellow fog, red snow and blue nice weather.

Beyazıt Mosque *(Beyazıt Camii)*

The mosque was one of the first new structures built after the conquest of İstanbul, probably at the request of sultan BEYAZIT I. The layout is similar to Hagia Sophia. The front courtyard with three lovely royal gates is followed by the main hall with a huge dome supported by four massive marble elephant feet and two porphyrite coumns. In the front and back there are two half domes, which make the square structure appear rectangular. The domes are decorated with patterns similar to those on nomadic tents. The marble *sultan's box* is lovely and the *cleansing fountain* may be the prettiest in İstanbul. A *medrese* (today a library) was also originally part of the Beyazıt Complex.

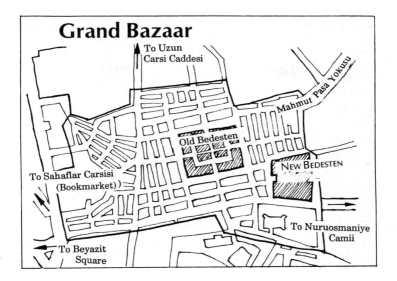

Grand Bazaar *(Kapalı Carşı)*

In this labyrinth of 4000 shops and boutiques, behind Beyazıt Square and the university, all types of merchandise are offered. You can get everything from copper, gold or other metal items, to jewelry, books, textiles, tools, porcelain, leather and carpets. But remember: everything that glitters is not gold, and not everything is handmade which claims to be. There is a system to this chaos: products of the same type are sold in the same street.

In the centre of the bazaar is a large hall topped by 15 domes, the *Eski Bedesten*, dating from 1461. Here the most valuable wares are sold because this part of the bazaar can be locked at night and is relatively safe from thieves. In *Sandalı Bedesten* we visited a lively carpet auction (Mondays and Thursdays).

The merchants attract business in true oriental fashion, inviting you into their shop with praise for their own merchandise and launching criticism against their "worthy competitors". Prices are difficult for an amateur to comprehend. In no case should you assume that everything is cheaper here than elsewhere. By the way, the first customer to make a purchase is said to bring luck, and therefore receives particularly advantageous terms.

OPEN: Monday to Saturday 8:00-19:00 h, closed on Sundays.

Nuruosmaniye Mosque *(Nuruosmaniye Camii)*

Close to the exit of the Great Bazaar, in a small oasis of shady trees, is the *Mosque of the Sacred Light of the Ottoman House* with a medrese, library and tombs. Unlike most mosques, there is a lot of bustle: beggars and musicians lend a touch of bazaar atmosphere.

Construction began in 1748 at the command of Sultan MAHMUT I. It was completed under his brother OSMAN III. For the first time, European baroque forms were used in Turkey. The large single-domed mosque consists of a lower story entered via marble stairs. The mimber is of green porphyrite. For once, the front courtyard is not four-sided, but horseshoe shaped.

The Burnt Column *(Çemberlitaş)*

On Divan Yolu, in front of Atik Ali Paşa Mosque, is the former land-mark of Byzantium. Emperor CONSTANTINE ordered erection of the column in 330 AD. It was made from seven red porphyrite cylinders, topped by a capital and an imperial statue of bronze. The column is said to contain nails and splinters from the true cross of Jesus Christ and the ax with which Noah chopped wood for his ark. Known as a fact is that the statue and one cylinder toppled during a storm in the 12th century. The six remaining drums were blackened by a fire. Quite early, an iron ring was set around the 36 m tall stump to protect it against new earthquakes.

Blue Mosque *(Sultanahmet Camii)*

History: SULTAN AHMET (1590 - 1617), at the age of 19 and ill with cancer, hired the ambitious architect MEHMET AGA, a student of SINAN, to build this tremendous mosque. By 1616 the building was completed; the sultan had completed his life's work. He died just a year later at the age of 27. Without knowing it, he had built himself a tomb comparable in size to the Taj Mahal or the Mausoleum of Halicarnassos!

Outer Appearance: No building dominates the skyline of İstanbul like the Sultan Ahmet Mosque. It is supremely situated across from the Hagia Sophia, which it clearly imitates. It is the only mosque in İstanbul with six minarets, for which Ahmet was obliged to donate a seventh minaret to the most sacred mosque in Mecca in order not to challenge its dominance. Its tremendous outer appearance leads one to over estimate the Blue Mosque. There is no revolutionary architecture involved. The Sultanahmet Camii is the last highlight and marks the completion of the great tradition of Islamic architecture.

OPEN: Sunrise to sunset.
SLIDE SHOW: On summer evenings a slide show presents the history of İstanbul in four languages.

No Gold, But Six Minarets

A lovely legend tells how the Blue Mosque came to have six minarets. When Mehmet Aga presented plans for the building to Sultan Ahmet, the ruler was enthusiastic. But the king insisted expressly upon four golden minarets! Mehmet Aga knew immediately that there was not enough money to realize the sultan's ambition. But it is not advisable to lock horns with a king. So Ahmet pretended to misunderstand the sultan and built six minarets (altı = six) rather than four golden minarets (altın = gold). Ahmet's sense of humor permitted the architect to keep his head.

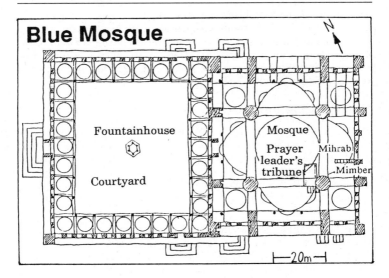

Blue Mosque

Fountainhouse

Courtyard

Mosque

Prayer leader's tribune

Mihrab

Mimber

—20m—

Front Courtyard: It is the most elegant part of the complex and has almost the same proportions as the mosque itself. The courtyard is surrounded by arcades resting on 26 granite columns carrying 30 domes. The three open sides each contain a monumental exit. The fourth side is the entrance to the mosque. In the centre of the courtyard is a hexagonal cleansing fountain.

Interior: Although the exterior of the Blue Mosque displays similarities to the Hagia Sophia, the interior differs greatly. The foundation is a 66 m square. Four massive columns, 5 m thick, so-called elephant legs, support the main dome which has a height of 44 m and a diameter of 22 m, almost the same size as the one in Hagia Sophia. Half-domes adjoin on each side, followed by smaller and still smaller domes. This creates a feeling of space much larger and lighter than its true proportions.

The Sultan Ahmet Mosque is known as the Blue Mosque for good reason. The interior is covered with blue-green İznik tiles, especially the columns. The dome is painted blue. Light filters in through 260 panes of dark-blue glass. Unfortunately, only the seven upper windows on the east facade are originals, all the others are copies!

The white marble pulpit (*mimber*) is an exact copy of the pulpit in the Great Mosque in Mecca. The prayer niche (*mihrab*) is decorated with

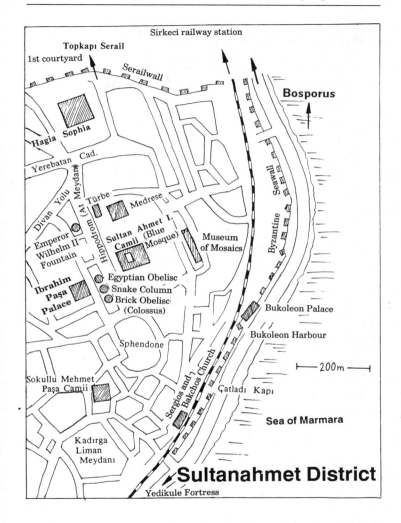

Sirkeci railway station

Topkapı Serail
1st courtyard

Serailwall

Bosporus

Hagia Sophia

Yerebatan Cad.

Divan Yolu

Türbe

Medrese

Emperor Wilhelm II Fountain

Sultan Ahmet I. Camii (Blue Mosque)

Museum of Mosaics

Byzantine Seawall

Ibrahim Paşa Palace

Egyptian Obelisc
Snake Column
Brick Obelisc (Colossus)

Bukoleon Palace

Bukoleon Harbour

Sphendone

——200m——

Sokullu Mehmet Paşa Camii

Sergios and Bakchos Church

Çatladı Kapı

Sea of Marmara

Kadırga Liman Meydanı

Sultanahmet District

Yedikule Fortress

costly stones including a piece of the Kaaba from Mecca. Another attraction is the proud cat which strolls through the mosque from time to time. If you see her, say hello for us!

A word of advice: Unlike Hagia Sophia, the Blue Mosque is still used for religious services. If you arrive in shorts, you will be offered a blue cloth to wrap yourself in. The mosque attendants can't always keep an eye on the visitors to ensure proper behaviour, so don't take pictures with flash, don't walk beyond the markers, do not disturb those who come to pray or meditate.

Side Buildings: Sultan Ahmet Mosque originally included a hospital and caravanserai. Both have been torn down. All that remains is the charity kitchen and the large square tomb of AHMET I in which his three sons and wife KÖSEM are also buried.

Museum for Turkish Carpets

At the southeast corner of the Sultanahmet District is the *Sultan Ahmet Köşk*, a small sultan's pavilion with a direct entrance to the mosque. Since 1978 it has housed the Carpet Museum. The exhibits are well worth a look. Most impressive are the large carpets with depictions of animals and the prayer carpets. Many of the displays have fallen victim to moths. The colours have faded under the feet of the faithful. But considering that many of the objects date from the 14th century, they are remarkably well preserved. Most of the carpets were used in mosques, particularly in the Great Mosque of Milas. Very valuable are the various green *Konya Ladik* carpets.

OPEN: 8:30-17:00 h, daily except Mondays and Tuesdays.

Mosaic Museum *(Mozaik Müzesi)*

Near the Blue Mosque is the Mosaic Museum. Don't expect the usual type of museum. In the garden of a former palace you'll see the ruins of ancient capitals and columns. Through a gate you enter a bazaar-like street where mosaic floors are displayed in several shops. The mosaics date from the 5th and 6th centuries, depicting scenes from daily life, e.g. the hunt or children at play.

OPEN: Daily except Tuesdays, 9:30-16:00 h.

Binbir Direk *(1001 Column Cistern)*

The covered cistern in Beyazıt holds almost 50,000 cubic meters of water and is second in size only to Yerebatan Sarayı. It is only 64 m long and 56 m wide, but with a height of 12.5 m it is higher than its competitor. Its name, 1001 Column Cistern, is an exaggeration: in reality there are only 224 columns.

By the way: many travel guides suggest that the key to the cistern can be found in the town hall (Belediye Sarayı) across the street. Despite our letters of introduction the door was not opened for us.

Hippodrome *(At Meydanı, Noble Steed Square)*

History: Built under Emperor SEPTIMIUS SEVERUS in 203 AD, then expanded by CONSTANTINE THE GREAT, the racetrack was a popular meeting place among Byzantine society. It was as important for the worldly life as the Hagia Sophia was for the spiritual. The fans - by no means just commoners - turned out in droves to root for the Reds, Greens, Blues, Whites, Purples, or Golds, each of whom would field a driver and team in the races. Over the centuries, teams were eliminated or merged together leaving only the Greens and Blues. They fought in battles which were not only restricted to the Hippodrome! The circus teams had their own divisions within the civil defense forces. The team captains were received by the emperor during the games. Otherwise they sought to differentiate themselves. The Blues represented the aristocrats and the Orthodox Church; the Greens were allied with separatists and heretics. They even dressed differently: for a number of years the Greens dressed and behaved like the Huns.

Sport and politics were closely related. A victory could be of far-reaching political significance. A sport festival at the circus in 532 AD quickly evolved into the Nika Uprising. The dissatisfied masses took offense at JUSTINIAN'S tax policy, resulting in days of street fighting with the Imperial Guard. Part of the Imperial Palace - predecessor to the Hagia Sophia - and half the city were set on fire. After all attempts at compromise and appeasement had failed, Justinian was ready to resign, but for the strength of Empress THEODORA. Speaking to her followers, she proclaimed, *"My motto is: the throne is the finest tombstone!"* Justinian took heart and sent his military commander BELISARIUS into the Hippodrome with his last troops. NARSES made liberal payments of cash to the Blues to ensure their support for Justinian. Together they killed 30,000 Greens in the Hippodrome. In keeping with tradition, the corpses were buried on the spot.

In the 12th century horseracing was prohibited. During the conquest of Constantinople by the knights of the 4th crusade, the Hippodrome was plundered. In the 16th century the Turks tore down parts of the structure to use it as building material. The *At Meydanı* (Noble Steed Square) was the scene of another bloodbath in 1826 when Sultan MAHMUT II ordered the execution of all 30,000 members of his elite Janissary Corps. Keep in mind when wandering through this friendly, clean park, that it is a mass grave!

Ruins of the Ancient Arena: The arena was originally 480 m long and 120 m wide. Around the rectangular racetrack, which joined a semi-circle at the Sea of Marmara side, were 30 rows of seats capable of seating 100,000 spectators. The arena was a place for chariot races, but also for political rallies, state receptions, and victory parades. The track was divided by the *spina*, a wall decorated with columns and obelisks, into two straightaways. The teams of horses raced down one track, rounded the turn at the markers and raced back up the opposite side of the spina to the start (for more about the horses see "Onyx eggs"/Cappadocia). Only two obelisks and the snake column remain.

Obelisk of Theodosius (*Dikilitaş*): Hewn about 1500 BC on orders of TUTMOSIS *III* (Egypt). It is not known how the transport to Constantinople was arranged 2000 years later. It is known that Emperor THEODOSIUS I (379 - 395 AD) had it ceremoniously erected upon the spina. The monolith of rose-coloured granite is 20 m tall and stands upon a 6 m tall pedestal which was added later. Notice the remarkable reliefs.

Snake Column (*Burmalı Sütun*): The oldest Greek relic in İstanbul. After the Greek victory over the Turks at Plataea in 479 BC, it was cast with bronze from captured Persian shields and placed before the Apollo Temple at Delphi. In 330 AD, Emperor Constantine ordered the column brought to his new capital.

The 5 m tall column (originally it was 8 m) depicts three intertwined snake bodies, the heads carrying a sacrificial bowl. The sacrificial bowl was lost in ancient times. The snakeheads were chopped off by a Polish ambassador in the year 1700 after a drinking bout. The scandal was hushed up. In the 19th century the remains of one head were discovered and are now on display in the Archaeological Museum.

The Wall Obelisk (*Örmelitaş, Colossus*): This obelisk is of truly colossal proportions. It is 32 m tall and cut of limestone. It was probably erected about 940 AD and was covered with plaques of gold-plated bronze, which were taken and melted down by crusaders in 1204 AD.

German Fountain *(Alman Çeşmesi)*

This very exotic fountain is at the Hippodrome. It was presented by Emperor Wilhelm II of Germany during his official visit to the court of Sultan ABDÜL HAMID II in 1898. The water is said to taste lovely.

İbrahim Pasha Palace *(İbrahim Paşa Sarayı)*

This is the largest private palace of the Ottoman Empire! It was built on the west side of the Hippodrome in 1524 by the Greek Grand Vizier IBRAHIM PASHA, who made a name for himself in the service of SÜLEYMAN THE MAGNIFICENT. When İbrahim - the sultan's son-in-law -

became too powerful, Süleyman followed the advice of his wife, ROXELANE, and had him murdered. The palace passed into imperial hands. For generations it served as a luxurious boarding school for pages; the audience hall housed the highest Ottoman legal court. In recent years the building has been restored. Today it houses an exhibit of Turkish and Persian miniatures, Seljuk ceramics and valuable Turkish prayer carpets.

OPEN: Daily except mondays 8.30-17.30 h.

Church of Sergios and Bakchos *(Küçük Aya Sophia)*

Below the Blue Mosque and the Hippodrome, toward the Bosporus - only the width of the coastal road separates the mosque from the water - is the *Small Hagia Sophia*. The church is dedicated to the two martyrs Sergios and Bakchos (Roman legionnaires) who served as the patron saints of Christian soldiers. Completed in 536 AD, the church was converted to a mosque in 1453.

The interesting layout of the central building served as a model for later mosques. A square rounded at the edges enclosed an octagon covered by a dome. The latter is not supported directly by the side walls, but rather by eight columns. This eight-column system with galleries between the columns and outer walls can be seen again in the great Hagia Sophia.

Hagia Sophia Museum *(Aya Sofya Müzesi)*

History: Constantine the Great was the first to erect a basilica here in 325 AD dedicated to the "great Truth". It was destroyed by an arsonist in 404 AD. The second Hagia Sophia was even larger: a triple-aisle basilica, dedicated in 415 AD during the reign of THEODOSIUS; it was destroyed in 532 AD during the Nika Uprising.

After restoring order following the Nika Uprising, JUSTINIAN had the church rebuilt with the goal of outdoing even Solomon's Temple. *"The Emperor ordered construction without considering the expense, recruiting the most skilled artisans from throughout the empire"* according to PROCOPIUS. Supervising a team of 100 architects (and more than 10,000 workers) were the mathematicians ANTHEMIUS of Tralles and ISIDORUS of Miletus. Construction took five years. But soon after the Christmas dedication in 537 AD an earthquake toppled the dome. Justinian would not be deterred; he ordered the younger ISIDORUS to begin restoration. In 563 the aging Justinian presided over a second dedication.

Additional earthquakes in 869 and 986 AD caused the western half-dome to collapse. The Armenian architect TERDAT repaired the damage just before the turn of the century; a third dedication of the church was held in 994 AD. In 1204 AD the church was plundered during the city's conquest by crusaders. Since 1317 sporadic reinforcement of the walls has been undertaken. While this was necessary, it has hardly enhanced the appearance of the church.

During the Turkish conquest of İstanbul in 1453 the church owed its rescue to sultan MEHMET II FATIH (the Conqueror). When the fighting was over he rode straight to Hagia Sophia and placed it under his protection. What he saw moved him so greatly that he ordered the immediate conversion of the church into a mosque. The mosaics were not damaged by iconoclastic Arabs, but simply covered with wood paneling. Several centuries later these were covered with a thin layer of plaster. In succeeding centuries the four minarets were added. The two large ones at the west corner were erected by SINAN.

During the following centuries only minor repairs were made. Not until 1847 did sultan ABDÜL MECIT I order the Swiss architects GASPARE and GIUSEPPE FOSSATI to conduct a complete restoration which lasted two years. This also brought the mosaics back to light. But the sultan ordered that they be covered again. Not until ATATÜRK ordered the Hagia Sophia to be converted into a museum, in 1935, were the mosaics again revealed for all time.

Around the Hagia Sophia: For almost 1000 years, until the construction of St. Peter's Cathedral in Rome, the Hagia Sophia was the largest and most important church in the Christian world. After its conversion to a mosque in 1453 it was equally revered by the Ottomans. Therefore it is not surprising that five sultans are buried inside. Two of them, MUSTAFA III and İBRAHIM III, rest in the converted baptistery of the church which is no longer open to the public (to the right of the main entrance). At the back of the garden is the tomb of sultan SELIM II (in the middle of the three tombs). Selim II was an exceptionally popular ruler who enjoyed both festivals and orgies. His death fit his lifestyle: in a state of drunkenness, he slipped and fell in the bath. The tombs of the two other sultans, MURAT III and MEHMET III, are also worth a look. In addition to the sultans, the tombs contain the remains of dozens of sons, daughters, grandchildren and favorite women.

The rococo *cleansing fountain* (1740), left of the entrance gate, is worth special notice. The painstaking detail is remarkable, particularly in the bronze filigree screen.

On the opposite side of the path, in front of the tombs, is the *Clock Pavilion*, built by the FOSSATI brothers in 1849. The court astronomers worked here around the clock.

Entrance Hall and Narthex: The bronze entrance gate with its marble facing probably dates from the 6th century. The "*Entrance Hall of Warriors*" received its name from the fact that guards would wait here until the emperor returned from religious service. The emperor would shed his street clothes and weapons here before entering the sacred church interior. Above the passage to the *narthex* (roofed vestibule) is the *orea porta*, one of the most beautiful gold-based mosaics with a model of the Hagia Sophia, and on the right Constantine the Great (founder of the Byzantine Empire) with a model of the city.

The narthex is huge: over 60 m long and 11 m wide. During the Christian era it was used in the opening ceremony of religious services. This is where the patriarch would greet the emperor, who would arrive from the entrance hall through the orea porta. The empress and her entourage, on the other hand, would ascend to the gallery via the entrance opposite the orea porta.

The narthex is entirely paneled with marble. The mosaic ornamentation of the chamber is remarkably well preserved. To the left, five bronze doors bearing signs of the cross lead to the *exonarthex* (outer entrance hall). It was the original entrance. To the right, seven doors lead into the main hall and the two side aisles under the galleries.

Most impressive is the central door - the only door with a bronze frame - called the *King's Door*. From here you have a breathtaking view of the nave and can admire the completely preserved *Royal Relief*. In the centre, Christ sits upon a jewelled throne. In his left hand is the gospel; the right hand is raised in blessing. At Christ's feet, Emperor Leo IX is kneeling. If you look closely, you will notice a special effect created by the artist: to emphasize the blessing, Christ's right hand is larger than the left.

The Galleries: Women were not permitted to enter the main hall of the Hagia Sophia. They were required to take their place in the galleries flanking the length of the main hall. The North Gallery contains an excellently preserved mosaic of *Emperor Alexandrus* (10th century); the South Gallery features the *deesis*, a mosaic of which only three heads remain (but they are very expressive). In the centre, Jesus is easy to recognize with his halo. He is flanked by John, the Baptist, and the Virgin Mary. They look across at the tomb of *Enrico Dandolo*, the Venetian doge who ordered the plunder of Constantinople in 1204 AD. Near the apse, a well-preserved mosaic depicts Jesus sitting on a throne between Empress Zoe and and her husband Constantine IX.

The Main Hall: This is the main attraction in the Hagia Sophia. The 80 m long room is dominated by the tremendous central dome. With a height of 56 m and a diameter of 33 m, it is one of the largest ever erected. The tip of the dome is as high as a 15-story building. Lengthwise, at both ends, it joins lower-lying half-domes. At each corner are smaller half-domes, called exedra domes. Although the dome was already known as a weight-supporting element (but not on this grand scale) the concept of half-domes and the two almost equally large secondary domes was quite revolutionary. The optical effect is terrific. The central dome does not seem to be supported by the heavy, almost invisible pillars, but rather to float.

The four main columns of green breccia were made of column remains from Ephesus. The exedra domes are supported by eight porphyrite columns brought here from Baalbek. Little remains of the original 16,000 sq m gold-based mosaics, except for the *apse mosaic* depicting the Virgin Mary. But the Ottomans decorated the room with their own symbols: a giant round *wooden shield*, covered with camel leather, dating from the 17th century (the calligraphy displays the names of the caliphs) and the long-legged *sultan's box* (built by the Fossati brothers). The splendid mimber, decorated with two flags, was donated by Süleyman the Magnificent in the 16th century.

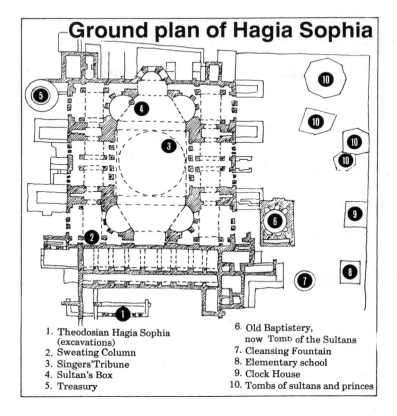

Ground plan of Hagia Sophia

1. Theodosian Hagia Sophia (excavations)
2. Sweating Column
3. Singers'Tribune
4. Sultan's Box
5. Treasury
6. Old Baptistery, now Tomb of the Sultans
7. Cleansing Fountain
8. Elementary school
9. Clock House
10. Tombs of sultans and princes

Two conspicuous *water containers* made of marble are in the front of the hall. sultan MURAT III (1574 - 1595) had them carved from a single piece of marble brought from Pergamon (they hold 1200 liters). They were filled with holy water and used for ritual cleansing.

In the northwest corner of the hall is another curiosity: the *Sweating Column*. When JUSTINIAN, while suffering from a headache, leaned his head against the cool surface of the column, his pain was immediately eased. The column was declared sacred. So many thousands of pilgrims have leaned their heads against the pillar that over the ages an actual hole, the "wishing hole" has been made. Recent investigations show that the column is siphoning moisture from a former cave beneath the church, which it then releases as "sweat".

Before leaving the main hall, have a look at the *omphalos*, the floor mosaic of colourful porphyrite before the prayer leader stands. On this spot, the navel of the world, the throne of the Byzantine Emperor is said to have stood.

OPEN: Tuesday - Sunday 9.30 - 17.00 h, admission: £0.28.

Yerebatan Sarayı *(Yerebatan-Cistern)*

İstanbul's largest cistern is directly across from the Hagia Sophia. The reservoir was built in the 6th century under JUSTINIAN. It held 80,000 cubic meters of water, brought to the city from the Belgrade Forest via a 19 km long aqueduct.

The Yerebatan Cistern, known locally as the "sunken palace" is 140 m long and 70 m wide - even larger than Hagia Sophia! It is supported by 336 columns, each 8 m tall.

The Sublime Porte and Alay Köşk

About halfway between Hagia Sophia and Eminönü is the Sublime Porte, a gate with a wavy baroque roof, which served as an entrance to the official residence of the Grand Vizier. Among foreign ambassadors, the "Sublime Porte" was synonymous with the seat of the Turkish government, since the Grand Vizier was the most powerful man in the empire - after the sultan.

The Alay Köşk, across from the Sublime Porte, is an alcove tower built into the wall surrounding the Topkapı Palace. From here the reigning sultan could observe goings-on in and about the Sublime Porte.

Irene Church *(Hagia Eirene)*

The first "Church of Sacred Peace" was built upon the site of an ancient temple dating from the pre-Constantine era. It was destroyed during the Nika Uprising and by an earthquake. Constantine V ordered reconstruction in its present form. During Ottoman rule the building was used by the Janissaries as an arsenal. Later it was converted to a military museum.

Today the Hagia Eirene is constructed as a triple-aisle basilica with an entrance hall and an unroofed front courtyard. Inside a porphyrite sarcophagus and a number of weapons are on display.

OPEN: Daily except Tuesdays, 9:30-17:00 h, admission £0.35.

Ahmet III Fountain *(Sultan Ahmet Çeşmesi)*

In front of the first gate of the Topkapı Palace is a splendid street fountain. It was built in 1728, at the command of the popular sultan Ahmet III, in Turkish Rococo style. The centre is four-sided, but the severe lines of the basic concept are relaxed with playful elegance: alcoves with fine ornamental screens (behind each of which is a fountain) and an expansive roof with low domes. At the top of the fountain are tiles and the inscription "*The sultan's wall enclosed the water here - astonishingly even the floods do not disturb its flow!*" There is more truth to the saying than the author imagined. The fountains are unused and dry today.

Topkapı Sarayı

You will need at least half a day for your visit to the Topkapı Palace. The complex contains priceless wealth. It is never boring: varied exhibits, unexpected views, cafés and quiet corners add to the charm.

History: MEHMET THE CONQUEROR erected the Topkapı on the site of the aged Byzantine Imperial Palace between 1459 and 1465. The harem took residence here during the reign of MURAT III (1574 to 1595). The pavilions in the fourth court were added later. On several occasions (1574, 1665, 1856), fire destroyed major parts of the complex, including the complete loss of the buildings in the first courtyard, with the exception of the Irene Church. The name *Topkapı Sarayı* (Cannon-Gate Palace) stems from the two mighty cannons guarding the entrance.

The Topkapı was more than the *sultan's residence*, it was the seat of the *divan* (the highest legislature), the most elite school in the empire, and of course the *harem*. The seraglio was divided into four courtyards. The first courtyard was open to the public and housed the domestic facilities. The second courtyard was open only to palace residents and visiting petitioners. The third courtyard was reserved for court officials and members of the government. The fourth courtyard belonged to the sultan alone, serving as his pleasure garden.

First Courtyard: The entrance is via the *Entrance of the Emperor beneath the Bird of Paradise* which lies behind the Hagia Sophia. As a deterrent against rebellion, the heads of executed prisoners were displayed in marble niches. Inside the courtyard itself, only the Irene Church remains.

Second Courtyard: Via the *Gate of Greeting* you enter the actual palace and museum. This is where everyone except the sultan lived. To the right of the wall was the *Executioner's Fountain* where the black-hooded craftsman would wash his hands after performing his service. The court is huge and confusing. Paths branch out in all directions between the cypress trees. This is where high imperial dignitaries would meet four times each week for the divan to discuss imperial business. During official receptions, 10,000 members of the Janissary Corps would take up position in the courtyard. To the left are the harem and the weapons collection. In the centre is the entrance to the third courtyard. To the right is the palace kitchen with its collection of porcelain and household utensils. Start your tour on the right.

The **Palace Kitchen** was established under MEHMET and later restored by SINAN. Notice the 20 chimneys. Up to 1200 cooks were employed here on festive occasions.

The *porcelain collection* is the world's second largest, outdone only by Beijing. The first grouping displays costly Chinese porcelain from Celadon (10th to 12th century, Sung Period). Celadon porcelain was popular among sultans for its lime-green colouring, but also because it was said to possess the unique property of discolouring upon contact with poisoned food (an invaluable asset to any Turkish prince or sultan). The adjoining section displays porcelain from the Yuan Dynasty (14th century). The central cabinets contain pieces from the Ming Dynasty (14th to 17th century). Well represented is the blue-white table setting preferred by sultan SÜLEYMAN. In addition to plates of all sizes, there are huge jugs, decanters, and platters (as large as wagon wheels). A number of pieces from the late Ming period (17th to 20th century) complete the Chinese collection. This tableware is more colourful (including yellow and green utensils), but less distinguished than those from the Ming period.

The adjoining *Japanese exhibition* holds some surprises even for experts. The *European exhibits* include splendid *Meissen*, excellent Sèvres, and some lesser-quality Limoges. The entire collection encompasses 12,000 objects in 10 rooms. OUTSTANDING!

The last two rooms of the palace kitchen contain a collection of *kitchen utensils* of interest to ethnologists and amateur cooks: everything from simple wooden spoons to large bronze pots and an original fireplace.

The northern end is reserved for changing exhibitions. During our last trip we had the misfortune to visit between exhibitions. On a previous visit we saw an excellent collection of Turkish silverware.

Third Courtyard: The entrance is via the *Gate of Good Fortune*, ornamented with columns and an inviting canopy. Coronation ceremonies and the annual acknowledgement ceremony for the Janissary Corps were held here.

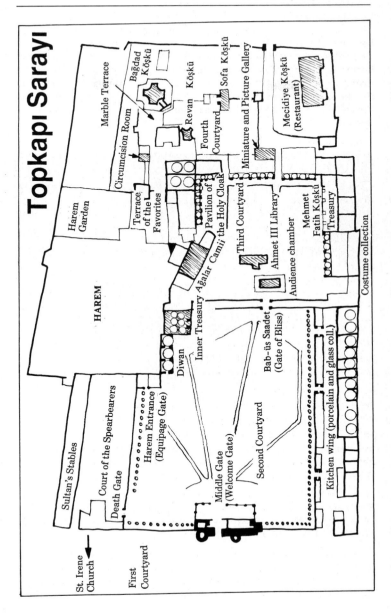

Topkapı Sarayı

Bağdad Köşkü
Marble Terrace
Circumcision Room
Revan Köşkü
Sofa Köşkü
Fourth Courtyard
Miniature and Picture Gallery
Mecidiye Köşkü (Restaurant)
Harem Garden
Terrace of the Favorites
Pavilion of the Holy Cloak
Third Courtyard
Ahmet III Library
Mehmet Fatih Köşkü
Treasury
Audience chamber
HAREM
Inner Treasury Ağalar Camii
Diwan
Bab-üs Saadet (Gate of Bliss)
Costume collection
Sultan's Stables
Court of the Spearbearers
Harem Entrance (Equipage Gate)
Death Gate
Middle Gate (Welcome Gate)
Second Courtyard
Kitchen wing (porcelain and glass coll.)
St. Irene Church
First Courtyard

Behind the gate, known because of its guards as the *Gate of the White Eunuch*, was the **Audience Chamber.** This is where the sultan received foreign guests and his minister, the Grand Vizier. He sat, or rather rested (the low height of the throne would require sitting in the lotus position), upon a throne ornamented with brocade and emeralds the size of eggs. Above the throne was a canopy graced with lovely engravings. The calligraphy featured passages from the Koran. The splashing of the fountain was designed to protect against eavesdroppers.

The *Library of Ahmet III*, featuring over 4000 Greek, Arabic and Turkish manuscripts, has been closed to the public for years. The public, however, is invited to view the *sultans' Garments Exhibit*. The collection is complete because the sultans' clothing was considered sacred and therefore carefully preserved. Several of the coats are splattered with blood - a number of sultans met a violent death.

The Treasury: Adjoining the collection of sultans' Garments. For many, this is the high point of their visit to Topkapı Palace. The priceless treasures include plunder, gifts from foreign ambassadors and dignitaries, and purchased objects.

* 1st Hall: The armour of Mustafa III made of the finest steel and ornamented with diamonds and gold paillette. The second case contains copies of the Koran adorned in pearl bindings. Nearby the ebony throne of MURAT IV. Also of interest are the golden water-

pipes from Van (18th century), several golden candlesticks, a cane dotted with diamonds (a gift of Emperor Wilhelm II), and a double-bladed dagger.

* 2nd Hall: The emerald stove with gold inlay dates from the 16th century, ABDÜL HAMID's emerald pendant (with three large gold-faceted, octagonal emeralds and a pearl chain), a tuft of feathers (17th century) with an 8 cm hatpin boasting valuable diamonds, a 31 cm dagger of sultan MEHMET IV (17th century), a sultan's crib of gold and emeralds. Equally of interest is the Topkapı dagger (18th century) which was featured in the film "Topkapı" starring NANA MOUSCOURI. The 35 cm instrument contains a clock with an emerald cover at the knob end. The knob also holds three other large emeralds. The grip and golden case are coated with diamonds!

* 3rd Hall: Gold and diamonds! Copies of the Koran are ornamented with rubies, opals, emeralds, golden incense and rosewater holders. In the two middle cases are two chandeliers of ABDÜL MECIT, weighing 48 kilos, containing a diamond for every sura in the Koran. The Koran has a wealth of suras, 6666 in all. And don't miss the golden ceremonial throne weighing 250 kg.
Spectacular is the *Spoon Diamond*, perhaps the most splendid object in the entire treasury, weighing 86 carats, surrounded by 49 diamonds in two rows. The jewel owes its name to the fact that the poor fisherman who discovered it traded the treasure for three spoons. That must have been the worst deal ever negotiated before the sale of Alaska to the United States.

* 4th Hall: Via an alcove balcony, featuring fountains and a tremendous view over the mouth of the Golden Horn, we arrive at the last hall of the treasury. Most splendid is the *throne* of Shah NADIR of Persia (a gift to sultan MAHMUD I). The Persians had no shortage of emeralds and pearls! Everything else is minor in comparison: the reliquary Shrine of the Prophet's Coat, carvings of ivory, sabres, rifles, other jewels.

Other Exhibits in the 3rd Courtyard: The *Gallery of Miniatures and Portraits* is mostly of interest to faithful Muslims. The adjoining *Watch Collection* is lovely. There are a number of gifts including a sphinx-shaped diamond watch, a present from Tsar NICHOLAS II, and a standing-pendulum clock in rococo style from England.

The *Exhibit of the Prophet's Sacred Coat* is also of greater interest to the Muslim faithful than to Christians. Still, where else can a non-believer view the most sacred relics of Islam? Of interest is the first copy of the Koran bound in gazelle leather, which OSMAN, founder of the Ottoman Empire, is said to have been reading with deep contemplation when death struck. Relics of the sacred Muhammad include a letter from the prophet, several hairs from his beard, a footprint and parts of his jaw. In the adjoining room is the most sacred of all relics, the *Coat of the Prophet*.

Pavilions and Belvedere in the 4th Courtyard: The *Revan Kiosk* was built in 1635. It is a smaller version of the Bagdad Pavilion, covered window-high with marble, and further up with İznik tiles. Walking past the fountain, we reach the Circumcision Hall. Be sure to have a look at the faiences. Adjoining is the *İftar-Baldachin*, built in 1640 by IBRAHIM I. Under the gold-plated bronze canopy, sultans would dine during Ramadan in the evening twilight after a long day of fasting, with a view of Gülhane Park and the Golden Horn!

The *Bagdad Pavilion*, built in 1699, was a copy of the Revan Pavilion. An arcade circles the eight-sided building offering beautiful views in all directions. Have a look inside at what a sultan calls home: four satin-covered benches of discreet dark-red colouring, a golden ball hanging from the ceiling, and a lovely ornamented bronze stove.

Wandering past the *Sofa-Kiosk*, one of the oldest wooden structures in the city (1704), we arrive at a building of white stone, *Medici-Kiosk*, built in pseudo-European style. Today it houses a good, but over-priced, restaurant. We recommend the self-service outside, with a nice view of the Bosporus and the mouth of the Horn.

Harem: Tours are offered every half-hour, but only in one or two languages. If you don't want to wait for an hour in the burning sun, check the times on the information board. The tour costs £0.70 extra, but it is worth it!

The harem (in Arabic "off limits") is a building complex of over 400 rooms, built at various times. The confusing maze covers 6700 sq m. Two mosques, a hospital, 10 Turkish baths, 12 storehouses, four kitchens, a swimming pool, and a number of lounges. It was home to the sultan's primary and secondary wives; the princes took residence after 1588. The complex was guarded by African slaves, the "Black Eunuchs".

The harem is entered through the *Wagon Gate*. After crossing the vestibule, we arrive at the guard room. Adjoining is the *Mosque of the Black Eunuchs*, featuring a lovely mimber with pearl inlay. Continuing on in the *Quarters of the Black Eunuchs* we pass along a long corridor with a fireplace at the end. On the wall to the right is the Ramadan Drum which woke the eunuchs for breakfast before dawn during Ramadan, and a bastinado for punishing insubordinate guards.

Past the *Princes' School* and the second guard room we come to the stone *Courtyard of the sultan's Women (kadınefendis)*. The private chambers of the sultan's kadınefendis lie to the right when entering the courtyard. They each consisted of a front room and a back room, the latter with a fireplace and fountain. The walls, of course, were covered with İznik faiences. The up to 500 women who resided in the harem at any time did not spend all of their lives here. They would be permitted to leave the harem, although only after achieving a mature age. They would then receive a substantial pension!

Next are the *Chambers of the sultan's Mother*. The dining room is particularly impressive: the ceiling is compartmented and inlaid with gold. The screened windows hold Chinese vases. In the centre is a splendid silver tray. The sultan's mother was the absolute dictator of the harem. Her orders had to be obeyed by all kadınefendis and even the prince. Her position was emphasized by a bed with gold inlay. The apartment also included a small prayer room with a niche.

The main attraction in the harem is the *sultan's Bath*. It consists of a lounge with a gold cabinet and white pillows, a hot-air bath, and a sweat bath. The entire facility is in marble. To protect the sultan at the only spot where he was truly alone, the sweat bath is secured with iron bars.

The *Banquet Hall* (Padishah-Hall), where the sultan could amuse himself with members of his harem, was probably built by SINAN. It has 26 windows. It is completely lined with delft tiles, a sign that it required complete renovation in the 19th century. The mirror is from Murano; the clock is from England. The sultan was enthroned in the centre beneath his canopy. On the sofas to the right sat the sultan's mother and his sisters. The kadınefendis made do on pillows in front. A female orchestra and dancers provided entertainment.

Continue on to the *Kiosk* of MURAT III. Lovely deep-blue tiles alternate with red flower patterns. The fountain with small jets of water served a practical purpose. As in the Audience Hall or in a spy thriller, it prevented eavesdropping upon government business. The dome is considered a masterpiece by SINAN.

Passing the library of sultan AHMET I, we reach the *Fruit Room* (18th century). This is an excellent example of Turkish Baroque, the tulip period. The walls are divided into rectangular fields and decorated with fruit and flower themes. sultan AHMET III was said to have had a poor appetite. The depictions were designed to stimulate his appetite.

The *Crown Prince's Apartment* provides the last high point in our visit to the harem. It was not discovered until 1965 when a piece of the ceiling was pierced during restoration work. The walls are again covered by faience with flower patterns predominating. In the second room, the fireplace attracts immediate attention with its wonderful goldsmithing, reminiscent of a minaret. The windows are decorated with the finest screening.

We leave the harem via the 46 m-long roughly-paved *Golden Path*, reminiscent of an old-town alleyway. This is where the harem women awaited the sultan when he returned from religious festivals or ceremonies. He rewarded them, and all those present, by tossing gold. The Gold Path leads through the *Birdhouse Gate* into the third courtyard.

OPEN: 09:30 - 17:00 h, closed Thursdays; Harem 10:00 - 16:00 h, admission £0.70, Sundays £0.35 (but it is crowded).

Archaeological Museum *(Arkeoloji Müzesi)*

The Archaeological Museum with its 34 halls, the adjoining **Ancient Oriental Museum** and the **Çinili Kiosk**, is one of the best of its kind in the world. It was founded in 1846, but international acclaim was lacking until 1896 when OSMAN HAMDI BEY brought the exhibits to the present location. The lower floor features sarcophagi from the Greek, Roman and Byzantine eras. The most famous object on display is the *Sarcophagus of Alexander* (4th century BC) which Osman Hamdi Bey discovered in Sidon.

In recent years the upper floor with its 17 halls has been opened to the public. It is accessible via a stairway in hall 3. The halls feature jewels, an extensive collection of Chinese and Japanese porcelain (but nothing compared to the collection in the Topkapı Seraglio), terracotta from Cyprus, Greek vases, glasses, coins (Greek, Byzantine, Roman, some of gold), the jaw of a snake head from the Snake Column in the Hippodrome (the only remains of the three snake heads) and bronze objects.

Faience Palace *(Çinili Köşk)*: Completed in 1466 under MEHMET THE CONQUERER; be sure to have a look at the tremendous - playful and airy - entrance hall. At one time, every room was completely decorated with tiles. Today, faiences from several epochs are on display.

As in every kiosk, four side rooms are grouped around a central hall. The idea is that at least two rooms will receive sunlight during the day. In a kiosk, every side room has the function of a living room or lounge. According to the mood of the owner, and the direction of the sun, any room might be in use.

Ancient Oriental Museum: Directly behind the entrance gate on the left is the building of the former Art Academy erected in 1883. Today it is flanked by two Hittite lions dating from the 14th century BC. After years of planning, the Ancient Oriental History Museum reopened in 1974 with outstanding exhibits.

OPEN: 09:30-17:00 h, closed Mondays, admission £0.35, on weekends just £0.18.

Gülhane Park

The park is below Topkapı Palace and the Archaeological Museum. The park entrance is a little above Alay Köşk on Alemdar Caddesi. It is the most popular picnic spot in İstanbul, not only due to its central location.

Directly behind the entrance is the *zoo*, featuring a curious collection of animals including a Holstein cow, a number of pet dogs, cats and rabbits along with traditional zoo animals like monkeys, lions and bears. Conditions in the zoo are less than humane (barred cages).

Otherwise the park offers lots of shade and family activities. A visit on Sunday is recommended. In the back of the park on a little hill is a small café with a nice view of the Bosporus and the Golden Horn. Nearby is the 15 m-tall *Goth Column* in honour of a victory by the Eastern Roman Empire against the Goths.

Cross the railway tracks (no danger) and the promenade (death-defying) to the adjoining **Seraglio Park** between the Golden Horn and the Bosporus. Here is the perfect setting for your vacation pictures (with the Bosporus Bridge in the background). Here also is a large *Atatürk Memorial* carved by the Austrian sculptor KRIPPLE (1926).

New Mosque *(Yeni Valide Camii)*

More accurately, this is the "*New Mosque of the sultan's Mother*". Construction of the mosque, located in Stambul at the end of the Galata Bridge, began in 1597. Unfortunate events (lack of funds, fire) delayed completion until 1663. Not only has the mosque been tarnished by the smoke and grime from the nearby *Eminönü* harbour; the architects, DAVUT AGA and others, clearly lacked the genius of SINAN.

The foundation of the Yeni Camii shows similarities to the Hagia Sophia. However, unlike the great church, the long axis is not emphasized; they built four half domes around the major dome and additional exedra domes in the corners to make the foundation square.

The large front courtyard boasts 20 columns supporting 24 vaults. In the centre is an enchanting ornamental fountain which is no longer used for washing (this function has been assumed by the faucet in front of the mosque). The tiles inside cannot be properly appreciated in the dim light. Of the original buildings in the complex, only two fountains, a tomb and a market hall remain.

Egyptian Bazaar *(Mısır Çarşısı)*

The Egyptian Bazaar was built in 1660 by the sultan's mother HATICE. It was financed with tax money collected from Cairo for the sale of Egyptian goods. It is located behind the New Mosque near Galata Bridge. We liked this L-shaped structure better than the Great Bazaar, because it is much more natural than its larger brother. Of course, there is no lack of neon signs, modern store-front windows or expensive shops.

The wares, also offered in the small streets surrounding the building, include spices, fruit, vegetables and fish. The latter are also sold by the docks near Galata Bridge. Birds are available on the square in front of the New Mosque. Be sure to visit one of the many old-fashioned tea houses.

OPEN: Monday to Saturday 8:00-19:00 h.

> **Restaurant Pandelli** on the second floor behind the barred windows above the entrance to the Egyptian Bazaar! Turkish food. The lamb (*Şiş Kebap* and *Döner Kebap*) is delicious.

Rüstem-Paşa Mosque

Rüstem-Paşa Mosque is just a few meters west of Yeni Camii in Eminönü. The husband of MIHRIMAH, daughter of SÜLEYMAN, chose SINAN as the architect. The mosque rises above a massive foundation of domed shop buildings, and is accessible only via a stairway. In front is an unusual vestibule complementing the mosque.

Particularly impressive are the *İznik tiles*. The bright red colour is characteristic of Armenian bolus, a clay rich in iron oxide. The rich ornamentation of these tiles lends the room a special charm.

Take a closer look at the pulpit: the lovely pearl inlay dates from the golden age of traditional Turkish woodwork.

Galata Bridge

In 1503, LEONARDO DA VINCI made a suggestion to sultan BEYAZIT II, *"Build a wooden dam and pump out all the water. Then build a bridge on stilts to Pera (Beyoglu) so that ships can still pass underneath"*. (Hans Thoma, *Türkei*, p. 232. Hallwag Verlag 1985). The suggestion was not realized. Not until the 19th century was the wooden pontoon bridge built on the Golden Horn.

The present pontoon bridge was erected between 1909 and 1936 by the West German company MAN. The bridge is 468 m long and 26 m wide, resting upon 22 pontoons. The centre portion is folded back every night from 02:00-04:00 h to permit ships to pass into the Horn.

Despite relief by a major highway which detours vehicles around the bridge, traffic is still chaotic. Lively bustle has turned the bridge, the square in front of the New Mosque and the piers in Eminönü into the heart of the city. Not surprisingly, fish grills and restaurants are located on the bottom story of the bridge. If you can avoid noticing the trash in the water, the food can be excellent.

Atatürk Bridge

This is the spot where sultan MAHMUT had the first bridge erected in 1836. It was replaced by a new bridge in 1912. The present pontoon bridge dates from 1940. Here too, the central section is moved away at night to provide large ships access to the docks in Kasımpaşa.

Süleymaniye Mosque *(Süleymaniye Camii)*

Set on a hill overlooking the southern bank of the Golden Horn, between the Atatürk and Galata Bridges. The mosque is dedicated to the tenth Ottoman sultan, SÜLEYMAN THE MAGNIFICENT. The famous architect, SINAN, constructed the building with the main facade facing Mecca. The mosque was designed to be viewed from the Galata side in its full splendor. Construction probably began in 1550.

The steep slope made construction difficult. A team of oxen, bringing stone from a quarry 1.5 km away, was only able to make one, perhaps two, trips daily. For the incline, additional oxen were harnessed, sometimes up to 20! Iron clamps were built into the facade to give it support. Over 3500 people helped with construction, half of whom were non-Muslim. Süleyman pressed the architect to increase his speed; the mosque was dedicated in 1557. Sinan himself was given the honour of officially opening the building.

A number of catastrophes have plagued the mosque. Two fires caused extensive damage. The Swiss engineer FOSSATI - invited here to supervise restoration of the Hagia Sophia - almost ruined the building by adding oil paintings. They were removed a short time later but with great difficulty.

The mosque once employed a staff of 275. Today there are nine in all: two prayer leaders, five prayer callers, a custodian and a gardener.

Minaret: The Süleymaniye Mosque is famous for its minarets - beside the two *Harem Minarets* with two ambulatories, the two *Mosque Minarets* boast three ambulatories. The total of four minarets symbolizes the fact that Süleyman was the fourth sultan after the conquest of İstanbul, while the total of ten ambulatories shows that he was the tenth sultan in the Ottoman dynasty.

Inner Courtyard: The large courtyard is paved with marble and surrounded by columned passages. In the centre is a simple *cleansing fountain* for the ritual wash.

Main Hall: The main hall of the mosque covers an area 69 x 63 m. 138 stained-glass windows (including several by the famous glass painter İBRAHIM USTA) provide light. The main dome rests upon four granite columns. It has a diameter of 27 m and a height of 53 m with a ring of 32 windows. Windows (64 x 50 cm) were built into the dome and corners to improve acoustics. The airholes in the dome keep the temperature stable and also aid the acoustics.

For years the mosque was illuminated with oil lamps and candles. Thanks to the stream of air, the lampblack was deposited in a room above the prayer niche without dirtying the mosque itself. Ink was produced from the collected lampblack. The ostrich eggs, hung in various places in the mosque, ward off spiders and their ugly webs.

Above the door leading from the courtyard into the mosque is an inscription providing information about sultan Süleyman, his forefathers and the construction of the mosque.

Süleyman Mausoleum: In the mosque garden is Süleyman's mausoleum. In the door, a piece of the Kaaba from Mecca has been inlaid. His wife ROXELANE is buried in an adjoining mausoleum. Outside the mosque is SINAN'S modest tomb.

Süleyman Complex (*Külliye*): Built around the mosque were seven medreses: five schools, a university and a technical college. Today a valuable library with about 100,000 volumes is housed here. The complex also includes a bath, caravanserai, a hospital, and an Imaret.

Subway *(Tünel)*

The *Tünel* is an underground cable railway, running from the foot of Galata Hill (Tersane Cad.) under Galata Tower to İstiklal Caddesi. İstanbul's only "Underground" boasts 612 m of track, while climbing 62 m vertically (incline: 26 %). It is also one of the oldest subways in Europe. It was put into service by French engineers in 1875.

Galata Tower *(Galata Kulesi)*

While the silhouette of its many mosques is the landmark of old İstanbul, Galata Tower dominates the European new town, Beyoğlu, on the other side of the Golden Horn. Once part of a huge fortress, it is a popular spot for local outings. Be sure to walk up the hill from the Golden Horn to the tower.

At several spots, stairs recall the time when the entire Galata Hill was accessible only on foot. Most of the stairs have now made way for roads; only the incline remains.

The *Observation Gallery* in the tower is accessible via an elevator. It offers a panorama second to none. Inside the tower are several pubs (café, taverne, restaurant, nightclub with belly-dancing performances).

OPEN: 10-24 h, admission £1.

Taksim

The city district and square of the same name is an important centre of public life in İstanbul. The rich and beautiful of this world meet in the luxury hotels. Fittingly, the neighbourhood boasts a number of expensive restaurants and pubs. In the amusement district along İstiklal Caddesi, big-city morals have replaced the strict traditions of the past. Neon signs invite you to dubious "amusements".

Taksim hosts many fine establishments including Cartier, Yves Rocher and Nina Ricci. No business of any importance can afford not to have at least a branch office here. It can be a real pleasure to promenade along - i.e. fight your way through - the shopping streets just looking at the people. You will see the rich in their fur coats who can afford to shop here; impostors who really can't afford to shop here; and normal people just here to watch the others shop. From Taksim Square, *Cumhuriyet Caddesi* (Republic Street) leads north. It is İstanbul's equivalent of Carnaby Street.

Dolmabahçe Mosque

Directly on the Bosporus is Dolmabahçe Mosque, designed by NIKOGOS, the son of the famous KARABET KALYAN. Ostensibly, the young architect was inspired by his predecessors, since the structure shows a number of styles including Baroque and Renaissance. There are a lot of special effects. Unlike most mosques, a large amount of light enters through the huge windows. This brings the marble-plated interior to full shine. The mihrab and mimber of red porphyrite make the bright interior seem almost modern.

Dolmabahçe-Palace

History: *Dolmabahçe* means "full garden". It describes a small harbour which sultan AHMET (1603-1617), patron of the Blue Mosque, ordered filled to provide land for a pleasure palace. The palace burned down several times before sultan ABDÜL MECIT I decided to build a new sultan's palace here in 1843. Topkapı seraglio was no longer good enough. The architect, KARABET BALYAN, supervised 13 years of construction before the sultan's dream was realized: a white palace right on the banks of the Bosporus. It served as the official residence until 1876 before becoming the seat of the first Turkish Parliament in 1877 (parliament was dissolved two months later). From 1923 until his death on 10 November 1938, ATATÜRK resided in parts of the palace. When he died, all the clocks in the palace were stopped, and now show the exact time of his death.

Since 1877 the palace has served as the official Turkish Government guest house. Among the guests: Empress EUGENIE of France, the Austrian Emperor FRANZ JOSEF, WILHELM II of Prussia and Germany, EDUARD VII, REZA PAHLEVI and King FAISAL of Iraq.

Facade and first impression: We were completely floored the first time we saw the palace. The sea-front facade is 600 m long! The mostly two-story building is divided into three wings. To the left (looking from the Bosporus) is the *Official Wing*, in the centre is the *Throne Hall*, and to the right the *Harem Wing*. The palace is surrounded by a lovely *garden* designed by the German architect SESTER. An elegant fence of marble screening and a splendid gate protect the seaside approach from unwanted visitors. A bit off to the side, on the access road to the entrance, is a lovely baroque *Clock Tower*. The palace itself is neo-classical (with a touch of Renaissance).

The complex boasts no less than 285 rooms and 43 salons. It contains 280 vases, 156 clocks, 4500 sq m of silk Hereke carpet, six baths, 36 chandeliers, 58 crystal candle holders. Construction consumed 14 tons of gold and 40 tons of silver and cost £350 million (at present-day exchange rates).

Tour: Disappointing! Visitors are scurried through the rooms. The guides give most of their effort to calculating how much gold has been viewed so far on the tour (see above) and urging the tourists to quicken their steps.

*　 **Ambassadors' Salon:** This is where the foreign ambassadors were received - or kept waiting. The ceiling was handpainted by French and Italian artists. The upholstery is of Hereke silk. The bear pelts were a gift from Tsar Nicholas II. The Hereke silk carpet spans 110 sq m.

* **Marble Bath**: There are three rooms (bath, dressing room, lounge) with a terrace in front. The dressing room and lounge are paneled with translucent alabaster, the bathtub is cut from a single piece of alabaster.

* **Atatürk's Death Chamber**: Atatürk could have found a nicer room to die in; there were enough to choose from.

* **Yellow Salon**: The assembly hall of the harem served as Atatürk's lounge. In this room, everything that glitters really is made of gold. The mirrors are decorated with gold reliefs and draped with expensive fabric. The cloths are interwoven with gold. The ceiling and console are richly coated with gold paint.

* **Bed Chambers of the Sultan's Wives**: During the 19th century, sultans were forced to make do with just three wives. The room of the sultan's favorite wife had a bed of walnut inlaid with gold plate. The second wife had to make do with a walnut bed inlaid simply with bronze. The third wife resided in a room decorated almost completely in white. The difference in rank is clearly visible.

* **Banquet Hall**: Certainly the high point of the tour. The huge chandelier weighs 4.5 tons and holds 750 candles. It was a gift from Queen Victoria. The room has floor heating and a gallery which was reserved for the sultan, other high dignitaries or an orchestra during festivities. Five sultans were crowned here, and Atatürk lay in state here before his burial.

* **Mosque**: Consists of two adjoining rooms. Notice the Bursa carpet with gold thread in front of the mihrab.

* **Garden**: This you can (and should) see without a guide. Be sure to complete your visit with some refreshment in the luxurious, but reasonably-priced, café. The waiters are very distinguished.

OPEN: 9:00-16:00 h, admission £0.70 for the half-hour tour or £1.35 for the hour-long tour. You must visit with a guide.

Military Museum *(Askeri Müzesi)*

The museum is 200 m north of the Hilton Hotel in Harbye, in the former Military Academy building. A visit is worthwhile even for our pacifist readers if only for a performance by the 20-man *Janissary Band* dressed in the uniforms of the elite Ottoman imperial guard. The displays include paintings, 16th-century cavalry equipment, sabres, rifles, and documents from the time of the struggle for independence.

OPEN: Wednesday to Sunday 9:00 - 17:00 h, the Janissary Band performs at 15:00 h, admission £0.28.

Naval Museum *(Deniz Müzesi)*

Founded in 1897, the Naval Museum has been housed (since 1961) in the old Tax Ministry building, located near Dolmabahçe Palace. Scattered among the retired PT boats in the garden are a few cannons.

Be sure to examine the Map of America by Admiral PIRI REIS dating from 1513, the boats with which the sultans were rowed to their Bosporus palaces, the cabin of Atatürk's yacht "Ertuğrul", and the wax figures of Turkish seamen.

OPEN: Wednesday to Sunday 10:00 - 17:00 h, admission £0.28.

Atatürk Museum *(Atatürk Müzesi)*

In Şişli, about 1 km north of the Hilton Hotel (Halaskargazi Caddesi), is a three-story building in which Atatürk resided after returning from the front in 1918. He held a number of conferences and meetings here before fleeing İstanbul in 1919 upon the arrival of international troops. In 1942 the city government bought the building and established a memorial.

For non-Turks the collection of pictures, documents, newspaper articles and Atatürk's personal belongings will have little meaning.

OPEN: 9:00-12:00 and 13:00-17:00 h.

Ortaköy Mosque

It is on a small peninsula, overshadowed by a suspension bridge spanning the Bosporus. Built during the reign of ABDÜL MECIT, it replaced an even older mosque. The architect, NIKOGOS BALYAN, created an interesting structure comparable to his other great work, the Dolmabahçe Mosque. However, here the different styles form a strong unity. The single-domed mosque profits greatly from its baroque flair. The slim minaret and colourful mosaics inside are lovely.

Bosporus Bridge

This is the longest bridge in Asia, the second longest in Europe (after the Scottish Humber Bridge) and the fifth longest bridge in the world.

A few **statistics**: Length: 1622 m, roadway height: 64 m above sea level, height of the pilings: 165 m, width: 33 m (six lanes). Construction consumed 55,000 cubic meters of reinforced concrete, 7000 tons of cable and about 17,000 tons of steel. The pilings are anchored 16 m into the bedrock.

The Bosporus Bridge was built in three years by the British Cleveland Bridge & Engineering Co. and Hochtief AG of Essen, West Germany at a cost of £50 million. Since its opening in 1973, on the 50th anniversary of the founding of the Turkish Republic, the bridge has been used by 100,000 vehicles daily. Although tolls are charged in one direction only, the bridge paid for itself within four years.

Traffic backs up during rush hour. For this reason a second suspension bridge is being built over the narrowest point, at Rumeli Hisari. The contract has gone to a Japanese-Italian consortium. The project is being financed by a £90-million credit from Japanese banks. Repayment is scheduled over seven years. No doubt this new bridge will easily pay off the loan.

Leander Tower *(Kız Kulesi)*

The Leander Tower is on a small island in the Sea of Marmara not far from the Üsküdar shore. About 500 BC a Greek customs station was built here. The present building dates from 1545. The tower serves as a lighthouse and a customs control station. The island is accessible by small boats from *Salacak İskele*. Take your time negotiating the price!

The name Leander Tower stems from a legend and a misunderstanding. It is said that Leander swam across the sea every night to visit his lover, the priestess of Aphrodite, Hero (which was of course prohibited). Unfortunately for the tower, it was the Dardanelles (Hellespont) which the brave youth swam across. At least, according to Lord Byron!

The Turkish name **"Girl Tower"** stems from another legend. A sultan was told that his daughter would die of a snake bite. In order to prevent this, he placed her on the island. Even there she was bitten by a viper smuggled onto the island in a basket of fruit. By the way, this story is frequently told in one form or another, wherever there is a tower/castle, water...and a young virgin.

Harbour Mosque *(İskele Camii)*

The İskele Camii was built in 1547 by the architect SINAN for MIHRIMAH, the favorite daughter of sultan SÜLEYMAN. It is located in Üsküdar, above the docks. This is one of the master's lesser works. The impression one has from outside is not complemented by the interior. The main dome is joined by just three - rather than the usual four - half domes. The weak light adds to the irritation. One can imagine why Mihrimah ("Sun and Moon") wanted this semi-darkness.

The nearby medrese now serves as a clinic. When leaving the mosque, at the bottom of the stairs, you will see a lovely *baroque fountain* built for AHMET III in 1726.

AROUND İSTANBUL

The Golden Horn and Eyüp

The Golden Horn is an arm of the ocean 11 km long, 800 m wide and with an average depth of 40 m, separating old Stambul from Beyoğlu.

It owes its name to the tides which shimmer with gold at sundown. According to legend, however, wealthy Byzantines poured their treasures into the inlet during the Turkish storming of Constantinople, to prevent them from falling into the conquerors' hands.

During the Ottoman era, the Golden Horn, along with the Bosporus, was a favorite excursion spot among İstanbul citizens of all classes. sultans regularly travelled via Eyüp to the furthest tip of the Horn. Splendid royal grounds were maintained at a spot where two small rivers, called the "Sweet Waters of Europe", flowed into the inlet. Both shores of the Horn were dotted with large, well-kept gardens, pavilions and small palaces.

And today? Dozens of ugly, run down factories are spread around the *Haliç*. Large amounts of untreated sewage are channeled into the water. The air is polluted. Don't expect to find any fish! The stench is horrid in many spots, particularly where a breeze passes over the once so golden tide (which happens frequently). Test your nose with a visit to the "Stinking Horn".

Coming-Going: Haliç-İskelesi (100 m from Galata Bridge heading towards Atatürk Bridge), £0.08, the return trip from Eyüp is half price (it is possible to go on to Üsküdar).

By Boat

You board at *Haliç İskelesi* near Galata Bridge. Small, regularly scheduled boats cruise hourly between five landings. The last stop is *Eyüp*. After casting off, the boat steers quickly toward Atatürk Bridge. On the left is Rüstem-Paşa Mosque with Sülemaniye Mosque in the background. The big factory about halfway down produces cigarettes. To the right is the hill of Pera, the modern European town with the Galata Tower. The Haliç Park is almost complete on both sides between Galata and Atatürk Bridges.

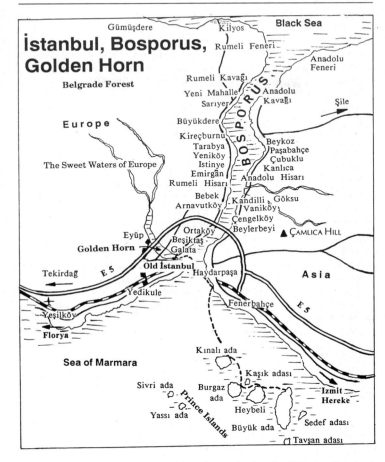

İstanbul, Bosporus, Golden Horn

Belgrade Forest

Black Sea

Gümüşdere
Kilyos
Rumeli Feneri
Anadolu Feneri

Rumeli Kavağı
Yeni Mahalle
Anadolu Kavağı
Sarıyer
Şile

Europe

Büyükdere
Kireçburnu
Tarabya
Beykoz
Paşabahçe
Yeniköy
Çubuklu
The Sweet Waters of Europe
İstinye
Kanlıca
Emirgân
Anadolu Hisarı
Rumeli Hisarı

BOSPORUS

Bebek
Kandilli
Göksu
Arnavutköy
Vaniköy
Çengelköy
Beylerbeyi
▲ ÇAMLICA HILL

Eyüp
Ortaköy
Golden Horn
Beşiktaş
Galata

Old İstanbul
Haydarpaşa
Asia

Tekirdağ
E 5

Yedikule
Fenerbahçe
E 5

Yeşilköy

Florya

Sea of Marmara

Kınalı ada

Kaşık adası

Sivri ada
Burgaz ada
İzmit
Hereke

Prince Islands

Yassı ada
Heybeli

Büyük ada
Sedef adası

Tavşan adası

The first landing is *Kasimpaşa* on the right bank. This is the spot where the besieging Turkish forces returned their ships to the water, after MEHMET FATIH ordered the fleet be pulled over Galata Hill in order to circumvent a Byzantine chain preventing direct access to the Horn by water. Today wharfs fill the district.

The boat then crosses the Horn to *Fener*. Here you can see a lovely park, on the left the Selim Mosque and on the right the red-brick college of the Orthodox patriarch. Adjoining is the plain Hagios Georgios Church, seat of the Patriarch. The park runs along the left bank to *Balat*, landing number three.

Haşköy is on the right shore. In the summer of 1986, a new layer of topsoil was laid for the park. But factory ruins still spoil the view. Haşköy seems to be a gathering point for dilapidated ferries, some of which are well worth a photo. Unfortunately the smell is horrible!

It smells better after the Haliç Bridge. To the left, an outcropping of land marks the landing at *Eyüp*. Last stop!

THE NEW MAN AND THE SEA

When BEDRETTIN DALAN assumed office in 1984 as mayor of İstanbul, he had harsh words for the Golden Horn. *"If you dip your finger in it, you will pull out only bones."* He promised to do something. *"By 1988 the Golden Horn will be as blue as my eyes."*

Dalan's £105 million program consists of three phases. The first phase is underway: 4000 buildings circling the Horn have been torn down. By resettling 250,000 residents, a strip of green covering 650 acres is being created. This is designed greatly to reduce the influx of pollution from surrounding industry.

During the second phase Atatürk Bridge and Galata Bridge are scheduled to be rebuilt. The intention is to restore a natural flow of water. At the moment the two pontoon bridges reduce water flow by 90 %. A £10 million contract with Thyssen has already been signed.

Phase three calls for construction of two large sewers which will redirect the sewage to new purification plants on the Bosporus. The relatively clean water will then be released into the Black Sea.

The situation in 1989: Dalans 3-phase-plan is far from completed, the Horn is dirty as before. Dalans project was disputed for years. *"I would much prefer to have electricity every day and running water than a clean Horn."* was the recent comment of one journalist. Dalan himself was a victim of the crushing defeat of the Motherland Party (ANAP) in the nationwide local elections 1989.

Eyüp and Eyüp Mosque

The spot has maintained its village atmosphere. Narrow streets with painstakingly preserved wooden buildings lend truth to the old saying that *"Eyüp is not İstanbul"*, as a local journalist explained. Eyüp is an intact community and not just a suburb of İstanbul, despite the growth of the metropolis. Well worth a visit.

The highlight of any visit is the *Eyüp Mosque*, the most sacred in all of Turkey. Only the mosques in Mecca, Medina and Jerusalem are more revered by Sunnite Muslims.

Its sacred status is due to EYÜP ENSARI, an advisor to MUHAMMAD and a banner bearer in the first Arab army to besiege Byzantium during the 7th century. Reportedly he was killed on this spot in 672 AD. MEHMET THE CONQUEROR visited the village in 1453 where he discovered the grave, whereafter he ordered the construction of an adjoining mosque. According to legend, one of his advisors prophesied that if he dug one meter under the prayer carpet, he would find the unspoiled corpse of Eyüp. And so it was!

The present mosque was reconstructed in 1800. Right up to the 20th century, coronation ceremonies for the Turkish sultans were held here. The Sheik of the Dervish Order residing in Konya would present the new Ottoman head of state with the sword of OSMAN, the founder of the dynasty.

The *front courtyards* of the mosque are particularly lovely. The first courtyard contains a splendid *cleansing fountain*. We pass through a gate into the second courtyard. Here, behind a huge plane tree, is the *tomb of Eyüp*, recognizable by its blue-green faience.

Only in recent years has the site been opened to non-Muslims in conformance with the dress code (covering legs and shoulders). Women are required to cover their heads. In order to avoid difficulties or misunderstandings, get permission to view the tomb from a Muslim, or better, have a Muslim show you the tomb and explain its significance. The interior walls of the eight-sided tomb are adorned with the finest İznik tiles. The banner bearer rests in a slightly raised wooden coffin.

The mosque itself is a less than spectacular domed building. The floor is covered with costly turquoise-coloured carpet, a gift from former prime minister MENDERES.

Don't miss a visit to the *cemetery* where a number of high dignitaries have found their rest. The only sultan's tomb, however, is not here, but halfway between the landing and the mosque complex by the large intersection (*Türbe Mehmet V, 1909 - 1918*).

CAFE PIERRE LOTI: Through the cemetery and after a twenty-minute climb we reach Café Pierre Loti, named after the French naval Lieutenant and author (1850-1923), who was sent to İstanbul to train the Turkish fleet and often came to this spot to write. The view across the Golden Horn to the Bosporus is great!

Bosporus *(Bogaziçi)*

A Bosporus trip is an absolute must on any visit to İstanbul. Currents keep the water clear, while the scenic countryside and enchanting villages on both shores make the cruise unforgettable.

"Bosporus" means "cattle ford". The strait owes its name to one of the many lovers of ZEUS (father of the gods), IO, who was a lovely priestess of Hera. In order to protect Io from the wrath of HERA (Zeus' wife), Zeus turned his lover into a cow. But Hera sent a horsefly, forcing Io, the cow, to flee and swim to the Asian shore.

Technically the Bosporus is a 31.7 km long river valley which sank during the Ice Age. At its narrowest point it measures only 660 m across, at its widest spot 4.7 km. Its average depth is no more than 70 m. A powerful current flows at 5 km per hour from the Black Sea to the Sea of Marmara.

The Bosporus is a tricky stretch of water, particularly during the winter when storms can kick up waves 1 m high, complicating navigation already hindered by zero-visibility fog and icebergs (!). The twisting strait creates eddies which have claimed many small fishing boats.

COMING - GOING: Slim, maneuverable steamers depart three times daily during the week from Eminönü (İskele 3 and 4), destined for the Black Sea (10:25, 12:10 and 14:10   h). There are five ships on Sundays. The schedule changes frequently, but is always posted at the pier. Board a half-hour before departure in order to get a good seat. As these are pure sightseeing tours, the price is expensive (£1.70). However, you are permitted to disembark at any stop and continue on with a later boat, making the cruise well worth it.

Beşiktaş is the first port of call for the Bosporus steamers. En route we pass the huge Karaköy wharf facility, the *Tophane* where

Ottoman cannons were cast, the *Dolmabahçe Mosque* and the *Dolmabahçe Palace*. Directly adjoining the landing is the *Naval Museum*.

The steamer now continues on to its first Asian port at **Beylerbey**. If you disembark here, be sure to visit the *Beylerbey Palace*. Then the strait is again crossed to **Ortaköy**. The *Ortaköy Mosque*, overshadowed by the Bosporus Bridge, is quite famous. There is always a lot going on in the small fishing harbour.

Passing under the Bosporus Bridge, we come to **Kuruçeşme** (an ugly village with coal reserves and piles of sand and rock) and on to **Çengelköy** on the Asian side which has an enchanting village square with tiny cafés and shady trees.

After the Bosporus Bridge we leave the city behind, cruising past typical Bosporus countryside with forested hills and tiny fishing villages. Worth special mention are the *yalıs*.

Yalıs are summer palaces of high Ottoman imperial dignitaries and wealthy İstanbulians, who, during the 19th century, were able to afford a cool refuge on the Bosporus from the sticky and stinking city heat. Unfortunately, real estate speculation during the 1960s brought down many of the yalıs. Strict laws, declaring almost the entire region as a historic landmark, have saved some of the loveliest palaces from the bulldozer or decay.

Most interesting are the "Red Yalı" in Çengelköy (also the largest), the "Amcazade Hüseyin Paşa" in Kanlıca, the oldest building on the Bosporus (built in 1698), the "Yalı of Count Ostrolog" in Kanlıca and the rose-coloured "Villa Bosporus" in Beylerbey.

Our cruise continues on to **Arnavutköy** (Albanian Village), one of the most beautiful spots on the European bank of the Bosporus. Side by side are crooked, narrow, three and four-story wooden buildings with balconies overlooking the harbour where colourful fishing boats ply their trade. A number of *seafood restaurants* populate the harbour promenade. Tip: Compare prices!

On a hill overlooking the village is *Robert College*, the first school of higher education in Turkey to admit women. Around the peninsula at Arnavutkoy, the currents are so powerful that sailing ships frequently had difficulty navigating the cape. A number of tragedies have occured here.

The next two landings, **Vaniköy** and **Kandilli**, are again on the Asian side. Kandilli is known for its yalıs and summer breeze. **Bebek** is certainly the most affluent village on the Bosporus. Directly on the shore, just before town, is the summer residence of the Egyptian ambassador. In the background you see a gently rising hill covered with groves of trees and dotted with villas. On the hill to the north the *Bosporus University* was founded in 1971. There are numerous, although expensive, seafood restaurants.

The impressive, 250 m long fortress, *Rumeli Hisarı*, overlooks the narrowest point of the Bosporus. It was built by 10,000 men in just four months in 1452 on orders of MEHMET THE CONQUEROR. Together with the *Anadolu Hisarı* castle on the Asian bank of the Bosporus, it was intended to close the strait to Byzantine shipping. Restoration was completed in 1953 as part of the 500th anniversary celebration.

Three massive towers, each with up to nine stories, rise above the fortress. Once upon a time, foreign ambassadors often languished in the northern tower. The southern tower is even more impressive with walls seven meters thick. Battlemented walls, reinforced by 13 smaller towers, connected the large corner towers. An *open-air theatre* has been set up in the courtyard inside. During the annual Art and Culture Festival, held in June and July, Shakespeare's plays are performed. During the summer the castle is lit up at night.

OPEN: 09:30 - 16:30 h, closed Mondays, admission £0.20.

The lovely little castle *Anadolu Hisarı* is at the point where the tiny *Göksü River* ("Heaven's River") flows into the Bosporus. A number of boats are attracted by the peace and quiet. The castle itself is considered the oldest Ottoman structure in the region, having been built in 1390 AD under BEYAZIT I. At the centre of the complex is a tall, square tower surrounded by a rectangular wall fortified with battlements and a triangular stronghold outside.

Just 200 m south of the Göksü confluence, the *Küçüksu River* (Little Water) flows into the Bosporus. At this lovely spot, on a meadow between the two rivers, sultan ABDÜL MECIT ordered the *Küçüksu Palace* built in 1856. The two-story, rococo palace was frequently used by ATATÜRK as a summer residence.

The zigzag course continues over to **Emirgan**, named after EMIR KHAN, a Persian prince, who surrendered the city of Eriwan without a fight. He was deported here for a time before becoming sultan MURAT IV's favorite drinking buddy. We especially liked the village square. By the way, the water at Emirgan is said to taste terrific, and make excellent Turkish coffee. Emirgan is famous for its *Tulip Garden*, which invites a visit, particularly in the spring. Over 1000 species of tulips are grown including the legendary *Black Tulip*.

OPEN: 8.30 - 17.30 h. Admission: £0.20.

Kanlıca is famous for its yoghurt, available everywhere at reasonable prices. Did you know that "yoghurt" is a Turkish word meaning fermented milk? **İstinye** on the European side boasts the prettiest harbour on the Bosporus, although its huge floating docks ruin the scenery. **Yeniköy** is an expensive residential community with luxury restaurants and night clubs. The next stop on the Anatolian side is

Çubuklu, famous for a monastery founded by St Alexander of the "Sleepless Order" about 420 AD, which prayed around the clock (in two shifts). Above the village is the *Palace of the Viceroy of Egypt*, a landmark familiar to generations of sailors.

The steamer plies on along the Asian bank to **Paşabahçe**, which is best known for its glass production. The village seems very industrialized. **Beykoz** has also been lost to the industrial age. *Joshua Castle*, set 200 m behind the village, dominates the scenery.

The ship now leaves the Anatolian shore, continuing without stops to the uninteresting last station, Anadolu Kavağı. Beyond Beykoz and Anadolu Kavağı is a closed military region. On the European side we can visit **Tarabya**. The narrow bay is very scenic and well worth a visit. The bay is spoiled by a 10-story hotel complex (*Tarabya Oteli*), a gathering spot for İstanbul's Arab community. Tourists were not the first to discover the pleasant climate here. Its name "Tarabya" (therapy) is a sure sign of that. European diplomats of the 19th century made Tarabya their residence. The Imperial German Embassy is still intact. The embassies of France and Britain burned down in the 1920s: their ruins are in lovely parks. In **Büyükdere** you will find a huge park, numerous villas, and loads of people - all out for your money. Also worth a look are the residences of the *Spanish and Tsarist ambassadors*. From here you can visit the *Belgrade Forest*, the largest forested region in the İstanbul area.

Our next stop is **Sarıyer**. The village is best known for its fish market. The Sarıyer fishermen are closest to the Black Sea and can bring in some impressive catches. Try one of the seafood restaurants in the harbour which are much more old-fashioned and natural than in Büyükdere or Tarabya.

Coming - Going: Get a local bus from Eminönü and Taksim. By dolmuş or bus you can continue on to the beach resort of Kilyos on the Black Sea (10 km).

Yenimahalle is a tiny fishing village with a castle and nice pubs. *Rumeli Kavagı* was an important landmark in ancient times! This is our last stop on the European side. On a hill, within a military zone, is a Byzantine castle. The paved road from İstanbul ends here. The military road is closed to civilian traffic. If you insist upon visiting the mouth of the river, you can rent a boat for a cruise out to *Rumeli Feneri* (light house). It is forbidden, however, to tie up on shore.

The last stop is **Anadolu Kavağı** on the Asian shore. The main attraction would certainly be the huge Genoese fortress above the village, if strict sailors would not insist that all visitors turn back. The roads toward the mouth (*Anadolu Feneri*) and toward Beykoz are closed. In short you are restricted to the village itself with its restaurants, stands, ice cream vendors and crowds of tourists. From Anadolu

Kavağı you can get a bus back to İstanbul, although you must change buses at Beykoz.

Belgrade Forest *(Belgrat Ormanı)*

The huge forest is accessible from İstanbul by bus or taxi. The cheapest route is with the Bosporus Line ship to *Büyükdere* and then by bus.

The name Belgrade Forest stems from the Serbian craftsmen and charcoal makers who were resettled here by BEYAZIT after the conquest of Belgrade in 1521. It is a lush beech and oak forest full of vines making it much more wild and impenetrable than the parks and ornamental forests of central Europe. It was never sacrificed for timber. In fact, the inhabitants of the village of Belgrade were forced to leave the region in 1898 when they began felling trees for personal use (there is a memorial plaque). The forest was an important source of water. Several aqueducts, some of which were built by SINAN, can still be seen. Even today, the city of İstanbul draws much of its drinking water from the wells of the forest.

COMING - GOING: By dolmuş and bus from Taksim to Bahçeköy, or by ship to Sarıyer and from there by bus to Bahçeköy. By local bus from Taksim (get off in Orman Fakültesi).

Çamlıca Hill *(Çamlıca Tepesi)*

The Spruce Hill (*Büyük Çamlıca*) is 270 m high, making it the highest viewpoint in the İstanbul region. If you are lucky enough to come on one of the few days with clear visibility, you can see along the entire Bosporus to the Black Sea and all the way across to the Sea of Marmara. Theoretically you should be able to see the Uludağ near Bursa, but air pollution makes this impossible! Still, the forested Çamlıca hill (easily recognizable by its TV tower) is one of the most scenic spots in the region. Restaurant there.

COMING - GOING: Hourly buses from Üsküdar (7 km to the northwest). Get off at Büyük Çamlıca.

Karaca Ahmet Kabristani

The largest cemetery in the Ottoman Empire! It is in the *Selimiye* district on the Asian side, behind Selim military base (one of the most crowded and most infamous Turkish prisons). The long rows of graves are well-kept. The cemetery is freely accessible to non-Muslims.

Üsküdar

A side trip into this Asian neighbourhood of İstanbul can be interesting. Üsküdar is accessible hourly from Eminönü, Kabataş or Beşiktaş (takes 20 minutes). Originally founded by the Greeks as *Chrysopolis*, the town is even older than İstanbul, with a turbulent history. Strategically located, directly upon the Bosporus, Üsküdar was once an important departure point for Asian traders. Because its location on a peninsula was difficult to defend, the town's development was frequently stopped by attacks. There are no buildings at all from the Byzantine era.

There is tremendous tourist activity during the summer months, with domestic tourists flooding the fish market. The town's landmark is the *Leander Tower*, visible from far and wide. Üsküdar is famous for its mosques around the landing. We enjoyed the bustle between the wooden buildings on narrow streets and the view of İstanbul.

Behind the harbour buildings is *İskele Mosque*. In the nearby *Yeni-Valide Mosque* notice the wooden front of the sultan's box. The mosque belongs to a complex including a mektep (Koran school) and imaret (charity kitchen). A real jewel is the *Semsi Ahmet Paşa Camii* whose light coloured marble is visible from far at sea.

The regional map at the harbour provides information on the surrounding area, whose park-like forests invite an outing.

Black Sea

The holiday villages of Kilyos and Şile are easy to reach from İstanbul and well known for their fishing. Tourists can expect a variety of seafood restaurants and also several clean, sandy beaches.

The Black Sea has special water conditions. A heavy influx of fresh water from the Danube, Dnieper and Volga Rivers keeps the salt content low, at only 2%. While surface temperatures range between 6 and 30 degrees Centigrade, the deep-water temperature is a constant 9 degrees. These temperature conditions prevent a water exchange, robbing water below 200 m of life-giving oxygen. For this reason the hydrogen sulphide content of the water rises rapidly at lower depths. Few forms of life can exist. There are plenty of fish in the relatively clean upper layers of water.

Kilyos

A lovely village 38 km north of İstanbul, 5 km west of the mouth of the Bosporus - only recommended on weekdays due to weekend crowds. The beach is large and relatively clean with adequate facilities (surfing, paddle boats, bicycles), but a bit expensive. The picture-postcard paradise of days past has been replaced by souvenir shops, boutiques and pubs. The inviting castle overlooking the village is in a closed military zone.

COMING - GOING: From Taksim Square by local bus every half hour (£0.50) or by Bosporus steamer to Sarıyer and from there by dolmuş.

A NIGHT'S REST: **Turban Kilyos Moteli**: Double £26.70, Off season 30 % cheaper. The usual standard with lots of sport and entertainment facilities, tel. 1 142 02 88. **Gurup Oteli**: Double £12.70; room with showers. Luxury furnishings, restaurant, nearby disco, tel. 1 142 01 94.

CAMPING: **Kilyos Camping**, a nice site with all the amenities. Electricity, kitchen, hot water, showers.

Şile

An ancient town (founded in the 7th century BC) set on the jagged coastline. Over the centuries it has been home to Hittites, Phrygians, Romans, Byzantines and Ottomans.

Şile has developed into a bathing resort much favoured by the people of İstanbul, particularly at the weekend; but it is not nearly as crowded as Kilyos. Şile is recommended for air travellers, who wish to wait in peace for their flight from İstanbul, or for those travelling around Turkey, who want to take a first look at the Black Sea before committing themselves. The lovely beaches *Aglayan Kaya, Şile Feneri, Ocak Ada* and *Kumbaba* can all be recommended. Şile boasts the tallest lighthouse in all of Turkey. It was built in 1858 by the French. The town is also known for its fine Silebezi cotton, which has recently been seized upon by international fashion designers.

INFORMATION: obtainable at the large car park by the mosque on the main road.

TELEPHONE AREA CODE: 9.1992

COMING - GOING: there are buses every hour from Üsküdar/İstanbul and vice versa. Duration of journey c. 2 hours for the 68 km. There are also buses from Üsküdar to Ağva.

A NIGHT'S REST

Those who look for a room up to midday Friday and from Sunday evening onwards will have a wide choice. Between these times, the place is flooded with weekend trippers from İstanbul. A selection:

Hotel Kumbaba: Double £21, open only during the summer. The hotel is beautifully situated on a sand bank, and normally accessible only via the hotel boat. Reasonable comfort, tel. 38.

Değirmen Oteli: Double £14, rooms with showers. There is a restaurant and disco adjoining. TV and a number of videos. Family atmosphere with the same guests coming each year. View of the harbour. The beach is accessible via some steps. tel. 148.

Deniz Hotel: Turn off to the left from the main road at the bus park (coming from İstanbul). The hotel is in a pleasant situation overlooking the sea and advertises "VIP Service". This means 1 grill room, 1 bar, 1 disco, 1 café. This VIP experience costs about £5 per person including breakfast. tel. 1427.

Seyhan Motel: The building in front of the Deniz Hotel. Jolly staff, breakfast included in the price and the same beautiful situation. Price and standard the equivalent of £1 below that of the Deniz. £4 per person. tel. 1050

Emek Pension: Friendly Reşat Ay runs this guest house at 23, Ihlamur Cad., a side road off the main road (sign reads Emek Pension 50 m). 40 guests can be accommodated in the single, double, three- and four-bedded rooms (3 of which have a shower) without any problem. Reşat Ay, however, believes that he can fit in 60 guests. Price with breakfast about £5 per person.

Yasemin Pansiyon-Restaurant: The friendliest and the nicest place, at the end of the main road before it makes a sharp bend, and high up above the harbour below. There are steep steps leading up to it. All double rooms complete with shower/WC and terrace and the cost per person, including breakfast, is about £7. At 1, Vali Muhittin Cad. tel. 1358

Tümay Pansiyon: A large, modern house in a dead safe position opposite the police station. Breakfast is taken in the café. Leisure activities on offer here include billiards and table tennis. Price as at the Yasemin, and in the same road, but at number 21. tel. 2144.

CAMPING: A very largeselection of sites, but only very few are up to Europ ean standards.

Kumbaba Camping, next to Hotel Kumbaba, accessible by the hotel boat. Adequate shade, modest comfort, showers, minimarket.

Akkaya Camping: Mr Karaoğlu is a lawyer, but he prefers to run a camping site, for he is a camping freak. This is by far the nicest site in the place. It occupies a position away from it all at the seaward end of a little valley; its own little beach is bordered by rocks and thus has an intimate atmosphere. Expert campers are in their element here, with an electricity supply, lockable refrigerators , kitchens, showers on the beach, and a minimarket. The sanitary facilities are immaculate, and the restaurant, with its attentive service, belongs to the upper price category. The tents are pitched on a small area of meadow behind the beach, and above them on the slope there are bungalows with a view of the beach. Price per person £2, cars and motorbikes £1 each, tent £1. Caravans and minibuses £2. Use of electricity supply £1. A bungalow with shower/WC costs about £15 for two people.

Coming - Going: The site is 10 miles to the east of Şile. Go in the direction of Kandira from Şile, and take the little side road which turns off towards Ağva/Sahil Yolu after about 2 1/2 miles. If you go down this little road for 7 1/2 miles you will pass through Kabakoz and come to Akçakese. From there, you approach the sea along a gravel track (signposted).

Camping Fener: On the eastern side of Şile; not as comfortable or secluded, but attractively situated in an area of meadow and near to Şile. The site is separated from the beach, to which there is general access, by a little road and an additional 55 yards. Friendly atmosphere, very clean sanitary facilities and kitchen. Restaurant of the middle category. Price per person £1, tent £1, cars half of this price and caravans about £0.50 supplement. How to get there: turn off from the main road between İstanbul and Kandira towards Şile in a seaward direction, at the sign which says "Şehir Merkezi" (at a barracks), and then turn right after that (signposted). The site is a few hundred yards down on the right.

Berlin Camping: Opposite Camping Fener; low standard, a completely cheerless place.

On the western side of Şile there are several sites strung out in a row, but there is almost nothing to choose between them. Situated along a gravel road above the beach, they are dull places with modest sanitation; only the restaurants boast any slight variations in style and are welcome at every point because they provide the only shade from the sun. Example of the prices here: Tents about £3 at the Bacanaklar Camp, while people, pets and vehicles are free.

Bathing

Those in a hurry can jump into the sea at the harbour of Şile, but no more than that - there is no beach there. To the west (left hand side), there is a long beach with numerous beach restaurants in the first part of it, and there is a long beach to the east (right hand side),too. The latter is also not so crowded at the weekend and is much nicer. Quiet beaches and bays can be found again and again in an eastwards direction.

Demirciköy/Gümüşdere

Near Kilyos, the beach is of fine, yellow sand (dunes), but frequently polluted by tar. Warning: dangerous undertows at certain sections of the beach! Much less crowded than Kilyos.

COMING-GOING: Minibuses from Taksim or Sarıyer.

Prince Islands *(Kızıl Adalar)*

A popular spot for outings, attracting lots of local visitors. The Prince Islands are called Kızıl Adalar (Red Islands) in Turkish due to the reddish quartz and iron content of their stone. Ships are always crowded!

The isolated location of the nine islands (between 18 to 30 km from İstanbul) attracted a number of monks who founded numerous monasteries, some of which are still in use today. Isolation is a thing of the past though, considering the long queues at Eminönü harbour. Be at the pier at least half an hour before departure time.

The cruise out is an experience in itself. Ghettoblasters blare out the latest hits - or last year's street performers show their skills, tea,

yoghurt and ice cream are hawked unceasingly. We reach the islands after a good hour.

Kınalı Ada: First stop; buildings are concentrated around the harbour. It takes some searching to find the tiny beaches. There is a good view from the highest point on the island (115 m above sea level), from where you can see monastery ruins on the neighbouring islands. A nice place for hikes.

Burgaz Ada: The extensive pine forests are easiest to explore by horse cart. The picturesque fishing village surrounding the harbour has been lost to tourism. Try an excursion up the 163 m high *Christos Tepesi*.

Heybeli Ada: The harbour houses a military academy and the "Savarona", ATATÜRK'S personal yacht. The harbour promenade is inviting. You can walk over to the *Theological Seminary* of the Orthodox Church in the hollow between the two highest points to the north. The same walk will take you past a 15th century Byzantine Church. However, you will need permission from the commander of the Military Academy (available at the gate).

Büyük Ada: The activity at the dock is hectic: ships unload masses of tourists. Crowds throng through the town filling every seat in its many restaurants.

Even if you share the pleasure with a couple of hundred other tourists, it is still worthwhile taking a ride on one of the 200 horse carts (parked behind the landing near the tourist information office); costs £1.70 for 30 minutes.

The best beaches are in the south and southeast of the island. There are facilities for surfing, waterskiing, or boat tours (£1.35). There is no charge for swimming, and the beach still has a number of quiet spots to discover, despite the crowds.

The island's claim to fame is its lovely old *wooden buildings*, some of which have become dilapidated in recent years. Others have been neglected by their owners in the hopes that the buildings, now protected as historic monuments, will need to be torn down, making room for new, more profitable structures. Fortunately, these are the exception. Still, tourism must take the blame for high prices: the local population can hardly afford to live on the island any more.

The other five islands are privately owned, closed military zones, or are not visited by tourist ships. The nice sandy beach on **Sedef Ada** is accessible by rented boat from Büyük Ada.

A sad event in the history of **Sivri Ada**, the most western of the nine islands, took place in 1910. All the stray dogs in İstanbul were captured and released on Sivri Ada, where they starved.

On **Yassi Ada** members of deposed Turkish governments and parliamentarians have been held prisoner by the military.

INFORMATION: By the landing on Büyük Ada. You can pick up a free map showing all the islands and providing information in English, German and Turkish.

COMING – GOING: Every two hours Eminönü; costs £0.70. In addition to the regular buses there are special express buses particularly between Büyük Ada and İstanbul. **Note:** Even on a trip of several days, your original ticket is still valid for the entire distance.

SHOPPING: Adequate, although more expensive than in İstanbul, no specialty shops.

SPORTS: **Büyük Ada**: Water sports on the beaches in the south and southeast: surfing, boat trips along the coast (£1.35), donkey rides on Isotepe (163 m above sea level) £0.80 for 30 minutes, swimming on all the islands served by steamer. **Heybeli Ada**: The swimming club boasts a 50 m pool, skindiving, surfing, waterskiing, sailing lessons.

A NIGHT'S REST: Since lodgings are expensive everywhere on the islands, you are advised to stay overnight in İstanbul. Still, an example from Büyük Ada: **Splendid Oteli**, Büyük Ada, Nisan Cad. 7, double £15, plus obligatory full board £12 per person, tel. 351/67 75.

FOOD: **Yalı Locanta**, Büyük Ada, at the harbour, good seafood, £3.35 to £6.70. There are approx. ten additional pubs on the promenade, varying in price.

Swimming

There are good beaches on the four largest islands with showers, restaurants and shops. You will find some quiet bays if you look for them.

Hereke

The small town, 25 km west of İzmit, has been known for its carpet weaving since the days of the Ottoman Empire. This is the home of the costly *Hereke Silk Carpets*, whose splendid colours and density of knots is not excelled anywhere in the world (honestly!). The reputation of local producers has been injured in recent years by a break with the traditional flower motifs: "*Hereke is prostituting itself!*" notes a well-known carpet merchant in Kuşadası. But the quality remains the same.

Do not expect to make a good buy. Most of the private producers are bound by long-term contracts with wholesalers. You may visit the government institute *Sümerbank*. A museum has been established in a pavilion built by the German emperor WILHELM II.

Sümerbank Hereke Müessesesi: Hereke, tel. 216 110 04.

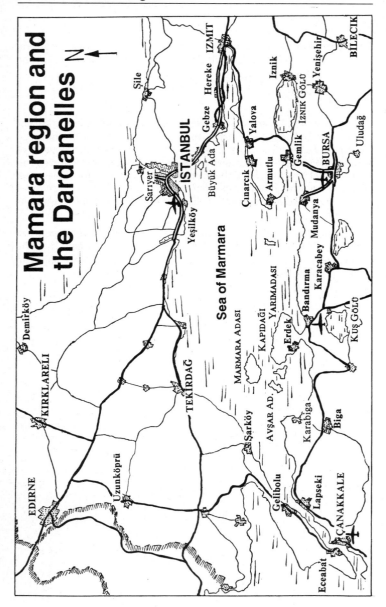

Mamara region and the Dardanelles

MARMARA REGION AND DARDANELLES

Europeans don't know much about Turkey. Towns are known primarily from the news or travel brochures: İstanbul, Ankara, Antalya, Kuşadası, İzmir, Troja, Ephesus. The Sea of Marmara may ring a bell, but who has heard of towns such as Bursa, Bandırma, Erdek and İznik? Streams of tourists flow past the Marmara region. Could there be anything of interest here?

Quite a bit, actually: *Bursa*, the "cradle of the Ottoman Empire", is an extremely diverse town with old Ottoman mosques, tombs of several sultans, healing waters, and the most modern ski area in Turkey. *İznik*, by the lake of the same name, was once capital of Byzantium. Then there is *Çanakkale*, where the strait is so narrow that one could almost touch Europe. And Schliemann's *Troy* is just a hop away.

Turkish vacationers have long since discovered the Sea of Marmara. This is evident in such crowded beach towns as *Erdek* or *Armutlu*. For ornithologists *Manyas National Park*, south of Bandırma, is a true paradise.

The region is no longer as wealthy as in ancient times. Regions outside of Bursa often lack infrastructure, water, electricity, schools and hospitals. Where tractors are needed, oxen work the fields. Villages are sleepy, poor, seemingly resigned. Emigration to İstanbul increases each year. Young people no longer see their future here. And Turkish economic policy, with its passion for mammoth prestige projects, has completely bypassed the region.

But those who remain have a better life than those lost in the Gecekondus of İstanbul. The almost perfectly flat region is very fertile. Wine, tobacco, olives, peaches and mulberry trees (whose leaves nourish silkworms) flourish here. The Marmara region and Thrace feed most of Anatolia! Nobody starves, and those who work the soil love it. Visitors are shown around with a smile, as we ourselves have experienced.

İzmit *(pop. 210,000)*

Today the town is a centre of heavy industry and toolmaking. Wharfs, refineries and cellulose plants pollute the air and water. Money is the first priority; there is no room for environmental concerns or a good image.

İzmit has few sights, but the great Sinan was here. He built the *Yeni Cuma Camii* in 1568.

COMING - GOING: **Buses** hourly to Bursa and İstanbul. Buses and minibuses to Adapazarı.
Rail: On the İstanbul-Ankara rail line; several trains daily.

A NIGHT'S REST: **Kozluca Oteli**, Ankara Cad. 152; Double £9, popular among backpackers, tel. 152 75.

Swimming: Swimming prohibited!

Around İzmit

Gebze *(pop. 65,000)*: A fast growing town, 50 km west of İzmit. The town boasts several remarkable mosques including *Çoban Mustafa Camii*, built in 1519 by Sinan. South of town on a hill are the ruins of what is reportedly the *Tomb of Hannibal*, the first tourist to cross the Alps by elephant.

Gölcük *(pop. 48,000)*: 10 km to the southwest. Turkey's great naval tradition continues to this day; see the navy's wharfs and piers.

Adapazarı *(pop. 140,000)*: A typical industrial town. Over 60 businesses have settled on the outskirts of town in recent decades. With advance registration, you can visit a railway-car factory of the Turkish Railway. Near town is the 16 km long *Sapanca Gölü*, a paradise for water fowl and water sport enthusiasts. The lake is surrounded by hills on all sides. There is a simple campsite on the southern shore.

In the nearby town of **Sapanca** (pop. 12,000) is the *Beş Köprü*, a bridge with nine arches (500 m long), built by order of JUSTINIAN. It was originally built to span a planned canal connecting Sapanca Lake with the Sakarya River. Fruit and tobacco are grown in the Sakarya Valley.

İznik _(pop. 17,000)_

İznik, a quiet town nestled within a city wall, is located on Lake İznik in a sparesly populated region. The clear blue of the lake and the green of the olive trees are the predominant colours.

This sleepy town, without any industry, is set in an enchanting region. Its importance belongs to the past. Local young people hanging about the streets and tea gardens are quick to approach any newcomer in the hope of becoming a guide. What else is there to do?

History

İznik was founded as Antigoneia in the 4th century BC by ANTIGONUS, a one-eyed commander in the army of ALEXANDER THE GREAT. In 305 BC LYSIMACHUS, founder of Pergamon, renamed the town for his wife NICAEA. In 281 BC the town was captured by the Bithynians. Along with the rest of the kingdom, it was passed to Rome by will and testament in 74 BC. An earthquake destroyed the town in 123 AD. HADRIAN ordered reconstruction.

In 325 AD the First Ecumenical Council was held here. The main issue was dogma: ARIANUS claimed that Jesus was not one with God, but rather god-like. This viewpoint was not accepted by the council. Arianus and his supporters were excommunicated.

In 787 AD the Seventh Ecumenical Council met again in Nicaea. This time the question was whether the _Bible_ prohibited the display of icons in churches. It was determined that depictions were permissible, bringing an end to iconoclasm. During the era of iconoclasm far more works of art were destroyed - particularly in Constantinople - than during the reign of Islam.

In 1074 AD, Nicaea passed into Seljuk hands. In 1097 it was conquered by the crusader GODFREY OF BOUILLON, inventor of the soup of the same name (honestly). The Byzantine emperor resided here briefly after being banished from Constantinople by the crusaders in 1204 AD.

In 1331, sultan ORHAN captured the town, bringing it under Ottoman control. The conquerors had trouble pronouncing the Greek name of the town ("eis nikaian" pronounced ayesnicayan) so they simply changed it to İznik. İznik eventually became famous for its wonderful faiences. After the conquest of Tabriz and Azerbaijan in 1514, sultan SELIM I resettled Persian craftsmen here, where Persian creativity was permitted to combine with traditional know-how. Over 600 kilns

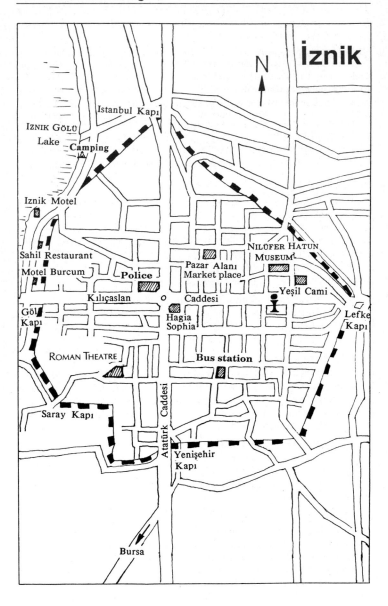

Iznik

N

Istanbul Kapı
IZNIK GÖLÜ
Lake   Camping
Iznik Motel
Sahil Restaurant
Motel Burcum   Police
Kılıçaslan   o   Caddesi
Göl   Hagia
Kapı   Sophia
ROMAN THEATRE
Saray Kapı
NILÜFER HATUN
MUSEUM
Pazar Alanı
Market place
Yeşil Cami
Lefke
Kapı
Bus station
Atatürk Caddesi
Yenişehir
Kapı
Bursa

were in use during the golden age of İznik craftsmanship. İznik tiles decorate mosques in Mecca, Medina, İstanbul, Jerusalem, Bursa, Sıvas, Konya and Manisa.

INFORMATION: Kılıç Arslan Caddesi 168. Not much help. The person we spoke with could only speak Turkish and was not willing to find a translator. No brochures, tel. 433.

TELEPHONE AREA CODE: 2527

COMING – GOING: Hourly connections during the day to Adapazarı and Bursa (£0.70). Two buses daily to İstanbul. Minibuses to Yalova (ferry connection to İstanbul), Gemlik and Bilecik. No rail service.

MEETING PLACE: Along the waterside promenade (Göl Kenarı) and - for men - the tea garden east of Hagia Sophia.

FESTIVALS AND EVENTS: In the 3rd week of September a large **Wine Festival** is held. The 1st weekend in October marks the **Livestock Fair** with traditional **wrestling**. The 28th of November is **Independence Day**.

EATING FISH ON LAKE İZNIK

As lodgings in İznik are substandard, you are advised to stay at a hotel in Bursa and visit İznik on a day trip (Bus 1 1/2 hours, 85 km). The ride is lovely beyond **Gemlik**. The bus turns into a small road, just wide enough for the bus, and drives along the southern bank of Lake İznik. Large olive plantations cover the slopes all the way down to the lake. Then the bus climbs thirty to forty meters up the bank where you have a great view of the lake (303 sq km).

Before İznik the drive goes along a stretch of lonely beach. Here you will find a number of seafood restaurants by the lakeside. They are rarely crowded. The waiter has time to provide proper service. When you spot the restaurant you want to eat at, give the driver a sign that you want to be dropped off. Don't worry: there will be another bus!

A NIGHT'S REST

Motel Burcum, Göl Kenarı (by the lake); double £7, four-bed rooms/breakfast £11, shower/WC in the hallway. Simple rooms, cot beds. Wonderful location, garden as in a first-class hotel, 50 m from the lake and beach, sufficient parking. Friendly staff, manager speaks good English, tel. 1011.

İznik Motel, Göl Kenarı 7 (on the lake); double £9. Lake in your front yard, 18 rooms, also singles, all with shower and WC. Not well kept, particularly the garden. Parking available, tel. 1041.

Babacan Oteli, Kılıç Arslan Caddesi 104 (near Hagia Sophia); double £5, showers in hall, simple furnishings, cold water. Lovely facade, view of the lovely townhall square. French and Turkish spoken, tel. 1211.

CAMPING by the lake is tolerated.

FOOD

Dallas Restaurant, at the south gate, first restaurant on the left. Seafood specialties, snack £1.60, seafood for two: £7.

Çamlık-Restaurant, at the southern end of Göl Kenarı (left of the lake gate), similar prices and quality to Dallas. Very energetic owner.

Other restaurants around "Burcum Moteli" and along Lefke Kapısı Caddesi. A good locanta is **Sahil Restaurant** on Lefke Kapısı Cad.

Sights

Walls and Gates: İznik was surrounded by a mighty ring of fortifications which is well preserved. Most of the 4400 m enclosure, only partially occupied today by the market square, dates from the Seljuk era. The oldest parts of the western wall date from Byzantine times. The inner wall was over 10 m tall and 6 m thick, with merlons, battlements and 108 towers. The lower front wall (15 m further) boasted 103 round towers and a (now dry) water moat.

Lefke Gate is the mightiest in town, 25 m wide and 40 m long. Designed as a Roman triumphal gate, it was later strengthened by Orhan. The best view is from the outside, from the cemetery. Inside is a new marble fountain from which you can drink without qualm. The *İstanbul Gate* resembles the Lefke Gate, not as large but better preserved. Be sure to look at the two masks on the inner wall.

Originally there were only four gateways into town: From **Yenişehir Gate** in the south, Atatürk-Caddesi leads to the **İstanbul Gate** in the north. Atatürk Cad. is crossed by Kılıç Aslan Cad. which leads from the lake to **Lefke Gate** in the east. At the intersection of the two main roads is Hagia Sophia Camii, site of the two ecumenical councils and once the main church in town.

Green Mosque *(Yeşil Camii)*: Built in 1378 - 1391 by HACI MUSA for a Grand Vizier of MURAT I. The tall, unusually wide, minaret is almost completely covered with İznik tiles as is the upper portion of the mosque. The mighty dome is just as impressive as the richly ornamented, triple-arched entrance hall. The vestibule is splendid and calligraphy decorates the windows. The interior, aside from the marble mihrab, is not well kept.

Nilüfer-Hatun Charity Kitchen *(Nilüfer-Hatun-İmareti)*: The İmaret was built in 1388 by MURAT I for his mother NILÜFER HATUN. The building probably served as a meeting place for dervishes. The building of rough square stone with an entrance hall boasting five arches seems inviting. The inside walls are coated with white tiles. The **Archaeological Museum** is worth a look. The highlight of the exhibits is a case with perfume bottles dating from Roman times.

OPEN: 8:30 - 12:00 and 13:30 - 17:30 h, admission: £0.20.

Roman Theatre: Built during the reign of HADRIAN, in the southwest corner of town. It boasted a huge inner frame as there was no slope to lean it against. It must have been very large. Little can be seen today: remains of a row of seats and traces of the palaestra, nothing more. The climb up the overgrown hill is dangerous.

Hagia Sophia *(Hagia Sophia Camii)*: Located in the centre of town at the crossroads of the two main streets. Recent excavations show that a church must have stood here at the time of JUSTINIAN. This is where the 7th Ecumenical Council was held. That church was destroyed in the 1065 AD earthquake and rebuilt as a triple-aisle basilica. The Ottomans converted it into a mosque which burned down in the 18th century and was never rebuilt. The ruins are not impressive. It is more fun to watch the two pairs of storks nesting on the stump of the minaret.

OPEN: 8:30 - 12:00 and 13:30 - 17:00 h, admission: £0.08.

Koimesis Church: This church, in the southeast of town, was built in the 9th century. The entrance hall was added in the 11th century. Once famous for its mosaics, it is only a ruin today.

Obelisk of Cassius *(Bestas)*: About 5 km northwest of town, at the edge of a hill, is the tomb of GAIUS CASSIUS PHILISCUS, featuring a 12 m tall obelisk on a pedestal.

THE VIEW FROM BARBER ROCK

The only spot from which you can look out over İznik and the lake is Barber Rock *(Berber Kayası)*, about 900 m from Lefke Gate. From the hill, on which lie the remains of a coffin supposedly struck by lightning, you can see most of the town wall.

Around İznik - Day trips

The drive from Gemlik to İznik (or vice versa) is popular among the connoisseurs of Turkey. There is hardly any traffic on this road which passes through an unimportant region. You drive along the lake passing through quiet villages and olive groves. Fishrestaurants, pleasantly situated in the shade, offer a variety of culinary delights. Even though there are no established beaches you can find many lonely stretches on the shore where you can sunbathe and take a swim in the lake (the water is not very cold).

Wash-day on Lake İznik

Tractors, minibuses and all sorts of jalopies cart large groups of women and their laundry to the shore in the morning. The wash-day is a reasonably pleasant day for the women they do the laundry together, spread it out to dry, talk, laugh and enjoy themselves until every piece is dry again. Then they (the women and the clean washing) are collected again and brought back to the villages, were the women take up their subordinate place in the hierarchy of the village once more.

Gemlik *(pop. 27,000)*

About 15 years ago, wealthy İstanbul residents discovered the protected Gemlik Bay, bringing an end to the pleasant atmosphere: 8000 apartments and vacation homes have gone up with little planning. In the nearby town of Narlı a new yacht marina is under construction.

The village has kept some of its charm. Lovely restaurants around the harbour jetty and the well-kept promenade invite a brief stay. Swimming is prohibited in the inner bay due to pollution.

In *Hasanaga* (4 km from town) and *Karacaali* are student camps of the Turkish Ministry of Education. Children from all over the country enjoy a ten-day holiday here. Stop by, visitors are always welcome.

COMING - GOING: Local buses from Bursa to Gemlik every hour, £0.15, but crowded. Tip: For twice the price, hop aboard a bus on the Bursa-İznik line and get off at Gemlik. Buses every 15 minutes from Gemlik to Küçük Kumla.

FESTIVAL: **Gemlik Tourism Festival** with local folklore, annually on the 1st of July.

A NIGHT'S REST

Therme Ilıca Otel, Ilıca Meykü, Gemlik; double £9. 62 Beds, clean, thermal bath, hot water in the rooms, tel. 2595.

Tibel Otel, Hamidiye Mah., Kumsal Sok. 18, Gemlik; double £13, 56 beds, comfortable, swimming pool, marina, tel. 1272.

Erdilli, Kaplıca Meykii, Armutlu; double £13. Clean, recommended, reasonable prices, tel. 39.

Karacaali Tur. Tesileri, Karaca Ali Köyü, Karacaali; double £8. Holiday village with sport facilities. Some rooms with showers, simple, tel. 40.

FOOD: In the restaurants on the waterside promenade. Recommended: **Liman Restaurant**, tel. 1192. **Böksör Restaurant**, tel. 1234 - 1919. **Rithim Restaurant**, tel. 2822.

Around Gemlik

Armutlu: 36 km northwest of Gemlik. The access road is unpaved, keeping tourism as low as the prices. The beach is rocky, but the water is clean.

Küçük Kumla and **Büyük Kumla:** 9 km northwest of Gemlik. A complete tourist centre with lots of sport facilities.

Karacaali: Hotel/Sport centre, about 15 km northwest of Gemlik.

PIGLETS IN GEMLIK

Leave Gemlik to the northwest. After two kilometers a road branches off toward the sea. Take it for 200 m and you will reach an idyllic garden restaurant (no name) shaded by maple trees. The spot is famous for its unusual bird songs; at any rate the little tweeters make a lot of noise. The cook will prepare a wild boar for his non-Muslim customers (the pigs can be seen in the restaurant pen). Enjoy!

BURSA (pop. 650,000)

The town is one of the nicest tourist centres in Turkey. After the stress of İstanbul, come visit the pastel-coloured facades, wood panelling, red-shingled roofs, and an almost intact old town.

Bursa is situated at the foot of the *Uludağ*. More than just the local mountain, it is a prime tourist attraction with the best and most crowded ski facilities in all of Turkey.

For religious Turks, Bursa is much more: this is the cradle of the Ottoman Empire and its first capital. The tombs of OSMAN and ORHAN are here. Several early Ottoman mosques are popular sights. European visitors should keep in mind that while flimsy clothes and shorts are the standard in beach resorts along the western coast, they are not appreciated here.

Bursa is also famous for its healing springs in the Çekirge section of town. These have attracted a number of wealthy Arabs in recent years. Çekirge is becoming increasingly more expensive.

Bursa, however, is not only a major tourist town, but also an economic and administrative centre. The provincial capital houses an outstanding university. Textiles and metalworking, the beverage company Uludağ and the car-maker Murat (a fiat-licensee) have set up shop in the flood plain north of town.

The *Nilüfer River* floods the fertile soil permitting rich harvests of Bursa peaches, quince, apricots, cherries, plums, nuts and sunflower seeds. Much of the produce is processed by the local canning industry. Industrial expansion after WW II was aided by the convenient proximity of the Sea of Marmara and the harbour at Mudanya.

The region is famous for its mulberry trees in which silkworms are nurtured for their wonderful *Bursa silk*, which experts consider second to none. The fabulous *Hereke carpets* seen in Ottoman sultans' palaces were made here!

History

Bursa is an ancient town. It is assumed that Phrygian tribes settled the castle hill in the 2nd century BC. The Roman historian PLINY the Younger names 185 BC as the year of its founding. A man named PRUSIAS is said to have founded the town upon the advice of the exiled Carthaginian commander HANNIBAL. The earliest existing record of the town dates from 74 BC, when NICOMEDES III willed the town to Rome. Governor PLINY restored the baths in Çekirge during the reign of TRAJAN. The thermal springs at Prussas, as the town was then called, were praised throughout the Roman and Byzantine world. JUSTINIAN built a palace here and supported silkworm breeding in the advantageous climate. The Byzantine court frequently visited the spa. In 950 AD the town was captured and destroyed by the Arabs. In 1097 the Seljuks took control.

Bursa's golden age began when a tiny Turkish tribe, the Ottomans, besieged the town for ten long years, forcing the Byzantine emperor (who was unable to raise a new army) to surrender the town in 1326. Bursa became the capital of the newly-founded Ottoman Empire until 1361 when the imperial court took new residence in Edirne.

The city thrived under the Ottomans. MEHMET I (1413 - 1423) left his mark by constructing the Green Mosque, Green Tomb and parts of the Great Mosque. Although the conquest of İstanbul would end the town's political importance, Bursa remained an important trading town. The population grew wealthy selling increasing amounts of silk (today 1500 tons annually). During the hot summer months, the sultans regularly sought relief at the foot of the Uludağ.

In the 19th century devastating fires and earthquakes hit Bursa. In 1920 the town was occupied by Greece before being liberated by Atatürk two years later. After WW II a number of industries built plants here including Renault (auto parts) and Murat (car assembly).

Bursa's Tombs and Their History

Bursa is a city of tombs. Resting side by side are the founders of the empire OSMAN and ORHAN. The father Osman, an illiterate old warrior, dreamed that from the breast of a sacred dervish, a halfmoon rose and then settled upon his own breast. Then suddenly a huge tree grew out of his stomach, which shaded the entire world. People settled under the tree and drank from fresh springs. Immediately upon awakening, Osman set out with his entire tribe (several thousand men, women and children). A few horses carried all his possessions: a barrel of salt, several boots, a number of weapons, a saddle, a decent tent. He marched upon Bursa, as his instincts told him that the conquest of this splendid fortified city would provide the foundation of his empire. The population must have laughed when he arrived with his ragged band of shepherds and warriors before the mighty gates. But Osman was stubborn; he would wait it out. This determination brought him victory and made believers out of the sceptics - among them his own son Orhan. Just before Osman's death, his son was able to report the fall of the town.

The tomb of BEYAZIT (or BAYAZIT). During his reign he was known simply as YILDERIM (lightning). Later he would be immortalized as BAJAZZO (straw sack), a clod in Italian comedy. He lives on today as the joker in every pack of playing cards. During the reign of his father MURAT, BEYAZIT scored a decisive victory against the Serbs at Amselfeld. Later he would defeat the Bulgarians, Hungarians, and a crusader army, which he pursued to Styria where he finally slaughtered them. Beyazıt was self-confident, well-educated and successful. In the end he met his match at the hands of TIMUR LENK, a Mongol famous for his brutality. Beyazıt was captured at the decisive Battle of Ankara in 1402. Timur took the pleasure of parading his captive in a golden cage through the streets of Bursa. The cultivated European rulers Charles IV of France, Henry IV of England, and the German emperor, were quick to praise the Mongols for turning back the Turkish tide.

Also buried here are KARAGÖZ and HACIVAT, the Turkish national comedians. They were beheaded on the command of sultan ORHAN for taking more interest in humour than the construction of their ruler's mosque. Orhan soon learned to miss the irreplaceable jesters. Turkish lore is filled with tales of the activities of the black-eyed Karagöz and his assistant. Those two would truly have deserved depiction on our joker cards.

INFORMATION: Cemal Nadir Caddesi, Tophane, tel. 27 513. English and French, good knowledge of the town, friendly. There are two other offices which we do not recommend because the staff speaks only Turkish and has few brochures to offer.

TELEPHONE AREA CODE: 241

COMING - GOING: The bus station is in the north of town, 3 km from the centre. Several buses daily to all parts of the country. Hourly connections to İstanbul and İzmir. Buses to Uludağ also depart from here.
Ship: Connections to İstanbul via Yalova (3 hours). Daily boats to Mudanya - İstanbul.
Air: No scheduled flights into the nearby airport. Ticket Information: Turkish Airlines (THY), Cemal Nadir Cad. 8a, Kocagil Apt., tel. 21866-111/67.
Cable Railway: The Cable Railway restarted service in December 1986 on the Uludağ (Teleferik) after a long interruption. From the valley station (see map) you can ride up to the midway station (£2.35 round trip) at Sarıalan, continue by chairlift (£2.35 round trip) to the hotels on Uludağ. The ride is a real experience. Every imaginable safety measure has been discarded. It is more like a ride at an amusement park than a serious cable railway. The Turks seem to enjoy it. The author feared for his life.

FESTIVALS: Annual **International Culture and Art Festival** in the Culture Park (7th to 31st of July). Every evening at 21:00 h international folklore groups perform (admission £0.35). **Uludağ Winter Festival** at the end of March and early April.

HOSPITAL: SSK Altıparmak, tel. 61 690. SSK Çekirge, tel. 68511-12.

MEETING PLACE: Along Atatürk Cad, in Tophane Café and in the Culture Park.

POLICE: tel. 113 15.

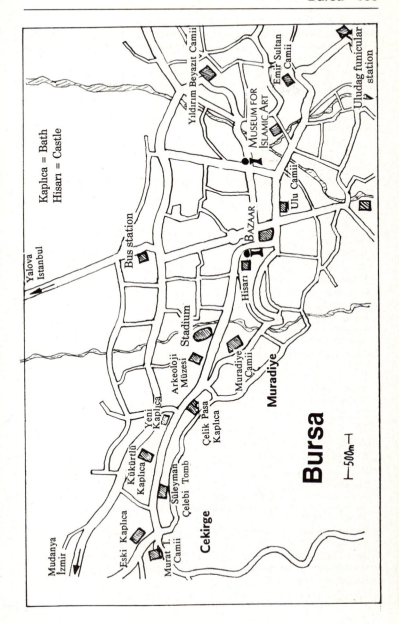

Kaplıca = Bath
Hisarı = Castle

Yalova
Istanbul

Yıldırım Beyazıt Camii

Emir Sultan
Camii

Uludag funicular
station

MUSEUM FOR
ISLAMIC ART

Ulu Camii

Bus station

BAZAAR

Hisarı

Stadium

Muradiye
Camii

Muradiye

Arkeoloji
Müzesi

Çelik Paşa
Kaplıca

Yeni
Kaplıca

Süleyman
Çelebi Tomb

Kükürtlü
Kaplıca

Eski Kaplıca

Murat T.
Camii

Çekirge

Mudanya
İzmir

Bursa

├─500m─┤

POST OFFICE: Next to the Kent Hotel, across from the bazaar.

SHOPPING: Of course in Atpazarı, the bazaar district. Here you will find your heart's desire. Almost European, modern shops have store fronts on Atatürk Cad., across from the bazaar.

TRAVEL AGENCIES: **Ottoman-Tur**, Cemal Nadir Cad., Kızılay Pasajı, tel. 10099-22097. **Nartur-Travel**, Altıparmak Cad. Uludağ Apt. 82/1, tel. 13207.

A Night's Rest

Günlüferah Hotel, Murat Cad. 24; double £24. Thermal bath and tennis court. tel. 179 00-1.

Hotel Akdoğan, Murad Cad. 5, Çekirge; double £21, thermal bath in the rooms! Free use of the thermal pool. tel. 60 610.

Kent Hotel, Atatürk Cad. 119, double £15, centrally located across from the Great Mosque and the bazaar, lovely breakfast room with ample buffet. Friendly staff, competent reception. tel. 18700.

Hotel Adapalas, Murat Cad. 21, Çekirge; double £15 (including breakfast), rooms with shower, very clean, tel. 61 600.

Hotel Yat, Hamamlar Cad. 31, Çekirge; double £15. Rooms with shower/WC. Several two-person thermal cabins (see Turkish Bath). Hygienic. Recommended! tel. 63 116.

İpekci-Hotel, Cancılar Cad. 38; double £4.35. Rooms with shower, simple furnishings. tel. 11 935.

Hotel Atlas, Hamam Cad. 35, Çekirge; double £5. WC in the hallway, clean.

Özğurt Oegrenci Yurdu, Maksem Cad. 46, per person £1.35. Bursa's first youth hostel, or so it is planned (the owner has applied for official status). There are 56 beds and a Turkish bath. Clean. The bunk beds seem dangerous, but are said to serve their function well.

CAMPING: **BP Mocamp Kumluk**, 10 km to the northeast on the main road to İstanbul. Warm water, minimarket, restaurant, swimming pool. Shade from several trees. Open: Mid May to end of October. tel. 13 995.

Mocamp Apollonia: 35 km west on Uluabat Gölü. Sanitation is reasonable, restaurant, relatively small. Open: June to end of September.

Food

Culinary specialties include: *Bursa Kebabı* (lamb, cooked on a vertical spit, served with bread and yoghurt), *Bursa peaches* (particularly juicy).

Restaurant Papağan, Murat Cad. 16, Çekirge. A large selection, English language menus. Lovely terrace with a nice view of the city. A lot of room. Specialties are huge servings of Cordon-bleu, Albanian liver and Turkish dishes. Cheap! tel. 12761

Tophane Café, below Hisarı Castle, a popular photo motif and a popular meeting place.

Canlı Lokantasi, Yeni Balık Pazarı 14. A well-known seafood restaurant. Atmosphere as in Genoa. Even the fish will dance on the table. A lavish meal costs £4.35 and up. tel. 13566.

Other cafés and locantas are along Atatürk Cad. and its side streets.

LA BELLO (*Atatürk Caddesi - Bridge Across the Gök Dere*)

La Bello is a gathering spot for Bursa's wealthy youth and affordable for European pocketbooks. One sits upon comfortable bast chairs at small glass tables. The furnishings are tasteful; the clientele has style; the bartender is as cool as the waiters. But don't worry: jeans and punks are also "Hoş geldeniz" (welcome)! The menu in two languages is covered with elegant leather. Through the large veranda doors, you have a view of a lovely stone bridge along which half of Bursa promenades during the afternoon. Simply perfect!

We recommend *İzgara Köfte* with very spicy chili, served à la nouvelle cuisine.

Sights

Yıldırım Beyazıt Mosque *(Beyazıt Camii)*: YILDIRIM BEYAZIT donated this mosque complex featuring eight independent buildings in 1390. It can be found 2 km northeast of town in a lovely neighbourhood. When crossing the town stream, *Gök Dere*, take a break to watch the carpet cleaners at work.

The centrepiece of the mosque is the richly ornamented *entrance hall* which seems to grow out of the main building. At the time of its construction, it was quite revolutionary. For the first time the emphasis upon the main gate at the entrance was lessened by continuous arcades. The interior of the mosque is disappointing by comparison. Aside from two lovely *mosaic windows* it is quite barren. The minaret collapsed during an earthquake in 1855 (a stump is visible by the entrance hall). Below the mosque is the simple tomb of the unfortunate Beyazit (see above), whose last remains were brought here in 1406.

Green Mosque *(Yeşil Cami)*: MEHMET I ordered construction of this Mosque between 1413 and 1421 by the architect İLYAS ALI. Its furnishings are among the most splendid anywhere in the Ottoman Empire. The architecture is equally interesting: two square main rooms are crowned by a single dome and separated from each other by a great arch. This creates a new sense of space, marking a revolutionary break from the century-old traditional pillar mosque (see Great Mosque). Because there is no entrance hall, the *stalactite portal* built into the rough outer facade is clearly emphasized; an example of excellent Seljuk work.

Via a smaller front room, we enter the first main hall with its lovely *cleansing fountain*. The fountain's remarkable mouthpiece is cut from a single piece of marble. Up three steps we reach the second main hall boasting a splendid, partially gold-plated *mihrab*, together with three lovely *mosaic windows* and a red *mimber*. The side walls are ornamented to a height of two meters with six-sided, green-blue İznik faience, hence the name "Green Mosque". The loveliest faience can be seen in the two prayer rooms left and right of the two main halls. Notice that all the tiling was once ornamented with a glazed pattern of golden stars. The mosque was seen as an earthly foretaste of life in heaven! The *sultan's box* is based upon a similar concept. The ceiling is dotted with stars, the walls with flower patterns.

Before you go, be sure to enjoy the view of town from the terrace in front of the entrance.

Green Tomb *(Yeşil Türbe)*: The octagonal tomb of MEHMET I was built in 1421 by HACI IVAZ. Like every building in Bursa, it suffered greatly in the 1855 earthquake, losing many of its faiences. The restoration performed in the 19th century must be seen as a success.

We pass inside through a lovely hand-carved cedar door (star patterns). The sultan's *coffin* and the pedestal on which he rests are ornamented with blue faiences inlaid with golden calligraphy. The white turban demonstrates the high rank of the deceased. In seven smaller coffins rest sons of the sultan, and his wet nurse. The unique prayer niche across from the entrance is completely covered with ceramics. The walls, too, are covered with tiles up to a height of two metres. A band of gold completes the transition to the barren upper portion of the room which has eight windows with blue mosaic glass and a 25 m-tall dome.

OPEN: 8:30 - 12:00 and 13:00-17:30 h.

Museum of Turkish-Islamic Art: Housed in the Green Medrese (*Yeşil Medrese*) since 1975. The Koran School was part of the complex founded by MEHMET I. In keeping with a long Seljuk tradition, three elongated arcades are grouped around the inner courtyard. On the southern side is the tall, domed teaching hall. Behind the arcades were the living quarters of the students.

To the right of the vestibule is the *Circumcision Hall*. This is where young Muslims would rest after the operation ceremony. In the east pavilion, valuable porcelain is on display including 12th century Seljuk plates (from Rakka). In the first room, shadowplay puppets of KARAGÖZ and HACIVAT are displayed.

In the *Teaching Hall* Bursa's famous printed silk and wooden stamps (for printing silk) are on display. Other treasures include weapons plundered from Persia, a golden copper decanter one meter tall, bathing utensils featuring two richly decorated sandals, and a towel of printed silk.

OPEN: 8:30 - 12:00 and 13:00 - 17:30 h, admission: £0.20.

Patiently waiting for customers

Bazaar Quarter (*Atpazarı*): The prototype of the cliché Oriental bazaar! Although established in the 14th century, the entire quarter burned down in 1957, and was then rebuilt. The market bustle remains undiminished.

At the centre of the bazaar is the *bedesten*, one of the oldest of its kind. Mostly jewellery is traded under its 14 domes. European ways have come to stay: bargaining is discouraged. In the surrounding alleys and the restored caravanserai, you can bargain to your heart's content. Here you can find true treasures: precious (but not expensive) silk handkerchiefs, finely engraved copperware, carpets. But remember, not everything that glitters is gold!

Great Mosque (*Ulu Cami*): The Great Mosque in the bazaar quarter was donated by YILDERIM BEYAZIT and built in 1396 - 1400. After winning the Battle of Nicopolis, the sultan vowed to build 20 mosques. On the advice of his Grand Vizier, he decided to build only one mosque, but with twenty domes. The Ulu Cami is a pillar mosque in the great Seljuk tradition. Rough on the outside, the interior features 12 mighty, rectangular columns, supporting the domes, and creating strict divisions.

The walls without tiles are decorated with calligraphy. In the centre of the mosque is a marble cleansing fountain with a glass dome overhead. Originally there was a hole in the ceiling above the fountain giving the feeling of a courtyard. Unique are the prayer niche with a stalactite hood, painstaking faiences from İznik, and wonderful calligraphy. It is flanked by two hour glasses. The mimber of cedar is the prettiest in all of Bursa.

By the way, the minarets are the only ones to survive the 1855 earthquake. The two large towers lost their entire coating of faiences. It is easy to see how popular this mosque is: never have we seen so many Muslims at prayer.

Castle Hill (*Hisar*): This fortress on Cemal Nadir Caddesi, in the centre of town, is the only remnant from ancient times. It was once a sultan's seat. Part of the fortress wall, dating from Roman times, can still be seen. Notice that in the north, where the fortifications face an extensive plain, it was necessary to build the wall twice as high.

Mausoleums of Osman Gazi and Orhan Gazi: The two tombs are beautifully located on the fortress hill surrounded by a lovely park with shady cypress trees.

OSMAN (1257 - 1326), founder of the Ottoman Empire, asked to be buried here. The colourfully ornamented tomb, crowned by a sarcophagus dotted with pearls, is an absolute must for any visitor to Bursa.

The same can be said for the tomb of ORHAN (1281 - 1362), who reorganized the realm as the second sultan in the Ottoman line. His tomb was set upon the ruins of a former monastery of which a few floor mosaics are inside the tomb. There are 20 additional sarcophagi inside the tomb including that of his wife NILÜFER HATUM.

If you have made the strenuous climb up to the tombs, be sure to visit the terrace-like outcropping in the north of the tiny park. From here you have a tremendous view over the roofs of Bursa and across the fertile plains.

Ottoman House Museum: The two-story building dating from the 17th century is across from the Muradiye Complex. The reddish interior exudes comfort of almost luxurious proportions. Notice the many hand made coal scuttles and the bright colours of the carpets.

OPEN: Daily 8:00 - 17:00 h, closed Mondays.

Archaeological Museum (*Arkeoloji Müzesi*): The plain-looking museum in the Culture Park houses some interesting exhibits: prehistoric and Hittite ceramics, an extensive coin collection, statues, inscriptive and depictive mosaics from Archaic, Hellenistic, Roman and Byzantine times. Terracotta and glass objects ranging from tiny perfume bottles to stately wine jugs. Equally of interest is the Library of Islamic Law.

OPEN: 8:30 - 12:00 h and 13:00 - 17:30 h, closed Mondays, admission £0.50, Sundays £0.28.

Atatürk Museum (*Atatürk Müzesi*): The white, three-story mansion served as a residence for Kemal Atatürk during his 13 visits to Bursa. The lovely furnishings, including a seemingly endless carpet and liberal use of precious woods, exude warmth. The exhibition also features documentation about the life and work of Atatürk.

Karagöz and Hacıvat Memorial: To the right on the road to Çekirge. It is a memorial dedicated to the two misunderstood heroes of Turkish humorous folklore, KARAGÖZ and HACIVAT (see Bursa and its Tombs).

After ORHAN realized his mistake in ordering the pair's execution, he arranged that they would live on - at least in stories, jokes, and skits. The result is the traditional *Karagöz Shadowplay Theatre* featuring puppets of fine leather. The best shadowplay can be seen in Bursa during the Culture and Art Festival, held annually in memory of the two comedians.

Tomb of Sultan Murat I: Murat's tomb seems very solid, an impression verified by the fact that the structure withstood the 1855 earthquake almost completely intact. MURAT I was the third sultan in the Ottoman dynasty, and the one who expanded the empire into the Balkans. After his death on the battlefield at Kozova, the sultan's remains were brought back to Bursa for burial.

The walls and ceiling of the tomb are paneled with marble. A large window and a magnificent crystal chandelier lend the hall a joyous tone. The seven smaller sarcophagi contain the remains of his son YAKUB CELEBI and his grandchildren.

Murat Complex (*Muradiye Külliyesi*): This picturesque oasis is a bit out of the way. Built by MURAT II, the last sultan to rule from Bursa, the park includes a small mosque surrounded by palms and cypress trees. The complex boasts a *medrese* and eleven eight- and six-sided tombs, including those of the sultan himself and of the rival of BEYAZIT II, SEHZADE CEM (1459 - 1495). Two of the tombs are always open on a rotation basis.

Thermal Baths: In Çekirge, 5 km west of town, are Bursa's famous thermal springs with water temperatures of 40 to 80 degrees Centigrade. They are collected and pumped to the spa hotels (see A Night's Rest). Treatment with the warm waters is recommended for rheumatism and diseases of the skin and joints. If you don't want to go through the whole treatment, visit one of the public baths.

New Bath (*Yeni Kaplıca*): The Hamam is halfway between the Culture Park and Çekirge, take the road across from Hotel "Palas" (the sign is difficult to see). The facility dates from the 16th century.

Old Bath (*Eski Kaplıca*): The famous Bursa bath is open round the clock - for men and women (in separate sections of course). The facility dates from the 14th century. The iron-rich water is a constant 38 degrees Centigrade. The bath is well known for its massages and wading pool. Be sure to plan at least two to three hours as the bath should be followed by a rest in the lounge.

OPEN (New and Old Baths): Daily 6:00 - 23:00 h (Wed. for women, Tues. & Thurs. for men). Admission (including towel): £0.35, double bath room £4.

Around Bursa

Uludağ

The 2543 m mountain is a National Park and ski resort all in one. The ski slopes are between 2000 m and 2500 m with three chairlifts, three other lifts, a giant slalom slope but not very competitive downhill slopes. There is room for 3100 guests in the surrounding hotels. Several bars and discos complete the scene. The season is January to April. If you aren't careful, you will end up in the local hospital. For more information see the only ski and surfing expert in Turkey, MUZAFFER ERGÖZ, Uludağ, tel. 2418/1062 (see Surf School Bodrum).

The huge (49,400 acre) *Kirazlıyayla* was established in 1961. The park features a number of picnic and camping areas, a network of hiking trails and several small hotels. The region is thickly forested. Brown bear, jackal, wild boar, wolves, vultures and eagles live here. Be sure to visit the mountain lakes *Karagöl*, *Buzlu* and *Aynalı* at 2200 m.

If you prefer not to climb, do what numerous Turkish families do and spend a pleasant day in *Sarıalan* - last stop of the cable railway and the valley station of the chairlift. Sarıalan boasts a restaurant, and more interestingly, a "Kendin Pişir, Kendin ye" or grill site. You buy some raw, marinated meat and rent one of the pre-heated grills. Just bring the coals to a glow and grill to your heart's content. If you don't trust the meat, then bring your own (impolite, but tourists are excused). Good advice and help, if necessary, are available from experienced Turkish grillers. Have fun!

If you prefer solitude, just walk a few hundred meters off the marked paths. You will have the world to yourself. The pre-alpine vegetation pleases hikers and the mouths of grazing wild horses.

COMING - GOING: **The cable railway** (valley station in Teleferik) costs £2.35 round trip and the **chairlift** £2.35 round trip. **Local buses** from Otogar £0.50, **dolmuş** from Atatürk Cad. (£10 for a 6-seater).

Mudanya *(pop. 11,000)*

This port town is 30 km north of Bursa (for which it is the main port). From here you have daily ships to İstanbul. There is also a lovely beach. Mudanya even has its place in history. In 1922 the peace treaty between Turkey and the Allied nations was signed here. There is a memorial plaque.

COMING - GOING: bus or dolmuş from Bursa; costs £0.70.

A NIGHT'S REST: **Köksal Hoteli**, Güzel Ali Mah.; June - Sept. Double £18. Right on the beach, tel. 29-52. Camping out is no problem.

Yalova *(pop. 44,000)*

This port town (70 km north of Bursa) is famous for its thermal springs and ferry port to İstanbul.

Yalova itself is hardly worth a stay: the beaches are polluted by the intensive shipping. Unfortunate currents bring sewage from the canals of İstanbul. There are no sights.

INFORMATION: İskele Meydanı 5, tel. 2108.

TELEPHONE AREA CODE: 1931

COMING - GOING: Hourly buses from Bursa. From İstanbul (Kabataş) you have seven ferries daily (takes 150 minutes) plus good bus connections. The last ferry to İstanbul: 18:30 h. Regular buses to Yalova-Yalova Kaplıca depart across from the ferry. Hourly minibuses to Çınarcık.

A NIGHT'S REST: **Ülke Oteli**, Rasim Yılmaz Cad., double £6, common showers. Simple furnishings, tel. 1680.

CAMPING: **Kumluk Mocamp**, Bursa Yolu.; tent £1.35, right on the beach, warm water, electricity, restaurant. Open only during the summer, tel. 13995.

Around Yalova

Yalova Kaplıca: 12 km southwest of town, the thermal springs of Yalova are beautifully situated in a forested valley. The iron and sulphur rich springs (65 degrees Centigrade) were known to the Greeks and Romans. CONSTANTINE and JUSTINIAN came for a cure, as did Ottoman sultans later. It is an open secret that KEMAL ATATÜRK had a special affection for the baths at Yalova; he ordered their modernization in 1928. The complex includes several hotels and restaurants, park-like forests and modern spa facilities. Treatments are offered for kidney ailments, blisters, nervous ailments and rheumatism.

Çınarcık: 16 km west of Yalova. The beach is lovely, but even more polluted than in Yalova! The town itself is pretty. Evening ferries (18:15 h) to İstanbul.

Bandırma   *(pop. 60,000)*

This port town is an important market for produce from the surrounding countryside. Unlike the town, the surrounding countryside is well worth a visit.

Kuşcenneti National Park/Manyas Bird Paradise

20 km south of Bandırma on the *Manyas-Gölü* (Lake Manyas) is Kuşcenneti National Park. Of Turkey's 180 bird species, a third can be seen in the park including pelicans, cormorants, heron, wild duck, nightingale and pheasant. The park's estimated 2-3 million birds can be viewed from observation towers.

Information brochures are available at the park entrances. The small museum gives a place of honour to the discoverers of this enchanting region, the German professor KURT KOSSWIG and his wife LEONORE. The park is sometimes swampy and damp.

Erdek   *(pop. 11,000)*

Few tourists are attracted by the sparse ruins of the Melesian town Kyzikos, but thousands flock to the large beach, Büyük Plajı.

Outside of town, around the *Kapıdag* peninsula, there are a number of easily accessible beaches. However, the once idyllic fishing village has been transformed into a tourist centre.

INFORMATION: Tourist Office Hükumet Cad. 6 - 8, tel. 1169, informative, English spoken.

TELEPHONE AREA CODE: 1989

COMING - GOING: Several **buses** and minibuses daily to Bandırma. The nearest railway station is in Bandırma.
Ship: Several boats daily to Avşa and Marmara; ferries to Erdek-Marmara-Avşa-İstanbul.

MEETING PLACE / FESTIVALS: The Erdek Festival is held in July. The meeting place is the beach promenade.

A Night's Rest

Yat Oteli, Kumluyalı Cad. 90 (Erdek); double £10, nice rooms, tel. 2308.

Çinar Oteli, Avşa; double £12, all rooms with shower/WC, by the beach, tel. 360.

Mermer Oteli, Marmara; double £7, recommended by the Tourist Office, right on the beach, clean sanitation facilities, tel. 21.

CAMPING: **Camp ground Ant**, 7 km south of Erdek, several shady trees, sandy beach, mini market, interesting clientele, squat toilets.

FOOD: Cheap pubs around the harbour.

Swimming

Kilometres of sandy beach run north and south of town. The beaches to the south are nicest. There are also excellent beaches on the islands of Avşa and Marmara.

Around Erdek

Take an excursion to the islands **Paşalimanı, Avşa and Marmara**, rising gently from the sea.

Marmara is 18 km long and 10 km wide and a perfect island to explore by bicycle. If you are lucky you can rent one by the boat landing. In the north of the island are several marble quarries which were worked even in ancient times. In the south there are a number of restaurants and pensions around the boat landing.

Like Marmara, the smaller islands of Paşalimanı and Avşa are a paradise for hikers. The wine made on Avşa is particularly good.

About 20 km southeast of Erdek is the large government farm **Karacabey Harası,** where research projects are carried out. These include the breeding of Merino sheep and fiery Arabian horses. Guided tours available by prior notification only.

If you are looking for a beach as yet undiscovered by international tourism, and are not deterred by a long drive, (80 km east of Karacabey), head for **Plaj**. The narrow, but kilometre-long beach hosts only a few Turkish bathers.

Balıkesir *(pop. 125,000)*

This provincial capital is an important industrial centre, railroad junction, and market for regional produce (tobacco). Cement factories pollute the air.

TELEPHONE AREA CODE: 661

COMING - GOING: Balıkesir is a **railroad junction**. Connections in all directions. Daily trains to Bandırma, İzmir and Eskişehir.
Hourly **buses** to İzmir and Bursa, several daily to Edremit. There is a daily **express bus** to Ankara.

A NIGHT'S REST

Molam Oteli, Yeşil Cad., double £10. Nice furnishings, clean, tel. 18075.

İmanoğlu Oteli, Orücüler Cad., moderate prices, tel. 171 44-113 02.

Yılmaz Oteli, Milli Kuvvetler Cad. 37, moderate prices, tel. 174 93-3.

Around Balıkesir

Lake Manyas: see Bandırma.

Çaygören Baraj: Dam, 65 km south of Balıkesir. Meeting place for water sport enthusiasts.

Çanakkale *(pop. 35,000)*

This provincial capital at the narrowest point along the Dardanelles is also the most southwestern point of the Marmara region. Traffic along the highway from the north (Europe) via Eceabat to Çanakkale is loaded onto a ferry here.

The town is set around the harbour. Every hour, huge ships load and unload masses of cars, engulfing the town in noise and exhaust fumes.

Few sights survived the destructive earthquake of 1912. You can't miss the military bases around the town. On Sundays off-duty marines fill the streets.

History

The history and name of the town (*Çanakkale* = pot palace - referring to its ceramic tradition) are very old. The territory was ruled by Persia in the 4th century BC. Two centuries later it was conquered by ALEXANDER THE GREAT. For years thereafter it was a bone of contention between the kingdoms of Pontus and Pergamon. In 133 BC it was defeated by the Roman Empire. It enjoyed a brief golden age during Byzantine rule.

After several attacks by Arab and Turkish armies, the town was finally defeated in the 15th century by SÜLEYMAN PASHA and added to the newly founded Ottoman Empire. Upon the conquest of Gelibolu in 1387, the Turks had gained the upper hand on the Dardanelles. During WW I, the Dardanelles was the scene of a bloody conflict when the Allies tried to force their way through the Hellespont (see Gallipoli).

INFORMATION: İskele Meydanı 67, tel. 1187. Near Hotel Anafartalar at the harbour, not very competent, little effort. Tip: At the reception of Hotel Anafartalar you can get equally good information!

TELEPHONE AREA CODE: 1961

COMING - GOING: Hourly **ferries** from Çanakkale. The larger ferries cruise to Eceabat, the smaller to the fortress of Kilitbahir.

Several **buses** daily to İstanbul, Bursa, İzmir. **Minibuses** to local regions leave at the Otogar.

TRAVEL AGENCIES: Several agencies around the harbour offer daily tours to Troy, e.g. **Troy-Anzac Seyahat Acentası**, Saat Kulesi Yanı, tel. 1447.

SHOPPING: If you are thinking about a souvenir, remember that in Çanakkale all you will find are over-priced items made for the tourist trade.

MEETING PLACE/FESTIVALS: Young and old congregate on the harbour promenade. The clock tower is the departure point for many tours. On August 15-18, the Çanakkale Truva Festival in Troy features folklore.

A NIGHT'S REST

Truva Oteli, Yalıboya Cad., double £20 (seaside), elegant entrance hall, narrow rooms, reasonable prices, comfort cannot compare with Anafartalar, but it is quieter: garden, bar, restaurant. tel. 1024.

Hotel Anafartalar, Kayserili Cad., double £15 (sea side/with balcony) £9.35 (land side/no balcony) large hotel by the harbour, ocean view, very clean, friendly service, competent reception, recommended, tel. 445 155.

Bakır Oteli, Yalı Cad., double £15. Reasonably priced, tel. 4088-89-90.

Tusan Motel, P.K. 8, Intepe (Güzelyalı), 16 km south of Canakkale, double £10. Well kept hotel, overlooking the ocean, restaurants, very clean, tastefully furnished. Good for longer stays. tel. 1416.

Gönül Pansiyon, Cevdetpaşa Mah. İnönü Cad. 21, double £7 and up, some rooms with shower/WC. Plain furnishings, tel. 1503-4597.

Konak Oteli, double £6. Rooms vary greatly, look first! Clean, tel. 1150.

Hotel Efes, behind the clock tower, double £5, simple, clean, tel. 3256.

Küyük Truva Oteli, comparable to Hotel Efes.

Bursa Otel, İnönü Cad. 147, per person £2.35. Simple, quite clean and cheap. Rooms without bath or WC.

CAMPING: **Şen Mocamp**, a good site in Kepez, 8 km south of Çanakkale, away from the road, right by the ocean. Address: Kepez Köyü, tel. 1961. Costs per person, trailer, tent (£1.15), bungalows, vacation homes available. Adequate shade! The beautiful sandy beach is the best in the region. Not recommended for long stays (tourists passing through).

Sun-San Camping Dardanos: For hardy souls who can do without proper sanitation and shade. But it is cheap: just £0.50 per person and tent. There is perhaps some hope: since 1988 there is a new owner.

FOOD: A lot of pubs, locantas and restaurants along the oceanside, none worth special mention. Try the rooftop restaurant (5th floor, great panorama, disco music, loud travel groups and package tourists) in **Hotel Anafartalar** and the fine restaurants **Yalova Liman**, **Entellektuell** and **Yalova Şehir**. The latter places more emphasis on presentation than food quality. These establishments have grown accustomed to day tourists. The most faithful customers are sailors whose interests are large servings and the price of beer.

LORD BYRON

When we speak of the Dardanelles, we must mention Lord Byron. He is the one who brought back to life the legend of Hero and Leander (see Leander Tower, İstanbul) by crossing the strait at exactly the same spot where Leander once entered the water.

George Gordon Lord Byron (1788 - 1824) was a fascinating figure in his own time. Few have succeeded so well as he in combining both life and work. His puritan contemporaries called Byron "*Leader of the Satan Movement*", fearing his bisexuality, indulgence, and unorthodox views of literature, life and politics. Others hailed him as the greatest poet of his time. "*Lord Byron is a truly great . . . educated talent, and there is hardly another to compare him to*", according to his admirer GOETHE.

Byron's fame is based upon the tales of "*Childe Harold's Pilgrimage*" (1812). The unhappy Harold wastes his talents and has fate against him. Much of English society could identify itself with the youth. In *Harold*, Byron was fierce in his condemnation of the exploitation of Greece, unleashing a romantic, philhellenic movement, which had consequences for the war of independence against Turkey. When the Turkish Empire conquered Missolonghi in 1826, brutally massacring its entire population, there was a storm of anger throughout Europe. Byron's martyrdom (he had come to support the Greeks in their fight for independence, but died of typhoid) was not in vain. Public opinion forced the Allied Powers to act. In the Treaty of Adrianople (1829), Turkey was forced to grant Greece its independence.

The myth of Byron continues today: "*Byron is a romantic in the full spirit of the classical age, a soldier and poet, a social lion who enjoyed fame and toiled under its pressure, a monogamous seducer of women with a touch of homosexuality, a genius with a taste for the trivial, a jester who awakens feelings with his charm, but then destroys them with sarcasm. . .*" (Hartmut Muller).

Sights

Ferry Harbour: The Çanakkale port is situated at the narrowest point along the Dardanelles. Ferries arrive at hourly intervals. The harbour facilities are surprisingly small. There is little handling of freight. A new marina is under construction 5 km to the north.

Sultaniye Kale: Sultan MEHMET II ordered construction of this fortress at the narrowest point along the Dardanelles in 1454. Together with the *Kilitbahir* fortress on the opposite shore, it was designed to defend and control access to the Sea of Marmara and the Black Sea.

Military Museum: The sultan's palace houses a military museum. Here you can see interesting artifacts from the battle of 1915 (see Gallipoli). In addition to several cannons, the battle's decisive mine-laying ship, the "Nusrat", is on display.

OPEN: Daily 9:00 - 12:00 h and 13:30 - 17:30 h, closed Mondays.

Archaeological Museum: Housed in a new building on the southern edge of town, featuring pieces excavated at the *Dardanos tumulus* and a wealth of ancient ceramics.

OPEN: Daily 9:00 - 12:00 h and 13:00 - 17:00 h, closed Mondays.

Swimming

Because the region around Çanakkale is a closed military zone, there are few beaches. The town beach is south of the castle. Nicer beaches are further away to the south, like "Şen Mocamp" in Kepez, or at Güzelyalı (beautiful beach) and on the islands of Gökçeada and Bozcaada.

Around Çanakkale

Nara: About 9 km north of Çanakkale at the second narrowest point along the Dardanelles (1450 m). During antiquity, Nara was called "Nagara". In ancient times the *Heptastadion Ferry* (the strait had the width of seven stadiums at this point) departed from here. Near Nara is the site of the ancient town of *Abydus*, which is mentioned in the legend of Hero and Leander.

Troja/Hisarlık: By far the most important historic site in the region (see Troy).

Lapseki: A sleepy spot on the east bank of the Dardanelles, across from Gelibolu, set in vineyard hills and olive groves. The ferry harbour seems a bit too large.

COMING - GOING: Buses from Çanakkale (45 km).

Bozcaada: A quite small, but enchanting, island at the end of the Dardanelles. Population 2000. Here we found the prettiest beaches between Fethiye and Marmara Island. Life on the island is modest. The local people have little inclination to go to any lengths for tourists which says a lot for them. On the other hand, nobody will complain if you watch them fishing, or even less if you enjoy seafood at one of the restaurants. This is much like the way Greek islands were before the word "disco" became part of the Greek language.

COMING - GOING: **Ferries** from Odunluk İskelesi (**buses** from Çanakkale to Odunluk, 70 minutes). Depart at 10:00, 13:00, 17:00, 21:00 h, costs £0.10 per person or £1.35 per car.

A NIGHT'S REST: In a **former Bozcaada school**, opened in 1986, with 36 simply furnished rooms and 80 beds, common showers, costs £2.70 per person. Similar prices at **Zafer Motel** in Alabey Mahallesi district.

Note: Permission from the governor is required before you may visit the island in this Turkish/Greek border region. You can conclude the formality at the harbour in Çanakkale. It will depend upon your appearance whether the process takes just two minutes or five hours.

Gökçeada: A quite large Aegean island (280 sq km, one of the few in Turkish hands) with a population of 5800. The lovely beaches are peaceful. Recommended for hikers, bike riders, painters, connoisseurs . . . (see Bozcaada).

In the middle of the island is the fairly large settlement of Gökçe Ada, surrounded by tiny villages including the lovely Aydıncık. Seafood restaurants and fresh fish can be found in all villages along the shore.

COMING - GOING: The **ferry** from Çanakkale sails daily at 15:00, returning at 8:00 h. The three hour cruise costs £0.40.

A NIGHT'S REST: **Dinmenle Tesisleri** in Kuzu Limanı, the harbour where the ferry docks. Double with bath £4, without bath £2.70. Excellent location, bungalows, clean beach at the front door, fresh fish in the adjoining restaurant. What more do you want?

Note: You also need permission from the governor to visit this island in the border region (see Bozcaada).

Gelibolu *(pop. 15,000)*: This picturesque fishing village is on an inlet at the northern entrance to the Dardanelles, surrounded by steep, jagged coastal scenery.

Gelibolu has frequently figured in historic events. In 405 BC, the Spartan fleet defeated Athens here and won the Peloponnesian War. In 1357, this was the first European town to be captured by the Ottoman Empire. This is also the home of PIRI REIS (1465 - 1554), the first geographer to draw a useful map of the world (on display at the Maritime Museum in İstanbul).

Sights include *Ulu Cami* (15th century), several early Ottoman tombs, the *Azepler Namazgahı*, an open-air place of prayer with a marble mihrab (1407) and a *Byzantine Fortress Tower* (8th century). There are ferries between Gelibolu and Lapseki.

COMING - GOING: **Bus** from Çanakkale 48 km, £0.50. **Ferries** from Lapseki, £0,40.

Eceabat *(pop. 5000)*: A ferry harbour across from Çanakkale on the European shore. The village is known for the fortress *Kilitbahir* (1462), the European sister to *Sultaniye Kale* on the opposite shore. The bulwark consists of three interlocking round towers, each 40 m in diameter. Later an additional tower was built which houses the small local museum today.

Gallipoli-Battlefield Peninsula

The 60 km Dardanelles Strait has been the site of fierce fighting since the days of Homer. A tale which begins with Xerxes' attempt to ferry troops, and ends during WW I with a famous sea battle.

Just after dawn on the morning of March 15, 1915, Vice-Admiral SIR JOHN DE ROBECK ordered the Allied fleet to proceed in full force through the Dardanelles Strait. By 15:00 h, three ships were out of action because the Turkish mine-layer "Nusrat" managed to lay 26 mines at the last minute, creating a seemingly impregnable barrier. The restored "Nusrat" is on display at the Naval Museum in Çanakkale.

March 18 is celebrated each year as a great victory. On both sides of the Dardanelles, huge painted plaques are displayed in memory of the event. An inscription by the poet NECMETTIN HALIL ONAN reads: *"Stranger, as you enter this land, remember an era came to an end here. Bow and listen. On this spot, you can hear the heartbeat of a nation."*

The Four Phases of the Campaign

The Allies' plan was to capture İstanbul, forcing Turkey out of the war, in order to gain ice-free access to Russia. At the same time a new front would be opened against Germany and Austria-Hungary. March 18 marked the first attempt to force access for the fleet through the Dardanelles. On April 25, 1915 British and French troops landed at Cape Halles, while Australian and New Zealand troops landed on the Anzac coast (Anzac = Australian and New Zealand Army Corps), today Arı Burnu.

On August 6, in the third phase, the British tried to push out of their positions in the north of Anzac and in Suvla Bay. This offensive ended in trench warfare.

In the fourth and final stage, the Allies were forced to perform a staged withdrawl. On December 19 and 20, troops were removed from Suvla Bay and Anzac while the Cape Halles position was abandoned on January 8 and 9.

GALLIPOLI: KEMAL PASHA ATATÜRK MAKES A NAME FOR HIMSELF

On April 25, 1915 at 4:00 h, Australian and New Zealand troops landed at Arı Burnu, opening the Anzac Operation. Fortunately for the Turks, powerful currents carried the attacking force miles off course, forcing the invaders to land in an unknown region. As the day went on, however, the attackers had regrouped and were storming up the hill. The Turkish defenders turned tail and ran.

The situation seemed hopeless when young KEMAL PASHA arrived at the battlefield at the head of a poorly-trained reserve division. He recognized immediately that the battle would be lost if the hill were surrendered, and the Turkish troops were abandoning the hill as quickly as possible. Hundreds stormed past Atatürk in retreat.

Kemal Pasha stopped the frightened soldiers, forcing them to lie down and secure their bayonets. The Australians began to fear an ambush and took cover. Hours passed before the attackers realized that the Turks were almost out of ammunition. By then reserves had arrived to encircle the bridgehead, stemming the land attack and leaving the hill in Turkish hands.

Had the allied force broken through, there would have been no way to defend İstanbul, bringing the war to an early end. And so the divisional commander and future head of state of modern Turkey defended his country with a bluff!

At several spots along the Gallipoli Peninsula, you will see memorials, monuments and huge military cemeteries.

Anzac Cove: In Anzac Cove, on "Anzac Day" in 1985, a memorial plaque was unveiled with a message from Atatürk addressed to the first delegation of Australian, New Zealand, and British veterans, who visited the battlefield in 1934:

"You heroes, who shed your blood and died, now rest in peace in a friendly land. There are no differences between the "Johnnies" and the "Mehmets"; we all lie together, side by side. Mothers, who sent your sons to us from far-away lands, dry your tears. Your sons now lie in our lap, resting in peace. They have become like brothers to us, in our country."

Lone Pine Cemetery: Named for the solitary pine tree, situated above Anzac Cove. Fighting was particularly fierce for this hill. In addition to hundreds of tombstones, there is a large monument in remembrance of the soldiers killed in action.

Turkish Memorial: A four-legged 25 m tall monument, visible from far and wide, at the tip of the Gallipoli Peninsula. It is dedicated to the Turkish martyrs of the Gallipoli campaign.

Chunuk Bahir: In Chunuk Bahir you can view reconstructed trenches from the August 1915 battle. The five columns of the memorial symbolize the hand of a soldier, reaching to heaven in prayer and thanks to the Almighty.

COMING - GOING: As the sites are difficult to reach with public transportation, we recommend you take one of the organized **day trips**. Check at one of the travel agencies in Çanakkale, e.g. Troy-Anzac Travel Agency, near the Clock Tower in Çanakkale, tel. 5047.

NORTH AEGEAN

One of the most interesting tourist regions in Turkey. World-famous excavation sites such as Troy and Pergamon alternate with lovely resort villages like Ören, Ayvalık and Foca. There is also the very Turkish Manisa or Sart, the capital of the legendary Croesus, whose people invented the coin.

The scenery is unspoiled: fishing villages and vacation towns; cotton, wheat, and tobacco fields; fig and olive groves. But like İstanbul to the north, İzmir attracts masses of workers, who end up living in the gecekondu settlements of the city.

Those left behind live from agriculture. Tourism provides jobs in only a few areas. In addition to cotton, tobacco and grain, wine is also produced.

This is a great region for tourists. The people are friendly, prices are lower than in the Southern Aegean, the infrastructure is good. In **Ören** and **Ayvalık** you can join the natives on the beach. If you are seeking solitude, try the area around **Assos**.

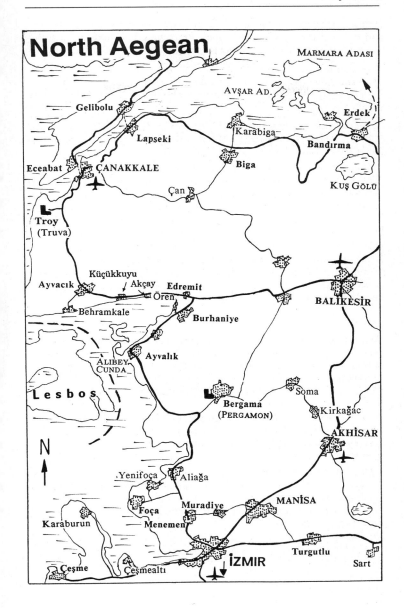

North Aegean

MARMARA ADASI

AVŞAR AD.

Gelibolu

Erdek

Lapseki

Karabiga

Bandırma

Eceabat

ÇANAKKALE

Biga

KUŞ GÖLÜ

Çan

Troy
(Truva)

Küçükkuyu

Ayvacık

Akçay

Edremit

Ören

Behramkale

BALIKESIR

Burhaniye

ALIBEY
CUNDA

Ayvalık

L e s b o s

Soma

Bergama
(PERGAMON)

Kırkağaç

N

AKHISAR

Yenifoça

Aliağa

Foça

Muradiye

MANISA

Karaburun

Menemen

Çeşme

Çeşmealtı

İZMIR

Turgutlu

Sart

TROY

Troy is certainly the best-known excavation site in Turkey. This is primarily a result of Homer's Iliad, but also because of the work of Heinrich Schliemann, a hobby archaeologist. He covered the already difficult excavation site with exploratory holes so thoroughly that later generations of scientists left frustrated, seeking their laurels elsewhere.

Adding to the difficulty is the fact that there are no less than nine Troys (there are also five Ephesuses), each built upon the ruins of its predecessor. On the site today, you can see remains of the first settlement, directly adjoining buildings from levels VIII and IX. It would be impossible to keep your orientation without the mostly reliable signs. For more information, see Sights.

The *Treasure of Priam* disappeared during WW II. For decades it was assumed that it had been shipped to the East. However, recent rumours maintain that the Americans secretly took possession of it. Two British journalists have announced the publication of sensational documents.

History

The history of Troy is lost in the mist of time and can only be reconstructed by filtering through the various levels of settlement. The work is difficult. CARL BLEGEN, leader of an excavation team from the University of Cincinnati, differentiates between nine major levels (I-IX), which he again subdivides into secondary levels (i.e. Ia - Ij). The Troy of Homer is level VIIa.

Troy I: The lowest level dates from 3000 - 2600 BC. This first settlement was not a town, but rather a castle with a ring of walls and protecting towers on the west side of the hill.

Troy II: Around 2600 - 2300 BC, Troy I was expanded to the south. Now encompassing 8000 square metres, the town sheltered over 3000 people. The walls were built of large rocks. Within this ring of fortification, some spectacular finds have been made. Schliemann discovered the *Treasure of Priam* here. About 2300 BC the town experienced a disastrous fire.

Troy III: After 2300 BC the survivors built a new, smaller settlement on the rubble. The ring of walls was repaired; smaller doors and gates were installed. The population lived in small huts and supported themselves primarily by hunting. This settlement was abandoned about 2200 BC.

Would you have been taken by the trick?

Troy IV and **V**: On the ruins of Troy III a new village took shape. In Troy V (2050 - 1900 BC) we can see Mycenaean influence. Mycenae was the first great Greek kingdom.

Troy VI: As new settlers were attracted to Troy V about 1900 BC, the town increased in size, although it was by no means large (200 by 300 m). The acropolis rose terrace-like. No evidence of a lower town has yet been found. Little is known of the inhabitants; they may have been Thracian or Aeolian Greeks. It is known that the town fell victim to an earthquake about 1300 BC.

Troy VIIa: Probably the "Ilion" of Homer. Soon after the disastrous earthquake, Troy was rebuilt. But only 100 years later (1200 BC) the town was again devastated by a fire. This event fits remarkably well with the story of the destruction of Troy (1184 BC). It is assumed that the town was conquered by Mycenaean Greeks, the true story of the Trojan War.

Troy VIIb: After the destruction of Troy VIIa, the hill was inhabited by Phrygians. Later the Dardanese settled here. The lifestyle of the new inhabitants differed greatly from that of their predecessors. For the first time buildings were grouped around a courtyard. Particularly interesting are vases with buckle patterns showing trade relations with central Europe (Lausitzer region).

Troy VIII: After the 8th century BC, the Phrygian settlement was transformed into a Greek colony. In 547 BC the Persian king CYRUS added the town to his kingdom. The temple of Athena dates from this period.

Troy IX: In 334 BC ALEXANDER THE GREAT took possession of Troy. The first port was built by LYSIMACHUS about 300 BC. In 190 BC, Troy came under Roman domination. It profited from its reputation as the birthplace of AENEAS, the founder of Rome. The tip of the hill was planed and decorated with splendid buildings including a new temple of Athena and a theatre. Under CAESAR the town doubled in size with the addition of a lower town. The population was now about 40,000. This late golden age of Troy ended with the invasion of the Goths in 262 AD.

In 1610 AD the Briton GEORGE SANDYS searched for Troy near the hill of Hisarlik to no avail. The Englishman FRANK CALVERT was the first to excavate at Hisarlik, but it was SCHLIEMANN who first proved the existence of Ilion. In the years 1932 - 1938 a University of Cincinnati program led by CARL W. BLEGEN conducted the most thorough investigation of Troy.

INFORMATION: The best information can be found in the Archaeological Museum in Çanakkale. In Troy (Truva) itself is a souvenir shop offering informative guides and maps of the excavation sites. Unfortunately, the local museum has been closed, and its exhibits sent to Çanakkale.

COMING - GOING: Minibuses from Çanakkale to Truva hourly from the Clock Tower in Çanakkale (£0.35), takes 45 min.
Taxi: Much faster, but more expensive (£2.75).

DAY TRIPS: Troy-Anzac Travel Agency, Xali Caddesi 2, Çanakkale, has the most experience offering Troy tours. Prices must be bargained; calculate 40 per cent cheaper in the off season.

POST OFFICE: In the souvenir shop you can get postcards with the special Troy stamp.

FOOD: There is a clean restaurant by the large parking lot at the main gate. The specialty, we read, is tomato omelette. We had a large plate of excellent rice (Pilav), well spiced. There are no refreshment stands on the grounds.

OPEN: Sunrise to sunset, admission £0.30 on weekdays, £0.20 on weekends.

Tour

Sad, but true: there are only a few remains of HOMER'S Troy.

After about a half-kilometre walk, visitors are greeted by a wooden horse, approximately 20 m tall. Warning: it is not the original! Since the summer of 1986, tourists are no longer permitted to climb the beast. Around the horse is a thick grove of pines, cooled by a sea breeze - a real oasis in the heat.

From here we climb into the hollow to the **East Tower** (Troy VI). On the left are the mighty walls of Troy VI sloping to the outside, hence safer against earthquakes. On the right, in a passageway behind the East Tower, are the walls from the Roman era (Troy IX), forming the boundary of the Athena district. We enter the town through the East Gate (notice the overlapping walls allowing optimal defence).

Continuing on we come to the **Lower Terrace**. On the left is a simple **rectangular building** (Troy VI), and behind the house 12 column stumps (probably from a temple). The other buildings on the terrace are roomy with sturdy walls, showing the affluence of Troy VI.

We follow the path to the top of the hill. Here you have a great view over the *Skamander Plains* (scene of Homer's duels), the *Dardanelles* and the *Gallipoli Peninsula*. If the weather is good, you can see the Turkish war memorial on the European shore. Of the **Athena Temple** only ruins of the paved terrace and a few column drums can be seen. Preserved are the well shaft and the northeast (corner) tower.

We climb down into one of Schliemann's exploratory holes. On the left, in the hollow, is the **Main Gate of Troy I**, with a small gate tower, recognizable by its small, irregular stones. This gate is 5000 years old!

On the right are the foundations of several **megaron houses** from Troy II. (These houses have elongated side walls. This type of building was the predecessor of the Greek temple with a column entrance hall.)

The path leads along the walls of Troy II and down the opposite side on a 5.60 m wide ramp. Looking back, you have a good view of the 6 m high sloping wall of Troy II. Up on the ramp was once a tremendous guard tower.

On the wall across from the ramp, Heinrich Schliemann found the *Treasure of Priam*. You leave the moat via a few stairs, climbing to the town wall of Troy VI. On the right is a destroyed **megaron** (site of numerous ceramic finds).

Continuing to the **Sacred Square**. Here an altar, a sacrificial pit and two shafts were discovered. One of the shafts actually served as a drain for sacrificial blood, the other was a well. The entire Sacred District is fenced and can only be observed from above. To reach the **Roman Bath** walk around the unexcavated hill of rubble.

Spectacular is the **odeon**, a hall for concerts and recitals. A little further is the **Dardanus Gate** (Troy VI) with its clearly visible sewage canal in the middle of the road. Directly adjoining are the sparse remains of a Roman **council hall**.

Around Troy

Everybody probably knows Troy. But do you know Alexander Truva (Alexandreia Troy)? And did you know that it is a fairly large town, not yet excavated, which is located between Troy and Assos? Alexandreia Troy was founded by the diligent Antigonus (one of Alexander's generals) who was also the founder of several other towns along the coast. The ruins of the town of Antigoneia (as Alexander Troy is also called) shimmer far off in the heat. The Apostle Paul stopped here to preach on his second missionary journey. The city walls, parts of the theatre and remnants of the baths are still visible today. What lies dormant underground is still a mystery.

The whole area between Troy and Assos, away from the main road, is charming and there is a lot more to see along the small road, although driving can sometimes be quite an adventure (recommended for car owners or very heat-resistant pedestrians only). Besides the already mentioned Truva, you can see the Apollo Stimeon or Smintheon, a small temple and a fountain, and many other ruins. The blue of the Mediterranean and the brown of the sun-parched hills dominate the scenery. You will also come across quiet villages,

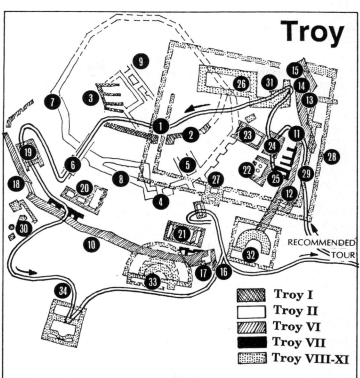

Troy

Legend:
- Troy I
- Troy II
- Troy VI
- Troy VII
- Troy VIII-XI

RECOMMENDED TOUR

1. Main Gate	18. Entrance
2. City wall	19. House
3. Megaron	20. Palace stock rooms
4. Entrance	21. Column house
5. Entrance	22. VI. F house with column base
6. Entrance and ramp	23. VI. C house
7. Entrance	24. VI. E. house
8. City wall	25. VII. Stock room
9. Megaron	26. Athena Temple
10. City wall	27. Temple entrance (Propylaion)
11. Entrance	28. Outer court wall
12. East tower	29. Inner court wall
13. Entrance	30. Sacred Square
14. Tower	31. Waterworks
15. Well	32. Parliament
16. Dardanos entrance	33. Odeon
17. Tower	34. Roman Bath

with broad main streets, and inhabitants who are actually still happy
to have strangers join them for some tea. People travelling with a
tent or a substantial holiday budget may want to stay a while in this
secluded area.

COMING - GOING: There are two possibilities: 1. Coming from Assos/Behramkale
take the gravel road towards Gülpınır/Tuzla. 2. Coming from the E87 via Ezine to
Odun (follow sign Alexandreia Truva) or towards Tavaklı.

A NIGHT'S REST / CAMPING: **Akkay II** right by Tavaklı on the ocean. Akkaya I is on
the Black Sea near Şile. Mr. Karaoğlu, the owner of both enterprises, wanted the
sites to meet European standards and therefore consulted the German Automobile
Club during construction. That is why this camp site has sanitary facilities for the
handicapped - probably the only ones in all of Turkey. There are ramps for
wheelchairs, the showers and washrooms have easy-to-reach basins and water
taps. The other sanitary facilities also represent a rarity for Turkey since they are, regarding installation, furnishings and cleanliness, comparable to Hilton standards.
The upper region of the site is very nice; the beach area is not quite finished yet.
There is a minimarket and a semi-luxury restaurant. Affiliated with the site is a hotel
which has nice rooms with balconies. Prices: £1.70 per person, £0.75 for a car or
motorcycle, £1.30 per tent, £1.80 for a caravan, £0.65 per child and for electricity.
No telephone yet. Address through Akkaya I, see Camping/Şile, p.181.

Assos

**Anyone who visits Troy might ask themselves why anyone
would want to build a town in such an awful spot - in the
middle of a barren region, far from the sea. The answer is
simple: fear of pirates.**

There was no such fear at Assos: the castle stands defiantly above the
beach, its lofty height providing a spectacular view of the entire
coastal strip, the island of Lesbos and the backlands.

From the village of **Behramkale**, at the foot of the castle mountain, is
a short footpath leading to the ruins of Assos.

History

Assos was founded at the time of the Trojan War and was capital of
the Lelegians. About 1000 BC, Aeolians, expelled from Lesbos, took
over the town. After annexation by Persia in 334 BC, Assos was liberated by ALEXANDER. Finally it was added to the Roman Empire in the

2nd century BC. In 1330 AD sultan ORHAN added the town to the Ottoman Empire. ARISTOTLE lived in Assos from 348 - 345 BC and founded a school of philosophy there. Many years later (58 AD) the Apostle PAUL founded a Christian community here. Assos was never of real importance.

After the founding of Alexander Truva (see Around Troy) the town always stood in the shadow of the neighbouring metropolis.

COMING - GOING: From Ayvacık by dolmuş (£0.35)/taxi to Behramkale, poor road. From Çanakkale 4 buses daily to Assos.

A NIGHT'S REST: **Motel Behram**, above the harbour, double £5. The facility consists of a motel, camping and restaurant by the water. Small pebble beach. **Assos Motel**, by the harbour, double £5.

CAMPING: Several private sites are located along a steep road next to the ocean. Tip: keep going until the last campsite. The owner organizes romantic evening boat rides (£0.70).

Motel-Camping-Kadırga: located about 7 km east of Assos on a long, sandy beach. Nice grounds with a good restaurant and passable sanitary facilities. The approach road will leave you pretty shaken up.

Sights

The massive walls and towers of the fortification - a circle with a perimetre of about 3 km - are fairly well preserved. At the highest point was the *Temple of Athena* with six Doric columns along the width and 12 columns along its length. The reliefs from this temple have been taken away to a number of museums (İstanbul, Paris). The agora and the city itself were built on the southern slope of the hill but there is little left to see of the famous agora. There are also the ruins of a *new temple* and a *Gymnasion*.

Küçükkuyu

The first of the three resort towns Akcay, Ören and Kücükkuyu, on the road heading south. It is also the nicest.

They have not managed to combine traditional Turkish life with the needs of mass tourism (that would be difficult anywhere). Turkey is pushed into the background, but the character of the village has not been completely destroyed. The best aspect of the village is its long sand/pebble beach.

A Night's Rest

Along the beach in the direction of Edremit are a number of motels. Recommended:

Gül-tur Motel: a double costs £10 in the elongated, clean motel with an efficient staff. Of course it has a garden, a swimming pool, a restaurant, a disco and surfboard rentals.

Tan Motel: tel. 132, similar prices, smaller, more pleasant and good service.

CAMPING: There are many camp sites along the coast and on the road between Küçukkuyu and Akçay but most of them are not very good.

SPORTS: Swimming (wonderful sandy beach, but dirty in mid summer), surfing (excellent wind conditions). Surfboard rentals in the following motels: Çavuşoğlu, Gül-tur, İda-tur.

Ören

A small collection of hotels grouped around two shops. Other shopping facilities are in the neighbouring town of Burhaniye (pop. 18,300).

Ören is not a town, but rather a typical resort village, popular among Turkish tourists. The sports facilities and super clean beaches will also please European guests.

COMING - GOING: From Burhaniye by local bus (2 km). Ferries across the bay to Akçay (£0.20).

A NIGHT'S REST

> **Turban Ören Altın Köyü**, reasonable prices, double £33 (half board), tel. 217 317. Actually a holiday centre with excellent sports facilities, 20 per cent discount in the off season. The rooms feature beach views. The restaurant (tasty dishes) is adjoining, disco and game hall, surfing possible.
> **Efem Motel**, double £10, tel. 21314. Right by the sea, lovely garden, well-kept, elongated building. Warm water sanitation, lovely dining hall.
> **Ada Moteli**, double £7, tel. 1225, simple bungalows with nice rooms right on the beach.

CAMPING: **Altın Camping**, (see Akçay, Altın Camp).

SWIMMING: Lovely sandy beach, right in front of the hotels.

SPORTS: Great facilities at Turban Akçay Altın Köyü holiday centre for surfing, sailing, waterskiing, table tennis, billiards, bicycle riding, rowing.

Edremit *(pop. 30,000)*

The town is located in a fertile channel, deposited by a river, excellent for growing olives, corn, grain and figs. The people of Edremit earn their livelihood with agriculture; they are not involved with the tourist trade which flourishes on the nearby coast. That is why things are quiet here; the excitement is at Akçay. For travellers the town is only of interest as a place to buy supplies.

COMING - GOING: From Edremit by local bus (10 km). There is a dolmuş every half hour from Edremit-Centre to Akçay. You are packed in like sardines.

A NIGHT'S REST: Edremit only has hotels in the cheapest category.

Akçay *(Population really just 7000)*

A phenomenon! Akçay does not have a lot going for it. The once sleepy fishing village does not have a strategic location, nor can its beach of sand and rock be considered attractive.

Still, Akçay is considered a real hot spot among Turkish families. If you like action, this is the place. If you came to see Turkey, you have come to the wrong place. During the Turkish holiday season it is totally overrun.

COMING - GOING: From Edremit also by local bus (only 10 km).

A Night's Rest

Lots of cheap pensions in town. Every halfway available room is rented for £4 and up, the rooms are not luxurious but clean.

> **Turban Akçay Tatil Köyü**, double £24, tel. 203. The usual standards you expect of a Turban holiday centre, with disco, restaurant, bar, sports. Particularly interesting is the surfing as wind conditions in the Gulf of Edremit are outstanding.

> **Asiyan Moteli**, double £9, tel. 1133, lovely and clean. Restaurant, swimming pool, lovely wooden balconies.

CAMPING: The camping facilities in Akçay itself (Güneş Camping, Saka Camping, Pat Camping) would hardly put even Turkish campers at ease. Question: Is it permissible to place a sign in a field, raise a fence, park a trailer as the office, and call it a campsite? I would call it fraud.

> **Akçay Camping**, on the road towards Çannakale. Frequented mostly by Turkish families staying for a few weeks and foreigners staying for one night only. Miniature beach, friendly people at the reception, restaurant serves breakfast. The sanitary facilities are clean in the morning but not at all so in the evening. Prices: £0.50 per person, large tent/car £0.75 each, electricity for a tent £0.20, for a caravan £0.35, caravans £1.70. tel. 3356-1445.

Altın Camp, tel. 201, 2 km from Burhaniye. Definitely the best site on the Aegean coast, but not cheap. Open year round with a fine sandy beach, good sports facilities including tennis, table tennis, rowing, waterskiing, and horse riding. This is a place for those who are willing to pay for their fun, but want to sleep cheap. Perhaps too well organized for our more chaotic travellers. Turkish teens are not permitted to stay on this site.

FOOD: Close your eyes and walk in any direction: you are sure to bump into a restaurant sign. The good and expensive spots are by the harbour; the cheaper locantas in the village. Don't be surprised if the food is better at the latter.

DISCOS: **Turban Disco** - so-so. **Eğe Disco** - a little better, lots of old Turkish folk songs.

Swimming

"About 10 km from Edremit is the Akçay beach, which caters almost exclusively to domestic tourism. Since the beach is rocky, international tourism is unlikely to settle here." That was our statement in the last edition. The beaches are still rocky, but it is questionable whether that alone will keep the tourists at bay.

SPORTS: In Akçay you have all the usual sports including skin diving and surfing. The holiday village Turban Akçay Altın Köyü, 2 km from Burhaniye (see Ören) offers a wealth of activities.

Ayvalık *(pop. 20,000)*

"This fishing village set on a scenic jagged coast, is appealing for its honesty and its warmth. This impression begins at the tourist information office. They are interested in more than just your wallet."

Our tip in 1987 is no longer quite true. Hotels have changed names and owners, deteriorating as new hotels are built. The scenery has been attacked by thoughtless development,moving into the surrounding beet fields.

And the tip about money needs revision: the price of food, drink and accommodation has risen unreasonably. Fast money has replaced friendly service.

Hugo Boss will be pleased to know that nowhere does he get as much free advertising as in Ayvalık. Every Turkish Mercedes and every Turkish teenager is wearing his logo on his/her bumper or chest. The symbol of a new age in which only mammon counts.

Settled originally in the 15th century, Ayvalık suffered a terrible earthquake early this century, and is now undergoing development as a holiday paradise. The 23 offshore islands boast seven kilometres of sandy beach for relaxation in an unspoiled environment. The strategy is to separate the intact old town of Ayvalık from the hotel complexes by the beach.

Think before booking a hotel room in town; it is a full 6 km to the beach. In **Çamlık** there are a number of good hotels, along with a lovely camp site, that have opened in recent years. 3 km further is the lovely *Sarımsaklı Beach*, where you can find almost everything. But a large number of people have discovered this.

Except for a well-preserved Greek Church (has pictures painted on fish skin), Ayvalık offers few sights. But this is a good departure point for trips to historic sites in the region, including Pergamon.

INFORMATION: Ayvalık Yat Limanı Karşışı, tel. 2122. Much better info from Ercan Kocelli, Tourism Director, on the road to Çamlık; it is hard to escape his enthusiasm.

TELEPHONE AREA CODE: 6631

COMING - GOING:
Bus £0.15 (6:00 - 23:00 h), frequently crowded.
Taxi: Be sure to bargain the price in advance! There is no taximeter.
Ferry to Lesbos: Mon, Wed, Fri 8:30 h (Note: Be there by 8:00 h), leaves from the customs office at the harbour, make reservations a day in advance at the tourist office. Price: one way £10, round trip £17.50, children 6 - 12 get a 50 per cent discount; cars £26, motorcycles £10, trailers £60.

BUS TOURS TO PERGAMON: 8:30, 10:00, 11:00, 12:00, 13:00, 14:30, 15:30, 16:30, 18:00 h (departure times), 45 km, 45 min., £0.60.

BOAT TOURS: Wed, Sat, Sun, groups of eight or more, boat rentals for one day (including captain), £1.80 per person, departs 16:00 h, returns at 20:30 h.

DAY TRIP : From Sarımsaklı you can head out by boat for £8.35; lots of stops to swim and for a meal in a nice restaurant.

FESTIVAL: International Tourism Festival from the 20th to the 22nd of July.

SHOPPING: In Ayvalık there are lots of small shops along the coastal road where you can find just about everything. In Sarımsaklı, however, you may have to do without.

TRAVEL AGENCY: **Eresos Tur**, Talafpaşa Cad. 67c, daily tours to Pergamon, Troy, Bursa, Ephesus; ship tickets to Lesbos, hotel reservations, tel. 1756. Or **Ayvalık Tur**, Bümrük Cad. 4(1)a, tel. 2740 with similar services.

A NIGHT'S REST

You will find only very simple pensions of the cheapest category in Ayvalık. Better lodgings, closer to the beach are located outside Ayvalık.

Hotel Ankara (Sarımsaklı), double £15 - £23, tel. 1195, restaurant, café, large facility by the beach.

Cam Motel, on the road to Çamlık just beyond Tourist Information. Double with breakfast £15. Garden with shady trees, clean showers, large rooms. 40 per cent off-season discount. tel. 1515.

Büyük Berk (Sarımsaklı), double £14, 112 rooms, some with a view of the ocean, terrace restaurant, swimming pool, bar, discotheque.

Sevo Motel (Sarımsaklı), double £12, lovely rooms, terrace with an ocean view, 100 m to the beach.

Çadır Otel (Çamlık), double £9, middle class.

Otel Ege (Sarımsaklı), bed & breakfast £4, half board £10.

Aytur Motel (Sarımsaklı), bed & breakfast £4, half board £8, full board £9.

Sehir Otel (Ayvalık), double, bath/WC on the hallway, £3.30, very simple.

CAMPING: **Ada Camping** (Alibey Peninsula), large, clean, room rental possible, sandy beach, clear water, sports (sailing, surfing).
Çamlık Belediye Camping (Çamlık), on the road to Sarımsaklı, shade, simple sanitation.

In Ayvalık the Tourist Information Office suggested the following hotels:
İpek Otel, Kıyı Motel, Sehir Otel and **El Otel**. Calculate £3 per person.
Recommendation in Çamlık: **Levant Pension**, £2.60 per person.
In Alibey: **Yıldız Pension** (£2.60), **Artur Motel** (£3)

FOOD

Şeytan Sofrası, see Ayvalık Tours.
Lale Restaurant (Alibey Cunda), Sahil Bayu Alibey Adası, inconspicuous restaurant, the specialty is seafood. Nicat Behil is an excellent cook! tel. 25.
Büyük Berk (Sarımsaklı), terrace, Sunday lavish buffet at a reasonable price, (£5 per person).
Belediye Gazinosu (Çamlık), appetizers change daily, delicate grill specialties, tel. 2251.
Bonjour Kafeteriya (Ayvalık), Atatürk Cad., excellent Turkish coffee.
Kafeteriya 83 (Sarımsaklı), Stranquai, very sweet, but good pastries.
Kösem Restaurant (Çamlık), good food.

NIGHT LIFE : The best disco is "Murat Reis". Otherwise lots of glitter but little action.

Swimming

There are lovely sandy beaches on Alibey Cunda, in Camlik and in Sarımsaklı; the latter is recommended, although it is plastered with umbrellas and chairs.

SPORTS: fishing, skindiving, riding, sailing, tennis, volleyball, minigolf, water-skiing, and surfing (Çamlık, Information/Rentals Hotel Büyük Berk).

Around Ayvalik

Alibey Cunda: A visit to Alibey Cunda peninsula is well worth your while. Its population has declined in the last 150 years from 5000 to just 2000 today. The first inhabitants (Greeks) named it "Island of Scent". Today the predominating smell is that of seafood restaurants. Remnants from Greek residents - windmills and church ruins - create a very unusual Turkish atmosphere. Plan an afternoon excursion to Cunda for grilled fish - try one of the 118 different types! And don't forget to order some rakı. We can recommend the following restaurants: "Canlı Balık", "Sadi Kaptan", "Saray Gazinosu".

COMING - GOING: **dolmuş** £0.10 (from the harbour), **ship** £0.10 (from harbour/Central Tourist Information Office), **taxi** £2.35.

A NIGHT'S REST: There are a few simple pensions and the Ada Motel with rooms and an area for tents.

Şeytan Sofrası: Between Çamlık and Sarımsaklı the road branches to the south. After the large Murat Reis Hotel, it climbs and twists through forest clearings to Şeytan Sofrası, "Devil's Valley". Here you have a beautiful view of the entire coastal region around Ayvalık and the chance to photograph an unbelievable sunset. If you are sure-footed, take the path to the south. There are no signs, but the path is easy to follow as you keep the coast in sight the whole way. After 45 minutes you reach the coast southeast of Sarımsaklı. From there you can head back by bus.

BERGAMA/PERGAMON *(pop. 38,000)*

This enchanting little market town in the fertile Selinus Plain is nestled at the foot of a jagged 400 m tall rock. White brick buildings with red tiled roofs huddle around the ruins of Kızıl Avlu.

Along Bergama's main road, Hükümet Caddesi, are a number of shops, including countless oriental carpet shops. The street is shared by donkey carts, honking taxis, women in traditional dress and tourists in colourful Hawaii shirts. A cloud of dust rises each time one of the buses from the Otogar passes through.

Bergama owes its fame to the German engineer KARL HUMANN who was here with a road construction crew in 1873. He noticed an unusual piece of mosaic lying in the straw of an ox cart. He bought the mosaic from the farmer and sent it to Berlin. Five years later, an excavation team led by Humann began digging on the castle mountain. After completing their work in 1886, they took the valuable mosaic from the Zeus temple back to Germany. It can be seen today at the Pergamon Museum in East Berlin.

History

The earliest known mention of Pergamon dates from 399 BC when the town was in Persian hands. Pergamon reached its importance during the conquest of western Asia Minor by ALEXANDER THE GREAT, when Alexander's general LYSIMACHUS appropriated 9000 talents (£35 million today) for his own personal use. Lysimachus stored the treasure at Pergamon, guarded by the eunuch PHILETAIRUS. The faithless guard asked the Syrian king SELEUCUS for aid. Lysimachus was killed in battle, but a siege of the town was unsuccessful, giving Philetairus possession of the treasure. By making alliances with his neighbours, shrewd maneuvers and generous gifts, he was able to consolidate his

position and pass the fortune on to his adopted son EUMENES who defeated the Syrians at Sardes (262 BC) and extended his realm.
Eumenes' nephew and heir ATTALOS I defeated the Celts in a battle at the Kaikos springs in 230 BC.

After the victory Attalos assumed the title of king. His fame spread throughout the Greek world. But he also established contacts with the rising Roman power in the Mediterranean. He beautified the town with construction of a library and the Temple of Athena.

Under Attalos' son, EUMENES II, Pergamon allied itself with Rome. With the aid of his powerful new ally, the Syrians were defeated in the Battle of Magnesia (Manisa, 190 BC). The Romans (divide and conquer!) turned most of the region over to Eumenes, their man in Asia Minor.

Eumenes II celebrated himself as the town's benefactor. During his reign the acropolis was given a secure town wall, a Gymnasion was built, and the Theatre Street laid from the Lower Agora to the Altar of Zeus .

After his death - his son was only 12 years old - the king's brother (an experienced general) assumed the throne. By a fortunate turn of events, he was able to defeat the Bithynian king PRUSIAS who agreed to peace after hard bargaining.

How Attalos Changed Fate

The Gauls, originally hired as mercenaries, had settled around the castle. They would knock on the gate annually to demand a tribute, until the king decided he had had enough. After taking heavy losses from the fights in the Kaikos Valley, the Pergamon army was beginning to disband. Taking the initiative, Attalos ordered the slaughter of a sacrificial animal, upon whose liver the word "Nike" (Victory) could be plainly seen. Assured of the blessings of the Gods, Pergamon's forces regrouped and - although outnumbered - sent the Gauls into flight. Evil tongues have claimed that the king aided the gods' judgement by writing the word backward on his signet ring and pressing it against the animal's liver at an opportune moment.

The last King of Pergamon, Attalos III, was one of a kind. He was very unpopular, particularly as he rarely left his palace, preferring to spend his time studying poisonous plants. He would conduct his tests on convicts. Additionally he suffered from persecution mania: he was always afraid of being poisoned and he armed himself with a battery of antidotes. When his lovely wife and his mother died in quick succession, it broke his heart. In his last will and testament, he gave his entire realm to Rome!

Under the Roman emperors Vespasian, Trajan, and particularly Hadrian, Asclepieion became one of the most famous spas in the ancient world. The town profited enormously, growing to a population of 150,000 along the plain. Pergamon was abandoned after an invasion by the Goths in 262 AD.

Information: Turizm Bürosu, Zafer Mah., İzmir Cad. 54, tel. 1862

Telephone Area Code: 5411

Coming - Going: Buses to İzmir (Note, the last bus departs at 18:00 h) and Bursa, plus minibuses to Ayvalık and Dikili (the last bus to Ayvalık leaves at 15:00 h!).

Shopping: There are dozens of carpet shops along the main road. Bergama is one of the best known carpet regions in Turkey. However, the best specimens are sold in İstanbul or Europe (made to order).

Festivals: **Bergama Festival** in Asclepieion (early June). A pop music festival with Turkish stars. **International Bergama Fair** (6 - 8th June).

A Night's Rest

Tusan Bergama Motel, Bergama - İzmir Yolu (crossroads), double £12. Good standards, best address, 6 km from town, restaurant, bar, Tel 1173.

Park Oteli, İzmir Cad., double £5. Partially torn down, very simple, not for everyone, tel. 1246.

Balay Otel, Bankalar Cad., £1.60 per person, simple, but clean, bath down the hall.

CAMPING: **Cleopatra Güzellik**, 2 guests £2.60, 3 km west of town. Poplar trees provide shade, simple sanitation, swimming pool, a few electric sockets. Small bungalows for rent (£5 double), tel. 1167.

FOOD: **Kardeşler Restoran**, Uzun Çarsı Caddesi. Good Turkish food.

Sights

Acropolis

Begin your tour of Bergama at the top of the castle hill. A visit to the acropolis is worthwhile if only to read the plaques with interesting information about all the major buildings (including sketches of the original appearance). From the **parking lot** (1) a ramp leads to the **Castle Gate** (3), of which little remains. Ruins of the town wall give a good impression of the former size. En route to the town gate, be sure to have a look at the ruins of the **Heroon** (2), a cult building in honour of the Pergamon kings. During the Roman era the interior is said to have been covered with white marble.

BORN OF NECESSITY - PARCHMENT!

When the Pergamon Library began to challenge even the great Library of Alexandria, the Egyptian king simply prohibited the export of papyrus. The Pergamese recalled the ancient Ionian art of making paper from animal skins (parchment!). The skins, however, were thicker than paper and difficult to roll. For this reason they were cut and bound within a leather cover as a book.

The extensive collection was later given by MARK ANTHONY to CLEOPATRA and shipped to Alexandria. Unfortunately it was all lost in the 7th century AD when the Caliph OMAR had it burned as "heretical".

On the left behind the entrance gate is the **Sacred Athena District** (4), which was enclosed on three sides by a double row of columns. The temple of Athena, built at the time of PHILETAIRUS, was in the centre of the district. The structure was flanked by six columns along its width and ten columns along its length. In the sacred district (*Temenos*) in front of the temple were a number of statues, many of which depicted the battle with the Gauls. The two rows of columns were richly decorated with weapons seized in battle. From the upper level of the north terrace you could reach the **library** (5) which is not very impressive looking at the moment, but is due for restoration by a German team as soon as the work on Trajan's Temple is completed. The great Pergamon Library, built during the reign of EUMENES II, was said to contain 200,000 books. To protect against moisture, the rooms were paneled with expensive wood. The large *Reading Room* (14 by 16 m) was probably over 5 m high and boasted a 4.5 m tall statue of Athena.

To the right of the path are the ruins of at least four **palaces** (6). They were simple buildings with a courtyard surrounded by a row of columns (peristyle). Each palace had its own cistern, the largest of which is still intact across from Trajan's Temple.

Across from the cistern is **Trajan's Temple** (7), one of the most interesting structures, currently undergoing restoration by a German team. The temple stood within a huge temenos (temple district), which like the Sacred Athena District, was surrounded on three sides by a double row of columns. Nine Corinthian columns have been restored along the northern colonnade. The actual temple boasted six columns along its width and ten Corinthian columns along its length, each 18 m tall! Reconstruction of the outer stairway is planned on the south side. After the restoration of Trajan's Temple is completed, it should be the main attraction of the castle mountain.

Following the marked path, we come to the northeast corner of the castle mountain. Inside the wall, you can see the **arsenal** (8), five long barracks in which lead balls were unearthed.

Through a hole in the wall you can walk out onto a small outcropping from where you have an excellent view of the **Northeast Wall**, which even today boasts 32 courses of stone. In the *Selinus Valley* are the ruins of a **Roman aqueduct**, part of the town's extensive water supply-system. The water was transported from *Madra - Dag* 45 km north of Pergamon through a triple-layer system of clay pipes made of 240,000 individual parts. The water flowed into a chamber on a neighbouring hill. From there it reached the mountain via a pressurized lead pipe (up to 300 psi). On the last rise, an elevation difference of 200m had to be overcome. And all that worked without the use of a single pump!

Entrance to the **theatre** (9) is from the theatre terrace. The Greek theatre was in the centre of town. All the other buildings on the castle hill were grouped around this cultural and social centre. 87 rows of seats rise from the theatre gallery on a 50 m incline. The royal box made of marble was located in the centre above the first side row. The other 10,000 seats were made of simple andesite. During the Greek era, the stage was made completely of wood and

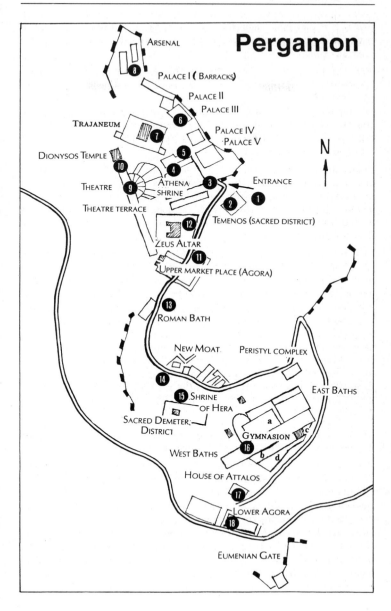

Pergamon

ARSENAL

PALACE I (BARRACKS)

PALACE II
PALACE III

TRAJANEUM

PALACE IV
PALACE V

N

DIONYSOS TEMPLE

ENTRANCE

THEATRE

ATHENA
SHRINE

THEATRE TERRACE

TEMENOS (SACRED DISTRICT)

ZEUS ALTAR

UPPER MARKET PLACE (AGORA)

ROMAN BATH

NEW MOAT

PERISTYL COMPLEX

EAST BATHS

SHRINE
OF HERA

SACRED DEMETER
DISTRICT

a

GYMNASION c

WEST BATHS

b d

HOUSE OF ATTALOS

LOWER AGORA

EUMENIAN GATE

erected only during the festival. At other times it was dismantled to reveal the **Dionysos Temple** (10). This small temple dominated the entire theatre terrace. Several of the long column drums and capitals are still intact.

The 250 m long theatre terrace was the shopping street and promenade of ancient Pergamon. The extreme slope required construction of a 12 m (three-story) high supporting wall crowned by a continuous hall of columns. Both sides of the street were occupied by shops and stands, a forerunner of the modern bazaar. At the southern end of the terrace was the **Upper Agora** (11), Pergamon's market place, surrounded by a hall of columns.

Below the market, two pine trees mark the location of the **Altars of Zeus** (12). Although only the foundations of the huge temple (34 x 34 m) remain, the spot invites one to rest. Shade from the two trees, combined with a sea breeze, which picks up over the hill, adds to the enchantment of this grove. The altar itself can be seen today in East Berlin's Pergamon Museum.

Follow the signs downhill along the well-preserved ancient road past the ruins of a **Roman bath** (13) and past the **New Moat** (14), whose most interesting parts can only be seen through a heavy iron gate. The upper (western) side of the moat forms the **Small Gymnasion**, consisting of a bath, a semi-circular Odeon and the Marble Hall (on the right). The Marble Hall was decorated with a statue of its founder, 18 reliefs and a floor mosaic. The entire complex probably belonged to a wealthy cult organization which used it for parties and entertainment. To the east are two small hot food stalls, and a store for oil and wine, recognizable by the semi-circular holes for the clay jugs. Beyond was the Podium Hall (24 x 10 m) and its entrance hall. The Dionysus Cult probably met here. The room was large enough for 70 people.

Participants at cult events sat around on pedestals facing the centre, and enjoyed the meals placed before them.

Behind the moat, the marked path moves off the ancient road and downhill to the large Gymnasion in the Demeter District. The **Sacred Demeter District** (15) was a 100-by-45 m terrace. The nine levels of seating had room for 1000 people. The entire district probably dates back to the time of the town's founding by PHILETAIRUS.

Here the *Eleusinian Mysteries* were introduced, which in Pergamon rivaled the Cult of Olympia. The primary force was seen as Hades, the underworld. An extremely formal and secret ritual was said to insure a better life after death.

The Demeter District is set across from the **Great Gymnasion** (16). The huge complex was set upon three terraces on the slope. The upper terrace, 36 m above the lowest, was closed to children under the age of 16. The middle was reserved for children 10 - 15 years of age, while the lower was a playground for smaller children. The Upper Gymnasion (16a) was the prettiest: 107 by 90 m, surrounded by a two-story column hall on three sides. It served as the palaestra for wrestling matches. There were baths on both sides of the palaestra. This is where the Latin phrase "*mens sana in corpore sano*" (a healthy mind in a healthy body) acquired true meaning. Each morning the boys would engage in running and exercises before bathing, and then turn to their lessons in philosophy, literature, mathematics and biology.

On the lowest floor of the **Middle Terrace** (16b) was a 210 m-long race track called the Basement Stadium which is no longer roofed. It was relatively narrow, and used for competitions. Via a completely intact roofed circular stairway, you can climb up to a point outside the town wall. To the east is the large **Town Fountain** (16c), and further west the triangular **Boys' Gymnasion** (16d), whose south side has collapsed. We now continue along the ancient road to the lower town.

There are few remains of the large **Lower Agora** (18). The grounds are overgrown and covered with Byzantine graves. Most interesting is the **House of Attalos** (17), a typical peristyle building. Further below, a good distance across the approach road, are the sparse ruins of the Eumenian Gate.

OPEN: 9:00 - 17:00 h (admission: £0.45).

Kızıl Avlu

Our next stop is Kızıl Avlu, the red hall, a monumental building you can't miss, directly on the road from Bergama to the acropolis. The tremendous brick ruin (58 x 26 m) was built by Emperor HADRIAN (2nd century AD) and was probably raised in honour of the Egyptian god Serapis. The lower portion was originally faced with marble and graced with a 12 m tall, colossal statue of the god. During the Byzantine era the hall was converted to a triple-aisle Basilica of St. John boasting an apse. The Arabs took down part of the building. Still intact are the two long pipes which channeled water from the Selinus River underneath the yard.

Archaeological Museum

The pride of the house are the Corinthian capitals. In the front yard are a marble statue from Pitane, a colossal statue of Hadrian from the Library at Asclepieion, busts of Socrates, Zeus, Vespasian, and Caracalla, an Aphrodite statue from Myrina and a splendid mosaic with a Medusa head. We particularly liked the three bronze statues from Asclepieion. And be sure to take a look at the model of the Zeus altar.

OPEN: 8:30 - 12:00 h and 13:00 - 17:30 h. Admission £0.50.

Asclepieion

West of Bergama, surrounded by military bases, is a field of ruins extensively explored by a team of German archaeologists. Asclepieion was one of the most famous spas of the antique world.

ASCLEPIUS

Originally he was a Greek doctor who served in Agamemnon's army during the Trojan War. According to legend he was granted a place among the gods on Mount Olympus after his death. His cult spread quickly, and at its peak boasted 200 shrines. The most famous was at Epidaurus, from where a man named ARCHIAS, after receiving treatment for a broken bone, brought the cult to Pergamon (4th century BC).

The methods of healing practised in Pergamon and elsewhere were a mixture of irrational and practical elements. The main portion of the treatment was incubation, sleep in the temple. This temple sleep was used to make a diagnosis. Asclepius would appear in the patients' dreams and prescribe treatment. But dreams, as we all know, can be confusing. Priests were employed to interpret the dreams. The fact is that the doctors practising at Asclepieion made a diagnosis. Their success rate was great, if we are to believe the sacred writings, even though an occasional fatality occurred.

The treatment usually consisted of a diet, baths, and exercises. Occasionally the gods demanded drastic treatment such as the drinking of diluted hemlock juice or chalk paste.

THE PATIENT ARISTIDES

Aristides, famous around town as an idler, was ordered by the gods on a cold winter night to smear himself with clay and run around the temple three times. Then he was told to wash off the clay at the ice cold Sacred Spring. While he, sick as he was, made it through the ordeal, the two friends who accompanied him through the treatment quickly gave up. The first gave up immediately. The other suffered a cramp on the second lap and had to be carried into the temple by four stout men.

From the entrance we cross the **Sacred Road** into the actual building complex. The Sacred Road is a colonnade, 18 m wide and several hundred metres long. A number of well-preserved column stumps can be seen on both sides. It ended at a large **Festival Square**, enclosed on three sides by columned halls and on the fourth by a gate, adjoining the Propylaeum. This is where new patients were ceremoniously received.

Via a stairway we arrive at **Asclepieion's Square** (120 x 92 m), which in its present form dates from the reign of HADRIAN (1st century AD).

To the right of the entrance stood the library. Today it is closed off with barbed wire and overgrown with weeds. In a niche here stood the great *Statue of Hadrian*, which you can see today in the Archaeological Museum. The splendid North Gallery stretches 120 m from the library to the theatre. The column hall was almost 10 m high. More than 20 columns have been restored, verifying the impressive size of the facility. In the northwest corner is the equally well-preserved theatre which could seat an audience of 4000. The theatre plays were used to cheer up the patients.

The adjoining West Gallery is badly damaged. The South Gallery (probably two stories tall) is completely destroyed. In the corner between them were toilets with running water.

After the Propylaeum on the left is the temple of ZEUS-ASCLEPIUS, the main temple in the district. This site is also closed because of danger from falling rubble. The large round building next door, the **Temple of Telesphoros**, is open to the public. The well preserved structure has two floors. In the cellar are three concentric rows of columns into which tubs were built. A stairway leads to the ground floor with its six semi-circular niches which once contained statues. The entire building was probably used by patients to avoid the sun or rain.

An underground passage leads from the Temple of Telesphoros to the Sacred Well. The passageway is still intact. Ghostly light filters down through holes, which can be closed. There is a dispute among experts as to whether the passage served a function in local rituals.

The centre of the entire complex was the **Sacred Well**. Recent studies, however, show that the slightly radioactive water has no healing quality. A second well, still faced with marble, is near the theatre. Take a drink.

MANİSA (pop. 110,000)

A lively provincial capital located between the foot of the Manisa Dağları (known as Sipylos in ancient times) and the Gediz River, which winds north of town through the fertile plain.

Manisa is just 40 km northeast of İzmir, but separated by a steep 675 m pass from the city. Few tourists find their way here. The local people are curious, interested, and helpful. Particularly friendly are the employees at the Tourist Information Office, who are ready to offer you tea and helpful hints.

History

HOMER tells that the Magnesians returning from the Trojan War founded two towns in the region: Magnesia at the Maeander (near Aydın) and Magnesia at the Sipylos (Manisa, 12th century BC). In the following years the Hitittes and then the Phrygians influenced the region. In the 7th century BC the Lydians took over the small settlement. But the unfortunate Lydian King CROESUS lost his realm - including Magnesia - to the Persians. The town became a toy for the superpowers. ALEXANDER THE GREAT marched into town after the Persian satrap surrendered without a fight.

In 190 BC the big Battle of Magnesia was fought between the rising Romans and Syria's King ANTIOCHUS III. The King of Pergamon and his cavalry provided the strategic edge for Rome. The Romans showed their appreciation by giving Manisa to Pergamon. But the Romans returned. In 133 BC the last King of Pergamon willed his entire kingdom over to Rome. Magnesia experienced its first golden age.

Neglected during the Byzantine era, the town was still able to resist the Arabs. After the fall of Constantinople to the crusaders, the Byzantine emperor JOHN DUKAS III fled here, making Manisa the capital of his greatly reduced Byzantine empire. When the Byzantine emperor returned to Constantinople, Manisa was lost to the Seljuk Duke SARUHAN BEY.

The Ottomans took the town in 1390. The peaceful and hard-working people of predominantly Greek origin were treated justly. This is where numerous Ottoman princes gathered experience before moving on to high politics in the capital. They remembered the town of their youth by sending generous donations, giving Manisa a second golden age in the 15th and 16th centuries.

Great bravery was demonstrated by the citizens in 1922, when they prevented the spread of fires set by the retreating Greek army. The fire was not permitted to engulf the mosques or most of the old buildings and so the old town structure was preserved.

INFORMATION: Doğu Caddesi 14, 3. Stock. English and French spoken, excellent advice, tel. 2541.

TELEPHONE AREA CODE: 5511

COMING - GOING: Manisa is on Route 15 from İzmir to Balıkesir and Bursa. There are **buses** every 15 minutes from İzmir (£0.45) over the pass where you'll see lovely mountain forests and tremendous views. Several buses daily to İzmir, Balikesir/Bursa, Afyon and Denizli.
Minibuses to Sardes and on to Salihli and Kula (see Sardes).
Rail connections to İzmir, Balıkesir and Afyon (several times daily). The railway station is 1 km north of town.

SHOPPING: Best on Murat Caddesi, where a market is held every Thursday. The lively, crowded, but unspoiled bazaar spreads for one kilometre east of Murat Mosque.

MEETING PLACE: The new, well-kept park on Doğu Caddesi. Still under construction in 1986 (pavilions, shady trees, lovely mosaics).

FESTIVAL

When AYŞE HAFSA SULTAN, the patroness of the sultan's Mosque and wife of sultan SELIM, fell ill one day, there was nobody in İstanbul who could help her. MERKEZ EFENDI, head of the hospital in the sultan Mosque Complex (which she also founded), treated her with a special syrup, *Mesir-Paste*, and brought about a cure. Ayşe Hafsa sultan was so pleased that she ordered the sultan Mosque to distribute this wonder paste annually among the people. This event is held every year at the end of April. The muezzin, dressed in his best robes and turban, throws candy filled with the syrup to the crowds. If you manage to get and eat one of these candies, you will be spared from illness, insect and snake bites for the coming year.

A NIGHT'S REST

Arma Oteli, Doğu Caddesi 14, double £11. Rooms furnished accordingly. Most rooms have showers and warm water. Recommended by the Tourist Information Office, tel. 1980 - 6290.

Günaydın Oteli, Sinema Park Caddesi 21, double £5. For the price you would expect more than a simple bed and dirty showers in the hall! tel. 2095.

Atlas Oteli: Dumlupğnar Caddesi 21, double £2 per person. Simple furnishings in keeping with the price, showers in the hall, friendly service, quiet. Also recommended by the Tourist Information Office. tel. 20 95.

FOOD

Safek Kebap Salonu on Cumhuriyet Caddesi below Doğu Caddesi. A simple kebap restaurant (lamb with garnishings), pleasant atmosphere, tender Şiş Kebap.

Şehir Restaurant near Fatih Park. Luxury restaurant with first class service and prices to match.

Sights

Murat-Mosque: The Murat-Mosque (*Muradiye Camii*) was built by the architect SINAN, at the command of sultan MURAT III, in 1583-1585. Most noticeable is the comforting brown colour of the walls and dome. As the muezzin explained (he kindly showed us the entire complex), 12 kilos of gold were used in the ornamentation. The *mosaics* and the shimmering green and blue *glass windows* are masterpieces made in İznik. Take a close look at the richly decorated mihrab and the costly, well-kept carpets. The front garden was lusciously green, despite the tremendous heat. The Ottoman tradition really shows here!

Manisa Museum: The *local museum* is in the kitchen for the needy and the medrese of the Murat Mosque. The *Archaeological Department* in the former charity kitchen features some exceptional finds from the region including mosaics from Sardes, statues, jugs, jewelry and tombstones dating from the Hittite, Greek, Roman and Byzantine eras. The oldest statue dates from about 3000 BC!

The *Ethnological Department* is located in the theological school (medrese). Of special interest are the well preserved antique carpets, including examples from Kula and Gördes (17th and 18th centuries). Be sure not to miss the caftans or the Koran books made with loving care. There is also a small weapons collection.

Oᴘᴇɴ: Tues - Sun 9:00 - 12:00 h and 13:00 - 17:00 h, admission £0.30.

Great Mosque (Ulu Camii): The stocky building with a minaret erected in 1366 is on a slope of the Syphilos, accessible via a stairway from the sultan Mosque and the Murat Mosque. It was built on the foundations of a Byzantine church whose ruins were fitted into the arcade (ancient columns with Byzantine capitals). The frescos inside are exceptional.

Sultan Mosque (*Sultan Camii*): The complex across from the Murat Mosque, consisting of a mosque, hospital, bath, charity kitchen and Koran school, was donated by Aʏşᴇ Hᴀᴛɪᴄᴇ, wife of sultan Sᴇʟɪᴍ I and mother of the great sultan Sᴜ̈ʟᴇʏᴍᴀɴ I. Especially nice are the two large minarets, the entrance hall with five pointed domes and the interior of the prayer niche. The annual Mesir Festival is held here.

Tomb of Saruhan Bey: Near the main square with the sultan and Murat Mosques is the tomb of Sᴀʀᴜʜᴀɴ Bᴇʏ (Saruhan Bey Türbesi) dating from 1348. Saruhan Bey conquered the town in 1313 making it the capital of his Seljuk principality which was absorbed by the Ottomans in 1390.

Tʜᴇ Tᴀʀᴢᴀɴ ᴏғ Mᴀɴɪsᴀ

His name was Aʜᴍᴇᴅᴅɪɴ Cᴀʀʟᴀᴋ and he was born in the then peaceful city of Bagdad. As a devout Muslim he fought in WW I against the British. In the War of Independence against the Greeks he was awarded the Independence Medal. After the war he settled in Manisa where he was quickly noticed because of his athletic build. He was not only the first jogger in Manisa, he was also one of the best mountain climbers in Turkey. When the "Tarzan of Manisa" died in 1963, the Manisa Tourist Association erected a bust in his honour.

Around Manisa

Syphilos National Park (*Spil Dagi Milli Parkı*): Syphilos National Park, surrounding Syphilos Mountain (1570 m), is a wonderful spot for hiking and camping. A lake, extensive forests, and a wealth of flora and fauna as well as cool, green valleys, invite you to stay a while. The forest consists of groves of olive trees on the slopes above Manisa; pine and oak trees are found in the backlands. It is said that the tulips in the sultans' gardens were imported from Syphilos. The fauna includes falcons, eagles, hawks, wolves, bear and jackal.

The main entrance to the park is 24 km south of Manisa on E 23. Taxi and dolmuş drivers know the way. There are two cafés there. A word about *camping*. A National Park warden informed us that it is officially prohibited, but tolerated if the visitors behave properly.

Relief of Cybele: About 7 km east of Manisa, on the road to Turgutlu, Sardes and Salihli, is a Hittite rock relief dating from about 2000 BC. Stop by a pond called Akpınar on the left side of the road and climb about 200 m steeply uphill. In a niche you can just discern the relief of a woman. It is assumed that this is a depiction of the Mother Goddess CYBELE who from this spot has a view of the Gediz Valley which she blessed with fertility.

Head of Niobe: To reach the rock relief, follow the İzmir Caddesi a kilometre west to a stream. Now climb up the hill on the left to a rock which greatly resembles a woman's head.

NIOBE

According to legend, NIOBE, mother of twelve, made fun of the goddess LETO, who only had two children, APOLLO and ARTEMIS. Apollo and Artemis took revenge in the name of their mother by killing all of Niobe's children. Thereafter her pain was so great that she asked ZEUS to turn her to stone.

Kula: A traditional village about 110 km east of Manisa on E 23 towards Afyon. Lovely wooden buildings, interesting shops, well-known carpet makers.

A connoisseur smoking his waterpipe in a café

Sardes

The ruins of the ancient town are near the two villages of Sart Mustafa (Gymnasion and Synagogue) and Sart (Artemis Temple) set in unspoiled scenic hills.

Both the Artemis Temple and the Gymnasion are enchanting, perhaps because, unlike in Pergamon or Ephesus, you can be alone with nature and your thoughts. You are clearly in the midst of an epoch long past. The Artemis Temple receives few visitors, despite its large parking lot.

History

The early history of Sardes is clouded with legend and mythology. The castle hill above the Artemis Temple was probably settled in the 12th century BC. The earliest known reference dates from the reign of King GYGES (680 - 652 BC), who founded the Mermnadian dynasty, making Lydia a great empire.

Gyges and his descendants expanded their military strength and economic power. The realm profited from its control of major trading routes and gold mined from the Paktolos River (*Sart Çayı*).

The Lydians invented the minting of coinage. The coins were stamped pieces of ore containing an officially guaranteed weight. Originally they were made of gold and silver alloys known as "electrum"; later pure gold and silver were also used. Lydians are also credited with the invention of dice and ball games.

The Lydian empire reached its height during the reign of its last ruler CROESUS whose wealth was legendary. After a shrewd attack, Croesus was defeated by the Persian king CYRUS II in 546 BC. Sardes was conquered and the Lydian region became an important outpost of the Persian empire. The beginning of the famous Persian Royal Road, providing paved access to the heart of the Persian empire all the way to Susa and Persepolis, was here. Every 5 km were rest houses, watch towers, horse stations. Well-trained messenger riders changed horses every four hours, enabling news to travel at a speed of 150 km per day! Still it could take weeks before a message from Sardes reached Persia.

The Persians managed to hold the town until the arrival of ALEXANDER in 334 BC. His descendants lost the town to Pergamon in 188 BC. In 133 BC the town passed to Rome along with the entire realm of Pergamon. In 17 AD it was destroyed by a tremendous earthquake. Reconstruction on a grand scale took place during the reign of TIBERIUS.

During the Byzantine era, Sardes was home to one of the first Christian communities. A number of fires during the early Middle Ages destroyed the ancient buildings.

GYGES, MIDAS, CROESUS AND HORRENDOUS LUCK!

The history of the Lydian empire is full of legends with one common denominator: the Lydians possessed endless luck.

GYGES, founder of the Mermnadian Dynasty, was originally the bodyguard of his predecessor CANDAULES. Perhaps he would have remained in this role if the king had not invited him to watch his wife during her evening toilet. Gyges was clumsy, however, and was discovered by the queen. What might have cost another man his head, was turned to his advantage: the queen asked the peeping Tom to kill Candaules, which he did. Gyges was crowned the new king and married the queen.

MIDAS was the Phrygian king who asked the gods to turn everything he touched into gold. The wish was granted. But then, every time the Phrygian tried to eat, he was forced to spit out a piece of 18 carat gold. After several days of fasting, he had turned everything to gold. The gods eventually heard the pleas of the starving man. Midas was told to wash his hands in the river Patoclus to remove the curse. And who managed to pick up all the gold dropped into the river? The Lydians, of course.

And then there was CROESUS. He consulted the Oracle at Delphi about his chances of success in an attack against Persia. Unfortunately he misjudged the oracle's advice: *"If you cross the border, a great empire will be destroyed!"* The Lydian set out and destroyed a great empire - his own. The Persian king ordered a large stake to be erected and had Croesus placed on top. But the fires were barely lit when the gods sent powerful rains. The Lydians were always lucky!

American archaeologists from Princeton University discovered the *Artemis Temple* in 1910. Teams from Harvard and Cornell Universities have been carrying out restoration since 1958. Some of the recent finds are on display at the Archaeological Museum in Manisa.

COMING - GOING: From İzmir get a **bus** toward Salihli, Alaşehir or Afyon and get off at Sart Mustafa. From Manisa, get a **minibus** toward Salihli. Heading back, stop a bus on the main road.
By Rail: The train station is in Sart Mustafa. Several trains daily to İzmir, but not every train stops in Sart!

Sights

Artemis Temple: A ten minute walk from the village of Sant Mustafa, through the village of Sart (remains from a dig). From far away you can see the archaeologists' storehouse and the over-sized parking lot. The temple was erected by CROESUS, destroyed by a Greek attack, and then rebuilt under ALEXANDER. The row of well-preserved columns along the east side (across from the entrance) provides a good impression of its former size. In fact, at 100 x 48 m, it was one of the four largest temples in Asia Minor. The two completely intact columns (each with a Roman and an Ionic capital) are both 17.3 m high.

Three periods of construction can be seen. During the first phase (4th century BC) a temple was built around the site of a more ancient Artemis altar (marked by a sign near the entrance). Not until the second phase (2nd century BC) was the tremendous row of columns erected (20 columns along its width and 8 along its length). The eight well-preserved columns on the east side date from this period. During the third phase of construction, under the Roman emperor ANTONIUS PIUS (2nd century AD), the temple was divided by a separating wall into two rooms: one for the worship of Artemis, the other dedicated to the empress FAUSTINA.

It is puzzling that several columns are completely intact, while others have completely disappeared. It is possible that this temple, like its counterpart in Didyma, was never completely finished.

Gymnasion and Synagogue: Although the well-restored Gymnasion complex is easy to spot on the road to İzmir, few tourists make a stop. The Gymnasion is a typical building dating from the late empire (3rd century BC). You approach the building from the entrance across a large lawn, the former palaestra, where you can see ruined columns. The marble court (Imperial Hall), 36 m wide, was rebuilt on a grand scale. The entrance is through a row of Corinthian columns. The exit is through an 8 m tall gate in the perhaps 25 m high monumental facade. Behind this is a well-preserved bath where you can recognize the basin and descending stairs, originally covered by a well-preserved column hall (50 x 50 m). The side rooms are equally well preserved and partially restored.

No less impressive is the *Jewish Synagogue* dating from the 1st century AD. The fine furnishings catch the eye more than its size. The many lovely mosaics are copies (the originals are in Manisa), but they are still worth a look! The square peristyle boasts a jug-like fountain in the centre surrounded by rows of columns. The columns are completely intact, but only a single capital remains. In the main hall, notice the two raised thrones with canopies, and the four out-standing mosaics featuring almost modern patterns (prisms). On the west side, four semi-circular rows of marble seats surround the sacrificial altar.

Continuing along the road toward Salihli, we see the ruins of a Roman stadium, an agora, a basilica, and a theatre.

Foça *(pop. 8000)*

On the peninsula, with its numerous small bays, you will encounter an upper level of touristic standards - measured by Turkish criteria. In the well protected harbour, once used by Phoenecian ships, simple fishing boats are berthed along-side luxurious holiday yachts.

Since the airport was relocated to the other side of İzmir the number of foreign visitors to Foça has declined. Club Méditerranée still holds the area in high esteem but the Club's guests usually stay on the Club grounds. Most of the visitors to Foça are either Turkish regulars or people in search of a reasonably quiet spot away from the bustle of the internationally famous holiday centres on the Aegean coastline.

Foça is located about 70 km northwest of İzmir. It was the site of ancient Phocaea which was founded in the eighth century BC by settlers from Teos. The Phoeceans were known for their extensive sea voyages. They ventured forth as far as the western Mediterranean where they founded Massilia, the present-day Marseille, in 600 BC. Many inhabitants fled Phocaea when it was conquered by the Persians in 540 BC. The town was later plundered by the Romans. In the eleventh century a branch of a Genoese trading company started quarrying alum here. Alum was a very sought-after substance in the Middle Ages; it was used for a variety of purposes e.g. as a dye for textiles, for the tanning of leather and to check bleeding (styptic pencil). Around 1550 the Genoese base was conquered by the Ottomans. Little is left to be seen of this eventful past - only a few wall remnants and the ruins of a thirteenth century Genoese fortress.

Foça is also called Eski Foça, Old Foça, as opposed to Yenifoça or New Foça. Yenifoça, built on the site of the repeatedly plundered ancient town of Phocaea, is located to the northeast of Foça. The quiet town of Yenifoça also lives on tourism but the beautiful beaches make up for that. Even though holiday villages have been built, you can still find simple and affordable hotels, pensions and camp sites.

The Turkish government has two military schools in Foça for land and sea service (Jendarma and Marines). That explains the numerous uniformed men in the streets (this is not valid for Yenifoça and the beaches - all men are civilians in bathing trunks).

TELEPHONE AREA CODE: 5431

INFORMATION: Turizm Bürosu at the entrance of town, Atatürk Mah., İlçe Girisi, tel. 1122.

COMING - GOING: Dolmuş or minibuses leave Konak Square in İzmir every hour. During the summer some buses run every 20 minutes, on weekends every 10 minutes.

FESTIVAL: Music, Folklore and Watersportsfestival, 20 - 22nd July.

A Night's Rest

Most of the hotels are in the upper price range. Smaller hotels can be found on quiet side streets.

Hotel Karacam: best lodgings in Foça, located on the coastal road. The hotel and grounds are appealing - genuine Turkish elegance. The rooms are large and light, almost luxurious. Café and restaurant. The prices are according to standard: during high season a single is £13, a double £18, 3-bed room £21. Showers/WC in all rooms, price includes breakfast. Address: Sahil Caddesi 7, tel. 1416.

Two additional middle class hotels are:
Hanedan Oteli, Büyük Deniz, Yalı Cad. 1, double £13, tel. 1579.
Sultan Otel, Özdere Köyü, double £12, tel. Gümüldurk 140.

Siren Pansyion: a comfortable, inexpensive pension on a side street off the beach road (sign). The owner is friendly and helpful and plans to increase the number of beds (13 at the present) by building onto the house (and not just by putting more beds in the rooms). Do-it-yourself kitchen, showers/WC in hall, breakfast available. The price for a bed is £2.30. Address: İsmet Paşa mahallesi 53 Sok. tel. 2443.

CAMPING: In Foça there is a large, overcrowded camp site which is not recommendable. The small space where you can put up tents in Yenifoça doesn't deserve to be called a camp site. Between Foça and Yenifoça there are numerous camp sites set in small bays. Here is the description of two of them:

Yonca Camping: About 9 km beyond Foça towards Yenifoça. This site has the best location - it is far below the road, has trees and a fairly long stretch of beach. However you can buy only only soft drinks and beer, and there are only a few simple and not too clean sanitary facilities. Prices: tent & people: £1.30, caravan & people: £2.30. The insolent employee at first named £1.30 as the admission price for swimming only, but then went down to £1.

Camping Imbat Obası: halfway between Foça and Yenifoça. A simple, shadeless site in one of the bays. Large restaurant (breakfast £0.65) and passable sanitary facilities. Prices: tent & people: £1.15, caravan £2.30, for £2.30 you can also rent a tent. 10 per cent reduction if you stay for more than one week. If you order fish you get a complimentary small bottle of Rakı (1988). Admission for swimming about £0.25.

Swimming

The beaches in Foça and Yenifoça are not the greatest: they are narrow, pebbly and, especially in Foça, overcrowded. Try the bays between the towns for an alternative. Many of them have been taken over by camp sites (admission is charged for swimming, see Camping) but some are still accessible free of charge (1988).

Around Foça

Yenifoça: The neat little town has 2000 inhabitants. The tourist crowds pass it by - some of the 200 hotel rooms are always available. The beaches are frequented mostly by people who are staying in the holiday villages nearby. Yenifoça has several minimarkets, a post office and a disco on the beach. The disco "Sev" is for couples only because the single male visitors caused too much trouble - disco fun Turkish style.

COMING - GOING: Good connections to Foça and back. At least one minibus per hour, in both directions.

A NIGHT'S REST

Palmiye Motel: Right on the beach promenade. The interior of the house, which is over 100 years old, was renovated a few years ago. There are leather lounge seats in the entrance hall and red and white tablecloths in the restaurant. The rooms are comfortably furnished in Turkish farmhouse style with showers/WC. One night incl. breakfast is about £5 per person. People travelling alone can stay in double or 3-bed rooms for the same price. English spoken. tel. 5434/6159.

Artun Motel: very quiet location about 150 m from the beach. The 2 to 4-bed rooms are large, have wall-to-wall carpeting and showers/WC. Mr. Artun, the proprietor, is very friendly and charges about £3.30 a night, per person. People travelling alone can stay in a 4-bed room for the same price since the motel is usually never booked up. Breakfast (extra) is served in a large day room. There is also a big balcony with a view of the sea and a refreshing breeze. tel. 5434/6436.

CAMPING: see Foça

FOOD: in a restaurant on the beach, of course. We recommend the **Can-Café** (good with a nice atmosphere) and the simpler **Sahin-Restaurant** (good).

SERVICE

Dinner time at the restaurant Sahin. The drought beer is already sitting in front of me, the food will arrive any second. The waiter serves my dish, shoots a quick glance at the beer and carries it off so swiftly that I don't even have time to object.

A minute later another beer is placed in front of me without explanation. After detailed inquiries I find out that, totally oblivious to me, a poor fly had come to death in my first beer.

Help us update

We've done our best to make this book as accurate and up-to-date as possible but travel developments are swift and things are always changing. We would greatly appreciate any contributions, suggestions, corrections, improvements or additions you may have for future editions.
Please write us:
Springfield Books Limited c/o Michael Muller, Norman Road, Denby Dale, Huddersfield HD8 8TH, West Yorkshire, England.

SOUTH AEGEAN AND LYCIA

This is the vacation spot in Turkey. Three international airports (İzmir, Dalaman, Antalya) funnel thousands of tourists here daily. The holiday slogan for this region is "Swimming and the culture of the ancient world".

The extremely popular village of Kuşadası is visited by 600 cruise ships a year. Marmaris is a town whose population increases tenfold in the summer. Bodrum with its crusader castle has the best surfing in Turkey. There are impressive ruins at Ephesus, but also at Priene and Milet and a huge temple at Didyma.

There are a lot of nice sandy beaches, many of which are crowded; others can be recommended, e.g. the Datça peninsula with Datça and ancient Knidos, Ören east of Bodrum, the Karaburun peninsula west of İzmir or Lake Köyceğiz.

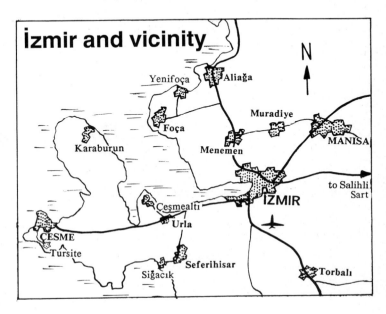

Things are quieter south of Fethiye. This is the beginning of Lycia, home of a puzzling people who left little other than tombs. The best rock necropolises can be found in Fethiye and Myra. Here too are ancient sites, including Xanthos and Phaselis, originally lovely fishing villages such as Kalkan or Kaş, and basically fantastic beaches like Ölü Deniz and Patara. The region is extremely fertile, wild, jagged and heavily forested. Many people, including Atatürk, consider it the most beautiful part of Turkey.

Now to the negative aspects: like nowhere else, tourism has left its mark. Kuşadası is over-built. Kemer, once praised as an example of positive tourism, has become one giant eye sore. Other towns, such as Bodrum and Marmaris, have lost their original appearance completely and look like all the other international tourist centres. Datça, Kalkan and Kaş, which were lovely and relatively unspoiled villages only a few years ago, have now joined the run on the money to be had from the tourists - the end of the race is not yet in sight. But long stretches of the coastline are sparsely populated and accessible only with difficulty or sometimes not at all. There are still hundreds of small bays that remain completely untouched making Lycia and the Southern Aegean still worth a visit.

İZMIR (pop. 1.500 000)

There are contradictory opinions about İzmir, Turkey's third largest city.

This is a city where unbearable heat mixes with dust and smog. A muggy wind carries the harbour smell through town. Noise from traffic jams mixes with the sound of jackhammers and sirens from police patrols and fire trucks. Beggars offer their outstretched hands and shoeshiners their services. It is easy to lose your way at night on the dimly-lit boulevards. Sometimes the city is hard to handle.

But then there is Smyrna, old İzmir! Smyrna figs, Smyrna carpets, the birthplace of HOMER, XENOPHANES, ANAXAGORAS and ARISTOTLE ONASSIS. It is a Greek city! Gavur İzmir, infidel İzmir, is what the Turks called world-famous Smyrna.

"Here the Greeks and Europeans rule. Of the 250,000 inhabitants, half are Orthodox, only a fourth revere the Koran, and the remainder are Shephardi, Armenian, Levantine and European", EWALD BANSE, ethnologist, wrote in 1915.

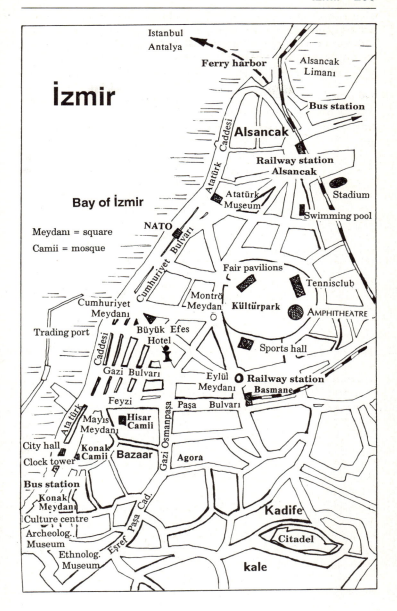

İzmir

Bay of İzmir

Meydanı = square

Camii = mosque

Istanbul
Antalya
Ferry harbor
Alsancak
Limanı
Bus station
Alsancak
Atatürk Caddesi
Railway station
Alsancak
Atatürk
Museum
Stadium
Swimming pool
NATO
Cumhuriyet Bulvarı
Fair pavilions
Tennisclub
Montrö
Meydan
Kültürpark
AMPHITHEATRE
Cumhuriyet
Meydanı
Büyük Efes
Hotel
Trading port
Caddesi
Sports hall
Gazi Bulvarı
Eylül
Meydanı
Railway station
Basmane
Feyzi
Paşa Bulvarı
Ata türk
Mayıs
Meydanı
Hisar
Camii
Gazi Osmanpaşa
City hall
Konak
Camii
Bazaar
Agora
Clock tower
Bus station
Konak
Meydanı
Culture centre
Kadife
Archeolog.
Museum
Eşref Paşa Cad.
Citadel
Ethnolog.
Museum
kale

Smyrna was the trading centre of the Levant and Europe's commercial base in Asia Minor. It was the western gate for the Ottoman Empire, where business boomed and fortunes were made. Lifestyles were comparable to Paris or Berlin during the Roaring Twenties.

Today İzmir is a very Turkish city. Smyrna is long forgotten; its priceless treasures are lost. The city still profits from its harbour, the second-largest in Turkey. The city is growing like a cancerous tumour, stretching 30 km along the *İzmir Körfezi*, the 54 km long and 24 km wide Gulf of Izmir.

Here is NATO's southeastern headquarter, from where the Mediterranean Sixth Fleet receives its commands. Each year Turkey's largest industrial fair is held in the Cultural Park. Import/Export are still the magic words of İzmir's success, along with cheap labour. In the belt of slums, living in huts surrounding the refineries, paperworks, and chemical plants, a new generation of beggars and day labourers is raised. Then there are others, who in the fashionable restaurants on the Kordon, enjoy a meal costing the equivalent of a month's pay for the average worker.

İzmir shows its true face. It is, in short, a modern Turkish city. Missing, however, are the fairytale pretenses of İstanbul, the pomp of Ankara and the pleasant climate of Antalya. Maybe that is a reason to visit İzmir.

History

The city traces its roots back to the third millennium BC. There is archaeological evidence that Smyrna was founded as an Aelian settlement on Bayraklı Hill, 4 km northeast of the present town centre (around 1100 BC). The name was derived from the myrrh growing there at the time. In the eighth century BC (while Homer lived here), Ionian Greeks from Kolophon took the town. In 575 BC, Lydians from Sardes captured the town and destroyed it.

Motivated by a dream, ALEXANDER THE GREAT ordered his generals, LYSIMACHOS and ANTIGONOS, to build a new town on Pagus Hill. They founded the *Kadifekale* (Satin Castle) at the top of the İzmir residential hill.

Under Greek and later Roman rule (from 27 AD onward), Smyrna was one of the greatest trading centres in the Mediterranean region. In the second century AD the population was over 100,000! During the seventh century, its Byzantine defenders withstood an Arabian siege. In the two succeeding centuries Smyrna was the bone of contention between the Seljuks and the crusaders, changing hands repeatedly. After a Mongol attack (1403) the town passed permanently into Ottoman hands under MEHMET. The name Smyrna was changed to İzmir. The Turks were able to defend the trading port successfully from Venetian attacks.

Ottoman domination of the town remained uncontested after the fall of the Venetian empire, and although it suffered from earthquakes, the plague and fires, it still remained the Ottoman Empire's primary trading port to the west; a trend which increased momentum with each rebuilding. In 1886 the *Gediz* River was redirected into a new riverbed, protecting the port from silt deposits.

An additional test was faced by İzmir at the beginning of this century. After a defeat in the Greek-Turkish War, the Treaty of Sèvres (1920) called for transfer of the town to Greece. However, an army of National Liberation under ATATÜRK reconquered the town on the 11 of September, 1922. Over 100,000 Greek and Armenian residents fled the city in panic, forcing their way aboard ships. Armenian commando units set fires to cover the withdrawal and a raging fire developed in the north of town consuming 30,000 buildings.

The Culture Park was built on the rubble of the Greek Quarter. In the second half of this century İzmir experienced new growth as industrial complexes were established in the north of town.

INFORMATION: Gazi Osmanpaşa Bulvarı 116 (in a passage of shops under Büyük Efes Hotel). A lot of info, at least four employees (friendly and well informed, speak English and French), tel. 14 21 47.

TELEPHONE AREA CODE: 51

COMING - GOING: Alsancak is the largest bus station from which **buses** and **minibuses** depart several times daily to all major Turkish cities and the surrounding region. A taxi from the bus station into town should cost at most £1.

By Local Bus: Warning, the local buses to Çeşme and Karaburun Peninsula no longer depart from Konak Square, having moved to Fahrettin Altay Meydanı, 4 km to the west. Only the downtown buses depart from Konak Square. Route 33 goes to Pagus Hill. Route 50 runs along the Kordon to the bus station. İzmir has an excellent bus system; waits are rarely more than 10 minutes.

By Rail: Alsancak Railway Station serves local routes. Trains to Aydin or Afyon (the two main lines) depart from Basmane Station. Both stations have seen better days.

By Air: The new Cumaovası Airport, 20 km south of town, opened in 1987. It has a number of advantages over the former Çiğli Airport: unlike its predecessor, it is not in a closed military region. The new airport is therefore accessible by private car, train and bus. Daily flights to Ankara, Adana, İstanbul and Dyarbakır. Several flights weekly to Malatya, Samsun, Sivas, Erzurum and Antalya. International charter flights usually depart from Dalaman Airport near Fethiye.

By Ship: Three times weekly, a Turkish Maritime Lines ship docks here on the İstanbul-Antalya route (toward İstanbul Tues, Thurs, Sun; toward Antalya Mon, Wed, Fri). Local ferries depart from Alsancak Limanı. The İzmir Körfezi is ferried every 20 minutes to Karsiyaka. A steamer departs Sundays from Konak Square to Urla (£0.20).

BOOK STORES: **Haşet Kitabevi**, Cumhuriyet Bulvarı 143/F, tel. 21 42 64. **NET-Bookstore**, a few steps further, across from the university.

CAR RENTAL: **Avis** on Şehit Nevres Bey Bulvarı 19/A, Alsancak, tel. 21 12 26. **Europcar** on Şehit Fehti Bey Cad. 122/F, tel. 25 64 98. **Hertz** on Cumhuriyet Bulvarı 123/1, tel. 21 70 02. and last not least **Budget** at Cumhuriyet Bulvarı 253/1, Alsancak, tel. 21 02 05.

EVENTS: İzmir does not have its own festival. The high point of the year is the Industrial Fair in early September. Cultural events are also planned to coincide with the fair.

MEETING PLACE: The Kordon with promenade and restaurants. The culture park with tea gardens and casinos (we recommend Göl Gazinosu by the pond), the luna park and the Kadifekale (especially on Sunday afternoons). The Atatürk Kültur Merkezi, İzmir's new culture centre at Konak Square. Open 8:30 - 17:30h, except Fridays and Sundays. Open evenings for special events (concerts, exhibitions). tel. 14 83 43. Ticket sales at the Karamürsel Store (rear passage way).

POST OFFICE: On Cumhuriyet Meydanı, including telegraph service.

TRAVEL AGENCIES:
MTIS (Milet Turizm Seyahat Acentası), Talatpasa Bulvarı 54. tel. 22 12 41. Day tours to Ephesus and Pergamon (£18).
Ramtur Turism Organization, Gazi Osmanpaşa Bulvarı 305. City tours for £7. Day trips to Pergamon, Ephesus, Priene-Milet-Didyma, Pamukkale (£18 to £30) tel. 14 70 65.
THY-Büro (Turkish Airlines), Gazi Osmanpaşa Bulvarı 112 (shopping centre under Büyük Efes Hotel). Thanks to a computer, you can book all Turkish flights (but no other airlines).
Yaşar Holding (Austrian Airlines Agent), Sehit Fethi Bey Caddesi 79 a, tel. 14 17 88.
Dutilh Tours Travel Tourist Transport (Swissair Agent), Cumhuriyet Meydanıel. 51-21 47 57.
Milet Riviera (Lufthansa Agent), Kızılay Caddesi 1 A, tel. 21 87 36.
Denizyolları Acentalığı, Yeniliman, Alsancak. Ship tickets and information on Turkish passenger ships, tel. 13 74 81.

TURKISH LANGUAGE CLASSES: Aegean University offers classes in Turkish. Ask in the "Tömer" (Turkish language department) on the campus of Eğe University.

TURKISH BATH: **Hoşgör** on Cumhuriyet Meydanı - 600 m behind Konak Square toward Çeşme and across from Kartas Lisesi - considered one of the best baths in all of Turkey. Open for women 13:00 - 17:00 h, for men before and after, open 6:00 - 20:00 h. **Hamam in "Büyük Efes Hotel"** is good and very expensive; also open to non-hotel guests. For details see "An Unusual Bathing Experience".

Shopping

Vakko, Atatürk Caddesi 226. The latest in clothing fads for the young people of İzmir. United Colours of Benetton and Lacoste, but cheaper than in Western Europe.

İzmir Bazaar: Stretching around Anafartaler Caddesi is one of Turkey's most beautiful bazaars. It thrives without neon lights and clean-swept streets. The shops are partly grouped according to merchandise, increasing both the competition and stress of the merchants. Bargaining, cursing and presentation are loud. Be sure to

Konak Square in the heart of İsmir

have a look in one of the workshops which are often right behind the sales stands. You are welcome everywhere!

Flea Market (Bitpazarı), 1369. Sok. Junk and second-hand goods are sold every day. Turkey is inexpensive and its flea markets are even more so.

İlhan Nargile İmalathanesi, Kızlarağası Karawanserai Z/15, tel. 14 02 79. The most famous manufacturer of waterpipes on the west coast. İlhan exports to Europe (i.e. France). The master pipe maker refuses to see his wares as decoration pieces. Each must be functional. He does not use plastic tubes, but rather real lamb leather. Without the middle man, the prices are cheap here, small pipes starting at £3.50. All sizes available. A visit, including the obligatory cup of tea and a chat (English), is well worth your while. The latest news: you'd better hurry if you want to visit the caravanserai because the building will soon be taken over by a hotel.

Haşet Kitapevi A.Ş., Cumhuriyet Bul. 143 (across from the University). A foreign (English, German, French) language bookstore. Available are travel guides and magazines (Rolling Stone and Melody Maker).

Karamürsel Department Store: Konak Square, one of the few real department stores in Turkey.

Döner Sermaye Müdürlüğü, (state owned souvenir shop) on Cumhuriyet Meydanı around the corner from Büyük Efes Hotel. Newly opened and just what you have been waiting for: a state-run souvenir shop with realistic prices but no bargaining.

A Night's Rest

Not that easy in İzmir, where real estate prices are sky-high. If you are short of cash, try around Basmane Station. Many pensions in the area have closed in recent years. Nobody knows what the future holds. Be sure to inspect the rooms and showers before accepting a room. The bad reputation of the area is legendary.

Filiz Pansiyon: a cheap pension with up to five beds per room. The house is built on a gentle slope and has a great breakfast terrace (sun and shade) and a marvelous view of St. John's Basilica and the sea. The young boss won't object to touring the discos in Kuşadası with you. The price is negotiable starting at £2 per person. Easy to find because it has signs posted. Address: Zafer Mah. Bademlik Nr. 10, tel. 1585.

Otel Soray, Anafartalar Cad. 635, double £5. Our cheapest recommendation (warmly recommended by the Information Office). Simple furnishings, but proper. Clean, friendly, tel. 13 69 46.

Otel Akgün, 1369 Sok. 64, double £5. We liked it, clean, cheap. tel. 13 55 63.

Sinlah Saray, 9 Eylül Meydani, double £5, showers down the hallway.

Özkaya Oteli, 1300 Sok. 8. Near the bazaar, showers/WC in the hallway. Lovely view of the town from the roof-top garden.

Antalya-Burdur Otel, 1396 Sok., double £5. Considered a hot tip. Clean with a roof-top restaurant. tel. 13 59 48.

Otel Bayburt, 1370 Sok. 1, double £7. A small, pleasant hotel near Basmane Station. A bit old fashioned but clean. People gather in the inner courtyard. Some rooms with shower/WC, tel. 12 20 13.

Otel Gar, 9 Eylül Meydani 787, double no bath £10, with shower £10.50, with bath £11.50. Very clean hotel, centrally located. tel. 25 45 45.

Atlas Oteli, Şair Eşref Bulvarı 1, double with bath £9, without bath £7. A pleasant hotel on a busy street. Rooms with shower/WC. Slow staff, clean, tel. 14 42 65.

Billur Oteli, Basmanı Meydanı 783, double £15. Popular among travellers. You have a nice view from the balconies over the station square, just a few metres from Culture Park, but loud. A great place for night people (open all night). Reasonably comfortable, tel. 13 62 50.

Otel Babadan, Gazi Osmanpaşa Bul. 50, double £17 (with breakfast). A bit small, tel. 13 94 40.

Otel Kaya, Gazi Osmanpaşa Bul. 45, double £23. Good location, showers, every comfort, carpets, and large closets. A nice reception hall and an adequate breakfast room.

Kismet Oteli, 1377 Sok. 9, double £32. Comfortable and air conditioned, tel. 21 70 50.

Büyük Efes Otel, Gazi Osmanpaşa Bul. 1, double £60. Hilton comfort, fairytale garden. İzmir's Number One, but not for long. Both a Hilton and a Sheraton are under construction. tel. 14 43 00.

CAMPING:

Mocamp Denizatş, a good camp ground in Gümüldür. The facility is part of the Denizatş Moteli, (double £23) the better of two motels in Gümüldür. Sanitary facilities are excellent, restaurant, mail service, disco adjoining. Carnival atmosphere, clean sandy beach.

BP-Mocamp İnciralti, like any BP-Mocamp. The site is 3 acres and very clean. Adequate shade from the trees. Mini market, restaurant and the unavoidable BP petrol station.

Food

İzmir's specialties include *Çipura* (gold bass) and *İzmir Köfte*, prepared with tomato sauce.

Klüb Orhan, 1469 Sok. 28. Excellent food, served with style, which you pay for. International and Turkish dishes. A club restaurant in Alsancak. Fish starts at £5.

Altav Lokalı, the most noticeable pub in İzmir, a pavilion, set over the water on pilings. The waiters wear sailor shirts, but are just as fast as their white-clad colleagues. The food and service is true poetry! Civilized prices (£6 for four courses, £5 for a juicy steak). You can select your meal from a menu (in English) or from the buffet. No charge for the sunset.

Deniz Restoran, Atatürk Cad. 188 B, tel. 22 06 01. Another first-class seafood restaurant on the Kordon, similar prices to above.
Other outstanding seafood restaurants can be found along Atatürk Caddesi. Same prices as at Altav.

Kordon Kebap Salonu, Atatürk Caddesi 150. A reasonably priced, but by no means cheap restaurant in a lovely location. This is the place to eat lamb. Şiş Kebap for just £1.60!
Other reasonable Kebapcis, Locantas and tea gardens around Basmane Station.

Tuborg Pilsen Beer Garden, Kadifekale. If you want a decent beer and a nice view, then come in the evening when the town lights up.

NIGHTLIFE AND DISCOS

Mogambo, Culture Park. Hottest disco in İzmir and best night club. tel. 25 54 88.

Regime, 1. Kordon (Atatürk Cad.). In 1986 it was officially termed the best discotheque in town.

Göl Gazinosu, Culture Park. Variety Program. Meals £10, tel. 13 99 22.

An Exceptional Bathing Experience In Hamam

One of İzmir's steep, ancient, stone stairways leads to what was once the main road along the Bay of İzmir. All traffic between Konkak and Çeşme funnelled through here before the shoreline was sacrificed for a new highway. Here it makes a bend leaving several of İzmir's old houses undisturbed. They seem like little lost toy houses compared to the new concrete apartment buildings. To the right a small shop displays its fruit and vegetables in the enormous heat. From here it is only a few steps into a tiny dead-end street where a narrow flight of stairs brings you to the entrance of a yellow-painted house.

8:00 - 12:00 h erkekler, 12:00 - 17:00 kadınlar, 18:00 - 22:00 h erkekler can be read on the sign next to the door, and above in plain red lettering on a white wooden plate: *HAMAM*. The quiet afternoon ends at this threshold. The door opens to lively hospitality. The air is warm and steamy, smelling of soap, moist wood, freshly bathed bodies, the clipclop of wooden bath shoes and the sound of many female voices. Fresh towels lie in large shelves on the opposite wall. The high-ceilinged, square entrance hall is encircled by a balustrade, behind which you can see into the upper, more private environs. A woman washes the lovely old tile floor. Another woman greets me with a smile and asks if I require a towel, soap or a ladle. She brings me a pair of wooden shoes and guides me to the dressing room separated by wooden walls from the hall. The room is lined with shelves and furnished with three large loungers. An old window with translucent glass and a deep sill is set in the wall.

I leave my valuables in a small locker at the desk, then dressed in just my slip I walk with my soap, washcloth and ladle into the front hall (covered halfway up with grey marble). In the back on the side are two marble loungers, in front four ladle spots are partitioned off. Daylight filters down from the top; it is pleasantly cool. Soapy water flows along channels in the floor, splashing out from under a wooden door. After three steps on the marble path I push the door open and walk in.

Warm steam greets me as the door closes. I am in a large rectangular room, crowned by a high dome. Tiny round windows allow light to filter through like white columns. Highlighted in the middle is a square platform, about hip-high, featuring a diamond pattern made of light and dark grey marble. The sound of splashing water and female voices echoes. Everything is made of silver-grey marble: steps, sills, partition walls in the corners, the many tiny basins along the wall. The marble is not polished, but shows long use along its surface. In the steamy light a number of women are sitting along the side, soaping themselves then rinsing repeatedly. They notice me and observe me with friendly curiosity.

The attendant leads me to a vacant niche, then turns to another woman who is lying on the side of the platform. The attendant starts rubbing her body with a course cloth until dark little balls come off her body. This procedure is called *kese*.

After pouring ladles of hot or cold water, which I mix in the ladle basins, over myself, my body has softened in the damp heat. Now it is my turn for "kese". I quickly lose my doubts in the friendly conversation, and am completely baffled by how much dirt is removed from my supposedly clean skin. The attendant tells me that she does not earn very much money because she is paid by her customers and not by the hour, yet she has been working here for many years. She is small, a bit stocky, but not fat; elderly, but agile, she wears only panties and a bra. Her long hair is bound by a scarf. Above all she is in a good mood. I enjoy letting myself be massaged and consent to having my hair washed because I answer every, often indecipherable question, with "yes".

I look around. An elderly woman has opened her braids and combs her long, grey hair. Two younger women soap each other's backs. An elderly woman spreads an herbal paste on various parts of her body, attracting the interest of the other women.

Women of every age, including girls and small children, enjoy this ancient bathing tradition. I will never forget the view of their wet naked bodies enveloped in steam on the marble steps, the sound of splashing water and excited chatter, the enchanting light filtering through the room, and the pleasant relaxation. The time passes peacefully. After about two hours the room begins to empty; I too leave. It must be cleaned before the men arrive I am told. I get dressed and ask the attendant how much I owe. About 1800 TL. I am 90 TL short but she lets me off paying the money without hesitation. There is a chorus of good-byes; the women all ask me to come again. I thank them and head out into the humid heat of İzmir.

Angelika Tuncay

Sights

Pagus Hill: In the south of town is Pagus Hill (*Kadifekale*), the most popular picnic spot in İzmir. Crowning the top is the Kadifekale (Velvet Castle), a fortress which dates back to ALEXANDER THE GREAT. The fortress itself is nothing special, but the view from the hill is spectacular: you can see the entire city, harbour and as much of the bay as the smog will permit. A number of clever businessmen seek to profit from this with tea gardens and open-air restaurants spread along the walls. Pagus Hill is accessible by foot via one of the few old town quarters to survive the 1922 fire (although it is run down today). The alternatives are Bus 33b (Konak) or a taxi (£2.75 from Konak Square).

Agora: The Agora, the market and public meeting spot dating from Roman times, is in the *Namazgah* section of town, not far from the bazaar. Its origin probably dates back to Hellenistic times. The ruins of the present-day buildings trace back to 178 AD when MARCUS AURELIUS ordered the construction of a new market hall to replace one destroyed by an earthquake. You can see the ruins of a 160 m long triple-aisled basilica in the north (across from the entrance) and 13 well-preserved Corinthian columns on the west side (including the capitals).

By the way: The marble statues of Poseidon and Demeter are now in the new archaeological museum.

OPEN: 9:00 - 12:00 h and 13:30 - 17:30 h. Admission £0.20, Sundays £0.10.

Konak Square: Konak Square (*Konaak Meydanı*) is the heart of the city. Here you'll find taxis, the central bus station, the *Konak İskelesi* (wharf), Karamürsel Department Store (the most modern in İzmir), the town hall and lots of green space where you may even stretch out to relax. There is a lot going on at all hours of the day!

Notice the rococo clock tower (*Saat Kule*), İzmir's landmark, depicted on the 500 Lira bank notes (which you rarely see). It was constructed for sultan ABADÜLHAMID II by his Grand Vizier, in honour of the sultan's twenty fifth anniversary on the throne in 1901.

Next to it is the lovely little Konak Mosque (*Konak Camii*), dating from 1754; an intentional copy of SINAN'S work, using miniature tiles. You must see it!

Also on Konak Square is the Atatürk Cultural Centre (*Atatürk Kültür Merkezi*), a daring and interesting modern multi-purpose building with space for exhibits, concerts, opera, and a music conservatory (see Meeting Spots).

She has been working here for years; only the colours change.
A carpet weaver in the fortress of İzmir.

Archaeological Museum: Since 1984 it is located in a new building on Birleşmiş Milletler Yokuşu, a curving street just above Konak Square. It gives a good impression with large front windows providing ample, but not too bright, lighting. The courtyard and rooms are designed to permit viewing of the objects from all sides, a great way to enjoy art. All captions are in Turkish and English. All exhibit rooms are spotlessly clean and air conditioned.

The splendid collection includes *sculpture* from excavation sites at Klaros, Çeşme, Milas, Sardes, Manisa, Pergamon, Milet, Ephesus and Didyma. We particularly liked Poseidon and Demeter, which originally stood at the Agora (second century AD), a sleeping Eros, statues of Athena, a Vestal Virgin and a Sophist (all fromEphesus, second century AD), and the head of Artemis (Didyma, about 140 AD).

Upstairs are items made of clay and terra-cotta, including pieces discovered in West Anatolia dating from the third millennium BC! We especially liked two large clay jugs from the Hellenic era (300 - 250 BC) and a number of Byzantine plates (400 - 1450 AD). Also lovely are the terra-cotta statues from the Roman era. Colourful display and information plaques make the museum very informative. Be sure to visit!

OPEN: 9:00 - 17:00 h, closed Mondays. Admission £0.60, Sundays £0.30.

Kızlarağası-Caravanserai (Kızlarağası-Han): There are still several caravanserais on the west coast, for example in Çeşme or Kuşadası. Most of them are in ruins or have been converted into luxury lodgings. This is not the case with Kızlarağası Caravanserai in İzmir's bazaar quarter (*Hisarönü*), although many İzmirers are no longer aware of the existence of this splendid complex.

The caravanserai consists of a large courtyard and a surrounding two-story building with wide arcades. It is one of the town's oldest wooden buildings (eighteenth century) and well maintained. Notice the large gate through which caravans from the east once entered the courtyard to house their camels for the night. The special attraction: a number of craftsmen have set up shop in the rooms. Some are true masters of their trade. Over a cup of tea you can ask questions (most speak English or German) and bargain leisurely. The quality ranges from satisfactory to excellent. We discovered the İlhan water-pipes all along the west coast.

The latest news: the craftsmen will be gone soon because this caravanserai will be turned into a luxury hotel in a few years. The municipal authorities are well aware of the fact that the craftsmen will need new premises and have made provisions for them: they can rent new workshops at twenty times the price of the old ones.

Hisar-Mosque (Hisar Camii): Built in 1598, the mosque is considered second in beauty only to Konak Mosque. However, in İstanbul we found two dozen mosques which might challenge that claim. The Greek town of İzmir was never a centre of religious culture.

Culture Park: Built in 1922 on the rubble of the former Greek Quarter, the large Culture Park (*Kültür Parkı*) is the Tivoli of İzmir. On hot and muggy summer days, people are attracted to the cool fountains and shady trees. But the Culture Park has much more to offer: a miniature train, a luna park including a rollercoaster, an observation tower, a pond, lots of greenery (335,000 sq m), a small zoo with all the standard animals (camels, elephants, predatory animals), a botanical garden, and no less than 13 tea gardens, restaurants, and casinos. The gym, stage and tennis courts are not usually open to the public. Everything is well tended.

Almost the entire west side of the park is occupied by the industrial fair grounds. Six fairs are held each year, including the *İzmir International Fair,* held for the 56th time in 1987. It hosts several hundred thousand visitors every year.

OPEN: 8:00 - 24:00 h. Admission £0.10.

Atatürk-Museum: The building at Atatürk Caddesi 248, right on the Kordon, the waterside road, was ATATÜRK'S residence during his visits to İzmir. On the first floor is a small ethnographic exhibit; the second floor contains the unavoidable display of relics immortalizing the great Turk.

OPEN: 9:00 - 12:00 h and 13:00 - 17:30 h, closed Mondays. Admission £0.10, on Sundays £0.03.

Republic Square (Cumhuriyet Meydanı) **and Kordon:** İzmir's showcase square is crowned by an equestrian statue of Atatürk. Here are the two most expensive hotels in town, the "Büyük Efes Oteli" and the "Etap İzmir", along with the post office. Take a break here to enjoy the view of the sea. Atatürk Caddesi, known to insiders simply as theKordon, is the town's promenade leading from Konak Square via Republic Square to "Altav Restaurant" by the ferry landing. Set back from the street are the NATO headquarters, the trading harbour and a number of first-class (not neccessarily expensive) restaurants. In the evening, young men leap over puddles to avoid staining their Gucci shoes...

Soccer in the Olympic Stadium: That's right, İzmir does have an Olympic Stadium. It can hold over 40,000 enthusiastic fans all cheering for ALTAY İZMIR, perpetual basement-dweller of the Turkish league. Atmosphere is included in the admission price, even if the team is playing poorly. Tickets are available at the Tourist Information Office or in the pubs around the stadium. Pick up your tickets several days in advance because the games are frequently sold out.

Swimming

Not recommended in the ocean due to pollution. Büyük Efes Hotel has an expensive swimming pool. The new indoor pool in Balçova Thermal Centre, a state-owned hotel complex (double £20) in Balçova, approx. 10 km west of Konak Square is recommended. The pool costs £0.50 for non hotel guests.

Around İzmir

Bayraklı: Approximately 8 km north of town are the hill and district of Bayraklı. This is where the most ancient remains of Smyrna have been discovered. Today you can only see the foundations of a Greek rotunda and the ruins of a seventh century temple. Up on the hill are the sparse ruins of the tomb of Tantalos, a 30 m by 25 m mausoleum, which was dismantled by thoughtless archaeologists in the last century.

Balçova: Leaving İzmir heading west on Cumhuriyet Bulvarı, you reach a crossroads after 10 km. To the right is İnciraltı (2 km); to the left is Balçova. Here you can visit the famous Agamemnon Hot Springs (*Agamemnun Kaplıcası*). There is also a funicular for a great view of İzmir.

İnciraltı: The main beach of İzmir which is hopelessly packed on weekends. The lovely sandy beach boasts lots of restaurants and bustle. The water is less than pleasant, plastic bags ahoy!

Teos: The Ionian settlement, dating from the 1st millennium BC is 74 km southwest of İzmir, near the village of *Sığacık*. The village was never of importance. It is only known as the birthplace of the poet ANACREON. The ruins were used as a quarry by the Genoese, who built a fortress in Sığacık, and by the local inhabitants so that little remains today. Most impressive are the ruins of the *Dionysos Temple* with its partially reset columns. To the east are the sparse remains of a *Roman odeion*. To the north, the ruin of a *Greek theatre* is wonderfully situated. Be sure to climb the hill which was once the site of the acropolis. From the top you have a nice view of the olive groves and town ruins, the filled in southern harbour, the Genoese fortress and Sığazıc village (an ancient breakwater shows that the coast line has hardly changed since ancient times).

LET'S TAKE KOLOPHON

When you visit the plains of Kolophon and Cumaovasi, it is easy to understand why horses have been bred here: no better country could be imagined! Horses from Kolophon were as legendary as the Arabian breed is today. The town's cavalry was also outstanding. STRABO wrote that the expression "Take Kolophon" in the ancient world carried the meaning, "kill them quickly". The Kolophons boasted more than just a powerful cavalry; they had a mighty fleet and packs of vicious dogs. The dog, they would explain to astonished strangers, is the most loyal ally, and he does not demand mercenary payment. Money was no object in the town. Trade, horse breeding and kolophonium (a pure resin harvested in pine plantations) made the people of Kolophon extremely wealthy. So rich, that they became spoiled: The men of Kolophon preferred to dress in perfumed purple-coloured garments!

Kolophon: About 3 km south of İzmir, a paved road turns off E 24 toward Cumaovası. Take this road to the village of **Değirmendere**. A bit to the south are the ruins of the Greek town Kolophon. All that is visible are the ruins of walls and foundations and several wall towers unearthed by German archaeologists in 1886.

Klaros: Following the road further south we reach Klaros, not a town but, like Didyma, a sacred site where APOLLO was revered. It was legendary in Roman times. The priests, if we are to believe the writings of TACITUS, which of course we do, did not even need to hear the questions of those consulting the oracle. All they needed was the name of the person; then they would withdraw into the *Sacred Spring* to drink and make prophecies.

Only the most sacred part of the Apollo Temple remains: two passages which join at right angles and separate again. This is where the priests went to consult the oracle and to drink from the inspirational sacred spring. A huge statue of Apollo once stood above the chamber, you can still see the ruins. The right arm must have measured 3 m.

Gümüldür: Just 2 km south of Klaros is Gümüldür, with a wonderful, long, sandy beach, and the scattered remains of **Notion**, once Kolophon's harbour (ruins of the agora, theatre and a temple). The water here, far from the Gulf of İzmir, is crystal clear. But others have discovered this too: motels and restaurants have already been established (see İzmir/Camping). You can reach the beaches (they start at Özdere and end beyond Gümüldür) by car. There are bays, pensions, holiday villages and simple camp sites which are mostly frequented by Turkish vacationers.

COMING - GOING: Buses from the Santral Garau in İzmir.

Karaburun Peninsula: This peninsula was populated by Greeks until 1922 but their villages are in ruins today. A narrow road leads to the tip of this sparsely populated, rough peninsula. It was strangely avoided by tourists and daytrippers, even those who know Turkey well, up until recently. It is on the road to Çeşme. "Cape Black" (literal translation) offers a truly lonely and lovely beach in *Mordogan*. But things are picking up in Karaburun: holiday villages are being built, a few simple camp sites and hotels have already opened up for business. Another camp site is situated about half way down the road to Karaburun and the hotel "Astoria" (medium price range) is right in Karaburun by the sea (Karaburun - İzmir, tel. 5449/1391). But the peninsula is still worth a visit. If you only want to visit the beaches be sure to bring your own food and drink. On the peninsula itself you will find nice villages, friendly people, nice locantas and it is still permitted to camp out anywhere you like.

> **ATTENTION!** The latest news: the governement in Ankara has drastically hiked up **admission fees** for museums, mosques etc. in 1989! Calculate about 5 - 10 times the prices given in this edition (depending upon the fame of the sights; for instance: admission for Hagia Sophia rose from £0.30 up to £3 !)

ÇEŞME

During the day everyone is at the beach. But things really get going at night: the main street, where driving is prohibited, turns into a lively tourist bazaar. The restaurants on the beach promenade offer tasty Anatolean dishes.

This former fishing village is located at the westernmost point of the Asian part of Turkey. The emblem of Çeşme is the Genoese/Ottoman fortress. The town has been a popular holiday spot for years because of its hot springs and the surrounding beaches. The water of the hot springs has a temperature of about 40 - 50 Centigrade and provides relief from rheumatism and ailments of the liver, kidneys and skin. A visit to this peninsula is still worthwhile. Tourism is firmly established here but it has not gone totally unchecked as in some places on the coast. Ilica is one of those touristy places without any atmosphere. It consists mostly of a beach, hotels, restaurants, shops, ice cream vendors etc.

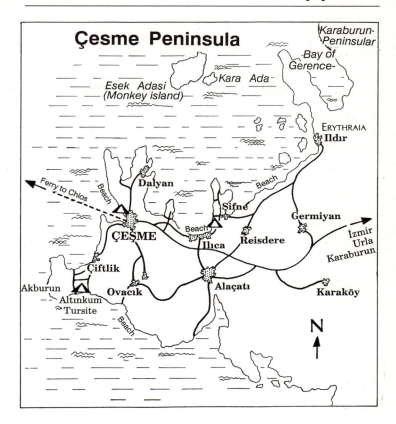

Çesme Peninsula

Karaburun-
Peninsular

Bay of
Gerence-

Kara Ada

Esek Adasi
(Monkey island)

ERYTHRAIA
Ildır

Ferry to Chios

Beach

Dalyan

Beach

Sifne

CEŞME

Beach

Ilıca

Reisdere

Germiyan

İzmir
Urla
Karaburun

Çiftlik

Akburun
Altınkum
Tursite

Ovacık

Beach

Alaçatı

Karaköy

N

History

Çeşme means fountain. Numerous fountains of Arabian origin are still being used by the townspeople for their daily water supply. Çeşme has a long history of tourism - it was a popular spa even in antiquity.

The Genoese, who wanted to protect their trade interests along the Levantine coast, built a fortress here in the fifteenth century tocontrol the narrow straights (10 km) between the mainland and the island of Chios. The Ottomans renovated the fortress in the eighteenth century according to their own taste and modified military requirements. In 1770 the people of Çeşme were witness to a historic event: nearly all the Turkish ships were sunk during a sea battle fought between the Russian and the Turkish fleet.

Many Greeks lived here until 1923. The only remainder of those times is the completely empty basilica on Main Street.

INFORMATION: İskele Meydanı 8. In the centre of town between the harbour and bus station, very accommodating. tel. 6653.

TELEPHONE AREA CODE: Çeşme 5492, Ilica 5493

COMING – GOING: Buses to Çeşme from İzmir (£0.70) do not depart from the central bus station in İzmir, rather from F. Altay Meydanı. The local bus to Altay Meydanı costs £0.35. Departure quarter-hourly (6:30 - 22:00 h). The scenery along the route is wonderful: vegetable markets right on the street, fish markets along the coast, families collecting clams in the waves. The bus station of Çeşme is located a little outside of town. Therefore, it is more convenient to get off the bus at the beginning of Main Street, where most of the locals also get off.

Ferry to Chios: During high season (July 14th - Sept. 10th) ships run every day between Çeşme and Chios (9:30 h, £10 per person).

ÇEŞME OR FESTIVALITIS

There are several traditional festivals held in Turkey: The St. Nicholas Festival in Demre, the camel fighting festival in Selçuk-Ephesus, traditional wrestling in July in Edirne or the Mevlana memorial festival in Konya. There are also an ever-increasing number of tourist events without historical tradition or any deeper meaning, many quite boring.

In the tradition-rich Theatre of Ephesus the first international beauty contest was held in Turkey in 1985. Already a "new" tradition (the fourth annual event will be held this year) is the Oceanic Festival in Çeşme. Don't expect hotdog surfing or high-masted schooners, this is a "Song Contest". The contenders this year were KAZINO from Belgium, SNAPSHOT from Denmark, CAROLINE from Monaco and TORE HANSEN from Norway. The latter sang "I was falling" which didn't knock anybody over. What - you never heard of it? Well you must at least know L. HARTZ, "a well-known cabaret singer" from England according to the program. Never heard of him either? But you surely do know the Special Guest Star from Germany JEAN FRANCOIS MICHAEL! With a line up like this Çeşme cannot be considered provincial. The coming Çeşme Festival is sure to be another great success.

BOAT TRIPS: Day-trips can be booked either at Ertürk (see travel agencies) or right at the harbour with private ship owners. When booking directly at the harbour the prices are between £5 and £10 depending on what kind of boat you take.

CAR RENTAL: There is an **Avis** office in the Kervansary-Motel to the right of the fortress, when facing it. tel. 276 06.

MOPED RENTAL: hard to believe but there is none.

FESTIVAL: 2nd to 6th July: Çeşme Oceanic Festival , a pop-music festival in İlica.

SHOPPING: You'll find few cheap knick-knacks but mostly quality jewellery, leather-wear, carpets, waterpipes from Eskişehir and Ottoman antiques on Main Street. The prices are fixed and fairly high.

TRAVEL AGENCIES: **Ertürk** is the largest agency in Çeşme located right across from the Tourist Information Bureau in front of the fortress. Here you can buy tickets for the boat to Chios. The agency also offers other day-trips. A small selection (prices include lunch): Ephesus £17 (Friday 8.00h); Pergamom £18 (Wednesday 7.30h); Pamukkale £25 (Monday 6.30h). Boat trips to the Monkey Island and to several bays are also being offered, prices depend on route and quality of the lunch and are anywhere between £8 and £16. tel. 261 47 and 262 23.

WATERSPORTS: The peninsula is an Eldorado for surfers due to the current from the Black Sea and a constant breeze. Off-shore diving is also very popular. Watersport equipment can be rented in İlica, on Altınyunus Beach, or at the Golf Hotel beyond Çiftlik. See there.

A Night's Rest

Çeşme is one of the most expensive places in Turkey. Therefore we will not even mention the expensive establishments. All lodgings, except for the Golf Hotel and the Hotel Rasim Palas are located in Çeşme.

Golf Hotel, ideal for people interested in sports. This completely isolated hotel has 52 double rooms and a camp site and offers the following sports facilities: a diving school, a surf school, a tennis court, a miniature golf course. A stable and several ping pong tables can soon be added to this list. The teaching staff are made up of certified diving and surfing teachers. The hotel grounds cover about 50 000 sq metres. There is a sandy sunbathing area, the beach itself, however, is pebbly. The camp sites are situated on partially wooded terraces. There is also a motel consisting of several small houses. Prices: double, incl. breakfast £10, half pension £13.50. Camping: person and car £1 each. A diving lesson, including diving equipment, is £15, ten lessons are £143. A surfing lesson is £5 per hour. Address: Çiftlik-Köy-Çeşme, tel. 549/26389.

İmren Oteli, İnkilap Cad., double £11. Good and clean, fits the price. Has an exquisite restaurant. tel. 6635.

06 Pansiyon-Holiday Inn, this pension, run by the Kara family, is located in a friendly, quiet "Pension Street" near the upper end of the nightly pedestrian precinct. The Kara family looks after its' guests lovingly and does everything to make your stay as pleasant as possible. Ample breakfast available (£1). You can get double or 3-bed rooms with or without shower/WC. Double £6.70. Address: İnönü Mah. Saç Sok 16, tel. 260 47.

Karakaş Pansiyon, the first building in the same street as 06-Pension. The proprietors are also very friendly and helpful. They are planning to increase the number of beds by building onto the house in 1989/90, so more guests will be able to enjoy the "ekstra kahvaltı". Double with shower/WC £6.70. Address: İnönü Mah. Saç Sok. 6, tel. 2 60 61.

Çeşme Pansiyon, right next to 06-Pansiyon, the last building on "Pension Street". We can also recommend this pension, quality and price similar to Karakaş Pansiyon. Address: İnönü Mah. Saç Sok. 18, tel. 260 29.

Ufuk Pension, double £7, shower down the hall, right by the ocean, clean. 150 m to the beach, kitchen facilities.

Sahil Pension, double £7, showers/WC down the hall, balcony, nice view.

Gül Pension, İnönü Mah., double £7, tel. 1696.

Hotel Rasim Palas (İlica), double £7.

Also recommended are **Kaptan Pansiyon** (tel. 6804) and **Çem Pansiyon** (tel. 6570).

Camping

If you have the courage to board a bus marked Turiste (£0.20) in Çeşme - the drivers are frustrated race-car drivers on the frequently unpaved roads - be sure you know which of the three camp grounds you want to visit. Only one of them offers mediocre comfort.

About half-way down the road is a site, separated from the beach by a dusty road. There is hardly a tree for shade! Not recommended!

Altın Kum Camp: The bus continues down the ever worsening road. Just before the end it turns to the left and after a couple of hundred metres stops in front of a group of haphazardly pitched tents and three very simple tin/straw hut restaurants. The sanitary facilities demonstrate that hygiene and cleanliness are not of primary importance. But the atmosphere is relaxed. In 1988, construction for a new camp site was going on right next door to Altın Kum Camp. We were not able to find out when it is planned to open.

Tursite (8 km from Çeşme): If you want some comfort, you must drive all the way to the end of the "main road". Here is the real Turiste camp site with an adjoining motel. The site is great for children and right next to the sea; the tiny motel buildings are slightly above the water. There is also a large, cheap restaurant, an administrative office and a small shop (just essentials). A camp doctor is always in attendance. Buses stop at the corner, every 20 minutes to Çeşme (£0.25), taxi (£2.35). Costs: adults £0.80, tent/caravan/minibus £0.45, motel £9 per night (including breakfast and lunch), free for children.

CAMP SITES in **Ilica**: Several sites near Ilica range from good to very good in quality, but you pay for it! The cream of the crop:

Ve Kamp, about 3 km beyond Ilica, signposted. The largest, most expensive and the best camp site on the peninsula. It takes about 1500 campers to fill up the 150.000 sq m site. But you don't suspect this size because the hilly grounds, covered with palms and conifers, are divided up into several sections. The owner thinks that the Turkish and the European way to spend a holiday clash, so he keeps the nationalities separated on the grounds. Each section has its own café, restaurant and sanitary facilities. The latter are tolerable and very crowded during the summer. The minimarket at the entrance offers a large selection of goods. The place also has its own beach and a hot spring. Prices: small tent (2 persons) £1, large tent (2 - 4 persons) £2.15, very large tent (4 or more) £2.75, caravan £2.15, electricity £0.40. Parking your car in the parking lot costs £0.60, next to your tent £0.30. Admission to the thermal bath is £0.70. You can also rent very simple wooden cottages. A 3-bed cottage is £5, a 4-bed cottage £6.15. If you're not staying at the site and just want to go swimming, you pay £0.80. tel. 314 16 and 324 03.

CAMPING in **Çeşme**: **Grup Camping**, on the northern end of the beach. A small, simple site with simple, small sanitary facilities. The biggest advantage for campers is that they're close to the centre of town.

FOOD

Sahil Restaurant (Çeşme), Cumhurriyet Meydanı. Prices are reasonable for Europeans. This middle class restaurant is mostly frequented by tourists, the quality has somewhat declined. Tel 1646.

Right next door is the **Sahil Pub** which belongs to the same proprietor but is simpler and therefore cheaper.

The restaurants on the quay promenade (near the post office and beyond) are better and more expensive. You can also have an excellent meal in luxurious surroundings in the restaurants of the large hotels. The prices are about £13 - £17 per person.

Inexpensive locantas and döner salons are on the main street. Two worth recommending are **Hassan Abi Lokantası** which has a large selection of common pan dishes and **Yedegör Döner Salonu** which serves various Döner Kebaps. Try the İskender Kebab with yoghurt.

İmren Lokantası, great fish and meze, tel. 6635.

Ildıri Balık Lokantası, here you can eat fish, away from the tourist bustle. It is right by the sea, shortly before the entrance to Ildır (see Swimming and Around Çeşme). It is not a fancy place but the owners take great pride in serving excellent sea food. The tables are set under a thatched roof, two metres away from the waves of the Mediterranean.

NIGHT LIFE

If you have the cash, you might join the fun in one of the following discos: **Altınyunus Disco**, **Bonjour Disco** and **Viking Disco** in Boyalik, or **Turban Çeşme Disco** in "Turban Tatil Köyü" in İlica. If you are worried about your finances, then visit Altınyunus Disco; it is the most reasonable.

Sights

Towering above everything is the castle right at the harbour. If you like a refreshing breeze from the ocean and a cool, damp fortress, then for £0.45 you can't go wrong. Astonishingly, you are permitted to climb just about everywhere after the motto: Falling is Not Permitted (children!). You can visit the **museum** which has a large collection of weapons (daily 8:00 - 12:00 h and 15:00 - 16:30h, except Tuesdays, admission £0.30, half price on weekends) and you have a spectacular view of the entire harbour area. Almost an attraction in itself is the harbour complex with its tiny streets of shops, numerous small, inviting pensions and cafés. The two mosques and the caravanserai (which has been converted into a luxury hotel) are nothing special.

Swimming

No matter if you just want to laze about or want some action - you'll find the right kind of beach for your taste. But don't expect to be alone anywhere. Attention all those sensitive to the cold: the water here, at the westernmost point of Turkey, is pretty chilly due to water from the Black Sea which flows through the Dardanelles into the Mediterranean.

Altınkum/Tursite Beach: This "golden sand" beach between dunes and the sea is the nicest and longest beach of the peninsula. And that is common knowledge. If you walk far enough you'll find small, quiet bays. Drinks and melons are sold on the beach. Turgut runs a simple restaurant at the beginning of the beach.

COMING - GOING: cross the bridge behind the harbour in Çeşme toward Çiftlik/Tursite (signposted). Turn left after about 9 km (sand path, signposted "Altınkum"). You can also take a minibus from Çeşme in the morning.

Ildırı Beach: 20 km from Çeşme, north along the coast, very inviting. A quiet pebble beach off the beaten path. Ideal for taking a dip while making a trip to Ildır/Erithraia (see Around Çeşme).

Dalyan Beach: Not to be recommended. This relatively small beach is crowded and surrounded by holiday villages.

Ilıca Beach: See Around Çeşme.

Altınyunus Beach: see Around Çeşme.

Alaçatı Beach: Take the turnoff before Ilıca, almost unspoiled by tourism.

Around Çeşme

Ilıca: A large tourist centre where a variety of activities are offered. The beach is just a few minutes from the bus station which runs parallel to the market street (promenade). Here you will find cheap drinks and provisions, the few stands and restaurants at the beach are infamous for their high prices. The beach right next to town is less than inviting (few showers/WC, dirty).

Altınyunus: The "Golden Dolphin Holiday Village" in Altınyunus, about 4 km from Ilıca (minibus £0.10) is very different. This almost futuristic complex is set in a lovely garden blocking the view of the sea, but don't let that deter you. Even if you don't lodge at this vacation village you may use the facilities (riding, surfing, sailing, fishing, water skiing, tennis, bicycles) at a reasonable price. Sign up at the reception in the main building.

COMING - GOING: Stop a bus on the road toward Çeşme, or to avoid the crowds, get a ticket (£0.35) in Ilıca.

Ildır/Erithraia: Ildır is a lovely, quiet village situated in a part of the ancient town of Erithraia. Stones from the ancient town were used for building and so you will find classic columns gracing a simple doorway and old reliefs on the facade of a stable. 300 people live in the seventy houses which are crowded closely together. Erithraia is also mentioned in the New Testament - back then it was a lively, modern city and had 300 000 people living within its 5 km city wall.

The town is not completely excavated yet. A few mosaics, coins and amphoras can be found in the museum. A continuous rainfall during excavations uncovered the mosaics of a Roman villa. The Roman and Greek stones of the town lie about in the sun, the agora is covered with tomato, melon and sesame plants. It is a nice place to have some tea and enjoy a view of the mountains but not very exciting if you're interested in archeology. New excavations by a Turkish team are due to start in 1989.

KUŞADASI *(pop. 15 000)*

Everybody is happy to leave İzmir's smog behind them. The desire for a pleasant sea breeze can be fulfilled in Kuşadası.

The village is not one of the most inviting on the Aegean. Town planning is not the strength of the community. Hotel complexes, holiday villages, camp grounds and discos sprout at will. Nobody comes to Kuşadası because of Kuşadası. They come to see the nearby historic sites (Priene, Ephesus), the lovely scenery, for some relaxation on the beach or for the cool sea breeze.

The town has a lot to offer: a half dozen excellent beaches, the largest yacht harbour on the Aegean, recreational facilities en masse, restaurants, shopping and night life. Kuşadası is a well-known port of call. Over 600 luxury liners dock here annually.

History

Little is known of its Greek past. Much more important is the fact that Kuşadası (Bird Island) was founded by Genoese and Venetian merchants in the thirteenth century under licence from Byzantium. The site for the new town (originally called Scala Nova) was selected because the old harbour near Ephesus had filled with sand. Medieval city planning is still visible in the pattern of streets in the old town. Not until the Ottoman era did the town become known as "Kusadasi".

INFORMATION: İskele Meydanı, right by the old harbour, English is spoken, not very helpful. Open daily 7:00 - 20:00 h. tel. 1103. If you plan to visit Kuşadası you can write and ask for information and a list of accomodation with phone numbers and prices in Lira and Dollars.

TELEPHONE AREA CODE: 6361.

IMPORTANT TELEPHONE NUMBERS: Police 1382, doctor 1470.

BIKE RENTAL: Mopeds cost £6 per day.

BUYING A CARPET: At one of the largest carpet dealers in Turkey, Bülent Erol (Üner Carpet Gallery), right by the harbour. Anybody can drop by for a cup of tea and a look at as many carpets as you'd care to see (without any obligation to buy). You can leave the shop feeling like an expert.

CAR RENTAL: A rented car is a great way to see the sights around Kuşadası. Turquoise Tours offers the following high season price (25 per cent cheaper in the off season)
Car (e.g. Fiat 131): per day £11 + £0.10 per kilometre; for two or more days there is no kilometre charge, but the daily rate is higher, e.g. three days with unlimited mileage £24.
Minibus: If you are travelling in a group, consider chartering a minibus: £16 per day

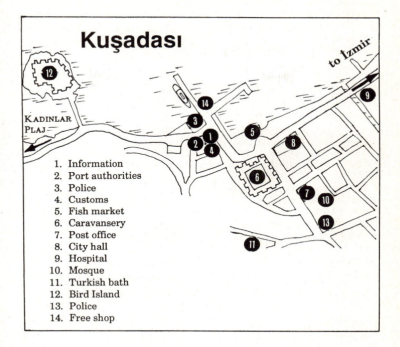

Kuşadası

to İzmir

KADINLAR PLAJ

1. Information
2. Port authorities
3. Police
4. Customs
5. Fish market
6. Caravansery
7. Post office
8. City hall
9. Hospital
10. Mosque
11. Turkish bath
12. Bird Island
13. Police
14. Free shop

plus kilometre charge, for multiple days £41 per day with unlimited mileage.
Other agencies include **Avis**, tel. 1475; **Europcar**, tel. 3607; **Budget**, tel. 3202. All have offices on Atatürk Bulvarı.

SAMOS TRIP: Several boats daily. Pick up tickets at a travel agency a day in advance; oneway £15.50; round trip (1 day) £17; return on a later day £28; cars (depending upon size £25 to £35. Passage takes 45 minutes to two hours (depending on boat size and power). The varying prices at the agencies are due to different exchange rates. The cheapest agency in 1988 was "Scalanova".

SHOPPING: At the bazaar in the centre of town. Lots of neon, little of value, frequently expensive and touristy. Kuşadası was the first town in Turkey where shopkeepers began putting price tags on their merchandise. Along Atatürk Bulvarı are a number of interesting shops. Most souvenir shops are open 24-hours a day.

TRAVEL AGENCIES: In Kuşadası a number of reasonable daytrips are offered (see Around Kuşadası). If you don't have a car, join a tour to Priene, Milet and Didyma offered by many agencies. Public transport involves a complicated and time-consuming changing of buses. If you lose your nerve and miss the last bus, it is easy to fall back on an expensive taxi. We found **Turquoise Tours** reliable, Yalı Cad. 10, right at the harbour. A selection:

Ephesus (all day), without refreshment, £13. Priene-Milet-Didyma (all day), with refreshment, £15. Pamukkale (all day), without refreshment, £17.

The tours can be booked directly at the agencies or through your hotel reception (usually without a surcharge). Participants are picked up at their hotels.

YACHT CHARTER: **Turban Kuşadası Marina**, Atatürk Bulvarı, tel. 1752. **Diana Turizm Seyahat Acentası**, Liman Cad. 3, tel. 1399 and 2969. **Grino Tours Seyahat Acentasıı**, Atatürk Bulvarı, tel. 2459.

A Night's Rest

As rooms are frequently booked in high season, contact Tourist Information (tel. 1103) a day or two in advance, open daily 7:00 - 20:00 h.

Hotel Kalyon (Kuşadası), double £10, 3-bed room £13, very clean, bath/WC in the room, recommended. Excerpt of a reader's letter: "One of the best tips of the book. When looking for a room you'd probably overlook this place. Nice furnishings, super clean, friendly staff, good location." Address: Kıbrıs Cad. 7, tel. 133 46.

Pansiyon Renk (Kuşadası), Liman Cad. Hottest tip for young people in Kuşadası and almost always booked. The international atmosphere compensates for the faults. tel. 1242.

Hotel Kotur (Kuşadası), about 1 km from town, not by the sea, double £10, shower/WC in the rooms, balcony, lovely terrace with a view of the town and the harbour, accommodating staff, recommended!

Balcı Pension (Kadınlar Plajı), 2 km from Kuşadası, double £5.30, good.

Kismet Oteli (Kuşadası), Akyar Mekji, double £28, tennis court, Tel. 2005.

Kuştur Tatil Köyü, 6 km to the north, double £27, a holiday village with all the frills, tel. 4110.

CAMPING

Yat Camping (right in Kuşadası): On the road, just behind the marina. Offers almost everything imaginable, but crowded.

BP-Mocamp: 5 km towards Selçuk, near Hotel Tusan. You need to do your shopping in Kuşadası as the camp store is too small. Noise from the coastal road detracts from the lovely location.

Camping Motel Adele: 7 km after Selçuk take a right (15 km from Kuşadası). This recommendable camp ground enjoys a peaceful setting. Very clean and lovely sandy beach. Restaurant and store.

Kücükoğlu Camping: 3 km from Kuşadası toward Söke. Built on a slope with a great view of the ocean. The numerous pines provide welcome shade. Moderate comfort and cleanliness.

FOOD

Dağ-Restaurant (Kuşadası), opposite the postoffice in the centre of town, accessible via several stairs. The specialty of this magnificent locanta is its excellent Köfte, but its other Turkish specialties are also good.

Oxalis (Kuşadası), one of the loveliest garden restaurants far and wide. Pleasant atmosphere and music (no charge), a large menu and reasonable prices. Motto: The customer is always right. Note: for large groups, reserve a table in advance.

NIGHT LIFE

Club Akdeniz Disco in "Club Akdeniz"; certainly one of the best discos in Turkey. Thanks to the international clientele, the atmosphere is like in Ibiza.

Hotel Martı Disco; also good. Great disc jockies with a good knowledge of English (rare) and good taste (even rarer). The clientele is very smart, including a number of wealthy older men with only one ambition.

Sun and fun on the beach

Sights

Harbour: The fishing port has evolved into a huge yacht marina with dock space for 600 boats ranging from simple Turkish "Gülef" to the most expensive luxury yachts.

Han/Caravanserai: Built by MEHMET PAŞA, by the harbour. Today it has been converted into a modern, very expensive 40 room hotel, with restaurants, bar and disco. A look inside is well worth your while, even for non-guests.

Mosques: The two mosques, *İcı* and *Hanım*, are in good condition since their restoration. Still, they are nothing special.

Town Wall: A wall with two gates was built to provide protection from an attack by land. Part of the southern ring can be seen by the police station.

Swimming

Kuşadası-Beach: In the centre of town, dirty, tucked in between the main road and the pedestrian promenade. Still large crowds. Not recommended!

Near town are a number of lovely strips of beach accessible by bus for £0.17. We can mention just a few:

Kadınlar Plajı: 2 km to the south. It used to be fairly clean and the sheer size used to reduce tourist concentration. But today the beach is too narrow, too crowded and too cramped. Showers/WC, lots of refreshments, surfboard rentals. No other recreational facilities.

Tusan Beach: 5 km north of Kusadası. At the hotel of the same name you can rent surfboards, sail boats, row boats as well as bicycles for a low price.

Altınkum Beach: See Didyma.

Kalamaki Beach: See Day Trips.

Güvercin Ada Plajı: By the the Bird Island dam, no changing cubicles, rocky.

Yavansu/Karova Plajı: 4 km south of Kuşadası, on the road to Söke, sandy beach.

Gücelçamlı Plajı: Zeus Beach, 2 km south of Kuşadası, sandy beach, shallow water, recommended.

Around Kuşadası

Pigeon Island: Visible from afar, the island - *Güvercin Ada* - is accessible via a dam. In and around the ruins of a Byzantine castle, no pigeons, but a number of cafés have taken residence. In high season the crowds of people are enormous. In 1985: 510,000 tourists visited Kuşadası, including 21,000 by ship. And not one failed to visit Pigeon Island.

Kalamaki Beaches: 30 km south of Kuşadası. A number of large and small beaches in a forested region, mineral springs near Cami Köyü, Dilek Peninsula (National Park).

Selçuk/Ephesus: See Selçuk/Ephesus.

Priene - Milet - Didyma: See Priene - Milet - Didyma.

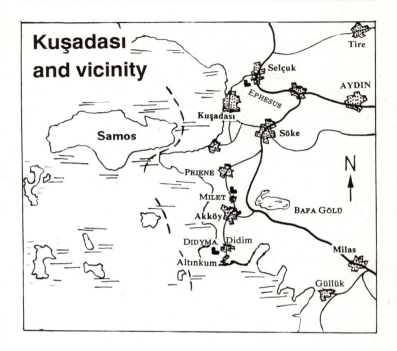

Pamukkale: See Pamukkale.

Söke: This village is your departure point for visits to Priene, Milet and Didyma (buses every 30 minutes from Kuşadası, £0.17). A lovely spot, but boring when staying longer.

Bafa Lake: A large fresh-water lake 45 km south of Kuşadası, on the main road. Two small camp grounds. Note: shopping is difficult.

CAMPING (southern shore): **Turgut Camping**, pebble beach, simple sanitary facilities, restaurant.

SELÇUK / EPHESUS

Ephesus (today Selçuk) was a metropolis when Athens was just a provincial town and Rome had yet to be founded. At its height the population numbered a quarter of a million people, an enormous number in those days.

Ephesus was the wealthiest town in Asia Minor, known as the "Bank of Asia". Its large harbour was the gateway to the wealth of Anatolia and Persia. But the Ephesians had more going for them than just money. It was the centre of the Artemis worship and a major pilgrimage site. The *Artemision*, a huge temple dedicated to Artemis, was one of the seven wonders of the world.

But fame and splendour run their course and the town was abandoned. Flooding by the *Kaystros* River did the rest, erasing every trace. Then, astonishingly, excavations between 1866 and 1922 brought Ephesus back to light. Much was destroyed, including the Artemision, but a lot remained preserved. Nowhere else in Asia Minor, and rarely elsewhere (e.g. Pompei), has such a complete town been excavated.

And something else: in 1891, Lazarists from İzmir, led by the visionary drawings of a nun, KATHARINA EMMERICH, who had **never** in her life visited the region, were able to pinpoint the building in which the *Virgin Mary* died, just 6 km from the excavation site. Vitality has returned to the town: commerce, religious faith, ruins, pilgrim sites bring in cash. At peak times about 6000 tourists clamber over the excavations and hundreds more visit the pilgrim sites.

History

The most ancient settlements of Lelegers and Karers were on the castle hill of Selçuk, northeast of the excavation sites, dating back to the second millennium BC.

On the western slope of the castle hill stood an ancient relic of the old Anatolian earth goddess CYBELE. In the eleventh century BC, Ionian settlers moved into the region. They allied themselves with the original inhabitants to protect the sacred Cybele sites and called themselves Ephesians. The Greek Artemis cult fused with the ancient worship of Cybele to form the cult of Artemis in Ephesus. The town profited from its location on several trading routes, with its harbour at the mouth of the Kaystros. It was one of the early mem-

Kureten Street

bers of the Ionian alliance. Ephesus was already famous as a pilgrimage town and wealthy enough to afford the tremendous Armetis temple.

When the Lydian CROESUS attacked in 550 BC, the people of Ephesus could think of no better defence than to fasten a rope around the Artemis temple and the entire town hoping from protection of the gods. CROESUS responded mildly, sparing the still uncompleted temple (to which he donated a relief and several columns), but he did insist upon plundering the town. The population resettled on the plain at the present-day site.

Without a wall or troops, Ephesus was a toy passing through the hands of the great powers. In 545 BC it fell to Persia but did not participate in the Ionian uprising. In 466 BC Ephesus changed sides, joining the Attian alliance, before bowing to the Spartans in 412 BC. By 386 BC it was again Persian, and remained so until the arrival of ALEXANDER THE GREAT in 334 BC.

Some years before that (356 BC), HEROSTRATES had set fire to the just completed Armetis temple in order to make his name immortal - he succeeded. When Alexander offered to pay for the complete cost of the temple reconstruction, the proud people of Ephesus refused with the clever reasoning that it would be wrong for one god to bow before another god. They proved capable of raising the money themselves. So the town prospered from the expansion of the temple asylum district, an area surrounding the temple in which any form of force or governmental power was prohibited. A number of wealthy individuals sought shelter from the law here, and demonstrated their thanks to the goddess with generous donations.

LYSIMACHOS, one of Alexander's generals, ordered the dredging of a new harbour (271 BC). Additionally, he secured Ephesus behind 9 km of wall and destroyed the neighbouring towns of Lebedos and Notion so their populations could be resettled here.

Around the year 200 BC, the town fell to Pergamon; in 133 BC to Rome. It thrived as the capital of the province Asia (population 25,000). Most of the structures visible today date from the Roman era.

About 262 AD, the Goths took their vengeance, destroying town and temple. Reconstruction was marginal, the harbour filled with silt. Trade moved to more convenient ports elsewhere. In 431 AD the third Ecumenical Council was held in the Duomo (cathedral) of St. Mary in Ephesus. Under JUSTINIAN the plains settlement was abandoned and the population withdrew to the castle hill. The Ottoman attack in 1426 leveled the town, despite heavy resistance by the Seljuks.

J.T. Wood was able to discover and excavate the Artemision in 1866. Since 1896 the Austrian Archaeological Institute has been digging here.

GREAT IS THE ARTEMIS OF EPHESUS !

For a change, something from the Bible (Apostle 19, 23-40). During his second missionary journey, Paul the Apostle arrived in Ephesus about 55 AD, where he remained for three years. His preaching evidently had great success. The silversmith DEMETRIOS, who earned a living producing Artemis souvenirs, reacted with great anger. The smith called a crisis meeting of his guild, accusing St. Paul of insulting the goddess and disturbing the peace. Masses of people took to the streets in protest, increasing in strength before entering the theatre (then under reconstruction). They raised their fists high and shouted "Great is the Artemis of Ephesus!".

The mob let off steam - few were even aware of the issue - and was not challenged by the authorities. Eventually one of the town councilmen made an appearance at the theatre, only to be insulted and whistled at. "*The greatness of Artemis is not in danger*", he shouted against a chorus of whistles increasing in intensity, "*nobody has attacked her. Anybody who is of other opinion should appeal to the town court. If this uprising continues, however, we will have to make a report to the Roman authorities, against whom we have no defence.*" Christians may be bad for business, but too many Roman troops would be even worse. The mob dissipated.

St. Paul, who had taken shelter from the mob, left Ephesus.

INFORMATION: Selçuk, Efes Müzesi Karşısı 23. Near the Museum. English spoken, large information plaques, tel. 13 26.

TELEPHONE AREA CODE: 5451

COMING - GOING: **Buses** several times daily to İzmir, Aydın and Denizli. Buses and minibuses to Kuşadası on the half-hour. No problem getting a dolmuş to Kuşadası (£0.45)
Train: Several connections daily to İzmir, Aydın and Söke. The station is in the northeast of town.

FESTIVALS: Camel fights are held in Selçuk in mid January. From the end of April to early May, the Great Theatre hosts the Ephesus Festival, featuring folklore and folkdance.

A NIGHT'S REST

Pamukkale Pansiyon, Mayıs Mh. Kaner Sok. 3, £5 per person with breakfast. Centrally located, the double rooms are in the new building with shower (hot water)/WC. On Mehmet İrdem's business card you'll read: rooms, restaurant, first aid. tel. 2388.

Güneş Otel, Kuşadası Cad. at İzmir-Aydın. Double £8. Loud, somewhat spartan.

Ak Otel, Kuşadası Cad. 14, double £13, excellent service, lovely garden, nice restaurant with a pergola, solar collectors and emergency water tanks on the roof. All 22 rooms have a telephone, balcony, bath. Rustic furnishings, tel. 5451/21 61.

Kalehan Pension, On the main street İzmir-Aydın across from the Shell petrol station. Double £11.50. 20 rooms with shower and warm water. Furnishings and cleanliness are satisfactory, but a little loud. Restaurant and bar adjoining. Sun terrace, tel. 11 54.

Tusan Moteli, Efes Yolu 38 (by the turnoff to the excavation site). Double £17. with swimming pool, very comfortable. An address for people with taste. Great location, shady, tel. 54 / 51 60.

CAMPING: The nearest campgrounds are in **Pamucak** on the coast, 9 km from town on the road to Kuşadası.

FOOD: A lovely tea garden is across from the museum not far from the Information Office.

We found the food excellent in the restaurant on Main Street 6 (secondary road to Kuşadası) at the corner of Kuşadası Caddesi (the road on which the museum is located), diagonally across from the Information Office. The restaurant has a tree-lined walk and fountains. The food is good and cheap. On Sundays you can change money here at an almost reasonable rate.

Sights

The main attraction in Selçuk/Ephesus is certainly the *excavation site*. Additionally, in Selçuk, you can see the ruins of the *Artemision*, the *İsa-Bey Mosque*, *St. John's Basilica*, the *aqueduct* and the *castle hill*. Be sure to visit the *museum* in Selçuk.

The Excavation Site

To the left of the access road is the **Vediusgymnasion**, donated by P. VEDIUS ANTONIUS, a wealthy citizen. The complex is large and maze-like. Coming from the road, you first see the *warm-water rooms*, recognizable by the partially exposed floor heating.

About 100 m further, on the hill above the parking lot, is the **stadium**, with the traditional length of 192 m, built by Emperor NERO. You enter the facility through the *ceremonial gate*, the only remnant. The stone spectator seating was taken away for construction of the fortress up on the hill. Be sure to have a look inside. The layout of the structure can still be discerned.

Right next to the parking lot is a **Byzantine Bath**, which, due to its complicated structure, is called "*The Drunkard's Bath*".

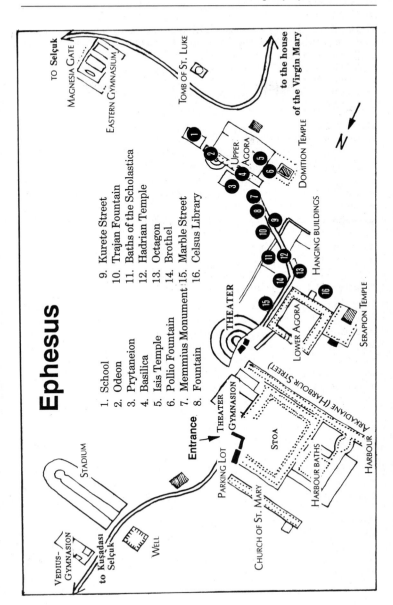

Ephesus

1. School
2. Odeon
3. Prytaneion
4. Basilica
5. Isis Temple
6. Pollio Fountain
7. Memmius Monument
8. Fountain
9. Kurete Street
10. Trajan Fountain
11. Baths of the Scholastica
12. Hadrian Temple
13. Octagon
14. Brothel
15. Marble Street
16. Celsus Library

A path to the left leads to the **Church of St. Mary**, also a duomo. Still visible are large sections of wall, columns, a baptismal basin and more. You will need some imagination to get the full picture. The triple-aisled basilica was probably constructed as an annex to a market building in the fourth century. The third Ecumenical Council was held here in 431 AD. In the seventh century, the rear section (from the road) was converted into a domed church and a baptistery. The front section became a buttressed cathedral.

Behind the official entrance on the left are the ruins of the **Gymnasium of the Theatre**, to the right **Verulans Square**, a 200 by 240 m courtyard with surrounding arcades which have yet to be completely excavated. Continuing on, you come to the **Arcadiane**, the harbour road, that lead from the theatre to the harbour (but ends in a thicket today). The 500 m long showcase street, renovated by emperor ARCADIUS about 400 AD, was lined on both sides by marble columns and arcades. It was the world's first street to be lighted at night! It is in excellent condition and the surface has been reconstructed. Many columns have been restored and placed at their original location by Austrian archaeologists. Walking down to the "harbour", you can see the still unexcavated ruins of the enormous **harbour bathhouse** on the right.

Highlight of a visit to Ephesus is the **Great Theatre**, built impressively on a slope, with a capacity for 24,000 spectators. Its origin dates back to LYSIMACHOS. Its present appearance, however, was shaped by the Emperors CLAUDIUS and TRAJAN. The diameter of the theatre is 130 m, its height 38 m. The spectators were seated in 66 rows of seats, divided in three tiers. Of the original three-story stage, only the walls of the first floor remain. A forest of columns separates the orchestra from the raised stage. The acoustics are very impressive, as is the view of the Arcadiane, down to the filled in harbour (which can be recognized by the lack of shrubs and the different colour of the grass).

Connecting the theatre and the Celsus Library is the **Marble Road**, once an avenue of arcades similar to the Arcadiane. The name of the road stems from its unusual surface of heavy marble plates. Some of the columns have been restored. On the right is the **Lower Agora** (110 m square), a market encircled by colonnades. The **Southern Gate** of the Agora, named "Mazeus Gate" and "Mithridates Gate" after its builders (two released prisoners) is well preserved. At the end of the Marble Road is the Celsus Library, built in 135 AD by C. AQUILA in memory of his father CELSUS (governor of Asia Province). The two-story structure featured a surrounding gallery on the upper floor from which you could look down to the reading room. The Austrian

The reconstructed fassade of the Celsus library

archaeological team has been able to unearth 850 of the original building blocks, representing about 80 per cent of the original building material. Over a period of eight years (1970 - 1978), utilizing a grant from the Viennese builder KALLINGER, the facade has been completely reconstructed. Even the statues have been returned to their original locations. Inside the library (it was impossible to reconstruct the gallery) are a number of informative plaques. The books were used by the Goths to heat the thermal baths - those barbarians.

Behind the Agora are traces of the **Serapion Temple** dating from the second century AD. The temple must have had tremendous proportions. Via an outer stairway, one passed into a columned entrance hall, supported by eight 14 m tall Corinthian columns, each weighing several tons. The gate to the interior was made of iron and so heavy that it was placed on rollers. The temple was used by the Ephesus-based Serapis cult for their ritual cleansing.

Kureten Street branches gently off the Marble Road and runs up to the Upper Agora. On the left, most guides point to a **brothel**. Actually, this was the site where a statue of the well-endowed god Priapus was found. In front of the house a footprint in marble points toward the entrance and there is a depiction of a rather tattered matron. Is this enough evidence? Across from the house are three **tombs**. Of interest is the **Octagon**, an eight-sided tomb, which was originally crowned with a marble ball. Further along on the left is the famous **Hadrian**

Temple (130 AD), which has been almost completely reconstructed utilizing the original parts. The arch between the two central columns is lovely!

Above are the ruins of the multi-story bath in the **Scholastica**. A statue of the patroness is preserved except for the head. Across the way on the slope is the new town excavation where several frescos have been discovered, including one of Socrates. The apartment buildings were up to six stories high. Again, on the left is the splendidly preserved **Trajan Fountain** dating from 114 AD, dedicated to emperor Trajan. Once upon a time the niches contained twelve statues. At the junction of the Kureten Street in the Upper Agora, on the left you see a fountain donated by the proconsul BASSUS and beyond the **Memmius Monument**, a memorial which was later converted into a fountain. Several pieces of sculpture are well preserved.

The **Upper Agora** (160 m by 58 m) was the political centre of the town in contrast to the trading centre in the Lower Agora. The path forks at the end of Kureten Street. Heading left we follow the north side of the Agora to the **Prytaneum**, the town hall. This is where the eternal fire burned, watched by the Kurets and Vestal Virgins. The huge Artemis statue, now on display in the Selçuk museum, was found in this building. Through an archway we enter the **Odeon** in which the town council met. The 27 rows of seats are well preserved. There was room for 1400 people. In front of the Odeon are the column remains of a 160 m-long triple-aisled **basilica** forming the northern end of the Agora.

Returning to the Memmius Memorial, we follow Domitian Street south past the **Pollio Fountain** with its reconstructed **arch**, to the tremendous foundations of the **Domitian Temple**. In the basement is an **Inscription Museum**. For each stone plate there is a plaque containing the original writing in Latin and an English translation. Read a few of the texts!

OPEN: 8:00 - 17:00 h, Admission £1, Sundays £0.50.

Even More Sights

Cave of the Seven Sleepers: If you have some time, visit the cave on the northeastern slope of the Pion (see map). During the persecution of Christians, seven youths are said to have taken refuge in the cave. Roman soldiers, who noticed their presence, sealed the cave entrance. The youths fell into a deep sleep lasting 200 years. By the time they awoke, Christianity was the accepted national religion, and they no longer needed to fear persecution. After their death, Emperor THEODOSIUS II buried them here and a pilgrim church was established.

Artemision in Selçuk: The Artemision is on the road to Kuşadası, a little outside of town. It is a half-hour walk from the excavation site (past the Tusan Motel). But there is little to see: a restored column, a few drums, lots of stones, a large pond, frogs, a family of ducks, and lots and lots of tourists; this is the ruin of one of the wonders of the ancient world.

Archaeological Museum in Selçuk: A selection of the most beautiful finds from the excavation site are on display.

Exhibit Hall from the Hanging Buildings: The portrait of a bearded man, Eros riding a dolphin, the seventh century BC statue of an Egyptian (!) priest, mosaic floors, fresco fragments, a marble fresco of Socrates, a head of Venus, a bust of Zeus.

Exhibit Hall of Fountain Statues: Notice the grouping of Polyphem and Odysseus from the Pollio fountain. Dionysos and a sleeping satyr from the Trajan Fountain. The figure of Androclos, the mythical founder of Ephesus is also from the Trajan Fountain.

Artemis Hall: The loveliest hall. Outstanding presentation (lights, background) bring two Roman marble copies of Artemis cult statues (the original must have been of wood) to life. The largest copy is 3.20 m tall. There is also a headless Artemis and fragments of a horse. The amulet hanging around the neck of Artemis is a fertility symbol, although experts differ as to whether it depicts genitals, breasts or eggs. Whatever its origins, the archaic influence is evident: her figure is a long way from the slim shape of the Greek goddess of the hunt Artemis (Roman Diana).

OPEN: 8:30 - 18:30 h, Admission £0.55, Sundays £0.30.

İsa-Bey Mosque and Aqueduct: The mosque on the southwest slope of the castle hill was built by the Seljuk sultan İSA BEY I of Aydın in 1375. The Syrian architectural style is rare in Turkey. Seen from the outside, the mosque is a rectangular block (57 x 51 m). Two-thirds of the interior is occupied by a courtyard whose arcades were destroyed during Ottoman attacks. The actual prayer hall is in the middle, crowned by two column-supported domes. The wooden roofs of the wings have been restored. The minaret has been destroyed. Of special interest are the granite columns supporting the domes (taken from the harbour thermal bath in Ephesus), the marble mimber and the wonderful stalactite portal. East of İsa-Bey Mosque is a recently restored *Byzantine aqueduct*, a popular breeding ground for storks. The water came from the south (Ortyga Forest) and from the Kuşadası region.

St John's Basilica and Citadel in Selçuk: With a length of 110 m and a width of 40 m, the basilica is one of the largest Byzantine churches. JUSTINIAN ordered the construction above the supposed grave of St.

John. In 1330 the church was converted into a mosque, before finding new use as a market hall. Later it fell during an earthquake. With financial aid from an American (a Mr. QUADMANN), partial reconstruction has restored several lovely columns and the southern longhouse arcade. A stone plaque commemorates the visit of Pope PAUL VI on 26 June, 1967.

Above St. John's Basilica is the Selçuk citadel. The Byzantines built the first fortress here. The wall crest and towers are in excellent condition.

Around Selçuk

The House Where the Virgin Mary Lived & Died (Meryemana): Head 2 km south of Selçuk on E 24 toward Aydın, then take a right. A road winds from the crossroads, past the eastern gate of the excavation grounds, about 6 km to *Panaya Kapulu*, the site of the house where Mary died.

In the mid-nineteenth century, a drawing by the German nun KATHARINA EMMERICH (1774 - 1824) depicted Mary's house and its location, although it was obvious that she had never visited the area. Using her description, in 1891, Lazarists from İzmir discovered the building on the Aladağ, 7 km south of Selçuk. It had formerly been a place of pilgrimage.

The building is a dome-topped stone structure dating from Byzantine times. Entering via an entrance hall, the aspse in the main chamber contains an altar with a black depiction of Mary. The room to the side is said to have been Mary's bed chamber. Directly under the building is a well which appears further down hill, flowing into a basin dating from the nineteenth century.

Whatever you think, a visit to Panaya Kapulu is worthwhile, if only for the restaurant and post office (for postcards!) located there.

Priene *(pop. 15 000)*

The setting is breath-taking: on a narrow rock terrace 130 m above the Büyük Menderes Plains.

Miles of fertile, ingeniously irrigated soil occupy a region once covered (3000 years ago) by the *Gulf of Latmos*. The sea ranged 20 km inland from the present-day coast, almost to the hill at Priene. North of town is a 250 m tall granite block, an outcropping of the *Samsun Dagi*. At its peak are the sparse wall ruins from an ancient acropolis.

The layout of the town is interesting. After Milet, Priene was the second town to be built in the "Hippodamian System" (chess-board fashion). The pattern is easy to see here. Visitors are quick to notice that all streets cross at right angles. Because Priene had already lost its importance in Roman times, all the architecture is Greek.

History

Ancient Priene was founded by Ionian settlers in the second millenium BC at some other location on the Gulf of Latmos (the exact location is unknown). The town played an important role in the Ionian Union as the *Panjonium*, meeting ground and the most sacred site in the union lay within it. Lydians conquered the town in the sixth century BC. A century later it fell to Persia.

Sand deposits closed the harbour, forcing the town to relocate on the high plateau. At the same time a new harbour was dredged at Naulochos, several kilometres downstream. The new settlement was built terrace-like on the slope overlooking the Menderes Plain: at the bottom the town wall and stadium (36 m up), further up the Agora (80 m), Athena Temple (100 m) and the Demeter shrine (130 m above the plain). The city treasury was almost empty when ALEXANDER arrived in 334 BC. He assumed the cost of construction of the Athena Temple and is thanked in an inscription of dedication - ancient advertising!

About 150 BC the town was entwined in the intrigue for succession to the Cappadocian throne and besieged on several occasions. Fire and plunder caused great damage. In 133 BC, the town passed into Roman hands. Sand deposits in the new harbour at Naulochos stripped the town of all importance. Priene was rediscovered in 1673, but excavations did not begin until 1868 when a British team, led by HUMANN (who discovered Pergamon) and WIEGAND, came. Sculptures and architectural parts were sent to İstanbul, the British Museum and to the Pergamon Museum now in East Berlin.

INFORMATION: No Tourist Information Office, no local guides.

COMING - GOING: From Söke, hourly minibuses to Priene. From Kuşadası and İzmir you can book organized day trips to Priene, Milet and Didyma (costs from Kuşadası £8.50). The town ruins are easy to reach on a narrow, well-built road.

A NIGHT'S REST / FOOD: Priene and the nearby village **Güllübahçe** have no lodgings. Camping out on the plain can be a problem (cultural site). By the parking lot at the east gate - small, often filled with buses - is a stand (postcards) and restaurant. Adjoining is a well containing water, brought here by an ancient aqueduct.

Sights

The entire town is crisscrossed with streets creating about 80 parcels of land of 35 m by 47 m (for major buildings several of these blocks were combined). The designer of the town was the famous HIPPODAMUS of Milet.

Theatre: From the parking lot, you pass through the ruins of the northeast gate on the so called *Theatre Street* for the 100 m walk to the theatre (dating from the third century BC), the most impressive ruin in town. It is relatively small, seating almost 6500 people in 50 rows. Right by the orchestra are five marble seats for honourary dignitaries. On the main axis is the altar of the God DIONYSOS. The ground floor of the stage building (renovated in Roman times) remains, as do the well preserved columns of the entrance hall. Behind the stage building are the ruins of a Byzantine church.

Demeter Shrine: From the upper steps of the theatre, a 40 m path leads to the ruins of the Demeter Shrine set in a pine forest. The building is in ruins but the layout is easy to recognize. The wall-enclosed district was entered from the east. The actual temple stood on the side. In front is a column hall with the stumps of three Dorian columns. In the southeast corner is a sacrificial pit. Little is known of the Demeter cult which originated in Egypt.

Athena Temple: Returning to Theatre Street, we continue on to the Athena Temple. Only the foundations remain of the most sacred site in town. The five restored columns and capitals (about 12 m tall and 1.2 m in diameter) are the main attraction.

Sacred Hall & Agora: From the Athena Temple, take the step path down to a lovely fountain. 50 m to the east is the magnificent Agora (128 m by 95 m) surrounded by a column hall on three sides. It was the centre of town and the trading centre. On the north side are the ruins of the Sacred Hall (116 m long and 12.5 m deep). The structure with two aisles boasts an outer row of 49 Dorian columns and an inner row of 24 Ionian columns. It was the political centre of the town with the official offices of the town administrators.

Apartments by the West Gate: Best preserved are the private homes by the West Gate. The buildings feature a rectangular courtyard around which an entrance hall, sleeping chambers and dining rooms are grouped. Particularly well preserved is the *Sacred House* (in which ALEXANDER THE GREAT was honoured) with pebble mosaics and two podiums for honouring the gods. In various other buildings you'll find remains of frescos and water basins.

Lower Gymnasium and Stadium: The Lower Gymnasium is accessible via stairs from the Agora. It is a classical example of Hellenistic architecture. Through a large gatehouse in the west, you enter a quadratic courtyard surrounded on all sides by Dorian columns. The North Hall (downhill side) has two aisles. Classrooms were below the rock outcrop. In the northwest corner (next to the step path) was a bath; the basins are easy to recognize with lovely encircling gutters and splendid lion-head fountains. Adjoining is the Epheben Hall where young students were taught. The marble walls are plastered over and over with graffiti.

The stadium east of the gymnasium is more than 191 m long and 20 m wide. To the west, individual starting blocks (in which the runners could place their feet) are well preserved. The racers started behind a barricade which was raised for everyone at the same time - similar to the starting gate at modern horse races. Due to the slope, all the spectators were seated on the north side. The stone bleachers in the centre and the column hall beyond are well preserved.

Bouleuterion and Prytaneon: Climbing back up to the Agora, we reach the Bouleuterion, the assembly hall of the town council, set in a small quadratic building. There are three sections of seats in ten rows of 16 (in the centre). About 650 members (one-tenth the population) could be seated. In front of the tribune is a metre high sacrificial stone upon which a sacrifice was made to the gods before each meeting. The entire building once boasted a wooden roof. Directly adjoining the Bouleuterion are the ruins of the Prytaneon, the official residence of the town administrators. You can still see a marble table and water basin in the courtyard, plus a stove in a side room where presumably the town's sacred fire burned.

Milet

During its golden age, Milet was the largest Ionian town with a population of 80,000. Over 90 colonies were founded by the people of Milet, particularly along the Black Sea coast.

A number of famous people lived in Milet: THALES who discovered the Thàles Circle; ANAXIMENES who thought air was the essence of the world; ANAXIMANDER who created the basis for the first map of the world; KADMOS who wrote the first historic chronicle; THIMOTHEOS, a famous and popular historian; HIPPODAMOS, the famous architect of the ancient world.

Ruins of the ancient settlement have vanished: The hippodamian chess-board town structure is no longer recognizable, most of the ancient Greek structures have disappeared. Only the ruins from the Roman era remain including the large *theatre* and the *Faustina Bath*. They are worth a visit.

History

Milet was supposedly founded in the fourteenth century BC by settlers from Crete. According to HERODOT, Ionians invaded the town in the eleventh century, killing all the men and marrying the women, who refused to speak to their new husbands. The town prospered quickly thereafter, and by the eighth century BC was founding its own colonies including Constanza (Roumania), Kertsch (Crimean Peninsula), Sinop, Samsun and Trabzon (Turkey). Milet reached its zenith as the spiritual and primary trading centre and the largest port of Ionia under the tyrant THRASYBULOS. This is also the era (sixth century BC) of Milet's well-known philosophers and historians; the Didyma Temple was built at this time. The town was by now strong enough to resist both Lydia and Persia. However, Persia's occupation of the straits and Egypt greatly reduced Milet's trade.

The Ionian towns attempted to rid themselves of Persian rule by way of an uprising, but Persia was too powerful and Milet and Didyma were plundered. After liberation from Persia in 479 BC, Milet joined the Attic Maritime League. In 401 BC the Persians returned. In 334 BC the town reluctantly submitted to ALEXANDER THE GREAT. In the coming centuries, Milet changed hands frequently: the Ptolemaics were followed by the Seleucids and Pergamese. About 200 BC the town was ruled by Rome, but it retained a certain autonomy and control of the Didyma Temple.

During the Roman Empire, the provincial capital flourished: CAESAR, ANTHONY and the Apostle PAUL paid visits. In this time the theatre was built.

After the Seljuk conquest in the twelfth century AD, Milet became a trading centre for the Dukes of Menteşe and site of a Venetian consulate. The İlyas-Bey Mosque dates from this period. In 1899, THEODOR WIEGAND began the first systematic excavation of the town. A German archaeological team began work in 1955.

INFORMATION: Day trips are organized from Kuşadası and İzmir (see Priene). From Söke, you can get a minibus to Altikum Plaj and get off at the village of Akköy. From there it is 5 km to the ruins. There is a large parking lot next to the theatre. Refreshments are available at a small stand in front of the theatre (shady seating). Here, too, you can get souvenirs, postcards and information.

Sights

Theatre: One of the largest theatres in Asia Minor. It was built here during the rule of Emperor TRAJAN (97 - 117 AD), on the site of an ancient Greek theatre. Although only the lower section remains, the huge semi-circular building, towering 30 m above the plains is quite impressive. The front section is 140 m long, while the upper walk is 500 m long! The seating, on three levels of 18 rows each, held over 15,000 spectators.

The 18 rows of seats in the lower level are well preserved. Notice the two columns at the centre of the lower level. They once supported the canopy under which the emperor would enjoy the show. If you look closely, you can see foot niches and at the end of every row a lion's paw as a symbol of power. Also intact are several access tunnels and the harbour stairs, which lead from the theatre to the Theatre Harbour. By the way, the prevailing winds blow from the orchestra pit into the ranks of spectators, providing outstanding acoustics. Towering over the theatre are the ruins of a Byzantine castle.

Lion Bay and Delphinion: From the Byzantine castle you have a great view of the ruins. Below the theatre are the Theatre Harbour and the Lion Harbour. These were the two most important of Milet's four harbours. We climb down to **Lion Bay** (recognizable by the tamarisk plants and swamps). The harbour entrance is marked by two well-preserved marble lions, which have sunk a good way into the swamp. There are plans to transport them to İzmir in the future. At the southern end of the harbour is the four-stepped pedestal of a harbour memorial, which was probably a stone ship at one time, in memory of the victory by Pompeius over pirates in 67 BC. From the harbour monument, a *colonnade* (Harbour Stoa) ran 160 m around the entire harbour to the Delphinion.

The **Delphinion** was a courtyard with a round marble pavilion surrounded by columns. It was dedicated to APOLLO DELPHINIOS, God of sailors, harbours and ships. Little remains beyond the overgrown foundations. From here the *Sacred Road*, upon which processions were held annually, runs south to the Didyma Temple.

Market Quarter: The 90 m x 43 m **North Agora**, which was once surrounded by columns lies west of the Delphinion. Together with the above-mentioned Harbour Stoa, it formed a trading centre boasting over 200 shops. The site is overgrown with tamarisk and algae. On the other side of the Sacred Road are the ruins of a *Hellenist hall* and a *Roman bath* (Capito Bath).

Between the North and the large South Market is the **Bouleuterion**, the town council hall, built in 170 BC. One entered through a gatehouse on the east side. Inside, rows of columns surround a courtyard where an altar was dedicated to Emperor Augustus. Behind that lies the well preserved meeting hall where 1200 council members were seated in 18 rows.

Across from the Bouleuterion is the **Nymphaeum**, a well house with a splendid three-story facade. It was donated by the father of TRAJAN. 27 gods, some of which served as gargoyles, were depicted in the niches of the main facade. The building housed public toilets and two water reservoirs. The first floor has been largely reconstructed. South of the Nymphaeum and the Bouleuterion is the **South Market**. It once covered 33,000 square metres, making it the largest market in the ancient world. Surprisingly, there have been no excavations of this site. The wonderful Market Gate has been re-erected at the Pergamon-Museum in East Berlin.

Baths of Faustina: This extensive facility, at the foot of the Theatre Hill, was built in 164 AD at the command of FAUSTINA, wife of Emperor MARK AURELIUS. It was equipped with hot, cold, and warm water basins and a sauna. The entire complex was paneled with marble. The *frigidarium* is particularly well preserved and you can see sculptures of the river god Maeander and of a lion. The 1.5 m deep basin and the stairs leading into the water are easy to recognize.

In a hollow next to the thermal bath are the foundations of a *stadium*. To the west is the still unexcavated *West Market*. South of the West Market is the excavation site of the *Athena Temple*.

İlyas Bey Mosque: The ruins of the İlyas-Bey Mosque date from the fourteenth century. It was built by the Seljuk Emir İLYAS of Menteşe.

After the earthquake of 1955, which completely demolished the village of Balat (west of the mosque), the mosque was rebuilt, but the interior remains empty. Still, it is worth a visit, if only for the quiet of the overgrown square, and for a look at the nesting storks.

Museum: Established in 1974 in the Theatre Harbour behind a small tea garden, featuring excavated finds. Nearby a caravanserai is undergoing restoration.

Altınkum/Didyma

Didyma, comparable in size to the Parthenon, is the largest ancient temple complex in Turkey. Unlike Milet or Priene, it was never a settlement.

The Oracle of the Apollo Temple at Didyma (the Turks call it simply *Didim*) was the most important in Asia Minor, second only in prestige to its counterpart at Delphi. The temple district was administered by Milet, with which it was connected via the 16 km *Sacred Road*, decorated with statues and sphinxes.

Altınkum is a faceless bathing resort, which has sprung up about 5 km to the south of Didyma; it serves mostly as a recreational resort for Turkish families. Its great advantage is its long, sandy beach (see under bathing).

History

The oracle and shrine already existed before the arrival of Ionian settlers in the eleventh century BC. In the seventh century BC the Miletians converted to the Cult of Apollo and built the Sacred Road to connect the sacred site with their town. The shrine itself consisted of a well, a laurel tree (said to mark the spot where ZEUS and LETO conceived the twins APOLLO and ARTEMIS), a crack in the earth out of which sulphuric gases rose and a small temple.

Since every pilgrim and advice-seeker left a small gift, there was soon enough money to build a larger temple. Before its completion, however, the temple was plundered and burned in 496 BC after an unsuccessful uprising against Persian rule.

At the end of the fourth century BC the architects PAEONIOS of Ephesus and DAPHNIS of Milet began reconstruction on an even larger scale. Although new pilgrims brought the temple immeasurable wealth, construction was still not complete after three centuries. That is not surprising if we keep in mind that just one of the 20 m tall columns cost £1.7 million (in modern-day terms), and the blueprints called for a forest of 122 columns. The building technique was much like that of the pyramids. Column after column was pulled up a ramp of sand and pebbles, then anchored into place. The ramps were later removed.

The Roman emperors lent great support to the project, but an attack by the Goths in 292 AD made it all in vain. After Christianity became the state religion, all work stopped. In 1493 the temple collapsed during an earthquake.

First excavations were performed by a French team in 1872. From 1905 - 1914 the temple was completely excavated by THEODOR WIEGAND.

COMING - GOING: Minibuses from Söke to Altınkum. Get off by the temple. Adequate parking for visitors by car.

A NIGHT'S REST (Altınkum): Simple pensions (starting at £3 per person), hotels and a motel.

CAMPING: **Orman**, 3 km before Didyma, right on the beach. Large, well-frequented site (also day visitors on weekends), with a restaurant. The sanitary facilities are not so good.

   Meltem: right next door to Orman. Small, and the sanitary facilities are not good at all.

FOOD: Directly adjoining the temple and across the street are simple restaurants which cater to mass tourism. We recommend the round restaurant at Altınkum Beach. In Altınkum there are a number of food stands.

Visiting the Temple Complex

The temple ruins are in a hollow, originally surrounded by a grove of trees. In front of the temple lay the famous *Head of Medusa*. The large temple (51 x 110 m) rests on a seven-tier pedestal, accessible via 13 stairs. We are now in the Entrance Hall (Pronaos) with five rows of columns. Although most columns have been reduced to stumps, you still have a tremendous sense of space because the stumps are over 2m tall. Only three of the 20 m columns are still intact. Two are side by side to the northwest, while a third is on the east side (which interestingly shows no sign of fluting - e.g. was still unfinished). Around the temple wall ran a double row of columns (called *dipteroi* = double-hall temple), the remains are still quite noticeable on the north side, while the south side shows only signs of work, but no column stumps.

On the west side you have an interesting sight: a toppled column, separated into cylinders, which you can crawl under to view from all sides. Keep in mind that each section with a diameter of 2.5 m, weighs three tons.

According to legend whoever looks at Medusa will be turned into stone

From the *Front Hall* we enter the *Central Hall* through a large gate (originally 5.6 by 14 m tall). The threshold is 1.4 m high, not permitting the faithful to step inside. The priests, who alone were permitted to enter the temple, would proclaim messages from the oracle from this threshold. The threshold is the largest stone block in the temple, weighing 70 tons!

The actual entrance to the *Adyton*, the inner court of the temple, was through two small dark tunnels. The inner court was originally planted with laurel trees. Around the courtyard was a wall 26 m tall, which is still intact up to a height of 10 m. At the west end is the foundation of a small temple, the *Sacred Shrine*, in which the well and the cult depiction of Apollo were located. An impressive stairway leads up to the Central Hall. On several stones in the courtyard are depictions (e.g. Pegasus) by builders and artists. The Persian influence is easy to spot!

OPEN: 8:30 - 19:00 h, admission £0.45.

Swimming

Altınkum Plajı (*Golden Sandy Beach*) does full honour to its name: fine, golden sand, changing cubicles available, clean water. If you are looking for peace and quiet: leave. Here is all the bustle of a carnival. And swimming is boring after a while because there are no waves.

Milas

A town with a great past. Agriculture flourishes today, while carpets are woven in a number of shops. The bazaar heralds the past. Milas is nice for a daytrip from Bodrum or as a place to visit while passing through.

History

In the fifth century BC, Milas was caught in a tug of war between Greece and Persia. In 392 BC it became the seat of the Persian governor of Karia. The HECATOMNOS dynasty (392 - 377 BC) gave Karia a golden age. The most visible works from that era are the Mausoleum of Halicarnassus and the Zeus Temple in Labraunda.

During the reign of MAUSOLOS, the seat of government was moved from the coast to Halicarnassus. After a rapid succession of rulers, Rome gave the administration of Mylasa to Rhodes in 188 BC.

During the Byzantine era, the town gained status as a bishopric. Later it was captured by the Seljuks and became capital of the Emirate of Menteşe.

INFORMATION: No Tourist Information.

A NIGHT'S REST:
   Pelit Pansiyon, Fenerburnu, Güllük Köyü, double £4, clean, tel. 14.

Sights

Firuz Bey Camii and Ulu Cami: In the old section of town, along the main road, is the Firuz-Bey Mosque, whose architecture resembles the Bursa Mosque. The Entrance Hall is followed by a wide Outer Hall, followed by the Main Hall with a dome. Notice the artistic ornamentation. The splendid Ulu Cami is in the centre of town.

Town Wall: At one time the entire town was surrounded by a wall. Today only the *Baltalı Kapı* ("Gate with the Ax" - the double ax was a symbol of Zeus) remains.

Gümüşkesen: The two-story marble Tomb of Gümüşkesen dates from the Roman era. The artfully worked ceiling is divided into quadrants that are geometrically arranged.

Becin Kalesi: Set on a hill, a little outside of town. This was the site of the original settlement.

Around Milas

Bafa Lake: See Kuşadası.

Zeus Temple of Euromos: The complex is easily visible from the road. Only half of the original 32 Corinthian columns remain, all connected with an architrave. Little is known of its history. It was probably the sacred temple of a town allied with Milas.

Zeus Temple of Labraunda: 15 km from Milas, accessible only via a gravel path (follow the signs), is the site of the Zeus Temple at Labraunda. Several excavated finds date from 600 BC, but the buildings were constructed on the command of the brothers MAUSOLOS and IDREUS (Hecatomnos Dynasty, fourth century BC).

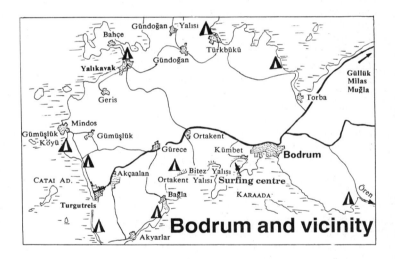

Bodrum and vicinity

Bodrum *(pop. 10,000)*

The centre of town, and its landmark, is the Castle of the Knights of St. John. It is situated on a peninsula overlooking the harbour and seems to protect the town with its shade.

The charm of the town begins with its preserved centre. The people of Bodrum realized that the construction of mammoth hotels would not make the town more attractive. The clever tourist office manager sells the town as a second Ibiza. The visitors here are crazier than elsewhere in Turkey. The tourist industry obliges. If you like action, this is the place to be.

History

The first inhabitants of Bodrum bay were Dorians (eleventh century BC). After the victory of King KYROS II, Halicarnassus, as Bodrum was then called, became Persian. Fate, however, played into the hands of a Carian-Greek dynasty. ARTEMISIA was a shrewd queen, who led her own troops in the campaign with XERXES against the Greek motherland. When this went awry, she abandoned Persia and became a member of the Delian-Attic Sea League.

This was also the lifetime of Bodrum's most famous offspring, HERODOT, a chronicler, who told the story of the war with Persia.

The Hacatomnos dynasty (the first ruling dynasty in Milas) under MAUSOLOS' rule transferred the seat of government to Halicarnassus and fortified the town. After Mausolos' death, ARTEMISIA, his sister and legal heiress, hired Greek artists and craftsmen to build a tomb in keeping with her brother's last wish. In 395 AD the town passed into Byzantine hands. After the brief period of Seljuk rule, it became the property of the Order of St. John. Bodrum was made a border fortress against the Ottoman threat. Unfortunately, the ambitious plans were greater than the economic resources, making it necessary to steal stone from the mausoleum for the castle.

INFORMATION: 12 Eylül Meydani (at the harbour in front of the castle). Open Mon - Fri 8:00 - 20:00 h, Sat - Sun 9:00 - 19:30 h.

TELEPHONE AREA CODE: 6141.

COMING - GOING: The bus station is centrally situated on Cevat Şakir Cad. Hourly buses to İzmir. Two buses daily to İstanbul (17:30 and 18:30 h). Once daily to Fethiye, Marmaris. You can take a dolmuş or a boat-dolmuş to the beaches.
Ferry to Kos, departs at 08:30 h, takes 90 minutes, returns at 16:30 h, costs £6.70 one way or £10 round trip, cars £26.70. Tickets are least expensive at Merhaba Travel Agency (direct sales).
Ferry to Datça, Wed, Thurs, Fri, Sat 8:30 h (takes 150 minutes), returns at 18:00 h, costs £4 one way or £8 round trip, advance reservations essential! The ship does not dock in Datça itself, but on the side of the peninsula facing Bodrum. When the ferry docks, there is a bus waiting (included in the price of the ticket), which covers the 8 km in 10 minutes. The ferry to Datça is a nice alternative to the bus, but not to be recommended for a real day excursion since it arrives in Datça at 12.15h and leaves at 15.30h.

Boat-dolmuş: The "water minibuses" also run between Bodrum and the nearby beaches (with nightclubs) at night.

BIKE RENTAL: At ERA Tours you can rent a bicycle for £0.70 per hour or £3.35 per day.

BOAT RENTALS are expensive.

BOAT TRIPS: are also possible without the assistance of a travel agency. There are several boats which offer trips in the harbour and on Cumhuriyet Cad. The cheapest offers are around the £3. The "Yaralı Ceylan" is recommended. Comment by a satisfied boat tripper: "Two-masted motor sailing boat built entirely of wood. Nice crew, and a good keyboard player on board. Probably better, but also a little more expensive than its competitors: £4 for a day trip to the various anchorages in the Bay of Bodrum."

DIVING CLASSES: At ERA Tours, for beginners and intermediate (costs £93.35 to £120 for six days).

TRAVEL AGENCIES: There are 20 travel agencies along the Bodrum promenade, most of which have boat trips as their specialty. There is little variety in the offers. You might consider:

Day Tour: Costs £1.70 to £2.35 aboard the "Daily Boat" which leaves the harbour each morning at 8:30 h. It cruises to some of the nicest spots along the coast, and you have time for a swim. Returns at 18:30 h, no meals.

A NIGHT'S REST

Halikarnas Moteli, at the end of the waterside road, double £30, luxurious motel, lovely location, full comfort, tel. 1237.

Grand Dolphin, Tatil Köyü, Gümbet, double £17, nice location, good sport facilities, tel. 2128 - 2409.

Hotel Gözegir, At the east end of the promenade, double £15, recommended, friendly service, a lot of "hotel" for little money.

Mercan Hotel: Centrally located on Cumhuriyet Cad., right on the beach in the middle of the bay. The hotel is an all-male undertaking, and even the chamber

maid is a chamber boy. Simple, pleasant, good quality and a nice view of the fortifications. Rooms with shower/WC. Single £7, double £11, and a room with
three beds costs £14. Address: 88, Cumhuriyet Cad. tel. 1111.

Aşiyan Pansiyon, Turgutreis, double £12 (full board), simple but clean, well kept.

Otel Çınar, Cumhuriyet Cad. 34, Bodrum, double £9 including breakfast, tel.
2638.

Yeşilclak Pansiyon, Gümbet, double £9, pleasant.

Otel Gurup, Belediye Meydanı, Bodrum, double £7, all right, tel. 1140.

Hünkar Pansiyon, Neyzen Tevfik Cad., £4 per person, simple, common showers, but clean, cheap for Bodrum, tel. 1833.

CAMPING: **Ocalyptus Camping**; Ortakent, by the sea, a good site on a lovely beach,
reasonable prices, costs £0.50 per person, £0.75 per tent, tent rental £5. Coming –
Going: From Bodrum toward Ortakent, then turn off by the Shell petrol station.

Zaferya Camping, Ortakent. A young staff manages an excellent site, right on the
beach. Adequate shade, restaurant, clean sanitary facilities, relaxed, international
atmosphere. They go to any lengths to fill the site, including advertising in buses.

Around the peninsula are a number of good camp grounds on the beach. Gümbet
has three (**Ayaz**, **Baba-Camping**, **Mocamp Ali**), of high standard, but crowded.
Additional sites along the north coast (turn off at Ortakent), see Turgutreis.

Food

Every evening, the promenade becomes a showcase for the rich and
beautiful. Have a look, there are a lot of interesting people. The side
streets have a bazaar atmosphere. This is where we enjoyed the best
ice cream which was probably made with mineral water rather than
tap water.

Restaurant/Cafe/Bar Bay Bilgutay, by the camp grounds of the same name in
Turgutreis, Abide Caddesi 33, cheap, nice ocean view, tel. 303.

The following pubs offer large selections, with prices typical of northern Europe:
Neşe, Kumbahçe Mah., Cumhuriyet Cad. 102, **Han**, Kale Cad. 29, **Agil Neyzen**,
Tevfik Cad. 104. Keep in mind: The best restaurants are in the centre of town;
east of Cumhuriyet Caddesi there are few good restaurants.

Sights

Mausoleum: This monument, 100 m inland from Tepecik Mosque,
was built by ARTEMISIA, sister and wife of MAUSOLUS. An idea of the
original size can be found in the texts of PLINY THE ELDER: The building
was 55 m high, with a 15 m tall pedestal-like lower building covering
a 33 x 39 m area around a cella (inner room of an ancient Greek or
Roman temple) upon which a colonnade with 9 x 11 columns was
built. A stepped pyramid formed the roof, crowned by statues of
Mausolus and Artemisia with a team of four horses. The mausoleum
is considered one of the seven wonders of the ancient world.
Earthquakes and the removal of rocks for the castle have left only
the foundations.

OPEN: 8:00 - 12:00 h and 15:00 - 19:00 h, admission £0.25.

St. Peter's Castle: The fortress was built by the Order of St. John, after it was forced to retreat from the Holy Land to the Aegean. In the centre are the French and Italian Tower (1431). In 1440 a wall was built around them, fortified with the German, English and Snake Towers. Also of interest are a number of finds which have been made off the Bodrum shore - from the holds of numerous sunken ships.

CEM, A HOLLYWOOD TRILOGY

Born in İstanbul and held prisoner in Bodrum, he died in Terracina (Italy) and was buried in Bursa. Great expectations (unfulfilled) marked the life of CEM, brother of sultan BEYAZIT and son of MEHMET FATIH, conqueror of İstanbul.

Mehmet Fatih failed to clarify the succession question, resulting in a battle between the unequal brothers near Bursa in 1481. CEM was defeated by BEYAZIT and forced to flee to Egypt where he was deported by the Mameluces.

Cem took an irreversible step by asking for aid from the Templar Knights, arch-enemies of the Ottoman Empire. Beyazıt, however, was shrewd. He contacted the knights and negotiated a contract to pay 45,000 ducats of gold annually - an unbelievable sum at the time - in return for the imprisonment of Cem on Rhodes and later in Bodrum (in the English Tower, where a memorial plaque hangs today). The Templar Knights eventually handed their lucrative prisoner over to the Vatican. Suddenly Cem was made an interesting offer: to lead a crusader army to recapture İstanbul. To end this threat, Beyazıt spared no expense: 120,000 gold ducats and a number of relics (including the lance tip with which Christ was stabbed and the sponge from the last refreshment). In return the Pope abandoned Cem. He died alone in Terracina in 1495. Rumours of his poisoning kept cropping up for a long time. In the end, a person, who might have made history, was reduced to a footnote - done in by the diplomatic games of his great adversaries.

Museum: Located within the castle walls. In the chapel and its side rooms you can view an interesting collection of underwater finds. Notice the *amphorae*, some up to 2 m tall. In a darkened room beside the chapel, a lovely collection of glass bowls and vases, rescued from the sea, are displayed. In the Italian and French Tower you can see the inventory of a Byzantine ship, which sank off the coast of Serge in 1025 AD. It consists of amphorae, coins and weapons. Beside a medieval knights' tablesetting, you can see Ottoman banners from several centuries, coats of arms from a number of the crusaders who resided here, and medieval weapons. There is an amphorae exhibit in the lower floor of the German Tower.

Theatre: The Halicarnas Theatre is on the hill behind Bodrum, on the road to Turgutreis. Built originally in the third century BC, the over-eager restoration team did not stick to the original plans.

Swimming

The situation in Bodrum itself looks gloomy in the true sense of the word - the colour of the sewage discharged into the sea here is brown, and the sea itself often takes on the same colour. All of the interesting beaches are in the surrounding area, see therefore under that heading.

Around Bodrum

Gümbet: The best-known surfing paradise in Turkey. Accessible from Bodrum by jeep-dolmuş (5 km), depart hourly (£0.17), hop aboard anywhere.

In Gümbet you will find everything which one expects at the "Eldorado of water enthusiasts". Surfing, sailing, diving, waterskiing, body surfing, or just take a dip in the sea or a hotel pool.

CLASSES: You can take internationally recognized classes in any of the above sports. Register at any of the travel agencies on the harbour road. Or just have a look at the beach and sign up afterward. For information, try **Muzaffer Ergöz**, Bodrum Sörf Okulu, Pk 122, tel. (6141) 12 47.

A NIGHT'S REST: We recommend **Hotel Sami**, double £19, wonderful garden, restaurant, American bar. There are many cheap rooms available, but don't expect too much of them.

Turgutreis: This tiny beach town is under transformation into a tourist centre. Atatürk, as usual, dominates the town centre, surrounded by tea gardens. There are several clean sandy beaches, but no sports facilities.

Dolmuş (£0.35) or minibus (£0.17) from Bodrum. Good connections to the numerous lovely beaches to the north (Gümüşlük) and in the south (Akyarlar).

CAMPING / A NIGHT'S REST / FOOD: The many camp grounds in the area are simple and clean, try: **Camping 86, Bilgutay Camping, Camping Akyarlar**. If you want to sleep in a bed you can chose between inexpensive pensions and hotels of the middle category. Restaurant: **Turgut Pokpolat**, Atatürk Meydanii (fish, köfte!).

Türkbükü: A lovely coastal village with a sandy beach, 25 km to the north. The beach at the neighbouring inlet at Gündogan is also pleasant. Dolmuş from Bodrum (£0.50). A longer stay is made possible here by the presence of several simple camp sites and accommodation of various categories.

Güllük: This coastal village is 30 km from Milas. On the road to the Bodrum peninsula, a road branches off after 10 km to Güllük where a clean bay invites a swim. Güllük, too, has made the transition from fishing village to bathing resort in the last few years; its infrastructure is geared to meet the requirements of tourists.

CAMPING / A NIGHT'S REST: Visit the pleasant and lovely camp grounds **Camping-Motel Gül Tur**, clean, adequate facilities, shade (olive trees). In **Motel Güllük** a nice double costs £7. Pensions offering good, clean rooms (prices start at £4 per person) can be found around the harbour and dockyard in Güllük.

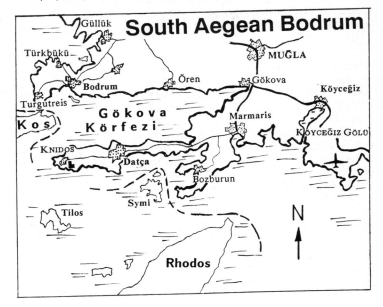

Marmaris - *(pop. 12,000)*

Those who go to Marmaris should know what they are letting themselves in for: 12,000 local people spend the winter nights here, but in the summer at least 70,000 tired people from the four corners of the earth collapse into their beds every night. What was once a sleepy fishing village has become the largest international tourist playground in Turkey.

The drive toward Marmaris is beautiful. Mountains, forested with pine and brush, stretch down to the sea.

Laurel, thyme and sage grow in this region. The *Benzoin Forest* produces the raw material for incense. The region around Marmaris is famous for its pine honey, which does not crystallize even after long storage.

Tourism is everything in Marmaris, which averages 300 days of sunshine annually. As Bodrum copies Ibiza, so Marmaris imitates Nice. Along the promenade you will find international painters, actors and musicians. A Coke is four times more expensive than elsewhere. All the same: If you don't mind crowds, are used to European prices and facilities, and like lovely beaches, then this is the spot. Marmaris' claim to fame is its wonderful bay!

History

Marmaris, founded around 1000 BC by Dorian immigrants, (formerly Phiscus) was once a trading port, gateway to Anatolia for traders from Rhodes and Egypt. In the sixth century BC, Phiscus came under Lydian rule. In 408 BC Marmaris, like all cities that had originally been founded by Rhodes, came directly under the jurisdiction of the island of Rhodes and remained thus, in spite of the coming of ALEXANDER, until the 2nd century BC. After that, it was occupied and reoccupied several times due to the changing balance of power until the Ottomans occupied the whole area in 1408; since then, Marmaris has been a part of Turkey. It declined in importance with the passage of time, but experienced the most gigantic upturn in its long history starting in the middle of the Seventies of this century - and the end is not yet in sight. There is still room in the Bay of Marmaris for new hotels; both the buildings under construction and those newly-finished attest to an optimistic view of the future.

INFORMATION: İskele Meydanı (way at the end of the promenade), very helpful and informative, Mon - Sat 8:30 - 18:30 h. tel. 1035.

TELEPHONE AREA CODE: 6121

COMING - GOING: **Dalaman Airport** (80 km away) offers a number of domestic flights each week. Detailed information available from the travel agencies or directly at the THY office at 30, Atatürk Cad. tel.3751/2. At departure and arrival times a bus goes to Dalaman Airport. The journey takes 1½ hours. Transfer costs: adults £4, children £2 (bookings can be made at the travel agencies). The taxi to Dalaman costs between £17 - 20.

Bus: The bus station is a little outside the centre, and connections are by the minibuses of the individual companies. There are good daily connections to İzmir, İstanbul and Ankara, and also to all nearby cities and bathing resorts both in the immediate vicinity and beyond, e.g. Bodrum, Fethiye, Datça and Köyçeğiz.

Dolmuş and **boat-dolmuş** maintain public connections to the beaches around Marmaris.

Crossing to Rhodes see Around Marmaris.

CAR RENTALS: **Hertz**, İskele Meydanı, tel. 2552. **Budget**, Kordon Cad., tel. 2898. **Euro-Car**, Liman Cad., tel. 2088.

BOAT TRIPS: are offered by travel agencies and by private individuals at the harbour. For more details see Around Marmaris/Day Trips.

FESTIVAL: A one-week International Yachting Festival is held in May, with exhibitions and lectures. The Music and Entertainments Festival follows in June. The favourite pastime of the hundreds of visitors is surfing, but there are also free musical and theatrical performances as well as exhibitions.

INTERNATIONAL BOOKS: Yeniyol, Demisar parajı

SHOPPING: Many of the house facades in Marmaris are completely covered by plac-ards, advertisements of all kinds and tourist goods. For simple souvenirs such as genuine carpets the rule is: prices are about 70 per cent above the normal level in the country, and many holidaymakers are as pleased as punch when they manage to get a reduction of 10 per cent by bargaining. And of course, you can get thyme honey everywhere.

SPORTS FACILITIES: **Skin diving** and **surfing**; small ships docked at the harbour pier take out swimmers and snorkel enthusiasts. However, they will only depart when the boat is full. Usually they offer day trips with several stops, cost £2 to £2.70. Some hotels and clubs (frequently luxury hotels) rent surfboards (e.g. "Hotel Martı"). Diving courses are also offered and diving equipment can be rented. Some boats in the harbour bring along surfboards for their guests (but it is expensive).

TRAVEL AGENCIES: An incalculable number offer their services. Apart from tickets, hotel bookings and other such services, they offer organised trips in every direction to suit all tastes. There is a choice of boat or bus and the range is huge. One address with a comprehensive selection of trips on offer is Yeşil Marmaris, at 11, Barbaros Ca. tel. 1033,1559 and 2290.

YACHT CHARTERS: In the El Dorado of yachting it has almost become a sign of good breeding to hire a yacht with captain and crew for a week - this is certainly the best way to enjoy the Turkish coast. The most reasonable offers start at around £67 per person per day, and increase according to the degree of luxury offered - there is no limit. An adequate selection of offers can be found at the travel agencies or directly at the yacht harbour from the captains or boat owners.

A NIGHT'S REST

Marti Tatil Köyü, luxury sport hotel, double £40.

Yavuz Hotel, Atatürk Caddesik double £23 to £27, well managed.

Hotel Anatolia, its great advantage is the fine location at the harbour opposite the Tourist Information Office, right where the motor road becomes a pedestrian precinct. A disadvantage for those who like it quiet: there is a lot going on here. Double with breakfast costs £15, and a 3-bed room £18. tel. 126 65 and 128 51.

Hotel Kalyon, İskele Meydanı, double £8, central location, but loud.

Sindi Pansiyon, Atatürk Caddesi, double £7, lovely lodging.

Pansiyon Hannimann, Liman Cad., £3 per person, very simple, but clean, inter-national clientele, relaxed atmosphere.

Otel Piana, Liman Cad., like Hannimann.

CAMPING: **Engür Camping**, a lovely site, 15 km south of Marmaris, on the next major bay. Easy to reach from Datça (signs mark the turnoff), costs: tent £1.65, £0.65 per person (children under 12 free), cars £0.30.

If you want to camp in Marmaris follow the coast to the east to several simple, small sites (**Altin Sahil, Karya Mocamp**). Heading west, a horrid road brings you to two sites, catering mostly to domestic tourism. Modest comfort (only an expensive stand for shopping). There are sites further away along the road to Datça (e.g. Amazon, see Datça Camping) and on the way to Bozburun.

TURBAN HOLIDAY VILLAGE: Located outside of town, this is the sports centre for the region. Costs (25 per cent cheaper in the off season): Bungalow for two people without ocean view £40.35, with ocean view £46.

FOOD: There are a number of restaurants along the promenade, offering a good selection of food. We recommend you try the restaurants in the nearby bazaar, where there are discoveries to be made. **Liman Restaurant**, near the water, offers a small but good selection of dishes. Just as good, but more reasonable in price, is the **Biran Restaurant**, three houses further on. It is cheaper to eat and shop on this road than in the immediate area around it.

Sights

Marmaris Kalesi: A medieval castle expanded by SÜLEYMAN THE MAGNIFICENT in 1522 and restored in 1985.

Marina: After its completion in 1988 this is the largest marina in the entire Aegean with dock space for more than 900 boats (Kuşadası 600, Bodrum 125). The docks dominate everything. Kordon Caddesi, the waterside road, runs along the harbour mole and is the meeting place in Marmaris. Most of the restaurants, bars and hotels are located here.

Around Marmaris

Day Trips Along the Coast: At the docks, a number of excursion boats make the same offer: "Just for fun"-cruises with swimming. Prices are never high: £2 to £5, depending upon whether food is included. Normally the ships depart at 10:00 h and return between 17:00 and 19:00 h. Moonlight cruises begin at 18:30 h and end around 22:30 h. It is very difficult to avoid the boat touts in the evening. In spite of an outward similarity in the prices, a calm comparison is recommended: there is a difference between a stay of 30 minutes or 3 hours at, for example, Dalyan Beach (see Around Köyceğiz). There is often live music on board, and here too the quality of what is offered can heighten or dampen the atmosphere.

Rhodes: The 3 ½ hour cruise from Marmaris to Rhodes costs £10 per person, cars are charged according to weight. The ferries are small, usually holding just one car, so get early reservations at one of the many agencies in the harbour.

Note: The official departure time is 8.00h. Crowds collect by the ferry at 9.00h. Actual departure time is at 10.00h (information from summer 1988). Question: How much time is actually spent on Rhodes?

Kaunos: See Around Köyceğiz.

Dalyan and Dalyan Beach: please see also under Around Köyceğiz.

An interesting boat cruise is offered here: you cross the lake, enter the canal, and visit ancient Kaunos.

Datça

"This up-and-coming beach resort, 80 km west of Marmaris on the Reşadiye Peninsula, seems familiar, friendly, clean and quiet". Thus we were able to report in the last edition of this book. Times are changing.

Datça, which was still a quiet Anatolian fishing village on the edge of the world and known only to few travellers several years ago, has become the favourite destination for those wishing to escape from Bodrum and Marmaris. There are still no large hotels and neither motor bikes nor cars can be hired here, but the writing is on the wall: minimarkets, souvenir shops, pensions and restaurants have sprung up everywhere in the village, and there are rows of yachts in the harbour. English is the vernacular here. A cynical tip from a tourist guide: Marmaris can no longer be recommended, but it's still nice in

Datça. You must hurry, however: in two years' time it could be too late.

The pebble beach at Datça itself is nothing to get excited about, but the surrounding region is lovely. The drive from or to Marmaris is exciting: Serpentine roads climb and fall on the narrow, extended peninsula, requiring full concentration by the driver, but rewarding with views of unspoiled gorges, inlets with sandy beaches, and barren, jagged cliffs. There are also numerous camp sites on the road to Datça far away from the bustle.

INFORMATION: Turizm Danışması, Belediye Binası İskele. The staff only speak Turkish and a little French, tel. 61 45 163.

TELEPHONE AREA CODE: 6145

COMING - GOING: Seven buses daily to Marmaris (takes 2 hours, wonderful route), the first at 6:00 h, the last at 19:00 h. Four buses daily to İzmir.
Taxi: Taxi stand across from Tourist Information. To Knidos and return (with a stay of one hour): £13.30.
Ship: Daily at 18:00 h, there is a ferry from Bodrum to Körmen Limanı, takes 2 hours, costs £8.35. From Körmen you have buses (included in the price) to Datça (20 min.). Ferries to Bodrum: 8:30 and 16:30 h, bus from Datça, 9:00 and 17:00 h ferries from Körmen Limanı.

MEETING PLACE: The disco in the Datça-Club.

SHOPPING: Across from the post office is a small fruit and vegetable market. Souvenir shops and small grocery stores on İskele Mah.

A NIGHT'S REST

Club Datça, at the north end of Datça, double £33. Large holiday village with its own beach, swimming pool, bar, restaurant, disco and a lot of sport facilities. The disco is the best far and wide!

Hotel Mare, on the beach near Club Datça, double £27 (half board or £18 without board if rooms available). A new three-star hotel with all the amenities, tasteful rooms, lovely lounge, dock.

Dorya Moteli, İskele Mah., 32 bungalow apartments, double £25. Lovely location on a cliff, surrounded by greenery. The apartments are nicely furnished, clean showers. The lounges are impressive, particularly the breakfast room with a nice view of the ocean, hotel beach. Friendly staff, charming dog, tel. 35-36.

Hotel Fudo, at the edge of town, double £17 (half board), conventional, clean.

İzci Pansiyon, İskele Mah. (harbour road), double £8. Its reputation is almost legendary. Terrace-like layout, very clean, each terrace with its own shower. Friendly staff.

Pansiyon Askin: In the style of the new trend on the Aegean coast of Turkey: a money-hungry pension with a friendly facade. Bar, breakfast on the terrace (£2). Money changed, boat trips arranged. Double with shower/WC £7. "Please don't bring any kind of food into your room." tel. 1406.

Huzur Pansiyon, İskele Mah., double £6, recommended by Tourist Information.

Cheap pensions worth recommending (£3 per person) **Kaya Pansiyon**, **Oya Pansiyon**, **Yale Pansiyon**. Showers in the rooms.

A bay near Datça

CAMPING:

There are numerous sites on the way from Marmaris to Datça; often situated in inviting bays and always amid the solitude of this sparsely inhabited peninsula. A selection:

Ilica Camping: Lovely grounds on a pebble beach behind the lake. Costs £0.60 per person and tent, camping bus £3. Showers, kitchen, electricity available, lovely restaurant, surfing. Small two-bed bungalows for rent £7, very clean.

Amazon Camping: about 30 km along the road from Marmaris to Datça, then to the right along 10 km of gravel road (signposted). Large, well-equipped site, not directly on the sea (a 10 minutes' walk or down the river by boat). Good restaurant, surfing school and hot water. Recommended.

Chen Camping: about 20 km beyond Marmaris. A large site on the road without its own beach (walking distance). Nice lay out and much-frequented.

Aktur Mocamp: about 50 km beyond Marmaris. The first sight of the beach is from above - and a joyful sight it is. The site itself is huge, with trees, a lot of leisure activities on offer and connections to Datça.

Camping Mustafa: On the Datça-Knidos road turn left at Reşadiye at the sign "Mustafas Gold Beach Paradise", then 2.5 km over a hazardous road to the site on the beach (camper trailers have made it!). Family atmosphere, good sanitation, shade, cooking facilities, surfing, boat rides (to Knidos) and skin diving. Small shop nearby.

FOOD: **Bambu Bar**, İskele Mah., in the marina. A lovely open bar with bamboo chairs and pergola. Your drinks are presented with style. Normal prices. In **Yunus Restoran** (best in the harbour) great seafood begins at £4.35, romantic atmosphere. Worth recommending is the excellent **Akdeniz Restaurant** in the harbour, meals begin at £4, good wine. The **Kösem Restaurant**, also on the harbour, is not a bad tip either. Other good restaurants are along İskele Mah. Good, reasonably priced Turkish food is offered by the **Durak Restaurant** near the bus stop/taxi rank. Prices are 20 - 30 per cent cheaper than in Marmaris and the service is 100 per cent better!

Sights

Most interesting is the small lake enclosed by a dam, which is filled by a mineral spring and pleasantly warm. A couple of kilometres walk beyond the lake is a Russian country cottage, erected for a film. It is now suffering from neglect.

Swimming

In addition to the beautiful private beaches at the Datça Club and Motel Dorya, Datça has two public beaches: a pebble beach (left of the harbour) and a stoney beach (right of the harbour). The beach to the east seems to be idyllic and ideal for families with children at first sight. Only a second glance reveals the sewage pipe. The best places to bathe on the peninsula are often the bays which are only accessible with difficulty. Thus, bathing excursions by boat are ideal.

Knidos

The town ruins, at the tip of the Reşadiye Peninsula, are a great day trip from both Marmaris or Datça.

The first thing you notice are two decrepit restaurants (by the large harbour), a rundown pension, a police station and a few bored village people who don't really know what to do. Still, you will soon like Knidos. The ruins could not be called spectacular, but the ancient culture combined with enchanting countryside makes this spot wonderful.

History

According to legend, Knidos was founded by Sparta (first documented in the seventh century BC). Within its territory was the Apollo Shrine, the centre of the Doric Alliance. Relations with the Greek homeland remained strong. On a number of occasions, people from Knidos consulted the Oracle at Delphi.

Knidos became famous as a bastion of science. The engineer SOSTRATES designed the lighthouse of Alexandria, one of the seven wonders of the ancient world. Local mathematician EUDOXES was a student of PLATO. In the fourth century BC the town was relocated to its present site, where a rectangular system of roads was installed. Knidos was allied with Halicarnassus and Rhodes.

COMING - GOING: There are boat excursions every morning from Datça to Knidos (departure: 10:00 h). There are stops to swim along the way, costs £5, negotiable in the off-season. Boats also arrive from Marmaris, but these cruises, arranged by travel agencies, are relatively expensive (up to £23.35).
Taxi: We were offered a round trip from Datça to Knidos for £13, including an hour of sightseeing. Don't expect anything cheaper.
Car: The road to Knidos is unpaved. Sturdy vehicles, if possible with four-wheel drive, should have no problem.

Sights

Harbour: Knidos had two ports, which today are simply bays. The smaller harbour served the navy, while the larger (145 m wide) was once fortified with a mole (now gone) and used by traders. Each harbour was connected by its own dam to the Triopion Peninsula.

Ancient Town: At the big harbour are the well-preserved ruins of the *Small Theatre* with a wonderful view across the harbour entrance and the Triopion Peninsula. Also preserved are ruins of an *odeion*, a *Doric hall*, a *Corinthian temple* and the *Large Theatre*.

Acropolis: On the rocky slope above the town is the acropolis with its well-preserved stone walls. Lost, unfortunately, is the *Aphrodite of Praxiteles* (350 BC), a larger-than-life Aphrodite statue, which was one of the most famous statues of the ancient world, attracting many visitors during the days of ancient Greece.

Köyceçiz *(pop. 8,000)*

During the day the little town, which is approached by a palm-lined avenue, slumbers around the pleasant central square in front of the lake. In the evenings, the chairs on the shore promenade are all taken - Köyceğiz and its lake are not only peaceful and pleasant from a distance.

Apart from peace, a serene atmosphere with a touch of southern charm, and good fish (trout, barbel), the village does not have much to offer. Those who are looking for attractions have come to the wrong place. The biggest tourist attraction are trips across the lake, to ancient Kaunos or to Dalyan Beach. Noteworthy perhaps is the fact that the inhabitants of Köyeceğiz live a life free from hectic, due to the lack of mass tourism, but do not have good neighbourly relations with the people of Dalyan, who are building up their village into a tourist resort.

Köyceğiz Lake

There was a time, many, many years ago, when the lake was a gulf. It became landlocked, and a lake was created. Today it has an area of 65 square kilometres, and is connected to the sea by a narrow canal. The lake is not fed in any way, but replenishes itself from springs, some of which are warm. Now for some good news: when the tide rises, sea water flows through the canal into the lake bringing along grey mullet and sea bass, which spawn in the calm waters. When the fish return to the sea after spawning, they are caught in the narrow canal, prepared in an appetising way, and eaten.

The Dalyan Delta, up to now, has always been a paradise for animals (except for the two types of fish mentioned above). Sea turtles lay their eggs here; otters, eagles, catfish, cormorants and pelicans have their rendezvous here. In 1987, the foundation stone for a hotel complex costing £10 million was laid (supported by the German Overseas Development Agency) in which 2,000 wealthy guests were to be able to enjoy their drinks at sunset. About 400 societies for nature preservation all over the world led a storm of protest, and public opinion slowly came round to joining them. The tourist giant TUI announced that it would not be sending any tourists to the Dalyan Delta, and Turkish Prime Minister Özal suddenly declared that a project of this magnitude should never be allowed to destroy the area. The building of the hotel complex was actually abandoned. The manager of a luxury hotel, when asked about the reason for this sudden change in policy, answered with charming naivety : "Well, because of the turtles."

The bad news: During the season, thousands of day trippers are rushed through the Dalyan Delta to the wonderful beaches of Dalyan. In the long run, this will certainly bring about as much damage as a large hotel would. They can still advertise the fact that the turtles lay their eggs here, and that there are 150 different species of birds to be found. The daily armada from Marmaris and lesser fleet movements from the little village of Dalyan will have the same effect in the long run as the hotel. And the trips to the turtle islands, which are offered on the quiet especially during the breeding season, are also a great favourite because the primeval looking shell of a sea turtle really does provide a wonderful subject for a photo.

INFORMATION: at the end of the main road, before the lake on the right. Turkish friendliness is expressed here through the medium of English; city map and an amusing map of the lake on demand. tel. 1703.

TELEPHONE AREA CODE: 6114.

COMING - GOING: 2 x daily to Marmaris, several times to İzmir and İstanbul, every hour to Fethiye and every half hour to Muğla. In addition to this, the airport bus from Marmaris to Dalaman and vice versa stops here.

BOAT TRIPS: There are half-day, whole-day or one-way trips by dolmuş to Dalyan Beach. Contacts can be made at the little harbour or in Paşa Parkı. The price of the tours is negotiable (about £12 for the whole day), and the trip to Dalyan Beach costs about £3.

A NIGHT'S REST

Özay Otel: To the right of the centre, on the lake shore. A sterile house with spartan rooms for the money: a double costs about £10.

Otel Deniz Feneri: At the end of the main road on the left. An attractive house right at the centre of action, and yet out of the way on Atatürk Square. Surrounded by greenery, small, simple and nice. Showers on each floor. £2 per person.

Ece Pansyon: A friendly little house in a side alley to the left of the main street, about 70 metres from the lake shore. Large, simple rooms, shower/WC on the passage, comfortable terrace with robust wooden tables. Do-it-yourself kitchen. The price is about £2 per person. tel. 1191 and 1075.

Derya Pansyon: two alleys behind the Ece Pansyon. The rooms are smaller, but the overall standard is higher for the same price. Well-equipped little do-it-yourself kitchen.

There are also numerous small pensions on the main road and all around it in both directions. As a rule, the prices are similar, but furnishings and atmosphere vary.

CAMPING: **Anatolia Camping**, about 1½ km to the west of the village (signposted). Separated from the lake only by a little road. A comfortable meadow camp site under tall trees and the grass is vigorously watered in the summer. This family enterprise is a quiet oasis and meets international standards. There is a self-service restaurant on the site and day trips on the lake are offered (about £10 per person including lunch. Guests who stay for more than 10 days go free). If they have not already been hired out from Marmaris, there are 10 surfboards, 5 sailing boats (for optimists) and also water skis. Amenities constantly available here: a playground for children and for everyone else, a volleyball court and several ping pong tables. Prices: adults £2, children up to 12 years of age £1, cars £1, tents £1.50, caravans £2, motor caravans £2. Motor bikes and boats £1 each, electricity supply £1. 10 per cent reduction is given on production of a camping carnet. Special rates for groups and school classes. tel. 1750.

FOOD/BREAKFAST: **Cınaraltı** is the last restaurant on the harbour mole (at Atatürk Square on the left hand side). Here, in what is certainly the best restaurant in Köyceğiz, you will receive friendly service and a meal including drinks and appetisers for about £4.

Breakfast is also available at **Paşa Parkı** on Atatürk Square in front of the lake and in the lokanta **Ali Baba**. Prices and quality are similar here, but Paşa Parkı has a nicer location.

Swimming

The greater part of the shore of the Köyceğiz Lake is covered with reeds and inaccessible. There is a small beach in Köyceğiz at Camping Anatolia, where a small swimming pool was built in 1988. The fresh water is very slightly salty, and the place is not breathtaking, but you have a view of the mountains instead of the sea while bathing for a change. The beach normally used for swimming is Dalyan Beach (see below).

Around Köyceğiz

Dalyan: Situated about 30 km from Köyceıiz on the canal from the lake to the sea. The rock graves on the other bank are a wonderful sight, visible for miles, and a little further on are the ruins of the city of Kaunos. The little village has taken up the tourist trade and is rapidly becoming a holiday resort. There are numerous restaurants (their speciality is, of course, fish) on the bank of the canal, and there is a large number of pensions, mostly new and of the standard usually found along the coast. Building is going on like crazy in Dalyan - new houses, extensions and new storeys are being built everywhere - so that the rapidly growing herd of holidaymakers can be accommodated. Souvenir shops, tourist agencies, and the numerous excursion boats complete the facilities offered to tourists here.

COMING - GOING: No problem here. There is a **minibus** to and from Köyceğiz.

BOAT TRIPS: A diverse, almost bewildering selection, but foreigners have everything explained to them at the Boat Cooperative (small office at the end of the quay).

A selection of the offers: To Kaunos and back with a "special boat" for £7 (per boat - the captain is never in a hurry). A five hour trip to Kaunos and beach costs about £14 in these boats and the additional journey to Sultaniye Hot Springs about £18. A whole day with a captain and his boat, where the itinerary can be planned freely, costs about £22. A boat-dolmuş to the beach is about £0.50 one-way. These boats leave when they are full, and the same applies to the journey back to Dalyan.

TRAVEL AGENCY: Dalyan is fully integrated into the coastal programme. **Yeşil Dalyan** organises excursions in the immediate area (Köyceğiz, Kaunos, Hot Springs of Sultaniye) and also to Marmaris, Ölü Deniz, Kaş, Pamukkale, and Ephesus.

A NIGHT'S REST: Numerous pensions, mostly new. Prices around £4 per person.

Kaunos: Can only be reached by boat. It is actually diagonally opposite Dalyan on the other side of the canal but all boats make a sightseeing detour through the delta. A few years ago, Kaunos was still a small, little-noticed ruined city without impressive remains. Kaunos has not changed; the ruins are still only "middling" as ruins go, but suddenly the whole world is going to Kaunos. Due to a lack of other, more attractive sights to visit (with the exception of Knidos), the ruins have been given such a build up by the tourist managers of Marmaris in recent years, that a trip to Kaunos belongs in every programme.

The boat trip from Dalyan is simply beautiful: passing massive, impressive rock tombs in the rock wall on the opposite bank of the canal (the oldest are Carian, the more recent are Ionic, and the newest is unfinished), the boat winds its way through little tributaries; in some places these are bordered by high reeds, in other places a flat plain opens out. The ancient city is situated near a weir. The acropolis is on the hill - those who take the trouble to climb up will be rewarded with a comprehensive view of the area from the ashlars of the fortification wall. The little Roman *theatre* is quite well preserved, as are the *baths* which date from a later phase of the Roman Empire. A little distance away from these is the small *Agora* - an attractive ancient circle in the scorched grass. The *nymphaeum,* a little behind the meeting place, is completely devoid of decoration, but also quite well preserved. Some of the stones and parts of columns bear inscriptions (in Greek) or simple reliefs (Roman). Kaunos was never important in history. Thus you should picture it, while it was inhabited, as a modest little country town. Kaunos was never a real city.

Dalyan Beach: It is actually called *Iztusan plaji* but only known as Dalyan Beach today. A sandy beach of the finest sort, 4 km long, which separates the delta from the sea. It is surrounded by water and thus only accessible by boat. The sea water is greenish - due to the delta - and not the usual turquoise blue and there are usually no waves. See also the box entitled "Köyceğiz Lake".

Sultaniye Hot Springs: Situated on a hot spring which feeds the lake. The baths were originally built by the Romans, architectural changes were later made by the Ottomans. Amongst other things, the water is good for those suffering from depression (results are not guaranteed).

Gümlük Ormanı: About 4 km east of Köyceğiz, on the main road, there is a signpost to one of the rare regions in which the Amber tree grows (also called Ambra or Gümlük in Turkish). This is the tree from which the precious Ambra oil is obtained. The area is marshy, because the trees require huge amounts of water.

Fethiye *(pop. 15,000)*

A lovely, amiable town. The adjective amiable can be dropped in summer - at that time, the inhabitants are hard-pressed in the service of the many holiday guests.

Fethiye is built on the site of the famous ancient city of Telmessos. But there are only a few rock graves left from the old city. All that remains of ancient Telmessos are the Lycian rock graves. The rest of the historic architecture was destroyed in the two heavy earthquakes of 1856 and 1958. A visit to the rock graves is heartily recommended, if only for the view of the picturesque bay and its forested shoreline. Here, in the south, there is only one colour for the water - turquoise!

If you are lucky you will see one of the huge ore freighters chugging through the bay. Turkey is the world's third largest producer of chromium ore, much of which is mined in the Lycian Taurus (20 km from the coast) and shipped out of Fethiye.

In recent years, however, tourism has developed into the biggest local industry, enhanced by the big, new Dalaman Airport (50 km to the northwest). Fethiye's popularity is based on its famous beach lagoon, *Ölü Deniz*, perhaps the prettiest in all of Turkey. This is a place for beach bums. If you are in possession of a huge beach towel, take an excursion to the beach at *Patara*, the longest beach in Turkey.

History

Fethiye was built upon the ruins of ancient Telmessos. The first recorded reference to Telmessos we have dates from the 5th century BC, when it was an important member of the Delian League. In the 4th century BC the town came under Lycian rule. Later it would fall to ALEXANDER.

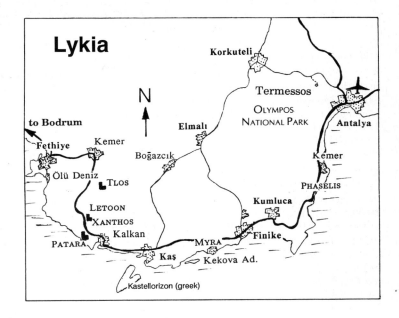

THE "TELMESSIAN" HORSE

Everyone has heard the tale of the Trojan horse. But who is aware that the troops of ALEXANDER THE GREAT used a similar ruse when capturing Telmessos? NEARCHUS, commander of Alexander's fleet, asked ANTIPATRIDES, ruler of Telmessos, for permission to dock in the harbour. He wished to return a number of imprisoned slaves and musicians to their home. Antipatrides granted permission after a quick inspection of the "crew".

In this way, Alexander's warriors were able to enter the town unhindered. Upon arrival they unsheathed swords from their flute cases and unpacked shields from their drums and baskets. The people of Telmessos could do nothing but surrender. For Antipatrides it was an embarrassment. But Alexander named him local governor. It is rumored that from that day on, Antipatrides kept away from street musicians.

After the death of Alexander, the town was annexed by the Ptolemaic dynasty (Egypt), who granted lifetime rights to exploit the city (called *dorea*) to honoured officials. Telmessos became famous for its Prophet School. The fame of the "Snake Men" spread far beyond Anatolia. A number of rulers came here in search of advice, including CROESUS and ALEXANDER.

In 197 BC the entire southern coast of Turkey was conquered by Syria. Telmessos surrendered voluntarily to ensure its local ruler the blessing of the new overlords. However, times were changing quickly. The Syrian King ANTIOCHUS was defeated by Manisa (190 BC), and Telmessos passed to Pergamon. Rome took over in 133 BC. In Rome's eyes, the town was little more than a pirate's nest on the jagged Lycian coast, unworthy of any development.

In the 6th and 7th centuries, the town was ravaged by Arab armies. It was neglected during the Ottoman era. After declaration of the Turkish Republic, the town was renamed Fethiye, ostensibly in honour of a pilot shot down during the war of liberation, FETHI BEY. (*Fethiye* also means "conquest", however, and so the name is more likely in remembrance of the conquest of İstanbul by the Turks in 1453). Fethiye profited greatly during WW II (chrome exports). It was completely destroyed by an earthquake in 1958, but then rebuilt as a model city.

INFORMATION: **Turizm Danışması**, İskele Karşışı, directly adjoining Hotel Dedeoğlu. Turkish, French. We have been more courteously received. tel. 1527.

TELEPHONE AREA CODE: 6151

COMING - GOING: **Buses** via Antalya to İzmir and İstanbul. Sizeable building operations were in progress on the coastal road to Antalya in 1988, and travellers had to reckon with a lot of dust and huge delays. **Dolmuş** connections throughout the region and quarter hourly to Ölü Deniz.
Ship: Every Tuesday a cruise ship of the Turkish Maritime Lines puts in at Fethiye (Antalya-İstanbul Route). Slow, pleasant, but expensive.
Ship Dolmuş from Fethiye and Ölü Deniz to the offshore islands.
Air: The nearest airport is Dalaman (50 km to the northwest), tel. 6111/24521. Regional flights, mostly from Antalya. Tickets for the bus to the airport are obtainable at the travel agencies.

MEETING PLACE: Everyone gathers along the waterside promenade. Or take a seat in a restaurant and watch the others promenade.

SHOPPING: A fruit and vegetable market is in the centre of town near the PTT. Except on Sundays, you'll find a rich selection of vegetables and sweet fruit. Have you ever tried Turkish bananas?

TRAVEL AGENCY: **Lykia Tour Service**, Otel Lykia, Marina. Here and in the Tourist Information Office you can book a number of day trips. Worth recommending:
Oniki Adalar Tur: This cruise visits the twelve offshore islands (9:30 - 19:00 h), costs £2.70 (meals not included).
Xanthos, Letoon, Patara: The three historic sites in the region are combined on this tour. If you have little time, this is the tour. Good guides! Costs £6. (without meals).
Patara, Xanthos, Kalkan, Kaş: Lycia the fast way, with a swimming stop, costs £6. (without meals).

A NIGHT'S REST

Dedeoğlu Otel, İskele Meydanı, double £11. By the harbour jetty, nice view from the upper floors. The rooms are not exactly comfortable (somewhat cramped), but adequate showers, lovely breakfast porch, bar. Safety last! You may see your keys hanging from your door when you return to your room. tel. 1707.

Lykia Oteli, Marina, double £13. More modern furnishing than the Dedeoğlu, view of the yacht marina, lovely garden, recommended, tel. 1169.

Meri Moteli, The only decent hotel in Ölü Deniz, by the lagoon, double £16.70. Lovely garden, private beach, restaurant, American bar, 180 beds. The guests are young, hip, international. Booked out in the summer, but they improvise, tel. 4389.

Pension-Restaurant White Rose, at the bus station. The owner is a helpful person and good, reasonably-priced food is available in the restaurant, more than just köfte and döner. Price for overnight accommodation £2 per person.

Holyday Pansiyon, Çarşı Cad. 91, double £3. An open secret among backpackers, relaxed atmosphere, 12 beds in 4 rooms, crowded. Common showers, terrace, full board possible, tel. 1696.

Can Motel, Çalış, double £13. 23 double and triple-bed rooms. Very clean. Rooms with shower and WC. Pleasant atmosphere, international clientele, surfboard rentals, tel. 1559.

Also recommended by the Tourist Information Office are the **33** (tel. 2275), the **Aygen** (tel. 1677) and the **Olimiyat** (tel. 3444). Phone in advance to be sure they have room.

CAMPING

Deniz Camping, Ölü Deniz (Belceğiz). The best known camp site on the bay, usually packed with international clientele. Heat, dirt, stray dogs, and banners from all over Europe.

Osman Çavuş Camp, Ölü Deniz. Next to the lagoon, plain furnishings, but clean. A quiet site with a friendly staff. The site runs along the beach. tel. 1430.

In Ölü Deniz there are a number of simple camp sites along the beach.

FOOD: Along the beach promenade are a number of restaurants. Prices far exceed the service. You are better off eating on Atatürk Caddesi, where you won't have an ocean view, but you will be well served.

NIGHT LIFE: Discos in "Hotel Lykia" and in Ölü Deniz in "Meri Moteli". The latter has action. This is where the international crowd gathers and two-year-old hits are played.

Swimming

The nicest beach is in **Ölü Deniz** (see Around Fethiye). The **Town Beach,** between the pier and the marina, cannot be recommended, neither can **Katrancı-Beach** (18 km to the northwest). Both are dirty.

Outstanding, however, is **Çalış-Beach**, 4 km to the northwest, clean with pebbles and sand. It has good facilities (pensions, restaurants, see above).

If you prefer it quiet, take an excursion to **Şövalye Island**. There is an hourly dolmuş boat (09:00 - 19:00 h, £0.35) from the harbour in Fethiye. On Şövalye you will find a lovely beach with dressing rooms, showers, toilets and restaurants.

Another inviting island is **St. Nicholas Island,** accessible by dolmuş boat from Ölü Deniz. The beach at **Gemile** has an outstanding reputation. And for fans of all that is superlative: make a daytrip to the beach at **Patara** (see Kalkan), the largest sand beach on the Mediterranean Sea (300 m wide).

SPORTS: You can rent a surfboard at the Can Motel in Çalış or at Sun Camping in Ölü Deniz. The prices are reasonable and the equipment is new.

"Bareboats" are yachts you can rent to skipper on your own, available at Kekova Yachting, Yat İskelesi (by the marina), tel. 1262. They speak English and are helpful. The boats look inviting. Of course you would have a larger selection in Bodrum, Marmaris or Kuşadası. The cost depends upon the size of the boat, calculate £500. to £1170. per week depending upon the size of the yacht (divided between 6 - 10 people, payable in dollars).

Hiking Tip: The Fethiye region is ideal for walks. Take a hike out to the ghost town of Kaya (two hours).

Sights

Lycian Rock Tombs: The attraction in Fethiye. The main group of tombs is along the rock wall on the east side of the present-day settlement. You will immediately notice the splendid tomb of AMYNTAS, a temple tomb in Ionian style (probably 4th century BC). Behind the two columns, which support an attractive architrave, is a richly ornamented pseudo-door which hides the tomb.

Around this tomb are a number of smaller rock graves, including several from the 6th century BC. The oldest resemble buildings from the region. It is easy to see that this necropolis was designed to be a city of the dead, in which the deceased could feel at home in the great beyond.

Lycian Stone Sarcophagi: Walk through town and you can see them everywhere: some are in a public square, others in a private garden. The finest sarcophagus is beside the town hall, near the post office.

Crusader Castle: Only rubble remains of a castle built by the Knights of St. John in the 14th century (built on foundations dating from the 4th century BC). A visit is not required.

Around Fethiye

Kaya Köyü: South of Fethiye, about half way to Ölü Deniz (in a valley, a bit off the main road) is the ancient Greek settlement of Kaya. As part of the population exchange following the Turkish War of Independence, 25,000 Greeks were resettled to the Peloponnese. This town with 3000 buildings became a ghost town.

Although the 1958 earthquake left its mark, a visit is still worthwhile. You are permitted to explore inside the houses, but beware of scorpions.

The importance of this attraction has not found universal acceptance. You may have to cut your own path in through the bushes.

Ölü Deniz: The actual beach lagoon (*Ölü Deniz* = dead sea) is about 15 km south of Fethiye, easy to reach on a well paved road. You may think you are in the South Seas - crystal-clear water, lovely, snow-white sand, jagged cliffs, Turkish wooden yachts at anchor. Admission £0.35 (includes umbrellas, beach chairs, and showers). It has recently become necessary to add that the beach is stretched to the limits of its capacity during high season.

The southern end of the beach (*Belcegiz*) is equally enchanting. Fearless explorers will notice that the large dunes begin here. The sand could not be cleaner in the middle of the Sahara, and there is no admission charge.

COMING - GOING: Dolmuş from Fethiye every 15 minutes (£0.50). The drivers compete for the world record in cramming paying passengers into one vehicle. On the steep road beyond Ölü Deniz the lamest donkey could keep pace. But the ride is fun.

Tlos: 42 km south of Fethiye is ancient Tlos. Its origin dates back to the 2nd millennium BC. Sources dating from the 14th century BC speak of a settlement called Tlava. During the Lycian era it was the mightiest town in the region. Its hill (crowned today by a Byzantine castle) controlled the entire Xanthos Valley. During the Roman Empire, Tlos experienced a golden age, and received the title "most glowing metropolis of the Lycian nation". This town was a bishopric during the Byzantine era.

The grounds are overgrown with poplar trees, brush, and grass. You will need a good eye to see the past. The castle hill, with its ruins of a Byzantine fortress and a Lycian rock necropolis, is easy to spot in the wall below the castle foundations. Despite the strenuous climb, a visit to the necropolis is well worth while.

In one of the temple tombs, you can see interesting reliefs depicting panthers, horses and the famous *Bellerophon Epic*.

Below the acropolis is the *Tlos Stadium* of which only a few stone seats remain. Running parallel is a 160 m long *triple-aisle basilica* which was once two stories tall. To the south are two *Roman baths*. Of the once tremendous chambers only a few, ivy-covered columns remain.

BELLEROPHON

BELLEROPHON, the son of the Corinthian king, was forced to flee from his father to this region where he asked IOBATES of Lycia for asylum. Asylum seekers were just as unpopular back then as today. Bellerophon was first required to kill a chimera (with the aid of the hippogriff PEGASUS, who ATHENA sent to his rescue). Then he was forced to do battle with Amazons. In the end he was deported anyway. Bellerophon was so angry he asked POSEIDON to flood the Xanthos Valley. As Bellerophon drifted toward Xanthos on the first wave of flood waters, the women of the town ran out to meet him, offering their charms if he would only spare the town. Our hero was distracted and lost his anger. Now Iobates changed his mind, deciding to marry one of his daughters to the refugee. After that Bellerophon probably was issued with a Lycian passport and all his problems were solved.

Off to the east, and easy to overlook, is the *theatre* in a grove of bushes. Its semicircular auditorium and 34 rows of seats (well preserved) formed the perfect model of a Roman theatre. Astonishingly, it was built upon a flat plateau, and not on the slope. It is easy to see why the construction required 150 years (documented).

Kalkan *(pop. 1000)*

There is an idyllic, fairy-tale atmosphere in this former Greek fishing village. This is not a place to seek excitement. But Kalkan is a wonderful spot to relax.

The village descends to the sea in several terraces. Whitewashed houses are nestled on a slope around a sleepy harbour. Not without reason is Kalkan considered by some to be the Portofino of Turkey. And Kalkan would win by comparison. Here tourism has already left its infancy behind, but there are still no signs of excesses, and the landscape is not yet characterised by large hotel complexes. The most ambitious project in the village, a modern yacht harbour, is being constantly persued. But the winter storms can be relied on to sweep away the harbour mole every 2 to 3 years. Thus, at the moment,

Kalkan presents itself as a pleasant little holiday village, where the inhabitants do not seem to achieve exactly what they set out to do.

Kalkan is a wonderful departure point for trips to the surrounding region, e.g. to the beach at Patara, to Kaş or even to Xanthos and Letoon. The lodgings might not satisfy the Queen, but the outstanding seafood in the restaurants might well make the royal table. So why not stop in Kalkan next time?

BEHIND THE FACADE

The inhabitants of Kalkan have sold off the greater part of the village to shrewd speculators in the tourist business from the large cities of Turkey. Vigorous building activities are going on in the open areas. At the moment, the level of tourism is modest here, compared with the other Turkish holiday centres on the Aegean and Mediterranean coasts. But if the boom continues, and it is expected to do so, the village will develop like Kaş or Datça, where more and more tourism of the middle category is being marketed. The vicious circle of the holiday business: freaks and globetrotters prepare the stage for managers in the tourist business all over the world. The houseowner, who at first rented out simple rooms to backpack tourists as a sideline, is pushed out or put paid to by a tempting financial deal from a businessman from İzmir. Of course holiday "specialists" can cosset their guests with the hot showers and bars that are a matter of routine to a much greater extent than a friendly village family, whose stand-up toilet is shared by all. Thus the backpack tourist with a small wallet is slowly disappearing - and a better class of client is moving in. Now big business can really begin but only a few become rich from it.

While the small managers engaged in the holiday business on the Black Sea Coast - the owners of camp sites, hoteliers and restaurant owners - look jealously at the Aegean and ask uneasily whether the waves caused by the flood of guests will also reach the Black Sea shores, the atmosphere on the coast of the Levant is slowly changing. Only a few of the local people are experiencing a concrete financial advantage from the mass invasions of the summer. The big money is shared out amongst a handful of businessmen in the big cities and a few international tourist companies. Most of the inhabitants of the Turkish coast have to look on impotently while their familiar fishing villages and little harbour towns become businesslike, disfigured tourist meccas where customs are introduced which are shameless by Turkish standards. The price level adjusts itself to the type of clientele, but the wages don't. The farmer who has sold his land and the fisherman who has sold his house have no perspective. Their sons have to find work as waiters or souvenir sellers and get only the tiniest crumb from the cake of tourism. So it is only understandable that the friendliness of the Turkish inhabitants along the coast has given way here and there to a certain resentment against the foreigners who they once welcomed with open arms. They have found out, in the meantime, that mass tourism has brought them no advantages. On the contrary: it has set off an avalanche, the damaging effects of which cannot yet be seen in their entirety.

The future of Kalkan has to some extent been preordained. The village will go the way that the partners in the leisure business have mapped out: the range of services offered to tourists will be mercilessly expanded and thankfully received.

TELEPHONE AREA CODE: 3215

COMING - GOING: Kalkan profits from its location on the İzmir-Antalya bus line.
Buses stop here twice daily, and pick up passengers, if they aren't full. The decision is made by the bus driver, not by the number of seats!

Taxi: Most fun is the donkey taxi, which a clever Kalkanese offered us at the harbour. Only for patient people. Easier to use the diesel version. Otherwise, numerous taxi drivers offer themselves and their vehicles for every kind of journey imaginable, both in the immediate vicinity and further afield. Prices are a matter of negotiation.

Boats: Available for charter in the harbour. Be sure to organize a group to fill the boat, otherwise it can be very expensive. Tip: let the best negotiator in your group handle the bargaining. The more people who participate in the negotiations, the higher the price will be.

Connection to Patara Beach: minibuses go to the beach every morning at around 10.00 h. Return journey at 17.00 and 17.30 h.

SHOPPING: Halil Sertcolik is a tailor with good taste and a deft needle. He also makes clothes to measure, and has his shop in the covered shopping passage, at 16, H. Altan Cad. tel. 1359.

A NIGHT'S REST

Deniz Pansiyon, Kordon Cad. 5, double £6, rooms with shower, great ocean view, tel. 1047.

Pasha's Inn, 10. Sok 8, double £15. A pension in the new style which has a bar and takes credit cards. They overdo the distinguished atmosphere, but the house is okay, tel. 1017.

Çetin Pansiyon: In the second row, as it were; a comprehensive view of the sea is still possible from the small, agreeable inner courtyard. Simple, clean rooms, mostly with a shower on the landing. The friendly proprietress ensures that there is a pleasant atmosphere here. Double £5. tel. 1094.

Erdem Pansiyon: modest, cheap, small, and in a quiet out of the way position, which is difficult to describe - you will have to ask. Pleasant rooms with balcony, but the dark bathroom on the ground floor is rather a weak point. £3 per person.

Other pensions are scattered throughout the whole village, there are no big hotels.

FOOD: The cheap restaurants, where the range of food offered comprises pizzas and hamburgers, are by the bus stop. A number of better-class restaurants, where prices are all at about the same level, compete with each other in the covered shopping passage. A common local speciality: various delicious appetisers for £2 as many of them as can fit onto the plate. The restaurant **Madımak**, on the way from the shopping passage to the harbour, is to be recommended: quiet, pleasant and good food, the prices are about the same as those at the restaurants in the shopping passage. There is a row of first class fish restaurants, in the upper price category, at the harbour. The swordfish in Kalkan is very tasty.

Swimming

Kalkan itself is less than spectacular. But this is only in reference to the tiny beach next to the harbour. The water is crystal clear. Not far from town, however, are several lovely beach inlets, particularly Patara (see below). But you must do without showers and toilets.

Letoon Beach: The name Patara Beach is used for the eastern end of the 5-mile-long sandy beach, while Letoon Beach is the name used for the western end. Less of an infrastructure here (two simple restaurants on the river before the beach; the first of these, on the other side of the river and reached by a bridge, is the nicer) and no public transport facilities. It is possible to pitch tents near the restaurants.

COMING - GOING: Proceed as for Letoon, then take the road to the left. After driving about 5 km on this bumpy gravel road you will reach the beach.

Bay of Kabutaş: The sea has dug a small sandy beach out of the steep coastline below the coast road from Kalkan to Kaş. This is a favourite destination for the excursion boats and cars can be parked up on the road.

Around Kalkan

Xanthos and Letoon

About 15 km north of Kalkan, in the *Esen Çay* valley of the ancient Xanthos River, are the ruins of the town of the same name. This was the mightiest of Lycian towns, and a member of the Lycian league in late Greek and Roman times.

According to HERODOTUS, Xanthos was founded by settlers from Crete. Archaeologists have unearthed evidence of a heroic battle waged against the advancing Persians in the 8th century BC, the story of which was passed down to us by HERODOTUS. "*The Xanthians of today are mostly descended from eighty families. These eighty families were absent during the siege by Persian forces and so survived.*" Their valiant defence impressed the Persians, who therefore declined to establish a military presence at Xanthos, leaving the town its autonomy. About 470 AD the town passed into Athenian hands and experienced a golden age.

After the takeover by ALEXANDER, in the winter of 334 BC, Xanthos was a bone of contention among the diadochi, falling temporarily into the hands of Rhodes, before achieving independence in 168 BC at the head of the Lycian League. In 42 BC the town was captured by BRUTUS (murderer of Caesar) who was on the run from OCTAVIAN. It must have been a terrible time! Xanthians committed collective

suicide in such numbers that Brutus was forced to offer a reward for each saved (!) Xanthian. Only thus were 150 citizens spared from death.

During the Roman Empire Xanthos prospered as a provincial capital. The town was a bishopric during the Byzantine Empire. Arab attacks during the 8th century wrecked the town, ending its importance.

The *theatre* in its present form dates from the 2nd century BC. While the seats are relatively well preserved, nothing remains of the two-story stage building. Directly behind the spectators' seats, at the same level as the stage building, rise the rectangular, pillar-shaped *Harpy Monument* and a *pillar sarcophagus*. The Harpy Monument is decorated with reliefs of sitting figures receiving fertility symbols (rooster, egg, pomegranate). These reliefs are considered the high-point of Lycian sculpture. The monument owes its name to the harpies on the sides (legendary figures, half-woman, half-bird). The pillar sarcophagus is a double tomb. Dating from Hellenistic times it has a pillar-shaped pedestal, which is hollow in the centre to hold the coffin. A second stone sarcophagus was later placed upon this pedestal.

Across the road is an interesting *Lycian tomb*, built like a house. The agora was located in front of the former stage building. Still preserved is a *Triumphal Arch* dating from the Reign of VESPASIAN and at the northeast corner the so-called *Obelisk*. The name is confusing as it is actually a tomb decorated with inscriptions on the exterior. The 250 lines of text laud the heroic deeds of the deceased.

Xanthos was robbed of one of its greatest monuments in the 19th century: the *Nereiden Monument*, a small Ionian temple set on a pedestal with marble inlay, and a masterpiece of Lycian masonry. It is on display in the British Museum today.

Letoon, 4 km from Xanthos, can be reached on foot or with your own vehicle (signposted). This was the most sacred shrine of the Lycian League.

Only the foundations of Letoon's three main temples remain. Excavations indicate that the western temple, facing the parking lot (30 x 15 m), was dedicated to Leto; the eastern temples were dedicated to Apollo and Artemis. It is unclear to which deities the smaller, central temples were dedicated. The large temples were once encircled by a row of columns, the stumps of which can still be seen by the Temple of Leto.

South of the main temples are the ruins of a *Byzantine church* which was destroyed in the 7th century. Further west are the remains of a gigantic Spring Temple, the *Nymphaeum*, which was built above a sacred well. Towering to the north are the column stumps of the *North Portico*, a splendid gate jutting out from a pond, providing access to the facility. Further north is the theatre with its well preserved rows of seats.

COMING - GOING: By **bus** or **minibus** from Kalkan toward Fethiye to the village of Kınık near the ruins of Xanthos. From there follow the signs along the country road to Letoon (4 km). If you want to avoid the walk, join a tour or take a taxi (costs £1.35)

LETO, THE MOTHER GODDESS OF LYCIA

LETO was made pregnant by her lover ZEUS. Zeus' wife HERA became jealous, forcing Leto to flee to Delos where she gave birth to the famous twins ARTEMIS and APOLLO. Later they settled in the region of Xanthos. Wolves showed them the way to the Xanthos River where Leto was able to wash and refresh her children. In thanks she renamed the territory (known until then as Termilis) "Lycia", after the wolves (*Lykos* means wolf). Since then, Leto has been revered as the Goddess of Lycia.

Ruins and the Beach Patara

Patara was one of the most important towns in Lycia and the main regional port. But since ancient times the town has battled against erosion sand which has clogged a tributary of the Xanthos River and threatens to close the harbour entrance.

Since the town was abandoned 800 years ago, the former harbour has been transformed into a sand dune. The beach is 8 km long and over 400 m wide. The sand is white and glowing hot. And the water is lovely! Powerful waves wash ashore in a comforting rhythm; the water is crystal clear; swimming is great. Two restaurants in front of the entrance to the beach offer food and drink, as well as showers and toilets. Drinks and snacks are sold and sun shades hired out on the first section of beach. But the beach is long, and those who feel the need for absolute peace can find a solitary little spot after a short walk along the water's edge.

Patara offers more than the prettiest beach in Turkey, and the largest along the entire Aegean, it is a place of archaeological interest. Nothing remains of the Apollo Oracle of ancient times, but other structures compensate.

We enter town through the splendid *Triumphal Arch* of METTIUS MODESTUS (100 AD). Few Roman structures in Turkey are so well preserved. Only the balconies are missing. Not a stone has fallen from the three arches or thick supporting pillars. The *theatre* presents a symbiosis of nature and craftsmanship unmatched in all of Lycia. In the orchestra, almost completely filled with drifting sand, luscious brush has taken command and has spread over into the rows of seats. Also of interest is an ancient *silo*, two *baths*, the foundations of a *lighthouse*, remains of *a town fortress wall* and a solitary *temple sarcophagus*. The spot's appeal goes beyond the ruins, to the wild steppe, lovely beach and a turquoise-blue sea. PAUL KLEE and AUGUST MACKE would never have gone on to Tunis if they had stopped in Patara along the way.

COMING - GOING: From Kalkan, it is 8 km northwest toward Kınık and Fethiye, then left toward the sea (signposted). In the morning there are minibuses from Kalkan (10.00h), Kaş and Fethiye, and the return trips are in the late afternoon (Kalkan 17.00 and 17.30h) The current departure times are posted at the final bus stop before the beach. Other possibilities are taking a taxi or hitchhiking (busy traffic).

A NIGHT'S REST / FOOD: The little village of **Gelemiş** is situated a short way before the ruins of Patara. For the sake of simplicity the village is also called Patara today. About twenty restaurants and pensions take care of the needs of those who are interested in bathing at Patara Beach. Apart from the meals and accommodation available there, it boasts no attractions of any kind, such as bars or souvenir shops, and the beach can be reached in 20 minutes on foot.

Kaş *(pop. 5000)*

The white facades of the Greek houses glisten in the sunlight. Attractive souvenirs vie with them for brilliance and the strong colours of carpets shimmer in the sun.

Within the space of a few years, Kaş has developed from a hot tip among backpack tourists to a favourite tourist resort. The place was known in antiquity under the name of *Antiphellos* and PLINY reported that its inhabitants lived mainly from the export of wood and sponges. Today, immaculate tourism of the middle category is marketed here. During the day, boat trips to the beaches and islands round about the resort are a favourite. In the evening, Kaş shows what it is able to do and that is giving its paying guests a carefree time.

INFORMATION: on the central square by the sea, Cumhuriyet Meydanı 7, tel. 1238

TELEPHONE AREA CODE: 3226

COMING – GOING: There are several buses daily to Antalya and Fethiye. Express buses to İstanbul and Ankara. The bus station is a large sand lot.
Dolmuş: Every one or two hours to Demre or Kalkan. There are ship dolmuşes to the offshore islands. The taxi stand is by the harbour.
Ship: Every 14 days (Saturday) a Turkish Maritime Lines cruise ship puts in en route to Antalya. It is usually late, so expect to depart on Sunday!
Bus to Patara: Tickets for the bus to the beach (£2) are sold, for example, at Kahramanlar Turizm (near Tourist Information). Departure 10.00 h, arrival 18.00 h.

BOAT COOPERATIVE: This association of small boat owners offers tours from the harbour. The prices are mostly a little lower than those quoted by the travel agencies.

EXCURSION TO MEIS: Called Megisti or Kastellorizo in Greek, for Megisti is a Greek island. These excursions were not being operated in 1988 because of the political tension between the two countries. There was complete uncertainty as to when this part of the tourist programme could be resumed.

FESTIVAL: Demre Santa Claus Festival in Demre (each year from December 6 - 8).

MEETING PLACE: The restaurants by the waterfront. There is no disco.

MOPED RENTAL: At Sima Travel Agency, costs £12 per day (plus petrol).Of course, there are also cars for hire here.

SHOPPING: The merchants of Kaş take account of the fact that the surrounding area is a paradise for divers, and offer any quantity of snorkels, masks and flippers.

TRAVEL AGENCIES: Kaş is firmly and officially in British hands. The travel agencies work exclusively together with British companies. **Simena Travel Agency**, Cumhuriyet Meydanı, offers the following day trips: boats to **Kekova**, **Simena** and **Teimiussu**: 9:30 - 19:00 h, £7 (see Kekova). Boats to **Kaputs Plajı**: 9:30 - 19:00 h, £8 including lunch. Excursions to the nicest beaches in the region.

Demre/Myra Tour: 9:30 - 18:00 h, £8, including a swim break. Excursion to **Gömbe**: 9:30 - 18:00 h, £10. Excursion into the backlands with fishing and a walk to a large waterfall.

In addition there are also whole-day excursions to **Dalyan/Kaunos** (Sundays, £16), **Fethiye/Ölü Deniz** (Mondays £14), **Xanthos/Letoon/Patara** (Tuesdays £14), and a 2-day trip to **Pamukkale/Ephesus** costs £43. A three-day "**mystery tour**" along the cost by boat costs £64 per person.

YACHT CHARTER: Simena Travel offers one week, including crew and catering, at £223 per person when there are 10 participants. Only drinks are extra.

A NIGHT'S REST

Hotel Lykia, Hükümet Cad., double £15 (including breakfast). Peacefully set with a splendid garden and a lovely rooftop terrace. 18 rooms, 43 beds, extremely clean, regular clientele returns every year.

Ali Baba Motel, Hastane Cad., double £6, or more expensive with shower. Rooms are clean, although the hotel is a bit dirty. Quiet, tel. 1126.

Antiphellos Pansiyon, Kücükçakıl Plajı, double £5, common showers, rooms of the usual standard, clean, pleasant.

CAMPING: **Kaş Camping**, Cukurbağ Cad.; £2 per person, relatively small, simple furnishings, a little cramped, tel. 10 83.

FOOD: **Eris Restorani**, Cumhuriyet Meydanı 7, adjoining the Tourist Information Office. The food (incl. fish) is good. Chickens walk around the table while you eat - not everyone's cup of tea.

Along the harbour promenade (rebuilt after the ravaging storm of 1985) are a number of seafood restaurants. Cheaper locantas can be found on Elmalı Caddesi running from the harbour to the bus station. There is a daily fruit and vegetable market by the station.

Sights

Sarcophagi: There are a number of sarcophagi scattered at various spots throughout town, most in poor condition. The loveliest ancient Lycian tomb is in the centre of town on Postane Sok. It is over 4 m tall.

Theatre: The Theatre of Antiphelos (1st century BC) is well preserved, but small with just 25 rows of seats. A visit is worthwhile if only for the lovely sea view.

Swimming

We cannot recommend *Küçük Çakıl Plajı*, in town east of the harbour (sewage, cramped, awful smell). The nicest beaches are *Büyük Çakıl*, 15 minutes on foot to the east, and *Liman Agzı*, accessible by ship dolmuş in 20 minutes. For Kabutaş-plajı see under Kalkan/Swimming.

Recreation

Kaş and the Kekova region with their underwater ruins are the perfect place for diving. The water is clear and warm. There are a lot of fish. Two underwater caves and a reef provide a few thrills.

The **Barracuda Club Gelsenkirchen** runs a diving school in Kaş. The diving instructor Ali Osman Çakıs and his assistant Adolf are well known in town. For more information, ask in Hotel Lycia. A week-long diving course with an experienced instructor and certificate costs £83.35. Individual instruction for advanced divers costs £8.35 (with own equipment excluding bottles) or £11.70 without equipment. Beginners classes have been offered since 1985. The school can accommodate up to 25 students, so it usually has vacancies.

Surfing: At Pamphilia Tours by the harbour you can rent a board for £6.35 per hour. A course with ten lessons costs £50.

Sailing: Simena Travel Agency on Cumhuriyet Meydanı rents sailboats, 11 m long, costs £20 per day.

Around Kaş

Kekova

The island faces Kaş. The easiest way to reach it is on an organized tour which will include the historic sites at *Simena* and *Teimiussa*. Kekova is famous for its *underwater ruins* along the north coast. In the crystal-clear water you can see a sunken settlement. The ruin of a church (apse) right in the Bay of Tersane is very picturesque. A number of inlets invite a swim.

Simena, like few other Turkish villages, projects you into a Greek Aegean settlement. However, the buildings are more grey than white. Everything seems neglected and poor. But we can easily recommend the seafood restaurant on the small harbour dam (seafood starting at £3.35). Rising above the village is a medieval castle, built upon ancient foundations. In the castle is a small theatre (capacity 300) hewn into the rock, without a stage. En route from the water to the castle, you pass a number of typical stone sarcophagi.

Teimiussa (east of the village of Ügacik) is a town of tombs, some in the water, others on the slope overlooking the coast. We particularly liked the "Gothic Sarcophagi", heavy stone sarcophagi with massive half-round iron or bronze tops, which you'll find throughout the necropolis.

Next to Kekova are two smaller islands, *Kara Ada* and *Toprak Ada*, which were once connected. In ancient times, large amounts of rock were carted away for use as construction material (little remains of the islands).

COMING - GOING: Üğacık (Teimiussa) and Simena are accessible by poor roads. Boats can be rented for £33.35 per day. Better still is the **dolmuş** to Kekova, costs £3.35, departs from the harbour at 9:30 h. Tickets available at Simena Travel Agency on the harbour square behind Tourist Information.

Myra *(Demre)*

Demre is a large agricultural centre where tomatoes are king. Coming from the north, along the narrow, serpentine coastal road, look down the jagged slope to the marshland plains below. Notice the areas covered with plastic. They are hothouses for tomatoes. The climate is excellent, providing three harvests annually.

Demre is famous for its native son, Bishop NICHOLAS OF MYRA (300 - 350 AD), whom children throughout the world honour as St. Nicholas. The bishop's church was renovated in 1862 on the orders of Tzar NICHOLAS I of Russia. A sarcophagus containing the saint's last remains was taken away to Bari in 1087 AD by Italian merchants. There are rumours that the Italians took the wrong sarcophagus (they dug it out of the floor, while pilgrims revered a coffin standing in the apse). What is certain is that the bones of good old Santa Claus have long since been spirited away. It is unlikely that the rubble, marketed today as the sacred sarcophagus, could be anything other than counterfeit (in the author's opinion). The museum in Antalya displays what it claims are jawbones and bone splinters from St. Nick (see Antalya/Museum). The triple-aisle basilica is a simple Roman structure with a number of additions dating from later epochs.

BUSY SANTA CLAUS

A poor man lived in Myra during the time of Bishop Nicholas. The man had three daughters and no dowry. The wealthy bishop decided to help. Modest as he was, the bishop stole to the house under cover of darkness, but all the windows and doors were locked. Finally he climbed up on the roof and threw a sack of gold down the chimney into the house. By chance, the girls had hung their stockings over the fire to dry, giving the gold a soft landing in the wool. Since this "lucky" event, children throughout the world have hoped to profit as much by hanging their stocking in front of the chimney or door on the 6th of December.

We don't want to steal from Myra's saint the honour of being Santa Claus, but there are other claimants. An employee at the French National Research Centre (CNRS) traced the family tree of that jolly elf. It seems that Santa Claus had no less than 30 fathers! The oldest of these was GARGAN, son of a Celtic god who cloaked himself in red and astonished children with presents. The ancient Romans knew how to profit from the event: during the Saturnalias (December 17 to 24) shops bustled in preparation for an exchange of gifts. Only later did our man from Myra pull the chimney and stocking trick.

"Santa Claus", as we know him, owes his popularity to the writer CLEMENT CLARCK MOORE (1822) who also invented the sleigh and reindeer.

The ancient town of Myra is located 1.5 km beyond Demre by the village of **Kocademre**. The first recorded mention of Myra dates from the 1st century BC when it was an important town in the Lycian League. The town prospered splendidly during the Pax Romana, but had no political importance. The settlement did not become famous until the 4th century AD brought reverence of St. Nicholas. Arab attacks forced the inhabitants to abandon the town in the 11th century.

Of interest are the public *theatre* (partially hewn into rock, notice the lovely frieze depicting theatrical masks) and the sparse remains of the acropolis. Most fascinating are the rock tombs of the **Lake Necropolis**. Between the steep vertical cliff walls are dozens of burial caves and cells, but also tomb buildings and tomb temples - similar to those in Fethiye. The prettiest tomb temples are decorated with colourful reliefs, some depicting warriors in full armor, battle scenes, or scenes from the life of the deceased. These reliefs are considered masterpieces of Lycian sculpture!

Finike *(pop. 8000)*

This port town makes its living primarily from the export of oranges grown on huge plantations. There are few sights of interest. But there is a wonderful, kilometre-long sandy beach.In recent years, Finike has endeavoured to pin its hopes on national tourism. The result: wide stretches of the miles of sandy beach have been built up.

TELEPHONE AREA CODE: 3225

COMING - GOING: Several buses daily to Antalya or Fethiye. Get a dolmuş to the surrounding towns, e.g. Lymira, Elmal and Demre and along the beach to Kumluca.

A NIGHT'S REST: **Şehir Otel**, Cumhuriyet Caddesi 37, double £5.35, common showers. Also rooms with shower and WC (more expensive), tel. 183.

CAMPING: A huge site on the beach (signposted).

FOOD: We can recommend the restaurants in the harbour. Best known is certainly the fish restaurant (due to the megalomaniac sign at its entrance). We preferred the Deniz Restaurant, by the Şehir Otel, where the local people eat.

Swimming

A lovely, clean beach runs from Finike to the industrial town of Kumluca (several kilometres long). A little outside Finike, the beach has not been built up.

Kemer

"Kemer 2000" is the name of the project: a tremendous recreational facility is under construction. Regional attractions include Olympus National Park, with its lovely beach, and Phaselis, an excavation site surrounded by forest.

You may hear whispers that the nicest thing about Kemer is the highway to Antalya! Responsible tourism is the key. Sewage and garbage-incineration facilities have been built. There is ample water and electricity. The hotels are supposed to fit into the countryside without disturbing the village structure. We were amazed.

The project close up: concrete and steel foundations, noise, the stink of diesel fuel, blocks of concrete in the harbour (destined to be part of the new marina docks), and in the middle of all this an old man on a donkey. This is what you can buy for US $30 million financed by the World Bank!

INFORMATION: Kemer, Yat Limanı 159, tel. 1503.

TELEPHONE AREA CODE: 3214

Around Kemer

Olympus National Park

This national park, south of Kemer, covers 173,000 acres. For tourists the beach is the big attraction. Ruins of ancient *Olympus*, whose roots can be traced back to the 2nd century BC, are sparse. There are ruins of a Byzantine church by the canal and a bridge column at the river, which seems not to have changed its course since ancient times. The theatre is in miserable condition; there is a lovely temple gate.

The beach: a lovely, long, sandy beach. The river with its crystal-clear masses of water easily replaces a shower. It is like the South Seas. But don't think you are the first discoverers. Lots of backpackers just roll out their sleeping bags (tolerated). There are a number of small restaurants and a very simple camp site. If you don't miss comfort, this is a great spot to rest up for a few days. Please: don't litter, respect private property and local customs. Only thus will the local people allow things to remain so nice. Otherwise you can expect police raids, barbed wire, and prohibitions sooner or later.

An hour northwest (approx. 5 km) from the ruins, and 250 m up on a slope, the *Eternal Flame* burns. Fed by natural gas, seeping from a crack in the earth, it has been burning for thousands of years (although less energetically in recent centuries). Once upon a time it was considered the location of the CHIMERA, a monster with the head of a lion, the body of a goat and the tail of a snake. Romans came here to worship VULCAN, the God of Blacksmiths.

COMING - GOING: Best by private car or hitchhiking. A good road branches off the coastal road to Antalya, 30 km south of Kemer near the village of **Ulupınar**. After 30 minutes, you arrive at Olympus.

Phaselis

"Here you will find cliffs, ruins, thick forests, lovely inlets, and the sea! The ruins of the ancient settlement have been excavated, but without destroying the region and leaving a field of archaeological rubble. The union of craftsmanship and nature is being preserved."

We were able to write this in our last edition with a good conscience. By now the tourist wave has rocked Phaselis. An excursion here is part of the standard program for any visitor to Kemer or Antalya. The result is that the lovely inlets are full of garbage and junk, as if all the trash in İstanbul had been dumped here. The forest is full of cars and buses. People are grilling on every corner. Trash is filtering ever deeper into the brush. The noise level equals Piccadilly Circus at rush hour. The crowning insult was the driver who offered to take us back to Kemer for £9.35 with the argument: "That is what it costs in Switzerland." At least the excavation field has remained unspoiled to this date. Tip: visit the excavation site (it is very lovely) and then move on quickly.

Phaselis is said to have been founded about 690 BC by a group of settlers from Rhodes. After forcibly evicting the original inhabitants, the town developed into a major Rhodian trading colony and was soon the main port along the Lycian coast. In the 6th century BC, it was taken over by Persia. With its conquest by Kimon (466 BC), the town became a member of the Attic League, paying the same tribute as Ephesus! With the death of ALEXANDER THE GREAT the town fell into the hands of the Egyptian Ptolemies, later the Syrians, and finally Rhodes. The town achieved autonomy in 167 BC after the Lycian uprising. In the 1st century BC the town became a hideaway for pirates. In 78 BC Rome put an end to the piracy and added the town to its empire.

Still recognizable are the town's three harbours. An aqueduct leads past the *North Harbour*, the large *South Harbour*, and the centrally located (and almost shut by sand) *Town Harbour*. A splendid *promenade* 24 m wide leads from the Town Harbour to the South Harbour.

Only the foundations (or a few ruined walls) remain of the buildings which once lined this "avenue". Notice the *theatre* dating from the 2nd century BC. It could hold 1500 spectators. Ruins of the stage building (the back was built into the fortress walls) give an impression of its original appearance. The *bath* is lovely, with its thin, still preserved arches which once supported the massive structure. Equally interesting is the *aqueduct*, which carried water from a grotto well, past the North Harbour, and south to a cistern (once located in the town centre), from where water was distributed to the buildings. It was reportedly one of the longest aqueducts in the entire Roman Empire.

INFORMATION: By the entrance to the archaeological site. Here there is a small souvenir shop. Open: 8:00 - 17:30 h.

COMING - GOING: There is an hourly dolmuş from Kemer. The turnoff is 10 km south of Kemer, from there it is 2 km to the archaeological site.
Warning: No camping at the archaeological site.

Once upon a time . . . - one of the lovely bays near Phaselis

---

Help us update

We've done our best to make this book as accurate and up-to-date as possible but travel developments are swift and things are always changing. We would greatly appreciate any contributions, suggestions, corrections, improvements or additions you may have for future editions.
Please write us:
Springfield Books Limited c/o Michael Muller, Norman Road, Denby Dale, Huddersfield HD8 8TH, West Yorkshire, England.

WEST ANATOLIAN BACKLANDS

A rough mountainous region with deep, wide valleys. The Anatolian high plains do not begin until Afyon. Few tourists find their way here.

But there is still a lot to see. The Sinter Terraces of Pamukkale, the ruins of Aphrodisias in a high isolated valley (one of the loveliest archaeological sites in Turkey), the lakes at Burdur and Eğridir, the poppy fields, and the Pillar Mosque at Afyon.

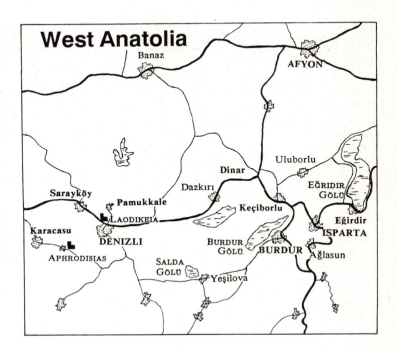

Rainfall is much more scarce here than along the coast. The climate is less friendly, as are the people. You have to win your friends. Tradition is very important. Strangers are welcome if they behave properly. There is no dependence upon tourism which bypasses the region, to the west along the Aegean coast or to the east via Ankara and Konya.

The best travel seasons in inner Anatolia are spring and fall. In the summer, temperatures rise to 40 degrees Centigrade and higher, and the sea is far away. In the winter the infrastructure collapses under masses of snow, and you are more likely to meet a wolf than a village elder.

Tip: Visit Afyon when the poppies are in bloom; it is an enchanting display of colour.

Denizli (pop. 150,000)

The provincial capital Denizli, on a plateau between tall hills, is a good departure point for visits to Pamukkale, Aphrodisias and Laodiceia, particularly as there are cheap lodgings in this bustling town.

The town itself is of little interest. It is a trading town and market for regional produce (fruit, cotton). Its historic buildings were lost in a series of earthquakes.

INFORMATION: İstasyon Cad. (at the station), English spoken, information material, Tel. 13393.

TELEPHONE AREA CODE: 621

COMING - GOING: Buses in all directions, hourly to Antalya, half-hourly to İzmir, 6 buses daily to Afyon. Large, roomy bus station, meeting place for backpackers. If you sit on the rose pots, you risk arrest.
Rail: Three trains daily to İzmir, a night train (Pamukkale Ekspresi) to İstanbul.

A NIGHT'S REST

Altuntur Oteli, Kaymakçı Cad. 1, double £15. Rooms with shower, quite comfortable and tastefully furnished, Tel. 16176.

Sarçıkaya Oteli, İstasiyon Cad. 72, double £7. Common showers, right by the station. Few foreign guests, Tel. 11760.

Etemağa Oteli, İstasiyon Cad. 34, double £7. Little comfort, but clean, Tel. 13851.

Kuyumcu Oteli, Delikliçınar Mey. 128, double £8, friendly owner, common showers, Presidential suite with its own shower, Tel. 13749 - 13750.

Around Denizli

Laodiceia: 6 km north of Denizli, founded in the 3rd century BC. Laodiceia prospered from wool production and processing, plus trade in textiles, and became one of the wealthiest towns in the region. For many generations, until its incorporation into the Roman Empire, Laodiceia waged a no-holds-barred war against its neighbour Pamukkale. Laodiceia is one of the seven Christian communities mentioned in the Apocalypse. In the 6th century AD, the town was destroyed by an earthquake. It was reconstructed, but never regained its former glory. Its final decline came with the Seljuk invasion in the 11th century.

Fairly well preserved is the *stadium* (350 m long, 60 m wide, built under VESPASIAN), one of the largest stadiums in Asia Minor. To the east are the ruins of a *bath*, built under HADRIAN. Little remains of the *theatres* and the *acropolis*. Of interest are the ruins of the *aqueducts*, near the villages of Eski Hisar, which once carried water here from Pamukkale.

Caravanserai Akhan: A perfectly preserved 13th century caravanserai, 8 km east of Denizli.

Aphrodisias: One of the most remarkable archaeological sites (see Aphrodisias).

Pamukkale

Its fame is based upon a chemical reaction: a hot spring (53 degrees Centigrade) contains a large amount of calcium bicarbonate.

As the water cools at the surface, the calcium bicarbonate is converted into carbon dioxide and calcium carbonate (chalk).

The carbon dioxide evaporates while the sinter chalk is deposited, clogging drainage channels. The water is forced to spread over a wide slope, forming snow-white sinter terraces. The huge basins, one above the other, are similar to huge bath tubs. From the bottom, the 100 m tall slope looks like a huge frozen waterfall.

The name Pamukkale is usually translated as "cotton palace", with reference to the cotton (*pamuk*) planted in the region or to the terraces resembling cotton balls. A better explanation was given to us by a friendly student working in the Tourist Information Office:

cotton is a synonym for white, as in "white as snow". Pamukkale (*kale* = palace) in this sense means "snow-white palace". By the way, the word pamukkale has become a synonym for the whitest of whites: car or kitchen appliance manufacturers offer a colour range from sky-blue, blood-red to pamukkale-white.

But there is a problem: the original pamukkale-white is turning black. Countless numbers of people are walking on the slowly regenerating sinter terraces. Water is increasingly diverted for use by motels and pensions. Car exhaust fumes do the rest. The result is that the terraces are becoming dirty, grey replacing white and black following the grey. Unless the terraces are protected in the near future (don't bet on it) this tourist attraction and natural wonder will be lost. Hindsight is more common than foresight.

History

The healing powers of the spring water have been known and cherished by neighbouring people for thousands of years. The Hittites and Phrygians erected altars here. But it was the Pergamon King EUMENES II who founded the town of Hierapolis as a counterbalance to the nearby Macedonian town of Laodiceia. Rivalry between the two towns was so great that it stunted the development of both. Not until their incorporation into the Roman Empire's Province of Asia did Hierapolis achieve importance. Its wealth was based upon wool processing. Hierapolis was destroyed by an earthquake in 60 AD but quickly rebuilt. It boasted a strong Christian community very early (Philip the Apostle died here in 80 AD). It was a bishopric during Byzantine rule. The town was deserted after the Seljuk invasion.

First excavations were made in 1887 by the discoverer of Pergamon CARL HUMANN. Systematic work began in 1957 with an Italian team under PAOLO VERZONE.

INFORMATION: By the parking lot, well-informed students, English spoken, Tel. 13532.

TELEPHONE AREA CODE: 621

COMING – GOING: Dolmuş from Denizli every ten minutes (£0.35). From Denizli you have a half-hourly bus to İzmir.

FESTIVAL: The Pamukkale Festival is held every year from May 25 to 27. The main attraction is traditional local Zeybek dancing.

FIRST AID: A small First Aid Station is situated by the parking lot.

MONEY EXCHANGE: At the reception of Tusan-Hotel, you can change traveller's checks, without a charge, at daily rates.

SWIMMING POOL: If you have had your fill of the chalk terraces, visit the swimming pool in Denizli (at the foot of the slope) or in Pamukkale (up on the terrace, admission £0.35). 100 per cent spring water or your money back!

A Night's Rest

Tusan Moteli, directly above the Sinter Terrace, west of the parking lot, double £33, the best price too, Tel. 13532.

Motel Koru, double £25. No worse than Tusan, but without the splendid location. Several swimming pools (Tusan has just one) and disco, Tel. 11323.

Yörük Motel, below the terraces, 100 m from the main road, double with breakfast £18, rooms with shower and toilet, very clean. The only hotel in the village; it boasts a swimming pool with its own well. Tel. 1073.

Pamukkale Motel, somewhat cheaper, double £18, built around the thermal pool. The faded elegance and pond can be visited for an admission fee.

Reasonable lodgings in Pamukkale Köyü, the village below the terraces:

Paradise Pansiyon, double £5. This address was recommended a number of times, even in İstanbul. The atmosphere is in fact international; English, French and German are spoken. But Hasan Hüseyin Özen does seem to be resting on his laurels. During our last visit he emptied the water from the swimming pool and refilled it. As a result, there was no water for showers or toilets for two days. And he would not permit even a symbolic wash in the pool. The atmosphere is more German than international, or more precisely, Bavarian. Tel. 34.

Ali's Pansiyon, double £5. A well-known cheap lodging, bargain. Sanitary facilities are very rudimentary, try washing in the water channel above the pension, Tel. 52.

Konak Sade Oteli, a lovely, old Turkish house, swimming pool with spring water. If Mehmet Semerci is in a good mood, he might organize a tour of the terraces! Tel. 7.

Pension Allgäu, on the main road. Upwardly mobile, clean, international, but not Bavarian (despite the name).

Camping:

Camping Kurtur, 5 km behind the necropolis. Shady. Three swimming pools of varied temperature.

Camping Mistur, Karahayit, not far from the Red Spring. We liked it. Cheaper than Kurtur.

Tip: At the pensions in Pamukkale Köyü, you can camp in the yards and use the sanitary facilities inside. The price is bargained individually.

Sights

Sinter Terraces: The main attraction in town. The completely sintered slope is over 100 m tall and 5 km wide. Over 100 basins offer - at least on weekdays - sufficient space for water lovers. While the large main basin below Tusan Hotel is flooded with tourists, there are far fewer crowds at the basins further down the main road. The spring continues to bubble as powerfully as ever. A water superintendent regulates the distribution of water with a series of locks. Each terrace is flooded at least once a week (for an entire day). The water is recaptured below the slope and channeled for irrigation of fields on the surrounding plain. The larger basins are illuminated at night, offering a lovely spectacle.

Baths and Museum: One of the first things you see by the parking lot are the ruins of the Great Bath of Hierapolis, whose large halls were once faced with marble. Since 1984 it has housed a small archaeological museum featuring finds excavated nearby. The museum complex also includes the Temple of Apollo, the Plutonium and the theatre (see below).

OPEN: 9:00 - 17:00 h, closed Mondays, admission £0.20.

Main Spring: Today, the main spring is located in the inner courtyard of the "Pamukkale Motel". It bubbles among palms in a lovely thermal pool containing ancient columns. The thermal pool is open to non-residents of the hotel for an admission fee. A bath in the 35-degree water is wonderful.

Apollo Temple and Plutonium: Little remains of the Apollo Temple. All you can see is a 2.5 m tall podium with a small set of stairs. A few parts of some capitals are still on the grounds, but the foundations of the temple can hardly be recognized.

Adjoining is the Plutonium, a grotto mentioned in the writings of STRABO and dedicated to PLUTO, God of the Underworld. The well once bubbled from inside this grotto. The large entrance hall was polluted with poisonous gases; uninvited guests (birds, even oxen) died. Only the priests could enter without risk: they crept along the floor, where oxygen collected at certain spots, and otherwise held their breath until they were safely through. The grotto has almost completely collapsed. Today you can see just one chamber with its arched doorway. The entrance is closed; sulphuric gases still escape!

Theatre: The well-preserved 2nd century BC theatre has been completely excavated in recent years. It boasts a width of 100 m. There are 20 rows of seats on the lower level and 25 rows on the upper level. Eight staircases lead to the balcony. Experts calculate that it could seat an audience of 10,000. The stage and stage building are just a rubble heap. The orchestra has been cleared.

St Philip Memorial Church: About 600 m north of the theatre is an eight-sided, 5th century building dedicated to St. Philip. The walls are approx. 2 m high; the foundations easy to recognize. The unusual form (octagonal without a visible apse) raises suspicions that it was never used as a church, but rather as a memorial to the martyr Philip and his seven sons who died with him.

Necropolis: Adjoining to the north of town is a city of the dead (necropolis) measuring 1 km across. Over 1000 tombs from every epoch stand here: stone sarcophagi, grave mounds, burial chambers, earthen graves with tombstones.

Red Spring in Karahayit: About 5 km to the north, easy to reach by private car, dolmuş or taxi, is the village of Karahayit with its Red Spring. The lively bubbles are powered by water temperatures of 80 degrees Centigrade. It washes out large amounts of iron, which are deposited on the rocks, providing the characteristic red colouring. Further down the water is captured in a large pool, where, cooled to a lukewarm temperature, it offers an inviting swim. Two restaurants help reduce the wait for a departing dolmuş. If you can withstand the heat, take a walk from the sinter terraces through the necropolis to the Red Spring. It is an unforgettable experience.

Aphrodisias

"Imagine entering a town so rich in archaeological treasures that sculptures roll at your feet, and marble heads fall from the walls or lie in irrigation ditches."

Such was the report of KENAN T. ERIM, leader of excavations at Aphrodisias, in *National Geographic Magazine*, six years after the beginning of excavations in 1967.

In fact Aphrodisias can be an unforgettable experience. The ruins of the ancient town do not compare with Ephesus or Pergamon, but they are located in enchanting mountain scenery at the foot of *Baba Dag*. The tallest of the surrounding mountains are covered with snow even in the summer.

The *Geyre Çayı* high plateau is particularly nice in the springtime when the heat is not so intense and flowers blossom among the ruins. The great advantage of Aphrodisias over Ephesus and Pergamon is its isolated position which keeps the number of tourists to a minimum. During the spring and fall, you can almost be alone with the ruins.

COMING - GOING: 12 km east of Nazilli, branching off the main Aydin-Denizli road (E 24) is a good road to Karacasu (25 km) and Tavas (74 km). Geyre is 38 km from the turnoff. From Nazilli you can get a dolmuş to Karacasu (autumn to spring) or to Aphrodisias (summer). In summer, patient people may wait at the turnoff for a passing tourist bus to stop.

OPEN: 9:00 - 12:00 h and 13:30 - 17:30 h, closed Mondays, admission £0.35.

History

Little is known. The oldest layers of settlement date from before 2000 BC. Not until the 1st century BC, however, did Aphrodisias grow into a town. The town's importance during the Roman era was based upon its Cult of Aphrodite and the School of Sculpture. As raw material for the School of Sculpture, marble of the finest quality was taken from a nearby quarry. Sculptures from Aphrodisias were displayed in Greece at Olympia, in Africa at Leptis Magna and on many squares in Rome.

The fall of the Roman Empire sent Aphrodisias into decline. The Cult of Aphrodite (the town was so sacred that it did not require a wall until the 4th century AD) was replaced by Christianity. The town was called Stavropolis (Town of Crosses) during the Byzantine era. It was a bishopric until the 12th century; after the Seljuk conquest it deteriorated.

Tour

The ruins are located within and near the village of *Geyre*, whose population was moved in the 1960s because they stood in the way of excavations.

Stadium: One of the best preserved stadiums in the whole ancient Greek world. With a length of 262 m and a width of 59 m, the facility was gigantic. Intact are the tunnel-like entrances at the outer ends of the semicircular sides and the 22 rows of seats around the track. Originally, a row of columns crowned the upper part of the stadium. The stadium could seat 30,000 spectators.

Propylaeum: Probably part of a great ceremonial gate dating from the 2nd century AD. The gate contained four rows of columns, of which two remain. Notice the artful fluting of the columns, the work of local masons! It is possible that this was the entrance gate to the sacred grove around the Temple of Aphrodite, whose columns can be seen in the background to the left.

Temple of Aphrodite: The famous Temple of Aphrodite was as important to Aphrodisias as the oracle to Delphi or the Artemision to Ephesus. Still standing are 14 columns and the front wall of the cella (inner room of the temple). Originally the cella boasted 13 columns along its length and 8 columns along both sides of its width. During the Byzantine era, however, the building was torn down to make room for a church. Only the surrounding column halls remain. For this reason it is almost impossible to determine the foundations of the original temple. North of the temple are the ruins of the *School of Sculpture.*

Bishop's Palace and Odeon: Southwest of the Temple of Aphrodite are the ruins of the Bishop's Palace. Notice the columns of blue marble. Above the east end of the Bishop's Palace you'll see a well-preserved odeon which was built in the 2nd century AD. The building, which was probably roofed in Roman times, was used for festivals and concerts. You can still see the nine lowest rows of seats (with lion's paws as a symbol of power), the orchestra (frequently picturesquely covered with a layer of water) and a narrow stage. The upper rows were made of wood. A wealth of statues and mosaic ornamentation from the building can be seen today in the museum.

Agora and Hadrian's Baths: South of the odeon stretches a small poplar forest, sprouting many rows of Ionian and Corinthian columns. This was the site of the town's *Double Agora*, two squares surrounded by column arcades, the economic and administrative centre of Aphrodisias.

Further west are the ruins of *Hadrian's Baths*, a typical Roman bath facility with cold-water baths, warm and hot-water rooms, plus a sauna. It is decorated with lovely mosaics; excavations are not yet completed. Notice the two marble baths in the caldarium (hot-water bath). South of Hadrian's Bath are the ruins of a 3rd century AD *triple-aisled basilica* measuring 100 m by 30 m.

Theatre: The rows of seats in this recently excavated theatre are completely intact. While the facility is Hellenic in style, it was rebuilt several times during the Roman era. The audience hall with marble seats was dug into the slope. The almost semicircular orchestra was deepened under MARCUS AURELIUS in order to improve the acoustics. The stage is intact. Of the stage building, a row of half columns is intact, as are several tunnel-like chambers. In one of these, imperial letters affecting the town were chiseled. At the west end of the theatre are ruins of the *Theatre Bath* featuring sections of rectangular columns, decorated with human figures in relief.

Museum: Even if you don't like museums, put aside your inhibitions and visit this tiny museum in the old village centre of Geyre. Keep in mind: Aphrodisias' claim to fame was its School of Sculpture.
A number of halls are grouped around an inner courtyard:

Imperial Hall: Busts of various emperors, princes, and muses. In the adjoining hall is a relief in honour of Zollos (1st century BC), depicting tributes to the honourable citizen Zollos.

Melpomene Hall: A large statue of Apollo and sculptures of the goddess of drama, Melpomene.

Odeon Hall: Statues of seated poets and philosophers excavated in the odeon. In the adjoining hall are unfinished sculptures from the sculpture studio.

Penthesileia Hall: The central grouping depicts Achilles, carrying the dying Amazon Queen Penthesileia from the battlefield. There are two versions of a satyr, cradling the young Dionysos in his arms.

Aphrodite Hall: Copy of the cult statue (the original was never found) from the Aphrodite Temple. Other statues depict important residents of Aphrodisias.

Inner Courtyard: Statue of a jumping horse, done in blue marble. Colossal statue of a woman. The torso of a horse.

Burdur *(pop. 45,000)*

This inconspicuous provincial capital is set in a wild and inhospitable steppe.

The town is primarily important as a market for the surrounding agricultural region. Rose oil and poppy seed are the main products. The town should be seen as a stopover. More interesting is *Burdur Gölü*, Burdur Lake (200 sq km), northwest of town. It is a well-known bird sanctuary.

History

Traces of prehistoric settlements have been discovered here. In Hacılar, on the southwest side of the lake, a row of tiny statues depicting gods was discovered. Experts dated them back to the 6th millennium BC! Unfortunately, these treasures disappeared into the vault of an unknown collector in İstanbul. The town itself was founded during Seljuk rule. It never played an important role as a city.

INFORMATION: Cumhuriyet Meydanı 4. English spoken. Tel. 10 78.

COMING - GOING: Last stop on the **train** route from Afyon, three trains daily to Afyon. In Dinar you have connections to Denizli. The station is very sleepy.
Bus: Good connections to Aydın, İzmir, Konya and Mersin. Several buses daily to Antalya, Afyon, Adana and Nazilli. **Tip**: If you can't get the right connection, just take a dolmuş to İsparta (30 km) where you have better connections in all directions.

SHOPPING: A nice souvenir is a bottle of rose oil. Enjoy a sample sniff from several bottles before making your selection. Warning: at the bazaar, it might be diluted. Otherwise we really liked the bazaar. No neon, no sterility, with all the nice and less praiseworthy scents. A must see!

A NIGHT'S REST: **Burdur Oteli**, Gazi Caddesi 37 A, double £10. Restaurant, double with shower is the rule (there are exceptions). The only hotel which meets European expectations, clean, friendly atmosphere.

Sights

Taşoda: A well - preserved royal seat of an Ottoman dynasty.

Ulu Cami: This Great Mosque dates from the 14th century, built by DÜNDAR BEY, a Seljuk sultan of the local dynasty. Don't expect too much.

Archaeological Museum: Features finds from the region, e.g. finds from the once inhabited Hacılar and Aglassos (Ağlasun). They are happy to see visitors.

Around Burdur

Burdur Gölü: Nearby Burdur Lake is a steppe lake rich in salt and sodium carbonate. It boasts a wealth of fish, and is a paradise for bird watchers and fishermen. Water sports are possible; camping is tolerated. The 5 km long *Çendik Beach* (only 2 km from Burdur) is popular, featuring dressing rooms.

Sagalassos: In Ağlasun (southeast of Burdur) are the ruins of ancient Sagalassos. Ruins of the theatre and acropolis are of little interest, but the rock graves in the necropolis are worth a visit.

Salda Gölü: Near the village of Yesilova is Salda Gölü, a lake completely surrounded by forest. It is a popular get-away spot for people from Denizli and Burdur (54 km southwest of Burdur).

İsparta *(pop. 90,000)*

This provincial town set at 1025 m is a local junction. This is where the north-south Afyon-Antalya route meets the Burdur-Eğridir route.

The town is known for its rose-oil production (extensive rose fields in the region and ovens for processing), and particularly for its daily carpet market.

The town was founded by the Seljuks, but never achieved real importance. In 1889 it was rocked by a terrible earthquake. Every building in town was destroyed. Reconstruction was done with great care. For excursions from İsparta we recommend Eğridir and Burdur Lake (see there).

INFORMATION: Yeni Hamam Arkası 2, Tel. 144 38.

COMING - GOING: Good **bus** connections in all directions, particularly with the local transportation company İsparta Seyahat. Several buses daily to Antalya, Afyon, Burdur, İzmir, Mersin, Aydın and Konya. Express buses in the evening to Kayseri and İstanbul.
   Train: A sleepy station on a secondary line to Afyon (which joins with the Bursa line). Three trains daily; change in Dinar to Denizli.

SHOPPING: Be sure to visit the famous carpet market. But be careful when buying at carpet auctions: these are rarely outstanding carpets. Most are household carpets from the surrounding region.

A NIGHT'S REST: **Gülistan Oteli**, Mimar Sinan Caddesi 31 B, double £12. Rooms with shower and WC. Plain for the price, Tel. 140 85. **Bolat Oteli**, Demirel Bulvarı 71, double £10. Most rooms with shower and WC, clean. Fun people at the reception, nice atmosphere, Tel. 189 98.

CAMPING: The nearest camp grounds are in Eğridir, on Eğridir Lake.

Sights

This bustling little town features white houses and an intact town centre. There are several lovely mosques and a quite modest Archaeological Museum.

Eğridir   *(pop. 12,500)*

This town on the shimmering green and fish-rich Eğridir Lake (fourth largest in Turkey, 468 sq km) is a popular destination for people from the surrounding region, and an open secret among travellers.

The town radiates old-fashioned Turkey. Narrow streets, lovely white houses, oriental smells. Parts of the enchanting town are inside an old Seljuk castle. The people are friendly and helpful to strangers. Guests are welcome everywhere.

History

Eğridir was founded by the Seljuks. It was the capital of the *Hamidogullari* dynasty which controlled a principality between Burdur Lake and Eğridir Lake in the 14th century. There was heavy damage during the 1889 earthquake.

INFORMATION: Çarsı İci No. 15/C, Tel. 32 81 / 13 88.

COMING - GOING: Amazingly good **bus** connections. Kontas Sehayat and İsparta Sehayat bus companies run routes from İsparta to Eğridir. There are buses every half hour to İsparta, and from there to all the major towns in West Anatolia (see İsparta).
Train: This is the last stop of the "Burdur Railway" line. Daily trains to Dinar and Afyon.

A NIGHT'S REST: **Eğridir Oteli**, by Tourist Information, double £7. Preferred by travellers, cheap. Furnishings without charm, warm water in the rooms, showers for the hardy, Tel. 32 81 12 19.

Even cheaper are **Ünal Palas Oteli** and **Barla Oteli** - high class dives. We can recommend the very clean **Kervan Oteli** and **Ankara Oteli** (double £5), also in town.

CAMPING: **Kervansaray Kamp Yeri**, 3 km east of Eğridir. Actually a restaurant with adjoining camp grounds. You are forced to use the sanitary facilities in the restaurant (definitely a minus). Price is negotiable. When bargaining, point out how awful the grounds look.

FOOD: Several restaurants beside Lake Eğridir. We can recommend **Eğridir-Restorani** (calculate £6.70 per meal) and the cheaper **Derya Restorani** (£5 and up). Be sure to try the inexpensive Eğridir shrimp.

Sights

Castle *(Kale)*: The castle was supposedly built by the Seljuk sultan ALAEDDIN KEYKOBAT (1220 - 1237), but its foundations are actually much older. There was a noteworthy symbiosis between the castle and the town: Eğridir maintained upkeep of the castle, while the castle protected the town for centuries. This relationship obviously deteriorated over the years.

Hızır-Bey Mosque *(Hızırbey Cami)*: The Hızır-Bey Mosque stands upon a large archway with a road running underneath. Notice the entrance gate. The mosque was built by the Seljuk sultan HIZIR, of the Hamidoğulları dynasty, in 1327 - 1329. The mosque burned down in 1815 and had to be rebuilt.

KEEP SPINNING!

Eğridir Lake is a typical shallow steppe lake, which was once a dry basin. Then it began to rain, causing rivers, streams, and ponds to overflow their banks, creating a new lake. People fled their homes taking refuge in the hills. One old woman refused to flee, despite numerous efforts to make her leave. She simply continued to spin wool. When it was impossible to wait any longer, one of those fleeing called out "Eğir dur" (keep spinning). That is how Eğridir Lake got its name.

Lake Eğridir and Islands: This large lake is surrounded by mountains on all sides. Its crystal-clear, greenish water invites a swim. There are no mosquitoes, but a lot of fish, especially crayfish. Each year 1200 tons are caught. They have a legendary reputation throughout Turkey for their tender, juicy meat.

For explorers: Visit the islands **Can Ada** and **Nis Ada**. If you don't like to swim, visit the **Yesilada** peninsula (accessible via a dam) which is called "green island" for a good reason.

BOAT RENTALS: You can visit the islands Can Ada and Nis Ada by boat. Rentals are available along the beach. Be sure to take your time, and drink tea, while bargaining for the price. The owner will praise the wonders of his boat, while you praise the Lord it has not sunk yet.

Swimming

Beaches with dressing rooms and toilets, some with showers to the northwest of town.

Around Eğridir

20 km south of Eğridir is **Kovada Gölü**, easy to reach via a paved road. This mountain lake (9 sq km in size, only 7 m deep) is surrounded by a forested (oak, pine) nature preserve. If you are lucky, you might see wild goats, deer or boars. Wolves and bears have also been reported in the swampy and impenetrable forest. You can fish, hike (please stay on the paths), and swim. Local people rent out boats, and for a price are happy to act as guides.

Afyon *(pop. 75,000)*

This provincial capital on a high plateau (1007 m above sea level) is an important road and rail junction. Outcroppings of the Sandıklı Mountains are nearby.

Afyon has had an exciting past. Phrygians, Pergamese, Romans, Byzantines, and Seljuks have left their marks. The Ottomans took over in the 15th century.

INFORMATION: Ordu Bulvar Cad. 22, Tel. 32

COMING - GOING: Daily **buses** to every major town in Turkey.
  Trains to İstanbul, İzmir, Aydın, İsparta, Konya, Ankara, Kayseri, etc.
A NIGHT'S REST: **Sener Oteli**, Ambar Yolu 72, double £7, simple rooms with shower, Tel. 2320.

Sights

Karahisar: The castle, built on a rock 226 m tall, offers a tremendous view.

Ulu Mosque: One of the major sights in town. It was constructed in 1272, completely of wood. *"The interior is a surprise: Forty wooden columns support a long, low wood roof. Its stalactite capitals are richly carved. The room radiates warmth and trust. The importance of the wooden columns to Inner Anatolia can be recognized by the white cow carrying a tent pole. This was the symbol of the Mongol ruler Genghis Khan. A reflection of this ancient veneration can be seen in this mosque."* (Hugo Föllmi). We could not have said it better.

İmaret - Mosque: Built in 1477 for GEDIK AHMET PAŞA, the Grand Vizier of sultan MEHMET. The portal, mimber, and furnishings are among the finest produced in Ottoman times.

Kuyulu Mosque: Also called Fountain Mosque. The minaret boasts a coat of glazed tiles (Seljuk era).

Around Afyon

Midas Tomb: Yazılhaya (on the Eskieğmir-Yapıldak route, 65 km, then on foot to Yazılhaya), is the loveliest Phrygian rock tomb.

Hüdayi: 65 km to the east (via Sandıklı, 10 km). The thermal bath (with 100 beds) has 60 to 80 degree water, featuring fluoride, bromide, and calcium content. Excellent for rheumatism, circulatory and stomach ailments.

AFYON = OPIUM

Afyon means opium. All around town are the largest poppy fields in Turkey, with blood-red flowers stretching as far as the eye can see. When the bulbs are ripe, they are sliced open, allowing a sticky juice to seep out, and this is when the problem begins.

Back in the 1960s, masses of freaks hung around the Hagia Sophia, in the Pudding Shop, and in lodgings along Yerebatan Caddesi and Divan Yolu. Then suddenly there was talk of an El Dorado on the high plains of central Anatolia, full of cheap, dynamite stuff. Bags were packed, cars chartered; a general exodus to the poppy fields began. After organizing and bargaining, a flourishing trade developed. You just took a Morris Minor or an old Opel, disassembled it, and filled the hollow areas with sweet juice. Then you put the thing back together any old way, and pushed it to the border in the 40 degree heat.

Then the professionals took over, the *French Connection*. Logistics were perfected, fast ships brought the goods to Marseilles or Naples, where they were refined for shipping to the United States. This attracted the attention of the American FBI, the FDA and the CIA to Afyon. A number of grim-faced individuals, dressed in ill-fitting suits, were seen patrolling the region. A financial agreement was struck with the Turkish government to prohibit the growing of poppies. But over 80,000 people lived by the poppy trade, and there were already enough unemployed in the Gecekondus of İzmir and İstanbul. So the officials took the money and no action.

Should you have the foolish idea of investigating one of Afyon's poppy fields more closely, you can expect a lot of trouble. Hands off, the olden days are gone. But nobody says what everybody knows: despite allegedly strict controls, a large portion of the crop is siphoned off into illegal channels. Business is still flourishing and its colour is that of the poppy blossom: blood red.

Eskişehir *(pop. 310,000)*

A provincial capital and industrial centre which sprang up during the industrial campaign following WW II. Most locomotives of the Turkish Railway are produced in Eskişehir.

There are textile factories, a sugar factory, and a stinking cement plant. Eskişehir is an important railway junction. There is no sign of tranquility. Eskişehir was once an important producer of pipes. The raw material, meerschaum, was found in great quantity in surrounding hollows.

Nearby is *Dorylaion*, a Phrygian settlement. Eskişehir itself did not really develop until late in the Ottoman era. Real growth began after WW II.

INFORMATION: İki Eylül Cad. 175 A, Tel. 17 292.

TELEPHONE AREA CODE: 221

COMING - GOING: From the bus station by the river, you have hourly connections to Bursa, Afyon and Ankara.
Good connections within the region (regional **bus, dolmuş**).
Rail: Direct connections to Ankara, İzmir, İstanbul (three trains daily) and Konya (once daily).

A NIGHT'S REST:
Şale Oteli, İnönü Cad. 71, double £8. Simple furnishings, friendly, Tel. 14 743.
Sultan Termal Oteli, Hamamyolu Cad. 7, double £8.50, most rooms with shower, thermal bath.

Around Eskişehir

Meerschaum Pits: To the left off the main road to Ankara (E 23) is a road leading to the villages of *Tokat* and *Karatepe* (follow the signs). Along the slopes are a number of meerschaum pits which may be visited without risk.

Küplü: About 60 km northwest of Eskişehir (National Road No. 200, meets National Road No. 600, take a right). This is the perfect backdrop for a film about the Ottoman Empire. The picturesque village with old, moss-covered, wooden houses is nestled on the slopes of a luscious river valley.

Bilecik: 2 km north of Küplü, 62 km northwest of Eskişehir. A little town, still intact, featuring lovely buildings of wood and stone dating from the 19th century.

SOUTH COAST

Almost one thousand kilometres of coastline spread out between Antalya and Antakya which is located near the border to Syria. On this strech you'll see many different sides of Turkey. Antalya is a modern, bustling, magnificiently decked out city and both an important economic and tourist centre. Antakya, on the other hand, the site of the ancient metropolis Antioch, is a quiet, slow paced town marked by Arabian influence.

And between you'll find very friendly people, ruins of all sizes from all ages, beach after beach and mountains whose foothills either form a steep coast with lovely bays or rise up precipitously directly behind the coastline.

More and more people have discovered the beauty of the south coast. So don't be surprised if you'll have problems finding a hotel room between Antalya and Alanya during the Turkish high season (July/August). The crowds thin out behind Alanya, after Mersin you'll find mostly Turkish vacationers who are joined by Arabs from neighbouring countries after Adana.

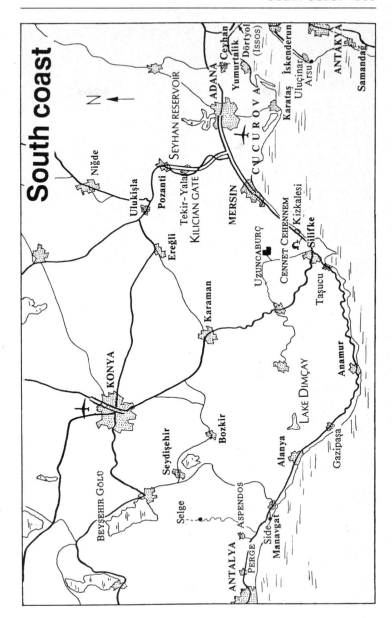

South coast

ANTALYA *(pop. 270 000)*

Framed by the 3000 m mountains of the Cilician and Lycian Taurus, Antalya is situated on rough rock, dropping steeply to the sea. Tourist guides heap praise upon the major tourist centre along the southern coast. You'll find mundane hotels, boutiques, long, white beaches, and exciting nightlife.

The city is one of the largest in Turkey. There was a tremendous building boom here in the 1960s and 1970s. As a result, the old inner city with its Ottoman buildings and narrow, shady streets is surrounded by modern suburbs, comparable to Ankara.

Antalya is more than a tourist centre, it is also the economic centre of a wealthy agricultural region producing fruit and vegetables. As soon as you leave the tourist centre of town, you'll find numerous artisans, workshops, and other small businesses - here there is no hint of tourism.

The old town and the centre have been taken over by tourism. In 1972 a program was begun to retain the old town's original appearance. Hotel towers were prohibited, and great care was taken in restoring old buildings. There is some controversy about the success, but the good intention is evident. This part of town may well have a new appearance in a few years after patina has covered the white walls. In the new centre of town - Atatürk Cad. and Cumhuriyet Cad.- palm-lined boulevards invite you to stroll past boutiques and shops. This is a good place to find stylish clothes and leather goods.

History

In Turkish history Antalya figures as a new city. It was founded in 158 BC by King ATTALUS of Pergamon as a harbour, and named "Attaleia" in honour of the king. After Pergamon was inherited by the Romans, the town took on a Roman appearance. Many prominent visitors have passed through the town including the apostle ST. PAUL and Emperor HADRIAN, in whose honour a gate was built (see Sights). A number of structures date from this era. During the 12th century the town was used as a military depot by the crusaders. In the 12th century the town was conquered by the Seljuks, who maintained control for a century before the Emir of Eğridir took control. In 1387, sultan MURAD I subjugated the town to the Ottoman Empire. From 1918 to 1921 the Gulf of Antalya was occupied by Italian troops. Of course it was Atatürk who forced their withdrawal. Today Antalya is a modern Turkish town, after a spurt of growth in the 1960s. In the last two decades, Antalya's population increased by 400 per cent.

INFORMATION: Cumhuriyet-Cad. 73, tel.117 47 & 152 71

TELEPHONE AREA CODE: 311

COMING - GOING: The bus station is on Kazim Özalp Cad.; several buses daily to major Turkish towns and smaller towns in the region. From the dolmuş station (Doğu Garaji/East Station) on Ali Çetinkaya Cad. you have regular connections to surrounding villages, including Lara and Manavgat (Side).
By Ship: Every 14 days a Turkish Maritime ship drops anchor in Antalya en route to İstanbul. The TML office (Türkiya Denizcilik Isletmeleri) is on K. Evren Bulvarı 405, tel.11120.
By Air: From Calkaya Airport (15 km east of Antalya) flights depart several times daily to several domestic airports. You can get a ride to the airport from the THY office at Cumhuriyet Cad. 73 (tel. 12830) in the centre of town. A taxi from the airport into town costs £3.30.

BIKE RENTALS: **Erman** in F. Altay Cad. 518 Sok.3, tel. 276 70, rents bikes, mopeds (50 cc), and motorcycles (250 cc). For one day you pay £5, £10, and £13 respectively. For three days the costs are £3.30, £8, and £12 resp. For seven days you pay even less: £3, £7, and £10.

CAR RENTALS: There are a number of rental agencies including **Avis** in Talya Hotel, Fener Cad. 30/D, tel. 16693 - 19483 and at the airport tel. 11202/364. **Budget**, Aspendos Bulvarı 50, tel. 25046, Fevzi Çakmak Cad. 57, tel. 26372 - 13845 - 13629 and at the airport, tel. 29680. **Inter Rent**, Atatürk Cad. 6-7, tel. 17644 and 10285. **Europcar**, Fevzi Cakmak Cad. 14/A, tel. 18879.

EXCURSIONS: Several travel agencies offer excursions to the surrounding attractions including Termessos, Aspendos, Perge, Side and Alanya. There are also 2 - 3 day tours, e.g. to Cappadocia. Most travel agencies are on Atatürk Cad. or Cumhuriyet Bulvari.

From the marina a number of boat trips are offered. The choice ranges from simple swimming trips to excursions to Kemer including lunch or dinner on board.
Three addresses:

Karpa Org. Kenan Evren Bulvarı Pasajı Kat. 2, tel. 278 65.

Pamfilya Tours, 30 Agustos Cad. 57, tel. 116 98.

Palm Tur, Kalekapısı Saatkulesi Yanı 53, tel. 131 22 and 120 62.

SHOPPING: A lot of leather and fashion shops can be found in the bazaar and on Atatürk Cad. Gold and silver jewellery is on display in many small shops.

A Night's Rest

There is a large selection of lodgings; even late at night you can get a room. European travellers prefer the lodgings in the old town. The better hotels are situated along the promenade and at the edge of the old town. Elegant sport hotels can be found in Lara, 12 km from town, right on the beach.

Simple, cheap hotels are located in town around the bus station and dolmuş station. There are pensions on the beaches in Lara and Konyaaltı which fill up quickly in the summer.

A clean single room costs about £4 without a shower, or £5 with shower; doubles cost about £2 more. There is no upward limit in the better hotels where you pay £9 for a single with WC/shower or £15 for a comparable double.

Kaptan Pension: Taxi drivers like to bring passengers to Kaptan in the old town and you won't regret it: sunny rooms, well kept, wall-to-wall carpeting, friendly service. Showers/WC some in rooms, some on the corridor. Trees in the garden provide shade, while evenings are cooled by the fountain. For about £3 upwards you can put together a delicious meal from a choice of about 20 - 25 dishes. Costs: single £5, double £9, breakfast £1. Address: Kılınçaslan Mah. Hesapcii Sok 63. tel. 118 333,

The Brothers: relaxed atmosphere, nice personnel, very well-kept, lovely garden and restaurant: very recommendable. For one person (incl. breakfast) about £5. Address: Sinan Mah. 1277 Sok. 3.

Atlas Pension: If you are out for the pulsating life of the new town, this is a pleasant, well kept pension, some rooms with WC/showers. Costs: single £4, double £6,50, breakfast £1. Address: Anafartaalar Cad. 10.

Sato Pension: In the old town, a distinguished pension in old fashioned style. The reception is huge and the room ceilings are unusually high. Showers/WC in the corridor. There are spacious double, 3-bed and 4-bed rooms available. Costs £5 per person, breakfast £1. Address: Çivarı Kılınçaslan Mah. Firin Sok. 120.

Adler Pension: A good tip: more modest, but with atmosphere. The landlady speaks German. The old house features an enclosed courtyard where you can have a drink, breakfast, or just relax. Breakfast costs £0.75, beds £2.75. Upon request, extra beds can be set up in the double or 3-bed rooms. Address: Barbaros Mah. Çivelek Sok. 16. tel. 117 818.

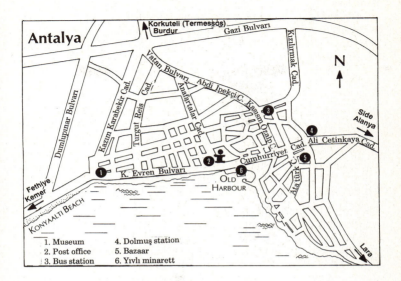

1. Museum
2. Post office
3. Bus station
4. Dolmuş station
5. Bazaar
6. Yıvlı minarett

Kamer Iki Pension: If you are looking for a cheap spot in the old town. The facilities (rooms, courtyard, WC/showers) are simpler than at the Adler, but service is just as friendly, and it is cheaper. Beds cost £2.30, breakfast £0.75. Address: Barbaros Mah. Üçkapilar Hesapcı Sok. 17. tel. 124 399.

CAMPING:

Bambus Camping: Off Atatürk Cad., on the steep shore near town. Heading toward Lara, it is off to the right after 2 km. The small camp ground has a few trees, it is crowded and loud. There is good swimming from the platform; stone stairs lead down into the sea. The sanitary facilities are okay. Costs £1 per person and £1.30 per tent. tel. 152 63.

Other camp sites are right by the beach at Konyaalti, crowded, loud. A new site was almost completed in 1988.

Food

At the harbour there are a number of spots catering to the tourist trade - and with the prices to prove it. Be particularly careful about pricing seafood dishes. The food is great.

Orkinos Restaurant (expensive): Harbour atmosphere, seafood specialties, meals begin at £10, outstanding service. Address: Kale Ici Yat Limani 22.

Sevil Çoban - Belediye Kösk Restaurant: Sounds like a public soup kitchen but it's actually a nice restaurant by the park. Spend £8 for an excellent meal with a view of the sea to aid digestion. Address: Parkici Belediye Nikah Salonu.

It is less idyllic, but cheaper and more *Turkish*, on the tiny "food street", a side street off Atatürk Cad. at Cumhuriet Cad. There is one pub after the other. So many tables fill the street that is is difficult to determine which table belongs to which restaurant. The food is great at about £3.30 per meal.

Sights

Yivli-Minare: The Seljuk minaret dating from the early 13th century is the city landmark, built by order of sultan ALAEDDIN KEYKOBAT I. The original Byzantine church was thereby converted to a mosque. For centuries, the rod-shaped brick tower served as a landmark for ships at sea. Only ruins remain of the medrese (Koran school) across from Yivli Minaret. Directly adjoining are the *Art Museum*, the *Old Library* and an *Ethnographic Museum*. Up at the square is the *Clock Tower*, whose foundations are built into the old town fortifications.

Old Town (Kaleici): Narrow, intertwined streets lead to the harbour where you'll find a number of well preserved Ottoman oriel houses. Lost in the jumble of buildings is another *clock tower*, and nearby the Ali Paşa Camii, a Seljuk mosque. The original harbour dates from the 3rd century, the enormous jetty from the Roman era. For 2000 years, this was Antalya's gateway to the world. Today the harbour serves only yachts and a few fishing boats. The biggest attractions are the boat owners at dinner with their families. Serious shipping has moved to the new harbour west of town.

Kesik-Minaret: Also in the old town is the "cut minaret". The 5th century Byzantine Panaghia church was converted (800 years later) to a mosque whose minaret has been cut off. Today the ruined interior of the mosque is filled with weeds and junk. If you go inside you'll only have one hand free, the other will be needed to hold your nose.

Hadrian's Gate: On your right coming from Atatürk Cad. The splendid, Roman-era gate is still well-preserved, as is the marble triumphal arch. It was built in 130 AD to honour a visit by Emperor HADRIAN. Even for the non-emperors of today, it makes a lovely entrance to the old town. It is plain to see that the elevation of the old town was several metres below that of the modern town. Closer to the sea, you can see parts of the ancient Roman town wall.

Karaalı Park: A sea of flowers flows down to the Mediterranean. Located at the end of Atatürk Cad., the park features a tea garden, restaurants, and a small zoo. The lovely grounds feature flowers, flowers, and more flowers - for a nice stroll high above the sea. Tip: come at sundown.

Hıdırlık Kulesi: The 17 m tall round tower in Karaalı Park certainly dates from the Roman era. It may have been part of an ancient fortress or perhaps a lighthouse or mausoleum. There is disagreement among the experts. People do like to climb up for the great view.

Archaeological Museum: In the west of town, just before the road descends to Konyaaltı Beach on the right; tell the dolmuş driver where you want to go. This is an outstanding museum whose exhibits from ancient times are second only to the National Archaeological Museum in Athens. The displays are scenically arranged to increase understanding. You begin the tour with stone fragments and charts depicting the Paleolithic period and end with Ottoman carpets (magic?) and Turkish art nouveau from the early 20th century. In between are exhibits from the bronze age, the Hittites, icons, and antiquity. There are rich finds from Pamphylia and Lycia, statues from Perge, sarcophagi. . . And near the icons there is a box covered with red velvet containing bone fragments and part of a jaw with the caption: St. Nicholas (Bishop of Myra until his death in 350 AD).

OPEN: Daily, except Mondays, 9:00 - 12:00 h, 13:30 - 18:00 h, photography is prohibited. Admission: £0.35, half-price on weekends, students free.

Swimming

ATTALUS did not take tourism into account when he founded Antalya on a cliff overlooking the sea. Both of the major beaches are outside the town.

Konyaaltı: A long beach of pebbles and sand, about 2 km west of town, easy to reach by dolmuş (the dolmuş stops at Cumhuriyet Cad. / K. Evren Bulvarı). The main road runs along the entire beach to the new harbour. The first 500 m are being converted to a camp ground and bungalow village. Adjoining are several small beaches between the camp sites, for some of which admission is charged (£0.15). But in return the beach is clean and there are showers. Every section of beach has a refreshment stand. The *free beaches* are very dirty. Keep going and the beach becomes less crowded until you reach the new harbour and a large oil depot. Across the street from the beach are numerous little hotels and pensions, usually catering to Turkish vacationers. The beach is very crowded in the summer.

Lara: The second beach is about 12 km east of town and easy to reach by dolmuş or bus (the dolmuş stops at Atatürk Cad., fare £0.30, beach admission £0.15). If there is too much noise and bustle in Antalya for your taste, then get a room out here. It is crowded in the summer; during this season arrange a room at the Antalya Tourist Information office before heading out.

More room is becoming available. Buildings are going up everywhere, generally vacation homes, but also a shopping centre featuring an ice cream parlor. The 750-bed *Club Hotel Sera* boasts five stars (double £60) and a casino, with Sera Car Rental next to the hotel entrance.

The beach begins to the left of Hotel Sera, first pebbles, then clean and well-kept sand. Toilets and showers are available; the water is crystal clear. You can get away from the crowds which gather at the beginning of the beach by walking a couple of hundred metres to the left. You can rent a surfboard at the beach, costs £14 per day or £40 per week. Be sure to bargain! There are several small cafés and restaurants along the beach.

A Night's Rest

Lara has lots of accommodation, most of it on the road above town. We particularly liked:

Motel Elmas: About 500 m from the road to Altinkum, the 30-bed hotel run by Kemal Elmas is shaded and cooled by trees all around the house. In short: an oasis in the midst of the bustle. Nothing special, WC and showers (with real warm water) in the rooms plus balconies with a view of the sea. The atmosphere is pleasant, but watch out: Mr. Elmas is a backgammon champion! On request, Kemal Elmas will take his guests to the airport (if he has time, that is, but this can usually be arranged). Costs: double with breakfast £5, single with breakfast £4. Address: Güzelyalı Lara Yolu, Tel 190 067.

CAMPING:

Motel Ekici Tesisleri, behind the beach to the left. This large, sandy, shadeless facility has friendly personnel, good sanitation, restaurant (not expensive, not bad), "müzik" and new bungalows. These cost £3.50 per day and can be shared by two people. Tents are also rented out, sleep two for £3.30 a night. If you stay in your own tent, you pay £1.60. tel. 20233.

Around Antalya

Düden Waterfalls: The upper falls are in a small park to the northwest, just a few kilometres from town, easy to reach by dolmuş. The Düden River roars through the park, providing a lovely background for Turkish picnickers. The lower Düden Falls, by the sea at Lara, are not as interesting.

Termessos

These ruins will take your breath away. Set way up in a mountain valley and difficult to reach, the ruins form surrealistic towers in the mountain forest. Burial chambers have been dug into the cliff walls. The theatre is right next to a deep gorge. Far below you see the plains of Antalya.

History: Invincible at 1000 m on Güllük Daği (Rose-Coloured Mountain), Termessos developed into a Psidian fortress. The inhabitants were known as Solimers: HOMER told of the town's proud, warlike people. Neither Alexander the Great nor the Romans were able to conquer Termessos. Alexander, who wanted to conquer the world, made a wide circle around the town. The Romans signed a peace treaty with Termessos, leaving the Termese relatively free within the empire's sphere of influence. The town had its golden age in the 2nd and 1st century BC. Most of the ruins date from that time. During Byzantine rule, the city lost its importance; in the 3rd century AD the city was destroyed in a powerful earthquake, then abandoned.

In 1842, Termessos was discovered by an English team led by SPRATT, FELLOWS, FORBES and DANIEL. During the 1880s, the German archaeologists Count LANCKORONSKI, NIEMANN, and PETERSEN conducted thorough excavations. Their work, especially the plans they drew, proved invaluable because some of the buildings have collapsed in the meantime and can be reconstructed today according to those plans.

ASYLUM SEEKERS

When Alexander the Great moved toward Perge, he kept well out of the way of Termessos - the heavily fortified and inaccessible town was too much of a challenge. When Alexander died in 323 BC, his chief generals squabbled over the division of his empire. Having lost the dispute, ALCETAS, fleeing the diadochus ANTIGONUS, sought asylum in Termessos. ANTIGONUS was determined to capture him, but. . .

The town council was not willing to go to war over ALCETAS, fearing destruction of the town. Against the wishes of the town's young warriors, it was decided to deliver ALCETAS to his fate. But ALCETAS thwarted those plans by killing himself. ANTIGONUS was satisfied with the death of his rival and withdrew. ALCETAS received a burial with full honours in the town walls.

History repeats itself, 2300 years later in Berlin (West): a young Turk causes the same trouble as Alcetas and kills himself in his cell the day before his extradition.

To the right of the ancient "Royal Road" into town is a *cemetery*. The Royal Road passes through several gates of both the ancient and modern *town walls* to the *agora*. To the left of the ancient *Town Gate* are the ruins of the *Gymnasium*, whose northeast wall is still intact. The agora is enclosed to the west by the *Stoa of Attalos*, to the north by the *Stoa of Osbaras*. To the east of the agora is the *theatre*, the best preserved structure of the town. The audience of 4000 - 5000 enjoyed performances and prizefights in addition to a fantastic view. Today, trees grow among the seats, and the stage building has collapsed into the orchestra pit.

The scenery is completely bizarre at the *necropolis,* 3 km southwest of the agora at the upper edge of the valley. The climb is worth the effort: hundreds of sarcophagi, large and small, simple and ornamented with reliefs, lie and stand among the mountain greenery, giving a good impression of the past.

COMING - GOING: Take E 24 from Antalya toward Burdur. After 12 km head left toward Korkuteli. It is another 14 km to the entrance of Termessos National Park (Termessos Mili Parkı, follow the signs). It is an additional 9 km from the park entrance to the ruins. The bus to Korkuteli will drop you off at the park entrance; from there it is a two-hour walk, or look for a ride with another visitor.

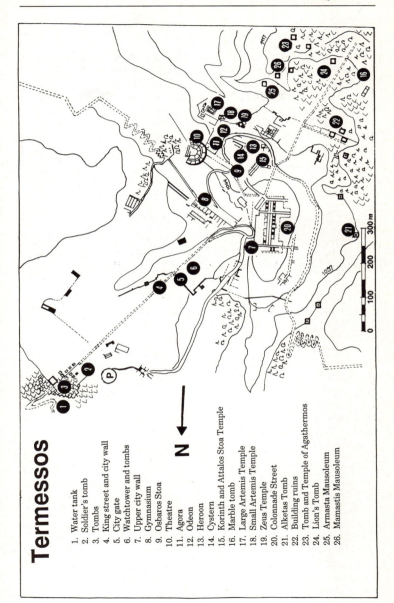

Termessos

1. Water tank
2. Soldier's tomb
3. Tombs
4. King street and city wall
5. City gate
6. Watchtower and tombs
7. Upper city wall
8. Gymnasium
9. Osbaros Stoa
10. Theatre
11. Agora
12. Odeon
13. Heroon
14. Cystern
15. Korinth and Attalos Stoa Temple
16. Marble tomb
17. Large Artemis Temple
18. Small Artemis Temple
19. Zeus Temple
20. Colonnade Street
21. Alketas Tomb
22. Building ruins
23. Tomb and Temple of Agathermos
24. Lion's Tomb
25. Armasta Mausoleum
26. Mamastis Mausoleum

N

> **ATTENTION!** The latest news: the governement in Ankara has drastically hiked up **admission fees** for museums, mosques etc. in 1989! Calculate about 5 - 10 times the prices given in this edition (depending upon the fame of the sights; for instance: admission for Hagia Sophia rose from £0.30 up to £3 !)

Perge boasts the largest stadium in Asia Minor. The theatre, the grounds of the ruined town and the huge necropolis enchant you despite the heat.

The founding of Perge followed a pattern seen throughout the Gulf of Antalya: Greek settlers selected a site on a steep table mountain with choice farmland at hand. A river was necessary to connect the town with the sea. The colonists did not want to be directly on the Mediterranean - coastal towns were plagued by pirates.

A brief history: Perge was founded about 1000 BC. In the 7th century BC, it was Lydian; later Persian. In 333 BC it surrendered to ALEXANDER THE GREAT without a fight. After his death it was absorbed by the Seleucid empire. The Romans conquered the city in 188 BC. It declined during the Byzantine era, probably because the harbour silted up.

One of Perge's most famous residents was the mathematician APOLLONIUS of Perge, known for his calculations of conic sections. The famous and the infamous have passed through, including VERRES, the insatiable Roman governor who plundered more than just Perge, and CICERO who condemned Verres in his "Speech against Verres". The apostles PAUL and BARNABAS both preached in Perge, which was one of Asia Minor's most important Christian communities during the early days of Christianity.

THE ARTEMIS OF PERGE

A goddess was the most influential personality in the history of Perge. As in Ephesus, the Cult of Artemis was the most important cult in Perge. From its inception, Artemis was the predominant motif on Pergian coins. But don't confuse the Artemis of Perge with the Greek goddess. On the most ancient coins she is known as Vanessa Preiia, Queen of Perge, and she is depicted as a rectangular block of stone with a human breast. The Artemis of Perge is an Anatolian mother goddess, encloaked with the name of a Greek goddess. Her sacred temple attracted pilgrims and rich offerings from far and wide, until it was plundered by Verres.

Up to the 19th century, Perge and its theatre remained largely intact. In 1922 the people of Murtunas renovated and expanded their village, using building material from the ruin.

To the right on the road to Murtuna is the *stadium*, with a length of 234 m, the largest in Asia Minor. Because the stadium was built on a plain, an additional structure had to be built to provide seating for 12,000. In the chambers underneath it (easy to see) there used to be shops. The arena with its seats is still intact and in good condition considering its age.

Across from the stadium is the *theatre*. The traditional ancient theatre is not well preserved. The much more ancient Greek theatre was converted to a Roman theatre during the 2nd century AD. Set on a hill outside the town, its seating capacity was 14,000.

Perge has impressive town ruins whose stones reflect its Greek, Roman, and Byzantine past. Besides the theatre and stadium, be sure to take a look at the *Town Gate*, the even more ancient *Southern Gate* with its two mighty round towers (very tall even for today) and the *Arcade Street* whose columns have been restored. A 2 m wide sewer runs down the centre of the street - on the left and right you can still see the shop walls. Scattered about are mosaic floors, altars, basilicas, thermal springs. . . Many excavation finds - sculpture from Perge and sarcophagi from the city of the dead west of town - can be seen at the Antalya Museum.

A Turkish-led excavation team began work here in 1946; it is still un-earthing interesting finds. However, no trace of the shrine of Artemis with the depiction of Vanessa Preiia has been found, despite count-less digs by archaeologists. It is probable that Byzantine Christians made certain that every trace of the Anatolian mother goddess was destroyed.

OPEN: Daily, except Mondays, 9:00 - 12:00 h, 13:30 - 17:00 h. **Admission**: £0.35, half price on weekends, students £0.07.

COMING - GOING: From Antalya, head toward Alanya; turn left in Aksu (16 km out-side Antalya) , follow the sign to Perge and Murtuna (2 km). Drive past the theatre to the parking lot on the left. Coming by bus or dolmuş, you have a 20 minute walk from Aksu.

Sillyon

Greek colonists founded Sillyon on top of a steep table mountain about the same time as Aspendos and Perge. Sillyon was an impor-tant centre during the Greek and Roman eras and a Byzantine bishopric. Today Sillyon is a quiet ruined town, only partly excavated, a minor tourist attraction. The horseshoe-shaped town gate is still visible, as are the fortifications, two ruined theatres, several temples, and various buildings. The Seljuk conquest also left its mark, includ-ing a small mosque and castle. Houses dating from the Greek era are quite lovely - they are dug into the rock and complemented by walls.

COMING - GOING: From Antalya to Alanya, just before Serik you take the road to Yanköy. From Yanköy, it is a short walk.

Aspendos

The theatre of Aspendos is an outstanding Pamphylian structure, the best preserved Roman historical monument in Asia Minor.

The history of the once great Pamphylian town echoes that of neigh-bouring towns. Founded by Greeks about 1000 BC, it was briefly un-der Lydian rule in the 6th century BC and, after the defeat of Croesus, under Persian rule. During the Persian wars the Pamphy-lians fought unenthusiastically for the Persians against their Greek compatriots. In 469 BC Aspendos - near the mouth of the Eurymedon - was the site of a land and sea battle in which the Greeks defeated Persia. Aspendos became a member of the Athenian maritime confederation until the defeat of Athens by Sparta allowed the Persians to return.

In 334 BC ALEXANDER THE GREAT entered the picture:

No, You Can't Have Our Horses!

Alexander prepared for his attack on Persia; Perge simply surrendered. Aspendos offered to pay tribute, but was unwilling to accept a Macedonian occupation. Alexander the Great was a reasonable man; he required only 50 gold talents and a substantial number of horses, all the same colour and size. An agreement was made and signed. But there was a rebellion in Aspendos due to the horse clause. The people of Aspendos were determined to break the treaty! They restored the town walls and withdrew to the acropolis on the hill when Alexander arrived to collect his due. Alexander occupied the lower town and demanded unconditional surrender, his 50 talents, and the most important towns-people as hostages. In the end the people of Aspendos accepted the conditions and surrendered.

During the Roman era, Aspendos experienced its golden age as an important trading centre. The staple of the economy was salt, collected during the summer months from a nearby lake. During the 2nd century AD, the *theatre* was built to hold 15,000 spectators on the east slope of the (naturally) steep table mountain. During the Islamic era it served as a caravanserai.

This theatre displays one of the major differences between Greek and Roman theatres: a Roman theatre is completely enclosed, while the audience at the Greek theatre could see the surrounding countryside behind the low stage.

Several rows of seats have crumbled over the centuries, the furnishings are largely gone, but overall the theatre doesn't seem to be in need of great repair. The intact ancient structure is still being used today for music and theatre performances from May 20 to 26 during the Antalya Festival. (Information: Tourist-Info Antalya).

On the plateau of the castle mountain is the *agora*, surrounded by the ruins of a *nymphaeum* and a *basilica* (whose entrance hall is still well preserved). From the northern edge of the hill, you can look down on the plains and see:

1. The overgrown ruins of a Roman *aqueduct*, originally 15 km long, parts of which still stand at its original height. The aqueduct is considered the most beautiful remaining in Anatolia.

2. The ruins of two *water towers* which provided the castle mountain with water.

OPEN: Daily, except Mondays, 9:00 - 17:30 h. Admission (new!): £1.70, half-price on weekends and for students.

COMING - GOING: Coming from Antalya, turn off E 24, about 5 km after Serik, left onto the road to Belkis and Aspendos (signs, 3 km). The road ends at a parking lot next to the theatre.

Side

Ruins covered by thick brush. Ruins rising out of the sand dunes. Columns along the road across from an ancient theatre. And then the parking lot, horns honking, buses, taxis, cars, people. A barricade hinders traffic, behind which the village of Selimiye is nestled in the shadow of the long-gone metropolis, Side. In English "Side" means "pomegranate".

A couple of centuries ago, only a few fishermen and farmers disturbed this ruined town. Today it is one of the tourist centres of Turkey's southern coast. The geographical features are ideal: ancient Side is situated on a headland surrounded by long, sandy beaches. Particularly along the eastern beach, the ruins rise up out of the dunes like a Hollywood set for a Greek melodrama. Side has been completely consumed by tourism. Outside of high season, Side is "closed", only a handful of restaurants, pensions, and hotels remain open.

Your first impression of Side in season is a crowded, over-priced tourist village. But once you've found a place to stay, you'll soon discover Side's attractions, designed to facilitate relaxation in every price category. The days pass quickly; while the evenings, away from the bustle of the "Column Street", are filled with the sound of pleasant conversation coming from gardens, terraces, and balconies. Another vacation day has passed.

History

This time the 7th century BC Greek settlers did not choose a table mountain, but sited the town on a rocky cliff. This exposed position and the expansion of the harbour made Side an important and wealthy harbour town. In the 2nd century BC, Side and its 60,000 inhabitants experienced a golden age.

The growth began when the town sheltered an illegal slave market run by Cilician pirates and participated in the profits in return for this hospitality. This trade came to an end when Pompey declared war on piracy with great success. The town quickly erected a monument and statue in honour of Pompey, and Side suffered no consequences. Several of Side's citizens then turned their investments to legitimate trade, and the town's wealth increased dramatically.

With the fall of the Roman empire, Side experienced its own decline. The town never recovered from repeated Arab attacks in the 7th century AD. The last inhabitants abandoned the site in the 9th century, moving to Antalya after a fire destroyed most of the town.

During the 1920s, Muslim ethnic Turk settlers from Crete established themselves here because Crete had once again come under Greek rule.

The economic rebirth of Side began in the 1960s when the local population discovered that tourism was a useful substitute for dealing with slaves or legitimate goods.

INFORMATION: The Tourist Office is about 2 km from town on the road from Side to Manavgat. It is pleasantly cool inside, the staff are friendly and ready to help with any problems. English, French and German spoken. tel. 265.

TELEPHONE AREA CODE: 2313.

COMING - GOING: Coming from Antalya, get a dolmuş from the dolmuş station to Manavgat (every half hour) or from the bus station. Then change to a dolmuş to Side (£0.20) or get a tourist taxi (£1.70). There are some direct buses to Side (£0.65).

BICYCLE RENTALS: Mopeds and bicycles can be rented by the hour, day or week. One of the cheapest is at the Subasi Motel, next to the post office along the west beach about 1 km from town. A one-seater moped costs about £7 per day, a two-seater £9. Compare prices and bargain.

CAR RENTALS: There are countless rental agencies on the Column Street and its side streets. Domestic and international rental firms compete, the former offer the best deals. Compare prices. You can take out a small Murat for £27 per day or pay £117 for a Mercedes 230 E.

DAY TRIPS: Several travel agencies offer Antalya tours (including Perge, Aspendos, Düden Waterfalls) and Alanya tours (Kervanserayi, Alanya). One of the cheapest agents is Şelale Tour, tel. 1066, costs £5. But there are also much more expensive tours. Be sure to compare prices. Two-to three-day tours to Pamukkale or Cappadocia cost £50 to £133.
Excursion boats depart from the harbour, e.g. to the Manavgat River and up to the waterfalls.

SHOPPING: The Column Street, the former main boulevard, running from the theatre to the harbour, is one tremendous tourist bazaar today. You can buy anything from jewellery, leather goods, carpets, colourful Turkish trinkets, and "Lacoste" shirts to groceries and toilet paper. International newspapers and magazines are also available. Tasty hand-packed ice cream is sold with a flourish at stands throughout town.

SERVICE

Occasionally you'll hear loudspeaker announcements which don't call the Muslim faithful to prayer. Drivers of improperly parked cars are reprimanded, but rendezvous are also announced, "Mr. Spinks from Colchester, your guest is awaiting you in Ali Baba Restaurant!"

A Night's Rest

The lodgings in Side are excellent. If you'd like a comfortable first-class hotel, try along the beach outside town, west (right) of the road. There are the modern hotels. It is an easy walk from here into town along the beach.

> You might try **Nuptün-Motel**, well-kept facilities, £27 for a double with the comfort and service you'd expect. tel. 8684.

There are countless small hotels and pensions in town. The nicest locations are along the steep coastline to the east where you have a lovely view of the sea (take the 2nd or 3rd left off the main road). Here you can escape the tourist carnival. A double with shower, balcony, etc. costs £13. There are a number of clean pensions where you can get a double with shower for under £7.

The cheapest and most simple lodgings are the pensions in town near the mosque (double £5). If you are short of cash, you might ask to sleep on the roof of one of the smaller pensions, costs £1.65.

> **Yalı-Motel**: Up on the cliff with a lovely view of the sea, east of town. Double with shower and WC £13. tel. 148.
>
> **Poseidon-Motel**: Heading toward the east beach, the next to last street on the left. Behind the inconspicuous entrance, featuring wrought-iron lamps, is a lovely garden with a bar, French café furnishings, a small fountain and a ping-pong table. In the evening, many guests gather on the roof to enjoy a last rakı. A 3-bed room with shower/WC, breakfast costs £9. tel. 1038.
>
> **Temple-Motel**: On the western beach a little out of town. Take a right at the post office just outside Side, follow the road to the corner shop on the right where you turn right. The facility is about 200 m from the sea, a quiet family-style place with a restaurant. Bungalows with showers, WC and breakfast cost £8. tel. 1179.
>
> **Pension Morning Star**: Our tip: very pleasant, with a lovely view, also on the east coast, right on the beach. Breakfast and non-alcoholic drinks in the covered, oriental **divan** on the first floor, or on your own balcony. Süleyman rents ten 3-bed rooms with wood panelling and showers, WC and balcony for £7. He is also very helpful. tel. 1134.
>
> **Pension Juvam**: seaside location next to the Morning Star; Hakan Öztürk, Süleyman's brother-in-law, rents out seven rooms with shower/WC and balcony. In addition, he also runs a small café by the name of Merhaba, along the steep coast. A double costs £7, a 3-bed room £9 and breakfast £1. tel. 1061 and 1151.
>
> **Pension Balcıoğlu**: The pension's name means "son of the honey seller", and the establishment is as friendly as its name. A quiet, white building on a small street near the eastern beach. The rooms are freshly renovated, showers and WC newly tiled. Guests gather to talk on the terrace. A 3-bed room with shower and WC costs £7. tel. 60.
>
> **Paradise Pension**: Down from the Pension Balcıoğlu; it consists of ten bungalows and is run by Hassan Özen and Metin Aktaş. Building was completed in 1988 - the paint is still shiny. The bungalows are simple, but have clean, tiled showers/WC. The complex has a coffee bar (a few tables and chairs), breakfast is available (£1) and a small restaurant is in planning. A bungalow with two beds

costs £7, with three beds £9. There is no telephone yet. Further assistance can be obtained at the Morning Star.

Pension Nar: Two streets from the east beach on a small dead-end road, simple, rustic, freshly whitewashed, pleasant. You can use the refrigerator and kitchen. Showers and WC in the hall; a 3-bed room costs £4.

Camping

The major camp grounds are in front of the main gate to the right of the road. Some are very loud and not very clean. Prices start at £0.70. In town, there are small camp sites along the east shore and the harbour where you can rent a two-person tent for £3, otherwise £2 for two people.

Mikro-Camping: Quaintly set in the ruins of a basilica (see map), well kept, small (see name). Two guests with a tent pay £3; a bungalow with breakfast costs £8. Guess the age of the owner's favorite aunt!

Kamelya-Camping/Bungalows: Not as idyllic and much louder. At the harbour, way on the right, across from the restaurant "Harbour Restaurant Ismail". But the bungalows are cheaper; per person with tent £1.30, bungalows for three people £3.30

Food

There are rows of restaurants along the Column Street and nearby. Many, however, have become cattle troughs for the tourist masses. Down by the harbour are a number of large restaurants where you can sit outdoors and watch the tourist bustle.

Aphrodite: On the right hand side of the harbour, worth recommending, reasonable prices. Try the swordfish. tel. 1171.

Yeni Afrodite: Better known to insiders as the "Soup Shop". Apart from soup, which is available into the early hours of the morning, you can get very tasty meat dishes (specialities of the house) for reasonable prices. The restaurant is located on the old market place, on the first floor over a carpet shop.

Better located, but more expensive, are the restaurants along the steep coastline on the left of the road.
Soundwave: One of the most expensive spots in town, 1 kg of the best fish costs £11.70.
Moonlight: In front of Yali Motel; the best spot in town.

If you have to watch your money and can do without tuxedoed waiters, enjoy a meal in one of the small pensions with an in-house restaurant - barbequed titbits in pleasant surroundings.

NIGHTLIFE:

The several discos in town quickly become boring, unless you are drunk or in love. The most expensive, but not much fun, is **Cin-Cin** on the square near the telephone booths. The nicest is **Nimfeon** up on the steep coast en route to the east beach. Still, there is lots of activity until the early hours of the morning as pubs and bars stay open late. And if everything else is closed, try the **Soup Shop**, next to Cin-Cin.

Sights

Side, with the largest theatre in Asia Minor, is - along with Pergamon and Ephesus - one of the major excavation sites in Turkey. The beaches and ruins attract streams of tourists to the ancient town. The picturesque scenery - bushes, dunes, and black rocks - put you in the mood to discover a long-lost civilization.

Aqueducts: These are the first ruins you will see rising out of the bushes along the road from Manavgat to Side. They are part of a 30 km long piping system bringing water from the source of the Melas (Manavgat Cayi) to the town. In rocky regions tunnels were cut through the rock, in the sandy plains freestone and mortar were used to build curved passageways and bridges were built across valleys and streams - all in all 24, with lengths of up to 400 m.

Nympheum (Nimfeon): Outside the town wall across from the main gate. It was considered the largest and loveliest in Asia Minor: 52 m long, 20 m high, 4 m thick, covered with marble and with a three-storey column-structure. In front was a paved courtyard surrounded by benches and stone steps. The basin, decorated with reliefs, contained 500 cubic metres of water flowing into the basin through lead pipes. A number of statues decorated the Nymph Temple.

Town Gate: This was the main gate of the town wall which is several kilometres long and now crumbling. The gate, like the entire wall, dates from Hellenic times and is a good example of a mighty ancient fortification. Because defense was not very important during the Roman era, the courtyard of the gate was richly furnished with pillars, statues and niches. Flanked by two hefty, rectangular towers (lovely ornamentation), it provided a splendid entrance into the town. Today it stands alone, looking rather helpless in spite of its defiant appearance.

Arched Gateway: This gate (triumphal arch) stands next to the theatre and not - as is customary - on a direct axis with the main gate. The straight run through town was probably blocked already by the *Temple of Dionysos* in front of the theatre, so it was decided to conceal the bend with a gate. The attic of the gate (destroyed) was crowned by an imperial quadriga of bronze (a four-horse chariot, melted). To the left of the archway the *Vespasian Memorial* was uncovered. It was an elegant spring or fountain building, and in its main niche stood a statue of the emperor VESPASIAN.

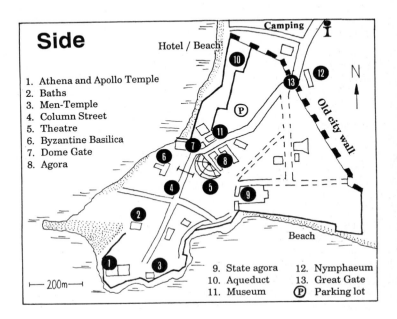

Side

1. Athena and Apollo Temple
2. Baths
3. Men-Temple
4. Column Street
5. Theatre
6. Byzantine Basilica
7. Dome Gate
8. Agora
9. State agora
10. Aqueduct
11. Museum
12. Nymphaeum
13. Great Gate
Ⓟ Parking lot

Camping
Hotel / Beach
Beach
Old city wall
N
⊢ 200m ⊣

Theatre: Side's landmark towers above every ruin and building in town. This magnificent "soup bowl" provided space for an audience of 15,000 - 20,000. Because Side was not built on a hill, it was not possible to construct the theatre on the slopes. Its walls - a rarity in Asia Minor - had to be built up all the way around. Construction was completed in the 2nd century BC using rocks from the "sea wall", which must have been considered obsolete. Besides performances, the theatre was a venue for public meetings and gladiator fights. The orchestra once contained a pool in which boat races were held. During an earthquake, the upper portion of the theatre was destroyed and the entire stage fell into the orchestra, which today is filled with rubble.

When the sun sank into the Mediteranean, the performers and gladiators were probably able to take a break because the sunset was a performance of its own. It's the same today, although the gladiators are long gone.

Column Street: You can still see a few columns at the theatre. For more info, see Shopping.

Agora: Bordered by the stage area of the theatre to the southwest, to the northwest the great Column Street. The square interior was lined with column halls containing exactly 100 columns on each side. Shops occupied the northeast and northwest sides. The street entrance was a tremendous gate (only the foundations remain) where the morning bustle took place. The agora was also the place where pirates sold their captives as slaves. In the northwest corner of the agora, next to the theatre, is a half-oval building. Once it was covered with a vaulted roof and served as a public toilet for 24 people.

State Agora: North of the theatre; on the way to the beach are the remains of a government building. The central room was probably used for festive occasions, while the two rooms on the left and right served as libraries or archives. Many statues once displayed in the niches have disappeared, a few can be seen in the Side museum. Only a headless torso has remained in its rightful spot throughout the centuries: Nemesis, the goddess of vengeance.

Athena & Apollo Temples: Just ten metres separate the two temples at the southern tip of the peninsula. The smaller temple is dedicated to Apollo, the larger one, in which people enjoyed the right of asylum, is dedicated to Athena. The temples were damaged by an earthquake and by the construction of the adjoining basilica. They are currently undergoing restoration. Columns are being placed back on their original pedestals at a rate of one per year. When the scaffolding finally disappears, this will again be a wonderful spot to watch the sunset.

Agora with kamel

Harbour: Its length was 450 m; you can still see where the moles used to be. It was always difficult to keep the shallow harbour basin free of mud and sand from the Manavgat River. Wealthy citizens bore the expense of dredging, for which they were remembered in inscriptions. These days are long gone: today the harbour is completely filled with sand.

Museum: North of the agora on the Column Street. The restored Roman bath dates from the golden age of Side in the 2nd century AD. You could spend hours in the garden among the weather-proof exhibits. The rooms of the bath contain more of Side's rich finds: statues, jewellery, reliefs, sarcophagi, and more.

OPEN: Daily 8:30 - 11:45 & 13:00 - 17:15 h, closed Monday. Admission (new!)£1.70, half-price on weekends and holidays.

There are many other ruins. From the upper deck of the theatre you will get the full picture with the aid of a map. In the museum and in numerous shops you'll find lots of interesting literature about ancient Side and Pamphylia.

Swimming

Western Beach: This is the beach where the major hotels and resorts are located. There are several kilometres of beach, in part well-kept, scattered trees provide shade. Since the hotels are set a bit back from the water, they are not a great bother. The entire beach is open to the public. Surfboards are for hire (£3.30/hour), as are umbrellas and loungers (£0.50). Here you'll find mostly European tourists. The prices in the tiny beach cafés are average. Since the bay is shallow with little wind, the beach is safe for children.

Eastern Beach: "This beach, which runs as far as the eye can see, is favored by Turkish families. It is prettier because of the ancient ruins on the horizon but there are no trees or other shade and it is less clean. You can rent an umbrella for £0.50. Here you can escape the masses of tourists - if you walk far enough." - thus we were able to report in the last edition of this book. The enterprising mayor has discovered that the beach is an additional source of revenue and has leased it out - supposedly only for a trial period. This "one year experiment" has endowed the beach with corrugated iron eating places and beach showers, which are certainly there to stay - for what is there, will remain. Particularly at the beginning of the beach, there are so many beach recliners for hire at £1 that there is often no room for a privately-brought bathing towel.

Around Side

Manavgat: A small town (20,000 inhabitants) on the Antalya - Alanya road, 72 km from Antalya, 3 km from Side. There is some industry and handicrafts, but this is primarily an agricultural market centre where farmers sell produce and pick up supplies. There is little to interest tourists, who are all busy in Side. A visit to the family tea garden at the dolmuş station (across the road, down by the river) is fun if you are waiting for your ride.

Manavgat Waterfalls: In Manavgat a small road leads to the "*Şelalesi*" (waterfall). After about 4 km there is a parking lot on your right. Behind it are the waterfalls, just narrow branches of the Manavgat, a 20 km long mountain river. Turks love this kind of place: cool shade underneath tall willow trees, with the constant roar of the light-green river and a view of the ruins built upon cliffs, almost reaching midstream. Tiny paved peninsulas with tables and chairs were built; here you can enjoy the favorite Turkish pastimes of eating and drinking in a pleasant atmosphere. Admission £0.07.

Seleucia: A tiny mountain village 11 km north of Manavgat. The ruins of ancient Seleucia are being excavated (since 1972). There are few visitors, which is astonishing, considering the lovely pinewood forest in which the ruins are located. Columns have been raised and an arcade restored - the archaeologists have worked hand in hand with nature. Seleucia is set on a table mountain, requiring just one defensive wall, to the south, where the slope is less steep. A 9 m tall building is visible on the plain below: it was probably a bath, built above a spring which still bubbles today. The function of the other buildings has still not been determined as they are too badly damaged. The temples and the agora of the small Greek town are remarkably well preserved. Small finds are on display in the Antalya museum. Little is known about the village's history. Historians are thankful just to have deciphered the name. Like many of the Seleucias in Asia Minor, it is derived from the Seleucids of Mesopotamia.

COMING - GOING: You have to walk the last kilometres to Seleucia. Dolmuş buses rarely drive down the road to Seleucia. A taxi costs about £7.

Selge: Kown as *Zerk* today, this is a tiny, picturesque village about 70 km northwest of Side. This village will give you an excellent impression of life in a Turkish mountain village. It is also a good departure point for hikes in the Taurus mountains. Since there are no hotels or pensions, be sure to bring a tent. In the summer, a visit to this village is quite strenuous due to the heat.

The main attraction are the ruins of ancient Selge which are even more isolated than those of Termessos. The ruins of the former town of 20,000 are spread out over three hills. The charm of the hill country makes this a worthy destination even for the less archaeologically inclined.

COMING – GOING: On the Alanya - Antalya road, turn off before Serik to Tasagil / Beskonak / Selge. It is about 6 km behind Beşkonak.

Tip: There are lots of tiny side roads leading off the Alanya - Antalya road into the interior. Even smaller, usually gravel roads, run off of these. Driving through the region, you'll pass mountain towns never usually shown on a map. *Çai* (tea) is served everywhere, and the romantic foothills of the Taurus quickly make you forget that the sea is around the corner.

Side - Alanya Route

From Side the road runs along the sea. Many empty beaches invite you to stop for a swim. At some spots you can drive across the beach to the water. To the left of the road, an hour's drive from Manavgat, is the fortress-like Sarapsa Hani, a caravanserai dating from the 13th century. It belonged to a chain of Hans along the caravan road connecting the Seljuk capital Konya with the then important harbour town Alanya. Shortly before Alanya the number of modern buildings along the beach increases and across the street you can see large banana plantations.

CAMPING:

About 25 km outside Alanya the hotel complex "Angora" is built on both sides of the road. Right after that is the **Alanya Motorcamp**, a relatively new, well kept camp site with new trees providing shade, a swimming pool, kitchen facilities you can use, a restaurant, and shop. Costs £4 for two people with car and tent. You can rent a 2-person tent for £3.50.

Next door is the well-kept, shady, **BP-Kervansaray-Motor-Camp** (two people/car £4, tent £1.50, camper £3), also well-equipped. It is shady, but also close to the road and loud. Tel. 1422.

These camp sites are preferable to those in Alanya itself, where you'll have to pitch your tent in a courtyard or on shadeless sand, and make do with poor sanitary facilities. And the swimming is not pleasant due to the sewage.

En route to Selge

ALANYA *(pop. 25.000)*

**Set on a gentle bay, Alanya is a small town with a lovely
centre. The white buildings spread up the slopes rising
behind the town. The 250 m high castle rock is the dominant
feature of the town. Crowning the summit, a Walt Disney-
style Seljuk castle looks down on the bay.**

Around the harbour there are shops both for tourist supplies and
household goods; a great place to window shop. Heading east or west
from the town centre you'll reach the beach after a few hundred
metres. Right underneath the castle mountain is the new harbour for
fishing boats and yachts.

Alanya's old town is spread around the castle mountain. It wasn't too
long ago that the walls of the *Alaye* - the present-day "upper town" -
ended at the harbour. The life of Alanya today is in the lower town;
the old town seems lost in quiet slumber.

History

Alanya dates back to the Greek colonial era. It was a minor fortress,
called Korakesion, on the border between Lycia and Pamphylia.
Little is known about its early history. In the 4th century BC it came
under Persian rule. It was the only town in 197 BC which successfully
defended itself against an attack by ANTIOCHUS III of Mesopotamia.

During the Roman era, Korakesion was an infamous pirate stronghold, plaguing coastal towns and merchant ships for a century.
DIODOTUS TRYPHON, the "Sensualist", started the piracy about 150
BC; the Roman general Pompey put an end to it once and for all in 67
BC in a sea battle off the shore of Korakesion. Two centuries later,
when MARK ANTHONY was arming for his attack on AUGUSTUS, he
gave the town and the entire region to his beloved CLEOPATRA. As a
result of this gift, the Korakesion forests were cut down to provide
wood for the Egyptian fleet.

During Byzantine rule and the succeeding Armenian era, the town
was called Kalonoros. The Seljuk sultan ALAEDDIN KEYKOBAT acquired
the town by trade in 1221 AD, and renamed it Alaiye. Under his rule
Alanya's importance increased. The sultan, whose court was in
Konya, designated Alanya as his summer residence and built a
harbour here because he loved the town and his empire needed a
military port. The sights of the town date from this period. However,

since Alanya does not have a natural harbour the town lost its importance after seventy years of Seljuk rule.

The town's revival began about 1960: increased tourism caused the original settlement around the castle mountain to expand to the foot of the 2647 m high Ak Dag. And the building boom continues.

ALL ABOUT CLEOPATRA (PART 1)

The Elizabeth Taylor of the turn of the millennium enjoyed a few carefree months with her Roman jet-set lover Anthony in Alanya. Just to make her feel at home, the then Roman-style castle was improved with a few extras. These included a tunnel running from the castle to the ocean: Cleopatra's tunnel. At the tunnel entrance a shower was installed: Cleopatra's shower. The tunnel opened onto a tiny bay sheltered by a mountain massif: Cleopatra's beach. Who wouldn't want their own beach in Turkey?

INFORMATION: Iskele Cad. 56/6, tel. 3231/1240. The staff is helpful and speaks English. Here you can pick up a free map.

TELEPHONE AREA CODE: 3231

COMING - GOING: The **bus** station is on Atatürk Cad., a bit outside town. There is irregular transportation into town, otherwise get a taxi (£1.35). It can be difficult to get a bus toward Anamur. Be sure to reserve your ticket early. Note: from the bus station you have direct connections to the Black Sea (Samsun).

The **dolmuş** station is in the town centre. You can get a dolmuş to Manavgat or Gazipaşa.

Ferry to Cyprus: You can make bookings for the ferry at the Tourist Information Office, where you can also pick up tickets for a direct bus to Taşuçu. The ship docks in Taşuçu near Silifke. For departure times and prices, see Taşuçu - Coming - Going.

AROUND ALANYA: The usual one to three-day tours are offered along the southern coast: Cappadocia, Pamukkale, the historic towns of Side, Perge, Aspendos, also trips to Anamur and "active excursions to the Taurus Mountains". There are also tours to "Discover the Real Turkey", or all-day "dreamlike" pirate tours (cost £17), where you go by boat to a secluded bay. Don't forget your bathing suit. There are lots of travel agencies; be sure to compare prices. One agent with a wide selection of tours is **Panel**, Kalearkasi Cad. 37, tel. 4151.

CAR RENTALS: **Avis** is at Iskele Cad. 68/5, tel. 4400 - 3278. **Budget**, Hükümet Cad. 135, tel. 3513.

HORSE CARRIAGES: You can take a tour around the town or use it just like a taxi to reach any destination. The carriages are twice as expensive as a taxi, a third as fast, but at least five times more pleasant. In the quiet of the night it is a real treat.

SHOPPING: In the streets around Kızıl Kule, you'll find lovely silver jewellery and long-standing carpet dealers with big, cool shops. Otherwise the old town is full of leather goods and tourist souvenirs. The specially tailored pants, salvar, are popular (baggy at the top). They are still worn today in Turkish villages. By the way, townspeople here consider tourists outfitted in these to be at least a bit strange. 'Villagers',

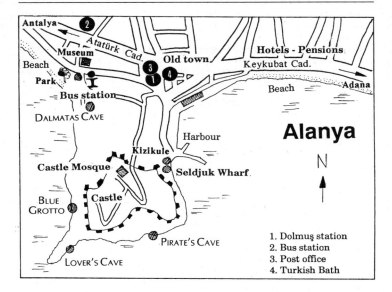

particularly those wearing a salvar, are considered by the westernized townspeople
to be real country bumpkins. Rural people, however, are amused by folklore tourists.

Tip: Mehmet Ali Genç is a tailor with a shop on Iskele Cad. 15 (a white cloth is
stretched over the street). He is willing to make you a pair of pants or other clothes,
using excellent cloth. He enjoys showing his photo album of satisfied customers.
That alone is worth a visit.

A Night's Rest

Alanya is even more geared to tourism than Antalya. There is a large
selection of hotels and pensions in every price category. The town has
the same number of beds as Antalya with only one-tenth the population. Still, in season, everything can be booked.

Good hotels costing £13 for a double with bath can be found along the
roads to the eastern and western beach. On the side streets, you'll
find cheaper pensions charging £6 to £7 for a double. The old town is
even cheaper, although the scene is louder, with more bustle.

OLD TOWN:
   Günaydin: Single £5, double £7, Kultur Cad., Tel 1943.
   Further west on Kultur Cad. are the small pensions **Atlas and Simsek**, double £7,
   pleasant, clean.

EASTERN BEACH
   Attila Güller: Single £5, double £7, bath, Pinarı Mah., Tel 1451.

Merhaba Motel: Double £13, Keykubat Cad., Tel 1251.
Cimen Hotel: Single £8, double £11, bath, Güller Pınarı Mah., Tel 2283.

WESTERN BEACH

Okan Pension: Nothing special besides a large tarnished safe upstairs, but it's okay for the price. Double £5.30, triple £7, plus £1 for each additional bed. Showers are in the hall, kitchen utilization costs £0.30 per day; everything you need is there. Address: Meteoroji Bitisiği, Tel 3210.

Özlan Pension: Hüseyin Avce worked for six years as a tram driver in Germany. He rents 80 beds in his nicely shaded house which appears to be much smaller than it is. WC and showers are in the rooms, the atmosphere is nice, costs £7. Address: Meteoroloji Yanı, Tel 2135.

CAMPING:

See under the Side - Alanya Route.

Food

In the old town are a number of tiny kebap places offering a variety of food at reasonable prices. Little "food streets" branch off of Gazi Paşa. The most exclusive spots, generally specializing in seafood, are right on Gazi Paşa.

The best and most expensive restaurant is **Mahperi** but others, e.g. **Siriu** and **Yönet**, can also be recommended.

Hotel Panorama: A ten-minute walk from the centre of town on the eastern beach. Don't be deterred by the expensive hotel lobby. You have a nice view of the illuminated castle mountain, great food (not expensive), and if you are lucky, Mahmuhd will wait on you. Mahmuhd organizes everything, even a Lucullian birthday surprise on short notice. Address: Keykubat Cad., Tel 1252.

Efes Beer Garden: Near the beach, shaded by old trees, unfortunately a number of videos have recently been installed.

Sights

Kızıl Kule (Red Tower): The huge, octagonal tower was built in 1225 AD at the harbour entrance. It was designed to protect the nearby shipyards. The five-story tower (46 m) was built around a column which served as a cistern. There is an ethnographic museum on the ground floor and the panoramic view from the roof terrace is beautiful. The tower was restored in the early 1950s. Admission £0.20, half price on weekends.

Terşhane (shipyard): This is where the sultan had his naval fleet built. The yard is 200 paces south of the Red Tower. Five vaulted roofed galleries, connected by archways, were chiselled 42 m deep into the rock and adorned with a lovely facade. The unique complex is over 50 m long. The shipyard is still used today, but not by the Turkish navy.

Tip: Don't be bashful about walking across the shipyard and climbing (easy) up the cliff at the end. The sea is clean out here; enjoy a refreshing swim after the sights.

Fortress: The town's landmark is a medieval castle dominating the ruins atop the castle mountain. You can get Bus 42 (bus stop next to the Tourist Information Office, departs hourly) for £0.10. Still intact are the tremendous walls, a Byzantine chapel, a mosque, a caravanserai, and a roofed bazaar. The main (most gruesome) attraction of the fortress is in the northeast corner, at the highest point on the castle mountain: the *adam ataçagi* (the spot where people are thrown down). Death-defying criminals were given hope: they were permitted a running leap. But there was no hope of clearing the rocks! Still, the view is wonderful. Admission to the fortress is £1.70 (new!), half price on weekends.

It is nice to take a long walk from the castle back into town, past the tiny Ottoman-period houses in the crooked streets of the upper town.

Museum: Diagonally across from the Tourist Information Office on the western beach. There is nothing special about the arts and crafts museum featuring exhibits from Greek to Ottoman times. The ethnological section, containing several splendidly extravagant books and examples of filigree work, is most interesting. The museum garden is an Ottoman cemetery with several hefty amphorae and tiny sarcophagi among the graves. Have a look when you get tired of the beach (500 m).

OPEN: Daily, except Mondays, 8:30 - 12:00 h and 13:30 - 17:00 h, admission £0.10.

Damlataş Stalactite Cavern: Just 40 m from the western beach at the foot of the castle mountain. Because of the constant interior temperature of 23 degrees C and the high carbon dioxide content of the air, the caves are considered beneficial for asthma. Strangers are informed at the entrance to the cave (in three languages!) that the engineer Mr. Ahmet Tokuş built a lockable door and handed the key over to Mr. Galip Dere. Exactly who is in possession of the key at the moment could not be determined. The author would be thankful for any information concerning this subject. But fortunately the cave is not locked during the day, making it a good spot to visit if you want to escape the heat of the sun. Admission £0.10.

Boat Trips

Be sure to take a boat ride around the castle mountain to the many caves and tiny bays among the vertical cliffs. A boat holding ten people costs £7 per hour.

The Phosphorus Cave is lovely with the clear water radiating green light. Jump into the water for a colourful swim. At the Lovers Caves, just two openings in a rock, your *Kaptan* might spin the following tale. In 1965 a German woman and her Turkish boyfriend disappeared in Alanya. Was it suicide - or murder? The Turkish police and the army formed search parties to look for the two lovers. After three months the two were discovered in the cave. They were in fine shape - a bit pale perhaps - and still very much in love!

The tour ends at Cleopatra's beach (see previous box). The original beach was buried in an earthquake and landslide. For an additional fee you can stop for a swim and a look in the tunnel.

Swimming

The eastern and western beaches are separated by the town and the castle rock. The water at the eastern beach is polluted by the sewage of the numerous hotels and pensions. Walk out a kilometre or more where the water slowly becomes cleaner.

The best swimming is on the west beach next to a small park near the Tourist Information Office. The rough-grained sand and the water are clean. Skin diving is interesting around the castle mountain with its numerous caves. Admission is £0.20 at the spots which are cleaned daily. You can rent an umbrella (£0.50) for some protection from the sun. Here too, you'll find lovely cafés. Take Bus 42 from the old town to get to the western beach.

Around Alanya

Aytap: About 15 km behind Alanya, in the direction of Anamur, you'll see the ruins of Aytap picturesquely embedded in the rocks of the steep coastline. Between the cliffs small, sandy beaches are accessible on foot from the road. Enjoy a quiet swim and the panoramic view.

Dimcay Regülatörü Lake: In the mountains, about 16 km to the north, with lovely picnic areas. A couple of restaurants offer freshwater fish. The river is spanned by a frightening suspension bridge which is a real adventure to cross.

Gazipaşa: This unspoiled Turkish town (population 10,000) has no tourist facilities except a few restaurants and pensions catering for a mostly Turkish clientele. The town's future lies in its beach. The town is framed by two hills. A river flows from the Taurus into the ocean. Completing the picture are a camp site, several restaurants, and refreshing peace and quiet after the bustle of the nearby tourist centres. A brightly-lit, brand-new, 3 km long avenue leads down to the beach.

COMING – GOING: Easy to reach by dolmuş from Alanya; 47 km down the road to Anamur.

CAMPING: **Camping Gazipaşa**, an intimate, quiet spot with family atmosphere, a kiosk, swimming pool, and restaurant. Tiny trees and tin roofs provide some shade. The sanitary facilities are good. Costs £1 per person/tent/trailer. Bungalows for 2 - 3 people cost £5, family bungalows £8. Tel (3236) 1631. There is an hourly bus into town (£0.07).

Alanya - Anamur Route

After Alanya the coastal road runs past long, empty, sandy beaches. Cilicia begins where the Taurus mountains reach the ocean. Classical Cilicia stretches from here to the Syrian border. Eastern Cilicia, around Mersin, is known as the Cilician Plain, a fertile region where the Taurus mountains move back from the ocean. The western mountainous region beyond Alanya is known as "rugged Cilicia". This is the poorest stretch of land with the lowest population on the south coast. The numerous ruins of ancient fortress towns, although unimportant, prove that the coastline was once much more heavily settled.

The road climbs into the mountains, providing a series of outstanding views. Cut deep between the cliffs are almost inaccessible little bays whose sandy beaches are a paradise for cross-country vehicles. Frequently the road moves inland, where old Turkish cemeteries sleep under the sweet shade of pine groves. This may well be the prettiest section of the entire southern coast. The ride by bus is £1.40.

CAMPING: There is a lovely site at Sehir, 65 km outside Anamur.

Forest Fires

At regular intervals, signs warn that it is prohibited to light fires in the forest. The fear of forest fires is easy to understand considering the hot, dry summers in the region. Turkey, particularly, has lost most of its forests forever. By the way, even a cigarette butt, thrown from a car window, has the same effect as a molotov cocktail.

Evening on the beach of Anamur

Anamur *(pop. 30,000)*

The small town is situated on a slope 4 km inland at the edge of an intensively farmed plain of alluvial soil. Anamur is famous due to the Mamure Kalesi, a picture-book medieval castle.

During the last 50 years Anamur has grown from an insignificant village to a small town. You will notice the straight modern streets but even though this quiet town is slowly beginning to look a bit worn, it is not very interesting for the visitor.

Because the town itself has little to offer, try to find lodgings on the beach or in İskele, Anamur's tiny harbour. Outside high season, Anamur caters only modestly for tourists, mostly Turkish families and western Europeans out to avoid the heat in the shady tea gardens on the beach. There are a few good pubs and hotels around the pier. Everybody gathers here in the evening.

But İskele has plans. Vacation apartments are being built for wealthy residents of İstanbul, Ankara and Konya.

INFORMATION: There is no Turizm Bürosu, despite what you may hear (1987).

TELEPHONE AREA CODE: 7571.

COMING - GOING: The **bus** station is on the road from Antalya - Silifke, about 1.5 km from town and 5 km from İskele. There are good **dolmuş** connections between Anamur and İskele (£0.07). There is no public transport from the bus station into town or to İskele; a **taxi** costs £1.

SHOPPING: You can pick up groceries at the market square on the end of Atatürk Cad. in Anamur. Near the market place there are shops, pubs, bakeries, etc.

A Night's Rest

Karan Motel: About 500 m to the east of the castle (7 km from Anamur) with its own restaurant and beach. The petrol station next door does not belong to the hotel. This is a pleasant, respectable hotel where you get what you pay for. All rooms with shower, WC, balcony and ocean view. Single with breakfast £8, double £13. Address: Bozdogan Köyü, Anamur. Tel 3564 or 1231.

Hotel Saray: A popular gathering spot for foreigners. Good value. Rooms with balcony, some with shower/WC. You can choose from singles, doubles, triples, cost £2.30 per person. Lounge. Address: Tahsin Soglu Cad. Tel 1191.

The following hotels are **in İskele**. All are near the ocean and offer about equal services.

Dragon Hotel: Very comfortable, popular, at the east end of town. Single with shower/WC £8, double shower/WC £12.

Eser Pension: A newly renovated building with a well kept garden, a pleasant roof terrace with a view of the sea. The ten doubles (£6) are OK, some with shower/WC in the room, others in the hall. Mrs. Eser, a former geography teacher, organizes tours to the caves near Anamur (see Around Anamur). Tel. 2322.

Yakomos Pension: Right behind the beach with an ivy-covered roof terrace. Ten doubles (£6), shower/WC. Tel. 2308.

Melin Pension: Eight doubles (£5) with shower/WC.

Meltem Pension: Double (£5) with shower/WC.

Camping

Yalı Motorcamp: About 4 km along a gravel road from the bus station in Anamur. Lovely sandy beach; the trees planted in 1984 receive lots of water, and have grown fast. The restaurant is good. There are not enough sinks; sanitary facilities are only average. There is a small market nearby, but no public transport. A taxi costs £1. The site is occupied primarily by European guests and mosquitos. Crowded during high season, but the crowds melt away along the kilometres of beach. Two people with one tent pay £2; a camping bus with electricity costs £3. Simple two-person wooden bungalows can be rented for £5; stone bungalows for three with shower/WC cost £8. Tel. 3471.

Camping Pullu: About 2 km from the castle towards Silifke. Set in a terrace-like pine forest, falling quite steeply to the ocean. Restaurant, kiosk, satisfactory sanitary facilities. Overcrowded in high season, particularly the beach. Caters for Turkish guests and mosquitos. Costs £0.80 per person. No telephone.

In İskele, there are several small sites between the beach and the road. They are simple, cater for Turkish guests, and cost about £0.60 per person.

Sights

Anamurium: At the western end of the bay, right where the Taurus hits the ocean, lie the town ruins which trace their roots back to the Greek era. Excavations are not yet complete, and you might rummage about the ruins. Be sure to wear sturdy shoes to ward off plants and thorns. A taxi from Anamur costs £2.

Mamure (Anamurye) Kalesi: The history of this castle dates from the pre-Seljuk era. The present complex was built by the king of Lesser Armenia to defend the coastal plain. Even earlier, this was a pirate stronghold before being used by the crusaders as a base and to store supplies. It passed on to the Seljuks, then to the Karamanidian Turks (a nomadic principality) and finally to the Ottomans. The facility is quite ordinary because it always served strategic purposes and was never used as a palace.

In front of the castle there is a small biotope containing water turtles, colourful dragonflies, and water snakes. The castle itself is the largest and best preserved medieval castle of the Turkish coast. It is pleasant to roam through the extensive, empty grounds right on the shore. The castle is divided into three courtyards, each separated by mighty walls. The mosque and bath house in the centre court are of more recent date, providing an oriental contrast to the romantic medieval castle in which they are encompassed.

It is nice to wander around the wall passages and battlements, or climb up one of the 36 towers to play lookout. From each of the towers you have a different view of the ocean, the cliffs, and the fortress, and each view is spectacular. Admission £0.07.

COMING - GOING:
Easy to reach by dolmuş from Anamur; 7 km on the road to Silifke.

Museum: The modern concrete building on the right side of the quay was completed in 1987. The museum features finds from the Anamurium excavations.

Swimming

STROLLING ALONG THE BEACH

A lovely walk leads west from the ANAMURIUM; after about 1 1/2 hours you reach Yali Camp. There is not one tavern along the way. The beach is deserted, serving chiefly as a source of sand and gravel for new construction. Occasionally a stream flows into the sea.

Keep walking west and you reach İskele after another 20 minutes. About 20 minutes beyond İskele there is a wide river which you can cross for just a few lira. Because the river water is several degrees cooler than the sea it is a delight to go for a swim here.

And after twenty more minutes, you arrive at *Mamure Kalesi* castle. The castle is about 7 km from Anamur.

The Bay of Anamur offers a long stretch of sandy beach. It isn't always clean, sometimes gravel-like. Several streams, and by the castle a river, flow into the sea. A lack of waves and a wealth of sandbanks

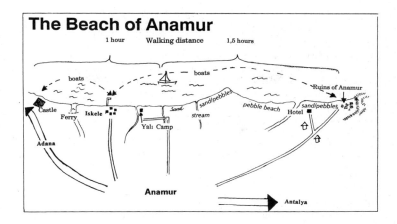

The Beach of Anamur

make this a good beach for children. During high season, the crowds thin out along the length of the shore (See above - Strolling Along The Beach).

Around Anamur

Caves: There are a number of caves in the karst outcroppings of the Taurus around Anamur; best known is *Kösekbüklo Amgarasi* (12 km). It is almost impossible to find without a guide (see A Night's Rest, Eser Pension).

Baraj Dam: Not on the tourist trail, but a nice place for a freshwater swim, 15 km from Anamur.

Softa Kalesi: This former Byzantine fortress, 25 km east of Anamur, is set on a ledge with battlements and massive walls. Easy to spot from a distance. The centuries have left little to see. Nearby is the ancient harbour *Arsinoe*.

Anamur - Silifke Route

Leaving Anamur, the coastal road runs above the picturesque rocky coastline along the slopes of the Taurus or winds through mountain forests. The route is dotted with inviting little bays boasting a hotel or pension. Usually they are located right on the road. After about 70 km, the road drops back down to the ocean at *Aydıncık*.

Aydıncık

There is little happening in this dreamy little town: a main road, a couple of pensions, a harbour where an occasional yacht comes in, and a few seafood restaurants. The water in the bay near town is a bit polluted. The eastern beach is nicest: a clean, sandy beach with a hotel where you can also rent cottages. An ideal place if you want some peace and quiet.

A NIGHT'S REST: **Hotel Ünbür:** The most exclusive hotel in town is right by the harbour. Newly built, a double costs £8. tel. (1046) 1115.

Pension Pinar: Representative of several comparable pensions. Located between the beach and the road at the east end of town. You have a view of the sea, a restaurant and simple sanitary facilities (in the hallway). Rooms (some with balcony) single (£2), double (£4), triple (£5). tel. (1046) 1065.

Above the town is *Kelendiris*, an ancient Phoenician settlement of which little is preserved.

For the next 45 km the road continues going up and down before descending to sea level at *Ovacık*, which consists of just a couple of buildings on the left of the road.

Ovacık

This peaceful village is very quiet, there are no pensions, no bars, no police station. The village itself is really called Büyükeceli; the name Ovacık refers to the entire region whose centre is Büyükeceli.

Note: Some maps show Ovacık/Büyükeceli to be right by the ocean with Aydıncık slightly inland. In fact, it is exactly the opposite with Aydıncık right by the ocean and Ovacık/Büyükeceli 2 - 3 km inland.

A NIGHT'S REST / CAMPING: **Hayat Motel:** About 2 km after Ovacık/Büyükeceli toward Silifke, on the beach, 200 m from the road. The tranquility of the bay and beach is almost undisturbed. The sand & pebble beach is ideal for children. There is a restaurant, and several trees provide shade. Muhamet Öztütüncü rents 12 beds, a triple with shower/WC costs £9, a double (shower/WC in the hall) £5. A tent and two campers pay £2. Trailer parking with electricity costs £1.60 plus £0.85 per person. Tel. (7598) 1021.

After Ovacık you continue through the mountains until the Taurus moves back from the sea near *Bogsak*. At Boğsak a white sandy beach is the site of the Intermot luxury motel and the unpretentious Gürbüzler Camping (no shade, but crowded in high season). In the bay of Boğsak there is an island boasting a wealth of sarcophagi, toppled tombstones, and medieval ruins which you can swim out to. From here on, the flat coastline becomes increasingly crowded, until, 10 km beyond *Taşuçu*, you reach Silifke.

Silifke *(pop. 25,000)*

A junction on the South Coast. This is where the old military road from Inner Anatolia joins the coastal road. Silifke is 15 km inland at the beginning of the Göksu Delta, a region crisscrossed with irrigation canals.

The town has flair - old fashioned two and three-story buildings line the streets, the town centre is full of bustle, the residential areas are pleasant. There is no modern satellite city; no modern high rises destroy the view. You can see the mighty castle and the blue water of the Göksu.

History

Ancient Seleucia was founded by the Greek general SELEUCUS I NICATOR about 300 BC. It is one of many towns founded by ALEXANDER THE GREAT'S former general. Its location on the main road between the coast and Inner Anatolia made Seleucia the most important town in rugged Cilicia. Since the 6th century the castle and town were successively controlled by the Byzantines, the Crusaders, the Byzantines, the Armenians, the Byzantines, the Crusaders, the Seljuks, the Karamaninians, and - last not least - the Ottoman Empire.

During the Roman era, the town was a major trading centre; during the middle ages it was briefly the capital of Armenian Cilicia; during the Ottoman Empire it was the seat of a provincial governor. Today it is a busy junction.

Silifke and the Göksu River played an important role in medieval European politics. During the 11th century, Emperor Frederick Barbarossa drowned just 10 km from town on his way to Jerusalem, creating the Kyffhäuser legend.

INFORMATION: Gazi Mah., Atatürk Cad. 1/2, Tel 151. Pick up the free map and info on local history and sights. Very friendly.

TELEPHONE AREA CODE: 7591.

COMING - GOING:

A large **bus** station and offices of the major bus companies are on the old Konya - Anatolia military road (see map). Buses to Kız Kalezi/Mersin depart right in front of the Tourist Office, as do dolmuş to Taşuçu.

By ship to Cyprus: Depart from Taşuçu, 11 km to the west (see Taşuçu / Coming - Going).

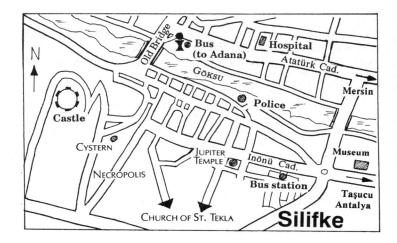

A Night's Rest

As a junction town, Silifke has a good selection of hotels and pensions.
Prices begin at about £2.30 for simple lodgings or £4 for rooms with
shower/WC. For £10 you can get a double in a modern downtown
hotel.

Eren Hotel: 30 beds in 16 rooms, double £7, Tel. 1289.

Cadir Hotel: 40 beds in 18 rooms; double £7. Tel. 1449.

Akdeniz Hotel: 56 beds in 29 rooms along long corridors, turquoise coloured,
like the ocean. Friendly atmosphere; quiet rooms facing the rear. Single £3;
double £4. A shower costs £0.30 extra, which is often the case in Turkey.
Address: Menderes Cad. 95. Tel. 1285.

Taylan Hotel: Tel. 1099. **Yeni Hotel**: Tel. 1094.

CAMPING: After Silifke, where the road reaches the sea, there is one camp site after
another. The best is probably **Akdeniz Mocamp**, although crowded in summer,
without shade, and just simple sanitation facilities. The prices are the same £0.60 per
person. Since none of the sites - including their beaches - look very inviting, keep
going at least until you get to Akkum. 25 km northeast of Silifke, behind Kız Kalesi is
the well-kept **BP-Motorcamp**, see Kız Kalezi/A Night's Rest.

FOOD: Good pubs around Atatürk Cad. and near the Roman Bridge.

Sights

The Romans left behind a tremendous *bridge* across the Göksu and a *Temple of Jupiter*. The *Archaeological Museum* (admission (£0.30) features ancient artifacts dating back to the Hittite era (2000 BC) and the standard ethnographic exhibits.

At the foot of the castle mountain is a Byzantine cistern containing a remarkable circular stone stairway. A medieval castle, *Camardesium*, projects its might above the town. The castle with its 23 towers is still intact and well worth a visit. Around the castle are a number of *rock graves* and the *necropolis*. The large mosque, *Ulu Cami*, was built south of the old stone bridge by the Seljuks on ancient foundations.

Swimming

Beaches are near Sacanoğlu. Camp sites and motels are right on the road with construction in full gear, plus there is noise from the coastal road. Cannot be recommended.

WOMEN TOURISTS - TURKISH MEN

Note: A Turkish police officer provided the following comments in a personal interview:

As Chief of Police, he sees women tourists travelling alone as a major headache. The Turkish press adds to the problem. Many newspapers like to print articles about women tourists who visit the country in order to "test Turkish men". The results are obvious.

Different backgrounds also lead to misunderstandings. If a woman in Turkey takes a man into her room, she loses all social protection. Few Turkish judges would see rape under such conditions - what happens behind a closed hotel door is private.

If the basis for rape can be proven, Turkish law can be severe. But frequently Turkish justice is much too slow. Friends and relatives of the victim have long since ended the matter. The perpetrator's corpse will wash up in some canal, while the police face a wall of silence. Conflicts in Turkey are frequently settled outside the bounds of the law.

Around Silifke

Merianlik: About 5 km from Silifke on the road to Antalya is an early Christian pilgrim town. According to legend, this was the home of St. Thekla (Aya Thekla), who was greatly admired by St. Paul. She is said to have disappeared into a cavern in the rocks. The legend spawned a cult and a "holy town" in the 4th century. The cult died out in the 6th century. Today only ruins remain.

Memorial: If you are travelling by car, take Route 35 into the Göksu Valley and Taurus. After 9 km you reach a memorial stone (donated by the West German government) in honour of Frederick Barbarossa. The following story is taken from the information brochure of the Tourist Information Centre in Silifke.

The True Story Of The Demise Of Frederick Barbarossa

While the bulk of his army fought its way forward in the mountains beyond the northern bank of the Göksu, the Emperor, accompanied by a small guard, took the rocky path right along the river. Although the river was running fast and deep, the small contingent forded safely. In the forest shade by the steep bank, the men stopped for breakfast. The difficulties and dangers of Anatolia were behind them. All that remained was an 8 km ride along comfortable forest paths to Silifke.

This 10th of June 1190 was another hot day. Frederick and one of his knights went into the river for a quick swim. The Emperor had just reached the middle of the river when he called out to his companion for help, and then drowned before the eyes of his horrified guard. A number of knights dived into the river and were able to drag his majesty onto the bank, but too late. Frederick Barbarossa was dead.

The drive is worth it, just for a view of the beautiful river valley and the plains. At some spots the Göksu cuts deeply into the rock, forming canyons. A great place to shoot rapids in a kayak. Above Silifke, the Göksu is still clean, ideal for taking a refreshing dip.

Taşuçu: The tiny resort village is 11 km west of Silifke on the coastal road. If you don't want to stay in Silifke, you can choose from a selection of good hotels and pensions slightly more expensive than in town.

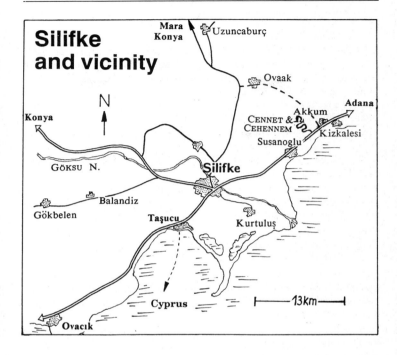

Silifke and vicinity

Taşuçu has a lovely harbour from which ships depart to Cyprus. This village at the southern tip of Aga Limani Bay has a long maritime tradition: once it was an infamous pirate stronghold.

Taşuçu is no place to swim since a huge paper factory began dumping its wastes here. The ships to Cyprus also leave their mark on the beach.

Coming - Going: The **bus** and **dolmuş** connections to Silifke are excellent (£0.17), a 20 minute drive.

By Ship to Cyprus: The hovercraft (Kibris-Express) "Barbaros" departs Monday, Wednesday and Friday at 13:00 h with 250 passengers to Girne on northern Cyprus. Costs £11.30, or students £8, children (4-12) £7, under 4 are free. A round trip costs £20 or double the child and student rates.

On Tuesday, Thursday and Saturday at 23:00 h the Ertürk ferry departs to Girne. One-way £8.60, students £7. A car (up to 500 kg) £7, (up to 950 kg) £9, (up to 1200 kg) £12. A bus (up to 4.25 m) £16, caravan £23.50. Round trip is double.

Book passage at the bus station in Silifke. Kibris-Express tel. 1691 - 2734. Ertürk tel. 1033 - 1325. You can also get a ship to Cyprus from Mersin (see travelling by boat).

A NIGHT'S REST: There are lovely hotels and pensions: turn left at the bus station before reaching the harbour.

Hotel Tastur: Upper middle class, tel. 1045.
Pension Arisoy: Dignified, tel. 1601.

Uzunkaburç: Ancient Olba, also called Diocaesarea, is 30 km north of Silifke on the road to Mara. The well-preserved town ruins date from the 3rd century BC, and give a good impression of an ancient Greek settlement in Asia Minor. Particularly interesting are the defense tower, the Temple of Zeus, the indoor road, and the necropolis. The ruins of Olba are by far the best on the Cilician coast. The Zeus Olbios Temple is the most ancient temple in Asia Minor with Corinthian columns.

A few kilometres east of Uzunkabuc, near *Ura,* are the ruins of another Greek settlement. The town is less well preserved, there are ruins of buildings, Byzantine churches, and the remains of a small castle.

COMING - GOING: Uzunkaburç is accessible by bus or dolmuş toward Kırobasi (via Yenıbahçe). Be sure to mention your destination when boarding.

Çennet & Çehennem (Heaven & Hell): These are two caves located 28 km east of Silifke. They played important roles in ancient mythology and are still considered sacred today.

They were created by an underground river which carved a system of caves in the karst, the roof of which partially collapsed, leaving circular holes with concave walls. The public is not permitted to descend into "Hell".

"Heaven", with its paradise of trees, is a popular spot for outings. Scraps of clothes are tied to many of the trees. A popular superstition, pre-dating Islam, holds that the former owner will enjoy luck and good health. I sacrificed a T-shirt.

In the ancient world, Çehennem was considered the entrance to Hades, the underworld. This belief continued into the Byzantine age. A chapel keeps the underworld at bay and guards the entrance. At the foot of the Çehennem is a small cave where you can hear the roar of the underground river.

Kız Kalesi

Its name means "Girl Castle", a picturesque island fortress 30 km east of Silifke and 100 m off the beach, surrounded by white walls and blue water.

Across on the mainland are the ruins of the neighbouring castle Korakesion. It crowns a mountain on the eastern edge of a sandy bay. Just west of the mainland castle is an impromptu Turkish Rimini - restaurants, pensions, shops, and afternoon video in the pubs. The high season bustle stays within bounds; one of the few such spots on the south coast. If you like it, stay a few days.

According to a legend, the island fortress was built by a sultan after he had received a prophecy that his daughter would be killed by a snake. The water castle seemed to be safe, but a snake made it across in a basket of fruit and fulfilled the prophecy.

The two castles were actually part of the harbour defenses for the town of Korykos. The castles date from the mid-12th century, and were once connected by a mole. They were built by Armenian kings.

Today you can take a boat to the Girl Castle, or just swim across.

THE ARMENIANS

"Four beasts of prey have a grip on the kings of Armenia: the lion symbolizes the Tartars who demand high tribute; the leopard the sultan who ravages the border regions daily; the wolf the Turks who sap his strength; and the snake the pirates who make the Christians in Armenia fear for their lives".

These are the words of a 14th-century chronicle, written at the beginning of the end of the Armenian kingdom. Over the previous 300 years, the Armenians had been driven from their land of origin in northeastern Anatolia by the Turks. Many refugees settled in Cilicia. They were able to establish their own region of Armenian rule independent of Byzantium. The successful strategy of the Armenian kings was later also employed by the Austrian Habsburg dynasty: they created alliances with Crusader kings along the Levant (Mediterranean) coast by establishing blood relations. Marriages between Armenian princesses and Germanic princes were popular. The result - aside from cute babies - was a happy mixture of Armenian high culture with early oriental renaissance.

The fun did not last for long. In the early 14th century, invading Mongols destroyed the Crusader kingdoms. The Armenians were left alone, surrounded by enemies. They withdrew to their castles and fortified towns, but were unable to withstand the continuous onslaught. In 1361 King PETER I of Cyprus conquered Korykos and its fortifications. In 1375 the Mamelukes captured the Armenian capital Anazarbus.

From that time on, the Armenians had to live under a series of foreign rulers, lastly the Ottomans. Before "the sick man of the Bosporus" finally died in the 1920s, he took most of the Armenians with him into his grave. The military government continued this policy: the Armenians who were lucky were deported but most of them were killed. Little remains in Cilicia to remind us of the former Armenian presence. The castles are the only testimony to their existence.

COMING - GOING: Buses and dolmuş from Silifke or Mersin. To get a lift back, just stand by the road.

A Night's Rest

In Kız Kalesi there are two categories of lodgings:

1. The best hotels, bungalows and pensions are right on the beach, reasonable prices. For a clean double with shower/WC you pay £8; the same for a small comfortable bungalow.

Kaya Pension: On the right side of the shopping street leading to the beach. Hot showers/WC in the room, each with a balcony facing the sea, clean. Double £8. tel. (7584) 1031.

2. Across the street, take the road at the mosque up to the right to the cheaper lodgings. Prices, furnishings, and cleanliness vary little. Try to bargain.

Pinar Pension: After the post office head up to the left, about 150 m on the left. Shower/WC in the hall, nothing special. Rooms are clean and sunny. The owner attended a hotel-management school, single £2.30, double £4.60. tel. (7584) 1154.

The cheapest rooms are in Akkum (1 km from the beach).

Zorlu: Clean, double £4.60 with shower/WC.

Next to the coastal road, in the Bay of Akkum, is a **camp site**.

CAMPING:

You can camp on the left or on the right of the beach in Kız Kalesi for £1. There is no shade; the sanitation facilities meet only Turkish expectations; crowded in season. The site below the mainland castle is a bit better.

BP-Motorcamp: 1 km from Kız Kalesi on the road to Mersin. A comfortable, shady site with its own stretch of rocky shore (reinforced with concrete in spots). Kiosk, restaurant, good sanitation. Four guests in a tent or a caravan pay £11; two people in a VW bus pay £6.

NIGHTLIFE: Kız Kalesi has some nightlife, with a disco right next to the beach. When a band plays in the evening at a beach restaurant, the fun reverberates along the beach. Families listen while relaxing on camping chairs. Dance groups churn to the rhythm. The nightly beach promenade is in full swing.

FOOD: Eat at one of the spots right on the beach. The seafood restaurant in Akkum is particularly good. Coming from Kız Kalesi, it is at the entrance to town on your left. The food selection and preparation is outstanding. You sit on a terrace above the sea.

Sights

First of all, the Armenian castles *Kız Kalesi* and *Korakesion*. Behind the mainland castle are the ruins of the town of *Korykos* spread over extensive grounds. Finally there is an *ancient cemetery* featuring sarcophagi and rock graves surrounding the ruins of Byzantine churches.

Around Kız Kalesi

Ayas: About 3 km from Kız Kalesi toward Mersin. Founded as Elaesa, later renamed Sebaste. This was once the residence of ARCHELAUS, king of Cappadocia. Most of the ruins are buried under sand dunes. You can see the ruins of a *theatre*, *temple*, parts of the *town wall*, and the remains of an *aqueduct*.

Kız Kalesi - Mersin Route

Continuing on toward Mersin, the coast finally joins the Cilician plains. Remains of the ancient world are strewn to the left and right of the road: ruined churches, house foundations, graves, aqueducts. This section of the coast was heavily settled in ancient times; it continued to function as an important economic and political centre until the fall of Byzantium.

The traffic is heavier here on the main road connecting Europe and Asia. Buses run every 20 minutes between Silifke and Mersin.

Erdemli

42 km beyond Silifke. The beaches are narrow and crowded with apartment buildings. Around the bus station there are simple hotels, cheap but noisy. Near Erdemli is *Sahil Camigi* national park with a large camp site in pine-covered sand dunes (tent £1, £0.30 per person). The place is crowded during the summer. On both sides of town are lovely bays with pretty beaches. Construction is in full swing.

Help us update

We've done our best to make this book as accurate and up-to-date as possible but travel developments are swift and things are always changing. We would greatly appreciate any contributions, suggestions, corrections, improvements or additions you may have for future editions.

Please write us:
Springfield Books Limited c/o Michael Muller, Norman Road, Denby Dale, Huddersfield HD8 8TH, West Yorkshire, England.

Mersin *(pop. 250,000)*

Mersin is proud to have the country's most modern mosque. Multi-story buildings line the arrow-straight boulevards. The heavy traffic is supplemented by horse carts waiting patiently for a green light. Hamburgers are sold right next to köfte while Turkish rock music is powered through the Luna Park by 1000 watt amplifiers.

Mersin has embraced the modern world. Most of the old buildings downtown have been torn down to make way for the new.

This is one of Turkey's newest cities. Turkey's third largest port has attracted a lot of industry including refineries, textile (cotton), and chemical factories. Turkey's largest silo complex is also located here. Mersin is not a tourist attraction since it is an industrial town.

History

Mersin is a town without history. It was founded 150 years ago near the ancient town of Solio. Several factors led to its rapid expansion (1890: pop. 9000, 1987: pop. 250,000). In the late 19th century the

British turned the Mersin region into an important agricultural centre. The Berlin - Bagdad railway required an Adana/İstanbul connection, while the proximity of Cyprus led to the expansion of Mersin's harbour. In 1954 the harbour was expanded to serve the million-plus population of Adana and the growing needs of the entire Cilician plains. Today, Mersin is the capital of Icel province.

TURKISH POLICE

The respect of the population for the police, or rather their fear of the police, is demonstrated by two examples.

I once asked a waiter in a small street café in Mersin if I could leave my backpack there while I did some sightseeing. The waiter refused, saying he already had trouble with the police and did not want to be accused of stealing the bag. I accepted this "excuse", took my bag and left.

Several weeks later, at the bus station in Konya, I tried to make an international call at about 01:00 h. A Turkish friend, with whom I had been traveling for several days, took my backpack to bring it to the bus. After just a few steps, two undercover policemen had him in handcuffs. It was difficult to convince the officers to drop the matter and release my friend. Perhaps it was a coincidence, but the incident in Mersin came to my mind.

INFORMATION: The main tourist office is off the beaten trail at the industrial harbour on İnönü Bul., Liman Giris Sahasi, tel. 11265 or 1270. Unfriendly. There is a more friendly office at the bus station at the exit to the taxis. A third small office is on the square by the new mosque, no telephone, friendly.

TELEPHONE AREA CODE: 741

COMING - GOING: Mersin has the most modern bus station on the south coast, a Turkish dream of plastic and concrete. Connections to all parts of the country. Into town, get a taxi or walk 15 minutes to the hospital (go out by the back entrance where the taxis are, turn right, and when you get to the large junction where you can see the hospital on your left, take a right). Here you can get a dolmuş.

CAR RENTALS: **Avis** has an office across from Atatürk Park next to the post office, address: Sahil Yolu Nail Göksu Ishane 75, tel. 23450 - 24813.
Europcar, address: Uray Cad. 33 Sok. 1/2, tel. 20017.

FERRIES TO CYPRUS: See Getting Around - By Ship.

A Night's Rest

There are a lot of good hotels in town. The cheap hotels around the bus station charge about £1.30 for a single, £3.20 for a double.

Hosto Oteli: Fashih-Kayabali Cad. No. 4, single shower/WC £7, double shower/WC £8 or £12. tel. 14760.

Hititer Oteli: Soğuksu Cad. 40, double £10. tel. 16327.

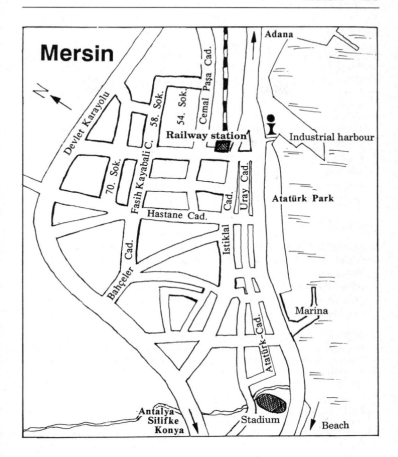

Hayat Oteli: Istlikal Cad. 88, single £5.30, double £8.30, some rooms with shower/WC. Breakfast £1.-. tel. 11076 or 12153.

Hotel Ocak: Istlikal Cad. 48, double shower/WC £8. Breakfast £1. tel. 15765.

Atlihan Oteli: Istlikal Cad., double £6. tel. 14308.

FOOD: There are lots of pubs on Istlikal Cad. or around the new mosque. Hamburger stands are everywhere.

Sights

Mersin has little to offer. You can enjoy the city atmosphere on the boulevards, or promenade along the sea in *Atatürk Park*. Next to the entrance to Atatürk Park is *Luna Park*, an amusement park complete with a ferris wheel and House of Horrors (you'll make it through without your valium) and other attractions. The most popular, of course, are the bumper cars.

Swimming

The tourist information office and most travel guides recommend the beaches west of town. The best advice is not to swim here at all, due to the heavy pollution. You run a major risk of infection. Head 50 km west and there is no problem.

Around Mersin

Pompeiopolis (Solio): 12 km northwest of Mersin, near the village of Viransehir. Founded by the Greeks as Solio, the town was destroyed by the Armenians about 100 BC. After the Roman takeover, POMPEY ordered its reconstruction. There is little to see beyond a short stretch of the column road once 450 m long. For centuries, the town has served as a rock quarry.

Yümüktepe: 3 km west of Mersin. Excavations have unearthed settlements dating from Neolithic to Hellenic and Byzantine ages. The hill was already fortified in the bronze age; the Hittites constructed a wall around it.

Mersin - Adana Route

At Mersin the highway leaves the coast and runs across the Cilician plains, also known as the *Çukurova*. After 27 km, off to the left (2 km) of the four-lane highway is *Tarsus*.

Tarsus

A dusty industrial town of 130,000 inhabitants. Public housing projects at the edge of town provide your first impression. The town centre is little different, with faceless buildings hiding the town's illustrious past.

History

Tarsus can truthfully claim 3000 years of uninterrupted habitation. As the gateway to the Cilician plain, it once held major strategic importance. During the early days of Christianity, it was famous as the birthplace of the Apostle PAUL. The greatest conquerors of all time all saw Tarsus as a keystone in their military ambitions: ALEXANDER THE GREAT, POMPEY, HADRIAN, Calif EL MAYMUN, sultan SELIM THE HARSH. But one woman topped them all.

ALL ABOUT CLEOPATRA (PART II)

It was autumn of the year 41 BC and Mark Anthony was getting nervous. He had heard great tales of the extravagant Egyptian woman, particularly from Caesar. Anthony had come all the way to Tarsus to meet the woman who could intoxicate an emperor. Suddenly there was movement among the crowd behind the barricades. As he gazed down the Knydos, Plutarch described the excitement.

She rode up the Knydos in a galley boasting a golden stern, purple sails, and silver oars. The rowers worked to the rhythm of flutes and harps. The queen, dressed as Aphrodite, lay stretched out on a lounge of gold brocade. She was fanned by lovely boys, dressed as cupid. Girls, dressed as nereids (sea nymphs) and the Three Graces, imitated the raising of sails and the motions of rowing. Clouds of perfume drifted from the ship across the river bank where thousands had gathered for the show.

The inevitable happened and it was not long before CLEOPATRA and MARK ANTHONY were more than just friends. They were able to enjoy several months of pleasure in Asia Minor before the reality of politics reclaimed their energy: the power struggle in Rome was on the agenda. 13 years later, after their political power plans fell through, the couple committed suicide in Alexandria.

Sights

There is little to see of ancient Tarsus; it lies buried under several meters of alluvial soil. A Roman *Town Gate* (Paul's Gate or Bitch Gate - *Kancik Kapisi*) is preserved along with the ruins of a *theatre*.

Just after Tarsus, E 5 links up with E 24. The roads across the fertile *Çukurova* plains are crowded with trucks headed for neighbouring Arab countries.

There are a number of villages in the Çukurova where Arabic is spoken. The farmers are called fellah and belong to the Alevitan sect. These farmers, who have specialized in growing garden vegetables, emigrated here from northern Syria in the 18th century (see box at Antakya).

MALARIA

When I first visited the Çukurova in 1978, I took malaria tablets. In 1977 there were 360,000 cases of malaria. Today, not a single case is reported. The cause was the irrigation of the cotton fields. In 1956 the Seyhan Dam, north of Adana, began operation. It provided enough water for irrigation. According to the motto "the more the merrier" water was pumped onto the fields, and swamps were created because of poor drainage: it was a perfect breeding ground for malaria mosquitoes.

The government responded by improving the irrigation techniques. The matter is still closely watched today. Rice production is prohibited as rice grows in pools of water.

Cotton pickers run the greatest risk of malaria. Usually this task is performed by Kurdish women "rented" by large landowners. The women sleep in simple tents next to the cotton fields.

Cotton pickers are paid about £0.04 per kilo. Good fields are usually harvested by local labourers. They can pick 80-90 kilos during a 12-hour day. When I tried my hand at picking, I only managed about half that - and was totally exhausted and had been bitten all over by mosquitoes. Most fields produce much less, 50 to 60 kilos per day or about £2.30. These fields are harvested by "mountain Turks" (migrant workers). Part of the wages are taken by the village elder or the large landowner who arranges the rental contracts for the female workers.

Officially the rental of labour is prohibited, but the southeast, particularly the region along the Syrian border, is frequently beyond the reach of the central Turkish government. The relationship between farmer and landowner is similar to serfdom. For political reasons - peace is needed on the border to Kurdistan - the central government does not interfere.

Adana - the city of gold

Adana *(pop. 1,200,000)*

Around the clock tower in the centre of town, artisans still work in tiny shops. Old Ottoman buildings on unpaved streets and countless mosques for the faithful convey a picture which no longer holds true for Adana. The traditional heart of this huge city is only a relic of the past.

The life of the city pulsates along the boulevards of modern Adana which surround the old town. Glass palaces and high rise buildings are the monuments of a modern, western city, which has outgrown the ruins of its oriental past.

Adana has grown to be the most important town on the south coast due to the fertile Çukurova plains and its location on both the Berlin - Bagdad railway and the road from Ankara to Syria.

After WW I, France was the occupying power. It emphasized city development. After joining Turkey in 1939, the city grew according to western-style planning. The outlying districts are very European with parks, villas, and apartment buildings.

Textiles are the major industry. The plan is to process cotton domestically. The canning industry is also important.

Adana is known as the "city of gold". Many Arabs are engaged in the production of gold jewellery. Browse through the numerous bazaar shops.

Note: The summer climate is horribly hot and humid. Turks who can afford it leave in August for the beach or the mountains.

History

Homer mentions Adana in the *Iliad* under the name of Cilica. The town has been settled since 7000 BC. ALEXANDER THE GREAT and others before and after him established a base here.

Although Adana has achieved real importance only in this century, it was a major trading town of the Roman empire.

In 1516 sultan SELIM III conquered the town from the Egyptian Mamelukes, bringing Adana into the Ottoman empire. In the 19th century the Egyptians recaptured the town briefly, leaving fortifications on the pass roads to the north.

After WW I, the Çukurova was given to France as part of Syria. The Turkish government took over in 1939.

Dikkat - Warning

Along the entire south coast from Antalya to Antakya, I experienced the Turkish people as friendly and helpful. Then I arrived in Adana. I had been warned in advance: be careful in Adana, the people are thieves and tricksters, out to waylay every tourist. The idea of a million men and women, young and old, all out to do evil, seemed to me to be just a silly prejudice of country folk against city slickers.

The business of the city is not cheating and theft, but a healthy mistrust is wise in Adana.

Another side of city life is its countless beggars and cripples. I have never seen so many poverty-stricken women and children as in the affluent city of Adana. No Turk ever mentioned them. They are ignored.

INFORMATION: Atatürk Cad. 13, tel. 11323. The tiny, inconspicuous wooden building is easy to overlook.

TELEPHONE AREA CODE: 711

COMING - GOING: You have excellent bus connections throughout Turkey and to the east, as all the major companies have offices at the bus station.

By Rail: Several trains weekly to Ankara/İstanbul, Syria and Iraq. The schedule is confusing. Be sure to ask how long the ride lasts and whether you can get reservations. The railway station is at the northern end of Ziapaşa Bulvarı.

By Air: THY Office, Stadyum Cad. 1, tel. 41545. There is a bus from the office to the airport in the south of town. Three flights weekly to Lefkose on Cyprus.

CAR RENTALS: **Avis** at Ziapaşa Bulvarı 11/B, tel. 33045 - 34824 or at the airport, tel. 18881/67 and 18882/67. **Europcar** at the airport, tel. 18881-71.

A Night's Rest

On Inönu Cad. there are lots of middle class and luxury hotels. The cheapest lodgings are on the side streets around the bazaar.

Adana Sürmeli Oteli Lüks: Experience real Turkish luxury for £30 single or £44 double. Address: Inönu Cad. 142. tel. 22701-4.

Koza Oteli: Single £14, double £17 with shower/WC, reasonable. Address: Özler Cad. 103, tel. 14657 or 18853.

Erciyes Palas Oteli: Single £7, double £10, breakfast £1. Some rooms with shower/WC, well kept. Address: Özler Cad. 53. tel. 18867.

Ağba Oteli: Single £9, double £14, shower/WC, clean. Abidin Paşa Cad. 1A, tel. 18743-5.

Duygu Oteli: Single £7, double £11, shower/WC. Address: Inönü Cad. 14/1, tel. 12425.

A number of cheap hotels charge £1 to £2 for a single and £1.60 to £3 for a double. As you'd expect they are loud, shabby, and frequently dirty. Many cheap hotels exist only a short time, or are constantly changing names for tax reasons.

CAMPING:

International is at the eastern beach, right on E 5 toward Çeyhan. The highway noise and pollution drifts over the small site, which is clean (even the sanitary facilities) with an expensive restaurant and a swimming pool. Costs £1.60 per person, tents £1.30. tel. 11904. There is no camping tradition in this part of Turkey, leaving this as the only site in town.

Food

The food in Adana is more heavily spiced than in the rest of Turkey, showing the Arab influence. The local specialty is Adana kebap, hot and spicy: peppered ground lamb, thinly packed around a metal skewer and grilled over wood coals. Enjoy it with Turkish bread and rakı (local tradition). There are also many other delicacies to tempt you to wash them down with some rakı.

Onbaşlar: Diagonally across from the Tourist Information Office. One of the best pubs in Adana, European prices. Luxury in Turkish restaurants is reflected in the service, not in the quality of the food. You can eat just as well elsewhere - and at lower prices.

Otobus: Recommended, on Sular Cad. Standard Turkish prices. The house specialties are home-made fresh sesame bread and Adana kebap.

Or just try the tiny pubs around the bazaar and Inönü Cad.

Sights

Taş Köprü: The sturdy, ancient stone bridge, dating from the days of Hadrian, has conveyed rush hour traffic 319 m over 16 arches across the Seyhan for the last 1800 years.

Ulu Cami Mosque: The medieval mosque in the centre of town dates from the Islamic era. The grounds, site of a Koran school, are surrounded by a high wall. The black and white marble and the cool, squat architecture are Syrian in style. Notice the mosaics in the mosque.

Luna Park: The amusement park has been coming to life in the evening for over 100 years. Some of the attractions seem even older. Most of the stalls attract customers with real American Marlboros as a prize for skills at shooting, throwing or gambling. Several cafés on the grounds serve as venues for local singers of varied reputation and skill. It is fun. Located on the bank of the Seyhan on Cemil Beriker Bulvarı.

Regional Museum: On display are remarkable finds ranging from the Hittite to the Roman eras. Everything was discovered in the surrounding region. The exhibits range from sarcophagi and countless sculptures to a bronze statue of a Roman senator and knick-knacks from antiquity: glasses, coins, jewellery, household goods, and a showy ring supposedly worn by Emperor AUGUSTUS .

OPEN: Daily, except Mondays, 9:00 - 11:30 h and 13:00 - 18:00 h, admission £0.30, no discounts. The museum is next to the bus station.

Ethnological Museum (Eski Müze): Set in an old mosque - originally a Christian church - on İnönü Cad. In the small garden are Ottoman graves and plaques. The interior features mostly carpets and Ottoman household utensils and, of course, the obligatory nomad tent. The building itself is the main attraction, conveying a timeless, peaceful atmosphere.

OPEN: Daily, except Mondays, 9:00 - 18:00 h, admission £0.15, students half-price.

Atatürk Museum: A trim little building across from Luna Park. In March of 1923, HE was in town and lived in this house. HE slept in this bed, in that bedroom. HE worked at this desk preparing Turkey's future. Numerous yellowing newspaper clippings and photos document the entire two weeks HE spent in Adana. One room puts all the others to shame: 15 gold-plated plaster busts stare at each other from opposite walls - HE is the largest and most golden bust.

OPEN: Daily 9:00 - 17:30 h, admission £0.05.

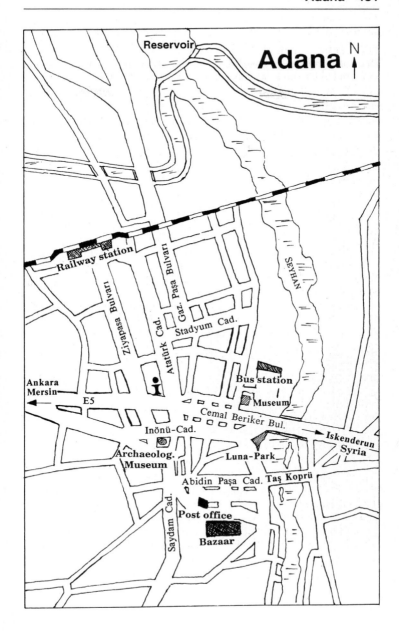

The museum is closely guarded and poorly visited: visitors are greeted by both soldiers and employees. Admission tickets must be procured from a locked room but first the key has to be found.

The town centre boasts lovely Ottoman buildings dating from the 18th and 19th centuries - some of which have been restored. If you have time in Adana, visit the "modern town" with its cafés, ice cream parlors, tennis courts, and pubs (around Atatürk Cad.) for a look at the new Turkey.

Around Adana

Seyhan Dam

If you are coming from the south coast and have had your fill of salt water, the Seyhan Dam can offer some relief. This large lake, which provides irrigation for the plains, is easy to reach by public transportation. This is a nice spot to paddle about and relax. Swimming is prohibited at the lower end of the lake due to the powerful currents!

The Cilician Gate

Tekir Yala

If you've had enough of beach hoopla, why not head northwest from Adana via the Cilician Gate (see above) to Tekir Yala (15 km outside Pozanti), a mountain resort where livestock once grazed. Just a few decades ago, this was open territory for nomad tribes. Only in the 20th century was the Turkish central government able to gain control of these mountains. At the top of the pass you can see the remains of an *Egyptian fort* dating from the 1835 war. The Turkish republican army scored its first victory over the French, who were trying to take Inner Anatolia, here in 1920. Near *Camalan* is a German military cemetery dating from WW I.

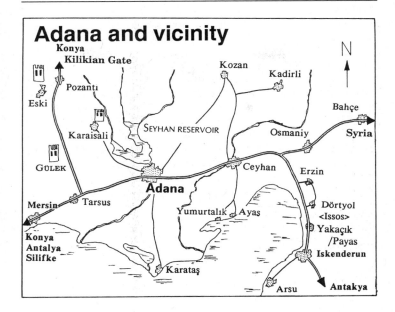

Adana and vicinity

Tekir Yala is a good departure point for hikes and mountain tours through the *Bolkar Mountains* (Bolkar Dağlari, 3500 m). You can still see nomads in isolated regions living according to century-old traditions.

In the high mountain regions, a few Lebanese cedars still thrive: these trees once covered the entire region. If you plan to do some mountain climbing - great fun - be sure to bring the proper equipment and a good map. The weather can change quickly during autumn. In the high mountains you are all on your own. Small mountain tours are also worthwhile.

Misis (Yakapinar)

A cosy little village on the bank of the Ceyhan River, 25 km east of Adana. The ruins of the ancient settlement, *Mopsuestia*, harmonize with the town. In the 13th and 14th centuries Misis flourished as a Genoese trading centre. In a *Mosaic Museum* you can see lovely mosaics dating from the 4th century.

OPEN 9:00 - 17:00 h, admission £0.15.

If Adana is too hot and muggy for you, head for the beach at *Karataş* and *Yumurtalik*.

Karataş *(pop. 7000)*

Except on weekends and during Turkish holidays, this is a peaceful fishing village at the southern tip of the Çukurova. Karataş was founded by the Greeks but their traces have been lost. The two post offices are a slight exaggeration. Karataş is Adana's closest beach. The main road parts by the tea garden, the right road leading to the beach and the left returning.

Magarsus (Mallus): 5 km west of Karataş, it features ruins dating from the Assyrian to the Ottoman empires. But there is not a lot to see.

COMING - GOING: The harbour town is 60 km south of Adana, accessible by bus or dolmuş (£0.30) from the bus station.

By Car: From Adana, leave town via Taş Köprü, turn right after the bridge. Later a sign announces another right. From here just follow the signs. The route reminds you of the Bavarian mountains, although the minarets are slimmer than baroque steeples.

A NIGHT'S REST

Hotel Mavikum Tesusleri: Right by the sea at the end of the main road. It isn't a high rise - the rooms are all in town house style. The hotel has its own swimming facilities (actually a pier). The adjoining restaurant is expensive (shark £6, lagos £8 per kilo). If you get a room without shower/WC you must use the restaurant facilities and have the author's sympathies. Single £4.30, double £8, no shower/WC; double shower/WC £12. A number of Arabs from Syria and Turkey stay here.

Hotel Balıkçı: From the main road take the last street before the sea to the right. The small hotel (20 beds) is clean, some rooms with balconies. Pleasant, quiet. Showers/WC are clean. Single £2.30, double £4. tel. 398.

Derya Pension: On Sol Çevre Yolu, turn left off the Adana road after the police station (follow the pension sign). Set several meters above the sea, away from the town. Quiet, pleasant. Double £5, shower/WC in the hall. tel. 235.

CAMPING:

Several camp sites are east and west of town; some right on the water, others up on the steep coastline. They all have little shade, rudimentary sanitation and a restaurant. The standard price is £0.60 per person. One site on the eastern beach has trees idyllically surrounded by barbed wire, same price.

To the western sites, follow the main road to the sea, then turn left toward the harbour. To the eastern sites: the same as to Derya Pension (see above) then continue along the road. The entrances are one after the other along the road.

Swimming: The beach is a disappointment. Sewage is pumped into the sea right next to the harbour. To the east the beach is rocky and little wider than your towel. Beyond that is a sandy beach - the dirtiest I have ever seen on the south coast.

Nobody considers themselves responsible for cleaning things up. But there are plans for major tourism development. Perhaps a dream but time will tell.

Ruins of a crusader castle in the harbour of Yumurtalık

Yumurtalık *(pop. 13,000)*

The knights of Rhodes left behind the Atlas Castle, facing the open sea, a picturesque background to the beach. Just beyond, ancient *Ayas* boasts countless ruins. As to Yumurtalık itself: a couple of roads, a small enclosed fishing harbour, a beach with restaurants, ruins, a mosque, and thousands of Adaners visiting on weekends.

Yumurtalık caters to Turkish tourists with lively bars, promenades, discos and good seafood restaurants.

COMING - GOING: 90 km south of Adana, accessible by bus via Çeyhan. Buses depart from Adana Bus Station. You might have to change buses in Çeyhan.

A NIGHT'S REST:

Turistik Tesisleri: Recommended, single £4, double shower/WC £11.
Hotel Öztur: A new building on the thoroughfare along the beach, nicely furnished. Large adjoining restaurant. Double shower/WC £8. tel. 167-168.

CAMPING: Right on the beach, but crowded, no shade, rudimentary sanitation. £0.60 per person, £0.60 per tent.

Swimming: The sandy beach is 600 m long and well kept. The sea is clean. To the west of the beach, below the steep cliffs, you can dive for sunken treasures.

Adana - Antakya Route

On E 5 beyond Adana. The highway is busy supplying the Iraqi wartime economy. Heavy trucks, machines, tractors etc. roll east. Police checks are frequent.

Hatay Province was governed by martial law (1987). Domestic Turkish politics - the mountain Turk (Kurdish) problem - are very evident. Fear of Islamic fundamentalism among Arabs to the south-east may also play a role. Even though tourists are treated courteously, I felt a bit uneasy looking at the machine guns.

The road through the Çukurova runs straight and flat past lovely villages. Light brown mountains rise above the plains to the east. About 50 km east of Adana, a sign marks the road to the right to Çeyhan.

Çeyhan *(pop. 75,000)*

The town is 4 km south from the junction of E 25 and E 5. The Çeyhan river marks the eastern edge of town. As the agricultural centre of the region, it is well off the tourist trail.

Old, low, brick buildings, in every conceivable colour, mark the centre of town. Large potholes in the roads hinder the flow of traffic as much as the bicycles and horse carts. European tourists still arouse curiosity. You might take a pleasant break for tea in the obligatory Atatürk Park under tall pine trees (on the road to Yumurtalık).

Around Çeyhan

Yılan Kalesi: The "Snake Castle" is a small Armenian fortress on the road from Misis to Çeyhan. Set on a solitary hill, it dominates the entire plain. Take a drive out, have a look at the ruins, enjoy the view, and marvel at tales of the legendary snake king who lived here once upon a time. . .

Tip: If you have your own car, and aren't in a hurry, drive from Adana via Yakapinar (Misis) and Sirkeli on the small road (off E 5) to Çeyhan; then head on either to Yumurtalık or back to the E 5. The route through the unspoiled Çukurova is lovely.

About 50 km beyond Çeyhan, the road branches off to Syria or straight on to İskenderun. 80 km southeast of Adana, 2 km east of E 5 is Dürtyol on the Plain of Issus.

Visas for Syria / Iraq / Iran

You are best off procuring these visas before leaving home as
conditions can change quickly in the region. If you are planning
to export cars to any of these countries, take care of the formalities before leaving Europe.

Dörtyol

To the left and right of the road, as it enters Dörtyol, is a large mili-
tary base. War has been traditional in the region since 333 BC when
ALEXANDER THE GREAT beat the Persian king DARIUS in the Battle of
Issus. This opened the route east for Alexander - all the way to India.

Dörtyol, set below the jagged Daz Dagi, is so rural that few of its
13,000 inhabitants have died of excitement. Dürtyol boasts a covered
bazaar and a Turkish bath.

The Issus battlefield is 11 km north of Dürtyol. Take the turnoff to
TURUNÇLU, cross the bridge and take the field path to the right to the
historical site on the PLAIN OF ISSUS. The organization and discipline of
40,000 Macedonian-led troops was superior to the brute might of
500,000 Asian troops, according to European history books. No wonder Darius didn't have a chance. Educated Turks are fond of
Alexander. They say he tried to unite east and west. The more practical local farmers like both Alexander and Darius: they say with a
grin that the soil here is fertile now. Today the fields cover the region
as they did before the battle - there is nothing to see. But if the
weather is right and you have the right sensitivity you can smell the
history.

Yakacık (Payas)

In Yakacık, 10 km south of Dürtyol, you can see a well-preserved
caravanserai with a mosque, medrese, bakery, and bazaar, dating from
the days of sultan Selim II. At the time the village was called Payas;
it was an important port and the last stop on the caravan route from
Mesopotamia to the Mediterranean.

The ruins on the hill across from the beach are part of a demolished
crusader castle which the Ottomans partially restored for military
purposes.

It is difficult to concentrate exclusively on the cultural events:
countless smoking chimneys just outside Yakacık prepare the newcomers for İskenderun.

The caravanserai of Yakacık

İskenderun *(pop. 170,000)*

You are unlikely to stop here unless you have relatives or business in town. İskenderun has nothing to make a stay worthwhile (although there is an airport near town).

Once called Alexandrette, the town 130 km south of Adana was founded during the rule of ALEXANDER (= İskender) THE GREAT. Syria (then a French protectorate) controlled the region from 1918 to 1939. Syria would still like to recover the town along with the entire Hatay Province.

İskenderun is dominated today by refineries and steel mills. The minarets seem lost among the steel mill towers. Business appears to be flourishing.

In the harbour, large ships lay at anchor, waiting to unload. İskenderun is a NATO port and, like Mersin, is busy supplying Iraq.

The good news last. In the background are the 2240 m high Amanos mountains.

CAMPING: İskenderun may be the site of Asia Minor's smallest camp ground. Near the harbour promenade, follow the blue signs. Costs £0.50 per person, £0.70 per trailer, tents are free.

Around İskenderun

Arsuz or **Uluçinar**. The fishing town 32 km south of İskenderun lives
from domestic and Arab tourism. The resort town consists primarily
of vacation homes and apartments with a few pensions and luxury
hotels. Countless seafood restaurants crowd both sides of the river.
The beaches are lovely, well kept, and an admission fee is charged. In
the summer people from İskenderun come here to escape the heat.

COMING - GOING: By dolmuş from İskenderun. The 30 km along the sea pass
   quickly. If you don't mind the filth, you might take a swim along the way.

   Tip: After Arsuz, the road runs a bit further, ending in the middle of nowhere. The
   area is lovely; find your own nice spot to swim!

A NIGHT'S REST: **Motel Yunus**; across from the post office, central, but relatively
   quiet, with the rooms facing the back. Caters to domestic clientele. 3-bed rooms
   (£9) and 5-bed suites (£13.30, two rooms). All rooms with shower/WC. Address:
   Akdeniz Cad. 12, tel. 9-881-11422 or 11423.

After İskenderun the road climbs with three lanes into the cool
mountains. *Belen* clings white to the steep mountain; the village ends
at a vertical cliff. At the mountain pass you can see the symmetrically
patterned Plain of Amik far below. Descending to the plain, the road
passes through fields and olive trees to Antakya.

Antakya *(pop. 135,000)*

**Jostling crowds of Arabs fill the tiny streets of the old town.
Bargaining for gold jewellery, the smell of leather - hundreds
of tiny shops fill traditional Turkish needs.**

Antakya is the modern-day name of ancient Antioch, which boasted a
population of 500,000 in the 2nd century AD. The town is no longer a
metropolis, nothing remains of its former buildings. The old town
presents a mixture of Arab architecture and French colonial style.
The crumbling facades of the art nouveau buildings show the wear of
time. Outside the old town, across the Asi River, is the new Antakya -
public housing projects and posh palaces built in classical Turkish
style. That side of the river holds Antakya's future.

The former Greek town of Antioch became an Arabian town over the
centuries. Language, architecture, clothes, and food show that
Turkey has not yet dominated Antakya's culture.

Antakya is no longer on a major trade route, and has lost its importance. Still, as a provincial town Antakya is charming.

History

The town was founded in the 4th century BC by SELEUCOS NICATOR and quickly grew into an important trading port on the eastern Mediterranean. By the 2nd century BC, the population was 500,000, making Antioch one of the most important cities in the world, following Rome and Alexandria.

Antioch was considered a fun city in ancient times, where people knew how to enjoy life. Puritans even spoke of Sin City. It was also a city which every empire wanted to control. It was ruled by Rome, Persia, Arabia, Byzantium, the Ottomans, France and finally by Turkey.

The world's first Christian congregation was founded here. It still exists today. During the first crusade, the Christian community helped the crusaders found the Duchy of Antioch.

With the fall of Rome, Antakya's decline began, culminating in its destruction at the hands of the Mamelukes in 1268 AD. During the Ottoman empire the ruins of the metropolis were crowned by a few hundred stone huts.

In the 20th century, the French and the British tried to establish military bases here. During WW I, İskenderun and Antakya were bombed repeatedly, then occupied by the French in 1918. After a plebiscite in 1939, the city came to Turkey.

Today, Antakya is a quiet administrative centre on the fertile alluvial soil, 30 km from the sea. The river is no longer navigable. The primary crop is olives.

STYLITES

The "pillar saints" really did exist. The most famous was ST. SIMEON STYLITES (the Elder), a native of the Antioch region. In 417 AD, as a 27-year-old man, he mounted his first pillar upon which he lived as an ascetic. For 42 years he meditated atop a series of columns, climbing down only briefly at infrequent intervals in order to mount an even taller pillar. The Christians were curious about this unusual form of asceticism. Large numbers of pilgrims came to worship in the presence of the revered soul. His influence grew and he became an authority rivalling kings and patriarchs.

If you travel from Samandag to Antakya, you can see the "wondrous mountain" to the south. At its peak are two ruined churches. Both are dedicated to ST. SIMEON STYLITES THE YOUNGER, who mounted a column at the age of seven, and remained on top praying until the end of his days.

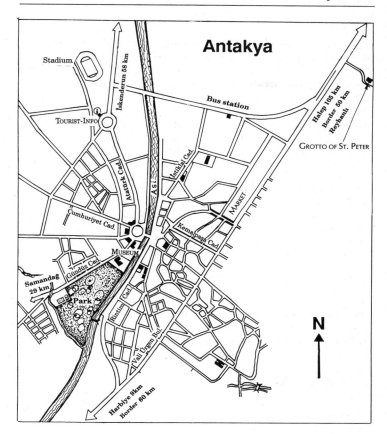

INFORMATION: Atatürk Cad. 41, Vali Urgen Alani, tel. 12636.

TELEPHONE AREA CODE: 891

COMING - GOING: Excellent connections include an hourly bus to Adana, plus direct buses to Ankara and İstanbul. There are also buses to Syria. Good dolmuş connections to every village in the region.

A Night's Rest

During the summer, Antakya attracts a lot of visitors from neighbouring countries who are fleeing the war or out to enjoy the relatively free nightlife.

Note: Casually dressed backpackers sometimes arouse mistrust if they try to check into one of Antakya's better hotels: visitors who present a shabby appearance at a hotel reception may spend the night as guests of the local police who will comb their belongings for drugs.

Atahan Oteli: Centrally located at the edge of the old town. A lot of Arab-style comfort with leather chairs, smoking tables, and hip baths. Double £10, single £8, breakfast £1.-. Address: Hürriyet Cad. 28, tel. 11670.

Divan Oteli: Good, preferred by western tourists, single £7, double £9, breakfast £1.-, Istlikal Cad. tel. 11581.

Hotel Kent: Centrally located on Köprübas (the small square by the river) at the edge of the old town. Loud, simple, shower/WC in the hall, costs £1.60 per person. tel. 11670.

Hotel İstanbul: Simple but appealing. A cheap hotel in Turkish green, with imitation marble in the oversized halls, and a proper reception. Double £2, Istlikal Cad. 14, tel. 11122.

İnçi Palas Oteli: Right next to Hotel İstanbul, same prices, tel. 11372.

FOOD: Enjoy good Arab food in the cheap little pubs on Hürriyet Cad. How about some kagit kebap and künefe for dessert?

Sights

Antakya was destroyed by more than just the hand of man. Earthquakes in the 16th and 19th centuries destroyed the last traces of its glorious years. However the present-day old town is one of Turkey's loveliest: French provincial charm combined with oriental flair.

Church of St. Peter: One of the few remaining sights is located 3 km above town on the road to Reyhanli and Halep. Its facade consists of three great arches built during the Duchy of Antioch in the 12th century. The church interior is a grotto in which early Christians gathered to worship. An altar stands against the front wall; an escape tunnel leads off to the side. It is said that the Apostle PETER preached here. He lived in Antioch for seven years, founding the Christian congregation here together with ST. PAUL and BARNABAS. St.Peter was the first bishop of Antioch. A service is held here each year on June 29, the date of St. Peter's death. Be sure to visit.

OPEN: Daily, except Mondays, 8:00 - 12:00 and 13:30 - 18:00 h, admission £0.30, half price on weekends.

Rana Köprüsü (Old Bridge): Its four arches once spanned the Orontes River; today they span the Asi. First constructed in the 3rd century AD, it has been restored several times.

QUIZ
A) Has the location of the bridge changed?
B) Has the name of the river changed?
Solution: see the next line.
Only B is correct.

Aqueduct: On Hastane Sok. (near the hospital). You can see the ruins of an aqueduct built by Trajan in the 2nd century AD.

Habibi Naccar Camii: On Kurtulus Cad. The mosque was originally built as a Byzantine church on the foundations of an ancient temple. The 17th century minaret completes the lovely example of Turkish baroque.

Archaeological Museum (Hatay Mozaik Müzesi): By the post office and town hall near Rana Köprüsü. The lovely Roman mosaics, found in the Antioch region, date from the 2nd to 5th centuries AD. The collection is unique and world famous. The mosaics are made of various coloured river pebbles, hence the colours remain undimmed.

OPEN: Daily, except Mondays, (sometimes in the afternoon) 9:00 - 12:00 and 13:30 - 18:00 h. Admission £0.30, half-price on weekends.

ALEVI HAVE LONG NOSES

The Alevi are an Islamic sect and members of an Arab minority in Turkey. They speak Arabic; few can speak Turkish. They originally came from the Syrian coastal region. Today they are settled in Hatay province, particularly in Samandağ and the surrounding villages. The Alevi support annexation of Hatay by Syria.

They also have their own quarter in Antakya. It is a ghetto in which no Turk would voluntarily set foot. Because "*Alevi are dirty and smell. Alevi have at least ten children in order to increase their numbers quickly and drive the Turks into the sea. Alevi want money for everything. Alevi have long noses.*"

In 1983 there were attacks against members of the minority in Antakya. The military intervened and restored order, at least externally. As the years pass, the Alevi still have long noses.

Around Antakya

Grove of Daphne: "Come on, let's go to Daphne!" The initiated know that this harmless sounding proposal is a polite way of discussing a bout of drinking in the formerly sacred grove. The people of Antakya maintain a long tradition. This is where APOLLO pursued DAPHNE, who sent the god packing in a most unusual way: at her own bidding, he turned her into a laurel tree. A while later, PARIS mused in this valley about which beauty he should give the apple to. The people of Antioch celebrated festivals in honour of various deities. ANTHONY and CLEOPATRA considered this the only spot for their wedding.

Near *Harbiye* (8 km south of Antakya), the grove is a popular picnic area during the day. Idyllic, sometimes a bit crowded. A stream feeds numerous tiny waterfalls, trickling through a forest of cypress and laurel trees, down to the valley.

Footbath & barbeque: picnickers place their tables and feet in the stream for a pleasant afternoon. It is easy to establish contact with Turkish families.

Samandağ: During the week, Samandağ is a loud bustling town complete with traffic jams. On weekends the town is dead. The beach is its claim to fame: this is the southernmost beach in Turkey.

On the coastal road 26 km southwest of Antakya is a long sandy beach, parts of which are dirty. The beach is a popular picnic spot for migrant workers traveling past in trucks. Camping outside official camp sites is prohibited in the entire province of Hatay, but you might be able to get permission from the local police.

COMING - GOING: Dolmuş from Antakya.

Çevlik: About 6 km north of Samandağ. There is a camp site and several family pensions. Turkish vacationers spend their summer holidays here, or come just for the day from Antakya; expect crowds. The sandy beach is strewn with plastic products of all kinds.

By the way: near Çevlik and Magarçık (between Samandağ and Çevlik) was the temporary capital of the Seljuk empire, *Seleucia Pieria*. All that remains are the ruins of an aqueduct and the underground water-supply system.

COMING - GOING: Dolmuş from Samandağ.

CAMPING: About 30 m from the beach, on the road. There is no shade; tents are also set up in the big, straw-covered restaurant. Costs £0.60 per person.

Yailadaği: There would be no reason to mention the town if it weren't the last Turkish town before the border to Syria. If all hell breaks loose it certainly won't happen in this place. The 6000 souls have little more to gossip about than who carried tea on a tray across the street.

2 km beyond Yailadaği, in a forest, is the last Turkish picnic spot before the Syrian border.

The route from Antakya to Yailadaği is worth a visit, even if you aren't planning to go to Syria. The road winds through unspoiled mountains past an occasional village or house. Trucks chug over the border from Syria, overloaded with grain. Herds of goats clog the street together with donkey riders. And you have a wonderful view of the jagged mountains.

COMING - GOING: Yailadaği is 55 km south of Antakya, easy to reach by dolmuş.

CAMPING OUT

If you have spent some time at the beach, you might feel the urge to pitch your tent by a mountain stream and spend some time in the mountains. Nobody will object. But: **Campfires are prohibited**. Forest fires are a constant danger in the southern Taurus. Where the forest has burnt down, erosion takes over. Reforestation is very difficult. The forest administration is strict about the fire prohibition. Violaters can count on stiff fines, in extreme cases even a prison sentence.

The last Turkish picnic area before the Syrian border

CAPPADOCIA

A poster featuring the bizarre rock formations in Cappadocia graces the wall of every real Turkish travel agency.

One of the wonders of the world is 300 km southeast of Ankara. The unique tufa landscape features underground towns and rock churches.

Cappadocia is the region within the tri-city area Kirşehir-Kayseri-Niğde. The unusual scenery stems from the Ercyes mountains, called ARGAIOS during antiquity and *Mons Argaeus* by the Romans. About three million years ago a volcanic eruption spread tufa ash throughout the surrounding region, leaving layers of varied density and colour. Erosion has left deep gorges. Where soft layers of tufa were deposited, the rock has been washed away over thousands of years leaving only the denser layers. These layers form the characteristic pyramids, or fairy chimneys, which add to the enchantment of the area. The process of erosion is still going on today. If you take a close look, you can see fairy chimneys beginning to emerge from the tufa. Will nature be able to continue its course despite the 5-star hotels being built?

History

A number of finds lead to the conclusion that this region was settled during the Hittite era. The name Cappadocia referred originally to a Persian satrap, later to a Roman province. In both cases, the region was much larger than present-day Cappadocia. Little is known about the settlement of the tufa region in the fifth century. It is possible that Cappadocian Christians, under the leadership of Basilius (the Bishop of Kayseri) came into conflict with the Byzantine religious hierarchy. Perhaps they then chose to withdraw to the less accessible valleys to live and work. A major wave of Christian immigrants arrived here in the seventh century due to the Arab and Sassanid attacks in Anatolia. The new arrivals learned to appreciate tufa as building material. The soft stone could be cut for housing. These stone dwellings proved to be cool in the summer and warm in the winter. The buildings and churches also provided suitable fortification in case of danger. Underground cities, such as Derinkuyu and Kaymaklı, were also built in response to attacks.

The Cappadocian Christians were finally able to relax in the eleventh century after the Seljuk empire conquered most of Anatolia. The new rulers believed in religious tolerance. This era was marked by the famous dervishes Hacıbektaş, Yunus Emre and Mevlana.

Later, under the Ottoman empire, the monasteries were closed and converted to stables and apartments. Many Christians chose to move. The last Christian residents of Cappadocia were forced to leave the region in 1923 as part of a population exchange between Greece and Turkey.

Since the 1970s, UNESCO has undertaken the task of protecting the relics of a thousand years of religious culture in Cappadocia. The breath of tourists passing through the narrow cave passages is enough to cause damage. Even worse are the flash cameras (prohibited, but tolerated) leaving a cumulative toll on the frescos.

ATTENTION! The latest news: the governement in Ankara has drastically hiked up **admission fees** for museums, mosques etc. in 1989! Calculate about 5 - 10 times the prices given in this edition (depending upon the fame of the sights; for instance: admission for Hagia Sophia rose from £0.30 up to £3 !)

Tourism

The best time to visit Cappadocia is spring or autumn, although the dry summer months are not as hot as on the south coast. Summer nights are cool; Cappadocia is at 1200 m above sea level.

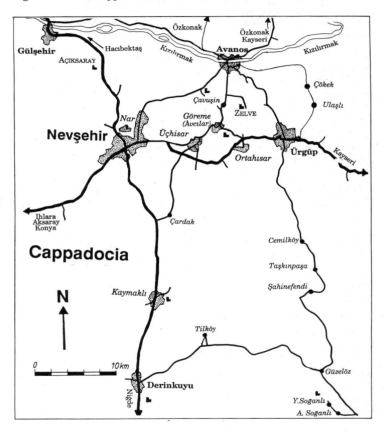

From December to February the fairytale landscape wears its winter dress. This is a time when empty hotels cater to Japanese tourism.

Tourism in Cappadocia is expanding quickly (500,000 foreign visitors are expected in 1989). This is particularly true in the classical tourist towns of Göreme and Ürgüp. Pension owners are expanding for the coming season. Those with 6 rooms are expanding to 12 and anyone with 12 rooms is adding a discotheque. They are building on, up, and into the rocks. Five-star hotels are planned along the main roads and some are already under construction, promising swimming pools, sport facilities and other luxuries.

The federal government is attempting to control hotel growth. In Nevşehir province (Nevşehir, Ürgüp, Göreme), there are 2200 beds at present with 4400 under construction. By the mid 1990s 38,000 beds are planned.

COMING - GOING: If you don't have your own car, take a bus to Nevşehir and head on from there to Ürgüp and Göreme. If you arrive in Nevşehir after dark, spend the night there. If money is no object, take Turkish Airways from İstanbul to Kayseri (which is also accessible by rail). See Nevşehir and Kayseri / Coming - Going.

Within Cappadocia (Nevşehir, Göreme, Ürgüp, Avanos), travel is simplest by dolmuş or local bus. Hitchhiking is relatively good during the day; distances are short, and traffic volume is heavy.

A taxi is your best bet late in the evening as prices are cheap. Drivers have established prices from village to village and hence do not use the taximeter. There is a good reason why the drivers do not like to use the metre: the passenger would have the right to insist upon paying only the taximeter price. It is advisable to check out the price before starting the ride.

ONYX AND ONYX EGGS

No souvenir shop in Cappadocia can do without a healthy selection of onyx products. The stone is excellent for making ashtrays, vases, jars, mortars and chess pieces. It looks much like alabaster, but is harder and of volcanic origin. Onyx is quarried near Hacıbektaş (50 km north of Nevşehir).

If you want to see the process of uncut stone being made into jewellery, visit one of the onyx factories in Uçhisar (on the road to Göreme), Ürgüp or Avanos. First the stone is cut with a water-cooled blade, then turned on a lathe causing a tremendous amount of dust which is harmful to the lungs. Then comes the machine polishing, first rough, then finer. Lastly, the onyx is polished with a chemical solution to achieve the desired shine.

The onyx eggs, which you can buy today for £0.60, played an important role in Roman chariot races in Constantinople during the early Byzantine era. Competitors carried eggs of different colours (which also represented various political parties: blue, green etc.). With each completed lap of the hippodrome, the driver would throw an egg into a basket. It was an almost foolproof method of keeping track of the leader, as long as the driver, at full gallop, did not miss the basket or toss in more than one egg . . .

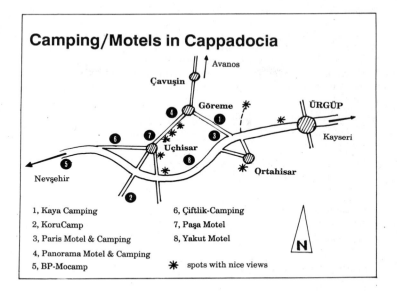

Camping/Motels in Cappadocia

1, Kaya Camping
2, KoruCamp
3, Paris Motel & Camping
4, Panorama Motel & Camping
5, BP-Mocamp

6, Çiftlik-Camping
7, Paşa Motel
8, Yakut Motel

✳ spots with nice views

A Night's Rest

Hotels/Pensions: Due to their central locations, Ürgüp and Göreme are excellent departure points for day trips to the surrounding region. During high season, in Cappadocia from June to September, it is not easy to find a room. Advanced reservations are advised for rooms in the middle and upper price categories. Luxury hotels are often booked months in advance by travel agencies. See local sections.

Camping/Motels: The development of Cappadocian tourism has increased real estate prices to the point where motel/camping may be advertised, but the owner is only interested in renting motel rooms. Service declines considerably in the off-season. Beware of tiny campgrounds on the outskirts of town. They are set up quickly, without much thought regarding sanitation, in the hope of making some fast money. Many camp sites have a swimming pool. The real luxury lies not in the concrete basin itself, but in how often the water is changed.

Most camp grounds are open from May to mid-October and are accessible by foot from the nearest village (see map). Or just get a bus or taxi.

Kaya Camping: Certainly the best camp site in Cappadocia, looking out over a valley full of fairy chimneys. Clean sanitary facilities, swimming-pool, bar, cellar restaurant. There is a charge for dogs: £0.60 per night.

Koru Camp: A lovely, shady site in a pinewood forest. Medium in size, simple sanitary facilities, but clean. Kitchen use (gas), restaurant open in July and August. A car is helpful since the site is isolated.

Paris Motel and Camping: A large facility with a swimming pool and garden restaurant. Sanitary facilities are adequate. Disco (folklore and belly dancing). Poor service in the off season (bad organization, unfriendly). The owner profits mostly from the disco's horrendous drink prices. He is known to clear all the individual travellers out of the hotel when a travel agency beckons.

Panorama-Camping and Motel: Very small. The motel has five doubles, and there is little tent space. Kiosk, cellar bar. Sanitary facilities are modest, but are due for renovation in 1988. The camping profits most from its unique location with a tremendous view of the Göreme valley. Very little shade.

Dinler Camping (former BP-Mocamp): A small spot for tents in a new orchard. Kitchen with a gas stove. Swimming pool. Restaurant at the petrol station. Little shade. Disadvantage: on the main road, loud petrol station. Well below the standards of the BP-Mocamp Chain.

Çiftlik-Camping: Medium-sized with little shade. Large, lovely restaurant offers evening programs (belly dancing, folklore, song). The owner has his hopes set on the motel under construction.

Mocamp Göreme: This small camp site profits from its lovely location. Little shade.

Paşa Motel: Luxury motel, double £20, including breakfast. Rooms are heated with shower/WC. Piped in music. Swimming pool under construction. A view of the Uçhisar mountains. Good, but expensive restaurant. The new facilities are reminiscent of an Arab desert settlement.

Yakut Motel: Despite the camping advertisment only motel service is offered. Double £12. Adequate. A small restaurant is in an old building.

NEVŞEHIR *(pop. 50,000)*

The town which bears the tulip on its coat of arms and whose main road (Lale Caddesi) means "tulip street" had its golden age during the tulip era of the Ottoman empire. The glorious days of the past have long since gone, leaving just a faceless provincial town.

There is no real centre of town. One can divide the town by imaginary lines using the two main roads as a guide. The most activity is in the southwest quarter, below the Damat-İbrahim-Paşa complex.

The bus station is very busy. Nevşehir is the main entrance way to Cappadocia and tries to profit from its position as a cross-country and minibus transfer point.

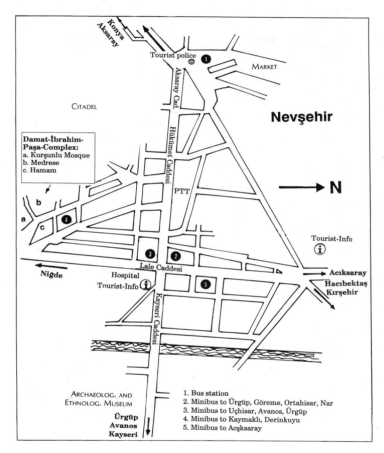

History

Scattered finds testify to settlement by the Hittites, Assyrians and Phrygians. Known as *Nyssa* during the days of antiquity, the town had no special history of its own, but was influenced by the course of classical Anatolian history: the Byzantines lost Nevşehir to the

Seljuks, who in turn were replaced by the Ottoman empire. Nevşehir flourished briefly during the early eighteenth century when the local-born DAMAT İBRAHIM PAŞA achieved the rank of Grand Vizier. Damat İbrahim Paşa, the leading politician of the tulip era, built the complex bearing his name and developed the town from a sleepy village into Nevşehir (meaning "new town").

INFORMATION: Kayseri Caddesi (right next to the hospital), Mon - Fri 8.30 - 18.00 h, (during the summer 20.00 h), tel. 2717. Helpful staff.

TELEPHONE AREA CODE: 4851.

COMING - GOING: **Buses**: to Ankara 7.30 - 19.30 h hourly (£1.30), to İstanbul nightbuses on the half hour 18 - 20 h (£3.30). Connections to Mersin (£1.60), Alanya (£3.30), İzmir (£3.30)).
Minibuses to Ürgüp, Göreme, Derinkuyu: See map for bus stop.

FESTIVALS & EVENTS: **Cappadocia Festival**, features folklore annually on 31st August to 1st September. The festival is celebrated simultaneously in Uçhisar and Göreme.

HOSPITAL: Lale Caddesi / Kayseri Caddesi; tel. 1200.

POST OFFICE: Hükümet Caddesi (across from Hotel Epok).

FOOD: Nevşehir's gastronomy leaves a lot to be desired. If you want good Turkish cooking, try à la carte in one of the luxury hotels. Smaller locantas can be found near the bus station and in the southwest of town.

TOURIST POLICE: In the pavilion at the bus station. Open round the clock. tel. 5039. The officers' language skills can be helpful in case of illness, finding lodgings, traffic accidents, theft, loss, etc.

TRAVEL AGENCIES: **Tulip Travel Agency**, at the bus station, tel. 1174. Full and half-day tours throughout Cappadocia, costs £7 to £10.
The agencies also rent cars, costs £18 to £45 per day.

A Night's Rest

Nevşehir is usually just a stop for one night upon arrival, since Ürgüp and Göreme offer cheaper hotels and pensions. There are a number of luxury hotels on Hükümet Caddesi which are frequently booked by travel agencies. There are a few cheap hotels around the bus station. You are advised against using the third-class hotels on the small side streets.

Epok Hotel, Hükümet Cad., double £23, including breakfast; new, luxurious hotel with every comfort. tel. 1168.

Göreme Hotel, Hükümet Cad., double £23, breakfast included; classic, somewhat old luxury hotel, tel. 1706.

Hotel Hisar, at the bus station, double £6, lovely hotel, with a Turkish-style lobby, clean rooms with tel., lovely breakfast room, well-kept. The only hotel in town below the luxury status yet respectable. tel. 3857.

Gürgenpalas Oteli, Aksaray Cad., near the bus station, double £3.30, modest, no comfort, breakfast served. tel. 1722.

İpek Palas Oteli, Aksaray Cad., near the bus station, double £3.30, very modest, no breakfast, tel. 1478.
Koç Palas Oteli, Hükümet Cad., double £3, tel. 1216.

Sights

Damat İbrahim Paşa Complex: Grand Vizier Damat İbrahim Paşa built the facility in 1727, featuring Kurşunlu Mosque with a lovely fountain in the front courtyard, a hamam and a medrese. The mosque was built in the classical Ottoman style : a central dome with architectural division of the interior by columns (round arch) and a clearly separated women's section. Toward the back: in the upper left is the honourary seat of Damat İbrahim Paşa, in the upper right is that of his entourage. The medrese, with its lovely courtyard, serves as a library today; the hamam is still in use.

Citadel: The fortress, set high above the town, dates from the Seljuk era and is most impressive when you are looking up from below. If you are up to the climb (start behind the Damat İbrahim Paşa complex), you'll find the view of the town to be disappointing. The flat, white roofs of the poor section of town seem reminiscent of a north African desert town. To drive up by car, head first toward Konya, then turn left at the industrial quarter. For the last stretch, ask for directions from the people on the street.

OPEN: Daily 9.00 - 12.00 and 13.00 - 18.00 h. Admission £0.30.

Museum: The modern state-run cultural complex on Kayseri Caddesi houses an archaeological and ethnographic museum, a gallery with changing exhibits and the cultural administration. Not worth a visit except for coin collectors and fans of Arabic script.

OPEN: 8.00 - 12.00 and 13.30 - 17.30 h daily. Admission £0.30.

Around Nevşehir

Açıksaray: 15 km outside Nevşehir you arrive at "Açıksaray" ("open palace"). The complex of churches and monasteries on the left side of the road looks exactly like that. You can wander through the palace chambers and the churches which include some of the oldest, dating from the sixth century, in Cappadocia. Rather than frescos, you'll see red wall paintings depicting bulls and other subjects. The bull is revered by many cultures due to its roar and its potency. However the symbol is rarely seen in Cappadocia. It is still uncertain what significance the bull had as a symbol for early Christianity.

COMING - GOING: If you don't have a car, get a minibus from Nevşehir to "Açıksaray" (toward Gülşehir).

Uçhisar

A tip for photographers! The first thing you notice at Uçhisar is the tremendous Swiss cheese like rock set at 60m over-looking the town. It was remodelled into a majestic castle which can be seen far and wide because the village is built on top of a hill.

The castle is pierced with passages and chambers, some completely blocked by fallen rock. Once upon a time about 1000 people lived here. The climb up, sometimes inside, sometimes outside, is not very difficult. At the top, the highest point in the region, you have a tremendous view of Ortahisar, Göreme, Çavuşin, all the way to Avanos. You can see the honey-combed cliffs of Uçhisar, the cone-shaped former apartments and pigeon stalls, the bizarre fairy chimneys in various stages of erosion in the background and, crowning everything, the 4000 m Erciyes Mountain. Admission £ 0.30.

Uçhisar itself is quiet. The town of 4000 has resigned itself to being bypassed by the tourism centred around the castle. Only a few carpet dealers, found around the parking lot, still hope to make some fast money. The majority of the population is engaged in agriculture, profiting from Erciyes' rich volcanic soil.

TELEPHONE AREA CODE: 4856.

COMING - GOING: Minibusses from the surrounding villages and Nevşehir.

FESTIVALS AND EVENTS: **Cappadocia-Festival**, annually on 31st August/1st September, featuring local folklore. The festival is celebrated simultaneously in Nevşehir and Göreme.

FOOD: **Hisar Restoran** and **Şeker Restoran**, both in the centre of town. The quality is just fast food, despite the long wait.

A NIGHT'S REST: There are two pensions, however neither can be recommended.

GÖREME

Göreme -
the name is synonymous with the centre of Cappadocia.

This is where you'll find the loveliest fairy chimneys and the most rock churches. The early Christians were attracted to the tufa formations where they could enjoy a largely undisturbed devout existence with plenty of natural hiding places.

Some etymologists see the name "Göreme" as a derivative of the Turkish *"göremezsin"* (invisible). Others cite historical evidence that the name stems from *"Korama"*.

Göreme refers to a village which just a few years ago was called Avcılar, a name still used by local people.

The tiny village is a nice example of harmony between nature and simple architecture. Available material was hewn and hollowed, creating rock apartments and buildings so lovely, you'd think this was an open-air museum. The village has managed to avoid the pressure of tourism. There are numerous little pensions, but no big hotels. In the çayhouse at the village square you can drink tea or the local speciality, apple tea (*elma çayı*). Donkey drivers can be heard cursing and on weekends the village loudspeaker system announces marriages and who has the honour of inviting the local people to a party . . .

TELEPHONE AREA CODE: 4857

COMING – GOING: By bus from the surrounding villages and Nevşehir.

FESTIVALS AND EVENTS: **Cappadocia-Festival**, annually on 31st August to 1st September, featuring folklore. The festival is also celebrated in Nevşehir and Uçhisar.

FOOD: It is not easy to find a good pub in Göreme. Recommended is **Maçan** ("Maçan" is the name for the village in Armenian), on the road to Avanos, just at the turnoff to the Open-Air-Museum. The lovely garden restaurant offers cheap food.

TRAVEL-AGENCIES:

The agencies **İdil** (Turtle) and **Rose**, both located on Main Street, offer day trips ranging from £7 - 10. These prices do not include the expensive admission fees charged for the various sights. Information about the local pensions is also available.

Gör-Tour, tel. 1211. Just car rentals. Prices vary greatly according to model and rental terms.

A Night's Rest

There are about three dozen pensions in town. Most advertise at the İdil (Turtle) and Rose travel agencies. You can sometimes bargain down the posted prices.

Saksağan Motel, on the main road to Uçhisar, double £13 incl. breakfast. Every room with shower/WC. A small, stylish motel, whose front is built into the tufa rock. Shady courtyard. Little noise. The owner has given each room the name of one of his son's rather than a number. tel. 1164.

Melek Pansiyon, on the main road to Avanos, turn right just before the turnoff to the Open-Air Museum. Double £12 to £14 with or without shower/WC. The owner is a Dutchman married to a local woman. The facilities were planned by a Dutch architect to harmonise with the local environment. Plans for expansion include a swimming pool. Melek Pansiyon is a nice spot for children, with children's tables and chairs, even a playpen upon request. And for adults there is a good selection of drinks. tel. 1463.

Fantasie Pansiyon, on the road to Avanos, a country house just behind the post office. Double £7. Uwe, the manager, is a young German who learned hotel management in a Turkish pension. Extras: ground coffee, espresso and funky music in the bar. The pension is a bit more expensive than average, but with well-kept rooms. Quiet. tel. 1417.

Sarıhan Pansiyon, on the road to Avanos, after the turnoff to the Open-Air Museum, up on the right. Double £5. A modest pension with large rooms, good for children.

S.O.S. Pansiyon, not easy to find. Take the path by the minibus station (see map). Ask. Costs £2.50 per bed. S.O.S. is the Turkish equivalent of a youth hostel. S.O.S. Göreme has 8 rooms with 22 beds. The rooms are all built into the rock. If necessary, beds can be placed in the bar and on the roof. S.O.S. offers a stoney camp site with five house-owned tents (no shade), or - cheaper still - you can pitch your own tent. You have a lovely view of a valley with fairy chimneys. You can do your own cooking, or let them cook for you. Washing machine available! tel. 1134.

Göreme Pansiyon, in the centre of town. Double 3.30. Very simple, friendly pension.

Sights

Open-Air Museum: The Open-Air Museum, featuring a number of churches and monasteries (1,5 km from Göreme), is undisputably the main cultural attraction in Cappadocia. In 1985 UNESCO declared it part of the world's cultural heritage.

The rock and cave churches of Cappadocia, many of which can be seen in the Open-Air Museum, vividly depict the century-long fears of the Christian community. The people dug into the tufa like moles, and it is easy to imagine them living in the numerous cliff caves. The churches were not only the sites of religious services, but also of burials. The countless tombs (stone hollows) in the churches demonstrate that the death cult was important to Cappadocian Christians.

Churches in Cappadocia have often been named by Turkish farmers as they settled the area (Church with the Apple, Church with the Farmer's Shoe, Dark Church, etc.). This shows how little is known about their history. An exact dating is impossible, only a rough judgment can be made based upon the drawings.

There are three types of churches:

1. *Geometric Style*: Ornaments, triangles and zigzag lines were painted right upon the stone using rags drenched in red paint. This style dates from the eighth century, the era of Byzantine iconoclasm, when the depiction of human beings was prohibited. Examples can be seen in the Barbara Church and the Church with the Snake.

2. *Free Symbolic Style*: Depictions of plants, animals and even human beings were either painted right on the rock or the rock was first plastered and the paintings applied as frescos. Examples can be seen in the Church with the Snake.

3. *Highly Symbolic, Figurative Style*: Frescos were painted using brushes. The themes were generally taken from the gospel or from legends of saints. Paintings in this style date from the eleventh and twelfth century and show great artistic talent. Good examples include the Dark Church and the Church with the Apple.

A number of the churches have been renovated over the centuries. In the Church with the Apple, the iconoclastic ornamentation can be seen under the lovely frescos where the plaster has been chipped away.

The frescos were often destroyed by thrown rocks - the vandals liked to aim for the eyes. This was part of a later Islamic-motivated iconoclasm.

The Tour

Elmalı Kilise (Church with the Apple): The first stop in the museum is a cruciform-domed basilica. You reach the richly painted interior through a gorge. The frescos (depicting the life of Jesus from birth to crucifixion, prophets, saints and scenes from the Old Testament) have been damaged by tourism - particularly by graffiti. Under the frescos you can see some of the ancient, non-figurative ornamentation.

Barbara Kilise (Barbara Church): Hewn into the same rock, just around the corner. The lack of figurative depictions (other than a few animals) shows the influence of iconoclasm. Later some of the ornaments were painted over. The symmetric axial depiction of the knights, George and Theodore, in battle with the dragon is a popular theme among Cappadocian Christians. One of the figures across from the central apse is the patron saint of the church.

Yılanlı Kilise (Church with the Snake): This church was originally built as a tomb. The ancient geometric patterns in red paint are still visible. The depiction of George and Theodore battling the dragon was added later, as was the trio of saints: Onophios (naked with a beard and breasts), Basilius and Thomas.

Refectory (dining hall): Well preserved, the table (chiseled from stone) has room for 40 - 50 diners.

Karanlık Kilise (Dark Church): As the name suggests, your eyes will have to adjust before you can enjoy the frescos (depicting biblical scenes) painted upon a dark-blue background. Due to the lack of light, they are in part well preserved. Artistically, they must be counted among the most valuable in the region. Art historians note that the costumes of the saints reveal fashions of the eleventh century Byzantine court.

Çarıklı Kilise (Church with the Farmer's Shoe): The name stems from the shoe-shaped hollow below the ascension picture. Although it has only two columns, Çarıklı Kilise is a cruciform-domed basilica. The badly damaged frescos date from the same period as those in the Karanlik Kilise.

OPENING HOURS Open-Air Museum: 8.30 - 18.30 h. New admission £2.30.

Churches outside the Open-Air Museum: After visiting the Open-Air Museum, take a walk through the lovely rocky scenery to see other early Christian churches in the region.

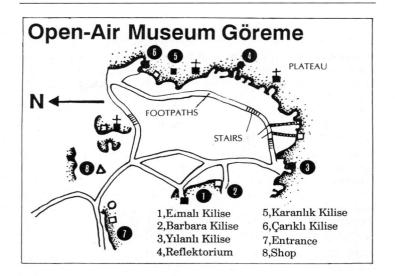

Open-Air Museum Göreme

PLATEAU

N ←

FOOTPATHS

STAIRS

1,Elmalı Kilise   5,Karanlık Kilise
2,Barbara Kilise   6,Çarıklı Kilise
3,Yılanlı Kilise   7,Entrance
4,Reflektorium   8,Shop

Tokalı Kilise (Church with the Buckle): On the road from the museum into Göreme (100 m from the museum on the right). It is among the largest churches in the region. Since restoration of the tenth century frescos, the church is never left unattended.

OPEN: 8:00 - 19:00 h daily (admission only with a ticket of the Open-Air Museum).

Meryem Ana (Church of St. Mary): On the left of the Tokalı Kilise a path leads past Eustachius Chapel through a tunnel to Meryem Ana. Before entering the church stop for a moment to take a look at the tremendous view. Kılıçlar Valley (Valley of the Swords) receives its name from the countless pointed rock formations. Meryam Ana Kilisesi itself houses well preserved frescos with extraordinarily bright colours.

Saklı Kilise (Church of St. John): About half way between the museum and Göreme, follow the sign to the right. A steep, narrow path leads to the church. The entrance was buried for centuries under rock before being unearthed in 1957. The frescos have bright colours and a unique feature: the painter used the Cappadocian countryside - note the fairy chimneys - as a background for biblical scenes. From the Saklı Kilise you have a tremendous view of the El-Nazar Valley with its famous fairy chimneys, whose forms have made many virtous young women blush.

St. Onophrius - the Saint with a Beard & Breasts

An intriguing depiction can be seen in Yılanlı Kilise. Beside Basilius and Thomas is the puzzling figure of Onophrius. Naked, with the face of a heavily bearded, elderly man, the body displays pronounced breasts and a very feminine stature. The sexually revealing section of anatomy is hidden provocatively behind a plant.

A number of solutions to the riddle have been offered:
Devout Christians venture that Onophrius was once a woman of such astonishing beauty that she asked God to have mercy upon her and protect her from the temptation of men. God granted her wish by changing her face and permitting the beard to grow.

The evil gossip counters that Onophrius, as a woman, was a shameless sinner who asked God for increased opportunities to indulge in her blasphemous lifestyle. As a punishment, God turned her into an old man.

Others believe that Onophrius was a homosexual. The painter wanted to expose this trait by giving him female attributes.

Çavuşin

Çavuşin is 3 km north of Göreme on the right heading toward Avanos. The village has nothing to offer except a view of a large collapsed rock face. A nighttime catastrophe in 1963, which cost many lives, has limited the village's touristic destiny.

Çavuşin once attracted pilgrims to its famous baptism church, probably the oldest church in the region. While some travel guides recommend a visit to the church, there is little to see, and you trample through the ruins at your own risk. The survivors of the catastrophe have rebuilt their homes at a safe distance.

Sights

Çavuşin Kilisesi (Çavuşin Church): Located outside the village on the Göreme - Avanos road. It is easy to recognize from the road because of its iron stairs. Right next door is the "Sultan" luxury restaurant.

The front hall of the Çavuşin Kilisesi has collapsed, leaving the frescos (arch-angels Gabriel and Michael) completely exposed to the sun. Entering the church via the iron stairs you come into a cylindrical vault with three apses whose paintings were completed in the tenth and eleventh century. Depicted is the complete evangelical cycle from the proclamation of the birth of Christ to his ascension. Admission £1.70

Around Çavuşin

Paşabağ: The most impressive fairy chimneys in all of Cappadocia can be found in the Paşabağ Valley (from Çavuşin toward Avanos, after 2 km turn right toward Zelve). Surrounded by orchards and vineyards, the tremendous chimneys frequently stand as pairs or triplets. Several were hollowed out centuries ago for use as monk's cells, chapels, tombs, or multi-story apartments.

Tip for photographers: the best light is in the afternoon.

Zelve

Boasting cave dwellings, churches and ruined monasteries, the rock village - made a museum in 1967 - is a must on any visit to Cappadocia. The ancient Romans chiseled out dwellings in the red tufa, an example followed by the Byzantines, Seljuks, and Ottomans. Christians and Moslems lived here in harmony until the Greek-Turk population exchange in 1923.

The last inhabitants evacuated Zelve in 1953 when a succession of rockslides made living in the caves too risky. Government aid was used to build Yeni Zelve (New Zelve), 2 km to the north. Don't bother to visit those mass-produced dwellings. Zelve is 5 km from Çavuşin, on the road to Avanos, 2 km down on the right.

The three valleys within the museum grounds invite tours which are not without risk. The triangular sign warning of rockslides on alpine roads is used here, right on the footpath, in all seriousness. With care

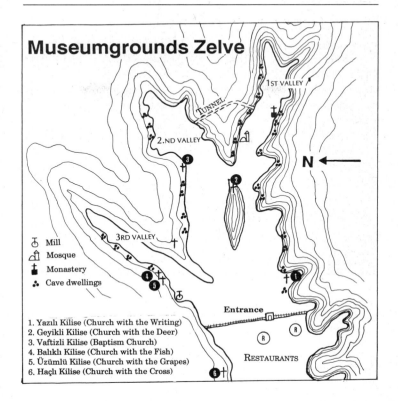

Museumgrounds Zelve

1ST VALLEY

TUNNEL

2.ND VALLEY

N

3RD VALLEY

Entrance

♉ Mill
🕌 Mosque
✝ Monastery
∴ Cave dwellings

R   R

RESTAURANTS

1. Yazılı Kilise (Church with the Writing)
2. Geyikli Kilise (Church with the Deer)
3. Vaftizli Kilise (Baptism Church)
4. Balıklı Kilise (Church with the Fish)
5. Üzümlü Kilise (Church with the Grapes)
6. Haçlı Kilise (Church with the Cross)

you can climb up to many rock dwellings or a half-ruined monastery with a tree growing out of the roof.

Sights include a well-preserved *mill*, plus a *rock mosque* with a tiny minaret. As in many Cappadocian villages, the muezzin has just enough space to do his duty within the four columns.

Best preserved of the Christian churches is *Üzümlü Kilise* (Church with the Grapes). The ornamentation dates the church back to the iconoclastic era of the eighth and ninth century.

The first and second valleys are connected by an ancient tunnel. The entrance to the tunnel in the second valley is easy to find due to the iron stairs. It is more difficult to find in the first valley - the entrance is in one of the hollows across from the monastery. Don't try to enter the tunnel without a flashlight. In the total darkness it is impossible to see steps, stairs or curbs and after a few steps you will have banged your head enough to turn around.

If you don't have a flashlight, wait for one of the young guides to light the way for you. Upon reaching daylight on the other side you will be happy to offer a small tip.

Near the museum entrance there are two small *garden restaurants* of which the lower can be recommended due to its shade and the good, cheap food.

Although you don't have much chance to spend money in Zelve, a number of mobile banks compete for your currency. All of the bank cars are bound to the official exchange rate.

OPEN: Daily 8:00 - 18:30 h. New Admission £1.70

Ortahisar

The quiet village built around a rock castle is Turkey's largest depot for fruit and vegetables. At the entrance to Ortahisar you can see the tremendous warehouses containing potatoes, apples, onions and other regional produce along with citrus fruit from the south.

Trucks arriving from Mersin dump tons of lemons in front of the cellar entrances. Teams of youths pack the fruit into cases which are stored underground in cool tufa caverns where a year-round temperature of 10 degrees Celsius is maintained. A million cases, each containing 20 kilos of lemons, lie waiting in Ortahisar. From here deliveries are made to all of Turkey and Europe. Local life in Ortahisar, away from the fields and warehouses, is concentrated around the village square with its few shops and an old tea house. Here old men spend the hours playing Tavla or sitting and dreaming.

The main attraction of the village is the **castle**, set on a rock 90 m high. It provided Cappadocian Christians with an ideal hiding place from Arab enemies. The cave dwellings remained intact for centuries and were inhabited until recently. But, as elsewhere in the region, life in the caves has become too risky, forcing the inhabitants to build a new settlement on the edge of town.

The climb is strenuous, but don't be deterred, the reward is ample (and you will get a good idea of your physical conditioning). Sweeten the climb by buying a bag of dried apricots at the entrance - three times the admission price, but still cheap. After working your way up the passages, stairs, ladders and other ironwork, you'll find a unique view. Across the jagged landscape you see the neighbouring castle of Uçhisar and you'll understand how important these fortresses were during dangerous times past. Wine grows where erosion has yet to remove the soil. Where nature has removed the economic basis of agriculture, it has sculpted an appealing landscape. There are some very bizarre tufa formations.

Admission £0.30

TELEPHONE AREA CODE: 4869.

COMING - GOING: Buses from Göreme, Ürgüp and Nevşehir.

A Night's Rest

Ortahisar is not the right place as a base for Cappadocian tours. Ürgüp and Göreme are much better. The two hotels mentioned below cater to fruit dealers and drivers, they offer little comfort at expensive prices.

Selçuk Otel (the sign on the house simply says "Otel"), at the village square, above the tea house, double £8, including breakfast. Each room with a shower, toilet in the hall, open all year round. Heated rooms, simple breakfast room. tel. 1352.

Otel Göreme, at the top of the village square, double £8, no breakfast, shower/WC in each room, modest. tel. 1005.

FOOD: Şehir Restoran, the tiny restaurant offers the usual fare (Şiş Kebabı, Saç Kebabı) and is not expensive. Like the hotels, it profits from guests in the citrus trade.

Sights

Churches dating from the early Christian era can be seen in Ortahisar itself and the surrounding countryside. However, they are frequently in ruins or used by local farmers as stables or barns.

Hallaçdere Monastery: This complex, probably of Armenian origin, is easy to find. Follow the *Pancarlık Valley and Churches* sign. After about fifteen minutes a footpath leads to the ruins badly damaged by erosion. Imagining that the yard was once the interior of a church will give you an impression of the size. The rich relief ornamentation of the facade is an Armenian trademark. In the main church of what was once a multi-story complex, depictions dating from the iconoclastic era can be seen. Later the apse was repainted with figures.

Balkan Church Centre: This collection of churches and monastery complexes is 2 km from Ortahisar. Follow the sign "*Pancarlık Valley and Churches*" below the village and walk uphill along a dry streambed until a path leads up to the right to the churches. The Balkan Church Centre has not been set up for tourism nor has it been restored. The few frescos are in poor condition.

Around Ortahisar

Aktepe and Kızılçukur: The place for landscape photographers! Leaving Ortahisar on the eastern arterial road via the straight extension of the Nevşehir - Ürgüp road, take the winding grawel road to Aktepe ("white hill"). The 3 km walk is best done in the morning when the heat is most bearable and the landscape most photogenic. Down to the left is the red tufa stone formation of Kızılçukur ("red gorge"), a valley with steep walls. From the lookout point at the end of the path, you can see the white tufa cones of Aktepe, a number of which have grown together with the mountain. To the west you can see beyond Kızılçukur to the El-Nazar Valley, with the famous rock castle of Uçhisar in the background.

Help us update

Help us update

We've done our best to make this book as accurate and up-to-date as possible but travel developments are swift and things are always changing. We would greatly appreciate any contributions, suggestions, corrections, improvements or additions you may have for future editions.
Please write us:
Springfield Books Limited c/o Michael Muller, Norman Road, Denby Dale, Huddersfield HD8 8TH, West Yorkshire, England.

Ürgüp *(pop. 10,000)*

This bustling town in the heart of Cappadocia attracts guests with its nightlife. The carpet dealers (galleries) on the main road stay open until late in the evening. Street restaurants are crowded; banks close their doors at 23:00 h.

You can't miss the town located at the foot of a tremendous rock, which is spotlighted at night, adding a touch of show to a place without any real sights. Climbing the mountain during the day provides a spectacular view of the town. A few caves on the southern rock face are still inhabited, others have collapsed and the refugees have found new homes in a state-financed catastrophe settlement which is on the left of the main road that crosses the Damsa Stream to Kayseri.

The small building on top of the rock resembling a tomb is said to have housed a library. A real tomb can be seen below. You can see the sarcophagus through the barred window. A Bey called Kılıç Aslan (probably not the famous Seljuk sultan of the same name) found his resting place overlooking the rooftops of Ürgüp.

Children playing up here among the ruins can show you the entrance to a tunnel leading 75 m to one of the many cave-like openings visible in the rock. The tunnel is dark and very narrow in places, making a flashlight helpful even if you have a guide.

INFORMATION: At the museum; Mo - Fr 8:30 - 18:00 h, during season every day, tel. 1059.

TELEPHONE AREA CODE: 4868.

COMING - GOING: Local buses from the surrounding villages and Nevşehir.

FESTIVALS & EVENTS: In mid-October, Ürgüp hosts an International Wine Festival under the auspices of the International Union of Wine Producers in conjunction with the Tekel monopoly administration and the town of Ürgüp. Over 140 wine producers from 70 countries compete for the gold, silver and bronze medallions.
The festivities include music and folklore along with films and presentations pertaining to wine.

HOSPITAL: (see map), tel. 1031.

MARKET (See map): Every Saturday farmers from the surrounding region sell tomatoes, potatoes and eggplant (the latter at £0.70 per kilo). At the livestock section sheep (£40) and donkeys (£35) change hands.

SHOPPING: **Bazaar of Handicrafts** (See map). The modern bazaar features arrays of jewellery, embroidery, kilims, onyx, etc.

TRAVEL AGENCIES: Competition between the agencies in town is heavy. There is little difference between the classic selection of daytrips and tours throughout Cappadocia.
The tours start at 9.00 h and cost between £7 - 10 (price includes transport and guide, admission fees are extra).

A Night's Rest

In Ürgüp you'll find all classes of hotels. If you want a little bit of luxury, be sure to book well in advance. Travel agencies frequently book an entire hotel forbus loads of tourists. Middle class hotels can be found in the centre of town or on the western arterial road. Cheaper hotels and pensions are located in the southeast of town. Several hotels have swimming pools (ask how often the water is changed!).

Turban Motel, just outside of town on the road to Nevşehir, double £28. The state-run motel is the most luxurious in Cappadocia: clean swimming pool with bar and lounge chairs, discreet music, drinks, good food. The bungalows blend in with the tufa landscape. Each room with shower/WC and telephone. tel. 2290.

Hotel Eyvan, on the Nevşehir - Ürgüp road before the entrance to town, double £23. A modern luxury hotel with restaurant, terrace and bar. Not so convenient for large travel agencies as it has only 54 beds. The rooms are built into the cooling rock. tel. 1822.

Hotel Asya Minor, on the Nevşehir - Ürgüp road, immediately after entering town, double £8. A small hotel with a sunny terrace and a small, quiet loggia. The owner will prepare dinner if you request it at midday. You can also cook yourself. Recommended for those planning to spend some time "at home". tel. 2029.

Hotel Konak, on the arterial road to Nevşehir, double £8. A lovely house with friendly, young management. The rooms are not large, but nice with shower/WC. The owner named his rooms after birds rather than numbering them: Pelican, Bülbül (nightingale) Kanarya... Tables are arranged in the shady courtyard. The lobby, a former stable, is occasionally used for carpet sales. tel. 1667

Göreme Pansiyon (Hotel Şato), across the street from Büyük Hotel, double £8. Göreme Pansiyon and Hotel Şato have been merged; the reception is in Göreme Pansiyon. The two establishments are furnished in modest oriental style. Rooms are equipped with a shower or tub, some with a balcony. Student discount (10 per cent), for groups over 10 people (20 per cent). As a last resort the camp site next to Göreme Pansiyon can be used, but it isn't very inviting. The owner also has a carpet shop on the main road. tel. 1022.

Peri Oteli, across the street from the north side of Büyük Hotel, double £5. Modest hotel, all rooms with shower/WC. Seating in the garden facing the road. The cellar restaurant features barbecue - the owner is an Australian woman. Food served in the evening. tel. 1055.

Hanedan Hotel, on the arterial road to Nevşehir, double £8. The rooms built into the rock are of varied quality. Inspect the room before you accept. Some are damp with a slightly moldy smell. The balconies facing the road are pleasant with the exception of occasional traffic noise. tel. 1552.

Hotel Eyfel, in southeast Ürgüp, double £5. Quiet, clean hotel slightly out of the way, with a small restaurant. tel. 1761.

Park Hotel, near the post office, double £12. Not recommended: it is loud, the rooms are not clean and price disputes often arise. tel. 1883.

Pínar Oteli, on the road to Kayseri, right by the bridge over the Damsa stream, double £12. All rooms with showers/WC. The hotel is a little bit dirty, and should not be recommended due to the noise from the street and the smell from the nearby stream. tel. 1054.

Erciyes Pansiyon, in the southeastern part of Ürgüp, double £4. A simple, quiet pension. Several rooms have balconies overlooking the garden. There is a small shower room (hot water costs extra!) and for a small fee you can have your laundry done. tel. 1206.

Food and Drink

CAPPADOCIAN WINE

Cappadocia is not only famous for its fairy chimneys and rock churches but also for its refreshing dry wines. The volcanic soil is extremely fertile providing it receives enough water; in some places irrigation is used. Around Ürgüp and Ortahisar you can see vines which are grown along the ground rather than up. Harvest time is in September.

Ripe grapes are processed in *wine factories* (*şarap fabrikası*) which can be visited in Ürgüp, Ortahisar and Uçhisar.

Turasan, located on the road to Nevşehir, below the Turban Motel, is Cappadocia's largest winemaker. Turasan has a dozen wine cellars, the largest of which stores 110,000 litres. After pressing and filtering, the wine is stored in underground tufa caverns for six to eighteen months. It is then distributed throughout Turkey.

You can buy a bottle of wine for £0.60 to £2 (set prices). Of course you are invited to test the white, red and rosé wines before making a purchase.

In the evening Turasan invites you to test their wine at folklore events. Admission of £1.60 includes drinks. You may drink as much as you can hold, but please no more! If you drink until you get drunk, you violate the unwritten laws of Cappadocian hospitality.

Try à la carte in the luxury hotels for good but expensive food.

Çirağan Restaurant, above the Hamam. This lovely garden restaurant has excellent food. The specialty - for which the Kayseri region is famous - is called "Mantı" (pasta filled with ground beef and yoghurt). The "Güveç" is also excellent. Good regional wines.

Restaurant Capadoce, behind Kayer Travel Agency. An average restaurant in the centre of town with tables set along the street. Good cheap food.

Restaurant Uğrak, on the busy road to Nevşehir. If you don't mind the dust and noise, you can get an unexpensive meal here.

İhlara Restaurant, set on the roof of the modern building housing the Bazar of Handicrafts. The food isn't anything special but it's a nice spot to down a glass of beer (on tap).

Restaurant Yaşar Baba, in the countryside on the road to Nevşehir, about 3 km from Ürgüp. The food is average, but you pay for the lovely location. A sunny terrace with a tremendous view of the tufa landscape is reached by walking through the rock on which the restaurant is perched. Very hot during the day.

DISCOS: **Armağan**, on the right side of the street at the turnoff toward Mustafapaşa. The disco, in the halls of a former camel stable features Turkish folklore plus familiar tunes.

Sights

Museum: The collection features regional finds: jewellery, candelabrum, weapons, tombs and ceramics from pre-historic, Greek, and Roman times. The most interesting object is the tusk of a mammoth, said to be 10 million years old.

OPEN: 8:00 - 18:00 h daily. Admission £0.30

From Ürgüp to Soğanlı

A trip for motorbike riders! The 45 km route to Soğanlı is an experience. The narrow country road runs through scenic countryside. Jagged rocky landscape is varied by pastures, gentle hills, forested valleys, dry river beds and a few villages.

If you don't have your own car, book a ride with one of the travel agencies in Ürgüp. Frequently the ride to Soğanlı is included as part of a day trip (Soğanlı and Avanos, Soğanlı and Derinkuyu). Costs are £7 including a guide tour through several churches in the Soğanlı Valley.

The first village, 5 km south of Ürgüp, is **Mustafapaşa**, formerly Sinasos, which had a mostly Greek population until the Turkish War of Independence (1921/22). Once in a while some of the old Greek inhabitants return to the village, only to cry at the sight of the dilapidated state of the once lovely buildings.

Be sure to visit the underground *Ayos-Vasilios* Church, one of the ancient churches in which the Greek population held services. It is located 1 km north of town at the edge of a plateau. The brightly coloured wall paintings are of recent origin. Islamic iconoclasts scratched out the faces in the twentieth century.

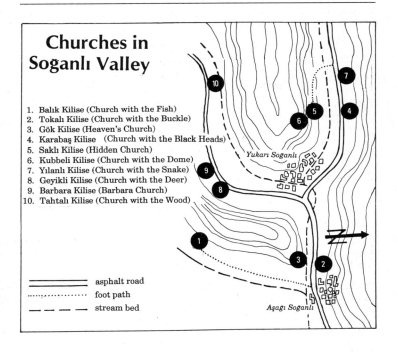

Churches in Soğanlı Valley

1. Balık Kilise (Church with the Fish)
2. Tokalı Kilise (Church with the Buckle)
3. Gök Kilise (Heaven's Church)
4. Karabaş Kilise   (Church with the Black Heads)
5. Saklı Kilise (Hidden Church)
6. Kubbeli Kilise (Church with the Dome)
7. Yılanlı Kilise (Church with the Snake)
8. Geyikli Kilise (Church with the Deer)
9. Barbara Kilise (Barbara Church)
10. Tahtalı Kilise (Church with the Wood)

Yukarı Soğanlı

Aşağı Soğanlı

========== asphalt road
·················· foot path
— — — — stream bed

You will find the Ayos-Vasilios Church locked. The key is kept at the information booth at the entrance to town. The person there provides both information and guided tours. The booth may not be occupied, in which case you have to be patient until he returns from a tour.

Just above the village are the ruins of a monastery complex containing the *Ayos Nicola* and *Ayos Stefanos* churches. Take the footpath behind the old cemetery up to the *Sinasos* church. Local children are happy to play guide, but don't forget to tip.

Cemil: the road continues to this terraced village in the mountains featuring a Greek triple-nave church (although there is little to see beyond the paintings above the apse). About 2 km beyond Cemil, in an overgrown region, is a former monastery whose lower rooms are used as stables by local farmers.

Via **Taşkınpaşa** and **Şahinefendi** you reach a high plateau, then the village of **Güzelöz**, and after 9 km a road branches to the right toward Soğanlı.

Soğanlı consists of two settlements: **Aşağı Soğanlı** and **Yukarı Soğanlı**. The upper village is the centre of town if a çayhouse indicates such. From here you can enter two valleys containing up to 200 churches, many of which have yet to be excavated. Some are known only to local shepherds, who hesitate to reveal the locations because they want to use the former churches as barns.

Notice the numerous pigeon holes in the slopes around Soğanlı. Unlike the familiar holes in Göreme, Uçhisar, Ürgüp or Zelve, these are marked with white. The ancient tradition of collecting pigeon guano still thrives. Every March the droppings are scratched out of the caves for use as fertilizer. Collecting this ecologically-sound form of fertilizer does have its dangers - the pigeon holes are hard to reach, and the rocks crumble easily.

In the Soğanlı Valley, the *Karabaş Kilise* and *Yılanlı Kilise* churches are locked. The key is kept by an attendant, who can be found at the Çayhouse, from where he can easily spot strangers on the road. The attendant will accept a donation for the churches and will offer his services as a guide.

The most interesting churches around Soğanlı include:

Tokalı Kilise (Church with the Broach): Accessible via 50 steps hewn into the rock. A number of tombs are found in front of the entrance (upon which visitors from the previous century have left their initials). The roomy rock architecture (three very long, high naves) is still well preserved. The frescos, however, have been completely destroyed.

Karabaş Kilise (Church with the Black Heads, locked): The name is deceiving: it is not the heads that are black, but the background on which the frescos have been painted. Give your eyes a chance to adjust to the dark before you enjoy the well preserved artwork. In the room furthest to the rear you'll find typical decorations from the iconoclast period.

Yılanlı Kilise (Church with the Snake, locked): The dark frescos are still discernible. On the right wall Abraham, Isaac and Jacob are depicted - each with four children representing the people of Israel. Across from them is Mary with two angels.

Kubbeli Kilise (Church with the Dome): Of greatest interest is the dome which is the hollowed tip of a fairy chimney.

ADMISSION for Soğlanı Valley: £0.60

If you have your own car, take a left after Güzelöz and drive back to Ürgüp via Derinkuyu. At Tilköy (12 km beyond Güzelöz), on the right side of the road, are the remains of a small caravanserai dating from the Seljuk era.

The Soğanlı - Derinkuyu - Nevşehir - Ürgüp route covers 87 km.

Avanos *(pop. 9300)*

"Even a blind man can find the way to Avanos if he follows the trail of broken pottery." This local saying hits the mark: Avanos   is   the   centre   of   Cappadocean   pottery production.About 300 pottery workshops process clay from the Kızılırmak ("red river") and red hills in the region.

Every imaginable object is produced: candlesticks coffee cups, figurines, jewellery, ashtrays, eggholders, and the famous clay pots in which the secret of a tasty Anatolian "*Güveç*" (meat and vegetable stew) lies hidden.

Avanos dates back to the Hittite era (1800 - 1200 BC). The Phygrians, Romans, Byzantines and Seljuks passed through here, although the historical traces are difficult to find.

What has remained is traditional pottery-making, using methods dating back 3000 years. Workshops in the upper village are proud to demonstrate how they work. Notice the ease with which the complicated shapes are formed. Frequently you will be invited to try your hand at the wheel. Amateurs, however, create only shapeless sausages, while the master laughs, watching without comment . . .
Ceramics are sold in many shops along the main road. Prices are low and the wares are generally practical.

After you've seen enough pottery-making, take a walk along the bank of the Kızılırmak. The river, with its source in the mountains between Sıvas and Erzincan, makes a tremendous bend west of Samsun into the Black Sea. It is the longest river in Turkey (915 km). In Avanos the soil has coloured the river red. If you are here in the evening, be sure to take a photo from the bridge as the sun sinks into the river.

It is local tradition for young couples to celebrate their engagement with parties (called "*binlik*" in Avanos). These are held on Sundays in August in the wine gardens by the river.

INFORMATION: There is only a branch of the Ürgüp information office and it is frequently closed. Little offered besides a list of hotels and the usual brochures.

TELEPHONE AREA CODE: 4861.

COMING - GOING: Buses from Ürgüp and Nevşehir.

FESTIVALS & EVENTS: The annual International Handicrafts Festival is held from 25 -
27th August.

TRAVEL AGENCIES:
Nevtur: Offers the usual Cappadocia tours. Day trips £7 to £10. tel. 1541.

FROM CLAY TO POTTERY

Mehmet, a member of an old potter family, gave us the
following recipe:
The clay is taken from the Kızılırmak river bed or from the
mountains and is ground and sifted in town. The raw material is
placed in a basin of water for an entire day creating a hunk of
clay. Using pedal-power the potter's wheel is turned. The art of
pottery-making is to shape the clay using only your hands. The
created product is dried in the sun for 20 minutes, then inside
for one week. Using a flat piece of iron, the object is polished
before being allowed to dry another week. Only then the object
is baked in a kiln for 6 hours. For the first hour a log fire is used
to heat the kiln. Wood chips are used for the last five hours.
Glazed objects are painted before being returned to the kiln.

A Night's Rest

Perhaps in the hope that Ürgüp and Göreme will be booked out, new
lodgings have been built here. Still, Ürgüp is much nicer.
The smaller pensions found in Avanos are modest, charging £4 to £7
per double. The most central lodgings are on the main (north) side of
the river (Çardak Pansiyon, Kervan Pansiyon). Quieter, less accessible pensions are on the south side.

Hotel Venessa, right by the bridge, double £25. An old luxury hotel, also booked
by travel agencies. tel. 1201.

Hotel Zelve, on the main road next to Nevtur. Double £15. A small luxury hotel in
the centre of town. tel. 1524.

Sofa Hotel, north of the bridge, across the main road. Double £13. Less than
pretty outside, inside is a lovely garden. A quiet old house. Recommended. tel.
1489.

FOOD: The restaurants in Avanos are not good. A few small locantas and kebapcis
can be found on the main road across from the minibus station.

Around Avanos

Sarıhan: The caravanserai, built in 1249, is 5 km east of Avanos. The richly ornamented entrance is well preserved. Large parts of the outer walls have been restored using the same local stone as in the thirteenth century. Trade took place under the arcades. The merchants slept in the section to the right while the animals were stalled on the west side across from the entrance. The mosque is above the entrance gate.

> All the caravanserais in Turkey date from the thirteenth century. These tremendous, fortress-like establishments were built along the trade routes at the main junctions: Konya (capital of the Seljuk empire) and Kayseri (junction to the east) are about a day's ride apart (30 km). Their function was very similar to motels today.

COMING - GOING: If you can't wait for the next caravan to Sarıhan, get a taxi in Avanos or ask at the minibus station (a dolmuş departs with four passengers). "Cappadocia Tours" in Ürgüp includes the yellow caravanserai on a half-day tour (Kızılçukur - Sarıhan - Özkonak, departs at 14 h in Ürgüp).

OPEN: daily 8:30 - 18:00 h.

Özkonak (underground town): The underground town (sign: *Yeralti Şehir*) is not as impressive as Derinkuyu or Kaymaklı and therefore has been spared from mass tourism so far.

The underground town, which once supposedly housed 60,000 people, was discovered by the muezzin of Özkonak, who dug too deep while working on his property. Excavations began in 1972. Five of ten suspected floors have been unearthed. The discoveries include a wine cellar with kegs (empty), a kitchen and a number of children's graves. The passages are narrow, and very dark despite illumination. Be sure to bring a flashlight.

The muezzin lives in the red building next to the old underworld entrance. Upon discovering the importance of his find he worked part-time as a guide. Now this job (financed only by tourist tips) has been turned over to his son.

COMING - GOING: To Özkonak get a minibus from Avanos or go by taxi. "Cappadocia Tours" in Ürgüp offers a half-day tour (Kızılçukur - Özkonak - Sarıhan, departs at 14 h in Ürgüp).

KAYSERI *(pop. 378,500)*

Located at the foot of the Erciyes volcano (the creator of the Cappadocian tufa scenery), the town is the historical capital of Cappadocia, although it has lost out on the expansion of the tourist and infrastructure development of the Nevşehir region. Kayseri is a central Anatolian city with the normal bustle.

Porters hurry through the bazaar with balls of cloth, cars seek passage through a mass of people, hawkers around the bus station sell chewing gum, notebooks, toys, and anything else that's salable. Kayserians are considered to be born traders (and not without cause). A local joke claims that the first Italian to make a bad deal here was Marco Polo.

Stroll through the old town where you'll see Kümbet (domed tombs). In numerous tiny shops you'll notice the red-coloured ham: Pastırma, dried beef tasting of garlic, Kayseri's culinary specialty.

History

The town has experienced the full brunt of Anatolian history. An early Hittite settlement has been discovered near Kültepe (20 km to the north). During the Roman era, Kayseri (Caesarea) was the provincial capital of Cappadocia. During the Byzantine era, the church leader Basilius worked here. In the Battle of Malazgirt (1071) the Seljuks captured the town, leaving impressive architecture behind, including the Hunat-Hatun Complex. Around 1400 Kayseri was destroyed by the Mongol prince Timur (the Lame). Mongol rule was succeeded by the Karamanlıs and later the Ottoman. The unfortunate town sank to insignificance until raised by Atatürk's republic to the status of provincial capital. Signs of new life include growing settlements on the outskirts of town and an underground shopping centre below Cumhuriyet Square in the town centre.

INFORMATION: at the Hunat-Hatun Complex. The staff are friendly and helpful. Besides the usual info, tips for mountain climbers are offered (Erciyes Mountain). tel. 11190.

TELEPHONE AREA CODE: 351

COMING - GOING: **Bus**: Kayseri is a junction with direct connections to almost every major town in Turkey. There are hourly buses to and from Ankara, Adana and İstanbul. For further information go to the travel agencies at the bus station. (See map).

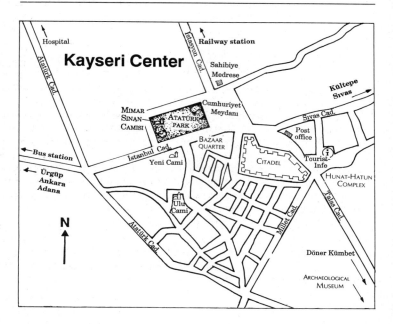

Rail: Kayseri is ideally situated on the rail network with connections at least once a day to most major towns, four times daily to Ankara. Prices are much cheaper than by bus, but it's not as fast.

Air: THY offers flights to İstanbul (Tuesday and Friday, £17). THY office, Sahabiye Mah., Yıldırım Cad., tel. 13947, reservations tel. 11001.

HOSPITAL: Devlet Yolu at Atatürk Cad., tel. 13222.

POST: Cumhuriyet Meydani, next to Hunat-Hatun Complex.

SHOPPING: In the bazaar you'll find everything from famous Kayseri carpets to pastırma. Even if you don't buy, it is a pleasant walk through the old partially covered bazaar (Bedesten).

A Night's Rest

In the old town there are hotels in every price category.

Turan Hotel, Millet Cad., double £20. Old luxury hotel with a roof terrace and Turkish bath. tel. 12506.

Sur Oteli, Cumhuriyet Mah., Uğur Sok., double £8. Right by the citadel, the hotel is popular among backpackers due to its central location. Beware of street noise when choosing a room. tel. 19545.

Kent Hotel, on Düven-Önü Square, double £7. Clean middle-priced hotel. tel. 12454.

Büyük Otel, İnönü Cad., double £7, rooms facing front are very loud. tel. 25340.

Çamlıka Oteli, Bankalar Cad., double £7. The modest hotel on the banking street is quiet at night. tel. 19426.

Hotel Berlin, Camikebir Mah., Melikgazi Sok., on the small road on the southeast side of Ulu Cami, double £7. Simple, quiet, centrally located. tel. 15246.

Food

There are small locantas throughout the centre of the city. The food is best in the luxury hotel restaurants. Kayseri specialties Pastırma or Mantı (leafy pasta stuffed with ground beef and yoghurt) are not so easy to find.

İskender Kebap Salonu, Millet Cad.; a three-story restaurant right next to the citadel (across from the Hunat-Hatun Complex), with good food at reasonable prices.

Merkez Lokanta, across from İskender Salonu, more modest, but the food is just as good.

Divan Pastanesi, also on Millet Cad., Kayseri's best pastry shop. Breakfast served.

PASTIRMA, PASTIRMA, PASTIRMA . . .

The famous spicy dried meat with a hint of garlic is not to everyone's taste. Connoisseurs quickly notice the delicate taste of Pastırma in Kayseri. A recipe for those ready to do it yourself: A fresh piece of beef (rump) is placed in salt (drawing the water in order to prevent spoilage). Then it is hung up to dry (sometimes in the sun) for several weeks. For the famous red coating a sauce containing garlic, peppers, cinnamon, and cumin is prepared in a vat. The exact amounts of the spices vary according to taste. The dried meat is laid in the sauce for several days before being hung in the sun for final drying.

Pastırma is served in millimetre thin slices as an appetizer. Or try it with fried eggs (yumurtalı pastırma): Heat a pan with butter, place slices of Pastırma in pan and top immediately with the eggs. Sprinkle fresh parsley on it to help avoid garlic breath.

Sights

Citadel (İç Kale): The impressive castle, built in 1224 under the Seljuk sultan ALLAEDDIN KEYKOBAT, is 800 m long and 200 m wide. It is made of black volcanic rock from the Erciyes mountain. The courtyard is under reconstruction since the Association of Goldsmiths and Traders plans a big market here.

Hunat-Hatun-Complex: Hunat Hatun is the name of the wife of the Seljuk sultan Alaeddin Kaykobat. The First Lady, who ordered construction of the complex, converted to Islam because of her marriage (like some of her counterparts in the twentieth century).

The most important part of the facility is the *medrese*, opened in 1239, one of the most beautiful examples of Seljuk architecture. Unfortunately the arcades have been glassed in recent years. Today the former medrese serves as an ethnographic museum. The quadratic rooms at both ends once served as student dormitories. Open-air classes were held on the square across from the entrance.

The museum exhibits include a Turkoman round tent (a yurta of cloth, felt and bamboo poles). The heavy stones hanging from the tent roof were intended to prevent a storm tearing it off.

In the back is an octagonal mausoleum containing the stone tomb of Hunat Hatun, plus two additional sarcophagi covered with green cloth. The smallest contains the remains of Hunat Hatun's granddaughter.

OPEN: 8:30 - 12:00 and 13:00 - 17:30 h, closed Mondays. Admission £0.70

Adjoining the medrese is the *Hunat Mosque*. An ancient tradition, nowadays rarely seen in Turkey, is still maintained: the muezzin himself climbs up and calls out to the people - using a microphone of course.

The third building is the lovely *Hunat Hamam*, a Turkish bath still in service.

OPEN: 5:00 - 23:00 h (Men), 8:00 - 18:00 h (Women). Admission £0.50, incl. massage £1.

Ulu Cami: Kayseri's "Great Mosque" has three entrances. It dates from the twelfth century and is considered an excellent example of early Seljuk architecture. The interior is made to appear less severe due to a number of columns. In the southwestern corner is a very old hamam (Kadı Hamamı).

Mimar Sinan Camisi: The mosque, dating from 1585 is at the western end of Atatürk Park. Until recently it was called "Kurşunlu Cami" (kurşun = lead) due to its lead-covered dome. It is said to have been built by the famous Ottoman architect Sinan (hence the name change). He also built the Süleyman Mosque in İstanbul and the Edirne Mosque. Sinan was reportedly born near Kayseri. Typical of the Ottoman style are the numerous slim columns, the domes and the round arches inside.

Sahibiye Medrese: Located at the north end of Cumhuriyet Square, built in late Seljuk style. Most interesting is the lovely geometric stone masonry at the entrance. The interior is full of souvenir shops.

Döner Kümbet: The most famous of Kayseri's numerous kümbets (domed tombs) is the Döner Kümbet (Turning Kümbet) on the Talas Caddesi. Of course the lovely mausoleum does not actually turn. The rich ornamentation and the cylindrical shape suggests this effect.

Archaeological Museum: Located near the Döner Kümbet. This is a must for anyone interested in Hittite or Assyrian culture. Excavated finds from the Hittite town Kanesh (Kültepe) are on display, however, many are on loan to the Museum of Anatolian Civilization in Ankara. Assyrian cuneiform writing is translated (for those illiterate in cuneiform) into French, German and Turkish. Even the assumed pronunciation is depicted.

OPEN: 8:00 - 12:00 and 13:00 - 17:00 h, closed Mondays. Admission £0.30.

Around Kayseri

Erciyes Mountain

The famous volcano, whose explosion 3 million years ago created Cappadocia's natural wonders, is long since extinct. There is snow all year round on the 3916 m peak. Skiing is good from mid December to April. A chairlift climbs from the *Dag evi* (Mountain House) on the Tekir Plain (2150 m) to Şeytan Deresi ("Devil's Stream", 2774 m).

Don't expect a ski and après-ski carnival. Erciyes is too hard to reach for wealthy Turks and the Europeans have their own mountains. The Turkish national ski team trains here if there is not enough snow on the Uludağ (2543 m) near Bursa.

Mountain Climbing: If you are serious about the subject, get some tips from the information office in Kayseri! They are well informed as to which routes fit with which season. Ask about the dangers when climbing from the north.

Hikers and nature lovers without sport ambitions can make it to the top, at least in summer. From the *Dag evi*, the climb up and back takes 12 hours. It's best to spend the night before your climb in the *Dag evi* and get some final tips from the house manager before setting out.

When the weather is clear, you have a tremendous view from the peak. To the west is Hasan Dağı, Cappadocia's other great volcano. To the south you can see the Taurus massif.

If you have your own car (or better, motorcycle), take a spin around the mountain. The scenery is surprising, and the mountain is extremely photogenic.

COMING - GOING: By **minibus** from Kayseri to Hisarcık, then on by local bus or by foot (3 hours) to Dağ evi (12 km).

A NIGHT'S REST:

Dağ evi, £4 per person. Since the establishment only has 60 beds (in 8 and 10-bed rooms), be sure to make reservations several days in advance. In the summer at Dağ evi (tel. 351/39439), in winter at: Beden Terbiyesi İl Müdürlüğü, Kayseri (tel. 251/28975). During the summer you must bring your own food. In the winter you can get full board (£10 per person).

A **sport hotel** is under construction adjoining Dağ evi.

ADDITIONAL DESTINATIONS IN CAPPADOCIA

Ihlara Canyon

It's not quite the Grand Canyon but you might be tempted to compare the two. Ihlara Canyon, about 100 km southwest of Nevşehir, is 15 km long with 382 steps running down the almost vertical cliff at the museum entrance. Looking up to the plateau from the bottom of the nature-rich valley of the Melendiz Stream you get a sense of nature's power.

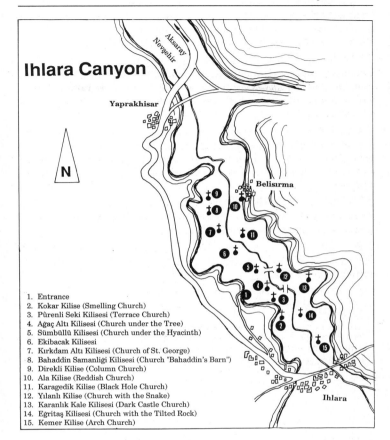

Ihlara Canyon

1. Entrance
2. Kokar Kilise (Smelling Church)
3. Pürenli Seki Kilisesi (Terrace Church)
4. Ağaç Altı Kilisesi (Church under the Tree)
5. Sümbüllü Kilisesi (Church under the Hyacinth)
6. Ekibacak Kilisesi
7. Kırkdam Altı Kilisesi (Church of St. George)
8. Bahaddin Samanliği Kilisesi (Church "Bahaddin's Barn")
9. Direkli Kilise (Column Church)
10. Ala Kilise (Reddish Church)
11. Karagedik Kilise (Black Hole Church)
12. Yılanlı Kilise (Church with the Snake)
13. Karanlık Kale Kilisesi (Dark Castle Church)
14. Eğritaş Kilisesi (Church with the Tilted Rock)
15. Kemer Kilise (Arch Church)

It is assumed that the once powerful Melendiz Stream eroded the rocky stretch for thousands of years before causing a collapse. Countless chunks of rock in the valley provide evidence of this violent natural event.

Since the eighth century, or perhaps earlier, Christians have settled here. The inaccessible canyon was a good hiding place in times of repression. Fifteen churches have been discovered in the valley.

Plan an entire day at Ihlara Canyon; the drive from Nevşehir takes an hour and a half. From Nevşehir, take the western arterial road toward Aksaray.

You reach **Ağzıkarahan** after 60 km , where a tremendous thirteenth century caravanserai on the side of the road demands a stop. The well preserved Seljuk motel (on the Konya - Kayseri Road) boasts a richly ornamented entrance. On one side of the court, which once contained a mosque, were kitchens, baths, and administrative offices. Travellers slept on the opposite side.

4 km after Ağzıkarahan the road to Ihlara Canyon branches off to the left to the mountain village of **Yaprakhisar**, where, well away from the centre of Cappadocia, you'll find tufa formations just like those in the Göreme region. There it was the Erciyes, here it was the Hasan Dağı, which showered the region with ash.

Continue on to the thermal spring at **Ziga** (known already in Roman times) and turn to the left before the village of **Ihlara**, following the sign *"Ihlara Vadisi"* ("Ihlara Valley"). It is not far to the modern complex featuring a restaurant, souvenir shops and the admission building to the canyon.

Churches in Ihlara Canyon

The best preserved of the rock churches are at the upper end of the canyon. The museum administration has constructed seemingly endless stairs (particularly when you're on the way up) onto the rock face.

Right at the bottom of the stairs is the *Ağaç Altı Kilisesi* (Church under a Tree). It is the oldest church in the canyon. Where the relatively well preserved frescos have been damaged, you can see more ancient paintings dating from the iconoclast era. The more abstract forms, e.g. quadratic mosaics, show Arab influence and date from the pre-iconoclast era.

A path on the left of the stairs leads to *Sümbüllü Kilise* (Church with the Hyacinth), in which non-figurative iconoclast art predominates. Outside you can see the arcades of a monastery complex to which the church once belonged. With a flashlight, you'll find a cave tunnel leading up from the ground floor and you'll also find more frescos.

Across from the Sümbüllü Kilise on the opposite side of the valley is the eleventh century *Yılanlı Kilise* (Church with a Snake). It is the largest and richest church in the canyon considering the still preserved ornamentation. Above the right wing is a depiction of

Constantine the Great and his mother Helena. In addition to numerous saints you can see an angel holding a scale, upon which the weight of sins are measured. The possible penalty is depicted upon another wall where four naked female sinners are ringed by snakes.

OPEN: Daily 8:00 - 19:00 h, admission £0.60.

Check the map if you want to visit other churches in the valley. Even if your visit to Göreme has given you your fill of Cappadocian culture, the descent into the canyon is worthwhile. A walk through the valley is unique. Bring a picnic lunch (the Peristrema Restaurant at the top is not recommended). If you dare, enjoy a bath in the chilling waters of Melendiz Stream.

COMING - GOING: From Nevşehir by bus to Aksaray, then on by minibus. You can book a day trip with Travel Agencies in Ürgüp or Göreme (£10 including transport and guide).

FOOD: **Peristrema-Restaurant** at the canyon entrance misuses its monopoly. The food cannot be recommended...

Derinkuyu (pop. 7,400)

Derinkuyu is 29 km south of Nevşehir, on the main road to Niğde. This is the site of the most famous underground town in Cappadocia. If you haven't seen Derinkuyu, you haven't been to Cappadocia.

Fifty underground towns are presumed to be in the region. Of the 36 discovered to date, only a few are open to the public. In the underground town at Derinkuyu eight stories have been unearthed so far, making it the largest in Turkey. It was accidentally discovered in 1963.

COMING - GOING: **Minibuses** from Nevşehir straight to the entrance of the underground town . You can also visit Derinkuyu on a half-day tour (£5) offered by travel agencies in Ürgüp and Göreme.

Sights

Underground Town: No matter how hot it is outside, the year-round underground temperature is 7 to 8 degrees Celsius, possibly colder further away from the ventilation shafts. A jacket or a least a sweater are necessary. A flashlight can also be helpful, although most of the passages are lighted.

A guided tour is not necessary if you don't suffer from claustrophobia. Follow the arrows or you risk walking in circles through the labyrinth of passages, stairs and chambers.

There is verifiable evidence that the first underground floor was used by the Hittites as a storeroom   for water and supplies. Additional excavations have shown that Cappadocian Christians built their earliest fortresses here in the late seventh century. The first two stories contained living and sleeping quarters and also churches. Escape routes were built including a tunnel - closed to the public - running 9 km to the neighbouring town of Kaymaklı.

The roundstone doors (kapı taşı), which look like millstones are interesting. They form a perfect barrier when rolled from the inside in front of the entrance. Communication with the outside world was through pipes 10 cm in diameter and 3 m to 4 m in length, running from the first two floors to the outside.

Most impressive was the ventilation system. Fifteenthousand tiny shafts supplied the upper level with fresh air from the outside. There were fewer shafts to the lower levels, but the system still functioned down to the eighth level. If you hold a burning cigarette to the intake shaft, the smoke flows down. Hold the cigarette to the ventilation shaft and the smoke goes up. (This experiment is no longer possible: smoking is now prohibited!)

The ventilation system with its 70 to 85 m deep shafts also provided water. Until 1962, the above ground population tapped water from the depths of the underground city.

OPEN: 8:30 - 18:00 h daily (£1.70).

ERICH VON DAENIKEN IN DERINKUYU

Erich von Daeniken, who made a name for himself in the 1960s with his books on extraterrestrial intelligence and its traces on our planet, paid a visit to Derinkuyu. This anecdote is told by Ömer Demir, an amateur archaeologist and member of the "International Society for the Investigation of Ancient Civilizations", author of a Cappadocia travel guide and a former employee of the Derinkuyu museum.

Erich von Daeniken discovered immediately that the "moles" of Derinkuyu could not have been human and that extraterrestrial beings clearly had a hand (if they have hands) in the building. Ömer Demir, a specialist in matters of underground towns, just laughed. Erich felt insulted and took his case to Ankara where he thought the Ministry of Culture and Tourism would certainly recognize the science fiction writer's expertise in matters of extraterrestrial affairs and Derinkuyu's early galactic inhabitants. "Derinkuyu - we don't know much about it, but we do have a specialist there - his name is Ömer Demir" was the reply he got.

role as a museum. The bell tower is separate from the main building, much like a minaret. Storks have been nesting on top for decades.

Cumhuriyet Cami: Coming from the north this mosque is on the left at the entrance to town. It was originally constructed as a Christian church in 1860. The sign over the entrance compares Atatürk with Mehmed the Conqueror, who converted the famous Aya Sofia in İstanbul into a mosque. The mosque's name "Cumhuriyet Cami" ("Mosque of the Republic") is, however, absurd. One of Atatürk's basic principles was the separation of church and state!

Around Derinkuyu

Kaymaklı: In Kaymaklı, 9 km north of Derinkuyu on the Niğde - Nevşehir road, is another underground town. It is open to the public. There are minibuses from Derinkuyu and Nevşehir.

A few tombs have been excavated on top of a hill under which the underground town (Yeraltı şehri) lies. The complex is not as large as Derinkuyu - in Kaymaklı just five stories have been unearthed. The architecture and infrastructure are similar. A disco has been opened on the second floor in Kaymaklı - a concession to tourism.

OPEN: 8:30 - 18:00 h daily (admission £1.70).

Nar Gölu (Pomegranate Lake): This lovely crater lake is about 25 km northwest of Derinkuyu, just off the park road running through the Ihlara Valley. A number of rock churches are situated on the southern bank. The frescos have disappeared under the smoke of the shepherds' fires.

Turkey's rural population associates Nar Gölü with hot sulphur baths. People (mostly poor) come from far and wide to seek relief from rheumatism. Since such a treatment is time consuming (unlike at Lourdes), most of the visitors establish residence near the baths from spring until autumn in a tiny tent village.

Nar Gölü is accessible only by car. But don't come for a swim - the lake is surrounded by a belt of reeds. Have respect for the sick seeking treatment and refrain from taking pictures.

Nar Gölü is difficult to find. People in the surrounding villages refer to it as "*Acigöl*". But if you ask for the way to "*Acigöl*", you will most likely be directed to the town of the same name which lies in the same direction. The name "Nar Gölü" is not known locally. It is an invention of the amateur archaeologist Ömer Demir of Derinkuyu, who coined the new name to prevent confusion with the village. A number of travel guides and maps have already accepted his new name.

COMING - GOING: Head past the post office in Derinkuyu then left at the first fork. Keep going straight, 24 km, to Gösterli (no sign). After another 2 km a dusty trail (just across from a lonely mountain cone) on the left leads up to Nar Gölü.

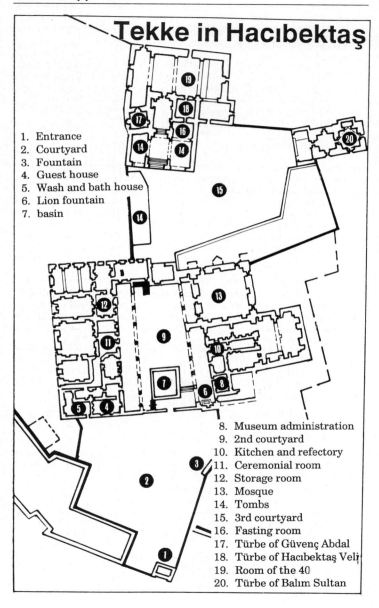

Tekke in Hacıbektaş

1. Entrance
2. Courtyard
3. Fountain
4. Guest house
5. Wash and bath house
6. Lion fountain
7. basin

8. Museum administration
9. 2nd courtyard
10. Kitchen and refectory
11. Ceremonial room
12. Storage room
13. Mosque
14. Tombs
15. 3rd courtyard
16. Fasting room
17. Türbe of Güvenç Abdal
18. Türbe of Hacıbektaş Veli
19. Room of the 40
20. Türbe of Balım Sultan

Hacıbektaş *(pop. 5,400)*

The town, named after Hacıbektaş Veli, the famous founder of a religious order, is located 46 km north of Nevşehir on the road to Ankara. It is the most important pilgrimage town for Anatolian Alewites. From here Hacıbektaş Veli (1247 - 1337) and his students preached a belief which has spread throughout Turkey, particularly in rural areas among the Alewitian minority.

There is little to see besides the *Tekke*, a dervish monastery (today a museum) of the Bektaşis. There is no mass tourism as in Mevlana Monastery at Konya. The monastery is visited primarily by pilgrims. The atmosphere in the complex with its courtyards, fountains and trees is very religious.

COMING - GOING: From Nevşehir by minibus (£0.80).
FESTIVALS & EVENTS: The Hacıbektaş-Veli-Festival is held annually from 16 - 18 August in memory of the order's founder.

HACIBEKTAŞ VELI - A WISE MAN WITH HUMOUR

Compared to other forms of Islam, the Bektaşitian teaching is quite revolutionary: Life is as important as the great beyond, art and science are revered ("The non-scientific route leads to darkness"), women are equal to men ("Countries which don't educate their women will not develop") and religious practice is left to the individual. Hacıbektaş Veli opposed both iconoclasm and the prohibition of alcohol. His translation of religious verse into Turkish did much to raise his esteem in the eyes of the rural people.

The Bektaşi Order was prohibited under Atatürk's government. The Tekke (dervish monastery) of Hacıbektaş was opened to the public in 1964 as a museum.

A number of legends surround Hacıbektaş, as the tales of his wonders have increased over the centuries.

The dervish is remembered in Turkish folklore for his enjoyment of life, making Hacıbektaş Veli a thorn in the eye of orthodox Islam. Veli, himself, thought little of orthodox Islam's rigid code of conduct. This led to a conflict:

Once upon a time, Hacıbektaş Veli visited a mosque to perform the Namaz, the ritual prayer. Without bothering with the prescribed previous washing, he strode right into the mosque. This was seen by his neighbour Ahmed Efendi. "Stop!" screamed Ahmed Efendi, "it is not possible to pray without washing yourself first!" - "Oh, really?" answered Hacıbektaş Veli, "I always do it this way - it is possible."

Sights

Hacı-Bektaş-Veli-Museum (Tekke): After passing through the large outer courtyard, you reach the inner courtyard surrounded by arcades on the left and right.

In a niche on the right is the *Lion Fountain*. This splendid object was built in Egypt during the sixteenth century and was given as a donation in the nineteenth century. The lion symbolizes Ali, the son-in-law of Mohamed, who the Alewites consider the rightful successor to the prophet.

To the right is the *aş evi* (kitchen and dining hall), a very important place. The kitchen chef was second in rank only to the Tekke administrator. New members of the order worked in the kitchen until they completed their training.

Among the kitchen utensils on display is a large black kettle. It was part of the booty won in battle against the Mongols. According to legend, it filled itself to overflowing in response to prayer by Hacıbektaş.

On the left is the *mihman evi* (guest house) for wandering dervishes and other visitors. Today is serves as the museum depot.

In the *maydan evi* (ceremonial hall) the solemn vows were made. Under the eyes of their peers, new members took the sacred oath to "be master over their hands, tongues and loins". Among the objects on display is a famous depiction of Hacıbektaş Veli with a gazelle and a lion on his lap.

The *kiler evi* (supply room) is of little interest. The leader of the Tekke once lived on the first floor. Today his chambers serve as a library.

The third court is even more peaceful. From here you reach the *türbe* (tomb) of *Hacıbektaş Veli*, a site drawing Alewite pilgrims from great distances. The high coffin is covered with green cloth. Medallions, calligraphy and flower patterns provide rich ornamentation. The tomb was built in 1344, seven years after the founder's death.

The small barren chamber, *çilehane* (fasting room) was used by initiates during their period of trial and fasting.

Behind the tomb is a large chamber, *ırklar meydanı* (room of 40). The primary exhibit is a 40-armed chandelier representing the 40 companions of Hacıbektaş Veli. Ceremonial dances were performed here by 40 dervishes. The dervishes moved in a circle to the polyphonic sound of music and choral singing. It is doubtful if the dance, for which the dervishes of the Mevlana Order in Konya are famous, does actually trace its roots back to the *mirac*, the ascension of Mohammed, as claimed. The group of 40 (companions of Mohammed) are said to have created this dance while enthralled by wine.

Further along in the third court is an ancient mulberry tree, whose branches are full of strips of paper and cloth representing the wishes of visitors to this sacred spot.

Open: 8:30 - 12:00 and 13:30 - 18:00 h, closed Mondays, admission £0.70).

ANATOLIA

If you have had your fill of sun and sea along the coast, visit the other part of Turkey - Anatolia. Good destinations are the cities of Konya and Ankara.

Bus connections from the coast to Anatolia are good. The cities are served by all major bus companies; the road system is relatively good. The drive from Adana to Konya takes 8 to 13 hours, depending upon the bus route.

If you are travelling from Adana to Konya or Ankara, be sure to take the route through the Cilician Gate and not along the coast via Mersin and Silifke. The route leads through enchanting countryside, changing as you move from the coast, across the mountains, and onto the Anatolian plateau.

As the road leaves the coast, it climbs and winds through the Taurus. First the slopes are rough and jagged, cut with deep gorges. Then the number of trees increases at the pass, as you drive through alpine scenery. When the road leaves the Taurus, you see the endless rolling Anatolian plain. Sun-bleached fields, squat clay houses, tiny whirlwinds of dust, and never-ending roads mark a change from the lighthearted coast to the melancholy of the arid plains.

If you stop to visit one of these small, poor villages you can sense the severity. The wind blows sharp and dusty. Buildings have small windows, walls enclose the yards, people seem more withdrawn. This is a land of flails, threshing boards, oxen wandering in an endless circle, single-axle carts with wooden wheels (screeching horribly). Little has changed in the last 3000 years.

It is often difficult to get a European-style lunch - the lokantas offer only simple food and tea. People are friendly, but reserved.

Life in Anatolia is still based on agriculture. Grain is grown and sheep are raised on the steppe. The major towns are located in the oases where vegetables are grown and fruit trees flourish.

KONYA *(pop. 500,000)*

This city is the conscience of Turkey - conservative in a religious sense - where the Ottoman tradition remains strong. Women at Konya University have finally achieved success in their demand legally to wear scarves in public buildings.

Konya serves as a centre for much of the surrounding Anatolian region. Although modern buildings are slowly pressing deeper into the old town, the spirit of the Ottoman Empire remains stronger here than anywhere else. Farmers bring their crops to market. Here are the workshops and repair shops, craft shops and small industry which support the entire region. The second source of income in Konya are the pilgrims and tourists. The traditional market town is on its way to becoming a venue for modern commercial fairs.

On the streets you can see tourists from Europe mixing with modern Turks, nomads from the high plains, veiled women, and Anatolian farmers. Be sure to respect the religious values of the people - in both dress and behavior. Many restaurants do not serve alcohol, and dining rooms are separate for men and women.

Unlike along the coast or in İstanbul, you will rarely see women walking alone. Pubs close early, and guards in brown uniforms keep a close eye on moral behavior.

History

As an oasis on the edge of the mountains, Konya was a perfect site for a settlement in the arid plains. There is evidence of continuous settlement since the early stone age. The town's castle mountain is *Hüyük* - a hill of rubble, created over thousands of years of habitation.

Four thousand years ago, the Hittite residents called their town Kuwanna; later the Phrygians would call it Kowania. There was also continuous occupation of the area during the Greek and Roman eras. During the Byzantine period Iconum (the Roman name) was a bishopric until the town was overrun and destroyed by the Arabs.

Under Seljuk rule, the town attained its full splendor. The arrival of the Seljuks, a Turkoman tribe pushing west from the Kirghiz steppe, marked the beginning of Islam in Anatolia. The empire built by the Seljuks, after their victory over Byzantium in the Battle of Manzikert in 1071, was the first Islamic inroad into Anatolia. For geographic and strategic reasons, Konya quickly became the capital of the new empire. The most splendid architecture dates from the sultanate of ALAEDDIN KEYKOBAT (1219 - 1236). Nothing remains, however, of the mighty walls with 108 towers which were erected at that time. Only one pillar remains of the one-time sultan's palace which was recently roofed with a concrete dome.

The most impressive architectural evidence of Seljuk rule are the caravanserais spread along the ancient trading routes. The largest existing caravanserai is *Sultanhan*, built in 1229 AD. It is on the road to Aksaray, 100 km east of Konya, and was built during the reign of ALAEDDIN KEYKOBAT.

In 1242 the Seljuks were defeated by the Mongols. During the Mongul era the viziers CELALEDDIN KARATAY and SAHIP ATA FAHREDDIN ALI were the most influential people in Konya.

Konya lost its importance during the reign of the Ottomans. The modern Turkish state established the city as provincial capital, and it grew to its present size.

THE ORDER OF THE WHIRLING DERVISHES

During the reign of sultan KEYKOBAT the philosopher CELALEDDIN RUMI founded the Mevlana Order in 1272 AD. It is better known as the Order of the Whirling Dervishes (Rumi was called *Mevlana* "Our Model" by his disciples). His teaching combined elements of Hellenic, Christian, Buddhist, and especially Islamic thought. His order achieved great influence in the sultan's court. The leader of the order was empowered to perform part of the ritual of enthronement by presenting the sword. This gave the order tremendous influence in the late Ottoman Empire, which it utilized shrewdly.

The order was very conservative and opposed any attempt to incorporate European social, political, or administrative forms in the Ottoman Empire. After the fall of the Ottoman Empire and the founding of the Turkish Republic, which the order tried to avert with all its might, it was prohibited by ATATÜRK in 1925, and its monastery was turned into a museum.

Sometimes, when visiting the museum in Konya, it seems as if the dervish spirit has come to life again. This is where modern politics mixes with Islamic tradition, which is no less radical than that of the Iranian mullahs.

The religious goal of the Mevlevis is the union of the soul with the Almighty, with Allah. This is achieved by ecstatic dance, to the accompaniment of a small orchestra - small drums, rebab (a two-stringed instrument without a neck), kemance, ney (an open-tubed flute), and a male choir. The dervishes would rotate in their flowing garments (the white costumes symbolized their funeral shrouds, the red cylindrical hats represented their tombstones) in an axis around the dance leader. The leader would turn in the opposite direction. This created a moving depiction of a star. This dance, known as *"Sema"*, sent the dancers into such ecstasy that they were in union with Allah. Dervishes are still dancing in Konya today: the *Sema* is performed annually in mid December at the **Mevlana Festival**.

INFORMATION: Mevlana Cad. 21, tel. 16255 or 11074.
TELEPHONE AREA CODE: 331

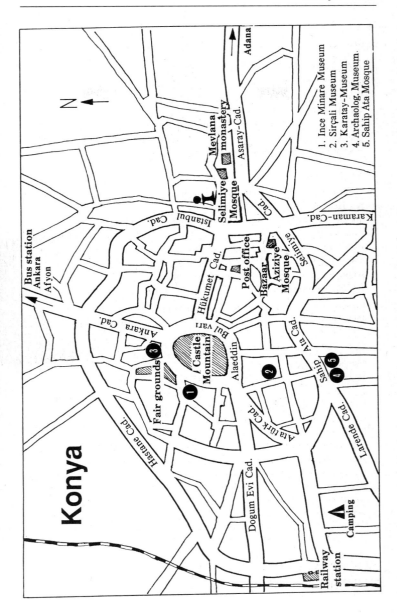

Konya

N

Adana

Meviana monastery
Selimiye Mosque
Asaray-Cad.

Istanbul Cad.

Karaman-Cad.

1. Ince Minare Museum
2. Sirçali Museum
3. Karatay-Museum
4. Archaolog. Museum
5. Sahip Ata Mosque

Bus station
Ankara
Afyon

Ankara Cad.

Hükumet Cad.

Post office

Bazaar
Aziziye
Mosque

Selimiye

Castle
Mountain

Alaeddin

Bul'vari

Ata Cad.

Fair grounds 3

1

2

Sahip
4 5

Hastane Cad.

Dogum Evi Cad.

Atatürk Cad.

Larende Cad.

Camping

Railway
station

A Night's Rest

If you prefer a central location, try lodgings on Hükümet Cad., Mevlana Cad., İstanbul Cad., or one of their side streets. There are cheap, simple pensions on the side streets off to the right of Hükümet Cad. (post office) and İstanbul Cad., costing £2.50 for a single and £4.50 for a double.

On the main roads Hükümet Cad./Mevlana Cad. are the best lodgings, single with shower/WC £7, or double with shower/WC £12. During festivals and fairs, rooms are difficult to find. We can recommend the following medium-priced hotels: **Saray-Hotel**, Mevlana Cad. 10, **Sema-Hotel**, Mevlana Cad. 8 and **Şahin-Hotel**, Hükümet Cad. 19 (more expensive).

Food

As mentioned above, do not expect to find alcoholic beverages in every Konya restaurant. Some travel guides suggest that if you insist, you will be served but that is not the case in Konya.
In Konya, hotels are frequently raided to make sure they don't serve alcohol. Tourists have nothing to fear, but your Turkish friends could pay a stiff fine. It is best if you refrain from drinking.

Along the main road Hükümet Cad./Mevlana Cad., there are a number of restaurants, which either offer a very limited menu, or have large European-style menus. I recommend the former. Food in Konya can be excellent, e.g. half a chicken with salad for £1, prepared in a small pub on Alaeddin Bul. There are a number of small locantas around the bazaar. If you like sweets, try the bakery and café next to the THY Office on Hükümet Cad.

Worth recommending is the restaurant **Zafer** on the southern slope of Alaeddin Hill. You can sit outside, and it is one of the few spots in town which serve alcohol. And the food is not bad.

On the castle hill, Alaeddin Tepesi, there are lovely tea gardens where young Turks gather. The obligatory video players are also there.

Fasting during the month of Ramadan is strictly observed in Konya. Many rstaurants are closed at this time.

Sights

Mevlana Monastery is a place of pilgrimage, and the primary sight in Konya. This is the resting place of the order's founder, his father, and his successor. The Monastery Museum is considered sacred by many believers; keep this in mind when visiting.
A number of MEVLANA'S personal belongings are on display in the monastery; hats, turbans and coats, plus several of his writings, written in the Persian language. Adjoining are monastic cells complete with furnishings, offering a glimpse of ascetic monastery life. This provides a contrast with the artistic objects, Koran scriptures, and valuable carpets on display in the monastery. You can also see dervish musical instruments including saz, flutes, violins and tambourines (Open: 9:30 - 18:00 h daily, Mondays 15:00 - 18.00 h).

Directly adjoining is the **Selimiye Mosque** dating from the reign of
SÜLEYMAN THE MAGNIFICENT (built about 1570) with two minarets.
Another interesting mosque is **Aziziye Mosque**, across the way in the
bazaar district. There are 14 mosques in the old town.

On the **Old Castle Hill** in the town centre is *Alaeddin Camii*, a 13th
century mosque, built by an Arab architect. The flat, wooden roof is
supported by 42 columns dating from Roman and Byzantine times.
Later a number of alterations were made. In Seljuk times, the palace
was located next to this mosque; today tea gardens are in its place.
Ruins of the ancient fortifications can still be seen on the castle hill.

The **Tile Museum** *(Karatay Müzesi)* is right next to the castle hill.
Inside, a number of lovely tiles from the Seljuk era are on display.

The **Museum of Seljuk Wood Carving** *(İnce Minare Müzesi)* is just a few
metres further on. The upper half of the minaret was cut off by a
thunderbolt - its name, *"Slim Minaret"*, no longer holds true. The
museum contains a lovely collection of statues and reliefs, depicting
people and animals.

The **Archaeological Museum** is a bit off to the side. The pride of the
exhibits are the sarcophagi dating from Roman times, including one
with reliefs depicting the deeds of HERCULES. There are also jewellery
and utensils from Hittite times (up to 3000 BC) and from earlier
periods of habitation.

Around Konya

Worth a visit is **Meram**, Konya's "garden". The town itself was not
built directly in the oasis; the green region was reserved for gardens
instead. Country homes and mansions eventually replaced the tiny
garden buildings. Today, this is a residential neighbourhood for the
wealthy, whose affluent homes are surrounded by lovely gardens.

Sille: A "carpet village" 10 km from Konya. There is actually little to
see, unless you are lucky enough to observe a girl hooking a carpet. If
you are thinking of buying a cheap carpet - sorry, no dice. The carpet
hookers do not own the carpets they make and cannot sell them.
They are hired only as home workers.

Karapınar: There is a volcanic field near this village, 100 km east of
Konya on the road to Adana. In the craters are small lakes filled with
sulphur-rich water. The scenery is bizarre and well worth a visit. If
you come with your own car, make a side trip into the steppe. The
paths through the fields can handle cars.

Beyşehir Gölü (Beyşehirv Lake): If you have had enough of city life, and would enjoy a swim, 95 km west of Konya on the road to Antalya/İsparta is a lake covering 650 sq km. The air is pleasantly cool, and the town of Beyşehir has a number of seafood restaurants (freshwater fish). This is a culinary delight after days of central Anatolian kebab. Drive 4 km along the lake from Beyşehir and you will reach a lovely beach with a small camping ground.

On the western shore of the lake, 60 km from Beyşehir, once stood the *Palace of Kubadabad*, which served as a summer residence for the Seljuk sultan ALAEDDIN KEYKOBAT. At the moment the grounds and its ruins are closed for excavation.

Çatalhöyük: This is a spot for those interested in prehistoric times. The settlement, excavated in 1961 by British archaeologist JAMES MELLAART, is perhaps the oldest town in the history of the world. 8000 years ago it was a Proto-Hattian settlement. There is little left to see in Çatalhöyük beyond the layout of the settlement. All the objects found were transported to Ankara for display in the Museum of Anatolian Civilization. There you can also see the reconstruction of a Proto-Hattian house with its entrance at the top.

Sultanhan: The largest and best preserved caravanserai in Anatolia, 100 km east of Konya on the road to Aksaray. If you are travelling along this ancient caravan route, be sure to stop for a closer look at its impressive architecture. The 120 m-long and 60 m-wide cara-vanserai was a Seljuk Grand Motel on the trading route to Kayseri. Passing through the impressively ornamented gate, you enter an inner courtyard with a mosque in the centre supported by four columns. In the halls to the left were a kitchen, bath, and shops. The three rooms right of the court, along with a five-aisled hall containing 32 columns, served as stables for the animals and a storehouse for wares. At dusk, endless rows of pack animals, swaying under heavy loads, would be lined up in the courtyard under the guidance of screaming drivers.

ATTENTION! The latest news: the governement in Ankara has drastically hiked up **admission fees** for museums, mosques etc. in 1989! Calculate about 5 - 10 times the prices given in this edition (depending upon the fame of the sights; for instance: admission for Hagia Sophia rose from £0.30 up to £3 !)

ANKARA   *(pop. 2,500,000)*

Like nowhere else in Turkey, the contradictions of modern life can be seen in the capital city.

Ankara was made the capital of Turkey with the founding of the Turkish Republic in 1923, and has grown rapidly ever since. There were two good reasons to make Ankara the new capital. First, İstanbul stood dangerously close to the military border. Secondly, ATATÜRK wanted a clean break with the Ottoman past. He saw Anatolia as the centre of the new Turkey, and thought that this was where the capital should be located. It should be a modern city free of ancient tradition.

Atatürk commissioned the German city planner HERMAN JANSEN to design a new capital in a town which had a population of just 30,000 in 1920. The main road is *Atatürk Bulvarı*, which begins below the ancient town centre - the fortress and castle mountain - leading to *Çankaya*, a modern, European residential district.

Today, Ankara consists of business, banking, and government administration. There is little industry. Only along the access roads can a few concrete factories be seen; they thrive on the city's rapid growth. Still, Ankara suffers from heavy air pollution. This is caused by its location in a valley, heating with brown coal, and the traffic.

City Panorama

Around *Ulus Square*, with its famous equestrian statue of Atatürk, is the old business quarter with bank buildings from the 1920s and 1930s and the bazaar. The old town stretches up the castle hill. To the south is the governmental district with its showcase buildings of the 1930s. Here you'll find the bustle of a major city. The cafés and fast food restaurants resemble those in any western country, but it is ten times more hectic. You can find your daily needs in the bazaar around Ulus.

In the most ancient part of the old town, below the castle, you might think you are in a small Anatolian town. Donkeys carry sacks, children play on the street, wool is bleached on the sidewalks, old men sit in front of small shops. It is very peaceful.

Heading south on *Atatürk Bulvarı*, we arrive at a green belt dividing the city. To the left is a park with lakes and a tea garden, with a sports stadium and horse race track in the background.

Across the train tracks is the modern city, Atatürk's Turkey. The roads fan out from Atatürk Bulvarı. To the left and right are modern business and shopping districts. The shops cater to European tastes, the streets have lost their bazaar character. At the centre of this district is *Kızılay Square*, built around a memorial in imitation Hittite style.

The boutiques on Atatürk Bulvarı could also be found in Munich, Milan, or Rome - and so could the prices. A T-shirt is twenty times as expensive as in the old town bazaar around Ulus. At the end of the boulevard is the diplomatic district, where fancy restaurants, bars, and apartment houses offer prices comparable to those in central Europe.

Within just a few kilometres we have moved from an Anatolian town to a western metropolis, but the people are the same. Just as you can expect to see western-clad people on the streets of the old town, you will find women dressed in traditional Anatolian costumes (perhaps of the finest silk) window-shopping the boutiques. In an air-conditioned bank, you might see an elderly Turk in cap and baggy pants being served by a young woman who could be found in any European city.

THE GECEKONDU DISTRICT

Standing on the castle mountain and looking east, you see countless tiny houses on the steep slopes, making up the Gecekondu District. This is the part of Ankara which Atatürk did not plan, but which just happened: poor sections of town which exist by right of Islamic law. According to the Koran, a person who builds a house on an unused parcel of land in one day becomes its rightful owner. That is why these buildings are called Gecekondu buildings (Gecekondu = "built overnight"). Many poor people from rural Anatolia, who came to Ankara to find work, found that they had no choice but to build such a shelter. These settlements can be seen around many Turkish cities. The government is forced to tolerate these districts built upon steep, barren slopes, where village activities, including the raising of fruit and vegetables, continues. The basic necessities can also be found here: simple shops, tea houses, locantas and barber shops. Two or three-room apartments are frequently crowded with three generations of an extended family. Many families are forced to survive on income from odd jobs, and children must help out by shining shoes or begging.

As their wealth increases, many families expand their dwellings bit by bit, building their tiny huts into lovely homes. The government has supplied the older districts with water and electricity, and built schools. New settlements are still being created on the outskirts of town, although the government tries to prevent it by every possible means.

History

Hittites lived here before 1200 BC. The name Ankara probably stems from the Phrygian settlement Ankyra, in 550 BC. Persia later conquered the town, and ruled until the arrival of ALEXANDER in 334 BC, which placed Ankara in the Greek sphere of influence. In the 3rd century BC, fearsome Celtic tribes were forced to resettle in the region. They made Ankara their capital, calling it Galatia. In the 2nd century BC, Asia Minor passed by right of inheritance into the Roman Empire. In 25 BC, Ankara was named capital of the central Anatolian province of Galatia.

In the 3rd century AD Ankara developed into the site of an important Christian community, seat of an archbishopric. Two councils were held here. Byzantine rule was shaken by Arab attacks in the 9th century, before being replaced by the Seljuk Empire. Crusaders recon

quered the town about 1100 AD, but the town remained Christian for only a century. In 1360, MURAD I conquered Ankara, placing it in the Ottoman Empire.

In 1401, TIMUR LENK - Tamerlane - conquered Ankara during his march west, disrupting the Ottoman Empire.

ONE SURVIVOR

According to historians, Timur Lenk hid his army in the endless pinewood forest around Ankara. Only one tree of this tremendous forest lives on today. It is called the Louis Pine, named for its "discoverer", located on Elma Dağ. The tree has been declared a natural monument, as a reminder of the once forested region which has been turned into steppe because of man.

After his victory, Timur took sultan BEYAZID prisoner and held Anatolia for 12 years. Sultan MEHMED I (1413 - 1421) managed to recapture Ankara.

After Greek troops invaded Anatolia in 1920, ATATÜRK founded the "Great National Assembly", and organized resistance with Ankara as his base.

As a traffic junction city, Ankara prospered, growing into a medium-sized town until it was named capital of Turkey in 1923.

506   Anatolia

INFORMATION: Gazi Mustafa Kemal Bulvarı 33, tel. 292930/95.
Small Tourist Information at the corner of İstanbul Cad./Cumhuriyet Bulvarı.

TELEPHONE AREA CODE: 4

COMING – GOING: **Bus station** on Hippodrom Cad. (easily accessible). Every agent
for Turkish bus companies has an office here. Buses hourly to every major town in
Turkey. Several companies offer rides to Iran or Arab nations. The major bus
companies have offices downtown around Gazi Mustafa Kemal Bulvarı and Kızılay.
Buses will take you from there to the bus station. "Blue buses" drive along Çankırı
Bulvarı at 20 minute intervals; they cost £0.15, you pay aboard the bus.

Taxi: The metre price from Ulus to the diplomatic quarter is £1.10.

Rail: Connection to all parts of the country. An express to İstanbul takes 8 hours. Be
sure to book advance reservations.

Flight Information: THY Office, Hippodrom Cad. (right off the Main Railway
Station), tel. 12 49 00 12 62 00. Buses to the airport from the THY (Turkish Airways
Office, ask about departure times there), costs £0.50. A taxi to the airport costs
£8.35 (bargain).

A Night's Rest

Lots of good, cheap hotels in the Ulus Quarter (old town). Public
transportation around town is excellent. Note: do not take a room
facing the road; Java motorcycles begin racing through town at 3:00 h
in the morning.

Olympiat Oteli, Rüzgarlı Eşdost Sok. 18 (by Çankırı Cad. 31), single with
shower/WC £7, double with shower/WC £9, very quiet hotel. tel. 24 30 88 - 24 33
31.

Taç Oteli, Çankırı Cad. 35, single £7, some without WC/showers, double £9,
some without WC/showers, tel. 24 31 95 - 11 16 63.

Otel Çetinkaya, Yıldırım Beyazıt Meydanı 3 (corner Çankırı Cad), single without
bath/WC £3, double without bath/WC £5.50, simple, clean.

Hotels in the upper price range can be found along Atatürk Bulvarı behind
Kızılay-Palaz, you pay £36 for a single, £24 for a double. The furnishings are
good, international newspapers are available.

Büyük-Ankara, Atatürk Bulvarı 183, one of the best hotels in town. The staff
speak English. tel. 34 49 20.

Bulvar-Palas, Atatürk Bulvarı 142, a single with shower/WC £36, a double with
shower/WC £24. Lovely hotel, nice place to stay, tel. 33 90 65.

Etap-Mola Oteli, Atatürk Bulvarı 80, medium priced hotel, centrally located, tel.
33 90 65.

Food

Eating, like sleeping, is reasonably priced around Ulus Square, with
fancy restaurants on Atatürk Boulevard.

If you are looking for classic Anatolian food, try the bazaar above Ulus
Square. Lots of small pubs are ready to demonstrate their skills.
On Çankırı Cad. are a number of nice pubs, some of which are quite

Akköprü

Hotels

Gecekondu district

Hippodrom

İstanbul Cad.

Kazım Karabekir Cad.

Canciri Cad.

Hotels

Cumhuriyet Bul.

stadium

GENÇLİK-PARK

Talat Paşa Bul.

Maltepe

Cemal Gürsel Cad.

ATATÜRK-
MAUSOLEUM

Necati bey Cad.

Atatürk Cad.

Ziya Gökalp C.

Yenisehir

modern shopping centre

airline offices

boutiques

embassy district

Ankara

Kavaklidere

1. Ulus Square
2. Castle
3. Roman Baths
4. Post office
5. Julian Column
6. Augustus Temple
7. Archeolog. Museum
8. Ethnograph. Museum
9. Hospital
10. Kizilay Square
11. Museum of Fine Arts
12. Bus station
13. THY office
14. Railway station

Syrian embassy

├─ 1 km ─┤

fancy with prices to match. On Ulus Square is a kebab stand clad in marble, snobbishness à la Ankara (corner Çankırı/Cumuriyet Cad.).

I really enjoyed the sweets in Ankara's outstanding bakeries. Have breakfast in one of these cafés.

Shopping

Visit the bazaar in the multi-storied shopping centres above Ulus Square. The selection caters to local consumers, and is remarkably cheap.

European-style clothes can be found south of Kızılay Square. Cheapest are the bazaar-like department stores left of Atatürk Bulvarı. You will find all the European brands of clothing, some very cheap. If they are extremely cheap, e.g. a Lacoste T-shirt for £1, they are probably fakes.

The high-class boutiques on Atatürk Bulvarı cater to an international clientele. Italian-style sneakers can cost £35, a price beyond the means of 90 per cent of the Turkish population. But window shopping is free.

Tip: If you plan to buy big, have the wares declared for export in one of the department stores. You can then bargain a 15 per cent discount (value-added tax rebate).

Meeting Places

The best places to meet people in Ankara, or just to watch people passing by, are the parks. Gençlik Park has lovely grounds with a small lake where you can rent a row boat. There are a number of tea gardens, stands, and pubs in the park where you can relax and watch. There is a nominal admission price to the park. A similar meeting spot is the small park on Kızılay Square.

The tea gardens up at the castle offer a lovely view, and are one of the quietest spots in this bustling city. This is where tourist meets tourist.

In the evening, you might head to Kavaklıdere (in the diplomatic quarter) to visit a disco or pub. Admission is about £2, but nothing special is offered. Never ask a Turkish woman to dance, no matter how she is dressed or behaves - somebody in the disco is certain to explode!

If this is all too complicated, go to Cebeci, in the student quarter. Here you will find a number of pubs, and meet some interesting people. By the way, students usually call it a night about 23:00 h.

Sights

Despite - or rather because of - its violent history, Ankara has few historic sights today. What the victor destroyed was rarely rebuilt.

White Castle (*Ak Kale*) in the north of town is the most ancient settlement in Ankara. The castle ruins date from Byzantine times, but the layers of rock in its foundations are certainly much older. Alterations made in the Seljuk, Mongol, and Ottoman eras can be recognized. Notice how columns and reliefs from Roman temples were incorporated. A tour of the castle might seem like mountain climbing, but the view makes it worthwhile.

Excavations of a **Roman theatre** are under way below the castle. While it is easy to observe the excavation, do not disturb the archaeologists at work. In the old town below the castle, notice the lovely old Ottoman buildings with their wooden frames.

Not far from the castle are the Temple of Augustus, Julian's Column and the Roman Baths. The **Temple of Augustus** is famous for the plaque containing an account written by AUGUSTUS just before his death. Nowhere else in the world is it so well preserved as here. The text was discovered by MOMMSEN in the 19th century. During the Christian era the temple was converted to a church. About 1400 AD a mosque, in honour of the town's saints, was built next door.

Julian's Column, 14.5 m tall, dates from 360 AD and was built to commemorate a visit by the Emperor JULIAN.

The **Roman baths** were excavated in 1926 when plans called for construction of defence ministry offices on the grounds. The baths were built in the 3rd century AD for public use. The foundations are easy to identify, including bathing rooms, dressing rooms, and swimming pools. Notice the ingenious installation of running water and floor heating. It is easy to imagine how nice this bath must have been.

The most interesting mosque is **Arslan Hane Camii**, built with donated funds in 1289. In the front courtyard is an ancient statue of a lion (arslan = lion). The wooden ceiling was supported by 24 columns with Roman capitals. Notice the decorative prayer niche and carvings.

A visit to Ankara is not complete without a stop at the **Atatürk Mausoleum**. Notice how Turkish pilgrims revere him as a saint. Leading to the mausoleum is an ancient 250 m showcase street lined with stone lions carved in Hittite style. Next to the mausoleum is a museum containing pertinent objects including Atatürk's car.

*Depiction of Hittite warriors
(Hittite Museum, Ankara)*

Museums

Ankara has many museums, all centrally located and easy to reach.

Hittite Museum (*Anadolu Medeniyetleri Müzesi*): One of the world's largest and most beautiful collections of pieces from early civilization. The museum is set in an old bazaar adjoining a caravanserai. The pride of the show are the Hittite stone reliefs in the central hall. But other cultures important to Anatolia are also represented, from early stone age tools to mother goddesses, gold jewellery, and animal depictions dating from early Greek times.

Ethnographic Museum: Here you can see arts and crafts from the Ottoman era. Furniture and jewellery from religious sites and private households provide an in-depth look into the Ottoman Empire. Be sure to pay a visit.

Museum of the Turkish Republic (on Ulus Meydanı): Dedicated to the liberation and founding of modern Turkey. There are two cannons in the garden. This is the building in which the first Turkish parliament met. On display are documents, pictures, maps, and weapons from the 1920-1923 war. You can look into Atatürk's simple office and the first meeting hall. The days of early Turkey are brought to life. Of special interest to the historically inclined.

Museum of Visual Arts: Here you can see paintings by major Turkish artists. Of interest to art enthusiasts are the works combining Turkish and European styles. Few of these artists are known abroad, making this well worth a visit.

MUSEUM OPENING HOURS: 9:30 - 12:00 h and 14:00 - 17:00 h, closed Mondays.

Hattuşa - *Capital of the Hittite Empire*

Almost nothing was known of the Hittites until the turn of the century. Even today, there is no agreement as to the origin of these Indo-European people who created the first high culture in Anatolia.

Credit for bringing forth the Hittites from the misty past must go to the German HUGO WINCKLER, a cuneiform writing expert with a position at a university in Berlin. His contemporaries viewed Winckler as a grouchy and eccentric pighead. Hugo Winckler did not like Anatolian cooking, and he could not put up with the hot climate. In 1906, the Berlin professor left his comfortable environs to lead excavation of the field of ruins already found near the present-day town of *Bogazkale* (also Boğazköy). Later he would prove that this was Hattuşa, capital of the Hittite Empire. Winckler's motivation was a clay tablet covered with cuneiform writing which had been sent to him in Berlin. Etched into the clay was writing in the Hittite language.

Eager to find more such tablets, Winckler motivated the village people to dig for the tablets at a feverish pace, more in line with treasure hunting than serious archaeology. Modern archaeologists can only shake their heads at his stupidity. But Winckler did manage to uncover thousands of the tablets: he had discovered the Hittite National Archives. Once the cuneiform was deciphered, it was easy to reconstruct Hittite history using the information from thousands of the clay tablets.

Most of the finds from the Hattuşa excavations - reliefs, vases, statues, bronze figurines - are on display at the Museum of Anatolian Civilization (Hittite Museum) in Ankara. A few of the objects can be seen at the museum in Boğazkale.

OPEN: 08.00 - 12.00, 13.30 - 18.00 h daily.

History: After a long military conflict with the previous inhabitants of Anatolia the Hittites, probably arriving from the east, founded their empire (Old Hittite Empire) in the 17th century BC. During the reign of the second king, HATTUSHILI I, a permanent capital was established at Hattuşa. It would remain the political centre of the empire for almost four continuous centuries.

In the 16th century BC the Hittites marched southeast and conquered Babylon. In the 14th century BC, after a long period of domestic squabbling, King SHUPPILULIUMA reconsolidated the realm as the New Hittite Empire. Treaties signed with Egypt, a superpower at the time, are preserved in cuneiform on clay tablets testifying to the glorious Hittite past. In the 12th century BC, the Hittite Empire was conquered by invading forces. The capital Hattuşa was destroyed in a tremendous fire.

The Excavations

The exact population of Hattuşa is unknown. At the time of the Hittite Empire's greatest territorial expansion, during the reign of King SHUPPILULIUMA (1380 - 1348 BC), Hattuşa was one of the largest cities in the Near East. If you want to walk all the way across this ruined city, calculate three hours. It is easier to take a taxi or drive yourself.

The first thing you see when approaching from Boğazkale is a large **temple complex**, which in Hittite times was divided by a road. Only the foundations of the temple's archives and magazine halls survive. It is known, however, that the buildings were several stories tall. Several thousand clay tablets inscribed with cuneiform writing have been discovered here and shipped away to museums for transcription. Remaining at the site are huge clay barrels - you will notice them immediately - some of which have a capacity of 3000 liters. It is not known what the Hittites stored in them.

From the temple complex a path leads south, up to the **town walls**, built upon a big, man-made wall of earth. Here, at the western end of the (still intact) southern bend of the wall, is the **Lion's Gate** with its two mighty stone lions. They were designed to protect the town from all evil. One of the statues is missing its head; the other is well preserved - except for the missing fangs.

The path leads along the town wall to **Yer Kapı** (Earth Gate), located at the highest and southernmost part of the town. This is the best spot for a look over the entire town. Posted left and right of the gate were two limestone sphinxes, one of which is now in İstanbul, the other in Berlin. The importance of Yer Kapı for the town's defence can be seen in a steep, 70 m long tunnel leading outside, at the outer end of which were seats for the guards. Notice how the tunnel was constructed: Unlike other contemporary civilizations, the Hittites had yet to discover the arch.

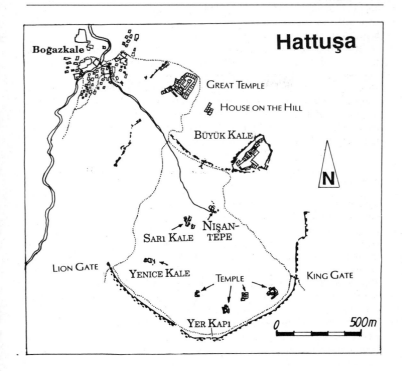

Further along the town wall we come to the **King's Gate**, named for the sculpture at its entrance. It was later discovered that the "gate watchman" was not a king, but rather a god. Visiting today, we see a painstakingly exact copy of the original, which is on display in the Museum of Anatolian Civilization in Ankara. It is the best preserved monumental sculpture dating from the New Hittite Empire.

At the King's Gate the path moves away from the wall, leading to **Büyükkale** (Great Castle), once the residence of the Hittite ruler, accessible via stone stairs. The castle is surrounded by mighty walls, which in the east follow the natural cliff. Inside the Büyükkale are a number of individual buildings separated by expansive courtyards. In addition to cult facilities and a large audience hall, this was the site of the national archives with thousands of cuneiform tablets. Most famous of these was the treaty between Emperors HATTUSHILI III and RAMSES II of Egypt in 1270 BC. This document, whose duplicate had been found at an excavation site in Egypt, was the key to proving that

Hattuşa was truly capital of the Hittite Empire.
Our tour ends above the entrance to the temple complex mentioned earlier.

The Rock Sanctuary at Yazılıkaya

Coming from Sungurlu, turn left at the entrance to Boğazkale and you are 2 km from the most famous Hittite religious sanctuary. In two natural rock chambers, open at the top, numerous reliefs were discovered, some of which were well preserved. In Hittite times a temple stood nearby.

In the largest of the two chambers you can see an entire parade of deities. By the hieroglyphics and more particularly their characters (winged sun, sickle moon, sword, club, etc.) it has been possible to determine which deities are depicted. On the opposite wall is a colossal royal relief depicting the Hittite King TUTHALIJA IV in priestly dress.

The entrance of the smaller chamber is guarded by winged demons with threatening claws. It is best known for its well-preserved reliefs depicting the "Twelve Gods". On the opposite wall a meeting of the Sword God and the above-mentioned Emperor Tuthalija IV is shown. Since the "Twelve Gods" and the Sword God belong to the underworld, it is assumed that this chamber served a cult of the dead.

Photo Tip: The best time to take pictures of the reliefs is from 12:00 - 13:00 h.

TELEPHONE AREA CODE: 4557

COMING - GOING: Daily buses from Ankara to Sungurlu with Sungurlu Ekspres and Es-Sungurlu. From Sungurlu to Boğazkale (28 km) by local bus (hourly 9 to 17 h), or by minibus or taxi.

A NIGHT'S REST / CAMPING:

Hitit Motel (Sungurlu), in the centre to the right of the road, double £6. Adequate comfort, all rooms with showers, swimming pool. A bit loud as buses depart in front of the hotel. tel. 1042.

Mocamp Aşıkoğlu (Boğazkale), at the entrance to town, double £6. Open March to October. Clean, modest rooms, lovely location, terrace, shaded seats in the garden. The camp ground behind the motel offered less than attractive sanitary facilities. tel. 1444.

Başkent Camping (Boğazkale), Left of the town entrance, turn left toward Yazılıkaya. There are plans to expand the mocamp. At the moment, it is a small, shaded area with sanitary facilities and a small restaurant.

FOOD: **Motel Asıkoğlu** (Boğazkale), at the entrance to town. The food is good. The dry white wine from Sungurlu tastes excellent.

LANGUAGE GUIDE

The Turkish language utilizes Latin characters. However, there are several letters which either do not exist in English, or are pronounced differently:

a, A	= **ah** as in b**a**r
e, E	= **eh** as in **e**nd
i, İ	= **ee** as in **i**diot
ı, I	= **uh** as in s**i**r
o, O	= **oh** as in l**o**rd
u, U	= **oo** as in bl**ue**
ü, Ü	= **ew** as in f**ew** or like the German "ü"
c, C	= **j** as in **j**ail
ç, Ç	= **ch** as in **ch**ange
g, G	= **g** as in **g**un. Never soft as in general!!
h, H	= **h** as in **h**eart
j, J	= **zh**, like a French "j"
s, S	= **ss** as in be**s**t or mo**s**t (sharply pronounced)
ş, Ş	= **sh** as in **sh**ort

The grammar is logical, but unlike Indo-European languages. Common among Ural-Altaic languages, which include Finnish, Hungarian, and Mongolian in addition to Turkish, is *agglutination*. The grammatical variations of a root word are formed by suffixes. These suffixes usually follow a pattern of vowel harmony; in other words they change according to the vowel in the preceding syllable. Short vowels are: a, ı, o, u, long vowels are: e, i ö, ü.

Sample Suffixes

Root + plural suffix "-**ler**/-**lar**":

kitap	book
otel	hotel
kitaplar	books
oteler	hotels

possessive suffix 1st person singular "-(i/ı/u/ü)m":

kitaplarım	my books

Where

In answer to the question "where?" ("*nerede*?") use the suffix "-**de**/-**da**":

in İstanbul	İstanbul'**da**
in the hotel	otel**de**

In answer to the question "where to?"("*nereye?*") use the suffix "-**e**/-**a**":

   to İstanbul   İstanbul'**a**
   to the hotel   otel**e**

In answer to the question "where from?" ("*nereden?*") use the suffix "-**den**/-**dan**":

   from İstanbul   İstanbul'**dan**
   from the hotel otel**den**

"with" is expressed with the suffix "-**li**/-**lı**/-**lu**/-**lü**":

   şeker   sugar
   şeker**li**   with sugar

"without" is expressed with the suffix "-**siz**/-**sız**/-**suz**/-**süz**":

   iş   work
   iş**siz**   unemployed (without work)

Order of words:

Usually at first the noun, then the verb:

   Bir otel nerede? - where is a hotel? (read as: "a hotel were is?")

General Expressions

yes	*evet*	eh-veht
yes(there is)	*var*	vahr
no	*hayır*	hah-yuhr
no (there isn't)	*yok*	yohk
is there ...?	*... var mı?*	vahr-muh
where is the/a...?	*nerede?*	neh-reh-deh?
and	*ve*	veh
or	*veya*	veh-yah
good	*iyi*	ee
bad	*fena*	feh-nah
pretty	*güzel*	gew-zehl
big	*büyük*	bew-yewk
small	*küçük*	kew-chewk
welcome	*hoş geldiniz*	hohsh-gehldee-neez
(answer:	*hoş bulduk*)	hohsh-bool-dook
good morning	*günaydın*	gewn-eye-duhn
good day, hello	*merhaba*	mehr-hah-bah
good evening	*iyi akşamlar*	ee-yee ahk-shahm-lahr
good night	*iyi geceler*	ee-yee geh-jeh-lehr
good luck	*bol şans*	bohl shahnss

good bye	*allahaısmar ladik!*	ahllah-hahuhs-mahr lah-deek
shortened to (departing person):	*alas maldık*	ahlahss-mahl-duhk
(staying person):	*güle güle*	gewleh-gewleh
thank you very much	*teşekkür ederim*	teh-sheh-kewr ehdeh-reem
thanks!	*teşekkürler! mersi!*	teh-sheh-kewr-lehr mehr-ssee
no thank you	*hayır, teşekkür ederim!*	hah-juhr, teh-she-kewr-ehdeh-reem
please	*lütfen*	lewt-fehn
pardon?	*efendim?*	eh-fehn-deem?
excuse me (after stepping on a foot)	*pardon*	pahr-dohn
excuse me (before asking for s.th.)	*affedersiniz*	ah-feh-dehr-see-neez
how are you?	*nasılsınız?*	nahssuhl-suh-nuhz
very good	*çok iyiyim*	chohk eeyee-yeem
of course	*tabii*	tah-beeh
all right (o.k.)	*tamam*	tah-mahm
perhaps	*belki*	behl-kee
good (closing a subject)	*oldu*	ohl-doo
How do you say this in Turkish?	*Bunun Türkçesi ne?*	boo-noon tewrk-cheh-see neh?
Do you speak English?	*İngilizce bilir misiniz?*	Eengee-lees-jeh bee-leer mee-see-neez?
I did not understand	*anla madım*	ahn-lah mah-duhm
How many Lira?	*kaç lira?*	kahch leerah?
give me	*bana verin*	bah-nah veh-reen
I would like	*istiyorum*	eest-yoh-room

Health

doctor	*doktor*	dohk-tohr
hospital	*hastane*	hah-stah-neh
band aids	*flaster*	flah-stehr
charcoal tablets	*karbon tableti*	kahr-bohn tah-bleh-tee
pain killers	*agrı hapı*	aree hah-puh

pain	agrılar	aree-lahr
head	baş	bahsh
eye	göz	gurz
ear	kulak	koo-lahk
tooth	diş	deesh
throat	bogaz	boh-ahz
chest	gögüs	gur-ewss
stomach	mide	mee-deh
back	şirt	sheert
heart	kalp	kahlp
liver	karaciger	kah-rah-jee-ehr
kidneys	böbrekler	bur-brehk-lehr
insect bite	böcek sokması	bur-jehk sohk

Numbers

0	= sıfır	suh-fuhr
1/2 (isolated)	= yarım	yah-ruhm
(in 1 1/2 etc.)	= buçuk	boo-chook
1	= bir	beer
2	= iki	ee-kee
3	= üç	ewch
4	= dört	durrt
5	= beş	behsh
6	= altı	ahl-tuh
7	= yedi	yeh-dee
8	= sekiz	seh-keez
9	= dokuz	doh-kooz
10	= on	ohn
11	= on bir	ohn-beer
20	= yirmi	yeer-mee
30	= otuz	oh-toos
40	= kırk	kuhrk
50	= elli	eh-lee
60	= altmış	ahlt-muhsh
70	= yetmiş	yeht-meesh
80	= seksen	sehk-sehn
90	= doksan	dohk-sahn
100	= yüz	yews
101	= yüz bir	yews-beer
200	= iki yüz	ee-kee yewz
300	= üç yüz	ewch yewz
1000	= bin	been
2000	= iki bin	ee-kee been
10.000	= on bin	ohn-been

Time		
yesterday	*dün*	dewn
today	*bugün*	boo-gewn
tomorrow	*yarın*	yahr-uhn
day after		
tomorrow	*öbürgün*	ur-bewr-gewn
hour	*saat*	saht
hourly	*her saat*	hehr-saaht
day	*gün*	gewn
daily	*her gün*	hehr-gewn
week	*hafta*	hahf-tah
weekly	*her hafta*	hehr hahf-tah
month	*ay*	ahy
year	*sene, yıl*	seh-neh, yuhl
morning	*sabah*	ssah-bahh
afternoon	*ögleden sonra*	ur-leh-dehn sohn-rah
evening	*akşam*	ahk-shahm
afterward	*sonra*	sohn-rah
the next	*gelecek*	geh-leh-jehk
when?	*ne zaman?*	neh zah-mahn?
what time is it?	*saat kaç?*	saht kahch?
at what time?	*saat kaçta?*	saht kahch-tah?

Weekdays and Months

Sunday	*pazar*	pah-zahr
Monday	*pazartesi*	pah-zar-teh-see
Tuesday	*salı*	sahluh
Wednesday	*çarşamba*	chahr-shahm-bah
Thursday	*persembe*	pehr-sehm-beh
Friday	*cuma*	coo-mah
Saturday	*cumartesi*	joo-mahr-teh-see
January	*ocak*	oh-jahk
February	*subat*	soo-baht
March	*mart*	mahrt
April	*nisan*	nee-ssahn
May	*mayıs*	mah-yuhs
June	*haziran*	hah-zee-rahn
July	*temmuz*	tehm-mooz
August	*agustos*	ah-oos-tohs
September	*eylül*	ehy-ewl

October	*ekim*	eh-keem
November	*kasım*	kah-ssuhm
December	*aralık*	ahrah-luhk

Travelling

airport	*havaalanı*	hah-vah-lah-nuh
harbour	*liman*	lee-mahn
centre of town	*şehir merkezi*	sheh-heer mehr-keh-zee
Tourist Infor mation Office	*turizm bürosu*	too-reezm bew-roh-soo
ocean	*deniz*	deh-neez
a good hotel	*iyi bir otel*	eeyee beer oh-tehl
square	*meydan*	mehy-dahn
street	*cadde*	jahd-deh
road, alley	*sokak*	soh-kahk
where?	*nerede?*	neh-reh-deh?
where to?	*nereye?*	neh-reh-yeh?

Questions on the Road

where is the/a...?	*nerede?*	neh-reh-deh?
train station	*gar / istasyon*	gahr/eestah-syohn
bus station	*otogar*	oh-toh-gahr
cheap hotel	*ucuz bir otel*	oo-jooz beer oh-tehl
police station	*karakol*	kah-rah-kohl
post office	*postane*	poh-stah-neh
bank	*banka*	bahn-kah
Turkish bath	*hamam*	hah-mahm
toilet	*tuvalet*	too-vah-leht
left	*sol*	sohl
right	*sag*	sah
straight	*dogru*	doh-roo
back	*geri*	geh-ree
here	*burada*	boo-rah-dah
there	*orada*	oh-rah-dah
nearest	*enyakın*	ehn-yah-kuhn
is it far?	*uzak mı?*	oozahk muh?
street, path	*yol*	yohl

Rail / Bus / Taxi

train station	*gar, istasyon*	gahr, ee-stah-ssyohn
train	*tren*	trehn
sleeping car	*vagonli*	vah-gohn-lee

couchette	*kuşet*	koo-sheht
dining car	*vagon-restoran*	vah-gohn-reh-stoh-rahn
conductor	*biletçi*	bee-leht-chee
bus station	*otogar*	oh-toh-gahr
bus	*otobüs*	oh-toh-bews
baggage	*bagaj*	bah-gahj
platform		
(also for bus)	*peron*	peh-rohn
departure	*hareket, kalkış*	hah-reh-keht,kahl-kuhsh
arrival	*varış*	vah-ruhsh
ticket	*bilet*	bee-leht
schedule	*tarife*	tah-ree-feh
stop	*durak*	doo-rahk
ticket window	*gişe*	gee-sheh
collective taxi	*dolmuş*	dohl-moosh
taxi	*taksi*	tahk-see

Air / Ship

airport	*havaalanı*	hah-vaah-lahnuh
flight	*uçuş*	oo-choosh
airplane	*uçak*	oo-chahk
ship	*gemi*	geh-mee
ferry	*feribot*	feh-ree-boht
dock	*iskele*	eess-keh-leh
small rowboat		
or sailboat	*kayık*	kah-yuhk

Accomodation

In the Hotel

a room	*bir oda*	beer oh-dah
two people	*iki kişi*	eekee kee-shee
a double	*çift yataklı bir oda*	cheeft yah-tahk-luh beer ohdah
room with bath	*banyolu bir oda*	bahn-yoh-loo beer oh-dah
room with shower	*duşlu bir oda*	doosh-loo beer oh-dah
Is there hot water?	*Sıcak su var mı?*	Suh-jahk soo vahr muh?
How much does		
it cost?	*Ne kadar?*	neh kah-dahr?
very expensive	*çok pahalı*	chohk pah-hah-luh

Can you show me a different room?	*Bana başka bir oda gösterir misiniz?*	bah-nah bash-kah beer oh-dah gur-steh-reer mee-see-neez?
all right	*tamam*	tah-mahm
cheaper	*daha ucuz*	dah-hah oo-jooz
the bill	*hesap*	heh-sahp
full board	*tam pansiyon*	tahm pahn-seeyohn
half board	*yarım pansiyon*	yah-ruhm pahn-seeyohn
breakfast	*kahvaltı*	kaah-vahl-tuh
butter	*tereyağı*	teh-reh-yahuh
coffee	*kahve*	kah-veh
tea	*çay*	chahy
milk	*süt*	sewt
sugar	*şeker*	sheh-kehr

Camping

Camp ground	*kamp yeri*	kahmp yeh-ree
tent	*çadır*	chah-duhr
shower	*duş*	doosh
site	*yer*	yehr
shady	*gölgeli*	gurl-geh-lee
kitchen	*mutfak*	moot-fahk

In a Restaurant

(call the waiter)	*Bakar mısınız!*	bah-kahr muh-suh-nuhz
breakfast	*kahvahltı*	kaah-vaahl-tuh
lunch	*öğle yemeği*	urleh
dinner	*akşam yemeği*	ahk-shahm yeh-meh-ee
meal	*yemek*	yeh-mehk
serving, portion	*porsyon*	pohr-syohn
fork	*çatal*	chah-tahl
knife	*bıçak*	bee-chahk
spoon	*kaşik*	kah-sheek
plate	*tabak*	tah-bahk
glass	*bardak*	bahr-dahk
bread	*ekmek*	ehk-mehk
water	*su*	soo
mineral water	*madensuyu*	mah-dehn-soo-yoo
ice	*buz*	booz
meat	*et*	eht
mutton	*koyun eti*	kohyoon ehtee
lamb	*kuzu eti*	koo-zoo ehtee
beef	*sığır eti*	suh-uhr ehtee

veal	*dana eti*	dah-nah ehtee
chicken	*piliç*	pee-leech
fish	*balık*	bah-luhk
the bill please	*hesap, lütfen*	heh-sahp, lewt-fehn
service charge	*servis ücreti*	sehr-vees ewj-reh-tee
tip	*bahşiş*	baah-sheesh
tax	*vergi*	vehr-gee
mistake	*yanlış*	yahn-luhsh
change	*bozuk para*	boh-sook pah-rah

Shopping

How much is it?	*Bu ne kadar?*	Boo neh kah-dahr?
That is very expensive!	*Çok pahalı!*	chohk pah hahluh
I will give you	*verecegim*	veh-reh-je-eem
I don't like it!	*Bunu begenmiyorum*	Boonoo beh-ehn-mee-yohroom
Is it old?	*Bu eski mi?*	Boo ehskee mee?
tax	*vergi*	vehr-gee
service charge	*servis ücreti*	sehr-vees ewj-reh-tee
book	*kitap*	kee-tahp
carpet	*halı*	hahluh
brass	*pirinç*	pee-reench
gold	*altın*	ahl-tuhn
silver	*gümüş*	gew-mewsh
leather	*deri*	deh-ree
copper	*bakır*	bah-kuhr
shop, business	*dükkan*	dewk-kahn
money	*para*	pah-rah
small change	*bozuk para*	boh-zook pah-rah
Turkish Lira	*lira*	lee-rah
dollar	*dolar*	doh-lahr
road map	*yol haritası*	yohl hahree-tahsuh
city map	*şehir planı*	sheh-heer plahnuh
pen	*kalem*	kah-lehm
lighter	*çakmak*	chahk-mahk
matches	*kibrit*	keeb-reet
a pack of cigarettes with	*bir paket*	beer pah-keht
filter cigarettes	*filtreli sigara*	feel-treh-lee see-gah-rah
without filter	*filtresiz sigara*	feel-treh-seez see-gah-rah

Shops

market	*pazar*	pah-zahr
bazaar		
(permanent market)	*çarşı*	chahr-shuh
chemist's shop	*eczane*	ehj-zah-neh
book shop	*kitapçı*	kee-tahp-chuh
bakery	*pastahane*	pahstah-hah-neh
grocery store	*bakkal*	bahk-kahl
travel agency	*seyahat acentası*	seh-yah-haht ahjehn-tah-suh

At the Post Office

pen	*açık*	ahch-uhk
closed	*kapalı*	kah-pah-luh
special delivery	*ekspres*	ehks-prehs
customs	*gümrük*	gewm-rewk
telephone coins	*jeton*	jeh-tohn
(large/small)	(*büyük, küçük*)	(bew-yewk, kew-chewk)
post cards	*kartpostal*	kahrt-poh-stahl
letter	*mektup*	mehkt-oop
stamps	*pul*	pool
air mail	*uçakla*	oochah-klah
Is there mail	*Benim için posta*	Beh-neem eejeen pohstah
for me?	*var mı?*	vahr muh?
my name is....	*Adım ...*	Ahd-uhm

Driving

General

driver's license	*ehliyet*	eh-hlee-yeht
insurance		
certificate	*sigorta kartı*	see-gohr-tah kahr-tuh
petrol station	*benzin istasyonu*	behn-zeen eestah-see-oh-noo
	/ benzinci	/ behn-zee-nee-jee
petrol	*benzin*	behn-zeen
diesel	*mazot*	mah-zoht
I'd like 15 liters	*15 litre süper*	15 leetreh sew-pehr
of super	*istiyorum*	eestee-yoh-room
motor oil	*motör yagi*	moh-tur yah-ee

lubricate	yaglamak	yah-lah-mahk
breakdown	ariza	ah-ree-zah
accident	kaza	kah-zah
service station	tamirhane	tah-meer-hah-neh
	/tamirci	/ tahmeer-jee
Where is a		
service station?	tamirhane nerede?	tahmeer-hah-neh neh-reh-deh?
it doesn't work	çalışmıyor	chah-luhsh muh-yohr
it leaks	damlıyor	dahm-luh-yohr
how much		
does it cost?	ne kadar?	neh kah-dahr?

Auto Parts

starter	marş	mahrsh
car battery	akü	ah-kew
turn signal	sinyal	seen-yahl
brakes	frenler	frehn-lehr
brake lights	stop lambaları	lahmbah lah-ruh
transmission	şanjman	shahnj-mahn
radiator	radyatör	rah-dy-ah-tur
clutch	debreyaj	deh-breh-jahy
dynamo	şarj dinamosu	shahrj dee-nah-moh-soo
motor	motör	moh-tur
tyres	lastik	lahs-teek
carburetor	karbüratör	kahr-bewr-ah-tur
spark plugs	bujiler	boo-jee-lehr
idle	boş vites	bohsh vee-tehs
put in gear	vitese takmak	vee-teh-seh tahk-mahk
reverse	geri vites	geh-ree vee-tehs

EATING OUT DICTIONARY

Appetizers ("mezeler")

Arnavut cigeri	fried liver with onions
Beyazpeynir	sheep's cheese
Börek	puff pastry
Çerkes tavugu	chicken meat in walnut sauce
Kabak dolması	stuffed pumpkin
Midye dolması	stuffed clams
Patlıcan salatası	mashed eggplant
Tarama	roe salad
Yaprak dolması	stuffed vine leaves

Soups ("çorbalar")

Dügün çorbası	soup with mutton goulash, egg, and lemon
Ezo gelin corbasi	lentil and rice soup
Haşlama	mutton in broth
İskembe çorbası	tripe soup
Yayla çorbası	yoghurt soup

Meat Dishes ("etli yemekler")

Bonfile	beef steak
Döner kebap	mutton roasted on a spit
Kuzu dolması	lamb stuffed with rice
Pirzola	lamb chops
Şiş kebap	grilled lamb
Şiş köfte	grilled meat balls
Çig köfte	spicy meatballs of raw ground beef
Lahmacun	ground beef on flat bread ("Turkish pizza")
Güveç	meat-vegetable stew
Taş kebap	lamb stew
Tavuk	chicken
Ciger tavası	fried mutton liver
Kabak dolması	zucchini stuffed with ground beef (Dolma-specialty: various vegetables stuffed with ground beef)

Rice Dishes ("pilav")

İç pilav	rice with liver and currants
Bulgur pilavı	cream of wheat
Patlıcanlı pilav	rice with eggplant

Cold Vegetable Dishes in Olive Oil ("zeytinyağlı")

İlmam bayıldı	stuffed eggplant in olive oil
Kabak kızartması	fried zucchini slices in yoghurt
Patlıcan kızartması	fried eggplant slices in yoghurt
Zeytinyağlı fasulye	white beans in olive oil and tomato sauce

Fish ("balık")

Alabalık	trout
Barbunya	red barbel
Dil balığı	sole
Hamsi	anchovy (fresh)
Karides	shrimp
Kılıç	swordfish
Levrek	perch
Midye	clams
Palamut	small tuna fish, bonito
Pisi	plaice
Sardalye	sardines (fresh)
Tarama	roe salad
Tranca	Aegean tuna fish
Uskumru	mackerel
Yengeç	lobster

Salad ("salatalar")

Cacık	yoghurt with cucumber and garlic
Çoban salatası	mixed salad with tomato, cucumber, onion
Patlıcan salatası	mashed eggplant
Piyaz	salad with white beans
Domates salatası	tomato salad
Salata	green salad
Kış turşuları	pickled salads in vinegar-water mixture

Side Dishes

Barbunya	red beans
Bezelye	peas
Salatalık	cucumber
Ispanak	spinach
Karnıbahar	cauliflower
Lahana	cabbage

Patates	potatoes
Sogan	onions
Beyazpeynir	sheep's cheese
Kaşar	mild yellow cheese
Hardal	mustard
Sarmısak	garlic
Karabiber	black pepper
Tuz	salt
Zeytin	olives

Dessert ("tatlılar")

Baklava	pastry filled with walnuts or pistachios
Helva	Turkish honey
Tel kadayıfı	pastry filled with walnut or pistachio soaked in syrup
Aşure	cream of wheat with walnuts and raisins
Krem karamel	baked caramel pudding
Muhallebi	pudding of rice flour and rose water
Sütlaç	milk rice
Revani	cream of wheat and syrup
Güllaç	waffles with cream and rose water
Ekmek kadayıfı	pancakes in syrup
Dondurma	ice cream
Peynir tatlısı	cheese cake

Preparation

Bugulama	steamed
Ezme(si)	mashed
Fırın	baked in oven
Haslama	boiled
Izgara	charcoal grilled
Tava	fried
Pişkin	simmered
Rosto	roasted
Soslu	with sauce
Yogurtlu	with yoghurt
Yumurtalı	with egg

Fruit ("meyve")

Armut	pear	*İncir*	fig
Elma	apple	*Karpuz*	water melon
Erik	plum	*Kavun*	honeydew melon

		Nar	pomegranate
Kayısı	apricot	*Portakal*	orange
Kiraz	cherry	*Şeftali*	peach
Muz	banana	*Üzüm*	grapes

Beverages

Ayran	joghurt-drink	*Adaçayı*	sage tea
		Kahve	coffee, mocca
Madensuyu	mineral water	*Şekerli*	sweet
Su	water	*Az şekerli*	lightly sweetened
Meyve suyu	fruit juice	*Bira*	beer
Elma suyu	apple juice	*Şarap*	wine
Portakal suyu	orange juice	*Beyaz*	white
Şeftali suyu	peach juice	*Kırmızı*	red
Limonata	lemonade	*Roze*	rosé
Süt	milk	*Rakı*	aniseed liquor
Çay	black tea	*Kanyak*	(Turkish) brandy

INDEX

Help us update

We've done our best to make this book as accurate and up-to-date as possible but travel developments are swift and things are always changing. We would greatly appreciate any contributions, suggestions, corrections, improvements or additions you may have for future editions.

Please write us:
Springfield Books Limited c/o Michael Muller, Norman Road, Denby Dale, Huddersfield HD8 8TH, West Yorkshire, England.

Notices